Germans and Poles in the Middle Ages

Explorations in Medieval Culture

General Editor

Larissa Tracy (*Longwood University*)

Editorial Board

Tina Boyer (*Wake Forest University*)
Emma Campbell (*University of Warwick*)
Kelly DeVries (*Loyola University Maryland*)
David F. Johnson (*Florida State University*)
Asa Simon Mittman (*CSU, Chico*)
Thea Tomaini (*USC, Los Angeles*)
Wendy J. Turner (*Augusta University*)
David Wacks (*University of Oregon*)
Renée Ward (*University of Lincoln*)

VOLUME 16

The titles published in this series are listed at *brill.com/emc*

Germans and Poles in the Middle Ages

The Perception of the 'Other' and the Presence of Mutual Ethnic Stereotypes in Medieval Narrative Sources

Edited by

Andrzej Pleszczyński and Grischa Vercamer

BRILL

LEIDEN | BOSTON

The research for this conference volume has been supported by the National Science Centre, Poland, under Polonez fellowship reg. no 2016/21/P/HS3/04107 funded by the European Union's Horizon 2020 research and innovation program under the Marie Skłodowska-Curie grant agreement No 665778.

Cover illustration: Statues of Margrave Hermann and his wife Reglindis at Naumburg Cathedral.
©Vereinigte Domstifter zu Merseburg und Naumburg und des Kollegiatstifts Zeitz, Bildarchiv Naumburg.
©Photograph: Matthias Rutkowski.

The Library of Congress Cataloging-in-Publication Data is available online at http://catalog.loc.gov
LC record available at http://lccn.loc.gov/2021019188

Typeface for the Latin, Greek, and Cyrillic scripts: "Brill". See and download: brill.com/brill-typeface.

ISSN 2352-0299
ISBN 978-90-04-41778-6 (hardback)
ISBN 978-90-04-46655-5 (e-book)

Copyright 2021 by Koninklijke Brill NV, Leiden, The Netherlands.
Koninklijke Brill NV incorporates the imprints Brill, Brill Nijhoff, Brill Hotei, Brill Schöningh, Brill Fink, Brill mentis, Vandenhoeck & Ruprecht, Böhlau Verlag and V&R Unipress.
All rights reserved. No part of this publication may be reproduced, translated, stored in a retrieval system, or transmitted in any form or by any means, electronic, mechanical, photocopying, recording or otherwise, without prior written permission from the publisher. Requests for re-use and/or translations must be addressed to Koninklijke Brill NV via brill.com or copyright.com.

This book is printed on acid-free paper and produced in a sustainable manner.

*This volume is dedicated to Grischa's mother, Renate Vercamer,
and to the memory of Małgorzata Pleszczyńska, Andrzej's wife.*

⁂

Contents

Acknowledgments XI
Abbreviations XII
Notes on Contributors XIV
Maps XXII

1 Introduction 1
   Andrzej Pleszczyński and Grischa Vercamer

PART 1
Zones of Comparison in Medieval Europe: Theory and Examples

2 Constructing Otherness in the Chronicles of the First Crusade 17
   Kristin Skottki

3 Alterity and Genre: Reflections on the Construction of 'National' Otherness in Franco-German Contexts 41
   Georg Jostkleigrewe

4 England – No Interest? How Anglo-Norman and Angevin Historians Perceived the Empire in the Twelfth Century 57
   Isabelle Chwalka

5 "… rogans eum sibi in auxilium contra superbiam Teutonicorum": The Imaging of 'Theutonici' in Bohemian Medieval Sources between the Ninth and Fourteenth Centuries 81
   David Kalhous

PART 2
Polish Views Regarding Germans in the Middle Ages – Hagiographical and Historiographical Sources

6 The Image of the Germans and the Holy Roman Empire in Polish Historiography until the 13th Century 101
   Andrzej Pleszczyński

7   The Perception of the Holy Roman Empire and Its People in the Eyes
    of the Polish Elites in the Middle Ages   119
    Sławomir Gawlas

8   Polish Hagiographic Sources and Their View of the Germans
    in the Middle Ages   167
    Roman Michałowski

PART 3
German Views Regarding Poles in the Middle Ages –
Hagiographical, Historiographical and Medieval German
Literature Sources

9   Poland and the Poles in Early and High Medieval German
    Historiography   185
    Volker Scior

10 Poland and the Polish People in Late Medieval German
    Historiography   195
    Norbert Kersken

11 Poland, Silesia, Pomerania and Prussia in the Empire's Hagiographic
    Sources   227
    Stephan Flemmig

12 Perception of Poland in Peter Suchenwirt's Heraldic Poems: Reflections
    on Dependence between Assessments and Genres   243
    Paul Martin Langner

13 Constructions of Identities and Processes of Othering. Images of Polish
    Characters, Polishness and Poland and Their Roles in Medieval German
    Literature   261
    Florian M. Schmid

PART 4
Regional Zones of Contact between Germans and Poles in the Middle Ages

14   Between Real Experience and Stereotypes: The Silesian People in the Middle Ages with Respect to Their Neighbors (in Historiographic Sources)   305
Wojciech Mrozowicz

15   Prussia I: '... *und das her konng mochte werdin czu Polan, und nicht von cristinlicher libe* ...' Historians within the Teutonic Order (Ordensgeschichtsschreibung) in Prussia in the Middle Ages with Regard to Poland   321
Grischa Vercamer

16   Prussia II: The Views of Late Medieval Historians in Prussia towards Poland   347
Adam Szweda

17   Kraków I: 'Ethnic' or 'National' Conflict in 14th Century Kraków?   357
Marcin Starzyński

18   Kraków II: '*Ad hoc traxit me natura* ...'. Social Stereotypes in Kraków and the Rebellion of Vogt Albert of 1311–1312   367
Piotr Okniński

PART 5
German-Polish Stereotypes in Modern Times as a Counterpart to the Medieval Period

19   Contemporary Stereotypes within German-Polish Relations: A Linguistic Approach   375
Jarochna Dąbrowska-Burkhardt

PART 6
Conclusion

20 Final Remarks: Germans and Poles in the Middle Ages: The Perception of the 'Other' and the Presence of Mutual Ethnic Stereotypes in Medieval Narrative Sources (10th–15th Centuries)   395
   Thomas Wünsch

Selected Bibliography   407
Index of Geographic Names and Historical (also Fictional) Persons   427

Acknowledgments

This volume is the outcome of a conference held in the Instytut Historii im. Tadeusza Manteuflla PAN in Warszaw during 24.–27. May 2018. The title was: "Germans and Poles in the Middle Ages – Perception of the Other and mutual Stereotypes" (conference report: https://www.hsozkult.de/conferencereport/id/tagungsberichte-8077). We would like to thank the former director of the Instytut Historii, Prof. dr hab. Wojciech Kriegseisen, and the director of the German Historical Institute in Warszaw, Prof. Miloš Řezník, for hosting and supporting the conference. We would futhermore thank all contributors of the confernce for their hard work and for their patience during the long editorial process. We are as well grateful to Larrisa Tracy and the board of Explorations in Medieval Culture for their feedback and for the chance to let us publish the volume within the series. Further thanks go to Philip Jacobs (editor from English Exactly), who did a great job by proof-reading the majority of the texts and translating three texts entirely, to Peter Palm for his excellent maps, to Marcella Mulder from Brill for her great support during the last months of editoring, to the anonymous reader of the volume for precise suggestions and very helpful comments, and to Pascal Weber, who assisted us at the very final stage with the index. Thanks to all of you!

Abbreviations

APH	*Acta Poloniae Historica*
Benessius, "Chronicon"	Benessius de Weitmil, "Chronicon"
Borgeni, *Annales*	*Annales Glogovienses bis zum J. 1493*
CDCC	*Codex diplomaticus civitatis Cracoviensis*
Chron. Ludovici quarti	*Chronica Ludovici imperatoris quarti*
Chronicon Aulae Regiae	*Petra Žitavského Kronika*
Dt. Chr.	Deutsche Chroniken
Ebonis vita Ottonis	*Ebonis vita sancti Ottonis episcopi Babenbergensis*
Ebran von Wildenberg	*Des Ritters Hans Ebran von Wildenberg*
FRB	*Fontes rerum Bohemicarum/ Prameny dějin českých*
FSGA	Ausgewählte Quellen zur deutschen Geschichte des Mittelalters. Freiherr vom Stein Gedächtnisausgabe
Herbordi dialogus	*Herbordi dialogus de Vita S. Ottonis episcopi Babenbergensis*
Iohannis Victoriensis Liber	*Iohannis abbas Victoriensis Liber certarum historiarum*
Johannes von Winterhur, *Chronica*	*Die Chronik Johanns von Winterthur*
KDMK	*Kodeks dyplomatyczny miasta Krakowa*
Korner, *Chron. Novella*	*Die Chronica novella des Hermann Korner*
MGH	Monumenta Germanie Historica
MPH	Monumenta Poloniae Historica
NS	Nova series
Ottokar, *Reimchronik*	*Ottokars österreichische Reimchronik*
Passio Adalberti. Redactio brevior	*S. Adalberti Pragensis Episcopi et Martyris Vita altera auctore Brunone Querfurtensi. Redactio brevior*
Passio Adalberti. Redactio longior	*S. Adalberti Pragensis Episcopi et Martyris Vita altera auctore Brunone Querfurtensi. Redactio longior*
Posilge	Johann von Posilge, *Chronik des Landes Preussen*
RBMS	Rerum Britannicarum medii aevi scriptores
Slecht, "Chronicon"	Richard Fester, „Die Fortsetzung der Flores Temporum"
SRP	Scriptores rerum Prussicarum
SRS	Scriptores rerum Silesiacarum
SSrG	Scriptores rerum Germanicarum
Twinger, *Chronik*	Jakob Twinger von Königshofen, *Chronik.*
Vita Prieflingensis	*S. Ottonis episcopi Babenbergensis Vita Prieflingensi*
Vita quinque fratrum	*Vita quinque fratrum eremitarum* [seu] *Vita uel Passio Benedicti et Iohannis sociorumque suorum*

ABBREVIATIONS

Vita sancti Adalberti	*Sancti Adalberti episcopi Pragensis et Martyris Vita prior.*
	A. Redactio Imperialis vel Ottoniana
VK	*Vita sanctae Kyngae*
VSMaior	*Vita sancti Stanislai Cracoviensis episcopi (Vita maior)*
VSMinor	*Vita s. Stanislai episcopi Cracoviensis (Vita minor)*
ZfO	Zeitschrift für Ostmitteleuropaforschung

Notes on Contributors

Isabelle Chwalka
(PhD, Mainz/Germany) finished her PhD at the Department of Medieval History at the Johannes Gutenberg University Mainz. Her doctoral work was focused on analysing comparatively the view of Anglo-Norman / Angevinian historians towards the Holy Roman Empire and the view of German authors towards 12th century England. She examines the influence of political, social and cultural constellations on the historians and their view about "others" and the interdependency between conceptions and perceptions. At present she works for the Department of University Development at the University of Applied Sciences Koblenz.

Jarochna Dąbrowska-Burkhardt
(PhD and habilitation in Zielona Góra/Poland) is a professor of German Linguistics at the University of Zielona Góra. She studies with a PhD-scholarship at the *Institut für deutsche Sprache* (Mannheim) and received her PhD in German Linguistics and Applied Linguistics from the University of Mannheim in the research field of national stereotypes (*Stereotype und ihr sprachlicher Ausdruck im Polenbild der deutschen Presse. Eine textlinguistische Untersuchung*, Tübingen 1999). In 2014 she concluded her *Habilitation* in German Linguistics and Philology at the University of Poznań (*Die gesamteuropäischen Verfassungsprojekte im transnationalen Diskurs. Eine kontrastive linguistische Analyse der deutschen und polnischen Berichterstattung*, Zielona Góra 2013). Her main research areas are discourse analysis, polito-linguistics, intercultural communication, research on stereotypes, culture-related linguistics, media linguistics and historical sociolinguistics, especially analysis of early modern chronicles. In 2004 she published a bilingual edition on the Town Chronicle of Grünberg in Niederschlesien (*Dawna Zielona Góra. Kronika 1623–1795. Das alte Grünberg. Chronik 1623–1795*, Zielona Góra 2004). Her research interests include the relationship between individual and collective language use and the process of meaning construction in different media during various time periods.

Stephan Flemmig
(PhD and habilitation in Leipzig and Jena/Germany) studied medieval and modern history, art history, and biology in Leipzig and Krakow. This was followed by a dissertation dealing with the medieval veneration of saints and then a *Habilitation* addressing the political history of entanglements in late medieval East Central Europe. In conjunction with these, there were longer research stays in Poland, the Czech Republic, Sweden, and Italy. Stephan

Flemmig is presently academic counsellor (*Akademischer Rat*) at the Friedrich Schiller University in Jena. His most important publications are: Hagiography and Cultural Transfer: Bridget of Sweden and Hedwig of Poland (*Hagiographie und Kulturtransfer. Birgitta von Schweden und Hedwig von Polen* (2011); The Mendicant Orders during the High Middle Ages in Bohemia and Moravia (*Die Bettelorden im hochmittelalterlichen Böhmen und Mähren*) (expected 2018); Between the Empire and East Central Europe: the Relationships among the Jagiellonians, Wettins, and the Teutonic Order (1386–1526) (*Zwischen dem Reich und Ostmitteleuropa. Die Beziehungen von Jagiellonen, Wettinern und Deutschem Orden (1386–1526)*.

Sławomir Gawlas
(PhD and habilitation in Warsaw/Poland) is professor of medieval history at the Institute of History at the University of Warsaw, Poland. He specializes in the history of Poland in the late Middle Ages, focusing his attention on the problems of political and economic systems; he is also interested in the question of social awareness in this period in East Central Europe. His most important publications include, among others: *O kształt zjednoczonego Królestwa: niemieckie władztwo terytorialne a geneza społeczno-ustrojowej odrębności Polski* [For the Shape of a United Kingdom: German territorial authority and the origin of Poland's distinctiveness in social and political system], Warszawa 2000; "Die Probleme des Lehnswesens und Feudalismus aus polnischer Sicht" in: Das europäische Mittelalter im Spannungsfeld des Vergleichs. Zwanzig internationale Beiträge zu Praxis, Problemen und Perspektiven der historischen Komparatistik, ed. Michael Borgolte, Ralf Lusiardi (Europa im Mittelalter, Abhandlungen und Beiträge zur historischen Komparatistik, vol. 1), Berlin 2001, pp. 97–123; "Der hl. Adalbert als Landespatron und die frühe Nationenbildung bei den Polen", in: Polen und Deutschland vor 1000 Jahren. Die Berliner Tagung über den "Akt von Gnesen", ed. Benjamin Scheller (Europa im Mittelalter, Abhandlungen und Beiträge zur historischen Komparatistik, vol. 5), Berlin 2002, pp. 193–233; Möglichkeiten und Methoden herrschaftlicher Politik im östlichen Europa im 14. Jahrhundert, in: Die "Blüte" der Staaten des östlichen Europa im 14. Jahrhundert, ed. Marc Löwener, (Quellen und Studien des Deutschen Historischen Instituts Warschau, vol. 14), Wiesbaden 2004, s. 257–284.

Georg Jostkleigrewe
(PhD, Erlangen/Germany; habilitation, Münster/Germany) is a full professor in medieval studies at the University of Halle (Saale)/Germany. His research fields cover the vernacular and Latin historiography of the High and Late Middle Ages and the role of symbolic communication in late medieval diplomatic contacts and court societies. He specialises in the study of French medieval history;

his specific focus is on the structures and interactional mechanisms within the French "political society" during the reigns of the last Capetians and the first Valois kings. During his time in Münster, he worked as a researcher in the Collaborative Research Center/SFB 1150 "Cultures of Decision-Making", investigating the development of scholastic notions of contingency and their embedding in internal discussions and conflicts at the University of Paris. His PhD was on the topic: Das Bild des Anderen. Entstehung und Wirkung deutschfranzösischer Fremdbilder in der volkssprachlichen Literatur und Historiographie des 12. bis 14. Jahrhunderts (Berlin 2008) (The picture of the "Other". Creation and effect of German-French Mutual Perception in the Vernacular Literature and Historiography of the 12th–14th centuries). In Halle, he focusses on the interdependencies between feud and other forms of conflict management on the one hand, and State formation on the other.

David Kalhous
(PhD., Faculty of Arts, Masaryk University, Brno, CZ) is currently Senior Post-Doctoral Fellow in the *Institut für Mittelalterforschung* ÖAW, Wien and associate professor in the Faculty of Arts, Masaryk University, Brno. His publications include *Anatomy of a Duchy. The Political and Ecclesiastical Structures of Early Přemyslid Bohemia* (Brill, 2012), "*Legenda Christiani and modern historiography*" (Brill, 2015), *Bohemi. Zu den Identitätsbildungsprozessen in Böhmen der Přemyslidenzeit* (bis 1200) (Verlag der ÖAW, forthcoming) and over 50 scholarly papers and articles. His interests concern early and high medieval history (mainly in Central Europe) with the focus on the beginnings of the organized polities and on identities, both in comparative scale. In his research, he combines the approaches of different disciplines (textual analysis, archaeology, codicology and palaeography) and cooperates especially with the Vienna-school (H. Wolfram, W. Pohl, H. Reimitz).

Norbert Kersken
(PhD, Münster/Germany) is a staff member of the Herder Institute for Historical Research on East Central Europe, Marburg. He specializes in the medieval history of East Central Europe and on the history of historiography in the Middle Ages. He is the author of various publications primarily on the topic of historiography in the Middle Ages. He wrote his PhD on "Geschichtsschreibung im Europa der 'nationes'. Nationalgeschichtliche Gesamtdarstellungen im Mittelalter" (Köln 1995) (Historiography in Europe of the 'nations'). He has published more than 100 scholarly articles in the fields of historiography and foreign policy in the Middle Ages (cp. http://opac.regesta-imperii.de/lang_de/suche.php?qs=Norbert+Kersken).

Paul Martin Langner

(PhD, Technical University in Berlin/Germany) is a professor of German Studies at the University of Pedagogy in Krakow. He studied Germanistik and Philosophy at the Technical University of Berlin and worked 15 years as the Manager of Cultural Affairs in Schleswig-Holstein, Berlin and Potsdam.

His main topics are area-studies in the Middle Ages: the concept of Tradition, performativity in religious drama, in law and court in the Middle Ages, the theory of images and Friedrich Hebbel dramas and theatre of the 19th Century. His last publication: Performative Elemente in den städtischen Gewohnheitsrechten (Performative Elements in Municipal Rights), Die mittelniederdeutsche Apokalypse unter der Perspektive zisterziensischer Frömmigkeit.

(The middle-low German Apocalypse from the Perspective of Cistercians Piety). Recently (June 2018) his book appeared on the perception of Polish knights in German poems of the High Middle Ages.

Roman Michałowski

(PhD and habilitation, University of Warsaw/Poland) is a professor of Medieval History at that university. He has published monographs and many articles on the Middle Ages including *Princeps fundator* (Arx Regia, 1993) and *The Gniezno Summit* (Brill, 2016) and is editor in chief of the important historical journal 'Kwartalnik Historyczny'.

Wojciech Mrozowicz

(PhD and habilitation, University of Wrocław/Poland) is a professor of Medieval History at the Institute of History of the University of Wrocław (Department of the History of Poland and Universal History up to the End of the 15th century). His scientific areas of research are concentrated around themes in the history of Silesia and Poland, as well as their relations with neighbouring countries. He also conducts research in the area of historiography (especially Silesian), hagiography (especially related to St. Hedwig), monasticism (especially involving the Augustinian Canons Regular) and codicology. He also has published source texts from the Middle Ages and the Modern Age in both Latin and German (among others the Chronicle of the Monastery of Augustinian Canons in Kłodzko and the Silesian Annals). He is the author or editor of over 350 texts related to this field. He collaborates with the Faculty of Manuscripts at the University Library of Wrocław, where he participates in the work of creating a catalogue of medieval manuscripts.

Piotr Okniński
(PhD, The Tadeusz Manteuffel Institute of History, Polish Academy of Sciences in Warsaw/Poland) is an associate professor of History. He specializes in comparative urban history of the Late Middle Ages. His PhD dissertation examines the establishment of municipal institutions in the urban community of Kraków in the 13th century. He has also written several papers concerning different institutional, social, and spatial aspects of the urban development in the Polish lands. He is currently working on a project focused on the communal self-identity of medieval Central European cities and the role of their governments in shaping official urban memory discourses.

Andrzej Pleszczyński
(PhD and habilitation in UMCS Lublin/Poland), Co-Editor of this volume. He is Professor of Medieval European History at Maria Curie-Skłodowska University in Lublin, Poland. His research interests include: myths, narratives, stereotypes, *topoi* especially in the area of the formation of opinions about peoples/nations in the Middle Ages in the sweep of Polish-Czech-German contacts in the Middle Ages. He is also interested in studying the influence of old conceptual clichés on the colloquial and scientific thinking about the past. His academic achievements comprise among other writings the monographs: *The Birth of a Stereotype. Polish Rulers and their Country in German Writings c. 1000 A.D.* (Brill, 2011); *Vyšehrad – rezidence českých panovníků. Studie o rezidenci panovníka raného středověku na příkladu českého Vyšehradu* (Praha: Set out, 2002); Przekazy niemieckie o Polsce i jej mieszkańcach w okresie panowania Piastów [German accounts about Poland and its inhabitants during the Piasts rule] (Lublin: UMCS, 2016), and a collection of studies: *Imagined Communities. Constructing Collective Identities in Medieval Europe* (Brill, 2018).

Florian M. Schmid
(PhD, German Linguistics and Literature, University of Hamburg) is currently a research assistant with teaching duties at the University of Greifswald, focusing on German Language and Literature of the Middle Ages and the Early Modern Period. He did his PhD on a study of the Nibelungenlied ('Wieder- und Weitererzählen. Strategien der Retextualisierung in der Fassung *C des ‚Nibelungenlieds' und der ‚Klage'). His publications include works on early prints, strategies of re-textualisation in heroic epics and negotiation and demonstration of power in German and Scandinavian literature. He has published articles as well on the construction of identity and the narration of space in heroic epics, performance and performativity in courtly epics, processes of scandalisation in regard to chivalric romances, perceptual and

interpretive patterns of the sea in verse epics, comedy in the Fastnachtspiel, text-image-relations in late medieval and early modern prose romances, constructions of knowledge and genealogy in medieval chronicles. He is currently working on projects dealing with literature as sources of information in early modern chronicles and the construction of internal worlds of literary characters in early modern prose romances.

Volker Scior
(PhD and habilitation Hamburg university) studied law, history and political sciences in Hamburg. After two scholarships from the Deutsche Forschungsgemeinschaft and two interim professorships in Hamburg and Eichstätt, he is now Assistant Professor of Medieval History at the Ruhr-University Bochum, Germany. He wrote his PhD thesis on the perception of otherness and strangeness in high-medieval Northern Europe (*Das Eigene und das Fremde. Identität und Fremdheit in den Chroniken Adams von Bremen, Helmolds von Bosau und Arnold von Lübeck, Berlin 2002*) and a second book on messengers as a means of communication in the Early Middle Ages (*Boten im frühen Mittelalter. Studie zur zeitgenössischen Praxis von Kommunikation und Mobilität*). His *Habilitation* text is in the process of being published. He wrote several articles on mobility in Europe and the Mediterranean, on letters and messengers between late Antiquity and the Late Middle Ages, and on the perception of foreigners and strangers in the Early and High Middle Ages.

Kristin Skottki
(PhD at the university of Rostock/Germany) is a *Juniorprofessor* of Medieval History at Bayreuth University. Her PhD thesis was published in 2015 with Waxmann under the title *Christen, Muslime und der Erste Kreuzzug. Die Macht der Beschreibung in der mittelalterlichen und modernen Historiographie*. She co-edited *Sprechen, Schreiben, Handeln. Interdisziplinäre Beiträge zur Performativität mittelalterlicher Texte* together with Annika Bostelmann, Doreen Brandt and Hellmut Braun (Waxmann 2017). She has published a number of articles on crusade historiography and theology, as well as on reflections about the role of modern academic historiography and medievalism. She is a member of the editorial board of the *Journal of Transcultural Medieval Studies* (De Gruyter). Her main research object is a host desecration case in a northern German town called Sternberg in 1492. But she is currently also involved in different projects addressing the challenges of Crusader Medievalism in recent political and violent contexts.

Marcin Starzyński
(PhD and habilitation in Krakow/Poland) is a historian-medievalist and works as habilitated doctor in the Institute of History at the Jagiellonian University in the Department of Auxiliary Sciences of History. His scientific interests include the socio-economic history of the Polish Middle Ages: the history of towns and townsmen, and the history of the Church in medieval Poland – in particular the history of religious orders. He had published books, e.g., *Das mittelalterliche Krakau. Der Stadtrat im Herrschaftsgefüge der polnischen Metropole* (Köln-Wien-Weimar 2015) and *Collegium minus* (Kraków 2015, co-author Dariusz Niemiec) and several articles: *Le cult de Saint Bernardin de Sienne en Pologne médiévale dans l'optique du Liber miraculorum sancti Bernardini de Conrad de Freystadt* (Paris 2014, co-author: Anna Zajchowska), *Last Tribute to the King. The Funeral Ceremony of the Polish King Kazimierz the Jagiellon (1492) in the Light of an Unknown Description* (Turnhout 2014), *Geschichte des Wappens der Cistercienserabte in Mogiła* (Heiligenkreuz 2012), *Il re, il vescovo ed il predicatore. Giovanni da Capestrano a Cracovia 1453–1454* (Roma 2011) and others.

Adam Szweda
(PhD and habilitation in Toruń/Poland) is a professor at the Nicolaus Copernicus University in Toruń/Poland. He did his PhD on the topic of "Families of the Grzymała coat of arms in Greater Poland in the Middle Ages" (1998) and his *Habilitation* in the field of the history of the Teutonic Order with a monograph titled "Organization and Technique of Polish Diplomacy in Relations with the Teutonic Order in Prussia in the years 1386–1454." The main fields of his interest are diplomacy in the Late Middle Ages, relations between Poland-Lithuania and the Teutonic Order in the 14–16th centuries and Prussian chronicles. He is the author or co-author of over 100 publications (books, articles and source editions). Many of them can be found at: https://torun-pl.academia.edu/AdamSzweda

Grischa Vercamer
Co-Editor of this volume. He is currently working as professor for regional studies (with special focus on the Medieval periods) in Chemnitz/Germany.

He studied medieval and modern history, German literature and the archaeology of Central Europe in Berlin and Edinburgh from 1995 to 2002. He did his PhD at the Freie Universität in Berlin on a topic taken from the late medieval history of the Teutonic Order in Prussia (until 2007). From 2008 until 2014 he worked as a research assistant in Medieval History at the German Historical Institute in Warsaw and as a lecturer in Medieval History at the Europa-Universität Viadrina in Frankfurt/Oder. In 2016 he submitted his *Habilitation* dealing with the perception of rulers and power among historians in the High Middle Ages in Frankfurt/Oder. From 2017 until 2019 he was working as principle investigator in an EU-project at the Tadeusz Manteuffel Institute of History of the Academy of Science in Warsaw/Poland on the position of a Professor of Medieval History. The project there addressed the perceptions of the "Other" in German and Polish relations as viewed by chroniclers in the medieval period (which is similar to the title of the present volume). From 2018 until 2020 he worked as a replacement professor for Medieval History in Passau/Germany.

His most important publications include: *Administrative, Social and Settlement History of the Commandry of Königsberg (Kaliningrad) in Prussia from the 13th–16th centuries.* [Siedlungs-, Verwaltungs- und Sozialgeschichte der Komturei Königsberg im Deutschordensland Preußen (13.–16. Jahrhundert), Marburg 2010 (672 pp., PhD)]; *Perceptions of the Good and Bad Use of Power by Rulers in England, Poland and the Holy Roman Empire as Reflected in the Historiography of the 12th and 13th centuries* (Hochmittelalterliche Herrschaftspraxis im Spiegel der Geschichtsschreibung. Vorstellungen von »guter« und »schlechter« Herrschaft in England, Polen und dem Reich im 12./13. Jahrhundert (Quellen und Studien des Deutschen Historischen Instituts Warschau, Bd. 37), Wiesbaden 2020. (Habilitation, 792 pp.)].

In addition, he has edited seven conference volumes and written about 30 scholarly articles (cf. http://opac.regesta-imperii.de/lang_de/suche.php?qs=Grischa+Vercamer) dealing with his research interests: German history, Polish history and the general history of Central Europe in the Middle Ages, the medieval history of military orders (esp. the Teutonic Order), the history of rule and power, the perception of the "Own" and the "Other" (Vorstellungsgeschichte), and lastly the history of chronicles and historiography in the Middle Ages.

Thomas Wünsch

(PhD in Regensburg/Germany, habilitation in Konstanz/Germany) is a professor of East Central Europe history at the university of Passau/Germany. He focuses in his research on the history and the culture of Poland, Bohemia, the Ukraine and Russia in Medieval and Modern periods. He has a wide variety of interests. His PhD has the title: "Spiritalis intellegentia. Zur allegorischen Bibelinterpretation des Petrus Damiani" (1991) and his *Habilitation*: "Konziliarismus und Polen. Personen, Politik und Programme aus Polen zur Verfassungsfrage der Kirche in der Zeit der mittelalterlichen Reformkonzilien" (Paderborn 1998).

Maps

MAP 1　　The Holy Roman Empire and Poland, 10th/11th century.
MAP DESIGNED AND © PETER PALM, BERLIN/GERMANY

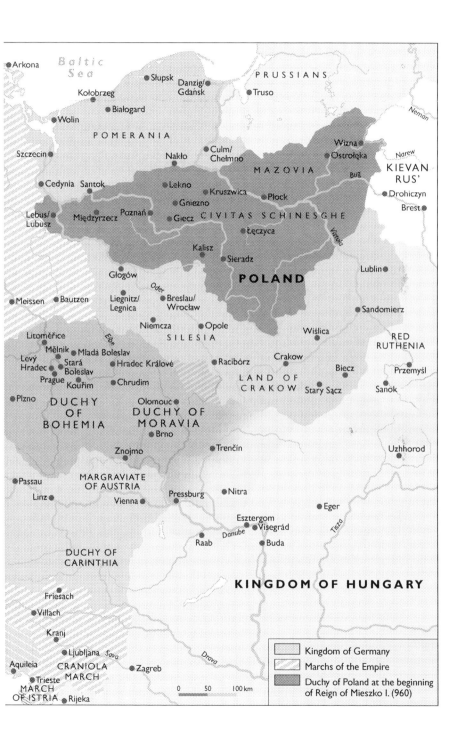

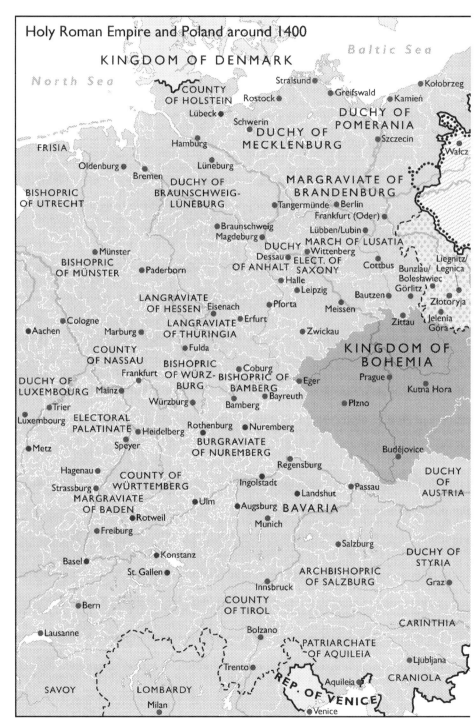

MAP 2 The Holy Roman Empire and Poland around 1400.
MAP DESIGNED AND © PETER PALM, BERLIN/GERMANY

CHAPTER 1

Introduction

Andrzej Pleszczyński and Grischa Vercamer

The topic of this volume[1] – extending beyond just the context of Germany/Poland – is currently trending, since in a globalized world, where all information and all consumer goods supposedly are just around the corner and are available at any time, many people seem to feel a longing for orientation and identity. It is therefore no coincidence that on the best seller list of non-fiction books (*Sachbücher*) of the leading German weekly newspaper *Die Zeit*, at the time of the conference in May 2018[2] we found many books dealing with foreign- and self-perception ('Othering'), such as Thea Dorn's "Deutsch, nicht dumpf" (German, Not Dull) or Isolde Charim's "Ich und die Anderen." (Me and the Others).[3] Moreover, one may surely assume that the problem is clearly wider in scope and also occurs elsewhere in Europe and within the global framework. People want and need an identity narrower than expansively belonging to the world, or even just to the European Union; they seek local and regional identities even when those are encompassed within supranational unions. We are witnessing a renaissance of national ideas.[4] This is not necessarily a bad thing, provided that strengthening your own national identity is combined with a further understanding and respect for other nations, ethnic groups, and individuals. Taking this in account, there is a lot to improve upon and learn from each other in Europe and elsewhere. While the 'western peninsula' of Asia may not be the worst example, all the same, the continent (Europe) is

---

[1] The research for this introduction has been supported by the National Science Centre, Poland, under Polonez fellowship reg. no 2016/21/P/HS3/04107 funded by the European Union's Horizon 2020 research and innovation program under the Marie Skłodowska-Curie grant agreement No 665778.

[2] This volume is the outcome of a conference held in the Instytut Historii im. Tadeusza Manteuflla PAN in Warszaw from the 24.–27. May 2018. The title was: "Germans and Poles in the Middle Ages – Perception of the Other and mutual Stereotypes" (conference report: https://www.hsozkult.de/conferencereport/id/tagungsberichte-8077).

[3] https://www.zeit.de/2018/18/sachbuecher-bestenliste-mai (27.9.2018).

[4] Which sometimes leads to nationalism – see e.g.: Greg Johnson, *Towards A New Nationalism* (San Francisco 2019); or the collection of studies: *Nationalist Myths and Modern Media. Contested Identities in the Age of Globalization*, ed. Jan H Brinks, Stella Rock, and Edward Timms, (London-New York, 2006).

divided by cultural and political barriers and behind them stand in most of the cases a basic misunderstanding,[5] sometimes even intolerance and racism. One of these European bi-national barriers persisting even into the present still seems to be the Polish-German one. Despite generally friendly actual relations between both countries, present animosities arising from historical experiences and, in many cases prejudices, can still be recognized. The memory of the tragic 'fresh history' in the 19th/20th centuries plays a major part within these bilateral *lieux de mémoire*. In the current situation of open-mindedness and broad Polish-German academic cooperation, it seems well worth the effort to rationally analyze and evaluate the mutual stereotypical perceptions in the more distant past, which we offer here for the Middle Ages, using examples from its written memories (chronicles, hagiographies) which are examined in the majority of the contributions to this volume. This is in view of the fact that it is specifically history which has created and continues to create stereotypes and prejudices that are influentially present even today.[6] Neither Germans nor Poles were unique in creating stereotypes that slandered the neighbor. Therefore, the volume comprises, besides the mentioned contributions about German-Polish perceptions, other articles as well on various mutual perceptions within Europe, especially those regarding Germans and the Holy Roman Empire from outside in the Middle Ages.

---

5 Malcolm Chapman, Jeremy Clegg, and Hanna Gajewska-De Mattos, "Poles and Germans: An international Business Relationship," *Human Relations* 57 (8), 2004, 983–1015; Jarochna Dąbrowska-Burhardt, "O języku niemieckim w Polsce. Stereotypy i wyobrażenia na przestrzeni wieków [About German in Poland. Stereotypes and ideas over the centuries]," *Lingwistyka stosowana* 23,3 (2017): 15–25.

6 Agnieszka Łada, *Barometr Polska-Niemcy 2013. Wizerunek Niemiec i Niemców w polskim społeczeństwie po dziesięciu latach wspólnego członkostwa w Unii Europejskiej* [Poland-Germany Barometer 2013. The image of Germany and Germans in Polish society after ten years of joint membership in the European Union] (Warszawa, 2014); Jarochna Dąbrowska, *Stereotype und ihr sprachlicher Ausdruck im Polenbild der deutschen Presse: eine textlinguistische Untersuchung*, Studien zur deutschen Sprache 17 (Tübingen, 1999). See also on a broader level: Richard F.M. Byrn, "National stereotypes reflected in German literature," in *Concepts of National Identity in the Middle Ages*, ed. Simon N. Forde / Leslie Peter Johnson / Alan V. Murray (Leeds, 1995), 137–153; David Lowenthal, "Identity, Heritage and History," in *Commemorations: The Politics of National Identity*, ed. John R. Gillis, Princeton, 1996, 41–57; Hans N. Hahn and Eva Hahn, "Nationale Stereotypen. Plädoyer für eine historische Stereotypenforschung," in *Stereotyp, Identität und Geschichte. Die Funktion von Stereotypen in gesellschaftlichen Diskursen*, ed. Hans H. Hahn (Frankfurt/M. 2002), 17–56; *Ethnic Images and Stereotypes – where is the border line? (Russian-Baltic cross-cultural relations); proceedings of the III International Scientific Conference on Political and Cultural Relations Between Russia and the States of the Baltic Region* (Narva, October 20–22, 2006), ed. Jelena Nömm (Narva, 2007); different contributions in: *National stereotypes: correct images and distorted images*, ed. Bianca Valota (Alessandria, 2007).

INTRODUCTION

Imagination is what usually stands at the start of stereotypical thinking, and it greatly simplifies and distorts reality. In 2011, a large exhibition took place in the well-known Martin Gropius Museum in Berlin/Germany and in the Royal Palace in Warsaw/Poland. The name was "Next door. Poland – Germany. 1000 years of Art and History" (German: *Tür an Tür. Polen – Deutschland. 1000 Jahre Kunst und Geschichte*; Polish: *Obok. Polska – Niemcy. 1000 Lat Historii w Sztuce*). The flyer for the exhibition proposed that the Germans and the Poles should deepen their knowledge of the others' country and develop cultural exchanges in order not only to understand the other side better – but also their own selves. Obviously, the intention was to propose digging more deeply into the mutual history of both countries, reaching back further than just the last two centuries. For example, in the preface to the catalogue, Bernd Neumann (then the German Federal Government Commissioner for Culture and Media) wrote:

> In the middle of Poland's EU Council Presidency, the exhibition shows that the history of German-Polish relations cannot be narrowed to the dark chapter of the crimes of Nazi Germany. For 1000 years, the neighborhood of the two countries was marked by cultural diversity, vivid exchange, and fruitful cooperation.[7]

Further on in the foreword, somewhat for the "other side", the famous politician and historian Władysław Bartoszewski, in his function as chairman of the scientific advisory board of the exhibition, wrote:

> Living next door is the story of many generations. This time [meaning a thousand years] is long enough to realize that we understand our history not only as a series of conflicts, but above all as the history of a community. This community left its mark on our intellectual and cultural heritage. These traces – as Karl Dedecius once aptly stated – are deep and enduring, but forgotten and hidden.[8]

---

7 *Tür an Tür. Polen – Deutschland: 1000 Jahre Kunst und Geschichte*, ed. Tomasz Torbus and Malgorzata Omilanowska (Köln, 2011), 7 [Translation by GV]. Original: „Mitten in der EU-Ratspräsidentschaft Polens zeigt die Ausstellung, dass sich die Geschichte der deutsch-polnischen Beziehungen nicht auf das dunkle Kapitel der Verbrechen des nationalsozialistischen Deutschlands verengen lässt. 1000 Jahre lang war die Nachbarschaft der beiden Länder geprägt von kultureller Vielfalt, lebendigem Austausch und fruchtbarer Zusammenarbeit."

8 Ibid., 9–10 [Translation: GV]. Original: „[...] Tür an Tür, leben, ist die Geschichte vieler Generationen. Diese Zeit [tousand years] ist lang genug, um zu begreifen, dass wir unsere

Even the small selection of different voices (*Blütenlese*) presented here will better sensitizes us to an important fact: The limiting of the history of relations for two large, coexisting cultures to merely their recent history narrows the view unnecessarily to just the very painful and dreadful experiences of the twentieth century.

It was this insight that gave rise to the idea for the planned volume, with most of the texts dealing with stereotypes and mutual perceptions of the 'other' by German and Polish historiographers throughout the Middle Ages (i.e. in this case from the 10th up to the 15th centuries) accompanied by a couple of other contributions reflecting on the same topic, but for other European regions. There is a serious gap in and *desideratum* for this research field about the medieval period because these types of studies are very rare.[9] Admittedly, we are not saying that there are already numerous studies devoted to this topic as it relates to Modernity, but at minimum there are plenty of shorter studies and also extensive scholarly dissertations on the stereotypes and mutual perception of Poles and Germans for the modern period.[10] However, there is

Historie nicht ausschließlich als eine Abfolge von Konflikten verstehen, sondern vor allem als die Geschichte einer Gemeinschaft. Diese Gemeinschaft hinterließ Spuren in unserem geistigen und kulturellen Erbe. Spuren, die – wie Karl Dedecius einst treffend konstatierte – tief und beständig, aber vergessen und zugeschüttet sind."

9   There are some older compendia on mutual relations in the Middle Ages: *Niemcy – Polska w średniowieczu: materiały z konferencji naukowej zorganizowanej przez Inst. Historii UAM w dniach 14–16 XI 1983 roku* [Germany – Poland in the Middle Ages: materials from a conference organized by the Institut of History of Adam Mickiewicz University, 14–16.11.1983], ed. Jerzy Strzelczyk (Poznań, 1986) – there are several interesting articles, but only the article of Henryk Samsonowicz really reflects on the perception of the Germans towards Poland. *Das Reich und Polen: Parallelen, Interaktionen und Formen der Akkulturation im hohen und späten Mittelalter*, ed. Thomas Wünsch (Ostfildern, 2003) – again: only 4 articles really reflect on the common history: Adam Labuda, Tomasz Jurek, Mieczysław Markowiec, Thomas Wünsch. The other 12 articles may be regarded as translation/ explanation of already established Polish research results for German readers. Jerzy Strzelczyk, "Deutsch-polnische Schicksalgemeinschaft in gegenseitigen Meinungen im Mittelalter," in *Mittelalter – eines oder viele?/ Średniowiecze – jedno czy wiele?*, ed. Sławomir Moździoch, Wojciech Mrozowicz, and Stanisław Rosik (Wrocław, 2010), 111–126 – this text is quite general and treats the problem in a very sketchy manner. Two books of Andrzej Pleszczyński, *The Birth of a Stereotype. Polish Rulers and their Country in German Writings c. 1000 A.D.* (Boston-Leiden, 2011); and: *Przekazy niemieckie o Polsce i jej mieszkańcach w okresie panowania Piastów* [German accounts of Poland and tis inhabitants during the reign of the Piast Dynasty] (Lublin, 2016), concern only the German perception of Poles in the Middle Ages and the scope of their analysis ends in the fourteenth century.

10   *Wokół stereotypów Niemców i Polaków* [Around the stereotypes of Germans and Poles], ed. Wojciech Wrzesiński (Wrocław, 1993); Tomasz Szarota, *Niemcy i Polacy. Wzajemne*

as well a clear imbalance between the historical research on German stereotypes about Poles versus the other way around (the Polish research is wider and deeper). This disproportion is even greater if we consider works related to the Middle Ages. Nor is it compensated for by studies on medieval literature and the opinions found in them.[11]

The deficiencies and imbalances in the studies of the mutual perception of these two large European nations in an important period of the birth of the literary and scientific traditions of both nations is a topic worthy of further attention even beyond the studies collected in this volume.

When speaking of stereotypes, we must consider two important and seemingly opposite pairings: 'Own/self' and 'others' are central terms in the discourse about stereotypes. Research in recent decades shows clearly that the perception of 'otherness' tells us quite a lot about the construction of the 'self'.[12] The assigning of stereotypes to others, therefore, only functions on the basis of an actual interdependence of 'self' – 'others', as the German literature scholar Alois Wierlacher rightly states.[13] It would certainly be wrong – specifically and especially for medieval history – to fall back on monolithic and static models,

---

postrzeganie i stereotypy [Germans and Poles. Mutual perception and stereotypes] (Warszawa, 1996).

11 For example, it can be mentioned here: Robert F. Arnold, *Geschichte der deutschen Polenliteratur*, vol. 1: Von den Anfängen bis 1800 (Osnabrück, 1900, repr. 1966), this publication collects information rather superficially; similarly: Hasso von Zitzewitz, *Das deutsche Polenbild in der Geschichte: Entstehung – Einflüsse – Auswirkungen* (Köln, 1991); better but still fragmentary are: *Deutsche Polenliteratur*, ed. Gerard Koziełek/ Gerhard Kossellek (Wrocław, 1991); Arno Will, *Kobieta polska w wyobraźni społeczeństw niemieckiego obszaru językowego od XIV do lat trzydziestych XX wieku* [A Polish woman in the imagination of the societies of the German-speaking area from the 14th to the 1930s] (Wrocław, 1983); or: Paul M. Langner, *Annäherung ans Fremde durch sprachliche Bilder: Die Region Polen und ihre Ritter in Dichtungen des Hochmittelalters* (Berlin, 2018); and older: Andrzej F. Grabski, *Polska w opiniach obcych X–XIII w.* [Poland in the opinion of foreigners 10th–13th cc.] (Warszawa, 1964); id., *Polska w opiniach Europy Zachodniej XIV–XV w.* [Poland in the opinion of Western Europe 14th–15th century] (Warszawa, 1968).

12 Elisabeth Ganseforth, *Das Fremde und das Eigene: Methoden – Methodologie – Diskurse in der soziologischen Forschung* (Aachen, 2016). For the state of the art in medieval research cf. the introduction of Volker Scior, Das *Eigene und das Fremde. Identität und Fremdheit in den Chroniken Adams von Bremen, Helmolds von Bosau und Arnold von Lübeck* (Berlin, 2002).

13 *Das Fremde und das Eigene*, ed. Alois Wierlacher (München, 1985); Alois Wierlacher and Corinna Albrecht, "Kulturwissenschaftliche Xenologie," in *Konzepte der Kulturwissenschaften: theoretische Grundlagen – Ansätze – Perspektiven*, ed. Ansgar Nünning and Vera Nünning, 5th ed. (Stuttgart, 2008), 280–306.

as found, for example, in Johann Gottfried Herder's conception of the issue when in 1791 he asked:

> Which people are there on earth who do not have their own culture?" He continues: "[...] the most natural state is therefore a people with a national character. For millennia, this [...] remains the same.[14]

According to this view, known today as Herder's *Kugelmodell* (sphere-model), each nation experiences bliss in its own culture, in peaceful coexistence with other peoples, yet it holds an unmistakable danger in itself, because it requires a clear culturally defined labelling of distinct peoples and nations. The social scientist Armin Triebel, therefore, warned in an article in 2012 that: "Cultures are not available for our observation as finished objects. Who the self is and who the others are, results from reciprocal processes of perceptions and collective identity formation."[15] He speaks of "intermediate spaces", which can easily be overlooked, if one does not see the 'own' and the 'other' as alternatives and in constant change relative to one another. If one spent his childhood in the Late Middle Ages in Poland, his student years in Paris and began his early career in Germany, he already has several layers of identities, even though he might have returned in his later years to Poland to serve at the court of the Polish king. It is precisely this that must be taken into consideration when viewing most of the medieval chroniclers and writers.

We know this, for example, about Jan of Czarnkau, the vice-chancellor of the Polish king Casimir III and one of the most important historiographers of Poland in the second half of the 14th century. He first served for many years as chancellor for the bishop of Schwerin in Mecklenburg/Germany. Did he feel one hundred per cent 'Polish' or possibly a little bit 'German' as well? That leads to the question: what, in this case, did 'German' mean at all? There might be different parameters to a national labelling; one of the most important factors in that discourse would seem to be the language. In an essay by Michael Wolffsohn, which was published in the summer of 2017 in the Berlin *Tagesspiegel* (a widely recognized newspaper in Germany) as part of a series

---

14   J.G. Herder, *Ideen zur Philosophie der Geschichte der Menschheit*, 2. Vols. (Berlin/Weimar 1784/91, repr. 1965), vol. I, 8 and 368 [Transl. GV]. Original: „Welches Volk der Erde ist's, das nicht eigene Kultur habe?", „[...] der natürlichste Staat ist also auch ein Volk, mit einem Nationalcharakter. Jahrtausendelang erhält sich dieser in ihm [...]."

15   Armin Triebel, "Autonomie der Kultur und internationale Politik," in *WIKA-Report* 1 (2012): 73, with reference to Georg Elwert, "Deutsche Nation," in *Handwörterbuch zur Gesellschaft Deutschlands*, ed. Bernhard Schäffers (Bonn, 2001), 123–134.

INTRODUCTION   7

in the newspaper dealing with the question "What is German?", he places far more emphasis on the dynamics and changeability of all parameters involved (geography, theology, economics, sociology, culture, etc.) rather than on the stability and static state of the same parameters.[16] But in terms of language, he emphasizes a certain degree of stability and cited the American political scientist Karl W. Deutsch, who saw a nation as a "community of communication." This model is referring not only to the spoken language but also to a set of non-verbal common rituals and customs in a given culture.[17] Nonetheless, the spoken language plays a major role.

Using that linguistic element as a criterion for distinguishing modern nations seems quite reasonable in so far as it finds its equivalent in the medieval period (at least for the High and Late Middle Ages).[18] It should be pointed out that in Polish the Germans are called "Niemcy". – The historical etymology points to "niemy", in English: "dumb or mute". That significance should not be underestimated: It means that the Poles once looked at the Germans as persons with whom they could not communicate.[19] That seems to be the reason for the Polish saying: "Jak świat światem nie będzie Niemiec Polakowi bratem" [As long as the world exists, a German will never be a brother to a Pole].[20] And indeed, the growing negative atmosphere in Poland against the Germans in the 13th century was caused by the difference in language in various contexts: church Masses were read in German, priests were trained in German, and so on. At this same time, we should not forget that a large influx of Germans into Poland took place (at the invitation of especially the Silesian princes).

16   Michael Wolffsohn, "Deutsch à la carte," in *Tagesspiegel*, Nr. 23147 (17.06.2017), 5.
17   Karl W. Deutsch, *Nationalism and Social Communication. An Inquiry into the Foundations of Nationality*, 2nd ed. (Cambridge/London, 1962), 96–100; id., *Nationenbildung, Nationalstaat, Integration, aus dem Amerikanischen übersetzt von Norman Gonzales*, Düsseldorf, 1972, 204.
18   Joachim Ehlers, "Was sind und wie bilden sich *nationes* im mittelalterlichen Europa (10.–15. Jahrhundert)? Begriff und allgemeine Konturen," in *Mittelalterliche nationes, neuzeitliche Nationen. Probleme der Nationenbildung in Europa*, ed. Almut Bues and Rex Rexheuser (Wiesbaden, 1995), 7–26.
19   Idzi Panic, *Zachodniosłowiańska nazwa „Niemcy" w świetle źródeł średniowiecznych* [The West Slavic name "Germany" in the light of medieval sources] (Katowice, 2007), 133–152.
20   Cf. Barbara Rodziewicz, „Póki świat światem, nie będzie Niemiec Polakowi bratem – językowy stereotyp Niemca (model archaiczny)" [As long the world is the world, a German will not be a brother to a Pole – the linguistic stereotype of a German (archaic model)], *Annales Neophilologiarum* 3, 2009, 129–35; also: Gerard Labuda, "Geneza przysłowia 'Jak świat światem nie będzie Niemiec Polakowi bratem,'" [The origin of the proverb 'As long the world is the world, a German will not be a brother to a Pole'] in *Polsko-niemieckie rozmowy o przeszłości* ed. id. (Poznań, 1996), 98–111.

These new settlers (in the countryside and in the cities) had a privileged legal position – in Krakow and Wroclaw they soon made up a large portion of the population. Although such privileges were natural for new settlers because they had to be attracted somehow, this caused a first "national" consciousness in Poland – masses were to be read in Polish, the "German element" (in the monasteries, for instance) was reduced intentionally, etc. The Gniezno archbishop, Jakób Świnka, († 1314) was a major player in this series of decisions.[21]

How do medievalists look on the 'self'/'other'-discourse (now that we have presented some modern views above)? In order to find answers, Volker Scior's dissertation is very helpful, bearing the title "Das Eigene und Fremde. Identität und Fremdheit in den Chroniken Adams von Bremen, Helmolds von Bosau und Arnolds von Lübeck" ("The 'Own' and the 'Foreign'. Identity and Strangeness in the Chronicles of Adam of Bremen, Helmold of Bosau and Arnold of Lübeck"). He stresses the point that in medieval studies there is no clear research consensus on 'own' and 'foreign', but it is nevertheless clear that 'foreign' always has its pivot point in 'non-foreign'.[22] In recent research, emphasis is therefore placed broadly on the medieval 'writer' (and his community). This means you get a more accurate picture of the author's attitude toward his described objects. Every medieval author and his construction of the 'other' (in Scior's conclusion) is unique to himself and therefore must be analyzed individually. Even just the geographical location of the writing creates differences: A German chronicler in Gdansk writing about the Poles very likely had many more contacts with Poles than an author sitting in Vienna – the former's picture of the Poles being more precise and detailed than the latter's. The concrete time period of the writing makes another difference: Jadwiga Krzyżaniakowa's verdict on this in her very helpful article "Poglądy polskich kronikarzy średniowiecznych na Niemcy i stosunki polsko-niemieckie" ("Medieval Polish Chroniclers' Attitudes Towards Germans and Polish-German Relationships"),[23] is clear; she writes that each generation of medieval writers had its own experience with the neighbor. The authors' attitudes developed unconsciously, often driven by stereotypes in the

---

21   Jerzy Strzelczyk, "Die Deutschen in Polen im Mittelalter," in *Identitäten und Alteritäten der Deutschen in Polen in historisch-komparatistischer Perspektive*, ed. Markus Krzoska and Isabel Röskau-Rydel (München, 2007), 36–37.
22   Scior, Das *Eigene und das Fremde*, 10.
23   Jadwiga Krzyżaniakowa, "Poglądy polskich kronikarzy średniowiecznych na Niemcy i stosunki polsko-niemieckie,"[Views of Polish medieval chroniclers on Germany and Polish-German relations] in *Wokół stereotypów Niemców i Polaków*, ed. Wojciech Wrzesiński (Wrocław, 1993), 15–72, at 15.

cultural memory of the respective nation.[24] People even today remember old medieval legends: for instance, in Poland there is the legend of Wanda and the German tyrant/emperor, which first appears in Vincent Kadłubek's chronicle on the Poles (around 1205).[25] An unnamed German emperor tries to conquer Poland but is, like all of his men, struck by the beauty of the Polish princess Wanda and then suddenly loses any ambition to subjugate her country. He asks his men to submit to Wanda and even commits suicide to make it easier for them to switch allegiances. This resembles modern national stereotypes: The strong German aggressor and the weak but pretty Polish lady, who dominates over physical aggression through her beauty.

'Germans/Germany' and 'Poles/Poland' – At what stage exactly may we apply these supra-regional, umbrella-like labels in the Middle Ages to ethnic groups actually living together in regional communities (e.g. Saxons, Silesians etc.)? They themselves had undergone different levels of development just back in the 9th/10th centuries, progressing from tribal structures to small principalities and tending to keep their regional identities (through customs, laws etc.). For the 'national level' we need to differentiate between labels coming from outside and the perception of identity from inside. Scholars such as Carlrichard Brühl, Jean-Marie Moeglin or Joachim Ehlers[26] clearly show for the German side that the heirs of the Frankish Empire – France and Germany – became concretely tangible as entities around 1025 (with the Salian dynasty). Very importantly, these supra-regional collective names served writers and observers from outside, making it easier to grasp a larger entity than when applied from inside. Obviously, only a very elitist circle of the highest nobility within these new state constructions had a notion of being e.g., 'Germans'. Especially in the case of the Holy Roman Empire, the kings and emperors also had to integrate the Burgundian and Italian parts of the Empire as well, which

---

24 Cf. Alberto Melucci, "The Process of Collective Identity," in *Social Movements and Culture*, eds. Hank Johnston and Bert Kladersmans (London, 1995), 41–64.

25 Cf. Jacek Banaszkiewicz, "Rudiger von Bechelaren którego, nie chciała Wanda. Przyczynek do kontaktu niemieckiej Heldenepik z polskimi dziejami bajecznymi" [Rüdiger von Bechelaren whom Wanda did not want. A contribution to the contact of the German Heldenepik with Polish fabulous history], *Przegląd Historyczny* 75 (1984), 239–247.

26 Carlrichard Brühl, "Die Anfänge der Deutschen Geschichte." in *Sitzungsberichte der Wissenschaftlichen Gesellschaft der Johann Wolfgang Goethe-Universität Frankfurt am Main* 10 (Frankfurt am Main, 1972), 147–181, 173; Carlrichard Brühl, *Deutschland-Frankreich. Die Geburt zweier Völker* (Köln-Wien, 1995); Jean-Marie Moeglin, "Die historiographische Konstruktion der Nation: 'Französische Nation' und 'deutsche Nation' im Vergleich," in *Deutschland und der Westen Europas im Mittelalter*, ed. Joachim Ehlers (Stuttgart, 2002), 353–377; Joachim Ehlers, *Die Entstehung des deutschen Reiches*, 3rd ed. (München 2010).

made a specific and solely German identification harder to develop. In the Polish case, the habilitation of Andrzej Pleszczyński from 2008 (translated into English in 2011) sums up the state of the research on early Polish identity to that point.[27] A similar sequence as to what manifested in Germany becomes visible in Poland: Regional communities from Lesser Poland, Silesia, Pomerania or Masovia, came into being during an earlier period, and then gradually from 963 onward they were subjugated by the Piast princes and incorporated into Greater Poland (namely by Mieszko I and Boleslav I). As a consequence, we can identify references to Poland in the early 11th century. Once again, we are dealing most of the time with very scarce source material such as short notes in annals, which gives us only an idea of the perception and self-identification of Polish nobles within the Polish population at that time. But at least we can state that at the beginning of the 11th century a notion arose of a larger unity that encompassed more than merely regional levels in the given countries. This happened well before the creation of most of the written records that serve here as sources for our inquiry.

It would be, in any case, a major fault to think too 'block-like' (here the Holy Roman Empire, there Poland). Naturally some national juxtapositions and comparisons can be found for the texts of the 10th–15th centuries, but the references to either 'region', or certain 'social groups' (knights, merchants, nobles) or 'individuals' (kings, archbishops etc.) in the narrations of the historiographical texts outweigh definitely the judgments of the writers about the other's nation. This is an aspect which has been surprisingly not clearly enough expressed or differentiated in many modern studies on the topic. Too often academics look through their own (nationally tinted) glasses rather than through the eyes of the medieval writers. We have to remember: Frequently in the Middle Ages, national-collective appellations were imposed first from the outside, as when Pope Gregory VII (at the time of the investiture dispute with Henry IV) spoke about the emperor for the first time as of the 'German king' (*rex Teutonicorum*)[28] – German chroniclers up to this time had not done so, because obviously they did not perceive themselves in that national way in the 11th century (as mentioned above). The regional link and identification

---

27 Andrzej Pleszczyński, *Niemcy wobec pierwszej monarchii piastowskiej (963–1034): narodziny stereotypu; postrzeganie i cywilizacyjna klasyfikacja władców Polski i ich kraju* (Lublin, 2008); and its translated and corrected edition: Id., *The birth of a stereotype: Polish rulers and their country in German writings c. 1000 A. D.* (Leiden, 2011).

28 Cf. Lutz von Padberg, "Unus populus ex diversis gentibus. Gentilismus und Einheit im früheren Mittelalter," in *Der Umgang mit dem Fremden in der Vormoderne. Studien zur Akkulturation in bildungshistorischer Sicht*, ed. Christopf Lüth (Köln, 1997), 155–193, 158.

INTRODUCTION   11

were much stronger for most persons in the Middle Ages, which the studies of Herbert Ludat clearly show for the Northeast-German-Polish contact zone (using information on the interactions between the Ekkardiner, as the dominant noble family in the 11th century in eastern Germany, and the Piasts) and as well the studies by Sławomir Gawlas or Tomasz Jurek of the Silesian perception of 'own' and 'other'.[29] One last aspect within this issue: Narrations about individuals of the other's nation should under no circumstances be transferred one-to-one to a notion of the entire 'other' nation or the entire people. Upon closer inspection, some of those narrations can be unmasked as colored by personal sympathies or antipathies. If for instance Thietmar, the Bishop of Merseburg (and also a famous chronicler), in the early 11th century portrays a predominantly negative image of the Piast prince Bolesław I,[30] then this is mainly due to the fact that Bolesław Chrobry (the brave) cooperated closely with the noble family of the Ekkardiners – a relationship made more intense through numerous marriage connections. The Counts von Walbeck, a family from which Thietmar himself stemmed, were clearly disadvantaged by these marital politics, for they were active in the same area. His negative image of the Polish king can be and was often easily mistaken for a national dislike of the Poles.

To speak of nations, regions, groups or individuals (with their *habitus*) means in all of the cases that one is referring to units which were linked by *cultural* similarities and behavior. Researchers working on these different units tend to form rigid categories that allow them to analyze and differentiate these units clearly from each other. But in recent years, the concept of cultural transfer has been the subject of many debates within historical research.[31] 'What constitutes culture at all?' – was asked. Would it not be better to understand it

---

29   Herbert Ludat, *An Elbe und Oder um das Jahr 1000: Skizzen zur Politik des Ottonenreiches und der slavischen Mächte in Mitteleuropa* (Köln, 1971); Sławomir Gawlas, "Ślązacy w oczach własnych i cudzych. Uwagi o powstaniu i rozwoju regionalnej tożsamości w średniowieczu," [Silesians in the eyes of their own and others. Notes on the emergence and development of regional identity in the Middle Ages] in *Ślązacy w oczach własnych i obcych*, ed. Antoni Barciak (Katowice, 2010), 41–67; Tomasz Jurek, "Między Polską, Niemcami i Czechami. Średniowieczny Śląsk i jego kultura," [Between Poland, Germany and the Czech Republic. Medieval Silesia and its culture] in *Tradycje śląskiej kultury muzycznej XIV* 1, ed. Anna Granat-Janka (Wrocław, 2017), 39–60.

30   E.g. *Thietmari Merseburgensis episcopi Chronicon* V/10, MGH SSrG. N.S. 9, 204. See also: Ludat, *An Elbe und Oder*, 18.

31   Cf. Michel Espagne, "Der theoretische Stand der Kulturtransferforschung," in *Kulturtransfer. Kulturelle Praxis im 16. Jahrhundert*, ed. Wolfgang Schmale (Innsbruck, 2003), 63–76 – with further literature.

dynamically rather than statically? How could it even be transferred into other regions or periods? Meaning: How might we measure and grasp culture at all? A glance into a major German encyclopedia makes it clear that at the least, the term 'culture' is used quite broadly:

> A creation produced by people at certain times and in enclosed regions on the basis of the abilities provided them for dealing with the environment and shaping it by their actions in theory and practice (language, religion [myth], ethics, institutions, state, politics, law, crafts, technology, art, philosophy and science).[32]

With such a diversity and variability, how can one dare to identify even the *transfer* of culture? Michel Espagne's general definition may help here:

> We start with the notion that cultural areas are not independent entities, but rather that their respective identities are the result of a multitude of interwoven threads. This working hypothesis naturally also has political implications. It culminates at the point where one has to emphasize the dimension of the 'foreign' in what is one's 'own', and in my case this is French cultural history. The 'foreign' and the 'own' are not complementary moments, but essentially identical moments of a single historical construct.[33]

He continues elsewhere: "The model of cultural transfer as an alternative to simple comparisons presupposes that the social carriers of cultural import are to be especially researched. These include, for example, the social groups that moved between Germany and France, artisans,

---

32 "Kultur," in *Meyers Enzyklopädisches Lexikon* 14 (Mannheim, 1975), 437 [transl. GV]. Original citation: „Das von Menschen zu bestimmten Zeiten in abgrenzbaren Regionen aufgrund der ihnen vorgegebenen Fähigkeiten in Auseinandersetzung mit der Umwelt und ihrer Gestaltung in ihrem Handeln in Theorie und Praxis Hervorgebrachte (Sprache, Religion [Mythos], Ethik, Institutionen, Staat, Politik, Recht, Handwerk, Technik, Kunst, Philosophie und Wissenschaft)."

33 Espagne, "Kulturtransfer – Podiumsgespräch," in *Kulturtransfer*, ed. Schmale, 15. Original citation: "Wir gehen davon aus, dass die Kulturräume keine eigenständigen Größen sind, sondern dass ihre jeweilige Identität das Ergebnis einer Vielzahl von Verflechtungen ist. Diese Arbeitshypothese hat natürlich auch eine politische Tragweite. Sie läuft darauf hinaus, im Eigenen, also in meinem Fall in der französischen Kulturgeschichte, die Dimension des Fremden zu betonen. Fremdes und Eigenes sind nicht ergänzende Momente, sondern im Grunde identische Momente eines einzigen historischen Konstrukts."

musicians, soldiers, wine merchants, bankers, high school teachers. In addition to social groups, books, sometimes complete libraries, are also to be understood as carriers of foreign cultural assets."[34]

These statements on cultural transfer blend fairly well with the issue as discussed above, namely, that the medieval authors in particular must be investigated and discussed in order to understand their perception.

To sum up: The mutual perceptions of (mainly) Germans and Poles in the Middle Ages in the eyes of medieval authors (chroniclers, authors of hagiographic texts, poets) has seldom been researched in the past and they form a *desideratum*. This volume consciously tries to create a counterpart to the modern period (which has been covered much better in this regard); our goal is to fill in the gaps. In order to do so in a proper way and to provide a certain level of comparability, the editors have added to the main body of texts on the German-Polish perception-contributions articles (see the first section: *Georg Jostkleigrewe, Isabelle Chwalka, David Kalhous*) that deal as well with the views towards the Germans of the medieval authors from England, France and Bohemia (the other neighbors of the Holy Roman Empire). The first article in this section (*Kristin Skottki*), within this set of 'wider articles', serves as a introduction to the whole issue in focusing on the Holy Land and the perception of (religious) 'otherness' during the crusades. These four articles serve generally, as mentioned above, to compare structural patterns of 'otherness'/'othering' to the German-Polish case. In the second and third section six contributions (*Andrzej Pleszczyński, Sławomir Gawlas, Roman Michałowski, Volker Scior, Norbert Kersken, Stephan Flemmig*) are offered as to the direct mutual perception of Germans and Poles in the medieval period in hagiographical and historiographical sources. In addition, in the third section we also shift from specifically historical sources to literary sources, with two authors (*Paul Martin Langner, Florian Schmid*) focusing on German medieval epics and poems and the views of the Poles contained in them. A fourth section connects five studies (*Wojciech Mrozowicz, Grischa Vercamer, Adam Szweda,*

---

[34] Espagne, "Der theoretische Stand," 64. Original citation: „Das Modell des Kulturtransfers als Alternative zum einfachen Vergleich setzt voraus, dass die sozialen Träger des Kulturimports besonders zu untersuchen sind. Darunter versteht man beispielsweise die sozialen Gruppen, die zwischen Deutschland und Frankreich pendeln, Kunsthandwerker, Musiker, Soldaten, Weinhändler, Bankiers, Gymnasiallehrer. Neben den sozialen Gruppierungen sind auch Bücher, manchmal vollständige Bibliotheken als Träger fremder Kulturgüter zu verstehen."

Marcin Starzyński, Piotr Okniński) on regional German-Polish contact zones in the Middle Ages (Silesia, Prussia, and examples of a town with both German and Polish residents: Kraków). In a fifth section one contribution (*Jarochna Dąbrowska-Burkhardt*) reflects on national stereotypes in the modern period between German and Poles to give some theoretical and modern background to the medieval material. There is one concluding reflection (*Thomas Wünsch*) serving as a final summary and theoretical overview of the presented material.

PART 1

*Zones of Comparison in Medieval Europe:
Theory and Examples*

∴

CHAPTER 2

Constructing Otherness in the Chronicles of the First Crusade

Kristin Skottki

1   The Times and Spaces of Others in History

Before the issue of the representation of Muslims in medieval European chronicles of the First Crusade[1] can be explored in greater depth, it is necessary as a first step to reflect more generally on the limits and possibilities of historiography in representing the 'other'. Reflecting on the spatial and temporal processes of identity and alterity construction in the creation of the medieval and the modern, the East and the West – or rather the Orient and the Occident – may help in understanding not only how medieval crusade chroniclers portrayed their opponents but also how modern historians can cope with their portrayals in a responsible manner. One of the most important insights from constructivist approaches for the conception of history might be that history only exists if someone in the present tries to make sense of what has happened in the past – this is not only true for contemporary historians, but also for medieval chroniclers. History (as an academic discipline) as well as modern and premodern historiography are always just *attempts* at reconstructing the past as plausibly and truthfully as possible, but it is impossible to recreate the past in its entirety.[2] The limits of reconstruction are not only set by the available source material, but also by the interests, agendas and perspectives of the historians and chroniclers who try to tell the story of a given historical

---

[1]   For recent studies on the portrayal of the early crusaders' Muslim opponents cf. Nicholas Morton, *Encountering Islam on the First Crusade* (Cambridge, 2016); Kristin Skottki, *Christen, Muslime und der Erste Kreuzzug. Die Macht der Beschreibung in der mittelalterlichen und modernen Historiographie*, Cultural Encounters and the Discourses of Scholarship 7 (Münster, 2015); Martin Völkl, *Muslime – Märtyrer – Militia Christi: Identität, Feindbild und Fremderfahrung während der ersten Kreuzzüge* (Stuttgart, 2011) and Armelle Leclercq, *Portraits croisés: L'image des Francs et des Musulmans dans les textes sur la Première Croisade. Chroniques latines et arabes, chansons de geste françaises des XIIe et XIIIe siècles*, Nouvelle bibliothèque du Moyen Âge 96 (Paris, 2010).

[2]   Ironically, this insight is not new at all, but can already be found in one the fundamental manifestos of early Historicism, see Johann Gustav Droysen, *Grundriss der Historik: Vorlesungen zur Geschichtswissenschaft und Methodik* (Leipzig, 1868).

phenomenon, and finally also by the limits and possibilities of the historiographical text type (in German: "Textsorte").

It is important to differentiate between the past and history – the first is what we are aiming at, but which is irretrievably gone; the second is what we are able to shape, to define, to 'make'. This understanding of history as a space for negotiating the meaning and relevance of the past for the present (and, not to forget, the future), is a necessary prerequisite to finally overcoming a positivistic reading of medieval historiography as a clear and undistorted mirror reflecting historical reality. This also accounts for the fact that historical narratives always entail processes of translation, explanation and – of course – representation, which are intimately bound to the agency and social contexts of the 'producers' of history (or rather: historiography).

History has no ontological status per se, it is a relational phenomenon; it is based on the process of relating one thing with another, that is, the present with the past.[3] If we take this strong connection between the past and present seriously, it is no wonder that assertions and judgements about the past are always (but often only implicitly) formulated as comparisons – comparisons between now and then, 'us' and 'them'. This means that representations of the past are by nature also statements about the present.[4] More importantly, constructions of identity and alterity (or 'otherness') are per se nothing that needs to be condemned: observing and creating criteria of equality and similarity as well as of difference and inequality when comparing one thing with another, as well as identifying continuities and discontinuities between a 'then' and the 'now', may well be understood as anthropological constants.[5] They are basal processes of structuring experiences of time, space and human encounters.

But historical experience teaches a different lesson: in most cases, statements about differences or inequalities also contain negative value judgements[6] and they may – metaphorically speaking – gain a life of their own if authoritative voices repeat and foster them continuously. This process of

---

3 Cf., for example, Chris Lorenz, "'The Times They Are a-Changin'. On Time, Space and Periodization in History," in *Palgrave handbook of research in historical culture and education*, eds. Mario Carretero, Stefan Berger, and Maria C.R. Grever (London, 2017), 104–133, and *Breaking up time: Negotiating the borders between present, past and future*, eds. Chris Lorenz and Berber Bevernage, Schriftenreihe der FRIAS School of History 7 (Göttingen, 2013).
4 Richard Utz called our attention to the very meaning of the word representation – it is re-*present-ation* (in German: 'Ver-gegen-wärtigung'; 'making present again'), see Richard Utz, "Coming to Terms with Medievalism," *European Journal of English Studies* 15/2 (2011), 102.
5 Cf. William S. Sax, "The Hall of Mirrors: Orientalism, Anthropology, and the Other," *American Anthropologist. New Series* 100/2 (1998), 292–299.
6 Note that negative value judgements are not necessarily restricted to the 'other' or the 'then' but may also serve to criticize the 'self' and the 'now'.

reification reaches its full extent when a community (or even a whole society) believes in the reality and genuineness of the value judgement as a statement about the nature (or the ontic status) of a thing. A perfect example for this would be the value judgements contained in the term 'medieval' – especially when used outside of academic Medieval Studies.

But an even greater challenge for medievalists is that their very research subject or reference value – the so-called Middle Ages – is an ephemeral phenomenon. Just like history in general, an epoch or a period of time has no ontological status per se, but functions as a grid to structure time and human experiences. As periods and epochs are nothing 'natural', they are by definition constructions based on qualifying certain historical events and developments as epochal, as periodic changes that mark the beginning and the end of an epoch.[7] Although it might sound objective, detached, and 'innocent' to say that the Middle Ages began around 500 AD and ended around 1500 AD, such a statement already contains a whole range of underlying assumptions, decisions, and value judgements. To choose this traditional dating is to stress the disruption of Roman antiquity as the beginning of the Middle Ages and to stress the fresh starts of the so-called 'Age of Discovery', Renaissance and Reformation as their end.[8] Not only does this dating reify the Middle Ages as a Western, Occidental or European (or Euro-Mediterranean at most) epoch, it also seems to confirm many of the negative images characterizing the Middle Ages since their invention as an epoch.

It is well known that the first ideas of a *medium aevum*, a dark and sinister period of time wedged in between a good origin and its rediscovery, were formulated by Renaissance artists already back in the 15th century and by Protestant theologians in the 16th and 17th centuries.[9] While the first ones were longing for the 'good style' of the ancients, judging medieval art as barbaric and Teutonic/Germanic, the others were longing for the true spirit of the pristine Christian community, assessing medieval church history as the age of papal tyranny. Keeping this in mind may help in remembering that 'The Middle Ages' never worked as a self-definition, as people in that period had very different ideas about and images of the structures of time and history.

---

7   Cf. Lorenz, "'The Times They Are a-Changin'," 120–124.
8   For the discussion of alternatives cf. for example *Alteuropa – Vormoderne – neue Zeit: Epochen und Dynamiken der europäischen Geschichte (1200–1800). Heinz Schilling zum 70. Geburtstag*, eds. Christian Jaser, Ute Lotz-Heumann and Matthias Pohlig, Zeitschrift für historische Forschung Beiheft 46 (Berlin, 2012).
9   Nathan Edelman, "The Early Uses of "medium aevum", "moyen-âge", Middle Ages," *Romanic Review* 29/1 (1938), 3–25.

The label 'Middle Ages' was and always is by its very nature a way to express and create difference and otherness. German historian Otto Gerhard Oexle coined an appropriate notion: the "divided Middle Ages" (German: *entzweites Mittelalter*).[10] He observed that, depending upon the self-perception and the perception of the present state of things, people tend to either represent the Middle Ages as a point of origin, as the roots of the present, stressing the *continuity as development* from medieval events and developments to our world today; or they tend to represent the Middle Ages as the 'other', the estranged (German: *fremdgewordene*) past which the modern world has overcome for good, stressing the *caesura, changes and divisions* between past and present.[11] Both ways of imaging the period can be filled with positive and negative judgements about the past – again depending upon the image of the self and the present. I would like to call this phenomenon 'the point of origin's uncanniness',[12] for the very reason that 'The Middle Ages' presents not the 'radical other' of Modernity, but rather the estranged past and the estranged self, or as John Ganim put it:

> Beneath its apparent stability as an idea, the Middle Ages repeatedly has been represented as both domestic and foreign, as both historical origin and historical rupture, as both native and 'native'.[13]

'The Middle Ages' is – more or less consciously – used as a secured space of negotiation and reflection of everything that is understood to be 'not modern'.[14]

But the issue is even more complex, as not only 'The Middle Ages' is an inherently Eurocentric concept of time and space, the same is also true for

---

10   Otto G. Oexle, "Das entzweite Mittelalter," in *Die Deutschen und ihr Mittelalter: Themen und Funktionen moderner Geschichtsbilder vom Mittelalter*, ed. Gerd Althoff, Ausblicke (Darmstadt, 1992), 7–28.

11   For a later English version cf. Otto G. Oexle, "The Middle Ages through Modern Eyes. A Historical Problem: The Prothero Lecture," *Transactions of the Royal Historical Society* 9 (1999), 121–142. Note that Oexle was convinced that it was possible to overcome this dichotomy. Max Weber was his favorite example for a 'better' historiographical approach to studying medieval history.

12   For the 'uncanniness' of the medieval cf. Kathleen Biddick, *The Shock of Medievalism* (Durham, 1998).

13   John M. Ganim, "Native Studies: Orientalism and Medievalism", in *The Postcolonial Middle Ages*, ed. Jeffrey J. Cohen, The New Middle Ages (New York, 2000), 123–34, at 131.

14   Cf. especially Kathleen Davis, *Periodization and Sovereignty: How Ideas of Feudalism and Secularization Govern the Politics of Time*, The Middle Ages Series (Philadelphia, 2008); Carol Symes, "The Middle Ages Between Nationalism and Colonialism," *French Historical Studies* 34/1 (2011), 37–46.

'Modernity' (and not-to-be forgotten 'Antiquity'). Now, 'Modernity', unlike 'Middle Ages' (and 'Antiquity'), serves as a hegemonic label of self-definition and is not simply employed to designate an epoch of European history. 'Modernity' is also used to name the spatial expansion of everything that is regarded as the 'achievements of Modernity' such as freedom, science, human rights, individuality and last but not least, secularism. This seems to confirm the claim that these achievements are not only European or Western by *origin*, but also by *nature*.[15] At the very same time, spaces *and* times of alterity are created by this notion – that is the pre-modern (or Middle Ages) and the non-European (especially the Orient/the East).

This point needs to be stressed: Although we can already find ideas of a dark and 'other' *medium aevum* in the 15th, 16th and 17th centuries, 'The Middle Ages' in the sense of an epoch was only established at the end of the 18th century, a time period which is now commonly referred to as the *Sattelzeit der Moderne* (the "saddle period of Modernity") – a term coined by Reinhart Koselleck, designating the century roughly between 1750 and 1850.[16] In this period, and especially during the 19th century, the triadic, secular vision of history (Antiquity, Middle Ages, Modernity) finally had not only overlain alternative models of periodization but even ousted them – the European model of history and time reached global hegemony. Also, it was exactly this period of Western expansionism which was the heyday of Medievalism and Orientalism as evolving discursive formations and of the institutionalization and professionalization of Humanities like history (in the form of Historicism), Medieval Studies, and Oriental Studies as corresponding academic fields. Since the end of the 18th century, not only the Orient became 'orientalized' but also the Middle Ages were 'medievalized' in the collective memory and consciousness of 'the West'. It was Kathleen Davis who most convincingly argued that the creation of the Middle Ages as 'the Other' was one of the major projects for the apologists of Modernity.[17]

One may then wonder why most discussions and debates about Modernity (or what is 'modern') on a first glance seem to lack references to the Middle Ages or to the non-European or non-Western world. But postcolonial critical intervention teaches us that this way of excluding and silencing 'the other' (or

---

15   Cf. the critique, for example, by Enrique Dussel, "Eurocentrism and Modernity (Introduction to the Frankfurt Lectures)," *boundary 2* 20/3 (1993), https://doi.org/10.2307/303341.
16   Reinhart Koselleck, "Vorwort," *Geschichtliche Grundbegriffe: Historisches Lexikon zur politisch sozialen Sprache in Deutschland*, eds. Otto Brunner, Werner Conze and Reinhart Koselleck (Stuttgart, 1972), xiii–xxvii, at xiv.
17   Davis, *Periodization and sovereignty*, 77–102.

'the subaltern') is one of the major strategies of colonialism for maintaining global hegemony.[18]

But what has colonialism to do with the creation or invention of 'The Middle Ages'? The indispensable prerequisite for understanding what postcolonial critical interventions aim at is the following: One needs to accept the notion that colonialism may not only be understood as a practice, as a certain type of rule, as a historical phenomenon of Western dominance in the age of Imperialism, but also as a discursive formation and a hegemonic epistemology.[19] Postcolonial studies of the last 40 years[20] have thoroughly shown that the process of 'Eurocentrification' did not end with the processes of formal decolonization in the first half of the 20th century at all, and that it may well have existed long before the 19th century. Because postcolonial interventions first and foremost are aiming at the conditions and premises of knowledge production, a number of philosophers and sociologists from Latin America have recently argued that we should seek to understand the logics of 'coloniality', that is the dominance of European culture as a universal cultural model with intimate ties to the ideas and ideals of Modernity and rationality.[21] Therefore, it seems more appropriate to call the discursive formation and hegemonic epistemology of colonialism 'coloniality'.

These observations may finally help to reveal the interconnectivity between coloniality as an epistemology and Medievalism and Modernism as well as Orientalism and Occidentalism as intersecting discursive formations. Anthropologist James G. Carrier defined Occidentalism as the self-image of the

---

18   Cf. as one of the classics of postcolonial critique on the inability of 'subaltern voices' to gain a hearing within the colonial power structures Gayatri C. Spivak, *Can the subaltern speak? Reflections on the history of an idea*, ed. Rosalind C. Morris (New York, 2010).

19   For a classical overview of colonialism as an historical phenomenon cf. Frederick Cooper, *Colonialism in question: Theory, knowledge, history* (Berkeley, 2005).

20   One might argue that the initial release of Edward Said's seminal study was one first important step toward establishing Postcolonial Studies as an academic field, cf. Edward W. Said, *Orientalism* (New York, 1978).

21   See for example Aníbal Quijano, "Coloniality and Modernity/Rationality," *Cultural Studies* 21/2–3 (2007), https://doi.org/10.1080/09502380601164353; Walter Mignolo, "Delinking. The rhetoric of modernity, the logic of coloniality and the grammar of de-coloniality," *Cultural Studies* 21/2 (2007), https://doi.org/10.1080/09502380601162647. For the sake of my argument I unfortunately will have to leave out most of the programmatic claims of those intellectuals. I am aware that transferring and transforming concepts and concerns from postcolonial studies and the Latin American de-coloniality project run the risk of white-washing (in the most literal sense) and belittling the political and emancipatory aspects of these interventions.

West against whose background the otherness of the Orient is created.[22] He pointed out that Orientalism[23] is always dialectically or contextually defined through Occidentalism. Accordingly, one could argue – taking up Oexle's notion of the "divided Middle Ages" – that Medievalism is always contextually defined through Modernism, i.e. the self-image of modernity. Therefore, it is no wonder that specific forms of Medievalism and Orientalism are inherent to Modernism and Occidentalism alike: Orient and Middle Ages both appear to be parts of the estranged self – the allegedly secular and rational West finds its distorted mirror image in the religiously determined, affective and, if nothing else, *medieval* Orient.[24]

On a more complex level, recent anthropological studies have argued that because alterity constructions are per se always dialectical, they do not deal with 'radical strangeness/otherness', but instead, the 'self' is reflected *as* and negotiated *in* the other. William S. Sax put it this way:

> I contend that difference making involves a double movement, where the Other is simultaneously emulated and repudiated, admired and despised, and that the source of this ambivalence is the recognition of Self in Other. That is to say, the Other represents a kind of screen upon which both the despised and desired aspects of the Self can be projected, so that the dialectics of sameness and difference is resolved into a kind of difference in sameness, the culturally particular apprehended only against the background of the generically human.[25]

If 'self' and 'other' are not so far apart from each other, as anthropologists like Sax have argued, then the real function of alterity constructions becomes visible: they work as strategies of dissociation, as tools for disentanglements. They actually can be understood as ways of disguising or denying connections, relations and entanglements – spatially and temporally.

---

22   James G. Carrier, "Introduction," *Occidentalism: Images of the West*, ed. James G. Carrier (Oxford, 1996).
23   Orientalism was most prominently criticized by Edward Said, cf. his definition in Edward W. Said, *Orientalism: Western Conceptions of the Orient*, Penguin Modern Classics (London, 2012), 3: "Taking the late eighteenth century as a very roughly defined starting point Orientalism can be discussed and analyzed as the corporate institution for dealing with the Orient – dealing with it by making statements about, authorizing views of it, describing it, by teaching it, settling it, ruling over it: in short, Orientalism as a Western style for dominating, restructuring, and having authority over the Orient."
24   Cf. John M. Ganim, *Medievalism and Orientalism: Three essays on literature, architecture, and cultural identity*, The New Middle Ages (New York, 2005).
25   Sax, "The Hall of Mirrors," 294.

Many anthropological studies have argued that most problematic master narratives dealing with non-European cultures and peoples are based upon a phenomenon that Johannes Fabian has called 'the denial of coevalness' or 'allochronism', which manifests itself as a spatialization of time.[26] It is a typical feature of these kinds of alterity constructions to position the research subject and the research object in different timescapes. The non-European 'other' is most commonly presented to be 'frozen' in a kind of timeless, ahistorical continuum, while in the case of Muslims and Islamicate societies, they are presented as living in a backward era of history, that is, the Middle Ages.[27] Obviously, two different strategies in creating the 'other' of European Modernity exist: The first one presents parts of the world as the 'nursery' of modern European culture, starting in the Middle East and North Africa (Mesopotamia and Egypt respectively), in some cases even with the 'Far East', and then following the alleged westward movement of civilization to northwestern Europe (and finally spilling out to North America) – these territories are used as spaces for negotiating and reflecting the 'self'; they form the time- and landscapes for Orientalism and Occidentalism. But those countries and parts of the world that are subsumed under the label of the 'global South' these days, especially Africa and Latin America, just have no place in this genealogy and therefore are indeed presented as the 'radical other'.[28] To the people in these parts of the world not only is coevalness denied, but even basic relevance and the existence of their own history – at least until their integration into the Modern world via bloody conquest and submission.[29] Only rather recently and slowly can attempts at overcoming the exclusion of the radical non-European history also be observed in Western academia.[30] It should be kept in mind that in the case of medieval history in general and crusade history in particular, we are dealing with alterity constructions that do not fall into the category

---

26   Johannes Fabian, *Time and the Other: How Anthropology Makes Its Object* (New York, 2002), with a new Foreword by Matti Bunzl. But cf. also the critical reassessment by Berber Bevernage, "Tales of pastness and contemporaneity: On the politics of time in history and anthropology," *Rethinking History* 20/3 (2016), 352–74, https://doi.org/10.1080/13 642529.2016.1192257.

27   Just cf. the affirmative view in Dan Diner, *Lost in the sacred: Why the Muslim world stood still* (Princeton, NJ, 2009).

28   This is the point where I disagree with most of the Latin American thinkers of De-coloniality, as they contend Latin America became 'the Other' of Western Modernity after 1492.

29   Cf. again Dussel, "Eurocentrism and Modernity (Introduction to the Frankfurt Lectures)".

30   Cf. the efforts to establish the Global History approach in university curricula, Geraldine Heng, "The Global Middle Ages. An Experiment in Collaborative Humanities, or Imagining the World, 500–1500 C.E.," *English Language Notes* 47/1 (2009): 205–16.

of radical otherness – these are timescapes shaped by ideas of identity and alterity as well as continuity and discontinuity from within the present day Euro-Mediterranean world.

To conclude this first part, the deliberate and reflected application of such concepts and terms like Orientalism and Occidentalism might be helpful in two different ways: not only may current concepts and methods help to shed new light on well-known sources and events and help to reveal details and aspects that so far have been overlooked or even ignored;[31] applying them to other times and spaces may also help to sharpen their profile by disclosing their own historicity and situatedness – by highlighting where they may fit and where not.

What follows from all that has been said above is that firstly, major differences between medieval alterity constructions and modern ones exist. Secondly, a rather banal insight from reflecting on the connection between Medievalism and Orientalism is – in regard to temporality – that in the time of the crusades, for example, the alterity label 'medieval-ness' for Muslims was, of course, not available. As the crusaders had no self-image containing an idea of their 'modern-ness', they could not use all the descriptive patterns which are so typical for (Neo)Orientalism[32] these days. Thirdly, in regard to spatiality, we should also keep in mind that for medieval European Christians the biblical and ancient Orient (i.e. the Middle East) was not only a place of longing, but for the period of the crusades even a part of their very own territory again. In modern times, on the contrary, the Orient has almost exclusively changed into the space of the 'others', especially Muslim others. This means that fourthly, the logics of 'coloniality', designating the dominance of European culture as a universal cultural model, intimately tied to the ideas and ideals of Modernity and rationality, was of course also not at hand in the period of the medieval crusades. If such an epistemology like 'coloniality' already existed in the medieval period, it obviously worked quite differently than the 'modern' one.

---

31   Gender Studies, for example, have helped to overcome general assumptions about medieval women lacking a voice or agency and about the timelessness of the concepts of female and male gender. In regard to the crusades cf. *Gendering the crusades*, eds. Susan B. Edgington and Sarah Lambert (Cardiff, 2001).

32   In this case the compound 'neo' in Orientalism refers to a change in perspective since in the age of globalization the existence of 'Orientals' (that is to say: Muslim communities) as part of the social reality of Western societies forms an important part of this discourse, especially since 9/11, cf. for example *Special Issue: Neo-Orientalism and Islamophobia: Post-9/11*, ed. Katherine Bullock (special issue), *American Journal of Islamic Social Sciences* 21/3 (2004).

2   What is in a Medieval Crusade Chronicle?

At first glance, the way Muslims were portrayed in crusade chronicles covering the First Crusade to the Levant at the very beginning of the 12th century seems to confirm all modern prejudices about medieval ignorance and stubbornness. The whole academic field of "Medieval Western Views (or Perceptions) of Islam" has shown over and over again, how 'wrong' and distorted Muslims and Islam were presented in most of medieval Western-Christian historiography.[33] Scholars working in this field have brought forward different arguments trying to explain these distortions, but most come to the conclusion that medieval historians simply all too often deliberately sacrificed historical accuracy for the sake of ideology.[34] 'Ideology' is here used to denounce the purpose of these accounts, that is, to provide future crusaders and larger Western Christian audiences with enemy stereotypes to justify their warfare, in other words, their crusades. These scholars certainly have a good point here. But what does this mean for our understanding of medieval historiography? To give it a name: Do the medieval chroniclers *lie* when they repeatedly promise to tell nothing but the truth, but then go on portraying their Muslim opponents as pagan idolaters worshipping a false trinity including "*Mahomet*" (i.e. Muhammad)?[35] I do really hope that this is not the case. On the other hand, I certainly do not want to exclude this possibility completely.

Another way to understand these accounts would be to assume that the chroniclers really did not know any better or, what might be worse, they did not want to know any better, therefore remaining stubbornly ignorant of the Islamic reality. Now, ignorance or deliberate distortion as two explanations for these misrepresentations both predominantly focus on the character of the author of a historiographical account. The author's knowledge or lack thereof is taken as the causal explanation for the accurate or inaccurate portrayal of Islam and Muslims in these accounts.[36] But I would like to argue that this

---

[33]   Cf. the classical studies by Norman Daniel, *Islam and the West: The Making of an Image* (Edinburgh, 1960); Richard W. Southern, *Western Views of Islam in the Middle Ages* (Cambridge, MA, 1962); John V. Tolan, *Saracens: Islam in the Medieval European Imagination* (New York, 2002).

[34]   Jean Flori, "La caricature de l'Islam dans l'occident médiéval: Origine et signification de quelques stéréotypes concernant l'Islam," *Aevum* 66/2 (1992), 245–56; Daniel, *Islam and the West*.

[35]   Even though images of a 'Saracen trinity' are usually only to be found in vernacular literature, cf. Norman Daniel, *Heroes and Saracens: An Interpretation of the "Chansons de geste"* (Edinburgh, 1984).

[36]   Cf. for example on William of Tyre's crusade chronicle, Rainer Christoph Schwinges, *Kreuzzugsideologie und Toleranz: Studien zu Wilhelm von Tyrus*, Monographien zur Geschichte des Mittelalters 15 (Stuttgart, 1977).

is a rather fragile or precarious approach, mainly because we know so little about the authors. For the larger part of the crusade chronicles it is a matter of fact that all the information provided about the reputed authors comes from the texts themselves. Here it would be a dangerous trap to buy into the self-fashioning and staging of the narrator, the authorial voice within the text as the actual author-writer outside of the text. A way to circumvent this dilemma might be to take a closer look at the forms and functions of these texts, at the limits and possibilities of the text type 'crusade chronicle', to find other, complementary explanations for the obviously incorrect portrayals of Islam and Muslims within them.

Crusade chronicles are a rather special and distinct type of text in medieval historiography. Monographic accounts of a very circumscribed subject of contemporary history are rather the exception. In the text type "*historia*" (to which almost all of the early Latin crusade chronicles belong) the events are not merely presented as matters of fact in a chronological sequence, but rather the emphasis is put on the interpretation of these historical events.[37] In this text type 'the narration of deeds done' ("*narratio rerum gestarum*") is structured to correspond with the historical-religious prior knowledge and expectations of the recipients, and the narrative is framed and interpreted on the basis of this specific knowledge. It is also important to remember that medieval historiography refers to more than just the empirical, rational reality – the appearance of saints, miracles, visions and God's own intervention into this world are portrayed as true and very real matters of fact. At the same time, the effort to decipher the transcendent truth and reality *behind* the historical facts always heavily influenced the epistemology of medieval chroniclers.[38]

The medieval master narrative, the big plot that was established by the crusade chroniclers in the early 12th century was that the First Crusade had been an almost unbelievable success and the 'good' (i.e. the crusaders) defeated the 'bad' (i.e. the Muslim adversaries). This is a very important observation. The chroniclers obviously would not tell this story otherwise, for while the First Crusade was full of trials and tribulations, in the end, the crusaders achieved

---

37   Richard W. Burgess and Michael Kulikowski, *Mosaics of Time. The Latin Chronicle Traditions from the First Century BC to the Sixth Century AD. 1: A Historical Introduction to the Chronicle Genre from its Origins to the High Middle Ages*, eds. Richard W. Burgess and Michael Kulikowski, Studies in the Early Middle Ages 33 (Turnhout, 2012), 189–268.

38   Laetitia Boehm, "Der wissenschaftstheoretische Ort der 'historia' im Mittelalter. Die Geschichte auf dem Wege zur 'Geschichtswissenschaft'," in *Speculum historiale. Geschichte im Spiegel von Geschichtsschreibung und Geschichtsdeutung*, eds. Clemens Bauer, Laetitia Boehm, and Max Müller (Freiburg i. Br., 1965), 663–93.

their goal – which was obviously to the great surprise of most crusaders. Another specific characteristic of these texts is that the success was not primarily attributed to the military superiority of the crusaders, but to God, who, again and again, was identified as the arbiter of man's fortunes and misfortunes. And in many cases, they went even further – portraying the crusade as the fulfilment of God's own will, exemplified in the crusaders' rallying cry "*Deus vult*" ("God wills it!").[39]

If it was God's own will that 'his people' from the West set out to liberate Jerusalem and the Holy Land from the unjust rule of a non-Christian adversary, this adversary had to be the enemy – not just in a military sense, but in a religious one as well. This is the theological or religious 'truth' of medieval crusade historiography: Muslims *had* to be portrayed as "*pagani*" ("pagans") or as "*inimici Dei*" ("enemies of God"). According to the religious/theological world view and foreknowledge of medieval Christians, only four kinds of people existed in this world: (good) Christians, Jews, pagans and 'bad Christians', i.e. heretics, schismatics and apostates. Those people who were neither Jews nor Christians had either not received the gospel yet or stubbornly rejected it (i.e. 'pagans') or had left the community of the true believers (i.e. heretics, schismatics and apostates).

This obviously also explains why nowhere in medieval historiography are the terms 'Muslim' or 'Islam' to be found, since according to the overarching religious framework, imagining a rival monotheistic religion with a truth claim of the same value as Christianity' was simply unthinkable" – or at least unrepresentable. Martin Völkl nevertheless recently mentioned two contracts between Sancho IV of Navarra and the Muslim ruler of Zaragoza (Ahmad I. al-Muqtadir) from the 1060s and 1070s in which Sancho does indeed refer to his heterodox counterparts as "*muzlemi*".[40] Four possible explanations for this extremely rare exception to the rule[41] might be: firstly, that unlike crusade chronicles, such diplomatic texts did not raise the claim to reveal the hidden, theological truth about the 'others'. Secondly, that these contracts were explicitly and exclusively addressed to the Muslim community of Zaragoza and therefore did not need to be in accord with the Christian framework. Thirdly, that a text type like a peace treaty or an accord about the dependent relationship of neighboring powers demanded a respectful and appreciative way of

---

39 Cf. Sini Kangas, "Deus Vult. Violence and Suffering as a Means of Salvation during the First Crusade," in *Medieval history writing and crusading ideology*, eds. Tuomas M.S. Lehtonen and Kurt Villads Jensen, Studia Fennica. Historica 9 (Helsinki, 2005), 163–74.
40 Völkl, *Muslime – Märtyrer – Militia Christi*, 190.
41 At least to my knowledge this is the only ever usage of this term in a premodern Latin Christian document.

addressing one's counterpart. Fourthly, that the religious model did not prevent medieval people from thinking of Muslims in other ways, especially if they had direct contact with them in a non-military environment.

But in regard to crusade chronicles, we need to face a double hermeneutical difference: In medieval historiography, the only model available and applicable for understanding and presenting *religious* alterity or otherness was the fourfold one mentioned above. Modern historians need to understand that the idea of religious pluralism or even different revelations of the same value was not acceptable for medieval Christians, as it seemingly questioned the universality of the Christian truth claim, that is, salvation is only possible if one believes in Jesus Christ as the savior of mankind. To tell the story of the crusades, the othering of Muslims as pagans or heretics, the presentation of their negative (!) religious alterity, obviously was an inevitable feature of these texts. But note that cultural and ethnic, or even supposedly biological (phenotypic and genetic) alterity played only a minor role (if at all) in the portrayal of the Muslim adversary – unlike in modern (Neo-)Orientalism and anti-Muslim racism.[42]

For example, the *Gesta Francorum* ("Deeds of the Franks") – the presumably earliest account of the First Crusade – contains a short passage usually referred to as "The Praise of the Turks".[43] Chapter Three of the *Gesta Francorum* describes the Battle of Dorylaeum on 1 July 1097, when the crusader army defeated the combined forces of Kilij Arslan (Seljuq Sultan of Rûm, 1092–1107) and Danishmend Gazi, ending with the following statement by the narrator:

> Quis unquam tam sapiens aut doctus audebit describere prudentiam, militiam et fortitudinem Turcorum? Qui putabant terrere gentem Francorum minis suarum sagittarum, sicut terruerunt Arabes, Saracenos et Hermenios, Suranios et Graecos? Sed, si Deo placet, nunquam tantum valebunt quantum nostri. Verumtamen dicunt se esse de Francorum generatione, et quia nullus homo naturaliter debet esse miles nisi Franci et illi. Veritatem dicam, quam nemo audebit prohibere: Certe, si in fide Christi et Christianitate sancta semper firmi fuissent et unum Dominum in trinitate confiteri voluissent, Deique filium natum de virgine matre, passum et resurgentem a mortuis et in caelum suis cernentibus discipulis

---

42 On the thorny question of whether 'racism' already existed in the Middle Ages, cf. Geraldine Heng, *The Invention of Race in the European Middle Ages* (Cambridge, 2018).
43 Edition and English translation:, *Gesta Francorum et aliorum Hierosolimitanorum. The Deeds of the Franks and the Other Pilgrims to Jerusalem*, ed. Rosalind Hill, Oxford Medieval Texts (Oxford, 1967).

ascendentem, ac deinde consolationem Sancti Spiritus perfecte mittentem et eum in caelo et in terra regnantem recta mente et fide credidissent, ipsis potentiores vel fortiores uel bellorum ingeniosissimos nullus invenire potuisset: et tamen gratia Dei victi sunt a nostris.⁴⁴

[Who – however wise or learned – would dare to describe the prudence, warfare and prowess of the Turks? (Who would dare to write about) those who thought they were able to fill with terror the Frankish people (at mere sight) of their arrows, just as they were able to scare the Arabs, Saracens, Armenians, Syrians and Greeks? But, if God wills, they will never become as able as ours. Veritably they claim to be of the same origin as the Franks and that no other man is naturally born to be a knight besides the Franks and themselves. (Now) I speak the truth which nobody will dare to hinder: Surely, *if* they had firmly held onto the faith in Christ and holy Christianity, *if* they had been willing to confide to the one Lord in his trinity, *if* they genuinely and wholeheartedly had believed that the Son of God was born by a virgin mother, suffered, was resurrected from the dead, ascended to heaven in plain view of his disciples, later sending them the all-encompassing consolation of the Holy Spirit and that He reigns in heaven as on earth, *then* you would not be able to find more powerful, braver and most ingenious warriors then them – but (nevertheless), thank God, the victory was ours.]

Although this passage provides many conspicuous details, only three will be of interest here: Already the anonymous author of the *Gesta Francorum*, probably not writing much later than in the year 1100, takes into account the differences between the new 'Turkish' rulers of Anatolia (i.e. the Seljuks) and those people whose territories they had recently conquered – be they Muslim ('Arabs' and 'Saracens') or Christian (Armenians, Syrians and Greeks). Their 'newness' might also be the reason why the anonymous author provides his readers and listeners with the probably 'invented' Turkish saying about the common origin of Turks and Franks, which seems to go back to an early Frankish '*origo gentis*'-tale, claiming that both peoples descended from the refugees of ancient Troy.⁴⁵ Interestingly enough, the authorial voice presents this myth of common

---

44 *Gesta Francorum* III, 9. All translations KS.
45 Cf. for example Alan V. Murray, "William of Tyre and the Origin of the Turks: Observations of Possible Sources of the 'Gesta orientalum principum',"in *Dei gesta per Francos: Études sur les croisades dédiées à Jean Richard*, eds. Michel Balard, Benjamin Z. Kedar and Jonathan Riley-Smith (Aldershot, 2001), 217–29.

origin not as a ridiculous claim, but instead confirms its veracity. Finally, the statement "si in fide Christi et Christianitate sancta semper firmi fuissent" ("if only they had firmly held onto the faith in Christ and holy Christianity") seems to imply that the Turks used to be Christians in previous times.

Such a notion was not totally strange or alien to medieval thought, as the anonymous author here used a heresiological explanation for the (contemporary) religious alterity of the Seljuks. Although it is not stated explicitly, it seems that for the anonymous author, the 'Turks' (just like the 'Saracens' before them) were led astray by Muhammad or other heresiarchs.[46]

What might be disconcerting here is that in many other passages of the *Gesta Francorum* the different Muslim adversaries still are called 'pagans'[47], which is obviously contradictory, as 'pagans' can hardly be Christian heretics at the same time. But maybe this incoherence is not a deficiency of medieval historiography, but even a strength or an advantage: It offers different and even conflicting explanations for the thorny issue of religious heterodoxy and therefore mirrors the very different attitudes and opinions to be found in medieval Christian society.

The apparently contradictory notion of the "Praise of the Turks" in the *Gesta Francorum* as well as the evaluation of the Muslim adversaries in most of the early crusade chronicles, praising the military prowess and chivalric behavior of some Muslim knights and noblemen on the one hand, and condemning their false religion on the other, should not be misunderstood as expressions of a schizophrenic attitude of medieval Christians towards 'the other'. The same is true for the juxtaposition of massacres and peace treaties, of conflict and coexistence between crusaders and the Muslim inhabitants of the Levant in the course and aftermath of the First Crusade.[48] All of this could be understood as an – again – schizophrenic coexistence of religious zealotry and secular pragmatism in the crusaders' mind.[49] But Nicholas Morton has recently argued for

---

46   Cf. for example John V. Tolan, "Anti-Hagiography. Embrico of Mainz's 'Vita Mahumeti'," *Journal of Medieval History* 22/1 (1996), 25–41.
47   Especially often in the last book, cf. for example *Gesta Francorum* x, 33.
48   Cf. Michael A. Köhler, *Alliances and Treaties Between Frankish and Muslim Rulers in the Middle East: Cross-Cultural Diplomacy in the Period of the Crusades*, The Muslim World in the Age of the Crusades 1 (Leiden & Boston, 2013).
49   This traditional view can be found for example in Marie-Luise Favreau-Lilie, "'Multikulturelle Gesellschaft' oder 'persecuting society'? 'Franken' und 'Einheimische' im Königreich Jerusalem," in *Jerusalem im Hoch- und Spätmittelalter: Konflikte und Konfliktbewältigung – Vorstellungen und Vergegenwärtigungen*, eds. Dieter R. Bauer, Klaus Herbers and Nikolas Jaspert, Campus historische Studien 29 (Frankfurt a. M., 2001), 55–93.

the importance of a religious framework juxtaposing the logic of 'Holy War'.[50] With the theology of creation, a religious model of equality was also at hand. According to natural law, Muslims and Christians alike were God's own creatures, therefore it should come as no surprise that crusaders and chroniclers were also able to describe their enemies as brave, noble and equally skilled on many occasions, in some cases even acknowledging their *cultural* superiority – or at least equality. Even in medieval crusade chronicles the Muslim adversaries were not reduced solely to their (negative) religious alterity. Another way to explain this observation, which Margaret Jubb fittingly has called "Enemies in the Holy War, but Brothers in Chivalry",[51] might be to relate it to William S. Sax's above-mentioned statement about the "recognition of Self in Other". While religious heterodoxy naturally had to be a despised and repudiated aspect of the Muslim other in the eyes of the crusaders, the Christian chroniclers and their audiences, they nevertheless 'recognized' shared values of military prowess and chivalric behavior which they obviously had in common with (some of) their noble and knightly Muslim adversaries – aspects they admired and emulated. And this is not only true for presumably lay audiences and writers – also clerical and monastic writers, commissioners and audiences of the crusade chronicles seem to have shared this ambivalent attitude, given that it can be found throughout the Occidental crusade literature.[52]

Re-evaluating the early medieval Latin chronicles of the First Crusade as a whole also makes clear that the enemy's religion was not a central issue to the chroniclers. It is probably due to modern day readers' fascination with the 'wrong' and distorted images of Muslims and Islam provided in the medieval source material as well as to the misreading of crusade history as a 'clash of civilizations' between Islam and Christendom that our vision of what at least the First Crusade was all about became rather blurred.[53] The fighting and killing were not – primarily – an attempt to exterminate the "Saracen infidels", but mainly to reestablish Christian rule over Jerusalem and the Holy Land. For some it was also a way to help the extremely endangered Byzantine empire.[54]

---

50 Morton, *Encountering Islam on the First Crusade*, 150–183.
51 Margaret Jubb, "Enemies in the Holy War, but Brothers in Chivalry. The Crusader's View of Their Saracen Opponents," *Aspects de l'épopée romane. Mentalités, idéologies, intertextualités*, eds. Hans van Dijk and Willem Noomen, (Groningen, 1995), 251–259.
52 An especially prominent example for this attitude is the portrayal of Saladin in Western sources, cf. for example Jonathan Phillips, *The Life and Legend of the Sultan Saladin* (London, 2019).
53 For an affirmative view of the latter cf. especially Thomas F. Madden, *The crusades controversy: Setting the record straight* (North Palm Beach, Florida, 2017).
54 Cf. Peter Frankopan, *The First Crusade: The Call from the East* (Cambridge, MA, 2012).

For a small number of high noblemen it was also a way to expand their own rule and territory.[55] But for most participants it was obviously a way to gain salvation, which is why most of the early crusade chronicles repeatedly stress the penitential quality of the crusade *for the participants* – rather than laying much emphasis on the religion or culture of the adversaries.[56]

3 Timescapes of Identity and Alterity in the Chronicles of the First Crusade

Early crusade ideology and crusade theology are indeed mostly concerned with the right or wrong behavior of crusade participants – right or wrong in the eyes of God, of course. It was again Nicholas Morton who convincingly argued that it was less the engagement with their heterodox adversary which shaped the crusaders' identity (as most models of medieval "othering" would have it), but more so the demand to behave and act according to God's will, following the role model of Christ (*imitatio Christi*) and finally to labor for one's own salvation.[57] The crusade chronicles, as well as many other medieval texts, provide a vast number of stories about Christians who fail to fulfil God's will, who dwell in sinful deeds and are described as being under demonic or even devilish influence. "*Infideli*", or "*increduli*" are labels which are not exclusively used to denigrate Muslims but are also used to describe 'bad' Christians – especially those crusaders who, directly or indirectly, defer or endanger the conquest of Jerusalem.[58] This observation also contains another lesson to be learned about medieval identity and alterity constructions – about the *performative character* of such ascriptions.

While it is almost a mantra of recent postcolonial and transcultural studies to highlight the fluidity and complexity of today's identity constructions,

---

55 Cf. as one example Jean Flori, *Bohémond d'Antioche: Chevalier d'aventure* (Paris, 2007).
56 This point was most prominently stressed by Jonathan Riley-Smith, cf. for example Jonathan Riley-Smith, *The First Crusade and the Idea of Crusading* (Philadelphia, 2009).
57 Morton, *Encountering Islam on the First Crusade*, 153.
58 Raymond of Aguilers's chronicle is full of such ascriptions, cf. my analysis in Kristin Skottki, "Vom 'Schrecken Gottes' zur Bluttaufe. Gewalt und Visionen auf dem Ersten Kreuzzug nach dem Zeugnis des Raimund d'Aguilers," in *Gewalterfahrung und Prophetie*, eds. Peter Burschel and Christoph Marx, Veröffentlichungen des Instituts für Historische Anthropologie 13 (Wien, 2013), 445–90. Cf. also for example William of Tyre who calls Arnulf of Chocques, the later patriarch of Jerusalem, "firstborn of Satan, son of perdition" ["primogenitus Sathane, perdicionis filius", William of Tyre Book x, 7], cf. the edition Robert B.C. Huygens, Hans E. Mayer and Gerhard Rösch, eds., *Willelmi Tyrensis Archiepiscopi Chronicon*, 2 Bde., CCCM 63 & 63A (Turnhout, 1986), 461.

people in premodern times are often portrayed as one-dimensional, unchanging characters trapped in the godly ordained estates of the realm. It seems to me that even in recent medieval studies too much attention is being paid to the ways medieval historiography portrays people as who they *are* (provenance, religious affiliation etc.) – but too little attention is given to the ways they are portrayed in what they *do*, how they behave, how they act. If Nicholas Morton is right with his observation of God being the positive 'other' defining the identity of the crusaders as being either 'good' or 'bad' believers (and I think he is), it is in perfect accordance with Christian theology to expect the believers to prove, maintain and *perform* their true faith through their actions, deeds and behavior – every single day. And this obviously also accounts for the image of the heterodox 'other', who was expected to perform his or her 'good' or 'bad' deeds as well.

Robert of Reims' crusade chronicle,[59] for example, allocates a lot of space to the story of a Muslim traitor called Firouz,[60] who presumably helped the crusaders enter the city of Antioch in early summer 1098. Even long before he received baptism, he is presented as a perfect example of "*fides*" (in both senses of the word, faith and faithfulness), because he did not break his promise and even stuck with the crusaders although (according to Robert's account) two of his brothers were killed by overzealous crusaders when entering the city. The authorial voice comments on Firouz' behavior with the following words: "Now truly, faith/fidelity came forth from an infidel, and from a stranger familiar and thorough love (came forth)." ["*Nunc vero de infideli processit fides, et de extraneo familiaris et integra dilectio.*"][61]

During the double siege of Antioch (lasting from October 1097 to June 1098) many Christian crusaders performed their 'infidelity' and 'disbelief' by deserting their fellow crusaders, but Muslim Firouz performed his faith and fidelity. This, as well as many other examples, exemplifies that the nowadays oft quoted catch phrase from the *Chanson de Roland* "Christians are right, and

---

59 *The "Historia Iherosolimitana" of Robert the Monk*, eds. Damien Kempf and Marcus Bull (Woodbridge, 2013); English translation: Carol Sweetenham, ed., *Robert the Monk's History of the First Crusade: Historia Iherosolimitana*, Crusade Texts in Translation 11 (Aldershot, 2006).

60 Other chronicles identify him as an Armenian Christian, cf. Robert Levine, "The Pious Traitor: Rhetorical Reinventions of the Fall of Antioch," *Mittellateinisches Jahrbuch* 33 (1998), 50–80; Kristin Skottki, "Of 'Pious Traitors' and Dangerous Encounters. Historiographical Notions of Interculturality in the Principality of Antioch," *Journal of Transcultural Medieval Studies* 1/1 (2014), 75–115.

61 *The "Historia Iherosolimitana" of Robert the Monk*, 56.

pagans are wrong"[62] does not meet the complexity of the identity and alterity constructions in medieval crusade chronicles. Although the religious alterity of the Muslim adversaries was definitely seen as a deficiency, the moral qualities of 'good' and 'bad' had to be earned or proved by acts and behavior – by Muslims as well as by the crusaders.

If, as stated above, (especially negative) alterity constructions mainly work as strategies of dissociation, as tools for disentanglements, they actually bear witness to connections, relations, encounters, and entanglements between self and other which had happened in the first place – this is the hidden historical reality medieval crusade chronicles indeed try to hide and disguise.[63] These strategies of disentanglement obviously also worked very well, as people seem to have believed in the truthfulness of the medieval Western portrayal of Muslims and Islam at least until the 18th century. And even today scholars experience difficulties in uncovering these hidden realities as the narrative accounts with their "active othering" are so much more appealing to modern readers than the arduous effort it takes to reconstruct the day-to-day lived experiences in all those spaces and places of the medieval world where Christians, Muslims and others dealt with each other on a daily basis.[64]

Coming back to the question of spatial and temporal constructions of continuity and discontinuity, there is also a lot to be learned from these texts. The crusades in the Eastern Mediterranean and the establishment of the crusader states exemplify a profound conceptual reappraisal of the "Self" and its origin which occurred during the 11th century – it is the combination of the *translatio salutis* idea with a retrieved sacralization of what was now called the "Holy Land".[65] In (most of) the crusade chronicles, the "Franks" (*gens Francorum*) or even the whole Latin Church are presented as the New Israel or as the heirs of Christ, whose duty it now is to free and protect its country of origin and heritage in the Levant.

62　La Chanson de Roland, laisse LXXIX: "Paien unt tort e chrestiens unt dreit", cf. Gerard J. Brault, ed., *La Chanson de Roland: Oxford text and English translation* (University Park, 1984).

63　Cf. for example Skottki, "Of 'Pious Traitors' and Dangerous Encounters. Historiographical Notions of Interculturality in the Principality of Antioch".

64　Cf. Daniel G. König, "Medieval Western European Perceptions of the Islamic World. From 'Active Othering' to 'the Voices in Between,'" in *Christian-Muslim Relations: A Bibliographical History Band 4 (1200–1350)*, eds. David Thomas and Alex Mallett, History of Christian-Muslim Relations 17 (Leiden & Boston, 2012), 17–28; Brian A. Catlos, *Muslims of Medieval Latin Christendom (c. 1050–c. 1615)* (Cambridge, 2014).

65　For the 'invention' of the Holy Land cf. Julie A. Smith, "'My Lord's Native Land': Mapping the Christian Holy Land," *Church History* 76/1 (2007), https://doi.org/10.1017/S0009640700101398.

While the biblical landscapes were of course always present in medieval Latin Christendom through liturgy and preaching, 11th century theology and pious practices saw a new emphasis on Christ's passion, on the idea of the "Imitation of Christ" (*imitatio Christi*) and therefore also a renewed enthusiasm for the historical vestiges of the life and passion of Jesus Christ – that is (besides contact relics like the "True Cross" etc.) the Holy Sites in Jerusalem and elsewhere in the Middle East. This new enthusiasm found its expression in a remarkable increase in pilgrimages to the "Holy Land" from the West during the 11th century, a development which was obstructed by the expansions of the Seljuks beginning in the second half of the 11th century and the ensuing conflicts between them, the Byzantine empire, and the Fatimids.[66]

Taking up this enthusiasm about the Holy Land, the crusade preachers presented the liberation of Jerusalem as the duty of each Catholic Christian (especially those who were able to bear arms).[67] Now, what makes the conquests in the Levant during the crusading period so distinct is that the Latin Christian contemporaries did not understand them as conquests of a foreign territory, but as a *re*-conquest of their very own heritage. As either "the Sons of the Apostles", "Christ's heirs" or as "The New Israel", the crusaders were understood to be the only legitimate rulers over the Holy Land. And the crusade chronicles bear witness to the process of legitimizing this claim by spatial and temporal constructions of continuity and discontinuity.

Most of these texts not only pay little attention to Islam as a religion, but they also largely ignore, or rather suppress the Islamic history of the Levant, as well as the Byzantine or Oriental Christian history of these territories. They exclude from their narratives the history of the Holy Land between the days of Christ and the Apostles until the entry of the crusaders into these territories – about 1000 years of history are silenced as insignificant. This might well be due to a lack of information – but we also find this strategy among those chroniclers who actually lived in the Levant, as for example Fulcher of Chartres,[68] Walter

---

66   Cf. John France, "Le rôle de Jérusalem dans la piété du XIe siècle," *Le partage du monde: Échanges et colonisation dans la méditerranée médiévale*, eds. Michel Balard and Alain Ducellier, Série Byzantina Sorbonensia 17 (Paris, 1998) David Jacoby, "Bishop Gunther of Bamberg, Byzantium and Christian pilgrimage to the Holy Land in the eleventh century (2005)," *Travellers, Merchants and Settlers in the Eastern Mediterranean, 11th–14th Centuries,* Variorum Collected Studies Series 1045 (Farnham, 2014), 267–285.

67   Cf. Georg Strack, "The Sermon of Urban II in Clermont 1095 and the Tradition of Papal Oratory," *Medieval sermon studies* 56 (2012), 30–45.

68   *Fulcheri Carnotensis: Historia Hierosolymitana (1095–1127)*, ed. Heinrich Hagenmeyer (Heidelberg, 1913)

the Chancellor,[69] and William of Tyre.[70] They would have had the chance to gather such information (and probably even knew much about this history), but they were obviously unwilling to include such contents into their crusade chronicles. Therefore, it seems more likely that this blank space of time was created deliberately to establish a narrative of undisrupted continuity between the days of the pristine Christian community and the contemporary crusaders. Raymond of Aguilers, for example, praised the conquest of Jerusalem in July 1099 in the following way:

> In hac autem die ejecti apostoli ab Iherosolymis per universum mundum dispersi sunt. In hac eadem die, apostolorum filii Deo et patribus urbem et patriam vindicaverunt.[71]

> [It was exactly today that (previously) the apostles were expelled from Jerusalem and dispersed throughout the whole world. On this very day (now) the sons of the Apostles took vengeance for the city and the whole fatherland of God and their forefathers.].

Another telling example for this constructed continuity is the renaming and reclaiming of the buildings to be found on the Temple Mount. Although the majority of crusade chroniclers were most probably aware of the fact that no Jewish or even Christian building had existed on the Temple Mount since the days of the Roman devastation in the year 70 AD, crusade chronicles stubbornly call the Dome of the Rock (*Qubbat al-Sakhrah*) "*templum Domini*" ("Temple of the Lord") and the Al-Aqsa Mosque is identified as "*templum Salomonis*" ("Temple of Salomon").[72] Converting both places into a church and a palace,

---

69 *Galterii Cancellarii: Bella Antiochena*, ed. Heinrich Hagenmeyer (Innsbruck, 1896).
70 Guillaume de Tyr, *Chronique.*, eds. Robert B.C. Huygens, Hans E. Mayer and Gerhard Rösch, vol. 1–2, (Turnhout. 1986). William obviously was an exception to the rule as he also wrote a history of the "Oriental rulers" of the Levant, but this text did not survive, so it is hard to guess how he portrayed the 'others' in this text, cf. Murray, "William of Tyre and the Origin of the Turks".
71 *Raimundi di Aguilers Canonici Podiensis: Historia Francorum qui ceperunt Iherusalem*, Recueil des historiens des croisades. Historiens Occidentaux 3, ed. Académie des inscriptions et belles-lettres (Paris, 1866), 300.
72 Cf. Benjamin Z. Kedar, "1099–1187: the Lord's Temple ('Templum Domini') and Solomon's Palace ('Palatium Salomonis')," in *Where heaven and earth meet: Jerusalem's sacred esplanade*, eds. Oleg Grabar and Benjamin Z. Kedar, Jamal and Rania Daniel series in contemporary history, politics, culture, and religion of the Levant (Jerusalem, Austin, 2009); Michelina Di Cesare, „How Medieval Christians Coped with the Islamic Past of the Templum Domini (The Dome of the Rocks) and Read 'Abd al-Malik's Inscription", *Annali*

respectively, claimed both buildings to be of biblical origin, denying the obvious fact that both buildings were built much later by the Umayyads.

A last example is the narrative presented in the crusade chronicle of Fulcher of Chartres. In its later chapters, covering the establishment of the crusader states up through the year 1127, the conquered territories are presented as the biblical landscape that needed to be restored and resettled by Western Christians, culminating in its most famous passage:

> Considera, quaeso, et mente cogita, quomodo tempore in nostro transvertit Deus Occidentem in Orientem. Nam qui fuimus Occidentales, nunc facti sumus Orientales. Qui fuit Romanus aut Francus, hac in terra factus est Galilaeus aut Palaestinus. Qui fuit Remensis aut Carnotensis, nunc efficitur Tyrius vel Antiochenus. (…) Quare ergo reverteretur in Occidentem, qui hic taliter invenit Orientem?[73]
>
> [Please, consider and think through the ways in which God has transformed the Occident into the Orient in our own days. Because we who once were Occidentals have now become Orientals. Someone who used to be a Roman or a Frank has become a Galilean or Palestinian in this land. Someone who used to be an inhabitant of Reims or Chartres, is now a citizen of Tyre or Antioch. (…) So why should someone wish to return to the Occident, if he has found an Orient in such a manner?]

In the latter parts of Fulcher's chronicle, the Latin settlers, that is the Franks of Outremer, are presented as the new "verus Israel", rightly reclaiming their original homelands as the fulfillment of God's will. It does so not only by concealing the previous 1,000 years of history, but by also identifying the Muslim adversaries at the frontiers of the crusader states with the pagan "gentes" which were already always present since biblical times, and threating (more or less) God's chosen people and the Promised Land.

The idea of the crusaders and especially the Franks of Outremer re-enacting the settlement of Israel in the Promised Land is also to be found in Robert of Reims's crusade chronicle. In Robert's version of Pope Urban's speech in Clermont he has him say:

---

dell'Istituto Universitario Orientale di Napoli. Rivista del Dipartimento di Studi Asiatici 74 (2014), 61–94.

73   Fulcheri Carnotensis, (II, 37) 747–749.

> Viam sancti Sepulchri incipite, terram illam nefarie genti auferte, eamque vobis subicite. Terra illa filiis Israel a Deo in possessionem data fuit, sicut Scriptura dicit que lacte et melle fluit.[74]
>
> [Set out for the road to the Holy Sepulchre; wrest that land from that nefarious people, and subject it to yourselves. That land which God had given into the possession of the children of Israel and of which the Scripture says that (it is a land) 'flowing with milk and honey'.]

These last examples show that at least since the beginning of the 12th century a crusade theology/ideology for the *settlement* of the conquered territories also was developed. This finally leads to the question of whether the First Crusade (and its aftermath) should be understood as a consequence of an early form of 'coloniality'.

Clearly, crusade ideology was not driven by the "dominance of European culture as a universal cultural model, intimately tied to the ideas and ideals of Modernity and rationality". If, at all, it was driven by the conviction that the crusaders not only had the superior religion, but that God himself was on their side – at least if they acted according to God's will. More importantly, according to the testimony of the early crusade chronicles what counted most for the crusaders was the *re*-establishment of (Catholic) Christian rule over the "Holy Land" – but hardly any attention is paid to the religious, legal and cultural status of the subjected Muslim (and non-Western Christian) communities living in the crusader states. No traces of a "civilizing mission" or even systematic attempts to convert the 'others' to Catholic Christianity can be found in these texts and in other historical documents.[75]

Sophia Menache, for example, has nevertheless understood Fulcher of Chartres's strategy of 'inverted inclusion' as an early form of modern Orientalism:

> The transformation of the crusaders from Westerners into Easterners in Fulcher's eschatology constitutes a conscious practice of erasing the 'other' by expropriating its identity. This was not, however, an act of including the Easterner into the crusaders' *Weltanschauung*, but rather a symbolic denial that further served to exclude the Easterners altogether.

---

74 *The "Historia Iherosolimitana" of Robert the Monk*, 6. Cf. Ex. 3:8.
75 But in other theatres of war, like the crusades in the Baltic, (forceful) mission also did play an important role, cf. *The Clash of Cultures on the Medieval Baltic Frontier*. ed. Alan V. Murray (Farnham, 2009).

The inverted inclusion of the Muslims became the last step on the long march of both including and, at the same time, erasing the infidel, for it was Christianity that defined the cultural boundaries of the West. In this way, in an almost embryonic 'Orientalistic' fashion, crusader society subordinated the East; indeed, it turned it into a part of the West.[76]

Although I generally agree with Menache's analysis of Fulcher's strategy of 'inverted inclusion', I would argue that this strategy only aimed at the *territory*, not the people who already lived in it. More importantly, this strategy did not work by stressing (and creating) the *otherness* of the territory and its inhabitants – which forms the main constituent of modern (Neo) Orientalism – but by stressing the Christian or biblical *identity* and *continuity* of the landscape.

But the major hermeneutical challenge has still not been settled with these observations. Just because the crusaders and their Christian contemporaries may well have understood the crusades as defensive wars and as a just *re*-establishing of their legal ownership, we as modern historians are not obliged to sympathetically adopt their arguments. We still have to face 'the point of origin's uncanniness' as the crusades – on an analytical level – were indeed expansionist wars conducted by Europeans/Westerners in a number of different theatres of war. Surely, they were not aiming at a worldwide Eurocentrification, but instead maybe (could one say) at a "Catholico-centrification" inside and outside of Western Europe with a variety of strategies like conquest, settlement, mission, expulsion, and persecution of dissenters? Focusing simply on the First Crusade and the early Latin crusade chronicles will probably not help to answer this question, but it might help to detect the specifics of medieval forms of alterity and identity constructions.

---

76 Sophia Menache, "When Jesus Met Mohammed in the Holy Land: Attitudes Toward the 'Other' in the Crusader Kingdom," *Medieval Encounters* 15 (2009), 66–85, at 85.

CHAPTER 3

Alterity and Genre: Reflections on the Construction of 'National' Otherness in Franco-German Contexts

Georg Jostkleigrewe

This contribution explores medieval images of 'national otherness' and the influences that shaped them. It focuses on French and German examples taken from historiographical and literary sources of the 12th, 13th and 14th centuries.[1] Its main interest is the study of the concrete perceptions and images of the 'other' that we find in our sources. The task is not only to highlight the (well-known) interdependence between identities and alterities;[2]

---

1 This contribution is based on my doctoral thesis published in 2008: Georg Jostkleigrewe, *Das Bild des Anderen. Entstehung und Wirkung deutsch-französischer Fremdbilder in der volkssprachlichen Literatur und Historiographie des 12. bis 14. Jahrhunderts* (Berlin, 2008). It also relies on further work on the topic which I have carried out since then, cf. especially Georg Jostkleigrewe, "Rex imperator in regno suo' – an ideology of Frenchness? Late medieval France, its political élite, and juridical discourse", in *Imagined Communities: Constructing Collective Identities in Medieval Europe*, ed. Andrzej Pleszczyński (Leiden/Boston, 2018), 46–82; idem, "Terra – populus – rex: La communauté du royaume vue de dehors. Regards allemands sur la France et les Français", in *Communitas regni: la « communauté du royaume » de la fin du xe siècle au début du xive siècle (Angleterre, Écosse, France, Empire, Scandinavie)*, eds. Dominique Barthélemy, Isabelle Guyot-Bachy, Frédérique Lachaud, and Jean-Marie Moeglin (Paris 2020), 31–50; idem, "Dekadente Schwächlinge und karolingische Helden. Zu den Problemen einer politischen Interpretation der deutschsprachigen Adaptationen des altfranzösischen Wilhelmszyklus," in *Das Potenzial des Epos. Die altfranzösische Chanson de Geste im europäischen Kontext*, eds. Susanne Friede, Dorothea Kullmann (Heidelberg, 2012), 217–235; idem, "Parler d'ennemi national au Moyen Âge? L'instrumentalisation d'invectives anti-anglaises dans les conflits internes de la cour française, " in *Ennemi juré, ennemi naturel, ennemi héréditaire. Construction et instrumentalisation de la figure de l'ennemi. La France et ses adversaires (XIVe–XXe siècles)*, ed. Jörg Ulbert (Hamburg, 2011), 23–33. – Since I have not participated in the scholarly discussions about medieval and modern 'medievalist' constructions of otherness in transcultural constellations, as to this topic, I would refer the reader to Kristin Skottki, *Christen, Muslime und der Erste Kreuzzug. Die Macht der Beschreibung in der mittelalterlichen und modernen Historiographie* (Münster, 2015), as well as Kristin's contribution to this volume.
2 For the relationship between 'identity' and 'alterity' and the application of these concepts to medieval perceptions of otherness cf. Volker Scior, *Das Fremde und das Eigene. Identität und Fremdheit in den Chroniken Adams von Bremen, Helmolds von Bosau und Arnolds von Lübeck* (Berlin, 2002), here especially 10–15, 17–27; cf. ibid., 9, note 1, a survey of relevant medievalist research. Since the publication of Scior's work, further theses have been

the particular aim of this contribution is to have a closer look at those processes which underlie the construction of concrete images of French and German otherness in medieval chronicles. Is it possible to interpret these images as part (and a result) of a coherent authorial vision of the French or German 'otherness' – or not? Are these images to be understood as 'tools' that were created to pursue specific political or historiographical goals – or not? And what is the relationship between these constructions of alterity and the historiographical and literary traditions in which they are embedded?

In order to propose answers to these questions, I will first outline the 'classic' approach which consists in interpreting the construction of alterity as a tool in the sense defined above: Constructing otherness as a means of asserting identities, of fighting one's enemies, and so on. I will illustrate this approach by two pertinent examples but will also highlight its problems and shortcomings. In the second part, I then discuss a different vision of how historiographical and literary perceptions of the 'other' emerge.

A clarification must be given regarding the notion of 'national' otherness referred to by the title. Like some other medievalists, I would hold that in the Middle Ages we observe collective identities which share a number of common features with modern national identities.[3] In this contribution, however, I will not address in detail the question of whether these medieval identities should be considered 'national' ones. If I refer to the construction of 'national' otherness in the text, this is simply to indicate that I am discussing identities and alterities on the level which we today would call national – that is, with regard to 'France' and 'Germany' and not with regard to regional, social, or religious identities within the Franco-German area.

---

published, which also throw light on the problem identities and alterities: David Fraesdorff, *Der barbarische Norden. Vorstellungen und Fremdheitskategorien bei Rimbert, Thietmar von Merseburg und Helmold von Bosau* (Berlin, 2005); Thomas Foerster, *Vergleich und Identität. Selbst- und Fremddeutung im Norden des hochmittelalterlichen Europa* (Berlin, 2009). Further insights in medieval perceptions of otherness will be produced by Isabelle Chwalka's doctoral thesis on Anglo-German images of the other (cf. also Chwalka's contribution to this volume). Perceptions of otherness also play a role in Andreas Bihrer, *Begegnungen zwischen dem ostfränkisch-deutschen Reich und England (850–1100). Kontakte – Konstellationen – Funktionalisierungen – Wirkungen* (Ostfildern, 2012).

3 On this topic, cf. more specifically Jostkleigrewe, *Bild des Anderen*, 38–41, with a survey of previous medievalist *prises de position* towards this question and ibid., "Terra – populus – rex". Cf. also Jean-Marie Moeglin, "Nation et nationalisme du Moyen Age à l'époque moderne (France/Allemagne)," *Revue historique* 301 (1999), 537–553; ibid., "Die historiographische Konstruktion der Nation – 'französische Nation' und 'deutsche Nation' im Vergleich," in *Deutschland und der Westen Europas*, ed. Joachim Ehlers (Stuttgart, 2002), 353–377.

1 The 'Classic' Approach: Constructing Otherness as a Narrative and/or Political Tool

1.1 *German Comments on 'French Expansionism'*

Up to now, the dominant approach to the perception of French and German 'otherness' in historiographical and literary texts has consisted of interpreting them as the result of conscious authorial constructions and as parts of a coherent historical vision. This approach seems well adapted to the study of a number of examples. For instance, from the end of the 13th century onwards, German authors regularly denounce the aggressive policy of the French king towards the border regions of the Roman Empire. To quote but one example: Probably in 1339, Rudolf Losse, counsellor to the elector-archbishop of Treves, exhorts the emperor Louis the Bavarian to honor his alliance with the king of England and go to war with France. In this view, attacking the French king would be fully justified (and probably successful) because of the notoriety of the injuries inflicted by the latter on the Empire. These injuries are later on specified as the "occupation" or usurpation of imperial possessions and rights, as well as the violent "oppression" of imperial vassals in the border region.[4]

Well into the 20th century, German historians interpreted such documents as evidence for French aggressions on the imperial border. In his 1910 habilitation thesis, the German historian Fritz Kern concentrated on the medieval "beginnings of French expansionism";[5] his work remained influential well beyond the nationalist period before World War I and the *Entre-deux-guerres*.[6]

---

4 Rudolf Losse, *Memorandum on the emperor's war on France*, ed. Edmund Stengel, Nova Alamanniae I, Nr. 581, 389sq.: "[Non] est imperatori propter paucitatem sue gentis diffidendum, cum nonnumquam multi per paucos victi legantur, tum propter imperii iustitiam et regis Francie iniurias notorie imperio irrogatas, tum eciam, quia imperii statum et potentiam naciones singule pertimescunt. [...] Item ad victoriam imperatoris faciunt iniurie per ..reges Francie diversimode perpetrate et primo occupacio bonorum et iurium imperii notoria. Item singulorum tam in regno quam in imperio sibi vicinorum oppressio violenta".

5 Fritz Kern, *Anfänge der französischen Ausdehnungspolitik bis zum Jahr 1308* (Tübingen, 1910). In this work, Kern identifies the French 'lust for expansion' as an important (and sometimes dominant) element of 600 years of European politics, cf. ibid., p. v: "Der Trieb Frankreichs, seine Grenzen zu erweitern, war während mindestens sechs Jahrhunderten ein Bruchteil der europäischen Politik und mehrmals ihre Dominante".

6 For a survey of French and German research on French 'expansionism' cf. Jean-Marie Moeglin, "La frontière comme enjeu politique à la fin du XIIIe siècle. Une description de la frontière du *Regnum* et de *l'Imperium* au début des années 1280," in *Faktum und Konstrukt. Politische Grenzen im europäischen Mittelalter: Verdichtung – Symbolisierung – Reflexion*, eds. Nils Bock, Georg Jostkleigrewe, Bastian Walter (Münster, 2011), 203–220, especially 203 sq., note 2; Georg Jostkleigrewe, "Entre pratique locale et théorie politique: Consolidation du pouvoir, annexion et déplacement des frontières en France (début XIVe siècle). Le cas du

In recent times, however, Jean-Marie Moeglin has argued convincingly that the French 'annexationism' denounced first by medieval contemporaries and then by modern historians is little more than a fiction: in fact, the Franco-imperial border remained astonishingly stable until the end of the 15th century. Except for some debatable cases –e.g., the annexation of the city of Lyons or the integration of the so-called 'Barrois mouvant' into the vassalitic structure of the kingdom – the French kings made little effort to alter the boundaries of their kingdom.[7]

Why then do we have all these complaints? The answer is: local conflict. All along the Franco-imperial border, there was a multitude of local parties which struggled for petty possessions on either side of the border. In order to fight their local enemies, they tried to obtain every possible support – from French officials, from French and imperial magnates, and sometimes from the emperor himself. Denouncing French aggression was a very pragmatic action in this context: It was a political tool that you used if you had not managed to get French help – and when you needed imperial support against those of your enemies who, unlike you, had gotten French help.[8]

Lyonnais et des frontières méditerranéennes," in *Annexer? Les déplacements de frontières à la fin du Moyen Âge*, eds. Stéphane Péquignot/Pierre Savy (Rennes, 2016), 75–96, especially 75–77. – Only recently, Kern's work has aroused the interest of French researchers working on the Franco-imperial border in the Lyonnais, cf. Alexis Charansonnet, "Sources administratives et négociation. Les tractations du roi, du pape et de l'archevêque concernant le rattachement de Lyon à la France (1311–1312)," *Francia* 39 (2012), 439–471, especially 439, note 2: "Disons-le tout net, les historiens de Lyon [...] semblent peu intéressés par la question de l'intégration au royaume capétien, comme si elle allait de soi et que l'Empire, par exemple, était devenu au tournant des XIIIe–XIVe siècles quantité absolument négligeable. [The work of] Kienast [...] et le vieil ouvrage de Fritz Kern, Die Anfänge [...], peu utilisé par les historiens français, démontrent pourtant le contraire".

7 Cf. especially Jean-Marie Moeglin, "Französische Ausdehnungspolitik am Ende des Mittelalters: Mythos oder Wirklichkeit," in *König, Fürsten und Reich im 15. Jahrhundert*, eds. F. Fuchs, P.-J. Heinig and J. Schwarz (Cologne/Weimar/Vienne, 2009), 349–374.

8 Cf. Moeglin, "Französische Ausdehnungspolitik" (cf. note 7), especially 353 (with regard to a characteristic example from the Ostrevant region): "Die Historiographie [...] hat für sicher gehalten, dass die dem Grafen von Hennegau von Philipp dem Schönen aufgezwungene Mannschaft im Jahre 1290 auch auf die reine Ausdehnungslust des Königs zurückzuführen wäre. So einfach ist es wiederum nicht. Zu bemerken ist zuerst die Tatsache, dass, wie an der lothringischen Grenze, der König nicht von selbst eingreift, sondern dass man ihn zu Hilfe ruft und auf seine alten Rechte auf Osterbant aufmerksam macht. Die Affäre fängt nämlich an, als die mit dem Grafen von Hennegau zerstrittenen Mönche von Anchin den französischen König zu Hilfe rufen". Cf. also Jostkleigrewe, "Entre pratique locale et théorie politique", which considers the question of French expansionism with regard to French frontier regions other than the Franco-imperial border, and develops a general approach to the problem which differs slightly from Jean-Marie Moeglin's.

Despite this somewhat cynical analysis, one cannot deny that these local conflicts and complaints, well before the humanist period with its German proto-nationalism, had an impact on the emergence of a somewhat negative perception of France and the French kingdom among a certain number of German medieval chroniclers. As early as the 1290s, the Alsatian author of what is called the *Ellenhardi Chronicon* summarises the conflicts in Upper Burgundy – that is, the region between Basle, Montbéliard, and Besançon – as part of a secular confrontation between *omnis Gallia* and *tota Theutunia*. It is debatable whether this passage – which was highlighted in the 1980s as early evidence for the existence of a German national identity[9] – is actually meant to refer to a conflict between 'France' and 'Germany'. As Jean-Marie Moeglin has pointed out, it is far more probable that the chronicler intended to depict a general conflict between the germanophone and the romanophone lords in Upper Burgundy – and that he was not referring to a conflict between France and the Empire.[10]

Nevertheless, later medieval readers of the *Ellenhardi Chronicon* understood its historiographical account in exactly this way.[11] For Ottokar of Styria, who writes about fifteen years later and who draws heavily on the Alsatian chronicles, the conflicts along the Lotharingian and Burgundian border form part of one great conflict between the king of France and the Empire. It is the king of

9   For a survey of the chronicles from south-western Germany which depict the border conflicts between the Empire and the kingdom of France at the end of the 13th century, cf. Bertram Resmini, *Das Arelat im Kräftefeld der französischen, englischen und angiovinischen Politik nach 1250 und das Einwirken Rudolfs von Habsburg*, (Köln/Wien, 1980), 116 sq. Among the relevant chronicles, cf. (apart from *Ellenhardi Chronicon*) especially the *Annales Colmarienses maiores*, 216. The German research has highlighted that the authors of these chronicles tend to interpret any conflict in the borderlands as a Franco-German or Franco-imperial conflict, cf. Rüdiger Schnell, "Deutsche Literatur und deutsches Nationsbewußtsein in Spätmittelalter und Früher Neuzeit," in *Ansätze und Diskontinuität deutscher Nationsbildung im Mittelalter*, ed. Joachim Ehlers, Nationes 8 (Sigmaringen, 1989), 247–319, here 271–2; Rolf Sprandel, "Frankreich im Spiegel der spätmittelalterlichen Historiographie Deutschlands," in *Kultureller Austausch und Literaturgeschichte im Mittelalter*, ed. Ingrid Kasten et al. (Sigmaringen, 1998), 35–45, here 37; Heinz Thomas, "Nationale Elemente in der ritterlichen Welt des Mittelalters," in *Ansätze und Diskontinuität deutscher Nationsbildung im Mittelalter*, ed. Joachim Ehlers (Sigmaringen, 1988), 345–376, at 364–5.
10 Jean-Marie Moeglin, "La Gallia entre la Francia et la Germania au cours des derniers siècles du Moyen Âge," in *Relations, échanges, transferts en Occident au cours des derniers siècles du Moyen Âge. Hommage à Werner Paravicini*, eds. Bernard Guenée/Jean-Marie Moeglin (Paris, 2010) 37–48, especially 40, note 8.
11 Moeglin, "Gallia entre Francia et Germania", 44, acknowledges this problem caused by the polysemic character of the medio-Latin term of Gallia (which may well refer to the kingdom of France).

France who stirs up rebellions and wars inside the Empire and who strives to subjugate the imperial vassals in the border area. This, at least, is the position of Ottokar and his *porte-parole*, the archbishop of Treves:

> Ich weiz wol den ungemach,/den mir der selbe grâve tuot,/daz vert niht von sin selbes muot:/in reizet darzuo/beide spât und fruo/ der Franzoisaere her.[12]

> [I know about the inconvenience / that the same count does to me / this does not stem from his own impulse / he is provoked to that / both early and late / by the French king.]

Due to his exposed position on the imperial frontier, the archbishop of Treves seems well qualified to judge the French ambitions:

> Ganzer frid noch staeter suon/zwischen Franzoisen/und den helden kurtoisen,/die dâ gehôrent ze Triere,/wirt nimmer ûf der riviere/der zweier rîche gemerke:/wande mit sîner sterke/der von Francrîch und mit gâb/dem rîche hât betwungen ab/sîner liute unde lande;/daz nieman sô wol erkande,/als swer datz Triere bischolf ist,/wande er ze maniger frist/ von in schaden dulden muoz.[13]

> [Firm and stable peace between the French and the noble warriors who owe their fidelity to Treves will never reign on the border between the two kingdoms, for the Frenchman [i. e. the French king] has used power and gift to wrench land and people from the Empire. No one knew this so well as whoever is bishop of Treves, for he often has to endure injuries from him.]

Ottokar of Styria thus develops a coherent vision of the relationship between France and the Empire – a relationship marked by French 'annexationism', by French lust for conquest. And as the latter quotation indicates, he fits this vision into the construction of a quasi-national image of France. It is the French no less than their king who are responsible for the grievances of the imperial

---

12 Ottokar, *Steirische Reimchronik*, ed. Josef Seemüller, MGH Dt. Chroniken 5 (Hannover, 1890/1893), v. 35.214–35.219.
13 Ottokar, *Steirische Reimchronik*, v. 39.766–39.777. Cf. also v. 39.732–39.738: "Der bischolf von Trier,/[...]/der meinte die rehtikeit,/wand im von herzen was leit,/daz der von Francrîche/rômischem rîche/sô vil des sînen vor hât."

vassals: The king – *der von Francrîch* – and the French – die *Franzoise* – become interchangeable.

The examples we have seen up to now fit very well with what I have called the 'classic' approach to medieval 'national' otherness in a Franco-German context. French 'expansionism' is a concept which contributes to the creation of a coherent historiographical vision of France and the French. Furthermore, this concept is often made use of in a purposeful manner as a political tool during local border conflicts. Therefore, the 'classic' approach is certainly not wrong in and of itself and is an approach that is helpful for understanding a number of German documents – and it would not be a surprise that there are comparable findings in French chronicles as well. I will briefly comment on one historiographical example which also focuses on the relationship between France and the Empire, though it highlights a different aspect.

1.2 The French King as 'Emperor in His Kingdom'

During the 13th century, jurists from within and outside France had developed the theory that the king of France was exempt from the Roman emperor's *imperium mundi* – indeed, that he was emperor in his kingdom. In a few French chronicles, this theory is made use of to explain the – political – relationship between France and the Empire. The most famous example is certainly the description of what is called the 'state-visit' of the emperor, Charles IV, to France in the *Chronique des règnes de Jean II et de Charles V*, a continuation appended to the *Grandes Chroniques de France*.[14] According to this chronicle, the emperor's visit was staged as an illustration of the theory of *rex imperator in regno suo*. This does not mean that Charles of Luxembourg was not welcomed in a most friendly manner when he came to France in 1378: The emperor was a close relative of the French king, and the house of Luxembourg had been a rather reliable ally of the French kingdom for many years. However, Charles was not allowed to perform any ritual of dominancy inside France; this point is made very clear by the chronicler who occupied a more or less official position as royal historiographer at the court of the French king, Charles V.[15]

---

14 For the description of Charles' visit to Paris cf. *Chronique des règnes de Jean II et de Charles*, ed. Roland Delachenal, 3 vol. (Paris, 1910–1920), here vol. 2, 193–277. For a comprehensive survey of the relevant scholarship, I refer to my latest article on the topic: Georg Jostkleigrewe, "Rex imperator in regno suo", especially 62, 66 sq., note 36 sq.

15 Concerning the authorship of Pierre d'Orgemont and his biography cf. Françoise Vieilliard, "Orgemont, Pierre d'," in *Lexikon des Mittelalters* 6, col. 1452 sq.; with regard to the specific partiality of Pierre's chronicle cf. Georg Jostkleigrewe, *Monarchischer Staat und 'Société politique'. Politische Interaktion und staatliche Verdichtung im spätmittelalterlichen Frankreich*, Mittelalter-Forschungen 56 (Ostfildern, 2018) especially 338.

The emperor was particularly forbidden to enter Paris on a white horse – an act which was interpreted as a sign of sovereign rulership. For his reception in Paris, he was therefore asked to mount a horse of dark color while the French king entered his capital on a white horse. In the illuminated manuscript written for the king of France, the reception of Charles of Luxembourg is portrayed accordingly: The emperor and his son, king Wenceslas, sitting on horses of dark color, accompany the French king who sits astride a white horse. The French king occupies the place of highest honor – in front of and between his two guests.[16]

This description of Emperor Charles' visit to Paris has been an enormous success principally among modern scholars. Most of them conceive of the relationship between France and the Empire in terms of "rex imperator"; they hardly ever neglect to refer to Charles sojourn in Paris as evidence.[17] Among medieval contemporaries, however, the *rex imperator*-theme played a less important role, as Chris Jones and I have shown in several publications: The concept is virtually absent from the vast majority of chronicles which comment on the relationship between France and the Empire.[18]

Why do I nevertheless refer to this quite exceptional representation? The reason is twofold: On the one hand, the historiographical description of Charles' visit to Paris is a striking example of a narrative which endeavors to fit the perception of the 'other' into a systematic construction of political identity and alterity – a legal one, in this case. On the other hand, the scholarly interest in *rex imperator* is paradigmatic for the shortcomings of the 'classic' approach concentrating on coherent and conscious authorial constructions of identities and alterities – regardless of the fact that the respective constructions represent only a small portion of the historiographical material. In fact, most medieval images of the French or German other do not conform to a conscious and

---

16   Cf. BnF, Ms. français 2813, fol. 470v.; see also: František Šmahel, *The Parisian Summit, 1377–78: Emperor Charles IV and King Charles V of France* (Chicago, 2014).

17   Cf., e.g., the companion by Jean-Marie Carbasse and Guillaume Leyte, *L'État royal* (Paris, 2004), especially 19–33, 40–47, which comments on the role of *rex imperator* as one of the juridical bases of – medieval and modern – French sovereignty; the authors also edit an extract from Théodore Godefroi's *Cérémonial français* which quotes the description of Charles' IV. visit to Paris in order to illustrate the juridical model of *rex imperator*.

18   Cf. Chris Jones, *Eclipse of Empire? Perceptions of the Western Empire and its Rulers in Late-Medieval France* (Turnhout, 2007), especially 223: "French jurist generally came to agree upon the principle [...] *rex Francie in regno suo princeps est*, a tag which became a staple of legal circles, though there is little to suggest it enjoyed more popular diffusion before the mid-fourteenth century. It is, for example, notably absent from chronicles written before 1350"; Jostkleigrewe, *Bild des Anderen*, 276–315, especially 308–314; ibid., "Rex imperator in regno suo".

systematic vision of identity and alterity, but instead were influenced by other factors – one of which will be discussed in the second part of this contribution.

2 Alterity and 'Genre'. The Impact of Tradition on the Perception of the Other

2.1 *France, Universal History and the Empire*

The focus of this second part is on the interdependencies between historiographical constructions of identity and alterity, on the one hand, and 'genre' traditions on the other. How are we to understand the relationship between historiographical 'genre' and the construction of 'national' otherness? Those scholars who follow the 'classic' approach outlined above tend to present this question in terms of a problem to be solved by the chronicler. In other words: The chronicler is expected to adapt the historiographical tradition – forming the framework within which he works– into a systematic vision of identity and alterity (such as those described above). To illustrate this problem, I will look to French universal chronicles and their impact on French perceptions of the Empire. In this connection, we will once more touch on the thorny question of *rex imperator* and its supposed impact on historiography.

At a first glance, the notion of French universal chronicles seems a *contradictio in adiecto* – a contradiction in terms. Medieval universal chronicles tell the story of the world's four universal monarchies – generally the Assyrians and Babylonians, the Persians, the Greeks, and the Romans. The final parts of these chronicles treat the history of the contemporary Roman Empire – i. e., the history of the German rulers, thus highlighting the universalistic vocation of their Roman emperorship. French chronicles, in contrast, focus not only on the history of the French kings but are generally said to highlight the specific and independent role of their most noble kingdom inside Christendom.

It has been asked how those French historiographers who wrote a universal chronicle coped with this apparent tension between the traditional orientation of the genre and the implications of their own, specifically French vision of history. A most significant representative of this approach is Mireille Chazan, professor emeritus at Metz, who has done substantial research on the perception of the Empire in French universal chronicles.[19] In particular,

---

19 Mireille Chazan, "Aubri de Trois-Fontaines, un historien entre la France et l'Empire," *Annales de l'est* 36 (1984), 163–192; ibid., "L'Idée d'Empire dans le *Memoriale historiarum* de Jean de Saint-Victor," *L'historiographie médiévale en Europe*, ed. Jean-Philippe Genet (Paris, 1991), 301–319; ibid., "Guillaume de Nangis et la translation de l'empire aux rois

Professor Chazan has analysed a set of eight continuations of the universal chronicle of Sigebert of Gembloux, the second redaction of which covers the period up to 1111.[20] Sigebert was a Lotharingian monk and a supporter of the Salian emperors in their conflict with the Gregorian popes.

According to Chazan, the French chroniclers who wrote continuations for Sigebert's works developed different strategies for coping with the universalistic aspirations of their model. One strategy consisted in claiming that the contemporary French kings were the true heirs of the universal emperors. They – and not the Romano-German rulers – perform the foremost tasks of the emperors – such as the protection of the Church and the leadership of the crusade movement. If Chazan is right, this is the strategy adopted by William of Nangis; William is one of the most important French historiographers of the late 13th century, and his works have been made use of for the constitution of what would afterwards be known as the *Grandes Chroniques de France*.[21] Another strategy consisted in claiming that the universal empire had come to an end and that the world had returned to a state of independent kingdoms. This is the vision of John of Saint-Victor[22] – a vision which is not equivalent to, but compatible with the jurist's concept of *rex imperator*.

As has perhaps become clear, I do not agree in every detail with Mireille Chazan; nor do other researchers. Chris Jones has shown, for instance, that the idea of a universal empire does not at all disappear from late medieval French chronicles,[23] as Chazan's position would at least suggest. Of course, Chazan's

      de France," in *Saint-Denis et la royauté. Études offertes à Bernard Guenée*, eds. Françoise Autrand, Claude Gauvard, and Jean-Marie Moeglin (Paris, 1999), 463–480; ibid., "La nécessité de l'Empire de Sigebert de Gembloux à Jean de Saint-Victor," *Le Moyen Age* 16 (2000/1), 9–36.

20   Cf. Mireille Chazan, *L'Empire et l'histoire universelle de Sigebert de Gembloux à Jean de Saint-Victor (XIIe–XIVe siècle)* (Paris, 1999).

21   Cf. in particular, Chazan, "Guillaume de Nangis et la translation de l'empire aux rois de France".

22   Cf. in particular, Chazan, "L'Idée d'Empire dans le *Memoriale historiarum* de Jean de Saint-Victor". – For John of Saint-Victor, cf. especially Isabelle Guyot-Bachy, *Le 'Memoriale historiarum' de Jean de Saint-Victor: un historien et sa communauté au début du XIVe siècle* (Turnhout, 2000); for his vision of universal history (and the role of the Empire therein), cf. especially John of Saint-Victor, *Traité de la division des royaumes, introduction à une histoire universelle*, eds. Isabelle Guyot Bachy/Dominique Poirel (Turnhout, 2002).

23   Cf. the carefully balanced conclusion of Jones, *Eclipse of Empire?*, 353–362, especially 362: "The eclipse of Empire in the late-thirteenth and early-fourteenth centuries is indeed a reality, but one largely restricted to the minds of modern historians. The inhabitants of France could conceive of a world in which the emperor no longer exercised universal temporal jurisdiction and the Roman Empire was no longer an institution associated with universal government. Indeed, they had conceived of such a world long before Aristotle's

approach is not wrong in itself: The question of how historiographical 'genres' are influenced or even transformed by authorial constructions of identity and alterity is certainly a pertinent one – and one that must be asked. What is to be criticised, however, is that Chazan does not put the question the other way around – that she never asks how the tradition of universal chronicles has influenced the French perception of the Empire. What can we learn if we adopt this inverted perspective – what then is the impact of genre traditions on identities and alterities?

2.2 The French Perception of the Empire – A Historiographical By-Product?

If we compare French and German chronicles, we observe that a great portion of news about the respective neighbor appears in the context of imperial (or: emperors') history.[24] As far as German chronicles are concerned, this is not astonishing: France or the French are mentioned because the German ruler meets the French king, sends ambassadors to the pope who has fled to France and so on. With regard to French chronicles, this same observation is somewhat more astonishing: A good deal of French chroniclers' news on the Empire is presented without any link whatsoever to French history. In the *Grandes Chroniques de France*, for instance, we find a number of passages which relate events that have occurred in the Empire and which are explicitly marked as "incidences" – as news that is important but does not belong to the main subject of the chronicle, which is the history of the French kings.[25]

Politics was read in the schools. Yet a form of universal temporal authority associated with the Roman emperor remained fundamental to the existence of a properly ordered Christian society. [...] As a consequence of the long vacancy that took place after the death of Frederick II it was certainly possible to imagine the world without an emperor, but such a world was, from a French perspective, hardly the best of all possible worlds."; Jones, ibid., and 238–257, even highlights the fact that Jean Quidort of Paris – who has long been considered a milestone of political thinking on the disappearance of Universal Empire – keeps a notion of necessary universal temporal authority linked to the Roman emperor; on this topic, cf. also ibid., "Diener zweier Herren? Jean Quidort und das Problem der königlichen Autorität," *Jahrbuch für Universitätsgeschichte* 19 (2016), 153–187.

24 Cf. Jostkleigrewe, *Bild des Anderen*, 63–84, with a detailed survey of the quantitative structures which mark the perception of the 'national' other in Francophone and Germanophone chronicles.

25 Cf. Jostkleigrewe, *Bild des Anderen*, 80 sq., on the importance of the 'universal history' context for the perception of the Empire in French chronicles such as the *Grandes Chroniques de France*; my findings are in patent opposition to opinions such as those presented by Albert Gier, s. v., "Institutionen und Legitimität im Spätmittelalter," in *Grundriß der Romanischen Literaturen des Mittelalters*, ed. Jean Frappier, vol. 11/1 (Heidelberg, 1987), 835–868, at 843: "Der Blick des Autors [der *Grandes Chroniques de France*] richtet sich

I would link this observation to the importance of universal chronicles in France. Because universal chronicles with their focus on the Empire form a relevant part of French historiographical writing, imperial history forms an equally relevant part in French historical thought – and this tendency influences even those works that originally focus on French (and not on universal) history. In other words: If French chronicles show a definite interest in imperial history, this is not because the French themselves are specifically interested in the Empire (they are rather not, I would say); it is the effect of a specific historiographical constellation.

Moreover, this constellation may be one of the reasons why we sometimes find astonishingly 'ghibelline' remarks in French chronicles. One example concerns the conflict between Manfred of Sicily and Charles of Anjou – the latter being the brother of the French king and ally of the popes and the one who chases the Hohenstaufen out of Sicily. In his account of Charles' wars in Italy, the French chronicler William of Nangis comments on the enmity between the citizens of Milan (who supported actually Charles!) and the Hohenstaufen – and yet the Milanese hatred is explicitly qualified as unjust, as *iniquum odium*. A later French translation even uses the wording of *tres felonesse haine* – of most treasonous hate.[26]

It is noticeable that this 'ghibelline' perception of imperial history had an impact on French authors outside the historiographical arena. One striking example is the lawbook of Philip of Beaumanoir. Philip was a royal bailiff and composed a famous compendium of the customary laws of his French homeland, *Clermont-en-Beauvaisis*. In this work, he refers to the story of the conflicts between the Hohenstaufen and the Lombard league – which he observes from an imperial point of view! The insurrection of Milan along with its Lombard allies is a treacherous act against the emperor, their lawful overlord. Philip

---

ausschließlich auf die Geschichte Frankreichs; und er verfolgt in erster Linie den Weg seiner Könige; Ereignisse in anderen Ländern werden nur erwähnt, wenn sie in irgendeiner Hinsicht für die französische Geschichte bedeutsam sind."

26 Cf. Guillaume de Nangis, *Vita Ludovici IX.*, MGH ss 26, 646: "Electus ad regnum Sicilie Karolus [...] misit Philippum de Monte-forti [...] cum sufficienti numero armatorum, ut viam Romipedearum, quam idem Poilevoisinus [sc. Alberto Pallavicini] obstruxerat, expediret et eum cum suis urbibus expugnaret. Qui cum adiutorio [...] marchisii de Monte-ferrato, et civium Mediolanensium, qui partem ecclesie fovebant et omne genus antiqui Federici, eo quod eos olim destruxerat et tres magos Colonie abstulerat, iniquo odio persequebantur, eos viriliter debellavit et negocium (....) cum adiutorio Dei satis laudabiliter expedivit." Cf. ibid. the 14th century French translation of Primat's lost chronicle used by Guillaume de Nangis: "[...] ceulz de la cite de Melen – qui soustenoient la part de l'eglise, et avoient en tres felonnesse haïne tout le lignage de l'anciën Federic, pour ce qu'il les avoit destruiz et oste leur les trois roys de Couloigne [...]".

then uses the story to explain why lords of every rank should severely punish those who foment treason.[27]

The traditional interest in imperial history may furthermore explain why most French historiographers observe the contemporary empire with not at all unfriendly eyes. At the very moment when John of Saint-Victor reflects on the disappearance of the Empire, another Parisian chronicler begs God to help Henry of Luxemburg in restoring imperial order:

> God help him (…) [and] guide him in a way that ensures the well-being of the Church, and support him in his wars so that peace may reign on earth.[28]

---

27 Cf. Philip of Beaumanoir, *Coûtumes de Beauvaisis*, ed. Amédée Salmon, 2 vol. (Paris, 1899/1900), here vol. 1, 448–50, §§ 885–6: "Une autre maniere d'aliances ont esté fetes mout de fois par lesqueles maintes viles ont esté destruites et maint seigneur honi et desherité, si comme quant li communs d'aucune vile ou de pluseurs viles font aliances contre leur seigneur en aus tenant a force contre li […]. [§ 886] Pour donner essample as seigneurs qu'il se prengnent pres de punir et de vengier teus aliances […], je vous conterai que il en avint en Lombardie. – Il fu que toutes les bonnes viles et li chastel de Lombardie furent a l'empereeur de Rome en son demaine ou tenues de lui, et avoit ses baillis, ses prevos et ses serjans par toutes les viles qui justiçoient et gardoient les drois l'empereeur, et avoient esté par devant tuit li Lombart mout obeïssant a l'empereeur comme a leur seigneur. Or avint qu'en l'une des bonnes viles avoit .III. riches Lombars a qui li baillis n'avoit pas fet leur volentés, ains avoit fet pendre un leur parent pour sa deserte par droit de justice. Li Lombart en furent meu par mauvese cause et pourchacierent malicieusement un homme soutil, malicieus et bien parlant. Cil […] ala par toutes les bonnes viles de Lombardie ; et, quant il venoit en une vile, il enqueroit .x. ou .xii. des plus fors de lignage et d'avoir et puis parloit a chascun a par soi, et leur disoit que les autres bonnes viles s'estoient acordees priveement qu'eles ne vouloient plus estre en obeïssance de seigneur et que la vile qui ne s'i acorderoit seroit destruite par les autres bonnes viles, et seroit chascune bonne vile dame de soi sans tenir d'autrui. Tant fist et tant pourchaça cil messages […] que […] en un seul jour et en une eure toutes les viles de Lombardie coururent sus a ceus qui estoient a l'empereeur et les pristrent comme ceus qui ne s'en donnoient garde. Et quant il les eurent pris, il leur couperent les testes a tous et puis establirent en leur viles teus lois et teus coustumes comme il leur pleut, ne onques puis ne trouverent empereeur qui cel fet venjast ne adreçast. Et par ce poués vous entendre que c'est grans perius a tous seigneurs de soufrir teus aliances entre ses sougiès, ains doivent tous jours courre au devant si tost comme il s'en pueent apercevoir et fere venjance selonc le mesfet si comme j'ai dit dessus".

28 Cf. *Chronique métrique attribué à Geffroy de Paris*, ed. Armand Diverrès (Strasbourg, 1956), v. 3683–3706: "En cele annee ainsi avint/Que l'apostoille Clyment Quint/Fist et crea empereeur/D'un riche et noble poingneeur/Qui conte de Lucebourc fu/Et roy d'Alemaingne refu/[…]/Et por le droit de son empire/mist soi et son cors a martire;/Et combien qu'assez i ait mis/Et perdu de ses chiers amis,/Touzjors persevere et guerroie./Dex l'aïde! si ne s'esmoie./Or le tiengne Diex en tel guise/Que le meillor en ait l'Yglise,/Et ainssi

Some years later, the author of the so-called *Manuel d'histoire de Philippe de Valois* mourns Henry's untimely death, for this emperor, "if he had lived, would have restored the cause of the Empire."[29]

A brief comment on these last quotations: I do not pretend that their authors are specifically interested in drawing a positive image of the Empire and the emperors. They refer to imperial history, because imperial history forms an integral element of their own historiographical tradition. If they seem to comment in a friendly way on the Empire, this is less because they are imbued with 'ghibelline' feelings, but because they are presenting it 'the normal way' – they accept the empire as they would accept any kind of legitimate rule unless it were to transgress its traditional limits and boundaries.

2.3   Frenchman or German – Charlemagne as an Indicator of National Consciousness?

Before concluding, I would briefly present a last example which once again highlights the issues that are at stake when we underestimate the impact of historiographical and literary traditions on the perception of the French or German 'other'. The example concerns how nationality was ascribed to Charlemagne by the Latin and vernacular writers from medieval Germany.

As is well known, Charlemagne is claimed as a German in some Latin texts from the 12th century onwards. In German vernacular texts, however, the Frankish emperor is considered a Frenchman until the end of the 14th century. Rüdiger Schnell, philologist and professor for Medieval German Literature, has interpreted these findings as a "discrepancy between Latin partisanship and vernacular indifference" which forces us to assume that the development of national consciousness was delayed among the vernacular authors who were less well educated than the 'Latin' intellectuals.[30]

---

maintenir sa guerre/Que pais en puist venir en terre". – On Geffroi de Paris, cf. also Jones, *Eclipse of Empire*, especially 361.

29   *Manuel d'histoire de Philippe de Valois*, ed. Gaston Raynaud/Henri Lemaître, Le Roman de Renart le Contrefait 1 (Paris, 1914 repr. Geneva, 1975), 293: "En celle année, morut le glorïeux empereur Henry, la mort du quel fut moult plainte par toute crestïenté; car on tenoit que s'il eült vescu son droit eage, il eust ramené la chose de l'Empire en bon estat."; – The *Manuel d'histoire* – a universal chronicle in French prose based on Bernard Gui's work – is not fully edited; most of it has been inserted in Renart le Contrefait and edited with this work.

30   Cf. Schnell, "Deutsche Literatur und deutsches Nationsbewußtsein," 317: "Die [...] deutlich sichtbare Diskrepanz zwischen lateinischer engagierter Parteinahme und volkssprachlicher Gleichgültigkeit zwingt zur Annahme von thematisch unterschiedlichen Kristallisationszentren des Nationsbewußtseins bei verschiedenen Bevölkerungsgruppen

In view of such opinions, I would maintain to the contrary that the 'French' Charlemagne we encounter in germanophone texts has little to do with the question of national consciousness. It is just another example of the influence of 'genre' traditions. In fact, the presentation of Carolingian history in German vernacular texts relies to some extent on translations of Old French 'Chansons de geste' – and in these French epics, Charlemagne is presented as a Frenchman. The fact that some 15th century vernacular authors break with this tradition and begin to claim Charlemagne as a German may be interpreted as an indicator for the intensification of national ideologies. On the other hand, the mere fact that their predecessors stick to the tradition should not imprudently be understood as evidence for anything whatever – except for the fact that these authors stick to the tradition.[31]

3   Conclusion

The conscious construction of 'national' otherness – i.e., the development of a coherent vision of 'national' otherness in its relationship to one's own identity-group – is indeed a phenomenon we observe in our sources; in the first part of this contribution, I have presented two relevant examples. Yet, the conscious construction of otherness is only one factor which influences the historiographical perception of foreign groups and peoples in the Middle Ages. In the Franco-German case, many traits which mark the image of the respective neighbour have emerged in an unintentional way; they represent not uncommonly a by-product of literary or historiographical traditions.

Historical research has mostly concentrated on those conscious and coherent constructions which fit into greater systems: Scholars have focused on those authors, for instance, who adhere to the *rex imperator*-theory and perceive a fundamental rivalry between France and the Empire – but not attended to those texts which present the Empire as a rather normal and inoffensive political entity. Research has focused on those exceptional authors who claim Charlemagne as a German – but not on those texts which portray the undoubted founding father of the Romano-German Empire as also a noble Frenchman.

The problem is that the exceptional (and more interesting) constructions which postulate a systematic rivalry between the French and German

---

und zur Annahme von soziologisch-bildungsmäßig bedingten Phasenverschiebungen in der Entwicklung des Nationsbewußtseins innerhalb einer und derselben Nation."

31   Cf. on this topic my doctoral thesis: Jostkleigrewe, *Bild des Anderen*, especially 157–170.

neighbors probably had a much smaller impact on medieval perceptions than the unsystematic and inconspicuous presentations which have been discussed in the second part of this contribution. We must therefore be cautious and should endeavor not to confuse the priorities of medievalist research on the one hand, and the characteristics of the mutual perception of medieval French and Germans on the other. It could be that our vision of the complex interplay between medieval identities and alterities is at least partly created by the specific presuppositions on identities and alterities which mark modern research – and modern research only.

CHAPTER 4

England – No Interest? How Anglo-Norman and Angevin Historians Perceived the Empire in the Twelfth Century

Isabelle Chwalka

1 Introduction

When analyzing Anglo-Norman and Angevin chronicles and annals from the 12th and early 13th centuries with regard to their comments about the Holy Roman Empire, it is possible to find abundant narrations about the German investiture controversy and the influence of the Empire on the Alexandrine Schism. Yet while Anglo-Norman and Angevin historians were well informed about developments in the Empire through many sources and they showed a critical perception of the Empire, it is astonishing that the headline ultimately reads "No interest?". Given this ostensible contradiction this article will reconsider the motives as to why Anglo-Norman and Angevin historians wrote about these events and will consider their *causae scribendi*. It will show that the Holy Roman Empire was hardly important at all for English historians and any interest they had was caused by the implications the Empire had for the church and the popes.

Pursuing an interest in perceptions and concepts about 'others' in the 12th century, it is possible to find abundant narrations about these in Anglo-Norman/Angevin and German historiography.[1] Analyzing 28 Anglo-Norman/Angevin chronicles and annals from 22 different authors from the 12th century, it is

---

1   This paper originated from my (soon to be published) Ph.D.-Thesis "Fremd- und Selbstwahrnehmung in der deutschen und anglonormannisch-angevinischen Historiographie des 12. Jahrhunderts", supervised by Prof. Dr. Ludger Körntgen, Johannes Gutenberg University Mainz, submitted in August 2018. The doctoral work was focused on comparatively analyzing the view of Anglo-Norman / Angevin historians towards the Reich and the view of German authors towards 12th century England. It examined the influence of political, social and cultural constellations on the historians, their view(s) about 'others' and the interdependency between conceptions and perceptions. The results of this present paper are based on the research for the chapters "4.1 Die Wahrnehmung des Romzugs Heinrichs V im Rahmen des Investiturstreits" and " 4.2 Die Wahrnehmung des Alexandrinischen Schismas im Angevinischen Reich".

possible to determine text passages about the Reich in 27 of them.[2] In just two of them there is only one entry about 12th century Germany, in 13 of them there are two to nine text passages, and in 12 chronicles there are more than 10 entries.[3] For comparison – in 36 analyzed chronicles and annals from

---

2   The only one of the 28 analysed sources without any such passages is the *Gesta Stephani regis Anglorum et ducis Normannorum*, ed. Kenneth R. Potter (London, 1955).

3   **One entry:** Richard of Hexham, *De gestis regis Stephani et de bello Standardii*, ed. Richard Howlett, Richard, Prior of Hexham (AD 1135 to AD 1139), *Chronicle, Chronicles of the Reigns of Stephen, Henry II., and Richard I.*, Rolls Series 82,3 (London, 1886, repr. 1964); *Annales Plymptonienses*, ed. Felix Liebermann, Ungedruckte Anglo-Normanische Geschichtsquellen (Strasbourg, 1879), 25–30; **Two to nine entries:** Eadmer of Canterbury, *Historia novorum*, ed. Martin Rule, Eadmeri Historia novorum in Anglia, et opuscula duo de vita Sancto Anselmi et quibusdam miraculis eius (London, 1884, repr. 1965); *Coventry Chronicle*, ed. Paul Antony Hayward, Medieval and Rennaissance Texts and Studies 373 (Tempe, 2010); William of Malmesbury, *Gesta Regum Anglorum*, ed. Roger A.B. Mynors, *Gesta Regum Anglorum. The History of the English Kings* (Oxford, 1998–1999); William of Malmesbury, *Historia Novella*, ed. Edmund King and Kenneth R. Potter, *Historia Novella. The Contemporary History* (Oxford, 1998); Henry of Huntingdon, *Historia Anglorum*, ed. Diana Greenway, *Henry, Archdeacon of Huntingdon, Historia Anglorum. The History of the English People* (Oxford, 1996); Robert of Torigni, *Gesta Normannorum Ducum*, ed. Elisabeth van Houts, *The Gesta Normannorum Ducum of William of Jumièges, Orderic Vitalis and Robert of Torigni* (Oxford, 1992/1995); Gervase of Canterbury, *Gesta regum Britanniae*, ed. William Stubbs, *The Historical Works of Gervase of Canterbury*, Rolls Series 73 (London, 1879, repr. 1965); Ralph de Diceto, *Abbrevationes chronicorum*, ed. William Stubbs, *Radulfi de Diceto decani Lundoniensis opera historica. The historical works of master Ralph de Diceto, dean of London*, Rolls Series 68 (London, 1876, repr. 1965); Richard of Devizes, *Cronicon de tempore regis Richardi primi*, ed. John T. Appleby, *The Chronicle of Richard of Devizes of the Time of King Richard the First* (London, 1963); Ralph Niger, *Chroncia Anglica (Chronica II)*, ed. Robert Anstruther, *Radulfi Nigri Chronica. The Chronicles of Ralph Niger. Publications of the Caxton Society* (London, 1851, repr. 1967). **More than ten entries:** John of Worcester, *Chronicon ex chronicis*, ed. Reginal R. Darlington and Patrick McGurk (Oxford, 2004–2007); *Winchcombe Chronicle*, ed. Paul Antony Hayward, Medieval and Rennaissance Texts and Studies 373 (Tempe, 2010); Symeon of Durham, *Historia regum*, ed. Thomas Arnold, *Symeonis Monachi Opera Omnia*, Rolls Series 75 (London, 1882–1885, repr. 1965); Orderic Vitalis, *Historia ecclesiastica*, ed. Elisabeth van Houts, *The Gesta Normannorum Ducum of William of Jumièges, Orderic Vitalis and Robert of Torigni* (Oxford, 1992/1995); Robert of Torigni, *Chronicle*, ed. Richard Howlett, *Chronicles of the Reigns of Stephen, Henry II., and Richard I.*, Rolls Series 82/4 (London, 1890, repr. 1964); Roger of Howden, *Gesta regis Henrici secundi Benedicti abbatis*, ed. William Stubbs, Rolls Series 49 (London, 1867); Roger of Howden, *Chronica*, ed. William Stubbs, *Chronica magistri Rogeri de Hovedene*, Rolls Series 51 (London, 1868–1871); Gervase of Canterbury, *Chronica*, ed. William Stubbs, *The Historical Works of Gervase of Canterbury*, Rolls Series 73 (London, 1879, repr. 1965); Walter Map, *De nugis curialium*, ed. Montague R. James (Oxford, 1983); *Annales Lewenses*, ed. Felix Liebermann, "The Annals of Lewes Priory," *The English Historical Review* 17 (1902), 83–89; *Annals of St. Osyth's*, ed. Henry R. Luard, *Annales Monastici 4. Annales Monasterii de Oseneia* (AD 1016–1347), *Chronicon vulgo dictum Chronicon Thomae Wykes* (AD 1066–1289), *Annales Prioratus de Wigornia* (AD 1–1377), Rolls Series 36 (London, 1869, repr. 1965); Ralph de Diceto,

within the Empire itself, ten of them do not mention England at all, and in eight of them there is only one entry, and two to nine text passages are found in 15 chronicles and annals. More than ten text passages are to be found only in two of them.[4] This broad statistical analysis is the basis for the quantitative

---

Ymagines historiarum, ed. William Stubbs, *Radulfi de Diceto decani Lundoniensis opera historica. The historical works of master Ralph de Diceto, dean of London*, Rolls Series 68 (London, 1876, repr. 1965); William of Newburgh, *Historia rerum Anglicarum*, ed. Richard Howlett, *Chronicles of the Reigns of Stephen, Henry II., and Richard I.*, Rolls Series 82,1–2/4 (London, 1884–1885); Ralph Niger, *Chronica Universalis (Chronica I)*, ed. Hanna Kraue, Radulfus Niger, Chronica. Eine englische Weltchronik des 12. Jahrhunderts, Europäische Hochschulschriften. Reihe III: Geschichte und ihre Hilfswissenschaften 265 (Frankfurt a. M. 1985); Ralph de Coggeshall, *Chronicon Anglicanum*, ed. Joseph Stevenson, *Radulphi de Coggeshall Chronicon Anglicanum*, Rolls Series 66 (London, 1875, repr. 1965).

4   **Those without entries:** Isingrim of Ottobeuren, *Annales Isingrimi*, ed. Ludwig Weiland, MGH SS 17 (Hannover, 1861), 312–315; *Annales Herbipolenses minores*, ed. Georg Waitz, MGH SS 24 (Hannover, 1879), 828–829; *Annales Babenbergenses*, ed. Georg H. Pertz, MGH SS 10 (Hannover, 1852), 4; *Annales Ratisponenses*, ed. Wilhelm Wattenbach, MGH SS 17 (Hannover, 1861), 579–588; *Annales Ensdorfenses*, ed. Georg H. Pertz, MGH SS 10 (Hannover, 1852), 4–8; *Annales Scheftlarienses maiores*, ed. Philipp Jaffé, MGH SS 17 (Hannover, 1861), 335–343; *Historia Welforum Weingartensis*, ed. Ludwig Weiland, MGH SS 21 (Hannover, 1869), 454–472; *Annales S. Petri Erphesfurtenses breves*, ed. Oswald Holder-Egger, Monumenta Erphesfurtensia saec. XII. XIII. XIV., MGH SSrG. 42 (Hannover, 1899), 46–48; *Annales S. Petri Erphesfurtenses maiores*, ed. Oswald Holder-Egger, *Monumenta Erphesfurtensia saec. XII. XIII. XIV.*, MGH SSrG. 42 (Hannover, 1899), 49–67; *Annales Brunwilarenses*, ed. Georg H. Pertz, MGH SS 16 (Hannover, 1859), 724–728; *Annales Rosenveldenses*, ed. Georg H. Pertz, MGH SS 16 (Hannover, 1859), 99–104. **One entry:** *Annales Herbipolenses*, ed. Georg H. Pertz, MGH SS 16 (Hannover, 1859), 1–12; *Die sogenannte Anonyme Kaiserchronik. Nach Vorarbeiten von Irene Schmale-Ott (†) und Franz-Josef Schmale (†)*, ed. Martina Hartmann and Ioanna Georgiou, MGH SS 33,2 (Digital edition in advance, 2016); *Annales Mellicenses*, ed. Wilhelm Wattenbach, MGH SS 9 (Hannover, 1851), 484–536; *Annales Aquenses*, ed. Georg Waitz, MGH SS 24 (Hannover, 1879), 34–39; *Annales Palidenses (Auctore Theodoro Monacho)*, ed. Georg H. Pertz, MGH SS 16 (Hannover, 1859), 48–96; *Annales Magdeburgenses* ed. Georg H. Pertz, MGH SS 16 (Hannover, 1859), 107–196; *Annales S. Petri Erphesfurdenses antiqui a. 1038–1163*, ed. Oswald Holder-Egger, Monumenta Erphesfurtensia saec. XII. XIII. XIV., MGH SSrG. 42 (Hannover, 1899), 3–20; *Annales Erphesfurdenses Lothariani*, ed. Oswald Holder-Egger, Monumenta Erphesfurtensia saec. XII. XIII. XIV., MGH SSrG. 42 (Hannover, 1899), 34–44. **Two to nine entries:** *Annales S. Disibodi*, ed. Georg Waitz, MGH SS 17 (Hannover, 1861), 6–30; *Annales Marbacenses qui dicuntur*, ed. Hermann Bloch, MGH SSrG. 9 (Hannover, 1907), 1–103; Burchard of Ursberg, *Chronicon*, ed. Oswald Holder-Egger / Bernhard von Simson, *Die Chronik des Propstes Burchard von Ursberg (Burchardi praepositi Urspergensis Chronicon)*, MGH SSrG. 16 (Hannover, 1916); Otto of St Blasien, *Chronica*, Franz-Josef Schmale, *Die Chronik Ottos von St. Blasien und die Marbacher Annalen*, FSGA 18a (Darmstadt, 1998); Ekkehard of Aura, *Chronicon universale*, ed. Georg Waitz, Ekkehardi Uraugiensis Chronica, MGH SS 6 (Hannover, 1844), 1–267; Otto of Freising, *Chronica sive Historia de duabus civitatibus*, ed. Adolf Hofmeister, *Ottonis Episcopi Frisigensis Chronica sive Historia de duabus civitatibus*, MGH SSrG. 45 (Hannover, 1912); *Annales Reicherspergenses*, ed. Wilhelm Wattenbach, *Magni Presbyteri Annales*

estimation and comparison of reciprocal perceptions in sources for assessing the significance of the remarks. With this statistical approach it is possible to combine the views of others in the sources and to ascertain characteristic patterns for distinguishing a collective awareness and a common reception of writers and their recipients. This approach is influenced by Hans-Werner Goetz, whose research about perceptions (*Wahrnehmung*) and conceptions (*Vorstellungen*) is well-rooted in the research about others.[5] Historiography is well suited for research about the perception of others, because historiographers do not only write facts, but interpret the past and reveal through this their own conceptions. The question of the function of the perceptions and descriptions of others is in the foreground, whereby influences on the authors' conceptions and the background to the writing, (e.g., political and historical occurrences or purchasers and audiences), should also be considered. "Self" and "Others" are relational categories, because one is defined through the other.

2   The Investiture Controversy

With the first statistical approach it can be determined that English 12th century historians focused especially on the occasion of the so-called Privilege from 1111, whereby Henry V captured Paschal II in St. Peter's and forced him

---

Reicherspergenses, MGH SS 17 (Hannover, 1861), 443–523; *Annales Admontenses, a. 1–1139*, ed. Wilhelm Wattenbach, *Annales Admuntenses*, MGH SS 9 (Hannover, 1851), 570–579; *Annales Admontenses, a. 1140–1250*, ed. Wilhelm Wattenbach, *Continuatio Admuntensis*, MGH SS 9 (Hannover, 1851), 580–593; *Annales Garstenses*, ed. Wilhelm Wattenbach, *Continuatio Garstensis*, MGH SS 9 (Hannover, 1851), 594–600; *Annales Pegavienses*, ed. Georg H. Pertz, MGH SS 16 (Hannover, 1859), 234–270; *Annales Hildesheimenses*, ed. Georg Waitz, MGH SSrG. 8 (Hannover, 1878); *Annalista Saxo Chronicle*, ed. Klaus Nass, MGH SS 37 (Hannover, 2006); *Annales Patherbrunnenses*, ed. Paul Scheffer-Boichorst, *Annales Patherbrunnenses. Eine verlorene Quellenschrift des 12. Jahrhunderts aus Bruchstücken wiederhergestellt* (Innsbruck, 1870); Helmold of Bosau, *Chronica Slavorum*, ed. Bernhard Schmeidler, MGH SSrG. 32 (Hannover, 1937); *Arnoldi Chronica Slavorum*, ed. Johann M. Lappenberg, MGH SSrG. 14 (Hannover, 1868); *Chronicon Stederburgense*, ed. Georg H. Pertz, MGH SS 16 (Hannover, 1859), 197–231. More than ten entries: Otto of Freising and Rahewin, *Gesta Friderici I. imperatoris*, ed. Georg Waitz and Bernhard von Simson, *Ottonis et Rahewini Gesta Friderici I. imperatoris*, MGH SSrG. 46 (Hannover, 1912); *Chronica regia Coloniensis*, ed. Georg Waitz, MGH SS 24 (Hannover, 1879), 1–20.

5 Hans-Werner Goetz, *Geschichtsschreibung und Geschichtsbewusstsein im hohen Mittelalter*, Orbis medievalis 1, 2nd ed. (Berlin, 2008), 415.

to warrant an investiture privilege.⁶ These events are reported in 13 of the English chronicles. That almost half of the analyzed chronicles report these events, reveals a strong interest of 12th century historians in this occasion.⁷ For comparison – Henry IV's quarrels with Gregory VII are reported in only five of the sources, the aftermaths of 1111 up to the concordat of Worms are reported in even fewer.⁸ These numbers confirm Hanna Vollrath's thesis that the events of 1111 received more recognition than Canossa, because the investiture controversy had already lasted several decades, England had had its own investiture conflict, and the interactions that were inherent to it caused the connections among popes, kings, bishops and monasteries to become stronger.⁹

---

6   With his journey to Rome in 1110/11 Henry V intended to achieve not only his coronation and the pacification of Italy, but he wanted a solution for the investiture dispute. In 1111 the Empire had been in conflict with the papacy for over 30 years over the matter which is called today (simplifyingly) the investiture controversy. While England and France had already solved the problem by 1111, there was still no solution for the Empire. On the occasion of the emperor's coronation a new effort was made. With the secret Treaty of Sutri – concluded between royal and papal representatives, but with no episcopal participation – a revolutionary attempt was made. Henry V would – from his coronation on – relinquish his participation in elections and investitures, whereas the bishops should renounce their prerogatives and finance themselves only through donations and the tenth. With the announcement of the treaty in St. Peter's right before the coronation, a huge uproar arose among the bishops and the aristocracy. Henry V seized Paschalis II and some of the cardinals. After several weeks of being held, the pope conferred on Henry the right to investiture by ring and staff. This privilege soon came to be called "Pravileg" and in 1112 was condemned as having been forced upon the pope and therefore wrong by a synod. For introductory literature, see Bernd Schneidmüller, "1111 – Das Kaisertum Heinrichs V. als europäisches Ereignis," *Die Salier. Macht im Wandel. Begleitband zur Ausstellung im Historischen Museum der Pfalz Speyer* 1, ed. Laura Heeg (Speyer, 2011), 36–45 and Carlo Servatius, "Paschalis II. (1099–1118). Studien zu seiner Person und seiner Politik," *Päpste und Papsttum* 14 (Stuttgart, 1979). The precise background for the papal proposal is still open. Both Servatius, *Paschalis II.*, 223–233 and Stanley Chodorow, "Paschal II, Henry V, and the Origins of the Crisis of 1111," *Popes, Teachers, and Canon Law in the Middle Ages*, ed. James R. Sweeney/ Stanley Chodorow (London, 1989), 3–25, at 4, presume that these ideas developed through the ideals of church reform of the past decades.
7   John of Worcester, *Chronicon ex chronicis*, 118–124; *Winchcombe Chronicle*, 516; *Coventry Chronicle*, 668; William of Malmesbury, *Gesta regum Anglorum* V.420–V.426, 762–771; Symeon of Durham, *Historia regum*, 242–247; Orderic Vitalis, *Historia ecclesiastica* X.1, 196–198 and XI.41, 172; Henry of Huntingdon, *Historia Anglorum* VIII.175, 554; Robert of Torigni, *Chronicle*, 92–93; Roger of Howden, *Chronica*, 167; *Annales Lewenses*, 87; Ralph de Diceto, *Abbreviationes chronicorum*, 239; Ralph Niger, *Chronicle* IV.1, 262–264; Ralph Niger, *Chronica Anglica*, 165.
8   John of Worcester, *Chronicon ex chronicis*, 18, 20, 22, 26, 28, 30, 36, 38, 40, 42, 62; Symeon of Durham, *Historia regum*, 200, 206–207, 211, 212, 219; Roger of Howden, *Chronica*, 128, 132, 136, 139, 144; Orderic Vitalis, *Historia ecclesiastica* X.1, 196; William of Malmesbury, *Gesta regum Anglorum* III.262, 484–III.266, 492 and III.288, 520–III.290, 524.
9   Hanna Vollrath, "Sutri 1046 – Canossa 1077 – Rome 1111. Problems of Communication and the Perception of Neighbors," *European Transformations. The long Twelfth Century*, ed.

In these 13 sources there is no standard account of the events of 1111.[10] In six of them there is only a short entry for 1111.[11] The *Annales Lewenses* and Henry of Huntingdon's chronicle narrate only the capture of the pope by Henry V, while the Winchcombe and Conventry chronicles as well as Roger of Howden add that peace was made. Only with Ralph de Diceto does one learn something about the background of the capture with a hint of an investiture privilege. Reducing the story to be about the capture shows that there did not exist an interest to the investiture controversy – an interest which should have been developed in the 12th century according to Hanna Vollrath – but rather an interest in the capture of a pope by an emperor – reducing the event to a spectacular scandal. It should be noted that the wording, except in the *Annales Lewenses*, is very similar. These five chronicles and annals use for their source the description in John of Worcester's *Chronicon*, or, like Roger of Howden, from Symeon of Durham's chronicle. But Symeon of Durham used John of Worcester's *Chronicon* for his chronicle. The other letters and resolutions

Thomas F.X. Noble/ John van Engen, Notre Dame Conferences in Medieval Studies (Notre Dame, IN, 2012), 132–170, at 151, 156, 158.

10   John of Worcester, *Chronicon ex chronicis*, 118–124; *Winchcombe Chronicle*, 516; *Coventry Chronicle*, 668; William of Malmesbury, *Gesta regum Anglorum* v.420–v.426, 762–771; Symeon of Durham, *Historia regum*, 242–247; Orderic Vitalis, *Historia ecclesiastica* x.1, 196–198 and xi.41, 172; Henry of Huntingdon, *Historia Anglorum* viii.175, 554; Robert of Torigni, *Chronicle*, 92–93; Roger of Howden, *Chronica*, 167; *Annales Lewenses*, 87; Ralph de Diceto, *Abbrevationes chronicorum*, 239; Ralph Niger, *Chronicle* iv.1, 262–264; Ralph Niger, *Chronica Anglica*, 165.

11   *Winchcombe Chronicle*, at 1111, 516: "Henricus imperator Romam uenit, Paschalem papam cepit et in custodiam posuit. Sed postea ad pontem uie Salarie ubi Paschalem festiuitatem celebraverunt pacem cum eo fecit"; Coventry Chronicle, at 1111, 668: "Henricus imperator Romam uenit, Paschalem papam cepit et in custodiam posuit. Sed postea ad pontem uie Salarie ubi Paschalem festiuitatem celebraverunt pacem cum eo fecit"; Henry of Huntingdon, *Historia Anglorum* viii.175, 554: "Henricus filius Henrici longeui, gener scilicet tuus, rex inuictissime, cui hec scribuntur, regnauit annis decem. Hic cum filiam tuam, cum pecunia incomparabili, duxisset, Romam peciit, et ui factus est imperator. Sed quomodo ceperit papam Paschalem dicere non attinet"; Roger of Howden, *Chronica*, at 1111, 167: "Henricus rex Teutonicorum Romam venit, Paschalem papam cepit, et in custodiam posuit, sed postmodum ad pontem, Via Salaria, ubi Paschalem festivitatem in campo celebraverunt, pacem cum eo fecit"; *Annales Lewenses*, at 1111, 87: "Paschalis papa Rome captus est ab Henrico imperatore"; Ralph de Diceto, *Abbrevationes chronicorum*, at 1111, 239: "Henricus rex Teutonicus Romam venit, Paschalem papam in custodiam posuit, sed postmodum ad pontem Viae Salariae, ubi paschalem festivitatem in campo celebraverunt, pacem cum eo fecit. Papa vero post lectum evangelium tradidit ei in oculis omnium principum privilegium de investitura episcopatuum, vel abbatiarum, tam per anulum quam per virgam, scilicet ut regni ejus episcopis vel abbatibus libere electis investituram conferat annuli et virgae, postea vero consecrentur electi ab episcopis ad quos pertinuerint."

inserted in John's and Symeon's chronicles were not copied. These six chronicles were not cursorily reported due to a lack of information, but rather they reduced the events to a focus on the scandal – the capture of a pope. There was no intense interest in the investiture conflict. The six chronicles and annals belonged to a second generation which dealt with 1111 and the investiture conflict, so there was a longer time lag. As a result of this distance to 1111, and as well to the own English investiture conflict, this particular conflict was apparently less noteworthy. The reduction to the capture shows that there did not exist an interest in the investiture controversy or privilege that was caused by their own or an English experience with the issue, but only an interest in the capture of a pope by an emperor.

These six annals and chronicles are in contrast to the first-generation historians, who were engaged in a detailed way with 1111, including both the ongoing conflict as well as the previous conflict between Henry IV and Gregory VII. John of Worcester, Symeon of Durham, William of Malmesbury and Orderic Vitalis wrote extensively about the events. To this end, they used for their narrations about the investiture conflict two sources directly or indirectly which were written in the Reich – Marianus Scotus' (Scottus) chronicle about the investiture conflict between Henry IV and Gregory VII and the description of Henry V's journey to Rome by David Scolasticus (Scotigena). But they did not just copy their sources but dealt intensively with them and had a critical view about their writings and opinions.

Marianus Scotus, a Benedictine monk from Ireland, who lived (after several sojourns in Cologne, Fulda and Würzburg) as a recluse in Mainz, wrote a chronicle, which was brought to England by Bishop Robert of Hereford.[12] William of Malmesbury, John of Worcester and Orderic Vitalis used his chronicle directly; Symeon of Durham did so indirectly by using John of Worcester's *Chronicon*.[13]

---

12   Martin Brett, "John of Worcester and his contemporaries," in *The Writing of History in the Middle Ages. Essays presented to Richard William Southern*, ed. Ralph H.C. Davis/ John M. Wallace Hadrill (Oxford, 1981), 101–126, at 110. There is not a standard and complete edition of Marianus Scotus' chronicle and its different recensions. The prevalent edition is *Mariani Scotti Chronicon*, ed. Georg Waitz, MGH SS 58 (Hannover, 1844), 495–562, especially 560–562.

13   William of Malmesbury and Orderic Vitalis refer to him in their texts. William of Malmesbury, *Gesta regum Anglorum* III.292, 524: "Sub isto imperatore regnante floruit Marinianus Scottus, qui primo Fuldensis monachus, post apud Mogontiacum inclusus, contemptu presentis uitae gratiam futurae demerebatur. [...]"; Orderic Vitalis, *Historia ecclesiastica* 2.III, 186–189: "Ioannes Wigornensis a puero monachus, natione Anglicus, moribus et eruditione uenerandus, in his quae Mariani Scotti cronicis adiecit, de rege Guillelmo et de rebus quæ sub eo uel sub filiis eius Guillelmo Rufo et Henrico usque hodie contigerunt honeste deprompsit. [...] Quem prosecutus Iohannes acta fere centum

In Marianus' chronicle there are several entries about not only Henry IV's conflict with Gregory VII, but also his conflict with Rudolf of Rheinfelden and the opposition of the German aristocracy. Marianus' attitude was not completely anti-Henry IV, which would be reasonable given his closeness to Siegfrid I, archbishop of Mainz, who crowned Rudolf of Rheinfelden and Hermann of Salm as anti-kings. But Gregory VII was the true and legitimate pope for him, even if most of the time he called him Hildebrand. Despite this background it is possible to understand his often-discussed entry about Canossa. Henry IV and Pope Gregory VII meet (*convenientes*), the emperor receives the lifting of the excommunication and the pope receives the apostolic seat from the emperor.[14] This description of the Road to Canossa was often described as negligible or digressive.[15] But due to Marianus' closeness to Archbishop Siegfried his sentence about Canossa should not be neglected; even more so it was his narration of the investiture controversy up to 1082 which became important for English historiography, especially for John of Worcester, Orderic Vitalis, William of Malmesbury, as well as for the other 12th century historians.

One historian who had the biggest influence on later historians in the 12th century was John of Worcester.[16] John used the Marianus chronicle extensively. In doing so, he copied not only the entries about the investiture controversy, but as well Henry's fight with the princes who opposed him. However, he adapted the Marianus chronicle to his needs, split the entries and re-arranged them. Therefore, it was possible for his readers to gain a good overview of German-related topics. Although he copied Marianus' entries quite meticulously, it became apparent – even if he did not explain the context – that he

---

annorum contexuit, iussuque uenerabilis Wlfstani pontificis et monachi supradictis cronicis inseruit in quibus multa de Romanis et Francis et Alemannis aliisque gentibus quae agnouit [...]". Orderic shows with this sentence that John of Worcester used Marianus' chronicle directly.

14 Marianus Scotus, *Chronicon*, to 1078, 561: "Heinricus ergo rex et Illibrandus papa convenientes mense Martio in Langobardia, rex a papa solutuionem banni, papa vero sedem apostolicam a rege accepit".

15 Very critical of Marianus' description are Rudolf Schieffer, "Worms, Rom und Canossa (1076/1077) in zeitgenössischer Wahrnehmung," *Historische Zeitschrift* 292 (2011), 593–612, at 605 and Harald Zimmermann, "Der Canossagang von 1077, Wirkungen und Wirklichkeit," *Akademie der Wissenschaften und der Literatur – Abhandlungen der Geistes- und Sozialwissenschaftlichen Klasse* 5 (1975), 135. Only Hanna Vollrath, "Lauter Gerüchte? Canossa aus kommunikationsgeschichtlicher Sicht, Päpstliche Herrschaft im Mittelalter. Funktionsweisen – Strategien – Darstellungsformen," in *Mittelalter-Forschungen* 38, ed. Stefan Weinfurter (Stuttgart, 2012), 151–198, at 190, refers to his closeness to archbishop Siegfrid I and suggests that Marianus' description should be read more closely.

16 Patrick McGurk, "Worcester, John of (fl. 1095–1140)," in *Oxford Dictionary of National Biography* vol. 60 (Oxford, 2004), 292–3.

regarded the goings-on under Henry IV in their entirety and reflected them precisely. Marianus Scotus had written in his entry about Canossa that there was a peaceful meeting with Henry IV and Gregory VII, while Henry received the lifting of the excommunication and Gregory received his seat. On the contrary, John changed this entry and commented on it. He shortened the second part of the sentence, referring to a mutual peace contract (*inuicem pacificantur*) and added *sed falso ut postea claruit*.[17] He considered Marianus' writings in their entirety and arrived at the conclusion that the sentence about Canossa was not wrong, but from a later point of view was misleading due to the ongoing conflict. John of Worcester perceived Canossa, even if he did not know the name of the place, as a peace between Henry IV and Gregory VII, but as a peace without value. Therefore, he did not want this to pass without comment.

Even more critical of the sources were the historians when considering David Scolasticus' (Scotigena) description of Henry V's journey to Rome. John of Worcester, William of Malmesbury and Orderic Vitalis used his now lost account for their information about 1111. William of Malmesbury refers to a David Scotigena, bishop of Bangor, in his *Gesta regum* about Henry V's journey to Rome.[18] David presumably was born in Ireland, became a master at the cathedral school of Würzburg, and came to Henry's attention, who then made him his chaplain.[19] At the emperor's command, David wrote a now lost account of the expedition. That John of Worcester used this account as well has been proven by Martin Brett and Rodney Thomson.[20] Orderic Vitalis does not mention David's name explicitly, but he did write that an *Irensis quidam scholasticus* wrote the account about the Italian expedition, though Orderic uses his source very freely.[21] John of Worcester reports – without narrating the background of the events or referring to Henry IV – that Henry V captured

---

17 John of Worcester, *Chronicon ex chronicis*, 30: "1100 Heinricus rex et Hiltibrandus papa conuenientes in mensa Martio in Longobardia, inuicem pacificantur, sed falso ut postea claruit".
18 William of Malmesbury, *Gesta regum Anglorum* III.420, 764: "Sed iter illud ad Romam magnis exercitationibus pectorum, magnis angoribus corporum consummatum Dauid Scottus Bancornensis episcopus exposuit, magis in regis gratiam quam historicum deceret acclinis".
19 Tilman Struve, "David Scholasticus," *Lexikon des Mittelalters* 3 (Stuttgart, 1986), 606–607.
20 Rodney Thomson, *William of Malmesbury* (Wolfeboro, 1986), 108; Brett, "John of Worcester and his contemporaries," 116–117. Vollrath, "Sutri 1046 – Canossa 1077 – Rome 1111," 158.
21 Orderic Vitalis, *Historia ecclesiastica* X.1, 198: "Quam grauis et periculosa hiemps pluuiis et niuibus glacieque tunc fuerit, et quanta discrimina in angustis et inaequalibus uiis et in transitu fluminum exercitus pertulerit, et qualiter imperator collectis uiribus urbem obsessam plus minis quam armis expugnauerit Irensis quidam scolasticus decenti relatione litteris tradidit."

Pope Paschal when he came to Rome, but that they had resolved the issue.[22] Henry vowed to release and provide security for the pope. In return Paschal promised Henry the right to invest the candidate with ring and staff prior to the episcopal ordination and that he would never excommunicate the emperor. In the end, John recounts that the peace was made at Easter and Henry was crowned as emperor.[23] Even though John compiled his source accurately, he does not follow David's narration blindly. William of Malmesbury criticized David's narration repeatedly for writing not as a historian but instead writing a panegyric.[24] John did not criticize David freely, but – because there is no hint of any panegyric for Henry V in his text – had to shorten David's text and praise. William even mocked David for comparing the capture of the pope with the biblical story of Jacob wrestling with an angel then insisting to be blessed.[25] Neither John nor Orderic Vitalis nor any other English historian repeated this image or any other praise for Henry V. Even if they worked with this German source and used the materials like the oaths and contracts from it, they did not follow it blindly, but chose what they adopted from it very carefully.

Despite their basis in good sources, their reflected handling of their sources and their lengthy entries about the investiture conflicts under Henry IV and Henry V, it is possible to say that the Holy Roman Empire was less important to English 12th century historians than the entries might at first sight cause one to presume. Though they provide descriptions of the actions of the emperors, their interest as historians was not in the figures of the emperor or because they were interested in the Holy Roman Empire, but because they were interested in the emperors' interactions with the popes. They take notice of Henry IV's quarrels with his sons, and they mention Henry V's wedding to Matilda, daughter of the English king Henry I. Especially with Henry V it is possible to find in some of the English chronicles lengthy entries about 1111 and the ongoing

---

22 John of Worcester, *Chronicon ex chronicis*, 118–124; several oaths and contracts were included.
23 John of Worcester, *Chronicon ex chronicis*, 118: "Heinricus rex Theutonicorum Romam uenit Pascalem papam cepit, et in custodiam posuit, sed postmodum ad pontem uie Salarie, ubi Pascalem festiuitatem in campo celebrauerunt, pacem cum eo fecit." This sentence was copied a lot by later historians.
24 William of Malmesbury, *Gesta regum Anglorum*, v.420, 762–64 and v.426, 770: "Sed iter illud ad Romam magnis exercitationibus pectorum, magnis angoribus corporum consummatum Dauid Scottus Bancornensis episcopus exposuit, magis in regis gratiam quam historicum deceret acclinis. [...] Ego interim, ne bonum uirum uerbo uidear premere, statuo indulgendum, quia non historiam sed panagericum scripsit. [...] Omnem hanc ambitionem priuilegiorum et consecrationis uerbo de scriptis prefati Dauid transtuli, quae ille, ut dixi, pronius quam deberet ad gratiam regis inflectit."
25 Genesis 32.26–29.

conflict with the popes up to the Concordat of Worms. But the majority of the entries, the quoted documents and letters, are always related to the popes. The interests of Orderic Vitalis, William of Malmesbury, John of Worcester, Symeon of Durham as well as later historians are primarily focused on church history and church leaders. Comparing the chronicles and annals with regard to their writings between 1070 and 1125, one should mention that besides entries about the investiture controversy, there are only a few short references to Henry IV and Henry V that have nothing to do with the investiture controversy. Though there was a direct connection between the Anglo-Norman and the Holy Roman Empire with the marriage of Henry V and Matilda, further news did not find its way into the chronicles. Even the marriage itself is only a marginal event compared to the conflict between the emperors and the popes. This interest can be explained by their clerical positions, but as well by the intense relationship the popes had with England after 1066 and the church-political developments in England.

Whereas it is only possible to determine that most of the 12th century historians wrote solely about events in Germany only if such were related to the church and pope, with Symeon of Durham's *Historia regum* it is possible to reconstruct the process of leaving out German news. John of Worcester's approach in commenting Marianus' description of Canossa has already been discussed. John had judged the Canossa meeting according to its meaning for the controversy and realized that there was not a lasting peace agreement. So he deleted half of the entry and wrote a commentary. Symeon's *Historia regum* (for the years 849 to 1119) is based in great part on John's chronicle.[26] Especially with the entries about Henry IV, Symeon's source becomes apparent.[27] Symeon copied great parts of John's annals but did not incorporate his entry about Canossa. Whereas John still depicted the meeting between Gregory VII and Henry IV and commented on the meeting, Symeon showed his judgment about this event simply by not copying it. The peace agreement proved not to be correct, as he had read it in John's chronicle, so he did not have to mention it. The Canossa entry was simply dispensable. This conscious elimination is even more plausible, because this was not the only entry he decided not to copy. Symeon copied all news about the conflict between Henry IV and

---

26 Bernhard Meehan, "Symeon of Durham (fl. c. 1090–1140)," in *Oxford Dictionary of National Biography* vol. 53 (Oxford, 2004) 581–2.
27 Symeon of Durham, *Historia regum*, to 1074, 200, to 1075, 206–207, to 1080, 211, to 1081, 211, to 1082, 211, to 1083, 211, to 1084 212, to 1101, 219. These entries are all compiled from John's chronicle.

Gregory VII, but not Henry's actions against the noble opposition and Rudolf of Rheinfelden. This is especially evident in a direct comparison:

John of Worcester, Chonicon ex chronicis, vol. 3, 36:	Symeon of Durham, Historia regum, 211:
Heinricus rex Hiltibrandum papam in Pentecostem Mogontie decernit deponendum, et Wigbertum Rauenne urbis episcopum in natale sancti Iohannis Baptiste pro eo facit papam. Ruodolfus rex Saxonum bello occiditur apud Merseburg, ubi et sepultus est idus Octob. Mogontia ciuitas magnum terre motum k. Dec. sensit, et sequenti anno ex magna parte incendio conflagrauit cum principali monasterio et aliis tribus. Heinricus rex hostiliter Romam aduersus papam adiit oppugnans eam non tamen intrauit.	*Henricus rex Hiltibrandum papam in Pentecostem Mogontie decernit deponendum, et Wibertum Ravenne urbis episcopum in natale sancti Iohannis Baptiste pro eo facit papam.* *Anno MLXXXIII Henricus rex hostiliter Romam adversus Hiltibrandum papam adiit, oppugnans eam non tamen intravit.*

Symeon chose not to copy the death of Rudolf of Rheinfelden as well as the news about an earthquake in Mainz. Only the text passages regarding Henry and Gregory remained.

3 The Alexandrine Schism

But the lack of interest in the Reich is not confined to the times of Henry IV and Henry V. In later decades of the 12th century it is possible to ascertain a lack of interest as well. The papal election of 1159 (following the death of pope Adrian IV) resulted in a double election. The following 18 years of schism shaped the government of Frederick Barbarossa until the peace of Venice in 1177.[28] Ottavian de Monticelli was supposed to be a friend of the Germans and a supporter of Emperor Frederick, and he had the support of the Roman

---

28   For a short outline of the schism: Odilo Engels, *Die Staufer* (Stuttgart, 1972), 87–95. Still an essential work: Timothy Reuter, *The papal schism, the Empire and the West, 1159–1169* (Oxford, 1975). New insights: Peter D. Clarke / Anne J. Duggan, eds., *Pope Alexander III (1159–81)* (Farnham, 2012). See also Johannes Laudage, *Alexander III. und Friedrich Barbarossa* (Köln, 1997); Werner Maleczek, "Das Schisma von 1159 bis 1177. Erfolgsstrategie und Misserfolgsgründe," in *Gegenpäpste: ein unerwünschtes mittelalterliches Phänomen*,

senate and public.[29] Cardinal Rolando Bandinelli was elected by the majority of the cardinals.[30] Rolando was known as a sharp opponent of Frederick I and his confident actions often opposed the Empire, as his role in the negotiations of Benevent and his dispute with Rainald of Dassel in Besançon had shown. Alexander III and Victor IV (Cardinal Rolando Bandinelli and Ottavian de Monticelli, respectively) took actions immediately after their elections to assure their positions.[31] Frederick also sought solutions to resolve the situation. Jochen Johrendt presumed that Frederick saw himself – despite his personal problems with Rolando – as *defensor ecclesiae*, his duty as emperor.[32] Frederick summoned the council of Pavia in February 1160, where he invited, besides the German and Italian bishops, bishops from other countries like from France and Angevin England as well. The desired effect of this council did not come to pass, because the resolution – the confirmation of Victor IV by 50 bishops – was not accepted. The Alexandrine party refused the decision of the council, because they felt justified in the cardinal's election and the lack of neutrality on the emperor's part.[33] Even in the Reich not everyone was happy with the decision and the process of the decision, so Alexander III had a couple of supporters.[34] But it was more problematic that France and Angevin England did not take part in the council. In fact, they summoned their own councils, first in London and then a joint council in July 1160 in Beauvais, where they acknowledged Alexander III.[35] A unanimous decision was not reached and to the end of the year 1160 the whole *orbis christianus* – except the Holy Roman Empire, Bohemia, Poland and Denmark – supported Alexander III.[36]

It is easy to infer from the number of entries about the emperor's action in the matters regarding the schism that there was great interest in how the

---

ed. Harald Müller and Brigitte Hotz (Wien, 2012), 165–204; Knut Görich, *Friedrich Barbarossa. Eine Biographie* (München, 2011), 316–23 and 389–461.

29 Görich, *Friedrich Barbarossa*, 322, pointed out that Frederick supported Ottavian's election with his attitude towards Rome and he probably approved the election. This would be his share in the genesis of the schism.
30 To Alexander III and the reasons for his election see Anne J. Duggan, "Alexander ille meus: *the* Papacy *of* Alexander III," in *Pope Alexander III (1159–81)*, ed. Peter D. Clarke and Anne J. Duggan (Burlington, VT: Farnham, 2012), 13–49.
31 Reuter, *The Papal Schism*, 12–16, 24–42.
32 Jochen Johrendt, "The Empire and the Schism," in *Pope Alexander III (1159–81)*, ed. Peter D. Clarke / Anne J. Duggan (Farnham, 2012), 99–126, at 104. See also Reuter, *The Papal Schism*, 26–27.
33 Laudage, *Alexander III.*, 121.
34 Johrendt, "The Empire and the Schism," 106.
35 Reuter, *The Papal Schism*, 41.
36 Reuter, *The Papal Schism*, 59.

Empire was dealing with the schism. There are entries about the schism in twelve of the 27 analyzed chronicles from the 12th century. Considering that eight of the chronicles and annals were finished before the outbreak of the schism, there are only seven historiographies that did not write about the discord of Frederick I and the schism. Especially Roger of Howden, Gervase of Canterbury, Ralph of Diceto, Robert of Torigni, William of Newburgh and the Winchcombe Chronicle include several text passages about it.[37] Historians with only a few entries – in quantity and length – were Ralph Niger with his two chronicles, Gervase of Canterbury with the *Gesta rerum Britanniae* and Ralph of Coggeshall, whose entries do not become lengthier until the Third Crusade.[38] However the number of further text passages about the Holy Roman Empire, e.g., Barbarossa's policy in Italy or the marriage of duke Henry the Lion and Matilda of England, argue against an overall interest.[39] In Roger of Howden's two chronicles, in Gervase of Canterbury's two works, in Ralph of Diceto's *Ymagines historiarum*, in William of Newburgh's *Historia rerum Anglicarum*, in the Annals of St Osyth's and in the Winchcombe chronicle there are only a few additional entries, which have nothing to do with the schism, but with the empire. The limited number of entries about Germany beyond the schism shows that the historians' perception of the Empire was determined by the schism in the period between 1159 to 1177. The schism was always at the forefront of the news.

Instead the chronicles have abundant passages about Pope Alexander III and his contacts with the English king, bishops, or Thomas Becket, with considerably more entries about that dynamic than about Germany and

---

37 The number of entries dealing with the Reich's involvement in the schism are: Roger of Howden, *Gesta regis Henrici secundi Benedicti abbatis*: 2 (127, 183–190); Roger of Howden, *Chronica*: 7 (vol. 1: 216, 219, 237–240, 244–248, 253, 253–255, 256–262; vol. 2: 137–143); Gervase of Canterbury, *Chronica*: 8 (166–167, 167, 171, 202, 204, 205–207, 247, 265–269); Ralph de Diceto, *Ymagines historiarum*: 6 (303, 306, 312, 318, 331, 421); Robert of Torigni, *Chronicle*: 8 (213, 213, 215, 216–217, 225, 230–231, 267, 273); *Winchcombe Chronicle*: 3 (530, 532, 538); *Annals of St. Osyth's*: 2 (171, 171); William of Newburgh, *Historia rerum Anglicarum*: 3 (117–121, 135, 144, 205–206).

38 Gervase of Canterbury, *Gesta regum Britanniae*: 1 (78); Ralph Niger, *Chronica* I: 2 (271, 282–283); Ralph Niger, *Chronica* II: 1 (167); Ralph of Coggeshall, *Chronicon Anglicanum*: 1 (19).

39 Other entries dealing with the Reich: Roger of Howden, *Gesta regis Henrici secundi Benedicti abbatis*: 1 (126); Roger of Howden, *Chronica*: 2 (vol. 1: 220; vol. 2: 101); Gervase of Canterbury, *Chronica*: 3 (171, 205, 205); Gervase of Canterbury, *Gesta regum Britanniae*: 0; Ralph de Diceto, *Ymagines historiarum*: 7 (308, 330, 353, 363, 397, 408–410, 416); *Winchcombe Chronicle*: 2 (530, 532); *Annals of St. Osyth's*: 0; William of Newburgh, *Historia rerum Anglicarum*: 2 (115–117, 132 ff.); Radulfus Niger and Ralph of Coggeshall are not further dealt with here because the shortness of the one's entries and the other does not get more detailed until the 3rd crusade, respectively.

Frederick I.[40] The majority of these entries were based on accounts of the council of Tours, correspondence about the Becket crisis, and the aftermath of the murder of Thomas Becket. The number of entries about contacts between England and Alexander III allows one to comprehend how close the contact between the different parties became due to the Becket crisis. This confirms Anne Duggan's thesis that with trying to neutralize the archbishop of Canterbury, the pope became more and more embedded in English politics by king Henry.[41] Alexander III was acknowledged as the legitimate pope by Henry II in July 1160; Frederick's actions and his support of the anti-pope were condemned. While there had still been a kind of routine interaction between England and Alexander III, despite having to act carefully so as not to lose Henry's support, the contact became closer with the controversy about the archbishop as the number of letters and legations do show.[42] So the empire and its actions in the schism were noted, but it was not the main focus for historians. Comparing this to the results as to the perceptions about the investiture controversy, again the Empire and the emperor were not in the historian's focus, but the church and the impact of the emperor's dealings with the church.

This result is supported by those places where entries about the schism and Frederick I can be found. The entries about the empire and the schism are not spread evenly through the years 1159 to 1177. Most of them are connected with the early years of the schism until Alexander's flight to France in 1162 – means

---

40   Entries dealing with contacts between Pope Alexander III and England: Roger of Howden, *Gesta regis Henrici secundi Benedicti abbatis*: 19 (7–9, 14–15, 15–16, 16–17, 17–19, 19–20, 20–22, 24, 28, 32–33, 69, 85, 112, 113, 117, 124–125, 135, 161, 181); Roger of Howden, *Chronica*: 34 (vol. 1: 221, 222–223, 224, 224, 230–231, 231–232, 235–237, 241, 241, 243, 243–244, 255–256, 276–273, vol. 2: 6, 7–10, 17, 17, 18, 18–20, 20–22, 22–25, 25, 25–28, 28–29, 32–33, 35, 36–37, 37–39, 58, 65, 73, 79, 98, 100, 105–117); Gervase of Canterbury, *Gesta regum Britanniae*: 0; Ralph de Diceto, *Ymagines historiarum*: 29 (vol. 1: 307, 309, 310, 310–311, 314–316, 316–317, 330, 331–332, 332–333, 334–335, 335, 335, 337, 337–338, 338, 339–340, 340–341, 341–342, 345–346, 347–348, 351–352, 369–370, 378, 387–388, 390, 390, 396, 406, 410); *Winchcombe Chronicles*: 5 (530, 534, 538, 538, 538); *Annales of St. Osyth's*: 4 (170, 171, 172, 177); William of Newburgh, *Historia rerum Anglicarum*: 1 (160–165). In addition to these entries dealing with contacts between Pope Alexander III, the English episcopacy and Thomas Becket, other entries can be found dealing with the development of the schism without referring explicitly to the Reich: Roger of Howden, *Chronica*: 4 (vol. 1: 219, 223, 231, 269); Gervase of Canterbury, *Chronica*: 2 (182, 197); Ralph de Diceto, *Ymagines historiarum*: 2 (vol. 1: 303, 318); *Winchcombe Chronicle*: 3 (528, 530, 530).

41   Anne J. Duggan, "Henry II, the English Church and the Papacy, 1154–76," in *Henry II: New Interpretations*, ed. Christopher Harper-Bill and Nicholas Vincent (Woodbridge, 2007), 154–183, at 182.

42   Hanna Vollrath, "Lüge oder Fälschung? Die Überlieferung von Barbarossas Hoftag zu Würzburg im Jahr 1165 und der Becket-Streit," in *Stauferreich im Wandel*, ed. Stefan Weinfurter, Mittelalter-Forschung 9 (Ostfildern, 2002), 149–171, at 160.

the early turbulent years with the disputed elections and the councils. There are only a few entries for the years 1165 to 1168 and after that, there is a long silence in the English chronicles about the schism until the peace of Venice. At the same time there were many entries about the papal relationship with England. While it is comprehensible that there are text passages about the outbreak of the schism and about the resolution with the peace of Venice, it can be seen that the entries for the years 1165 to 1168 were inserted only due to the Becket-crisis.

The term 'Würzburg oaths' is linked to the assembly of 1165 in Würzburg. Previously there was the death of Victor IV and then the election of the new anti-pope, Paschal III, which caused new disturbances.[43] Due to the growing opposition of some bishops, Frederick wanted to secure the princes' obedience to Paschal III and unify the Holy Roman Empire again. The main adversaries were the archbishop of Salzburg and Konrad I, archbishop of Mainz. Frederick I himself swore never to acknowledge the schismatic Rolando or any other person elected by Rolando's party, but to support instead Paschal III in everything.[44] Most of the princes took part in this oath. In Würzburg there were Angevin delegates as well. For a long time there was the presumption that Henry II wanted to switch his obedience, because Frederick's newsletters of this event announced English envoys had sworn to support Paschal III and abjure Alexander III.[45] The reason of this change has been seen in Henry's conflict with Thomas Becket, his exile in France, and his contact with Pope Alexander. The treaty's basis has been identified in Rainald of Dassel's journey to England and the marriage agreements for two of Henry's daughters with

---

43   Recently, with the latest findings, Vollrath, "Lüge oder Fälschung?," 150–171. Cf. Reuter, *The Papal Schism*, 124–136; Johrendt, "The Empire and the Schism," 113–117, Görich, *Friedrich Barbarossa*, 407–411. Outdated Gerhard Rill, "Zur Geschichte der Würzburger Eide von 1165," *Würzburger Diözesangeschichtsblätter* 22 (1960), 7–19.

44   Görich, *Friedrich Barbarossa*, 409.

45   Barbarossa's report on the Würzburg Oaths has been handed down in four different letters and circulars, see MGH DD FI:480–483, 395–402. A letter of John of Salisbury to John of Canterbury – in which he refers to the oaths of the English ambassadors – is also considered as a recognition of this circular, see for this *Letter No. 177 to John of Canterbury, bishop of Poitiers*, in *The Letters of John of Salisbury* 2, ed. W.J. Millor and H.E. Brooke (Oxford, 1979), 178–185. An anonymous letter to Alexander – which is handed down in two versions – also speaks of the Oaths: MTB 5, letter 98:184–188 and letter 99:188–191. These authors have the opinion that Henry II wanted to switch his obedience: Reuter, *The Papal Schism*, 131 and Marshall W. Baldwin, *Alexander III and the Twelfth Century*, The Popes through History 3 (New York, 1968), 100. Maleczek, "Das Schisma," 201, somehow qualifies this judgment by stating that the change of obedience appeared to be imminent. Laudage, *Alexander III.*, 159–160, however, points out that there have been doubts about the description of the process and especially about the unity in the German episcopacy.

Duke Henry the Lion and one of Frederick's sons. Hanna Vollrath has been able to clarify in her article "Lüge oder Fälschung" that the Angevin envoys swore mutual assistance. Frederick rephrased the truth in the newsletters and made active support in his politics regarding them.[46] Vollrath even calls the newsletters a propaganda letter.[47]

While it is not possible to find any comments about the oaths in German historiography, there are three English historians who wrote about them. Two hints about the oaths can be found in Roger of Howden's Chronica. Roger inserted many of Thomas Becket's letters as well as papal, royal, or other letters in his account of the Becket-crisis. Therefore, there is a letter from the archbishop of Canterbury to his bishops explaining the excommunication of John of Oxford, who had sworn an oath to the schismatics and with that revitalized the schism in Germany.[48] Thomas Becket does not mention in his letter the Würzburg assembly explicitly and he does not mention that this happened on Henry II's order. Presumably, Thomas Becket was referring to the anonymous letter *Epistola amici ad Alexandrum papam*, a letter with two different versions, written by a supporter of Alexander III.[49] Roger of Howden inserted a second letter to Alexander III, in which Becket repeated his explanations for the excommunication because of the envoys dealings with the schismatics

---

46   Vollrath finds the sudden change of obedience implausible, as the majority of bishops in England had been in favor of Alexander III and his recognition had been pursued since 1160. With a sudden change of obedience –happening without consultation – Henry II would have destroyed the unstable balance in England. Also, after the circular and further letters came up, there had been immediate denials from the English side. She doubts, however, that the letters to Alexander came from Thomas Becket, otherwise Henry II would have been shown much worse. She suspects a personal enemy of Rainald of Dassel to be the anonymous author. Recently, Vollrath's considerations were criticized by Duggan, "Alexander ille meus," 30 (especially annot. 88) – however not definitely refuted. Duggan thinks it quite possible that Henry II played a double game and changed his plans again. She does not hold Vollrath's argument to be valid that there were not 50 English bishops Henry could have contributed as a bargaining chip, as there were 21 bishop seats in England and Wales and 27 in Henry's possessions on the continent.

47   Vollrath, "Lüge oder Fälschung," 171.

48   Roger of Howden, *Chronica*, to 1165, 237–240, at 238–239: "Denunciamus etiam excommunicatum, et excommunicavimus es nomine Johannem de Oxenford, qui in haeresim damnatam iudicit, praestando juramentum schismaticis; per quem schisma jam fere emortuum in Alemannia revixit; communicando etiam nominatissimo illi schismatico Reginaldo Coloniensi; et quia contra mandatum domini papae, et nostrum, Salesberiensis ecclesiae decanatum sibi usurpavit".

49   The title of this letter is not the original one but was created later. See Laudage, *Alexander III.*, 160 annot. 48. For the long version / letter version see MTB 5, letter 98:184–188, for the short version / protocol-version see MTB 5, letter 98:188–191.

being detrimental to the church.⁵⁰ Nevertheless, it should not be ignored that these explanations were only a small part – only a few sentences – of these letters. The Würzburg oaths were not of central interest for Roger of Howden. The author was more interested in outlining the conflict between Thomas Becket and Henry II, Becket's measures after his appointment as papal legate for England, and the excommunications of Vézelay in 1166 – a year after the Würzburg oaths – with the following synod of London and an increased communication among the archbishop, the Angevin episcopacy, Henry II, and Pope Alexander III.⁵¹ The Würzburg oaths were not the center of attention, but instead the Becket controversy.

But yet in Ralph de Diceto's far more detailed description of the oaths, it was not his intention to describe the developments in the Empire explicitly. In his *Ymagines historiarum* he inserted the so-called protocol of the letter in a shortened version, referring to a letter having Pope Alexander as its source.⁵² Ralph's version was orientated to the protocol, but there are some changes.⁵³ So he did not write that 50 English bishops would join Paschal's party or that Angevin envoys swore an oath. Rather he mentioned the demand of the bishop of Magdeburg, that Rainald of Dassel should abjure Alexander for all times and should be ordained by Paschal. The Cologne archbishop protested, but he had to swear by imperial order. After that, Frederick and other participants of the assembly did the same. There is no entry that the envoys swore an oath as well. Besides not mentioning the envoys' oaths, he reported this as taking place in 1168, three years after the assembly and two years after the excommunications

---

50   Roger of Howden, *Chronica*, to 1166, 253–255, at 254–255: "Nominatim autem excommunicavi Johannem de Oxeneforde, qui communicavit schismatico et excommunicato illi Reginaldo Coloniensi; quique, contra mandatum domini papae et nostrum, usurpavit sibi decanatum Salesbiriensis ecclesiae, et in curia imperatoris pro schismate renovando, praestitit juramentum. Similiter et Ricardum de Yvecestre denunciavimus et excommunicavimus, eo quod inciderit in eandem haeresim damnatam, communicando famosissimo schismatico illi Coloniensi, machinando et fabricando omnia mala cum schismaticis et Teutonicis illis, in perniciam ecclesiae Dei, maxime ecclesiae Romanae, ex pactis contractis inter regem Angliae et ipsos; et Ricardum de Luci et Jocelinum de Balliol, qui regiae tyrannidis fautores et haereticarum illarum pravitatum fabricatores exstiterunt [...]".

51   Frank Barlow, *Thomas Becket* (Berkeley, 1986), 147–150. To the discussion about the legality of the excommunication see Richard Helmholz, "Excommunication in Twelfth Century England," *Journal of Law and Religion* 11,1 (1994/1995), 235–253, at 242–243.

52   The protocol is a shortened version of the Epistola amici ad Alexandram papam. Laudage, *Alexander III.*, 160 annot. 48, presumes that the protocol was written by a German eyewitness. For the long version / letter version see MTB 5, letter 98:184–188, for the short version / protocol-version see MTB 5, letter 98:188–191.

53   Ralph de Diceto, *Ymagines historiarum* 1, to 1168, 331: "Alexandro papae scriptum est in haec verba".

of Vézelay.[54] The author's access to sources, like papal or royal letters or letters from Gilbert Foliot or Thomas Becket was very good, so a conscious concealment of the oaths has to be assumed. This assumption is confirmed by the following letter of Gilbert Foliot to Pope Alexander affirming that Henry was loyal to him and would never turn away from him.[55] Though there is not in the present text any notice about a possible change in obedience, Ralph emphasized the loyalty of Henry II to Gilbert Foliot. Ralph de Diceto was, even if he respected the archbishop – Charles and Anne Duggan as well as John Mason presumed he tended to Becket's side – absolutely loyal to Henry II and Gilbert Foliot, a close friend and patron.[56] In his *Ymagines historiarum* he tried to find a balance between all the different sides.[57] So he showed "editorial tact" by concealing the presence of some of his friends in Würzburg and he could be assured that a change in allegiance would not happen, because this event had happened three years prior to his writing.[58] With the following letter of Gilbert Foliot as well as his assigning it to the year 1168, Ralph could explain that Gilbert, even when he was excommunicated, always remained loyal to the king and to the true pope, and did not ill-advise his king as the archbishop of Cologne had done; instead, he had been a moderating influence in the Becket crisis. Ralph de Diceto was informed about the Würzburg oaths, but his text passages were not a narration about the events and the English connection to them. Rather he wanted to depict Gilbert Foliot's and Henry II's conduct and their loyalty to Pope Alexander. So here again, the Becket crisis was the center of attention and the Würzburg oaths were not seen as an important event in the schism, but as part of the Becket controversy.

A description of Würzburg is most detailed in Gervase of Canterbury's *Chronica*. Gervase recounts there the marriage of Henry the Lion with Matilda

---

54   For the excommunications see Ralph de Diceto, *Ymagines historiarum*, 318.
55   Ralph de Diceto, *Ymagines historiarum*, to 1168, 332: "in primis asserens mentem suam a vobis se nullatenus avertisse, nec id unquam propositi mente concepisse, quin dum vos sibi patrem rebus ipsis cognoverit, vos ut patrem diligat, et sanctam Romanam ecclesiam ut matrem veneretur et foveat, et sacris jussionibus vestris, salva sibi sua regnique sui dignitate, humiliter obtemperet et obediat".
56   Charles Duggan / Anne J. Duggan, "Ralph de Diceto, Henry II and Becket with an Appendix on Decretal Letters," in *Authority and power: studies in medieval law and government presented to Walter Ullmann on his seventieth birthday*, ed. Brian Tiernay / Peter Linehan (Cambridge, 1980), 59–81, at 63, 75; John F.A. Mason, "Diceto, Ralph de," in *Oxford Dictionary of National Biography* vol. 16 (Oxford, 2004) 40–2.
57   Duggan, "Ralph de Diceto," 69: "At critical phases, he appears to seek a balance in the choice of texts, to discuss the arguments of each side."
58   Duggan, "Ralph de Diceto," 70. Ralph was a friend of Richard of Ilchester's, one of the excommunicated persons.

and about the meeting of the Saxon duke, the archbishop of Mainz, the Cologne archbishop (*Coloniensis electus*) and the bishop of Liège and their offer to help the English king against the French by joining Paschal's side.[59] Henry II treated them respectfully, but did not accept their offer.[60] Then Gervase adds excerpts from the so-called protocol. Here again Frederick intended to make peace with Alexander III, but suddenly Rainald of Dassel appears and promises that 50 bishops would join the imperial party if he abjures Alexander III. As confirmation he presents the two Angevin envoys. After the emperor's and the other participants' oaths, the envoys themselves swear.[61] Differently from the other descriptions, Gervase now makes mention of an assembly in London, where the public as well as the bishops should abjure Alexander III, but the episcopacy refuses to do that. As a sign of the legitimacy of their action, God lets Paschal die.[62] Here Gervase takes up information from William of Canterbury's Life of Thomas Becket.[63] William related in chapter 43 that Henry wanted to turn away from Alexander due to the latter's support of Thomas Becket. So, he sent the envoys to Würzburg.[64] As a further affront to the pope, Henry enacted

---

59   Gervase of Canterbury, *Chronica*, to 1168, 205: "Venerunt interea ad regem Angliae nobilissimi Alemmanniae et specatbiles legati, dux scilicet Saxonum gener regis, Maguntinus archiepiscopus, Coloniensis electus, et Leodicensis episcopus, cum multa ambitione et fast missi ab imperatore Frederico, multa ex Alemannis adversum francos spondentes auxilia, multisque temptantes moliminibus qualiter regem Angliae in scismatis sui partem inducerent, et ob favorem ipsius regnum Francorum cum bellico apparatu intrarent".

60   Gervase of Canterbury, *Chronica*, to 1168, 205: "Rex autem praedictos legatos cum multo suscepit honore, responsis prudentibus et blandiloquiis satisfaciens, ipsosque abeuntes prosecutus est multis gratiarum actionibus preciosis honoratos muneribus".

61   Gervase of Canterbury, *Chronica*, to 1168, 206: "Juraverunt etiam duo clerici nuntii regis Angliae in persona regis".

62   Gervase of Canterbury, *Chronica*, to 1168, 207: "Per totiam etiam Angliam ex praecepto regis a populo juratum est, quod ad praeceptum regis faciendum omnes forent parati; unde et congregatio episcoporum, et abbatum, et aliarum personarum ecclesiasticarum apud Londonias facta est. Sed et supprior et monachi Cantuariensis ecclesiae ex imperio regis jussi sunt ibidem adesse. Cum autem super hoc juramento faciendo convenirentur episcopi, et ipsi tam detestabile juramentum contra Deum et Alexandrum papam praestare noluissent, dilatum et infatuatum ets tam iniquum et enorme negotium, et quisque ad sua repedavit. Homo proponit sed Deus disponit. Homo proposuit scismaticum exaltare, sed Deus disposuit, immo et deposuit eum, nam in brevi Paschalis ille defunctus est. Imperator tamen caeterique scismatici, jam duobus defunctis, tertium falsum papam substituerunt".

63   There is not much information about William of Canterbury, Benedictine monk in Canterbury. He was present at Thomas' murder and wrote after that a life of the late archbishop and a collection of his miracles. Presumably he wrote the Life between 1172 to 1174.

64   William of Canterbury, *Miraculorum gloriosi* (MTB, I), cha 44, 52: "Unde dolorum suum in fide vindicaturus, clericos duos misit ad imperatorem alemannorum fredericum, qui coacto concilio de pace Romanae ecclesiae tractabat, mandans, quod si nomen et

supplements to the Constitution of Clarendon and took actions against family members of the archbishop. Furthermore, the public should abjure Alexander III.[65] Gervase softened William's strong attitude against Henry II, because he wrote his *Chronica* many years after the murder of Thomas Becket and he had seen that Henry had never changed his obedience in the schism and regretted the murder of the archbishop. Again, neither the Würzburg oaths nor the empire and the schism are the center of attention, but the Becket controversy instead. The oaths were only seen as a further act in the conflict between Henry II and Thomas Becket.

The exception in these statistics is Robert of Torigni and his chronicle. In eight entries he refers to the Empire and Frederick's actions in the schism; in six entries he reports about further developments of the schism; then there are twelve entries about news in the empire – but there are only two entries about Alexander's relationship to England.[66] So, was he the one who was deeply interested in Germany? Robert of Torigni joined the monastery of Bec in 1128 and became prior in 1149.[67] In 1154 he became abbot of Mont-Saint-Michel, an office he had until his death in 1186. Being a member of the two most prominent monasteries in Normandy, he lived in the center of political events. Henry II visited Mont-Saint-Michel in 1158 and 1166 – Van Houts presumed that Henry II and Robert may have previously met in 1147– and Matilda, Henry I's daughter,

---

obedientiam Alexandri papae abjuraret, participem se schismatis haberet cum episcopis et archiepiscopis suis".

65   William of Canterbury, *Miraculorum gloriosi* (MTB, I), cha 46, 55: "Abjurante itaque populo, militibus, proceribusque beati Petri successorem Alexandrum per vicos, per castella, per civitates, ab homine sene usque ad puerum duodennem [...]". These supplements have rarely received attention. David Knowles, Anne J. Duggan, and Christopher N.L. Brooke, "Henry II's Supplement to the Constitutions of Clarendon," *The English Historical Review* 87 (1972), 757–771. *Councils & Synods, with other Documents relating to the English Church* 1/II, ed. Dorothy Whitelock, Martin Brett, and Christopher N.L. Brooke (Oxford, 1981), 926–939. Paul Brand, "Henry II and the Creation of the English Common Law," in *Henry II. New Interpretations*, ed. Christopher Harper-Bill and Nicholas Vincent (Woodbridge, 2007), 215–241, at 230.

66   Entries in Robert of Torigni's *Chronicle* dealing with the Reich's involvement in the schism: 8 (213, 213, 215, 216–217, 225, 230–231, 267, 273); entries dealing with the Reich without references to the schism: 12 (195, 199, 201, 213, 220–221, 222, 224, 234, 240, 253, 266, 270); entries dealing with the schism without references to the Reich: 6 (204, 215, 219, 222, 239, 239–240); entries dealing with the papal relationship with England: 2 (235, 263).

67   Antonia Gransden, *Historical Writing in England c. 550 to c. 1307* (London, 1974), 261–263, here 261; Elisabeth van Houts, "Le roi et son historien: Henri II Plantagenêt et Robert de Torigni, abbé du Mont-Saint-Michel," *Cahiers de civilisation médiévale* 37 (1994), 115–118, at 115.

as well.[68] He saw himself as even a kind of mentor to the empress.[69] He actually became godfather to Eleanor, Henry II's daughter.[70] His strong relationship to the royal family is clearly visible in his works. As Henry's retainer, Henry II was a patron of Mont-Saint-Michel – he would not write critical comments about the king. This explains why there are only two entries about Pope Alexander's relationship to England and none about the Becket crisis with the murder in 1170 and the subsequent penance by Henry II.[71] Nevertheless, Robert wrote in detail about Frederick I, his Italian journeys, and his interventions in the schism. In doing so, Robert of Torigni could develop a strong contrast between the English king as a deeply religious man, always loyal to Alexander III, and the Holy Roman emperor, who supported the anti-pope. So Robert criticized Frederick for the *discordia inter regnum et sacerdotium* [...] *propter schism Octaviani*, while Henry was *devote semper Romanam ecclesiam*.[72] Henry II fulfilled the *officium stratoris* respectfully when he met Alexander III – a side blow to Frederick Barbarossa and the frictions about this service in Sutri 1155.[73]

---

68   Gransden, *Historical Writing*, 261; Van Houts, "Le roi et son historien," 117, who explains the contact and the mutual agreement – upon other terms – with the acknowledgement occurring quickly and without difficulties.
69   David Bates, "Robert Torigni and the Historia Anglorum," in *The English and their Legacy, 900–1200. Essays in Honour of Ann Williams*, ed. David Roffe (Woodbridge, 2012), 175–184, at 177. After Matilda's return to England she was always called "empress" pursuant to the marriage to her first husband, Emperor Henry V.
70   David S. Spear, "Torigni, Robert de (c.1110–1186)," *Oxford Dictionary of National Biography*, vol. 55 (Oxford, 2004).
71   Spear, "Torigni, Robert de"; Gransden, *Historical Writing*, 262–263. One of the entries where Robert refers to Pope Alexander III is about papal legates coming to England for Henry II's penance after the assassination of the Archbishop of Canterbury. Robert of Torigni depicted that Henry – without hesitation and despite his stay in Ireland – received them in a friendly and honouring manner. See also Robert of Torigni, *Chronicle*, 235–236.
72   Robert of Torigni, *Chronicle*, 213 to the support of Henry II for Alexander III while Frederick I destroyed with Octavian the peace between *regnum* and *sacerdotium* zerstörte: "Discordia inter regnum et sacerdotium adhuc perdurante propter schism Octaviani, quem rex Romanorum Fredericus secum in Italia habebat, Alexander papa Romanus, confidens de regibus Francorum Ludovico et Anglorum Henrico, qui devote simper Romanam ecclesiam fovent et venerantur, ad cismontanos marina expedition circa Pascha venit, et apud Montem Pessulanum in Provincia debita honorificentia susceptus est".
73   The English king did the strator service, 215: "Exinde, parvo spatio temporis interjecto, Ludovicus rex Francorum et Henricus rex Anglorum super Ligerim apud Cociacum convenientes. Alexandrum papam Romanum honore congruo susceperunt, et usi officio stratoris, pedites dextra laevaque frenum equi ipsius tenentes, eum usque ad praeparatum papilionem perduxerunt. Quo mediante, Deo favente, pax inter eos firma restituta est". In the 12th century it became common to welcome the pope by holding the reins of the papal horse and holding the stirrup for dismounting. Meeting Hadrian IV in Sutri

Robert also described the *ultio divina* for Frederick's behavior with the catastrophe of the fourth Italian campaign, the death of archbishop Rainald of Dassel, and the death of many counts and soldiers.[74] While for many twelfth century historians, the Becket controversy was prominent in the sixties and seventies of the twelfth century and they depicted the papal actions in detail, the schism was for Robert of Torigni the possibility for concealing the crisis and to depict Henry II as an ideal king by reporting continuously and extensively about the Empire. The number of entries about the Empire evolved not through an interest of Robert of Torigni in it or that he conceded the Empire a certain kind of position among European kingdoms, but rather to depict Henry II as a true king compared to Frederick Barbarossa.

4   Conclusions

The analysis of the entries about the Holy Roman Empire in Anglo-Norman and Angevin sources shows that simple statistics can be misleading in the examination of sources. The introductory statistic makes clear that there are more entries about Germany in Anglo-Norman or Angevin sources, much more than references to England in German 12th century historiography. But the detailed analysis with the case studies – the perception of the investiture controversy and the perception of the Alexandrine Schism – shows that large numbers do not mean that English historians were interested in German politics. Especially if the numbers of the perceptions of the other are compared to perceptions of other contacts such as the perception of Alexander III in

---

1155, Barbarossa refused to do that, so the pope did not give him the kiss of peace. This caused severe conflicts between the empire and the papacy. See also Görich, *Friedrich Barbarossa*, 241–246.

74   The punishment for Frederick's behaviour shows itself in the catastrophe of the fourth expedition to Italy, 230–231: "Circa Pentecosten, Fredericus imperator Alemannorum, missis exercitibus suis, multos Romanorum occidit, ipse ab eisdem similia recepturus. Circa mensem Julium per semetipsum Leoninam Romam obsedit et cepit, et quaedam juxta ecclesiam Beati Petri destruxit, scilicet porticum et alia nonnulla. Antipapam etiam Widonem de Creme Romam adduxit, et per manum ipsius uxorem suam in imperatricem fecit coronari. Subsecuta est e vestigio ultio divina. Nam Karolus, filius Corradi, qui ante Fredericum imperaverat, consobrinus ejus, mortuus est, et Rainaldus, archiepiscopus Coloniensis, cancellarius ejus, cujus consilio multa mala faciebat, et episcopus Leodicensis, et multi alii tam episcopi quam consules, similiter perierunt. Dicitur enim quod, crassante mortalitate, xxv. Milia hominum de exercitu suo mortui sunt. Longobardiae civitates, quae sunt numero xxv., Mediolanum reaedificant et ab imperatore desciscunt, praeter Papiam et Vercellas".

the Becket controversy. Consequently, the perception of Germany can be perceived as marginal. Most of the time the historians had a multitude of sources about events in the Empire. With the investiture controversy they even had sources which were written in Germany. But they did not simply copy them without reflection but evaluated the descriptions and arranged the information in fit their own perception of events. They could be very critical with their sources, as the example of David Scolasticus and his report about Henry v's journey to Rome shows.

But both case studies – despite the statistics – show that the Holy Roman Empire was less important for the twelfth-century historians than it is often presumed, the interest laying primarily in the pope and the church. With the Investiture Controversy what the popes had to suffer at the hands of the Holy Roman Emperor was interesting; for the Alexandrine Schism the focus lay primarily on the Becket crisis, with the schism as a kind of background information. They even often copied the information about the Empire only, as Symeon of Durham's chronicle shows us, if it was combined with the church. The perceptions of Germany in the twelfth century by Anglo-Norman and Angevin historians were mostly seen through papal lenses.

CHAPTER 5

"… rogans eum sibi in auxilium contra superbiam Teutonicorum": The Imaging of 'Theutonici' in Bohemian Medieval Sources between the Ninth and Fourteenth Centuries

David Kalhous

"Who established Germans to judge over the nations?", asked John of Salisbury in 1160 in one of his letters and in years following, he criticized the "German tyrant", emperor Frederick I Barbarossa (1152–1190).[1] Was his criticism of "Germans" unique? Moreover, who were the "Germans", whom he complained about so severely? Thanks to Eckhart Müller-Mertens, we better understand the genesis of the term "Thiudisco" with its beginnings in Carolingian Italy, where it was first used as an adjective to comment on "barbarians" from beyond the Alps. "Thiudisco" meant "popular/folkish" and was similar to the Slavic term "Němci", "dumb" or "mute" people.[2] Within the borders of the East Frankish kingdom, it was not used regularly until the second half of the eleventh century. At that time it signaled allegiance to the papacy, which started to use that adjective to weaken the universal claims of the king and emperor, Henry IV

---

1 Cf. "Quis Teutonicos constituis iudices nationum?," in John of Salisbury, *Letters 1. The early letters, 1153–1161*, eds. and transl. William J. Millor, and Harold E. Butler, Christopher N.L. Brooke, Oxford Medieval Texts (Oxford, 1979), 207, Nr. 24; and id., *The letters 2. The later letters, 1163–1180*, Nr. 68: "Teutonicus tyrannus" or "Nonne Teutonicus tirannus nominis sui fama nuper orbem perculeret et fere subegerat regna vicina …".

2 Eckhardt Müller-Mertens, *Regnum Teutonicum. Aufkommen und Verbreitung der deutschen Reichs- und Königsauffassung im früheren Mittelalter*. Forschungen zur mittelalterlichen Geschichte 15 (Berlin, 1970); also Heinz Thomas, "frenkisk: Zur Geschichte von theodiscus und teutonicus im Frankenreich des 9. Jahrhunderts," in *Beiträge zur Geschichte des Regnum Francorum. Referate beim Wissenschaftlichen Colloquium zum 75. Geburtstag von Eugen Ewig am 28. Mai 1988*, ed. Rudolf Schieffer (Sigmaringen, 1990), 67–95; idem, "Theodiscus – Diutiskus – Regnum Teutonicorum. Zu einer neuen Studie über die Anfänge des deutschen Sprach- und Volksnamens," *Rheinische Vierteljahrsblätter* 51 (1987), 287–302; idem, "Regnum Teutonicum = diutiskono richi?," *Rheinische Vierteljahrsblätter* 40 (1976), 17–45. For the Late Middle Ages, see Len Scales, *The Shaping of German Identity: Authority and Crisis, 1245–1414* (Cambridge, 2012). The term "Theutonic" is Roman already.

(1056–1106).³ Soon the term became widespread over Europe, and even the inhabitants of the Holy Roman Empire, who spoke with different Germanic dialects, started to call themselves not only Saxons, Swabians, or Bavarians, but also *Theutonici*.⁴

Discussions about nations and nationalism in the Middle Ages have never led to any convincing results – the reason might be, for one thing, that theorists mostly did not work with medieval sources and based their conclusions on secondary literature and, for the other, specialists were too keen to take over those theoretic conclusions as given premises of their own research. This led to a vicious circle. Consequently, it makes better sense to analyze concrete strategies of identifications and sources of social cohesion, rather than to discuss them on a theoretical level.⁵

In my paper, I will focus on the image of *Theutonici* in selected high medieval historiographical sources from Bohemia. The first is the chronicle written by Cosmas of Prague between 1117–1125, which was preserved in 15 manuscripts (until one was destroyed by fire in 1870); it strongly inspired most of the medieval Bohemian chronicles, histories and annals.⁶ Its importance is supported by the fact that it was continued by an anonymous canon of a Prague chapter in 1140⁷ and by an anonymous monk of Sázava twenty years later.⁸ Although highly respected in modern times, two other texts remained

---

3   Müller-Mertens, *Regnum Theutonicum*.
4   For an extended discussion of the "birth" of Germany and France cf. Carlrichard Brühl, *Die Geburt zweier Völker. Deutsche und Franzosen (9.–11. Jahrhundert)* (Böhlau, Köln u. a., 2001).
5   Among many others, Benedict Anderson, *Imagined communities. Reflections on the Origin and Spread of Nationalism* (London, 1983; repr. 2006), 9–47; for modernism of nationalism: Anthony D. Smith, *The Ethnic Origins of Nations* (Malden-Oxford-Victoria, 1986; repr. 2005) for its long history.
6   For manuscripts cf. Bertold Bretholz in his edition of the Chronicle Cosmas Pragensis, *Chronica Boemorum*, ed. idem, MGH SSrG. N. S. 2 (Berlin, 1923), XLV–LXXXV, or David Kalhous, "The piece that fitted in different puzzles. Chronicle of Cosmas Pragensis (ca. 1120) and its manuscript context," (forthcoming); for the latest analysis of the text cf. Lisa Wolverton, *Cosmas of Prague: Narrative, Classicism, Politics* (Washington, DC, 2015).
7   Kanovník Vyšehradský, *Pokračování Kosmovo* [Cintinuatio of Cosmas], ed. Josef Emler, FRB (hereafter cited as FRB) 2 (Praha, 1874), 201–237; for the latest analysis cf. Lukáš Reitinger, "Psal tzv. Kanovník vyšehradský opravdu na Vyšehradě? První Kosmův pokračovatel v kontextu dějepisectví přemyslovského věku," [Did the so-called Vyšehrad Canon really write in Vyšehrad? Cosma's first successor in the context of the historiography of the Přemyslid age] *Český časopis historický* 113 (2015), 635–668, who proved its author was a canon of St.-Vitus cathedral chapter, and not of a collegiate chapter in nearby Vyšehrad.
8   Mnich Sázavský, *Pokračování Kosmovo* [Continuatio of Cosmas], FRB 2, 238–269; for the latest analysis cf. Marie Bláhová, "Sázaver Geschichtsschreibung," in *Der heilige Prokop, Böhmen*

nearly unknown to the medieval audience, but will be analyzed here, are: the chronicle of the Premonstratensian Bohemian province written by the abbot, Gerlach of Milevsko (ca. 1210), and the *Gesta* of the king, Vladislav II, penned by Vincencius, a canon of the Prague chapter (†1167). Both texts can be read together in one medieval manuscript compiled by Gerlach himself.[9] Henry the Woodcutter, chronicler of the peripheral Cistercian monastery Žďár (Saar), compiled his text ca. 1300 and it did not affect many medieval readers either.[10] Yet, all these text enable us to bridge the gap between the chronicle of Cosmas, also known predominantly from later manuscripts, and other Bohemian medieval "bestsellers", the chronicles of what is usually referred to as 'Dalimil', which articulates the requirements and fears of Bohemian nobility after the Přemyslid dynasty died out 1306,[11] and of Přibík Pulkava of Radenín, a clergyman and courtier who was asked by the emperor, Charles IV (1344/6–1378), to write a new chronicle for him.[12] Both of these fourteenth-century chronicles were translated into all three languages used in the Czech lands in that time: Dalimil's rhymed chronicle from Czech to Latin and twice to German, Přibík's from simple Latin to Czech and German. In total, they are known from more than fifty medieval manuscripts – fourteen copies of what is called 'Dalimil' and nearly forty of the chronicle of Přibík Pulkava.

Let us start with Cosmas of Prague. His use of the term *Theutonicus* is mostly descriptive and neutral; it just helps him label that group of people. However, these 'neutral' notes do reveal that he relates *gens Theutonicorum* to a specific

   und Mitteleuropa. Internationales Symposium Benešov – Sázava 24.–26. September 2003, ed. Petr Sommer (Praha, 2005), 185–204.
9 Vincencius, *Letopisy*, FRB 2, 403–460; Jarloch, *Letopisy*, ibidem, 461–516; for the latest analysis cf. Anna Kernbach, *Vincenciova a Jarlochova kronika v kontextu svého vzniku. K dějepisectví přemyslovského období*, [Vincent and Jarloch's chronicle in the context of its origin. On the historiography of the Přemyslid period] Knižnice Matice moravské 28 (Brno, 2010).
10 Henry the Woodcutter, *Chronicon domus Sarensis Maior*, ed. Jaroslav Ludvíkovský, Chronica domus Sarensis maior et minor (Třebíč, 2003).
11 *Tak řečený Dalimil, Kronika* [So-called Dalimil, ed. Jiří Daňhelka and col., col. 1–3 (Praha, 1988–1995). Cf. Éloïse Adde-Vomáčka, *La chronique de Dalimil: les débuts de l'historiographie nationale tchèque en langue vulgaire au XIVe siècle* (Paris, 2016).
12 Přibík Pulkava z Radenína, *Kronika* [the Chronicle], ed. Josef Emler, FRB 5 (Praha, 1893), I–XX, 1–326. Cf. Marie Bláhová, "Přibík Pulkava z Radenína, Kronika česká," [Přibík Pulkava from Radenín, The Czech Chronicle] *Kroniky doby Karla IV.*, ed. Marie Bláhová, (Praha, 1975), 572–580; Marie Bláhová, "Offizielle Geschichtsschreibung in den mittelalterlichen böhmischen Ländern," in *Die Geschichtsschreibung in Mitteleuropa. Projekte und Forschungsprobleme*, ed. Jarosław Wenta (Toruń, 1999), 21–40.

territory,[13] and that he recognizes its specific language.[14] Also calling *Theutonici* a *gens* means that they were probably understood by Cosmas as a group having a common origin[15] – just a few years earlier, narratives about the mythical origins of different ethnic groups within the Holy Roman Empire had started to circulate.[16] In the chronicle of Cosmas, *Theutonici* are represented by their elites.[17] This also means that for Cosmas, there were also *Theutonici* of humble origin.[18] To him, it also seems to have been easy to recognize the *Theutonici* either as individuals,[19] or as a group.[20] Although they might have lived in

13   Cosmas, *Chronica* I. 40, 73: "Hisdem temporibus Teutonicis in partibus fuit quidam comes valde potens, cognomine albus Otto, sanguine de regio prodiens stemmate patrio".; ibid., II. 18, 110: "[...] occidentalem vero, que est versus Teutonicos, dat Conrado, qui et ipse sciebat Teutonicam linguam".; ibid., III. 3, 163: "Eodem anno fuit mortalitas hominum, sed maxima in Teutonicis partibus; nam redeuntibus predictis episcopis de Magoncia, dum transirent per quandam villam nomine Amberk, parrochia[le]m ecclesiam quamvis satis amplam, que est sita extra villam, non potuerunt intrare, ut audirent missam, quia totum eius pavimentum usque ad unum punctum erat cadavere plenum.".; ibid., III. 4, ed. Bretholz, 164: "Eodem anno tanta fuit commotio, immo divina compunctio in populo Hierosolimam proficiscendi, ut perpauci in Teutonicis partibus et maxime in orientali Francia per urbes et villas remanerent coloni [...]".
14   Ibid., I. 34, 61; ibid., II. 29, 123.
15   Cf. n. 21 and 27.
16   Cf. David Kalhous, *Bohemi: Prozesse der Identätsbildung in frühpřemyslidischen Ländern (bis 1200)*, Forschungen zur Geschichte des Mittelalters 24 (Wien, 2018), 89–91.
17   Cosmas, *Chronica* II. 10, 97: "[...] Teutonicorum ... nobilita.; ibid., III. 18, 182: ... ex Teutonicis proceres [...]".
18   Cf. also n. 27.
19   Cosmas, *Chronica* II. 25, 118: "[...] comites Severum, Alexium, Marquardum Teutonicum [...]"; ibid., II. 28, 123: "[...] clericus nomine Hagno, vir Teutonicus, philosophie domesticus, Tulliane eloquentie alumnus".
20   Ibid. II. 9, 95: "[...] hec verba solvit ora: 'Licet extruant muros silvis altiores, licet elevent turres sublimes usque ad nubes, uti frustra iacitur rete ante oculos pennatorum, sic nihil valent contra Teutonicos obpugnacula Boemorum. Aut u si ascendent super nubila aut si includant se inter sydera, Perditam et miseram gentem nihil ista iuvabunt.".; ibid., II. 35, ed. Bretholz, 132–133: "Venerat dux Wratizlaus cum Boemiis simul et Teutonicis, qui erant presulis Ratisponensis; ast alia de parte Otto et Conradus adiungunt se cum suis omnibus qui sunt in tota Moravia militibus. [...] Iussit Teutonicos a dextrum irrumpere cornu, fratres vero suos Conradum et Ottonem ordinat pugnare in sinistra ala.".; ibid., III. 15, 178: "Nam Borivoy collecto exercitu occurrens eis castra metatus est supra duos colles iuxta oppidum Malin, paratus in crastinum cum eis committere bellum. Teutonici vero non longe ex altera parte rivuli Wyzplisa applicuerunt castra, ita ut uterque ab utrisque possit e videri exercitus.".; ibid., III. 22, ed. Bretholz, 188: "Quem remittens ad patrem omne debitum, scilicet tria milia talentorum, compatri suo Zuatopluk dimisit et precepit, ut paratus sit secum in expeditionem contra seviciam Ungarorum; quia rogatu quorundam Teutonicorum illuc proposuerat ultum ire necem Hierosolimitanorum, quos illa gens ob crudelitatem suam alios gladio interemit, alios in servitutem redegit.".; ibid., III. 25,

Bohemia for a long time, for Cosmas and his contemporaries, they still remained 'those', 'foreign': this is well documented by the alleged speech of Kojata, son of Vsebor, against the princely chaplain and canon of Litoměřice-Chapter Lanco, whom prince Vratislav II of Bohemia (1061–1092) presented to the nobility and freemen as his candidate for the Prague bishopric:[21]

> ... Even if your brother displeases you, why do you sully our clergy, not just a little but equally skilled in learning, with this German? Oh, if you had as many bishoprics as you could find chaplains born in this land worthy of a bishopric! Do you think that a foreigner will love us more and desire better for this land than a native? Indeed, human nature is such that anyone, wherever his land, not only loves his people more than a foreign people but would even divert wandering rivers into his country if he could. We prefer, therefore, that a dog's tail or the dung of an ass be placed on the holy seat rather than Lanzo. Your brother, Spytihněv of blessed memory, who expelled all the Germans from this land in one day, knew differently. The Roman emperor Henry IV yet lives and long may

---

194: "Quadam similiter die plus quam mille viros ex electis militibus a predicto rege ad hoc directos, quatenus per insidias aut pabulantes scutarios caperent aut super incautos Teutonicos noctu irruerent, dux Zuatopluk preagnoscens, ubi inter paludes latitabant, repente irruens, omnes usque ad unum, velut pisces missa sagena captos, alios interfici, alios in eculeo suspendi iusserat, paucis vero accepta magna pecunia vitam concesserat."; ibid., III. 48, 220: "Eodem anno quidam ex Teutonicis infra terminos Boemorum in silva, ad quam itur per villam Bela, in prerupta rupe edificant castrum. Quod audiens dux Wladizlaus acceptis tribus scaris ex electis militibus repente ex inproviso irruens obtinuit castrum, ubi in primo accessu missis de muro sagittis vulnerati sunt, non tamen ad mortem, duo milites ducis, Oudalricus filius Wacemil et Olen filius Borsa. Illos autem Teutonicos, qui erant in castro capti, nisi comes Albertus superveniens multis precibus et innata sibi sagacitate liberasset, procul dubio iam dux h in eadem silva omnes suspendi iusserat. Eiusdem anni fuit hiemps nimis ventosa et calida et aquarum inundatio magna."; Cf. also annot. 27.

21 Ibid., II. 23, 116: "Aut si tibi displicet frater tuus, cur sordet nostratum clerus non modicus, scientia eque preditus ut iste Teutonicus? O si tot habeas episcopatus, quot cernis capellanos hac in terra progenitos episcopio dignos! An putas, quod alienigena plus nos diligat et melius huic terre cupiat quam indigena? Humana quippe sic est natura, ut unusquisque, quacumque sit terrarum, plus suam quam alienam non solum diligat gentem, verum etiam si quiret, peregrina flumina in patriam verteret. Malumus ergo, malumus caninam caudam aut asini merdam quam Lanczonem locarier super sacram cathedram. Frater tuus, beate memorie Zpitigneu, aliquid sapuit, qui una die omnes Teutonicos hac de terra extrusit. Vivit adhuc Romanus imperator Heinricus et vivat; quem tu temetipsum facis, cum eius potestatem usurpans das baculum et anulum episcopalem famelico cani; certe non inpune tu et tuus episcopus feret, si Koyata filius Wsebor vivet." – Wolverton, *Cosmas of Prague*, 142–143.

he live; usurping his power, you act against yourself when you give the episcopal ring and staff to a hungry dog. Surely you and your bishop will not go unpunished if Kojata, son of Vsebor, lives.

Paradoxically, the nobleman who appreciated Spytihněv's attack on Germans in Bohemia appealed to the authority of the Roman emperor. Although *Theutonici* often play the role of the aggressors in the chronicle, the ethnicity of individuals does not necessarily influence Cosmas' attitude towards them: Marcus, provost of the Prague cathedral chapter, is one of the few other colleagues of Cosmas remembered in his chronicle, and he is immensely praised for his character, wisdom, or for the reform of the cathedral chapter. According to him, Marcus exceled over all people who lived in that time in Bohemia:[22]

> ... he gave his chaplain Mark the provostship of that same church. By the measure of human birth, Mark descended from a noble family of ancestors originating from the German people. He was mighty in wisdom before all the men whom the Czech land then contained.

Cosmas, too, welcomed the election of a foreigner as bishop of Prague. He expected, that Hermann, who was not born in Bohemia, would be able to remain impartial exactly because of his foreign origin and would prefer the interests of the church before the interests of his family and friends:[23]

> The duke, astonished at the unanimity of his own will and Wiprecht's, said: 'Your heart and mine hardly think differently. Because he is a foreigner, this will profit the church more. His kin will not exhaust it, the care of his freemen will not burden it, a crowd of his relatives will not despoil it. Whatever he brings from wherever he comes from, his bride and mother church will have the whole of it. Therefore, I order that he be bishop of Prague.'

---

22 Ibid., II. 26, 119: "[...] dat Marco capellano suo eiusdem ecclesie prepositura, qui secundum hominis genituram nobili ortus erat attavorum prosapia ducens originem de gente Teutonica, pollens sapientia pre cunctis, quos tunc habuit terra Boemica." – Wolverton, *Cosmas of Prague*, 145.

23 Ibid., III. 7, 168: "Tunc dux ammirans suam et eius unanimem voluntatem ait: 'Haud aliter cor tuum atque meum sapit. Et quia hospes est, plus ecclesie prodest; non eum parentela exhauriet, non liberorum cura aggravabit, non cognatorum turma despoliet, quicquid sibi undecumque veniet, totum sponsa eius et mater ecclesia habebit. Hic ergo faciam Pragensis episcopus ut sit." – Wolverton, *Cosmas of Prague*, 189–190.

After all, even though the attempt of Vratislav II to promote his chaplain Lanco is severely criticized and Cosmas works here with negative stereotypes possibly widespread among secular elites, primarily it is an attack on the ruling prince, not on that clergyman, who is depicted glowingly.[24]

However, Cosmas did not present *Theutonic* solely in 'neutral' terms (language, territory, elites), but also came up with negative stereotypes when he regards *Theutonici* as "proud by birth" and mentions their "disrespect towards the Slavs and their language".[25] In another chapter of his chronicle, Cosmas speaks about "Theutonic foolishness".[26] Here, Cosmas echoes John of Salisbury's criticism. Paradoxically, although Conrad I, prince of Brno and Znojmo (1061–1092), asked his brother Vratislav II for support against "Theutonic pride", they both hired an array of warriors from the bishop of Regensburg.[27]

A specific case is represented in the story about Prince Spytihněv II (1055–1061), who acted to banish from his realm all "of the Theutonic tribe" including his own mother:[28]

---

24 Cf. n. 20.
25 Ibid., I. 40, 73: "Perpendit enim in natam Teutonicis superbiam et, quod semper tumido fastu habeant despectui Sclavos et eorum linguam."
26 Ibid., III. 15, 177: "Preterea unde cumque potuit, non paucos sibi in auxilium acquirit Teutonicos, qui pro sui stulticia estimabant in Boemia auri et argenti pondera fore in plateis sparsa et exposita."
27 Cosmas, *Chronica*, II. 35, 131–132: "Nam cum frequenter Conradus ad marchionem huiusmodi de compescenda mitteret verra et ille tumido fastu despiceret eius verba, supplex adiit fratrem suum Wratizlaum ducem Boemorum, rogans eum sibi in auxilium contra superbiam Teutonicorum. Qui suis quamvis non diffidens viribus tamen Ratisponensis episcopi unam scaram ex electis militibus precio/ conducit sibi in auxilium." – cf. n. 19.
28 Ibid., II. 14, 103–104: "Prima die qua intronizatus est, hic magnum et mirabile ac omnibus seclis memorabile fecit hoc sibi memoriale; nam quotquot inventi sunt de gente Teutonica, sive dives sive pauper sive peregrinus, omnes simul in tribus diebus iussit eliminari de terra Boemia, quin etiam et genitricem non tulit remanere suam, de qua supra meminimus, Ottonis natam, nomine a Iuditham. Similiter et abbatissam sancti Georgii, Brunonis filiam, eliminat, quia hec olim antea eum verbis offenderat acerbis. Nam dum pater eius Bracizlaus reedificaret menia tocius urbis Prage per girum et hic supradictus heros a patre sibi concessam Satc haberet provinciam, forte exiit, ut cum suis circa sancti Georgii claustrum componeret murum. Et cum nullo modo recte poni posset murus, nisi destrueretur fornax abbatisse, qui ibi forte stabat, iactata fune in media, tunc aliis hoc facere cunctantibus accessit natus herilis et quasi risum sibi faciens cum magno cachinno iussit eum deicere subito in torrentem Bruznicam dicens: 'Hodie domna abbatissa calidas non gustabit placentas.' Quod agnoscens abbatissa exiit irata de claustro et valde moleste eius dicta ferens sic eum yronicis aggreditur et confundit dictis: 'Nobilis, insignis, vir fortis et inclitus armis, Quam magnas turres nunc expugnavit et urbes Et sibi famosum fert de fornace triumphum, Timpora iam lauro victricia cingat et auro. Clerus multimodas campanis personet odas, Dux quia deiecit fornacem miraque fecit." – Wolverton, *Cosmas of Prague*, 131–132.

On the first day on which he was enthroned, he did a great and marvelous thing, memorable for all ages, as a memorial to himself: as many as could be found of the German people, whether rich or poor or pilgrim, he ordered all of them banished at once from the land of Bohemia within three days. Not even his mother – the daughter of Otto, named Judith, about whom we spoke above – would he allow to remain. He likewise banished the abbess of St. George, the daughter of Bruno, because she had once earlier offended him with sharp words. For when his father, Břetislav, rebuilt the walls of the whole burg of Prague in a circle, and the aforesaid hero held the province of Žatec by his father's grant, he happened to come with his people to construct a wall around the cloister of St. George. Now, it was in no way possible to position the wall correctly without destroying the abbess's oven, which happened to stand there. With a rope thrown in its midst, others hesitating to do it, the master's son approached. As if making a joke to himself, he ordered the oven thrown down suddenly into the stream (Brusnice) with a great guffaw, saying, 'The Lady Abbess will not enjoy hot cakes today.' Seeing this, the abbess came out furious from her cloister and, taking his words very badly, attacked and confounded him with these ironic words: 'What a noble, distinguished, powerful man, renowned in arms! Much as he stormed great towers and burgs, now he brings off a famous triumph over an oven. His victorious temples are now wreathed with a golden laurel. Let the clergy resound with various melodies and bells, because the duke has thrown down an oven and done a wondrous thing. Ah! It is shameful to say that he is not ashamed to have done this.' The man stiffened in his body, and his voice choked in his throat. Indignant, he restrained his rage with a groan.

Cosmas confirms in the story that *Theutonici* represent for him not just members of the elites, but also people of humble origin. He, however, does not directly celebrate the prince, who was responsible for their punishment.[29] His story about abbess of St. George monastery, which he includes as an explanation of Spytihněv's action, is mere sarcasm towards that prince, although the latter's image in the chronicle is otherwise positive – as it also confirms the description of his looks.[30]

To sum up, for Cosmas, *Theutonici* were clearly recognizable as an ethnic group, which spoke its specific language, inhabited primarily clearly defined

---

29 For an interesting interpretation combining gender and power aspects conf. Wolverton, *Cosmas*, 148–151.
30 E.g. among the latest Wolverton, *Cosmas*, 117, 139–141.

territory and consisted of elites, but also people of humble origin. Their origin is for him an important indicator of their identification, as well, since he still perceives *Theutonici* who had lived for a long time in Czech lands as the "others", which makes them e. g. also possible to be identified and to be expelled. Although his image of *Theutonici* is negative in part, he does not share any sentiments about the Slavs: the worst enemies of the *Bohemi* in his chronicle are the Slavic speaking Poles.[31] There is also a question as to what extent Cosmas represents the feelings and sentiments of all inhabitants of the Přemyslid *regnum*? As Patrick Geary once mentioned, ethnicity could have been even in the Early Middle Ages a useful tool for labeling either enemies or allies in concrete political situations, or within a social conflict.[32] That does not mean that it is just a result of authorial manipulations and deliberate decisions by the historical actors, or that it was active over time and that it must have been important to the same extent for all social strata. As ethnicity (and different layers of identity in general) are often activated by conflict, the probability of ethnic identification is simply higher among elites who represent a polity, which might be a product of that conflict. Among their clients (and later subjects), other, more localized identifications most probably prevailed.[33]

Whereas Cosmas' continuators, Gerlach of Milevsko, or Henry the Woodcutter shared his basic categorization of "Theutonici" (territory,[34]

---

31   Barbara Krzemieńska, "Polska i Polacy w opinii czeskiego kronikarza Kosmasa." [Poland and Poles in the opinion of the Czech chronicler Cosmas] *Zeszyty naukowe Uniwersytetu Łódzkiego, Nauki humanistyczno-społeczne* 15 (1960), 75–95.

32   Patrick J. Geary, "Ethnic Identity as a Situational Construct in the Early Middle Ages," *Mitteilungen der Anthropologischen Gesellschaft in Wien* 113 (1983), 15–26.

33   For the importance of different identifications in fourteenth-century Czech lands cf. František Šmahel, "The Idea of the 'Nation' in Hussite Bohemia: an Analytical Study of the Ideological and Political Aspects of the National Question in Hussite Bohemia from the End of the 14th Century to the Eighties of the 15th Century," *Historica* 16 (1969), 143–247; 17 (1969), 93–197. For the wider central-European context František Graus, *Die Nationenbildung der Westslawen im Mittelalter* (Sigmaringen, 1980) and Scales, *The Shaping of German Identity*.

34   Canonicus, *Continuatio*, 216: 1133, "[…] in Theutonicis partibus[…]"; Vincentius, *Annales*, 413, a. 1142: "Rex autem Conradus Wissegrad ueniens cum processione in die sancto pentecostes honeste suscipitur et honestissime a duce W[ladizlao] et domina Gertrude sua sorore, predicti ducis coniuge, Teuthoniam feliciter revertitur." – ibid., 423, a. 1156: "His itaque peractis domnus imperator ex consilio suorum principum Veronenses in gratiam suam recipiens per Ueronam Teutoniam cum trihumpho feliciter reuertitur." – Gerlacus, *Annales*, 464 a. 1170: "[Qui recuperata terra nec non et gratia patris, in Teutonia postmodum] peregre mortuus est." – ibid., 506, a. 1184: "Interea Fridericus in Teutonia exercitum colligebat per amicos suos." – ibid., 516, a. 1198, "Itaque Boemi Teutoniam ingressi mox circa Wirtzburc uersi sunt in sedicionem, et orta inter eos graui simultate, militares uiri fere omnes relictis domnis suis baronibus abierunt retro et redierunt in Boemiam."

language,[35] people,[36] elites,[37] origin),[38] they follow him in the use of negative stereotypes only in exceptional moments. One example is the Sázava-addition to the Chronicle of Cosmas, which mentions the "Theutonic" origin of an abbot installed by Spytihněv II.[39] We are told that he was an awful person, and his origin seems to be a complement to that characterization. Consequently, he was forced to leave the monastery by the long since deceased St. Procopius, who threatened him in his dreams.

For the anonymous Prague canon, Conrad III is not only "rex Romanorum", but also *rex Theutonicorum*.[40] Another Prague canon Vincencius mentions *Theutonicorum cantus*.[41] For him, *Theutonici* seem to be all the German speaking subjects of the emperor, yet his enumeration of different *nationes* under

---

35   Cf. n. 42.
36   Canonicus, *Contintuatio*, ed. Emler, 215, a. 1132: "[...] dum ad quendam locum Omberk vocatum venirent, ibi cum Theutonicis foro praedicti loci pugnaverunt."
37   Vincentius, *Annales*, 438, a. 1158: "totius Teutonie principes."; Canonicus, *Contintuatio*, ed. Emler, 223, a. 1135: "Haec cum dixisset, cuncti principes Theutonici inanimiter responderunt, nullum imperatori adeo fidelem et familiarem ut ducem Sobieslaum, et cum prius pro infideli et inimico coram imperatore reputatus fuerit, in hoc praesenti negotio amicissimus et fidelissimus eius fautor liquido patuit." Gerlacus, *Annales*, ed. Emler, 474, a. 1179: "Mortui sunt in eo proelio Zezema comes, pater domni Hroznatae, et Aghna, et alii multi, comes Witcho captus, capti etiam Teutonici maiores natu ex his, qui in adiutorium Friderici venerunt, multi quoque ex eis occisi, residuique nasos praecisi ludibrium mundo sunt effecti."
38   Cf. annot. 38.
39   *Gründung des Klosters Sázava*, ed. Bertold Bretholz, in Cosmas, *Chronica*, 2, 248: "Memoratus namque dux Vito abbate cum nepote suo Emmerammo et fratribus, quos unitas caritatis concordaverat, in terram Hunorum per egre proficiscentibus, propria fautorum suorum consiliaria diffinitione utens in loco illo abbatem genere Teutonicum constituit, hominem turbida indignatione plenum. Ubi dum nocte prima adventus sui ex more ad matutinalem sinaxim pergens foribus ecclesie appropinquaret, apparuit vir sanctus Procopius infra ianuam oratorii appodians et dicens ei: 'Unde tibi potestas hic degendi? Quid queris?' At ille: 'Potestativa', inquit, ducis maiestas et eius primatum inconvulsa sublimitas mee possibilitatis regimini hoc cenobium usque ad finem vite mee tradidit.' Cui sanctus pater: 'Citissime', inquit, 'sine confusionis verecundia discede, quod si non feceris, ultio divinitus veniet super te'."
40   Canonicus, *Contintuatio*, ed. Emler, 230, a. 1139: "Eodem tempore dux Sobieslaus levirum suum Belam, regem Pannoniae, convenit, nam idem rex Bela filiam suam filio regis Theutonicorum Conradi tradebat. Hae nuptiae in festo penthecosten celebratae sunt." Ibid., 236, a. 1142: "Pragam vero metropolim civitatem ingressi cum Theobaldo, munitiones firmaverunt, Wladislaum propere ad regem Theutonicorum pro auxilio adipiscendo direxerunt.... Evolutis igitur paucis diebus pro dolore et afflictione non computatis, regis Theutonicorum Conradi conductorumque eius Wladislai ducis et episcopi Zdiconis [...]"; for Theutonicae partes, cf. ibid., 214–217: 1132, 1133.
41   Vincentius, *Annales*, 451: 1161, "[...] id clamor ad astra Theutonicorum cantibus[...]".

the emperor's command does not allow any further specification.[42] Henry the Woodcuter more than once made his reader aware of the different etymologies of toponyms in the surrounding region and argues for their Slavic origin.[43]

It is not possible for in this context to deal with the chronicles of Pulkava and Dalimil in detail,[44] since the number of instances in which the *Theutonici*, or "Němci" are mentioned exceeds one hundred in Dalimil, and sixty in Pulkava. Because of that, I will merely focus on their strategies for identifying and "othering", which will be compared with those of the authors previously mentioned.

For Pulkava, *Theutonici* were also clearly recognizable through their language.[45] They lived in a certain area.[46] In one instance, he calls them (along with the *Boemi*, or *Lombardi*) a *natio*;[47] in another place, he identifies *Theutonici* and Saxons.[48] He is not particularly critical of them, only in one instance when he speaks about their "tyranny".[49]

For a start, "Němci" are "bad guys" in the chronicle of Dalimil and are always responsible for the failure of "Češi". Once a prince or king of Bohemia decides

---

42 Ibid., 452, a. 1162: "Imperator interea cum Boemis, Theutonicis, Lonbardis et aliarum nationum plurima militia Mediolanum circumire non desinit, fruges eorum, vineas et arbores fructiferas destruit, pecudes, armenta et quae potest eis aufert, castella, turres, quas potest, eis destruit, ex eis, quos capere potest, capit, suspendit, interficit". Ibid., 454, a. 1163 "Imperator autem Theutonicorum, Papiensium, Cremonensium et aliorum Lonbardorum collecta militia, Mediolani suo residet pro tribunali, quid de tanta urbe faciendum sit, consilivm querit". Ibid., 452, a. 1161, "[...] plurimi Alamannie episcopi [...]".

43 Henry the Woodcuter, *Chronicon*, 44: "Hoc in Latino resonat quasi castra gygantum: / ober enim Sclavice Latine sonat quasi gygas,/ Teutunici castrum tamen hoc Oberzez modo dicunt.; Sic Sar est Sclavicum, sonat hoc plantacio recens,/ quamvis Teutunici sar dicant gramina grossa, / Sar non Teutunico, sed de Sclavico trahit ortum."

44 For the manuscripts cf. Eloise Adde-Vomáčka, "Environnement textuel et réception du texte médiéval. La deuxième vie de la Chronique de Dalimil," *Médiévales* 73 (2017) 169–192.

45 Přibík Pulkava, "Kronika," ed. Josef Emler, c. 39, 49: "[...] Conrado, qui et linguam theutonicam optime scivit, [...]".

46 Ibid., c. 63, 87: "illius Sobieslai ducis, exul in partibus Theuthonicis [...]"; ibid., c. 63, 86: "[...] Theutoniam feliciter est reversus [...]" ; for contemporary example of defining borders by language in pragmatic literacy cf. Codex diplomaticus et epistolaris regni Bohemiae, V/2, nr. 679, 317.

47 Ibid., c. 65, 102: "Imperator interea cum Boemis, Theutonicis, Lombardis et aliarum nacionum [...]".

48 Ibid., c. 77, 165.

49 Ibid., c. 77, 165: "Fuit insuper dictorum Theutonicorum tirannide Boemia multum lesa [...] eiectis inde Saxonibus et Theutonicis supradictis liberaretur ab eorum [...]; ibid., c. 78, 169: [...] eiecit edictum sub pena capitis, ut omnes Theutonici de regno exirent [...]"; ibid., c. 78, 169: "Quoniam agri per regnum Boemie propter Theutonicorum tirannidem aliquibus temporibus [...]".

to follow their advice, *regnum* declines, since, according to Dalimil, the "Němci" always seek the extermination of the "Češi". His hatred for "Němci" is so strong that he would prefer the daughter of a Czech peasant rather than a "German princess" be a future Bohemian princess;[50] or he hails the king who has asked even Jews to kill "Němci".[51] Who are "Němci", or "Češi" in that chronicle is revealed in the synonyms used for them: "německý/český jazyk", "German/Czech language":

> And he (the emperor) made himself aware of Soběslav, a brave man, who was ready to die for the honor of his people (jazyk), and started to treat him with respect/ ... Once the German people in Bohemia rise,/ our dynasty loses its honor,/ as they (the Germans) betray the land and princes/ and because of them, our crown will be taken to Germany/; Germans, at the beginning, pretend to be nice,/ but once their numbers increase,/ they stop respecting their lord/ and look for a lord from their own country.[52]

It signals that the language became for Dalimil an important source of identification, which could have superseded other social differences and might have been used as a synonym for all those who speak it.[53] That belonging to "Němci", or "Češi" is inherited by blood might connote "kinship", which in one instance is possibly used for "Czechs":[54]

---

50   Cf. n. 60.
51   So called Dalimil, *Kronika* 1, ed. Jiří Daňhelka and col., c. 80: "O královu Václavovu boji s Němci/ Král Václav ščedrý ovšem bieše,/ ale Němče v zemi plodieše. [...] A když Němče potkachu,/ nos jemu uřezachu. [...] Němci Čstibora míle s synem přijechu/ a bezpečenstvie jemu dachu; velmi jej čstiechu. Pak toho i s synem královí proradichu/ a do Prahy jě svázány poslachu. [...] Král židóm ku brani pokynu řka: 'Zbijete-li jě, nepočtu vám za vinu'. Židé tajně oděnie a lidu dobychu,/ a když na ně křižovníci udeřichu,/ židové křižovníky pobichu/ a na dvě stě tehdy Němcóv zbichu".
52   Ibid., c. 68: "A ten, znamenav Soběslava, muže udatného, že jest hotov za svého jazyka čest umřieti, poče sě k němu dobřě jmieti; [...] Když německý jazyk v Čechách vstane,/ tehdy našeho rodu vše čest stane;/ neb zradie zemi i kniežata,/ pro ně bude nášě koruna do Němec vzata./ Němciť sě najprve krotie,/ ale, jakž sě rozplodie,/ tehdy o svéj hospodě netbají.'; z své země pána sobě hledají."; cf. ibid., 97: "O Albrechtovi, říšském králi, vrahu českém/ Na léto vrah český Albrecht do Čech poče jíti, chtě překotem český jazyk zahladiti./ Chlapi s kosami s ním jdiechu,/ ti vše obilé sieci chtiechu,/ aby Čechy hladem sě rozlezli/ a Švábi by u pustú zemi vešli".
53   Cf. Jaroslav Mezník, "Němci a Češi v Kronice tak řečeného Dalimila," [Germans and Czechs in the Chronicle of the so-called Dalimil] *Časopis Matice moravské* 112 (1993), 3–10, here especially 6. The equation language = nation has most probably Biblical roots.
54   Dalimil, *Kronika*, c. 63: "V radu poče Němce pojímati,/ pro to bratr jeho Vladislav jě sě naň hněvati. Pojem jej do komňaty samého,/ veče: 'Báťo, třeba mi s tobú mluviti cos tajného'. Veče: 'Báťo, proč druhem sě nekážeš, že Němcóm jíti z dvoru nekážeš?/ Či nepomníš, co

> He started to invite the Germans to his council/ and because of that, his brother Vladislav became annoyed with him. He invited him into his chambers/ and told him: Lord, I need to talk to you privately. Lord, why do you not order the Germans to leave your court?/ Don't you remember all the bad things they brought about?/ How the Germans betrayed our kin ... But Bořivoj was not able to follow this policy / and started again to invite the Germans into his land.

Even though "Němci" also lived in Bohemia, where they came as settlers, or experts especially during the thirteenth century, they had their own basic territory – therefore, they could be invited to Bohemia, or repelled:

> After him, Spytihněv, his son, became prince,/ who immediately showed his anger towards Germans/ and in three days, he expelled them from the land.... After he weeded all Germans from the land/ and all other foreigners/ as nettle from a garden ...[55]

A good relationship with the Germans only leads to troubles, in the view of Dalimil:

> He began to defame the Czechs and the numbers of Germans started to grow in the land.... As he started to persecute his brother and invited the Germans into the land./ Once the Poles noted / that the Czechs did not respect their prince,/ they attacked their land / and thoroughly devastated it./ The Czechs with their prince defeated them,/ but once they did that,/ they also expelled their prince from the land,/ saying: "To you, Czech souls smell,/ go off to Germany, you German muzzle.[56]

---

jsú nám zlého učinili,/ kako jsú Němci náš rod zradili? [...] Ale Bořivoj neumě té milosti schovati/ i jě sě opět Němcóv v zemi zváti."; it might also mean "dynasty".

55 Ibid., c. 48, 553: "Po tom by syn jeho knězem Spytihněv,/ ten inhed Němcóm zjevi svój hněv. / Ve třech dnech vše Němce z země vypudi. [...] Když vyple z země vše Němče/ i vše jiné cizozemče/ jako z zahrady kopřivy/[...]"; cf. Ibid., 69: "Ten počě mluviti,/ že, by jměl moc, chtěl by z Čech vše Němče vypuditi. Větší menšie namluvichu,/ tak Stanimíra knězem učinichu./ Ten počě Němcóm do Čech nedati/ a káza všěm nosy řězati./ Ale když sě ve vše tvrzě uváza,/ milost, již k Němcóm jmiešě, pokáza./ Jě sě Čechóm dolóv hlav puditi/ a Němče v zemi ploditi./".

56 Ibid., c. 69: "Ten počě na hanbu Čechóm mluviti/ a Němcóv sě jě v zemi ploditi. [...] Neb ten počě bratra následovati a Němče mocně v zemi zváti./ Polené, když to znamenachu,/ že Čechy svého kněžě netbachu,/ na zemi udeřichu/ a škodu velikú učinichu./ Čechy na ně s svým knězem míle jidechu/ a bojem jě udatně podjidechu./ A když jě pobichu,/ kněžě z země vypudichu/ řkúc: 'Tobě smrdí česká dušě,/ náhle do Němec, němečská kušě!'"; Cf. n. 53.

Pavlína Rychterová convincingly argues that this strong identification with the language has its roots in the contemporary situation, when the Přemyslid dynasty, which was originally the important source of identification for the Bohemian nobility,[57] died out and contemporaries had to refocus on other sources of identification.[58]

Surprisingly, this chronicle was also translated from Czech into German and transferred to prose during the fourteenth century, most probably by a Prague burgher of German origin.[59] This man was, of course, not just a translator; he also had to deal with Dalimil's feelings towards Germans and burghers. As Vlastimil Brom has clearly demonstrated, the translator found an effective solution for his problem: when "Němci" is mentioned in a negative context, it is transformed into *vremde*, "foreigners"; they remain *Teutsche* in neutral contexts. (The Latin translation follows mostly that German prose-translation – "Teutschen" are exchanged for "alienigenae".)[60] The story mentioned above of Udalrich and Božena provides us with an excellent example of his translation practices. Whereas in the Czech version, we read:

> I prefer to be happy with a Czech peasant woman, / rather than to marry a German King's daughter,

the translator into German writes:

> Vil mer wil ich lachin da/ mit einer bemischin půrin,/ wen eines fremden koniges tochtir gewin. (Bohemian peasant girl rather than daughter of a foreign king)[61]

---

57 That it was not its unique source of identification is demonstrated in Kalhous, *Bohemi*, c. 3. 2.

58 Pavlína Rychterová, "The Chronicle of the so-called Dalimil and its concept of Czech identity," in *Historiography and Identity VI: Historiographies in Central and Eastern Central Europe Between Latin and Vernaculars, C. 1200–1500*, eds. Pavlíny Rychterová and David Kalhous, (Turnhout, forthcoming).

59 Vlastimil Brom, "The rhymed German translation of the Old Czech chronicle of so-called Dalimil and its specific identification models compared to the original text," in ibid. (forthcoming)

60 Conf. e.g. Anežka Vidmanová, "Nad pařížskými zlomky latinského Dalimila," [Above the Parisian fragments of the Latin Dalimil] *Slovo a smysl: časopis pro mezioborová bohemistická studia* 3, č. 5 (2006), 25–67; http://slovoasmysl.ff.cuni.cz/node/97 (last access 9-11-2018).

61 Dalimil, *Kronika*, c. 42, 493: "Radějí sě chcu s češskú sedlkú smieti/než královnu německú za ženu jmieti"; *Di tutsch kronik von Behem lant: die gereimte deutsche Übersetzung der Alttschechischen Dalimil-Chronik. Rhymed German translation of the Old Czech Dalimil Chronicle*, ed. Vlastimil Brom (Brno, 2009), 274–275.

Yet, both author and translator admit that the "German princes" might teach Udalrich's children "deutsch" and that it might cause "ein groz zcweiunge/ vnd dem lande zcu hant/ ein recht virderbnize bekant".[62] The prosaic German version of the chronicle not only mitigates ethnic conflicts in the chronicle, but also reduces animosity towards the burgers, which is so well documented in its original version.[63]

> A common 'peasant' doesn't give you of his own will anything for free; / reassuring you that you are his master, he is seeking a suitable moment: / As soon as he frees himself of you, / he will have you pay everything back to him with interest. / Now you can see, my lords, whether yours is a right decision / to give castles in (our) land to Germans.

This is transformed as follows:

> Dem prager gibt man sin willin, /waz er mit dem elbogin stillin /vf wundirlich mag gehebin, /daz wil er nur von im gebin. /Dristunt spricht er: 'Her' /biz im sin will nit ver /kumbt bi nacht adir tag, /ob er nimer mag, /dich also vbir windin. /Ir herren, ir mogt nv vinden, /ob er gutis ratis sit: /Gebt den fromden in Behem wit /husir vnd gute burgen, /dar vf si vch irwurgen.

Offensive 'peasant', or 'villain' are replaced with neutral "Prager", and "Germans" with "fromden".[64]

From our perspective, it is important that both authors have come up with different definitions of what it meant to be "Němec", "teutsch". Whereas the high medieval Czech chronicler followed Cosmas of Prague and defined the "Němci" by their origin and language and ascribed them affiliation towards other "Němci" without taking into consideration their birthplace, his German counterpart – by switching out "Germans" in the original so-called Dalimil for "foreigners" – largely adapted and transformed that categorization; for him, the border led through those who lived in Bohemia and those who came from outside. The source of identification was for the translator the land, and not the language.

---

62   *Di tutsch kronik von Behem lant*, 276–277.
63   Dalimil, *Kronika*, c. 98: "Chlap svú volú tobě ničs nedá,/ pánkajě tobě, svého času hledá./ Moci-liť bude kdy s tě býti,/ kážeť své i s lichvú zaplatiti./ Juž vidíte, páni, dobré-li jste rady,/ dávajúce Němcóm v zemi hrady".
64   Based on Brom's *Di tutsch kronik von Behem lant. The rhymed German translation*.

This is, however, not a completely new strategy. If we return back to an earlier time, to the chronicle of Gerlach of Milevsko, written at the beginning of the thirteenth century, we can follow a similar pattern. Of course, Gerlach identified himself with the Christian community, *civitas*,[65] or with his Premonstratensian order.[66] But, although Gerlach was born in the Rhineland and came to Bohemia in his late teens, he included himself among the *Bohemi*:

> After the consecration of Bishop Henry in that summer, our noblemen, motivated by a long-lasting hatred, started to persecute Duke Frederick and then expelled him from the land. Then they elected Prince Conrad, also called Otto, of Moravia, about whom we spoke a lot, and with him, they besieged and captured Prague.[67]

"Bohemian" identity was in his case, as well, based on identification with the land and its polity, not necessarily with the language.

Both strategies of identification and "othering" reflect the interests of different social groups and their seeking of, or struggle for legitimacy. Both also remind us remarkably of two different models of nationalism, which are traditionally associated with Western, or Central and Eastern Europe respectively and labeled with moral epithetes. Whereas positive Western "civic nationalism" is based on the identification with the state and every citizen is theoretically a member of a national group, in the case of negative "ethnic nationalism",

---

65 Gerlacus, *Annales*, 467, a. 1175, "Pro his et aliis operibus misericordiae credimus eum invenisse misericordiam apud patrem misericordiarum, domnum deum nostrum. Ibid., 499, a. 1184, Verum inter haec quis putas fuerit affectus in nobis videntibus aegrotare patrem nostrum, et talem patrem, qui per euangelium omnes nos genuerat".

66 Gerlacus, *Annales*, 486, a. 1178, "[...] tum in omnibus ecclesiis nostri iuris [...]"; ibid., 488: 1178, [...] secundum disciplinam ordinis nostri[...]".

67 Gerlacus, *Annales*, 481, a. 1182, "Igitur post consecrationem episcopi Henrici eadem aestate Bohemi, nostri maiores natu, persecutionem diutinis odiis conflatam excitaverunt in ducem Fridericum et eiicientes eum extra terram mille persecutum opprobriis, Kunradum Moraviensem, qui et Otto, de quo supra multa diximus, sibi eligunt in principem, cum quo Pragam multo tempore obsident et tandem obtinent." Cf. Ibid., 470, a. 1175, "Inde profecti sequenti die natalis domni inciderunt custodias Mediolanensium, a quibus omnes quidem nostri in fugam conuersi, multi uero sunt capti atque in Mediolano tamdiu tenti, quamdiu speraretur, quod uitam suam possent pecunia redimere, quod ubi desperatum est, dimissi ad terram suam sunt redire permissi. Reliqui uero, qui tale discrimen euaserant, mercede nautica stagnam transfretantes Cumanum per aliam uiam et inmanissimam in Alpibus niuem reversi sunt in Ratisponam ac deinde in terram suam. Redditi uero suis delitescebant, ubi poterant, nec usquam audebant apparere curiae, quamdiu Zobezlaus dominabatur Boemie".

it is the shared origin, culture and language which are determinative of the nationality. Medieval people were not citizens, but subjects. This analysis of selected sources of Bohemian origin shows that these definitions of belonging and these strategies of identification were pre-modern and might have been established as a result of a conflict among different social groups in one region. They might well have found different definitions of belonging a useful tool for confirming or disproving the legitimacy of others.

PART 2

Polish Views Regarding Germans in the Middle Ages – Hagiographical and Historiographical Sources

∴

CHAPTER 6

The Image of the Germans and the Holy Roman Empire in Polish Historiography until the 13th Century

Andrzej Pleszczyński

The question of Polish opinions about Germany in the Middle Ages is still a poorly researched area; the same is true as to German opinions about Poland in the same period. This adds to the weight and significance of to the conference that has given rise to this collection of articles. Although there are works which, to a greater or lesser extent, address the subject formulated in the title of this paper, they were written relatively long ago, during a time when historiography was heavily influenced by tendencies to "nationalize" analyses of the past, however distant. Today, we are in a position to attempt to achieve the greatest possible objectivity.[1]

Not only is the question of the perception of the Germans and the medieval Roman Empire in Poland intriguing, but it also has a considerable multifaceted significance. It is enough to mention here that the oldest writings have always constituted a kind of reference basis for more recent texts and views, including modern ones.

The matter does not merely concern literary tradition. Opinions about strangers say a lot about the people who formed such judgments.[2] Therefore,

---

1 Cf. a summary of older Polish research in: Jadwiga Krzyżaniakowa, "Poglądy polskich kronikarzy średniowiecznych na Niemcy i stosunki polsko-niemieckie," [The Views of Polish medieval chroniclers on Germany and Polish-German relations] in *Wokół stereotypów Niemców i Polaków*, ed. Wojciech Wrzesiński, Acta Universitatis Wratislaviensis. Historia 114 (Wrocław, 1993), 15–72. The problem has not been exhausted in: Andrzej Pleszczyński, *The Birth of a Stereotype. Polish Rulers and their Country in German Writings c. 1000 A.D.* (Boston-Leiden, 2011); and: ibid., *Przekazy niemieckie o Polsce i jej mieszkańcach w okresie panowania Piastów* [German sources about Poland and its inhabitants during the Piast rule] (Lublin, 2016); also: Jerzy Strzelczyk, "Deutsch-polnische Schicksalgemeinschaft in gegenseitigen Meinungen im Mittelalter," in *Mittelalter – eines oder viele?/ Średniowiecze – jedno czy wiele?*, ed. Sławomir Moździoch, Wojciech Mrozowicz, and Stanisław Rosik (Wrocław, 2010), 111–126; or: Thomas Wünsch, *Deutsche und Slawen im Mittelalter: Beziehungen zu Tschechen, Polen, Südslawen und Russen* (Munich, 2008).
2 For more on the subject e.g.: Alois Wierlacher, "Mit anderen Augen oder: Fremdheit als Ferment. Überlegungen zur Begründung einer intellektuellen Hermeneutik deutscher Literatur," in *Das Fremde und das Eigene: Prologomena zu einer interkulturellen Germanistik*

the question is vital. Before it is explored in more detail, a word of explanation is in order about why the 13th century constitutes a dividing line in this discussion. Very briefly, the close of the 13th century ended the era during which the Piast state had emerged, and it was subsequently divided into several sovereign provinces. In the 14th century, the Kingdom of Poland came into existence and the new state soon began its expansion towards the east; it also became involved in confrontations with the Teutonic Order. Facing problems that were entirely different from the ones which had existed earlier, the Polish elites changed quite considerably, and simultaneously their views about the world were also transformed.[3]

The subject of this paper, even though it has been narrowed down from a broader one, is still relatively extensive and multifaceted, so it can only be presented here in the manner of a sketch. The structure of the discussion will mainly be based upon chronicles, while information from the Polish annals will also provide some help. The sources will be presented and analyzed chronologically; only the references which are most important for the subject will be discussed.

In view of this introduction, to begin our actual reflections we should remark that our knowledge about this subject concerns almost only the elites. We know very little about how Germans were perceived by ordinary Poles during the earlier period of the Middle Ages, because prior to the 14th century we have no appropriate text that could confirm any given perception. Only the old ethnic terms are evidence of some general assessments or value judgments. For instance, the Polish and Slavic word "Niemcy [Germans]" is connected with the inability to understand because it denotes people who do not or cannot speak, unlike the Slavs, and whose words are comprehensible.[4] It happened that for a very long time this term was used to denote all the inhabitants of

---

(Munich, 1985), 3–28; Elke M. Geenen, *Soziologie des Fremden. Ein gesellschaftstheoretischer Entwurf* (Wiesbaden, 2002), 28–38.

3   This change is poorly understood in Polish historical thought, although the Piast and Jagiellonian orientations are noticed, but the first is treated only in terms of hostile resistance to Germany and attachment to the so-called western territories, the latter is seen as the idea of Polish patronage over the Ruthenian and Lithuanian territories and friendly neutrality towards Germany. The issue is present only in political thought without serious reference to older history – see e.g.: Jacek Kubera, "Polska 'piastowska' vs 'jagiellońska'. Odmienność wizji relacji z Niemcami jako determinant poglądów na polską politykę zagraniczną" [Poland of the 'Piasts' vs of the 'Jagiellonians'. The different vision of relations with Germany as a determinant of views on Polish foreign policy], *Acta Politica Polonica* 38/4 (2016), 65–80.

4   Aleksander Brückner, *Słownik etymologiczny języka polskiego* [Etymological Dictionary of the Polish Language] (Warszawa, 1985), 360; Krystyna Długosz-Kurczabowa, *Wielki słownik etymologiczno-historyczny języka polskiego* [A great etymological and historical dictionary of the Polish language] (Warsaw, 2008), 446–447.

Western Europe, because all ordinary people in Poland and also in Slavdom could not distinguish the westerners from each other.

This seems to say much about the difficulties for the Poles to have any objective knowledge of their western neighbors. Although the sources were written solely by clergymen from the circles associated with those in authority, their opinions were in some way influenced by the above-mentioned cultural strangeness between the Poles and the Germans. This influence can easily be seen in the oldest known chronicle written in the Polish lands.[5] Its author is unknown, but in Poland he was traditionally believed to have come from France, so he was given the name Gallus Anonymus.[6]

In his chronicle, references to the Germans and their country are relatively rare and more modest than the information about other neighbors of the Piast state: Rus, Hungary and Czechia (Bohemia); only the pagan Baltic people receive markedly less attention. This phenomenon is accompanied by the conviction, expressed in Anonymus' text, that although Poland respects the Empire as the supreme authority in the Christian world, the Piast state has no strong ties to the system headed by the emperor. Poland belonged to a different political structure, which was poorly connected to the so-called West as represented by Germany, but was instead more closely linked with the Slavic countries and Hungary.

This way of thinking can already be noticed in the preface to the chronicle, where, while enumerating the western neighbors of the Piast country, the author only laconically mentions Saxony.[7] At the same time, Anonymus devotes considerable attention to the position of Poland within the Slavic lands, the northernmost areas of which it supposedly covered; he also writes about, in rather great detail, the lands of the southern Slavs.

---

5 *Galli Anonimi chronicae et gestae ducum sive principum Polonorum*, ed. Karol Maleczyński (Kraków, 1952); English translation: *The Deeds of the Princes of the Poles*, eds. Paul W. Knoll, Frank Schaer (Budapest, 2003); more about this edition: Jacek Banaszkiewicz, "O nowym łacińsko-anglojęzycznym wydaniu Galla i samej jego kronice," [About the new Latin-English edition of Gall and his chronicle itself], *Roczniki Historyczne* 70 (2004), 205–15; about the chronicler: Thomas N. Bisson, "On Not Eating Polish Bread in Vain. Resonance and Conjuncture in thee Deeds of the Princes of Poland (1109–1113)," *Viator. Medieval and Rennaissance Studies* 29 (1998), 275–289; Piotr Oliński, "Am Hofe Bolesław Schiefmunds. Die Chronik des Gallus Anonymus," in *Die Hofgeschichtsschreibung im mittelalterlichen Europa: Projekte und Forschungsprobleme*, ed. Rudolf Schieffer and Jarosław Wenta (Toruń, 2006), 93–105.

6 Lately on this subject: Tomasz Jasiński, *O pochodzeniu Galla Anonima* [On the descent of Gall Anonym] (Cracow, 2008); cf.: Johanes Fried, "Kam der Gallus Anonymus aus Bamberg", *Deutsches Archiv für Erforschung des Mittelalters* 65 (2009), 497–545.

7 *Galli Anonimi chronicae*, 7; *The Deeds of the Princes*, 13.

Following the organization of this work and reading the part devoted to Mieszko I, we notice that it contains no information concerning the role played by Germany in the Christianization of the country – there is only a reference to Princess Dobrawa, who was supposed to have been "a very good Christian".[8] As a matter of fact, however, from a general point of view, we notice that the chronicle does not mention any "helpers" as far as the baptism/conversion of the country was concerned: neither the Czechs, nor even the papacy. Anonymus' reports about Mieszko I's reign are very limited. It was only the times of the next ruler, Bolesław Chrobry (the Brave), which receive more extensive coverage, including references to the issue in question. The second of the historical Piasts was an extremely important figure for Anonymus: the chronicler's depiction of Bolesław the Brave became the portrait of a model monarch. It is significant that the extraordinarily detailed description of Bolesław the Brave's reign does not contain a single word about his dozen-year-long heavy battles with Henry II. The notation that Bolesław "brought the uncontrollable Saxons under control with such might that he marked Poland's borders with iron posts in the Saale river in the middle of their lands"[9] may be a certain echo of the wars. However, it was one thing to refer to the Saxons as Bolesław's enemies; to refer to the German King and Emperor Henry II in this way would have been quite another.

One could also surmise that the conflict was "forgotten" due to the logic of the narrative constructed by Anonymus. After all, the author clearly intended to present Bolesław the Brave as Otto III's friend in his description of the magnificent welcome extended to the emperor in Poland in 1000. What was referred to as the Congress of Gniezno plays an important part in the narrative of the chronicle. The description of the event is extraordinarily detailed. Emperor

---

8   *Galli Anonimi chronicae*, 15; *The Deeds of the Princes*, 29; see also: Jacek Banaszkiewicz, "Dąbrówka 'christianissima' i Mieszko poganin (*Thietmar, IV, 55–56, Gall I, 5–6*) [Dąbrówka 'Christianissima' and Mieszko the Pagan]," in *'Nihil superfluum esse'. Studia z dziejów średniowiecza ofiarowane profesor Jadwidze Krzyżaniakowej*, ed. Jerzy Strzelczyk and Józef Dobosz (Poznań, 2000), 85–93; more broadly about the problem of a woman influencing the pagan to baptism, e.g.: Martin Homza, "The Role of Saint Ludmila, Doubravka, Saint Olga and Adelaide in the Conversions of their Countries (The Problem of 'Mulieres Suadentes', Persuading Women)," in *Early Christianity in Central and East Europe*, ed. Przemysław Urbańczyk (Warsaw, 1997), 187–202.

9   *Galli Anonimi chronicae*, 16–17; *The Deeds of the Princes*, 33, see also: Gotthold Rhode, "Die eisernen Grenzsäulen Boleslaws des Tapferen von Polen. Wege einer Legende," *Jahrbücher für Geschichte Osteuropas* 8/3 (1960), 331–253; the author tried to find out historical and philological (339) grounding of Anonymus' words, but he did not notice their symbolic meaning, which reveals the exaggeration of the chronicler's statement, because driving in his border marks in the middle of the enemy's country meant the enemy's humiliation or even his mastery of the earth marked in this way – see: Jacek Banaszkiewicz, "Unity of spatial order, social and tradition of the origins of the people," *Przegląd Historyczny* 3 (1986), 445–66.

Otto, whom the chronicler calls the Red (Rufus), came to St. Adalbert's tomb "for prayer and reconciliation and also to meet the famous Bolesław".[10] It is unclear what is meant by "reconciliation" since the earlier text does not mention any feud.[11]

It is neither possible nor necessary to elaborate on the chronicler's description of the meeting in the year 1000 – this is a separate subject in itself. However, it needs to be mentioned, in connection with the problem discussed here, that Anonymus emphasizes the fact that Bolesław was proclaimed king by Otto III, not by the pope, who supposedly merely confirmed the Emperor's conferment of the title at some later date.[12] Nevertheless, the significance of this statement, which might imply that Bolesław the Brave and his country were somehow more subordinate to the Empire, is in many ways weakened by the chronicler. First of all, while discussing the precious gifts offered to the noble guest, he stresses that Otto received them all as a goodwill gesture and not as a tribute due to him.[13]

This is an important distinction since the payment of tribute indicated the payer's lower position and implied dishonourable submission,[14] from which the chronicler openly dissociates himself. It seems that by contradicting the views about the Piasts' submission to paying tribute to the German Empire, which were familiar to him, Anonymus in a determined way attempts to emphasize the high esteem accorded to Bolesław the Brave by Otto III. After a lengthy passage describing the magnificence of the Piast court, the chronicler observes that the Emperor was so impressed by the Polish ruler's generosity

---

10 There is a large literature on the issue; lately the subject was summarized by: Roman Michałowski, *The Gniezno Summit. The Religious Premises of the Founding of the Archbishopric of Gniezno* (Leiden, 2016) – polemical comments in relation to many of these interpretations can be found in: Dariusz A. Sikorski, *Kościół w Polsce za Mieszka I i Bolesława Chrobrego. Rozważania nad granicami poznania historycznego* [Church in Poland under Mieszko I and Bolesław the Brave. Considerations on the boundaries of historical cognition] (Poznań, 2011), 332ff.; see also: Knut Görich, "Ein Erzbistum in Prag oder in Gnesen?," *Zeitschrift für Ostforschung* 40 (1991), 10–27; Gerard Labuda, "O badaniach nad zjazdem gnieźnieńskim w roku 1000. Spostrzeżenia i zastrzeżenia," *Roczniki Historyczne* 68 (2002), 105–56.

11 *Galli Anonimi chronicae*, 18–19; *The Deeds of the Princes*, 35–37.

12 Johannes Fried, *Otto III. und Boleslaw Chrobry. Das Widmungsbild des Aachener Evangeliars, der "Akt von Gnesen" und das frühe polnische und ungarische Königtum* (Stuttgart, 1989).

13 *Galli Anonimi chronicae*; *The Deeds of the Princes*, cf.: *Die Annales Quedlinburgenses*, ed. Martina Giese, MGH, SS rer. Ger. 72 (Hannover, 2004), 510–12 – where it was written that Bolesław Chrobry had gathered a proper tribute for the emperor, but Otto did not want the tribute. The source suggests vaguely that this was due to the pious moment and respect for the burial place of Saint Adalbert.

14 Pleszczyński, *The Birth of a Stereotype*, 65–71.

that he believed the number of gifts offered by the latter to be a miracle.[15] This is a significant statement since we know that at that time a ruler's power and even his position in the hierarchy were assessed according to his wealth and generosity.[16]

Therefore, the chronicler's position towards the institution of the Empire is characterized by considerable ambivalence: on the one hand, he realizes the emperor's political and legal significance – he considered the ruler of the empire as a grantor of the crown that Boleslaw Chrobry had received; on the other hand, he avoided writing at length on the existence of numerous and serious links between the Piast' state and the Empire ruled by the Ludolfings and later the Salier dynasties.

The mentioning that "Mieszko [II, the son of Boleslaw Chrobry] had already married the sister of Emperor Otto III during his father's lifetime, and begotten a son by her, Casimir (that is, Charles), the restorer of Poland"[17] is therefore Anonymus' characteristic way of descibing the oldest Polish-German relations. The chronicler did not write about the meaning of this marriage, and what lay behind the second name of the grandson of Bolesław Chrobry, which obviously refers to the great Frankish emperor. He also never mentions the name of Rycheza – not the sister, but in fact the niece of Otto III,[18] although he had a very positive opinion of her.

---

15   *Galli Anonimi chronicae*, 21; *The Deeds of the Princes*, 39; Gert Althoff, "Symbolische Kommunikation zwischen Piasten und Ottonen," in *Polen und Deutschland vor 1000 Jahre*, ed. Michael Borgolte (Berlin, 2002), 305–306, suggested that this description was an ironical overstatement. But it is very doubtful – see: Jacek Banaszkiewicz, "Gall as a Credible Historian, or why the Biography of Boleslav the Brave is as authentic and far from grotesque as Boleslav the Wrymouth's," in *Gallus Anonymous and his chronicle in the context of twelfth-century historiography from the perspective of last research*, ed. Krzysztof Stopka (Cracow, 2010), 19–33.

16   See e.g.: *Widukindi res gestae saxonicae*, ed. Albert Bauer and Reinhard Rau, FGST 4: Quellen zur Geschichte der Kaiserzeit (Darmstadt, 1975), 16–183, here 62: "Deinde [king Henry I – A.P.] videns adolescentem [of count Giselbert] valde industriam, genere ac potestate, divitiis quoque clarum, liberaliter eum coepit habere, ac postremo desponsata sibi filia nomine Gerberga affinitate pariter cum amicitia iunxit eum sibi, sublegato omni ei Lotharii regno."

17   *Galli Anonimi chronicae*, 40: "secundus Mescho [...] qui iam vivente partre sororem tertii Ottonis imperatoris uxorem acceperat, de qua Kazimirum, id est Karolum, restauratorum Polonie, procrearat"; Cf.: *The Deeds of the Princes*, 73; see also: Kazimierz Jasiński, *Genealogia Piastów* [Genealogy of the Piasts] (Wrocław, 1992), 129.

18   Eduard Hlawitschka, "Königin Richeza von Polen – Enkelin Herzog Konrads von Schwaben, nicht Kaiser Ottos II?," in *Institutionen, Kultur und geselschaft im Mittelalter. Festschrift für Josef Fleckenstein zu seinem 65. Geburtstag*, ed. Lutz von Fenske, Werner Rösener, and Thomas Zotz (Sigmaringen, 1984), 221–244.

Though she gave her son a liberal upbringing, and governed the kingdom as honorably as a woman could, she was driven out of the kingdom by traitors who bore her ill will. [And later] [these villains] were afraid that he [i.e. Casimir] would take revenge for the wrong his mother had suffered, so they rose up against him and forced him to quit the kingdom of Hungary. [Then] the neighboring kings and dukes rode roughshod over the portion of Poland nearest each of them, adding the cities and castles near the borders to their dominions or capturing them and leveling them to the ground.[19]

But there is not a word about the Germans. Apparently, Anonymus did not want – and it seems that he had to know about it – to make references to the wars of Mieszko II with Konrad II, the German intervention in Poland, and the discontinuation of the Piast monarchy brought about by the Empire's ruler. Instead, he made the emperor a patron of Casimir in a certain sense. So after leaving Hungary, the son of Rycheza Rycheza, Polish Duchess and Queen, niece of Otto III (d. 1063) "set out with great joy and hastened to the land of the Germans [*regio Teutonicorum*], where he joined his mother and the emperor"[20] (who is not mentioned by name).

Casimir remained some time among the Germans [*apud Theutonicos*] ... [but soon] decided to return to Poland, [although] the emperor made his plea, by begging him to stay with him and by offering him a quite splendid duchy.[21]

This briefly described attitude of Gallus Anonymus to the "German question" can be confirmed when we read further passages of his work, with its descriptions of the reign of the next Piasts: Bolesław the Generous and Władysław Herman. Regarding the first of these – let us remember, who was crowned (which outraged the German court)[22] – the chronicler does not mention that he became an opponent of the emperor, although there is no mention as well

---

19 *Galli Anonymi cronicae*, 41; *Deeds of the Princes*, 77–79.
20 *Galli Anonimi chronicae*, 42; *Deeds of the Princes*, 77.
21 *Galli Anonimi chronicae*, 44; *Deeds of the Princes*, 81.
22 *Wiponis gesta Chuonradi II. imperatoris*, ed. Werner Trillmilch, FSGA 11: Quellen des 9. und 11. Jahrhunderts zur Geschichte der Hamburgischen Kirche und des Reiches (Darmstadt, 1978), 522–613, 42.; *Die Annales Quedlinburgenses*, 578.

that the pope supported him at the coronation, what is usually stressed by Polish historiography.[23]

Also the relations of Władysław Herman to the Empire are described very laconically by Gallus Anonymus: the prince would marry a (nameless!) sister of Henry III (in fact IV),[24] and one of the daughters of this marriage "got married to one of the compatriots [of her mother]".[25] That is all.

A significant change occurs in the narrative of the chronicle only at the moment when Anonymus' account comes to the times of Bolesław Krzywousty (the Wrymouth), and specifically the war he waged against Henry V. The chronicler calls him emperor, although in the year 1109 the German ruler had not actually succeeded in being crowned in Rome. Our author in fact seems to equate the position of the Roman-German king with the imperial title, or even fails to recognize the existence of the institution of the German Kingdom, hence we have his manner of counting German monarchs according to the order of their taking over the Roman throne – Henry IV is for him the third member of the dynasty bearing this name, and Henry V – the fourth.

This circumstance is important to our considerations, because it reveals that the addressees of all his opinions concerning the emperors were by no means the German rulers – as usually referred to in literature, especially Polish[26] – but the emperors whose center of power was (in Anonymus' opinion) in Rome.

Let us now turn to the description of the aforementioned struggles of the Polish and German rulers, when Henry V entered Poland in 1109 with his army. An important reason for the war, the chronicler writes, was that the Polish duke Bolesław the Wrymouth firmly refused to pay a tribute to Henry and to yield to

---

23   Especially the older – see e.g.: Jerzy Wyrozumski, *Historia Polski do roku 1505* [History of Poland up to 1505] (Warszawa, 1983), 98; but differently: Tadeusz Grudziński, *Bolesław Śmiały-Szczodry i biskup Stanisław* [Bolesław Bold-Generous and bishop Stanisław] (Warszawa, 1986), 62; and Krzysztof Skwierczyński, *Recepcja idei gregoriańskich w Polsce do początku XIII wieku* [Reception of Gregorian ideas in Poland until the beginning of the 13th century] (Wrocław, 2005), 63.

24   It was Judith of Swabia (1054–1105?), the youngest daughter of emperor Henry III – Mechthild Black-Veldtrup, "Die Töchter Heinrichs III. und der Kaiserin Agnes," *'Vinculum Societatis'. Festschrift für Joachim Wollasch*, ed. Franz Neiske (Sigmaringendorf, 1991), 36–57.

25   *Galli Anonymi cronicae*, 64; *Deeds of the Princes*, 117.

26   In principle, every synthetic account of Polish history, even at the academic level, shows the war of 1109 as a fight between the Piast state and the German state. Simultaneously, often in the past, the bridge was mistakenly laid down between the early medieval battles, Poland's conflict with the Teutonic Knights, and modern wars – see e.g.: Gerard Labuda, *Polska granica zachodnia – tysiąc lat dziejów politycznych* [Poland's Western Border – A Thousand Years of Political History] (Poznań, 1971).

his will.[27] Anonymus, however, attributed to Bolesław a declaration that if the emperor had amicably asked for money or armed support to be given "in aid of the Church of Rome", he would have "received no less aid and counsel [from Bolesław] than Henry's "forebears did from ours [i.e. the Polish]".[28]

The above mentioned ambivalent attitude of the chronicler towards Germany appears here again, when he admits the general subordination of Poland to the Roman Empire, which is confirmed here by the recognition of Poland's ruler as Henry v's "vassal" (*miles*).[29] Anonymus opposed, however, closer relationships between the two monarchies, for that could be used as justification for the Empire's interference in Poland's internal affairs. This was obvious for the chronicler, which is why the emperor, when he "proudly", and "overwhelmed with anger"[30] enters the land of Piasts, is presented as tyrant, a ruler violating natural law. Bolesław the Wrymouth decided, therefore, to fight "for Poland's freedom (*pro libertate Poloniae*)", because he did not want to pay a tribute and bear the disgrace of bondage.[31] In Anonymus' view, he did that justifiably and successfully. In contrast, the emperor acted dishonestly, e.g. he allegedly took hostages (as warranty of truce) and then used them perfidiously as "live shields" for his troops. Despite all adversities, the Piast warriors bravely resisted "the aggression of the Germans,"[32] and did it successfully because the German monarch behaved like a tyrant. The Polish duke, even in the opinion of the subjects of Henry v (sic!), appeared to be an appropriate ruler, fighting in defense of the order of the world.[33]

It is worth noting that even the nature of the land owned by Bolesław became, in the opinion of the chronicler, a mode of defense for its rightful ruler: swamps and forests hindered attackers from moving around the country, and flies and fierce peasants (*rustici mordaces*) attacked the enemy.[34] Especially

---

27 In fact, there were many reasons for the conflict: Zbigniew Dalewski, *Ritual and Politics. Writing the History of a Dynamic Conflict in Medieval Poland* (Boston-Leiden, 2008) 13–40; Przemysław Wiszewski, *'Domus Bolezlaï'. Values and social identity in dynastic traditions of medieval Poland (c.966–1138)*, (Leiden-Boston, 2010), 297ff.

28 *Galli Anonimi chronicae*, 130: "quodsi bonitate, non ferociate pecuniam vel milites in auxiliam Romanae ecclesiae postulasse non munus auxilii vel consilii forsan apud nos, quam tu antecessores apud nostros imperatrares"; cf. *The Deeds of the Princes*, 227–29.

29 *Galli Anonymi cronicae*, 130; cf. *The Deeds of the Princes*, 227ff.

30 *Galli Anonimi chronicae*, 125; also: 130; on the anger of the ruler see: Gerd Althoff, "Ira regis. A History of Royal Anger," in *Anger's Past. The Social Uses of an Emotion in the Middle Ages*, ed. Barbara H. Rosenwein (Ithaca/London, 1998), 57–74.

31 *Galli Anonimi chronicae*, 130, 134; *The Deeds of the Princes*, 227, 233.

32 *Galli Anonymi cronicae*, 131: "impetus Alemanorum".

33 *Galli Anonymi cronicae*, 139; *The Deeds of the Princes*, 233.

34 *Galli Anonymi cronicae*, 140; *The Deeds of the Princes*, 245.

this last element of Anonymus' topical structure, sometimes interpreted as a manifestation of the "patriotic uprising of the Polish people" (sic!),[35] reveals clearly how much the chronicler idealized his story, in order to give Bolesław the qualities of a perfect ruler.[36] As a result, even the warriors of Henry V came to admire the virtues of Bolesław, acknowledging the watchfulness of divine protection over him and putting together a song in his honor.[37]

No wonder that the emperor, who "had thought to crush Poland's ancient liberty,"[38] could not face such a great monarch and he only "had his triumph in returning from Poland, when memorably he brought back mourning for joy, and corpses for tribute."[39] Again, however, there is a certain ambivalence in relation to the emperor: the chronicler does not shy away from painting his portrait in dark colours; he writes about him as an illegal invader, a perfidious man who did not hesitate to send hostages to their death.[40] Bolesław "feared him little when he was around, but without a doubt even less when he was not there."[41]

However, in another place in his work, our author states that the Polish ruler had concluded: "Let friendship with the emperor be framed,/ Fraternal concord, too, as justly aimed".[42] These words placed in the hymn – the prologue to the last book of the chronicle – were left without any justification, simply a comment in the main text of the chronicle, perhaps because the writing of the work was interrupted between 1113 and 1114 and it was never resumed. However, if that was the situation, one can say that for the chronicler, the ruler of the Empire turned out to be a negative hero when he was fighting with Bolesław; but when the situation changed, that former perfidious person

---

35 In the past: Wyrozumski, *Historia Polski*, 102; but again, similar statements have been published not so long ago – see: Henryk Samsonowicz, Andrzej Wyczański, and Jerzy Tazbir, *Historia Polski* [History of Poland] (Warsaw, 2007), 55; where, when commenting on the phrase of the Anonymus, one reads about the "early form of patriotism".

36 Who, according to the old topos, should control the nature of the country – more about it e.g.: Henry A. Meyers and Herwig Wolfram, *Medieval Kingship* (Chicago, 1982), 236.

37 *Galli Anonymi cronicae*, 138ff.; *The Deeds of the Princes*, 241–243.

38 *The Deeds of the Princes*, 247; *Galli Anonymi cronicae*, 141: "libertatem antiquam Poloniae subigere cogitavit"; Cf.: Sławomir Gawlas, "Der Blick von Polen auf das mittelalterliche Reich" in *Heilig – Römisch – Deutsch. Das Reich im mittelalterlichen Europa*, ed. Bernd Schneidmüller, Stefan Weinfurter (Dresden, 2006), 266–285, at 273.

39 *Galli Anonymi cronicae*, 141, 143 – see: Wiszewski, *Domus Bolezlai*, 319ff.; also: Marita Blattmann, "Ein Unglück für sein Volk. Der Zusammenhang zwischen Fehlverhalten des Königs und Volkswohl in Quellen des 7.–12. Jahrhunderts," *Frühmittelalterlich Studien* 30 (1996), 80–102.

40 *The Deeds of the Princes*, 251; *Galli Anonymi cronicae*, 134.

41 Ibid.; *The Deeds of the Princes*, 251.

42 Ibid., 219; *Galli Anonymi cronicae*, 125.

became a desirable political partner with whom a friendly relationship (*amicitia*)[43] would elevate the importance and prestige of the Polish ruler.

There is one more thing to be noted and considered here. In the chronicle, several different names are used for Germans. Thus the term *Alemanni* is used when describing a situation of conflict with the Polish ruler and it espresses something negative: fight, aggression; the usual word "Teutons" (i.e.: Germans), on the other hand, is found in neutral or favorably inclined texts. It should also be added that the term was rather vague and, as a rule, the chronicler uses the words Saxons [and Saxony] to refer to Poland's western neighbours, just as the country, Germany – Teutonia, did not exist in the chronicler's accounts,[44] for to him the nation – the Teutons, German people, were associated generally with the Roman Empire and the highest authority in the Christian World. But, as mentioned above, in situations of hostility and war, this term is replaced with *Alemanni*.

The style of referring to the Germans as *Alemanni* in situations of conflict was copied from Gallus Anonymus (along with much other content) by the first Polish-born chronicler of Poland's history, who lived about one hundred years later.[45] Like his predecessor, Vincent Kadłubek (pol. Wincenty) was not

---

43   On the phenomenon see: Gerd Althoff, "Amicitia [Friendship] as relationship between states and people," *Debating the Middle Ages: Issues and readings*, ed. Lesster K. Little and Barbara H. Rosenwein (Oxford, 1998), 191–210; Verena Epp, *'Amicitia'. Zur Geschichte personaler, sozialer, politischer und geistlicher Beziehungen im frühen Mittelalter*, Monographien zur Geschichte des Mittelalters 44, (Stuttgart, 1999); and eadem, "Rituale frühmittelalterlicher amicitia," in *Formen und Funktionen öffentlichen Kommunikation im Mittelalter*, ed. Gerd Althoff, Vorträge und Forschungen 51 (Sigmaringen, 2001), 11–24.

44   Which is somewhat natural, because we can speak about the existence of the German nation only in the modern period. The terms "Germany" and "German" in relation to the Middle Ages are artificial and we use them out of necessity – more about the problem: Joachim Ehlers, "Schriftkultur, Ethnogenese und Nationsbildung in ottonischer Zeit," *Frühmittelalterliche Studien* 23 (1989), 302–317; To a large extent, this comment applies to all European nations – see: Bernd Schneidmüller, "Reich-Volk-Nation: Die Enstehung des Deutschen Reiches und der deutschen Nation im Mittelalter," in *Mittelalterliche "nationes" – neuzeitliche Nationen. Probleme der Nationenbildung in Europa*, ed. Almut Bues (Wiesbaden, 1995), 73–101.

45   *Mistrza Wincentego zwanego Kadłubkiem Kronika polska / Magistri Vincentii dicti Kadłubek Chronica Polonorum*, ed. Marian Plezia, MPH, nova series 11, (Kraków, 1994); the Latin-German edition: *Die Chronik der Polen des Magisters Vincentius*, ed. Eduard Mühle, FSGA 48, (Darmstadt, 2014); more about the chronicler and his work: Jacek Banaszkiewicz, *Polskie dzieje bajeczne Mistrza Wincentego Kadłubka* [Polish fairy tales of Master Wincenty Kadłubek] (Wrocław, 2002); and collections of studies: *'Onus Athlanteum'. Studia nad kroniką biskupa Wincentego* [Studies on the chronicle of Bishop Wincenty], ed. Andrzej Dąbrówka and Witold Wojtowicz (Warszawa, 2009); or: *Writing History in Medieval Poland. Bishop Vincentius of Cracow and the 'Chronica Polonorum'*, ed. Darius von Güttner-Sporzyński, (Turnhout, 2017).

particularly interested in the Germanic countries or the Empire.[46] He only mentions them in connection with Polish affairs and these references do not present a uniform portrait of the country or its inhabitants.

The first reference which is interesting for us can be found in the introductory part of Kadłubek's chronicle, what is called the "legendary history". It is well known in the Polish tradition since it includes stereotypical content which was later elaborated on in both popular culture and the old historiography. According to the "legendary history", a clash between German aggressiveness and the Polish idea of sovereignty was supposed to have occurred as early as at the dawn of the country's history. At some vague time around the beginning, Krakow and the Polish country were allegedly ruled by Wanda, the daughter of Krakus [Krak, Grakch], the legendary founder of the city and country. The chronicle, whose author was appointed Bishop of Krakow, was written from the perspective of the new capital and the Gniezno tradition was not included.[47]

Wanda was supposedly so beautiful that "some Lemannic [= Aleman] tyrant", the ruler, possibly the emperor of the *Alemanni*, wanted to marry her and in this way gain the Krakow throne "intending to annihilate the people (i.e. the Poles)". Wanda refused and the tyrant amassed a mighty army and invaded Poland. However, in the field of the decisive battle, Wanda's exquisite beauty made the *Alamanni* soldiers unwilling to fight with her troops and the tyrant himself committed suicide.[48] The story entered into the repertoire of the Polish national myths, and each author who retold it knew more about "Wanda, who did not want a German". This is a separate matter, on which we need not focus. What is important here is that the idea of sovereignty was positioned at the very beginning of a presentation of the history of the country and juxtaposed with the inclinations of the "Lemannic [Aleman] tyrant", who must have embodied the medieval Empire.[49]

However, the Empire as a political entity was not necessarily perceived in the same way as it is seen today, i.e. it was by no means associated with all the

---

46 This issue has recently been developed by Michał Tomaszek, "Die Wahrnehmung der Kaiser bei Vinzenz Kadłubek," in *Verwandtschaft – Freundschaft – Feindschaft: Politische Bindungen zwischen dem Reich und Ostmitteleuropa in der Zeit Friedrich Barbarossas*, ed. Martin Wihoda and Knut Görich (Köln, 2018) 53–68.

47 See the introduction to the Polish edition of the chronicle, *Mistrz Wincenty zw. Kadłubek, Kronika polska* [Master Wincenty called Kadłubek, The Polish Chronicle], ed. Brygida Kürbisówna (Wrocław-Warszawa-Kraków, 1996), I–CXXXI.

48 *Magistrii Vicenti dicti*, 12–13; the wider topic context of the story in: Banaszkiewicz, "Rüdiger von Bechelaren".

49 *Magistrii Vicenti dicti*, 12.

Germans since the Saxons, for example, are treated separately. Furthermore, Kadłubek did not always treat the institution of the Holy Roman Empire with hostility or animosity. The spirit and content of the account of Otto III's arrival in Gniezno are the same as in Gallus Anonymus' chronicle.[50] Another similarity between the two works is that Kadłubek's whole chronicle also does not include any information about Bolesław the Brave's dozen-year-long war with Henry II.

A certain ambivalence about the Germans can only be seen when the Bishop of Krakow writes that the reason for the animosity which the Polish felt towards Richeza, considered to be Emperor Otto III's sister, was that she supposedly elevated her compatriots (*Teutari*) above the local inhabitants, which allegedly led to her exile from Poland.[51] This entry could be the first trace of some competition between indigenous nobility and German newcomers for high church and secular positions that clearly became the case in the 14th century.

It is only in the account of the war between Bolesław the Wrymouth and Henry V in 1109 that we find a more detailed description of the Polish-German struggle. In his pompous, grandiose style, Kadłubek again refers to Bolesław the Wrymouth's enemies using the same terms he chose previously in the case of legendary Wanda's suitor. Henry V's invasion into Poland is described as *furoris impetus Lemanici* [a furious attack by the Alemanni].[52] The term *Lemanni* continues to be used in the course of the narrative in the chronicle, which in fact is a stylistically modified version of the account provided by Gallus Anonymus. There is only one new addition, namely the description of a battle allegedly fought between the Polish and German armies near Wrocław, in what is called in Polish *Psie Pole* [Hundsfeld; Dogs' Field]. The name supposedly originated from the fact that after the battle there were so many corpses "of sad Lemannia [=Allemannia]" in the field that before anyone managed to clear them, packs of dogs from the neighborhood feasted on the dead and "were driven into some wild frenzy".[53] Undoubtedly, this is an allusion to the frenzied aggression mentioned at the very beginning of the story of the war of 1109 and, at the same time, about the "Aleman tyrant".

At that point, a description of the subsequent events in the history of the country could no longer be based upon Gallus Anonymus' chronicle, which ends about the year 1100. The next passages reflect Vincent Kadłubek's own

---

50 *Magistrii Vicenti dicti*, 39f.
51 *Magistrii Vicenti dicti*, 45f.
52 *Magistrii Vicenti dicti*, 103.
53 *Magistrii Vicenti dicti*, 106.

views on the relation of the emperor to the Polish Duke Bolesław. It is intriguing that in the account of Frederick Barbarossa's invasion of Poland in 1157,[54] the emperor was called the Red Dragon (*draco russus*).[55] It is unclear how this should be interpreted given that the term was also unclear to later historiographers. They omitted it when rewriting Vincent's accounts in subsequent compilations of the country's history. From the perspective of the Bishop of Krakow, the Red Dragon was, however, an extremely gentle ruler. The Emperor did not, in fact, wish to invade the country of the Piasts or become involved in the local dynastic dispute, but he had to do so, as he was being besieged by requests from Władysław II, who had been exiled from his country, and also from the latter's wife, who was a relative of Frederick's.[56] As a matter of fact, Kadłubek holds Agnes of Babenberg in great respect, depicting her as a very energetic, ambitious and proud woman. These traits are emphasized by the nickname "tigress", which is given to her by the Krakow chronicler.[57]

The concise description of Frederick Barbarossa's campaign does not contain any scenes of violence or fighting. None took place; still, as we know, this fact would not have prevented the chronicler from inventing some if he had wished to do so. Beguiled by Władysław, Frederick sought only to force the recognition of Władysław's right to the Polish throne. When this failed, the Emperor supposedly entreated and persuaded Bolesław the Curly, the Grand Duke at the time, to grant provinces in Poland to Władysław's sons.[58]

There are no references in the chronicle to the threat which Poland faced in 1172, when Frederick prepared an invasion in order to support Władysław's son, Bolesław the Tall, and defend the rights of Bolesław to a certain territory in Poland.[59]

A final work which will be discussed here is what is called the Wielkopolska or Great Poland Chronicle.[60] It was created at the end of the 13th century on

---

54   On the historical context of the war: Magdalena Biniaś-Szkopek, *Bolesław IV Kędzierzawy – książę Mazowsza i princeps* [Bolesław IV the Curly – Duke of Mazovia and princeps] (Poznań, 2009), 132ff.; Robert Holtzmann, "Über der Polenfeldzug Friedrich Barbarossas vom Jahre 1157 und die Begründung der schlesischen Herzogtümer," *Zeitschrift des Vereins für Geschichte Schlesiens* 56 (1922), 42–55; Knut Görich, *Die Ehre Friedrich Barbarossas. Kommunikation, Konflikt und politisches Handeln im 12. Jahrhundert* (Darmstadt, 2001), 358.

55   *Magistrii Vicenti dicti*, 124.

56   Kazimierz Jasiński, *Rodowód Piastów śląskich* [A Lineage of Silesian Piasts] (Kraków, 2007), 2: 255–59.

57   *Magistrii Vicenti dicti*, 120–124.

58   *Magistrii Vicenti dicti*, 121.

59   *Regesta imperii – Friedrich I* IV, 2, 3, Nr 1995 – online edition: http://www.regesta-imperii.de/regesten/4-2-3-friedrich-i (14.07.2018).

60   *Chronica Poloniae maioris*, ed. Brygida Kürbis, MPH. Series nova 8 (Warszawa, 1970).

the basis of Vincent Kadłubek's chronicle, but it contains a great deal of new information not included in any other sources. The Wielkopolska Chronicle only became known through just two copies, which were created about a hundred years later and in places differing considerably from each other. The chronicle is a compilation, and includes texts from many previous annals as well as numerous subsequent annotations; it is therefore often difficult to establish the order in which its particular parts were written.[61] The facts that its author is unknown and that it is impossible to find the original accounts make it difficult for us to assess the relationship to Germany and the Germans who are mentioned in this source.

As far as the topic in my title is concerned, however, some of the content of the Wielkopolska Chronicle differs from the previously mentioned restrained comments from the Polish historiography and takes on a rather anti-German tone. Nonetheless, some passages can also be found which seem friendly towards the Germans. This results from the fact that the Chronicle is a compilation and was handled by many writers, which is why it contains annotations by various authors.

A brief review, conducted chronologically, would begin with the "legendary history". It does not contain much information that is different from what is included in Kadłubek's chronicle; however, the differences are highly significant. Kadłubek's megalomaniac and imperial-sounding disquisition is embellished here with the information that the vast country of Lechites extended up to Bavaria, and then after the victory over the army of Iulius Ceasar, Bavaria itself was handed over to Lestek, the ruler of the Lechites (old Poles) as the dowry for Iulia, a daughter of the Roman Emperor, whom he married.[62] Accordingly, the chronicler also adds concise information about the Slavs from beyond the Oder, from the East and from the Balkans, as if these groups had once belonged to the proto-Polish ethnic community.[63] The story of "Wanda-who-did-not-want-a-German" given here makes clear reference to the king of the *Alemanni* and not some mysterious "Lemanni".[64]

The above information is evidently at variance with statements such as "the Slavs and the Germans were supposedly descended from two brothers,

---

61 Edward Skibiński, "Kronika Wielkopolska," [The Chronicle of Greater Poland] *Vademecum historyka mediewisty*, ed. Jarosław Nikodem and Dariusz A. Sikorski (Warszawa, 2012), 260–265; see also: Henryk Łowmiański, "Kiedy powstała Kronika Wielkopolska" [When the Greater Poland Chronicle was created], *Przegląd Historyczny* 51/2, (1960), 398–410.
62 *Chronica Poloniae maioris*, 11.
63 *Chronica Poloniae maioris*, 4–7.
64 *Chronica Poloniae maioris*, 9; besides, the story as constructed puts more emphasis on the combat values of Wanda's forces and speaks of the pledge of loyalty and homage to the Queen of Lechites made by the Alemanni warriors.

Jan and Kus, the descendants of Japheth, as was claimed by Isidore in Book I of Etymologies[65] and Martin in The Roman Chronicle.[66] Or, inhabiting lands neighbouring those of Slavs, the Germans have frequent contact with them and there are no other nations as kind and friendly to each other as the Slavs and the Germans. Also, since the people used Latin, the name Ducz was created, from which later [arose] the name *Teutoni*, and also [the people using Latin created] the name *Slaw*, from which the Slavs were named, Germans, who were also called brothers".[67]

The parts of the Chronicle which describe the historical epoch up to the end of the 12th century were, in fact, mostly re-written from Vincent's work. The story of Agnes of Babenberg is clearly embellished. She is no longer a "tigress"; she is a demonic *femme fatale*. In the chronicler's view, it was her pride, uncontrollable ambition, and intrigues which led to the blinding of *comes* [castellan] Piotr [Piotr Włostowic], known as Dunin [the Dane], then, in turn, to the outbreak of the civil war and, finally, to the destruction of the country's unity.[68]

The account of the country's history in the 13th century contains quite overt accusations against the Germans, especially the ones living in Poland.[69] Thus, there is information, repeated from the annals, about disputes resulting from the fact that the Germans refused to pay Peter's Pence.[70] These reports are accompanied by comments that they (the Germans) held high church and secular positions that should have been occupied by the locals. Such matters were mainly raised during the synod in Łęczyca by Jakub Świnka, the Archbishop

---

65   It is about Isidore of Seville and his 'Etymologiae' – *The Etymologies of Isidore of Seville*, ed. Stephen A. Barney (Cambridge, 2006).

66   Martin of Poland (also called: Martin of Opava) – the author of *Chronicon pontificum et imperatorum* – see: http://www.geschichtsquellen.de/repOpus_03363.html (14.07.2018).

67   *Chronica Poloniae maioris*, 6–7: "Scire autem dignum est, quod Slawi et Theutonici a duobus germanis Japhet nepotibus Jano et Kuss dicuntur orte habuisse [....] Theutonici cum Slauis regna contingua habentes simul conversacione incendunt, nec aliqua gens in mundo est sibi tam communis et familiaris veluti Slaui et Theutonici. Sic eciam per Latinos ducz a quo Theutonici et Slav a quo Slawi, germani qui et fratres sunt appellati".

68   *Chronica Poloniae maioris*, 49–52.

69   In the situation of rivalry for dignity and offices, a proverb was born: 'Jak świat światem nie będzie Niemiec Polakowi bratem' (As the world is the world, a German will not be a brother to a Pole) – see also: Labuda, "Geneza przysłowia 'Jak świat światem nie będzie Niemiec Polakowi bratem", 98–111.

70   Such accusations were often raised by Polish bishops. They became a subject of discussion especially during the synod in Łęczyca in 1285, called by the Archbishop of Gniezno, Jakub Świnka, At this synod laws were issued ordering preaching be done in Polish. This decision had an anti-German effect; see also: Strzelczyk, "Deutsch-polnische Schicksalsgemeinschaft," 118.

of Gniezno, who was well-known for his exceptionally anti-German attitude.[71] A Czech chronicler, Petr Žitavsky [Peter of Zittau] wrote that the hierarch tended to deride the Germans by claiming that they had "dogs' heads" (*canina capita*).[72]

Although the author of the Wielkopolska Chronicle did not resort to such insults, there are numerous negative comments about the Germans in his work. A report re-written from the annals of the Poznan Archdiocese is an example of this. It is an account of an attack by the Duke of Silesia, Bolesław Rogatka, on Tomasz, the Bishop of Wrocław:

> driven by infernal rage and persuaded by the Germans whose advice he took, the Duke, like a thief and scoundrel, [...] ordered that the bishop, while asleep in his bed, should be captured once his door was broken down, robbed of all his possessions and stripped of his clothes. He gave him lame excuses, among which the important one was that he (the bishop) had extorted money from him so as to give it to the Germans. And seeing that he (the bishop) was not used to riding a horse, as he was already quite heavy, the Germans made him ride at a trot, wearing only a shirt and short pants, devoid of other clothes. A pauper took pity on him [and gave him] a coarse gown, very tattered, and an old pair of shoes.[73]

It should be emphasized here that in the original account in the annals, the pauper who offered the gown to the bishop was a German. This piece of information is missing from the chronicle.[74]

The Wielkopolska chronicler, again re-writing from the annals, criticized Duke Bolesław Rogatka for "having been the first to bring the Germans to Poland and having granted them lands and towns to gain their support against his brothers, with whom he constantly fought. He also separated Żytawa, Zgorzelec, and many other cities and towns from the Duchy of Silesia by giving them to strangers, which was a disgrace. Who cannot see that the Germans are

---

71 Maciej Maciejowski, *Orientacje polityczne biskupów metropolii gnieźnieńskiej* [Political orientations of bishops of the Gniezno archbishopric] (Crakow, 2007), 33ff.; Tadeusz Silnicki and Kazimierz Gołąb, *Arcybiskup Jakub Świnka i jego epoka* [Archbishop Jakub Świnka and his epoque] (Warsaw, 1956).

72 *Petra Žitavského Kronika Zbraslavská*, [Petr of Žitava, The Chronicle of Zbraslav] ed. Josef Emler, FRB 4 (Praha, 1884), 82; on-line: http://147.231.53.91/src/ (14.07.2018); assigning animal features to strangers, or some imperfections of the body that make them non-human was not something special in the situation of expressing fear, dislike or even hatred.

73 *Chronica Poloniae maioris*, 105–106.

74 *Annales capituli Posnaniensis 965–1309* [The Anal of Poznań chapter], ed. Brygida Kürbis, MPH, NS 6 (Warszawa, 1962), 41. – Cf.: Strzelczyk, "Deutsch-polnische Schicksalsgemeinschaft," 116.

brave and courageous men?"[75] In the annals German knights who served the Piasts are praised, especially by the Silesian Piasts,[76] and in this final question there is a hint of disagreement with such favorable opinions. This also corresponds to the chronicler's description of the war fought by Przemysł II, the Duke of Greater Poland, against Brandenburg in 1271. The account stresses that the 16-year-old Duke of Greater Poland easily defeated the Brandenburgians, seizing two of their major castles.[77]

As far as the information on the 13th century is concerned, the Wielkopolski chronicler does not provide any serious historical reflection. He does not explicitly express criticism of Duke Rogatka for giving Lubusz (germ. Leubus) to the Archbishop of Magdeburg in return for the latter's support in Rogatka's wars with his brothers. There is also no information about the emergence of Brandenburg and the beginning of its expansion into the territories to the east of the Oder, which led to Poland being cut off from Pomerania, the old fiefdom of the Piasts and, ecclesiastically, the land under the jurisdiction of the Archbishopric of Gniezno. Furthermore, the chronicler does not offer any reflection on the emancipation of Pomerania from Poland and the fact that it became a fiefdom of the Empire at the close of Frederick Barbarossa's reign. The Chronicle does not mention numerous key facts which have been taken into consideration by modern historians analysing the subject of the relations between the Piast states and the German states and with the Empire in the 12th and 13th centuries.

To briefly summarize the question discussed here, it can be observed that the historiographical works written in Poland recognized the Empire's authority over the Piast state, but solely as a factor in unifying Christians. The Germans and their countries were interesting to the chroniclers only in connection with Polish affairs. In the 13th century, arrivals from the West started to compete with the locals for posts and positions, which led to the emergence of stereotypes that attributed qualities of "non-humans" to the foreigners: character traits that emphasized possessiveness, greed for money and devilish perversity, as well as having physical features similar to dogs.

75 *Chronica Poloniae maioris*, 93–94.
76 Marek Cetwiński, "Polak Albert i Niemiec Mroczko. Zarys przemian etnicznych i kulturalnych rycerstwa śląskiego do połowy XIV wieku," [A Pole Albert and A German Mroczko. An Outline of ethnic and cultural changes of the Silesian knighthood until the mid-fourteenth century] in *Niemcy – Polska w średniowieczu*, 157–169.
77 *Chronica Poloniae maioris*, 128.

CHAPTER 7

The Perception of the Holy Roman Empire and Its People in the Eyes of the Polish Elites in the Middle Ages

Sławomir Gawlas

The way in which the Holy Roman Empire was perceived by Polish intellectual elites in the Middle Ages is a broad and for many reasons complex research field. Analyses of various aspects of the Polish-German or, more broadly, the Slavic-German neighbourhood were carried out since the beginning of critical historiography in the nineteenth century.[1] For quite obvious reasons, they did not have a strict symmetrical character, and the studies in general amounted to questions about the scope and mechanisms of the influence of German culture on the development of the Polish lands. Quite often the accompanying discussions were looking in the field of past events for substitute arguments relevant to contemporary political conflicts. Manifestations of dislike, provoked by intense contacts and especially by the inflow of foreign settlers, were gladly exposed. Therefore, the importance of the confrontation with the newcomers was emphasised as part of the formation of national identities in the Slavic-German borderlands. But their role was variously interpreted. On the one hand, the strong feelings aroused by the aliens were perceived as a reasonable reaction to the threat of German expansion (*Drang nach Osten*).[2] On the other hand, however, expressions of hatred against newcomers were emphasised as evidence of an unrestrainable ethnic egoism of the Slavs. This was contrasted with the explicitly moderate attitude of the Germans. Hatred

---

1 Discussions and a broad literature on the subject of German-Slavic contacts are presented in: Thomas Wünsch, *Deutsche und Slawen im Mittelalter. Beziehungen zu Tschechen, Polen, Südslawen und Russen* (München, 2008); cf. Jan M. Piskorski, *Polska – Niemcy. Blaski i cienie tysiącletniego sąsiedztwa* [Poland – Germany. The light and shadow of a thousand-year-old neighborhood] (Warszawa, 2017). In this study, I refer only to the most representative and recent publications.
2 *Stosunki polsko-niemieckie w historiografii, część pierwsza: Studia z dziejów historiografii polskiej i niemieckiej*, [Polish-German relations in historiography, part one: Studies in the history of Polish and German historiography] ed. Jerzy Krasuski, Gerard Labuda, and Antoni Walczak (Poznań, 1974); cf. Klaus Zernack, "Die deutsch-polnischen Beziehungen in der Mittelalterhistorie aus deutscher Sicht," in *Polen und Deutschland vor 1000 Jahren. Die Berliner Tagung über den "Akt von Gnesen"*, ed. Michael Borgolte and Benjamin Scheller (Berlin, 2002), 29–42.

against them lacked real grounds, so it was treated as evidence of a culture gap (*Kulturgefälle*) between the West and the East, and implied German moral superiority.[3] The analyses were based on the testimony of textual sources which were specifically chosen to prove the formulated statements. Yet be that as it may, the testimonies did actually exist. The radical extinguishing of political instrumentalisation in discussions on history (that had been ongoing since the 1970s) has not automatically led to a verification of the opinions established in the literature on the subject. What should be emphasised is a surprising circumstance in the above context, namely, that there has been comparatively little research on the problem of the image of the German Reich in Polish medieval sources. The accumulated knowledge is scattered and there are only a few more extensive studies.[4] They focus mainly on written chronicles, and are synthetic in character. And their main emphasis is on the early modern and – especially – the modern period, which is in direct contrast to the great interest and insight found in the publications on the perception of Polish lands in foreign medieval sources.[5] A main difficulty in outlining the subject is the necessity of taking into account various source-related problems essential to a thorough interpretation of chronicle texts, which in fact, however, cannot be exhaustively discussed within this present article. Neither does space allow any more comprehensive reflections on the method of research into external

---

3   Interpretations confirming moral superiority are presented by Erich Maschke in his otherwise substantive publication: Erich Maschke, *Das Erwachen des Nationalbewusstseins im deutsch-slawischen Grenzraum* (Leipzig, 1933). A radical position was taken by Kurt Lück, who was strongly involved in the Nazi movement: Kurt Lück, *Der Mythos vom Deutschen in der Volksüberlieferung und Literatur. Forschungen zur deutsch-polnischen Nachbarschaft im ostmitteleuropäischen Raum* (Posen, 1938). Lück concentrated on early modern times and collected a rich and full documentation of a variety of prejudices in folk stereotypes of Germans, comparing them, among other things, to the devil. An open attitude and reasonable acceptance of German superiority was demonstrated only by segments of the Polish elites. It was against this background that the primitive opinions of the majority of Poles became more conspicuous, as they rejected the reality, not wanting to remember centuries-long German cultural work. The author with great zeal and an equal amount of exaggeration searched for all traces of German blood in the origins of outstanding people in Polish history.

4   Teodor Tyc, "Niemcy w świetle poglądów Polski piastowskiej," [Germany in the light of the views of Piast Poland] *Strażnica Zachodnia* 4, no. 7–12 (1925): 1–23 (repr. id., *Z średniowiecznych dziejów Wielkopolski i Pomorza. Wybór prac*, ed. Jan M. Piskorski (Poznań, 1997): 279–301); Maschke, *Das Erwachen*; also: Grabski, *Polska w opiniach*, 25–80. The most comprehensive analysis is: Jadwiga Krzyżaniakowa, "Poglądy polskich kronikarzy średniowiecznych na Niemcy i stosunki polsko-niemieckie," [Views of Polish medieval chroniclers on Germany and Polish-German relations] in eadem, *"Nie ma historii bez człowieka". Studia z dziejów średniowiecza* (Poznań, 2011): 241–94.

5   Grabski, *Polska w opiniach obcych*; id., *Polska w opiniach Europy*; Pleszczyński, *Niemcy wobec pierwszej*; id., *Przekazy niemieckie o Polsce*.

opinions and their theoretical justifications. To satisfy these criteria, a detailed analysis would require a separate and substantial volume.

In general, it may be said that the image of the German Reich was influenced by several factors. It was shaped by the character of the mutual contacts, and the way the conflicts were presented by the Polish side and the defence of their own interests. A basic mechanism of medieval international relations was matrimonial policy, omnipresent on the level of both states and aristocratic families. Polish rulers were constantly confronted with the ambitions of ruling dynasties in the neighboring countries. In the late Middle Ages, they were entangled primarily in the rivalry of the Angevins, Luxembourgs, Wittelsbachs, and Habsburgs. This rivalry had a great impact on foreign policy. As far as it was possible, and which depended on having children, rulers participated in a continuous diplomatic game. From this point of view there is no doubt that with regard to their own interest, both the milieus of the Polish royal court and the intellectual elites had a good grasp of the real problems of the Empire and they formulated ideological concepts. This is explicitly shown in chronicle narratives despite the fact that this knowledge was substantiated to only a limited extent in the sources, since it was constantly being transformed in line with the aims of its own policy and the methods of its justification. They were situationally conditioned, while at the same time were rooted in past experiences. From the early beginnings of the Polish state, the collective Polish identity was being shaped in confrontation with the emerging German community of memory which in the eleventh century adopted a scholarly assertion as to the ancient origins of the Empire.[6]

Crucially important for the functioning of collective memory was the development of the literate culture. Participation in this culture required an adoption of the heritage of Latin culture, together with its knowledge of geography and universal history. At the same time, however, the written text in chronicles irreversibly changed the rules for how knowledge about the past functioned. Oral testimony was brought up to date every time it was being told.

A lack of interest resulted in a fading into oblivion. The literalised collective memory accumulated narratives of earlier events that were increasing with the passage of time. Once recorded, the stories were hard to erase or ignore. Their update was mainly a new interpretation. Written down in Polish chronicles, stories of contacts with the Empire were becoming a permanent element in Polish collective memory and were constantly influencing anew the way of presenting

---

6 Sławomir Gawlas, "Pytania o tożsamość średniowiecznych Polaków w świetle współczesnych dyskusji humanistyki," [Questions about the identity of medieval Poles in the light of contemporary discussions in the humanities] in *Symboliczne i realne podstawy tożsamości społecznej w średniowieczu*, ed. Sławomir Gawlas and Paweł Żmudzki (Warszawa, 2017), 54–67.

later events. Thus, the image of the Holy Roman Empire was under pressure from the cognitive schemes developed and established in earlier texts, and they had within their framework a great impact on the shaping of worldviews. It could even be said that the episodes included in chronicle writings were to a large extent a component of the stories that constructed a Polish historical identity and sense of sovereignty. It seems therefore necessary to reach more deeply into the past and outline here some of the constructive elements for the image of the German neighbour in Polish medieval chronicles. A fundamental methodological procedure is to follow the changing versions of events that had been described earlier by their predecessors. Its importance is further underlined by the very frequent practice of passing over in silence inconvenient, contemporary events. This procedure, however, cannot be applied in a comprehensive way.[7] I will, therefore, put emphasis on the emergence of new plots.

From the Empire's perspective: as a state, the Polish lands (from the very beginning of their state autonomy) belonged to the set of dependent countries. The actual forms of this subjection were almost constantly changing. In the twentieth century, their interpretation in legal and public terms became a matter of heated dispute loaded with political overtones.[8] In this context, there was reference made to a distinction between the vassal feudal subjection and that of tributary one. Its additional hidden aim was to defend an extension of Poland's state sovereignty. In the latter case it was supposed to be greater, and as such – better suited the image of the historical roots of Polish state independence. The meaning of the sources and the limited scope of the information they contain do not lead to unambiguous conclusions. Despite this fact, however, it should be noted that in the most recent literature on the subject, the general opinion seems to prevail that it was the norm for emperors to impose feudal bonds as the principle that would govern their relations with neighbouring countries.[9] Yet, Polish rulers in general did not provide military support for the Italian wars

---

7 The application of methodological standards in the research on the functioning of the Empire's image within public space requires an analysis of source texts – not on the basis of their critical editions, but through a careful scrutiny of the consecutive versions in individual manuscripts – in accordance with the rule that each copy is a separate narrative. The cognitive advantage of this method is demonstrated by Piotr Węcowski, *Początki Polski w pamięci historycznej polskiego średniowiecza* [The beginnings of Poland in the historical memory of the Polish Middle Ages] (Krakow, 2014).

8 The problem itself and the positions taken in the literature on the subject, seen in a concise way: Sławomir Gawlas, "Der Blick von Polen auf das mittelalterliche Reich," in *Heilig – Römisch – Deutsch. Das Reich im mittelalterlichen Europa*, ed. Bernd Schneidmüller and Stefan Weinfurter (Dresden, 2006), 266–85.

9 Jarosław Sochacki, *Stosunki publiczno-prawne między państwem polskim a Cesarstwem Rzymskim w latach 963–1102* [Public-legal relations between the Polish state and the Roman Empire in the years 963–1102] (Słupsk-Gdańsk, 2003).

and seldom participated in convocations of German princes. The possibility of resolving the dilemma between the tribute and being a feudal liege depends to a great extent on the general opinion about the legally set feudal rules that were applied to contacts with the eastern neighbours before the internal transformation of the political system of the German Reich in the twelfth century. Doubts about this matter, in my opinion, are justified.[10] More light on the nature of the mutual relations has been shed by the analyses of symbols of public ceremonies accompanying political compromises at meetings of emperors with Piast princes.[11] It should be emphasised here that members of the Polish elite tried to maintain close contacts with the Saxon aristocracy, and quite frequently also with the imperial court and the Bamberg cathedral associated with it. Without going into details, we are justified in thinking that the possibility being blocked from rising in status within the Reich served to strengthen the sense of being distinct among the Polish political elites.[12]

The first Polish chronicle written in the early twelfth century includes a description of the contemporary family tradition of the Piasts,[13] prepared by the well-educated newcomer known as Gallus Anonymous.[14] The way of presenting the successive historical episodes which make up the narrative suggests that specific facts were drawn from the decades-long circulation of

10   Cf. *Das Lehnswesen im Hochmittelalter. Forschungskonstrukte – Quellenbefunde – Deutungsrelevanz*, ed. Jürgen Dendorfer and Roman Deutinger (Ostfildern, 2010).

11   It applies mainly to the conventions at Merseburg in 1013 and 1135, and a *deditio* ceremony at Krzyszków near Poznań in 1157; cf. Zbigniew Dalewski, "Lictor imperatoris. Kaiser Lothar III., Soběslav I., von Böhmen und Bolesław III. von Polen auf dem Hoftag in Merseburg im Jahre 1135," *Zeitschrift für Ostmitteleuropa-Forschung*, 50, no. 3 (2001): 317–336.

12   Factors indicating the attempts at direct references to the monarchies of Charlemagne and Otto, as well as the Biblical heritage of the Old Testament kings in the ideological programme of the first Piasts are presented by Zbigniew Dalewski, "W poszukiwaniu poprzedników – pierwsi Piastowie i ich wizja własnej przeszłości" [Searching of predecessors – the first Piasts and their vision of their own past], in *Przeszłość w kulturze średniowiecznej Polski*, v ol. 1, ed. Jacek Banaszkiewicz, Andrzej Dąbrówka, and Piotr Węcowski (Warszawa, 2018): 23–58.

13   *Galli anonymi Cronica et gesta ducum sive principum Polonorum / Anonima tzw. Galla Kronika czyli dzieje książąt i władców polskich*, ed. Karol Maleczyński, MPH N.S. 2 (Kraków, 1952); English translation: *Gesta principum Polonorum / The Deeds of the Princes of the Poles*, ed. Paul W. Knoll, Frank Schaer, and Thomas N. Bisson, Central European Medieval Texts 3 (Budapest/New York, 2003, repr. 2007). The introduction includes basic information, but does not contain the current state of research. I refer henceforth to the critical edition.

14   The most recent state of the discussions of source studies are in: *Nobis operique favente. Studia nad Gallem Anonimem*, [Studies on Gall Anonymous] eds. Andrzej Dąbrówka, Edward Skibiński, and Witold Wojtowicz (Warszawa, 2017); cf. Tomasz Jasiński, *Gall Anonim – poeta i mistrz prozy. Studia nad rytmiką prozy i poezji w okresie antycznym i średniowiecznym* [Gall Anonim – a poet and master of prose. Studies on the rhythm of prose and poetry in the ancient and medieval periods] (Kraków, 2016).

information within oral memory.[15] Its existence restricted the literary freedom of the chronicler, while still leaving plenty of room for his creative invention when he was unable to refer to any given knowledge at his disposal. In this place we can omit the question about the historical truth of the chronicle's details, since what is really important is the fact that the image created in the chronicle initiated the continuity of Polish literary tradition, and thus the collective memory. For this reason, the chronicler's opinion about the German Empire needs to be described in more detail.

The Empire was represented by the emperor – *imperator Romanus* or *cesar*. In the mental geography of the author, Poland formed a northern part of Slavdom, neighbouring Saxony and Bavaria.[16] There is also a collective name for the German state used in the text – *regio Teutonicorum*.[17] More frequently used were the names of its people: *Alemanni* or *Teutonici*, who had participated in invasions and raids into Poland. Contrary to the Bohemians (who were born robbers – *naturaliter raptores*), they inspired respect rather than dislike. It was the Saxons who earned their collective characteristic as the immediate neighbours: indomitable Saxons – *indomitos Saxones*. Prince Boleslaw the Brave (Bolesław Chrobry) put iron stakes in the middle of their land to mark the boundaries with Poland. In the time of Charlemagne King of the Franks (*Karoli Magni, Francorum regis*), those Saxons who rebelled against his rule and did not want to convert to Christianity emigrated in boats to barbarian and pagan Prussia.[18]

Contacts with the Empire are more fully described in the chronicle on two occasions: the congress at Gniezno in 1000, and Emperor Henry V's invasion of Poland in 1109. The two events became a permanent feature of the Polish chronicle tradition. The emperor was held in high esteem, and it was within his authority to grant the royal crown. On his pilgrimage to St. Adalbert tomb, *Otto Rufus imperator* was received by Prince Bolesław the Brave in a manner suitable for an emperor – "ut regem, imperatorem Romanum ac tantum hospitem

---

15   Jacek Banaszkiewicz, "Gall Anonim – tradycja historyczna Piastów jako wykład o początkach rodu-dynastii i Polski, w planie podobnych realizacji dziejopisarskich XII stulecia," [Gall Anonim – the historical tradition of the Piasts as a lecture on the beginnings of the family-dynasty and Poland, in a context of similar historiographic realizations of the 12th century] in *Przeszłość w kulturze*, 241–267. Jacek Banaszkiewicz, *W stronę rytuałów i Galla Anonima* (Kraków, 2018).

16   Adam Krawiec, "The Concept of Space in the Chronicle of Gallus Anonymus, the Mental Geography of its Author and their Significance for the Controversy on his Place of Origin," *APH*, 112 (2015), 25–46.

17   *Galli anonymi* I-18, 42.

18   *Galli anonymi* I-6, 16; II-42, 111–112. The topic was not elaborated upon in the old Polish historical texts, but appeared in later German chronicles.

suscipere decens fuit". The richness and power of the host practically forced the emperor to elevate the prince to the throne: "such a great man does not deserve to be styled duke or count like any princes, but to be raised to a royal throne and adorned with a diadem in glory" – "in regale solium glorianter redimitum diademate sublimari". So, the emperor took his own diadem (*imperiale diadema*) and put it on the prince's head, and gave him "as a triumphal banner a nail from the cross of our Lord with the lance of St. Mauritius" – "pro vexilio triumphali clavum ei de cruce Domini cum lancea sancti Maurici dono dedit". In return for the emperor's favour Bolesław gave him the martyr's arm – "sancti Adalberti brachium redonavit".[19] The message of this description is clear: Poland became a kingdom – regardless of the actual crowning of its rulers. They were to be equal partners, with the precedence of the prestige for the emperor being understood. The chronicler initiated the practice of a meticulous writing down in chronicles of all marriage connections between the Piasts and the imperial family. When his father was still alive, Prince Mieszko II had married the *sororem tertii Ottonis imperatoris*, while her son Kazimierz was *matre imperiali puer*.[20] Over the next centuries the Gniezno congress was updated through further interpretations.[21] In time, these were used to construct the idea of the restoration of the kingdom, that served as the principle for the unification of the Polish lands in the thirteenth century.[22]

While describing Henry V's interference into internal Polish affairs, the chronicler gives a detailed account of the emperor: "Henricus imperator IIII, Rome nondum coronatus, secundo quidem anno coronandus". This, of course, did not concern the course of the expedition itself. On the basis of his imperial power (*imperatori legibusque Romanis*), the emperor allegedly demanded three things of as his vassal (*sui militis*), Bolesław the Wry-Mouthed (Bolesław Krzywousty): divide his kingdom and give half to his exiled brother Zbigniew, pay annual tribute of three hundred marks, and provide military reinforcement. He met with an outright refusal. The expedition of the angry emperor was full of dramatic episodes that through the chronicle's account entered the collective mythology of the Poles. Thanks to their bravery and God's help, the emperor's expedition ended in total failure. His plans to obtrusively crush Poland's ancient liberty were thwarted by the Righteous Judge – "quoniam superbe libertatem antiquam Polonie subiugare cogitavit, iustus iudex illud

---

19   *Galli anonymi* I-6, 19.
20   *Galli anonymi* I-7, 40, I-18, 41; Queen Richeza was not the emperor's sister, but his niece.
21   Węcowski, *Początki Polski*: 341 et seq.
22   Wojciech Drelicharz, *Unifying the Kingdom of Poland in Medieval Historiographic Thought*, Kraków 2019; earlier Polish edition" Wojciech. *Idea zjednoczenia królestwa w średniowiecznym dziejopisarstwie polskim* (Kraków, 2012).

consilium fatuavit".[23] The struggles described at length are presented as the defence of the freedom of the land that had been frequently attacked and yet had never been completely subjugated by anyone – "multociens impugnata, nunquam tamen ab ullo fuit penitus subiugata".[24] Looking in retrospect, it could be said that, regardless of the actual historical events and circumstances, the self-stereotype of successful defence in its contacts with the Holy Roman Empire became a constant element in the Polish identity.

The motif of full sovereignty was elaborated upon in the early thirteenth century in the Chronicle of Poland by Master Vincentius Kadłubek, bishop of Cracow.[25] He modifies the meaning of the events recorded by his predecessor, revealing a strongly anti-German bias, and he supplements the origins of the Piast dynasty with his own reflections upon the earlier history of the community of pre-Poles – the Lechites. He bases his account of them on mythical, fictional plots drawn from oral history, but which he transforms with great literary erudition using Plato's *Timaeus* and Justin's *Epitome*.[26] The narrative was constructed employing an elaborate rhetoric characteristic of the "difficult style" – *ornatus difficilis* – and a sophisticated vocabulary full of rare and uncommon neologisms. To correctly grasp its meaning requires knowledge of substantial source literature.[27] The Empire in contact with Poland evidently became more German in character. As to his terminology, the chronicler uses a collective term *Lemani*, and only occasionally *Teutonici*. He also mentions Bavaria and Saxony, and princes in general (*Lemanorum principes*). In his narrative, the Germans appear several times, mainly as invaders: proud, tall, of iron strength, and as numerous as the locusts (*Lemanorum locuste*), full of fighting fierceness (*furor Teutonicus*). Set against this background, the bravery of the Poles is made to look even better. A battle near Wroclaw in 1109 was turned into a crushing defeat of the emperor, who escaped – thus saving his life. Instead of tribute, there was a battlefield with heaps of dead bodies being eaten by dogs, and for this reason the place was called "Dogs' Field" (Polish: *Psie Pole*, German:

23 *Galli anonymi* III-2-15, quotations: 129–130, 141–142.
24 *Galli anonymi* I-incipit 8.
25 *Magistri Vincentii dicti Kadlubek Chronica Polonorum /Mistrza Wincentego zwanego Kadlubkiem Kronika Polska*, ed. Marian Plezia, MPH N.S. 11 (Kraków, 1994); translation to German with the Latin text and introduction presenting a survey of the state of research: *Die Chronik der Polen des Magister Vincentius*, ed. Eduard Mühle, FSGA 48 (Darmstadt, 2014).
26 Jacek Banaszkiewicz, "Mistrz Wincenty i naśladowcy – wizje najstarszych dziejów Polski XIII–XV wieku," [Master Vincent and followers – visions of the oldest history of Poland in the 13th–15th centuries] in *Przeszłość w kulturze*, 271–306.
27 *Onus Athalanteum. Studia.*

Hundsfeld) – *Canium Campestre*.[28] The chronicler thus reverses a contemptuous comparison of pagan Slavs with dogs present in early German chronicle texts.[29] The terms describing the battlefield and a pejorative characteristic of the neighbours were preserved in the memory of the Polish chronicles.

Master Vincentius also changes the interpretation of Otto III's meeting with Bolesław the Brave in Gniezno. The emperor wants to honor the martyr St. Adalbert. Having seen the greatness of his host, he confirms his sovereignty. There was no royal elevation of any kind, and during the meeting of equal partners there is only an exchange of headgear: for a diadem instead of a helmet. It could be no other way, since it was already his predecessor, Mieszko I, who had been called the king. New meaning was given to marriages with German princesses who were accused by the chronicler of being proud, contemptuous of local people, and surrounded by German newcomers. Vincentius generally condemns women's meddling with matters of power. Their apparent gentleness was only a cover for their untamed fierceness – "est enim omnis mansuetudo feminea omni severitate truculentior, omni truculentia seuerior". Such a reflection is added to the description of the intrigues engaged in by Władysław II's wife Agnes, a sister of Emperor Conrad III and aunt of Friedrich I. Also, the wife of Mieszko II, Richeza, behaves in a similar way (none of these wives are mentioned by name). There is even a suggestion made that the latter might not have been Casimir I's mother, but instead his envious stepmother, and her intrigues resulted in the banishment of herself and the ruler.[30]

The chronicler is very familiar with new components of the imperial ideology of his times. This applies especially to a more precise definition of regalia as the sole prerogatives of supreme power and the reception of Justinian's codification as the imperial law, together with their consequences for the justification of universal power.[31] It is evident that Master Vincentius did not like Frederick I Barbarossa whom he calls the "red dragon" – *rufus draconus*.

---

28   In a document contemporary to the chronicler, the name: *Psie Pole* (literally: "dogs' field") was put down as the settlement *Pzepole* inhabited by the *Teutonicis* – in a charter of grants made by Prince Henryk I for the St. Vincent Monastery in Wrocław in 1206; *Schlesisches Urkundenbuch*, vol. 1, ed. Heinrich Appelt (Wien, 1971), 73, no. 101. The German name of the village – *Hundsfeld* – is regarded as a calque of the Polish version. The etymology of the term is unclear, however, since originally it could denote only "infertile soil", that was later interpreted as a battlefield because of its new inhabitants. Cf. Józef Domański, *Nazwy miejscowe dzisiejszego Wrocławia i dawnego okręgu wrocławskiego* [Local names of today's Wrocław and the former Wrocław district] (Warszawa, 1967), 34–35.
29   *Magistri Vincentii* III-18, 106; cf. Maschke, *Das Erwachen*, 10 et seq.
30   *Magistri Vincentii* II-14; III-26 and 29, quot.: 119.
31   Cf. Sławomir Gawlas, "Das Problem der Fürstenmacht zur Zeit von Vincentius Kadłubek," in *Macht und Spiegel der Macht. Herrschaft in Europa im 12. und 13. Jahrhundert vor dem*

He is assisted by princes – *principes* – sometimes called *senatus*. With the use of rhetorical figures, the chronicler camouflages the fact of the emperor's successful expedition, and contrary to reality, he suggests that the emperor's intervention in 1157 ended in failure. As regards the return of his nephews, the Polish supreme Prince Bolesław IV the Curly gives in only later, at the emperor's request. In fact, there is relatively little real information about the German Reich in the narrative. The chronicler has a very poor opinion of the princes seeking the emperor's assistance, and by way of example quotes the information that Bolesław the Tall is suspected of such intentions and wanted to sell Polish freedom to the Germans – "hic namque nostram Lemannis renundare libertatem". During a discussion about the succession to the supreme prince's throne, Bishop Pełka of Cracow rhetorically admits that Pope Alexander and Emperor Frederick had the authority to establish and abolish laws – "ius habent et condendi et abrogandi iura", but what was of decisive importance was the will of people (*cives*), that is of the Cracow magnates. Such are the words he puts in the mouth of the emperor himself, who surrounded by princes (*senatus*) considers, contrary to his interests, to decide on the choice of the Polish ruler:

> nec Polonis eligendi principem posse adimi potestatem quia nihil interest inutilem habeant an nullum [...] – imperatorius apex sententiat.[32]

> [The Imperial Majesty judged that the power to elect their own prince cannot be taken off the Poles because it is not important whether they will have an useless prince or none at all.]

In any case, the emperor's authority was justified under divine right – *ius divinum*. The actual polemics over the authority of the German emperor are transferred by the chronicler to the times of legends and are constructed into an ancient history of the Polish kingdom stylised in the form of an empire established by Krak – *Graccus*. After his younger son had been expelled, it was beautiful and wise Wanda who was entrusted with the rule and who gave the name to the Vistula River – *Wandalum flumen*. When a certain Lemmanic tyrant (*quidam Lemannorum tyranus*) tried to take her throne (*imperium*) and to destroy her people – he was struck by the virtue (*virtus*) and majesty of his female opponent. Then, praising her charms, he resigns from a battle and throws himself onto his sword. The image of the queen is the opposite

---

    Hintergrund der Chronistik, ed. Norbert Kersken and Grischa Vercamer (Wiesbaden, 2013), 273–308.

32   *Magistri Vincentii* III-30 124; IV-21 177; IV-12 152–153.

of German princesses and the bad wives of other monarchs. Later chronicles present other versions of the story of Wanda who is depicted as preferring to die childless rather than marry a German invader. In time, Wanda became so popular that she made her way into popular folklore.[33]

Later on, under the rule of people of lower social status, there was an expedition by Emperor Alexander of Macedonia. *Imperatrix Polonia* proudly refuses to pay tribute and successfully opposes his invasion. The dynasty established by Lestek I reconstructs the Polish empire which includes the territories of the Lusatian Serbs and probably also of other Polabian Slavs. Lestek III defeats Julius Cesar three times. The latter gives Lestek his sister Julia as a wife together with Bavaria as her dowry. Julia is sent away after the emperor claims the province back. Lestek's successor, King Pompiliusz, takes over the Slavonic monarchy – *Slauie monarchia* – and is assigned *ducatus, alias comitias seu marchia, nonullis regna* to his bastard brothers. Through the instigation of his jealous wife, the monarch poisons his brothers. The dynasty, so contaminated by the crime, comes to an end, and the empire collapses, bringing down the glory of Poles – *omnis Polonorum gloria*. The meaning of the expanded story about victories over ancient emperors and the glory of the ancient Polish empire consists in ideological polemics, with the Prophet Daniel's idea of the wandering of universal monarchies,[34] being adapted at that time to the needs of the German historical memory. In a vernacular version written down in the *Annolied* or Song of Anno, and later in *Kaiserchronik* (Imperial Chronicle), rulers of the German Reich were the continuators of ancient empires and direct successors of Julius Cesar.[35] Master Vincentius argues that already in ancient time, the Poles had not recognised this universal superiority and paid no tribute. Consequently, questioning the imperial powers, he conscientiously takes note of the manifestations of such powers in the successes of Polish rulers. The boundaries of the empire were renewed by Bolesław the Brave who subjected the neighbouring peoples, including the Saxons. When fighting off an invasion of Emperor Henry IV, the chronicler reminds the reader of the earlier refusal

---

33 *Magistri Vincentii* I-7, 12–13; cf. Jacek Banaszkiewicz, *Polskie dzieje bajeczne Mistrza Wincentego Kadłubka* [Polish fairy tales of Master Wincenty Kadłubek] (Wrocław, 1998), 65–153; Violetta Wróblewska, "Wanda," in *Słownik polskiej bajki ludowej*, vol. 3: *P–Z*, ed. Violetta Wróblewska (Toruń, 2018): 287–290.

34 Werner Goez, *Translatio imperii. Ein Beitrag zur Geschichte des Geschichtsdenkens und der politischen Theorien im Mittelalter und in der frühen Neuzeit* (Tübingen, 1958).

35 *Magistri Vincentii* I-9 14; I-17 23; I-19, 27; cf. Gawlas, Pytania o tożsamość: 58–67; Grischa Vercamer, "Imperiale Konzepte in der mittelalterlichen Historiographie Polens vom 12 bis zum 15. Jahrhundert," in *Transcultural Approaches to the Concept of Imperial Rule In the Middle Ages*, ed. Christian Scholl, Torben R. Gebhardt, and Jan Claus (Frankfurt/Main 2017), 321–366.

to pay tribute to Alexander of Macedonia. In short time, he attributes almost imperial power to Bolesław the Wry-Mouthed, understood in terms of his freedom to make and depose kings. Commenting on his successful intervention in Bohemia, the chronicler notes that it incited hatred among the Germans:

> Quod illi aput Lemannos plurimum conflauit inuidie, quod imperatoriam sibi uendicaret quasi maiestatem, cum in regnis contiguis arbitratu proprio quos mallet deiceret potenter, quos mallet potenter sublimaret.[36]

> [That brought him a lot of resentment among the Germans, that he acted almost as Imperial Majesty, when he deposed or raised whom he liked in the neighbouring realms at his own discretion.]

The use of memory preserved in writing about past events to defend the sovereignty of Poland against the Empire, the interpretation of contacts with the Empire in national terms, and attributing to the Germans an envy at Polish successes became a constant feature of later chronicles. On the other hand, although the clearly overzealous image of an imperial sovereignty of its own in ancient Poland had not been forgotten, it was not continued in descriptions of later events. That Master Vincentius introduced to his narrative various fictional plots was made possible by the prevalence in the twelfth century of oral memory accounts over written versions. In the following century, however, the situation changed due to the rapid development of literary culture. The vision of the past recorded in the chronicle is the actual beginning of the Polish chronicle tradition. Its further development took place under new external and internal conditions. The collapse of the authority of the supreme prince residing in Cracow and the increasing political fragmentation of the Polish state were changing the scale of the ideological aspirations of the growing number of the Piasts. An important factor was the implementation of Gregorian reforms and the strengthening of papal control over the Polish Church under Pope Innocent III.[37] As for relations with the Reich, of special importance was the elimination of the possibility of enforcing the imperial superiority as consequence of the dual election after Henry VI's death. When there were

---

36   *Magistri Vincentii* III-20, 107.
37   Wojciech Baran-Kozłowski, *Arcybiskup gnieźnieński Henryk Kietlicz. Działalność kościelna i polityczna* [Archbishop of Gniezno, Henryk Kietlicz. Church and political activity] (Poznań, 2005), 94 et seq.; cf. Mikołaj Gładysz, *Zapomniani krzyżowcy. Polska wobec ruchu krucjatowego w XII–XIII wieku* [Forgotten Crusaders. Poland and the Crusade Movement in the 12th–13th centuries] (Warszawa, 2002), 144 et seq.

internal conflicts, Polish princes began to seek protection from the pope.[38] It was accompanied by a more effective collection of the so-called Peter's Pence (*denarius sancti Petri*). Constructing an alternative to the imperial ideology account of Polish history lost its political relevance. It was replaced with the concept of a direct dependence of the Polish lands on the Chair of St. Peter and the protection accorded by the Roman Church, which were developed into a political doctrine. The development of this special bond with the papacy and its functioning in the late medieval period occurred in the period of a rapidly increasing importance of written documents in public life. The existence of source materials has made it possible to thoroughly examine this topic in the scholarly literature.[39]

In 1253, Innocent IV invoked the submission of Polish princes (*principes Polonie*) to the papacy as having existed since the time of the adoption of Christianity and the paying by the Polish people, in token of this submission, of an annual tax called *denarius sancti Petri*. Thus, the pope commanded legate Opizo, abbot of Mezzano, to provide all of them with protection against threats, especially any from Wilhelm of Holland – *infeudationes, distributiones aut occupationes de terra Polonie inveneris, tam a carissimo in Christo filio nostro W[ilhelmo] rege Romanorum illustri quam ab aliis factas*.[40] Over next years, ideological interpretations of the consequences of the papal protection were further elaborated, only marginally taking into account imperial claims. Special bonds reflected in the payment of Peter's Pence were included in the programme of the defence of the political unity of Polish lands that was given a national and at the same time an anti-German character. The most credible evidence is a 1285 letter of Archbishop Jakub Świnka of Gniezno to the cardinals. He emphasises the community of interests resulting from the submission of the Polish people – *gens Polonica* – to the Roman Church. By paying Peter's Pence, as "special sons of this Church" (*speciales filli eiuisdem eccclesie*) they were justified in expecting its effective help. The occupation of Polish frontiers by German princes damaged also its interests for the latter recognised imperial authority as superior – *quia dum fines Polonie per principes Theutonie occupantur, qui principes subsunt imperio et sic fines occupati devolvuntur ad imperium, et ob hoc ecclesia Romana proprio dominio frustratur*. This is also the case when German knights and settlers did not want to pay Peter's Pence – *Theutunici tam*

---

38 Johannes Fried, *Der päpstliche Schutz für Laienfürsten. Die politische Geschichte des päpstlichen Schutzprivilegs für Laien (11.–13. Jh.)* (Heidelberg, 1980), 289 et seq.

39 Changes in the function of Peter's Pence are presented in detail in: Erich Maschke, *Der Peterspfennig in Polen und dem deutschen Osten*, 2. ed. (Sigmaringen, 1979), here: 47 et seq.

40 *Kodeks dyplomatyczny Wielkopolski* [The diplomatic code of Greater Poland], vol. 1, ed. Ignacy Zakrzewski (Poznań, 1877), no. 314, 278.

milites quam coloni penitus solvere contradicunt, et sic ecclesia Romana privatur similiter iure suo. They were respecting the custom of their own people and not that of the land they had settled in. Also, the German Franciscans ousted the Polish brethren and joined the Saxon province. The archbishop expected help in defending the unity of the Polish ecclesiastical province – *Polonia sicut prius non Saxonia censeatur.*[41] This specific ideological alliance with the papacy in a certain way excluded Poland from participation in the imperial struggle for *dominium mundi* and was something that was commonly known. In the oldest collection of Polish customary laws compiled in the early fourteenth-century in the Teutonic State, its German author stresses the fact that the Poles were taken under the protection of the pope to make easier their Christianisation and in consequence they were not subject to the emperor:

> dy Polen, von ir cristenheit anegende, habin dem romysche stule des bobistes undirtenik gewesin unde nicht dem keyser, wen sy der romysche stul in synen schirm inpfing, dorch daz ze erste gernir cristen wordin.

> [From the beginning of their Christianity, the Poles had been subjects to the Holy Roman See and the Pope and not to the emperor. Only because the Holy See received them under his protection, they wanted to become Christians.]

For this reason, Polish courts did not derive their authority from the emperor's power:

> unde wen ir gericht von dem keyser in dy werlt nicht enkunt alz dutscher vursten unde richter tut.[42]

> [that is why their court of justice cannot judge in the name of the emperor in the world like German prices and judges do.]

This change in perception of the Holy Roman Empire was caused in great part by the transformation of internal conditions within the region of Central Eastern Europe according to the principles of the German colonization that

---

41   *Ibid.*, vol. 1, no. 616, 574–575; cf. Bronisław Nowacki, "Arcybiskup Jakub Świnka – budziciel i propagator polskiej świadomości narodowej," [Archbishop Jakub Świnka – the awakener and promoter of Polish national awareness] in *1000 lat archidiecezji gnieźnieńskiej*, ed. Jerzy Strzelczyk and Janusz Górny (Gniezno, 2000), 107–120.

42   *Najstarszy zwód prawa polskiego* [The oldest deception of Polish law], ed. Józef and Jacek Matuszewski (Łódź, 1995), § 1.1 and 2.1, 59.

intensified at the end of the twelfth century. It has been the subject of numerous different studies. In the situation of the actual absence of German kings, the freedom of action of East German princes increased. There was a significant change in the character of contacts between the Polish lands and the German Empire. Instead of political confrontation with the imperial ideology, there was an intensification of border conflicts and direct contacts with the arriving German merchants, peasants and knights. The changes are more evident due to the richer and more diverse body of sources, but mainly because of the development of the legal functions of charters in social life. In comparison to the earlier chronicles, a marked change occurred in the terminology which became more standardised – there was almost exclusively one term used: *Theutonici*, and *Theutonia*.[43] Source references in documents are abundant. What had a great uniforming impact on the status of any newcomers, regardless their ethnic origins, was the emergence in 1220 of the term: *ius* (*mos*) *Teutonicus/corum*.[44] This change in terminology can also be seen in chronicle records, more frequently in the thirteenth century. They also contain almost exclusively the term *Teutonici*, mainly in descriptions of military conflicts with Brandenburg, but also of events with the participation of Germans living in Poland.[45] From this perspective, the image of the Empire was focused on the nationality of its inhabitants.

An increasing confrontation with German settlers in the first half of the thirteenth century as they were flowing into the Polish lands emphasised the differences which were obvious for ordinary people in their daily lives.[46] These

---

43 The terminology appeared in the founding charter of Lubiąż monastery of 1175 – *Schlesisches Urkundenbuch*, vol. 1, no. 45, 28: monks came "de Portensi cenobio, quod est in Theotonia super Salam fluvium". Lands were to be cultivated by "Theotonici" who "ab omni iure Polonico sine exceptione sint in perpetuum liberi".

44 Jan M. Piskorski, *Kolonizacja wiejska Pomorza Zachodniego w XIII i w początkach XIV wieku na tle procesów osadniczych w średniowiecznej Europie* [Rural colonization of West Pomerania in the 13th and early 14th centuries against the background of settlement processes in medieval Europe] (Poznań,1990), 81 et seq.

45 Due to the vicinity of Brandenburg, most references are in the Greater Poland annals: of the Poznań Chapter and Gniezno Chapter – *Annales Poloniae Maioris*, ed. Brygida Kürbis, MPH, series II-6 (Warszawa, 1962), as in the index. A more meticulous use of the records from Polish annals of the 13th century requires taking into account the fact that a majority of the annals have survived in later copies that were subjected to various updating measures. The Greater Poland annals have been preserved within the framework of a collection of historiographic texts called the Great Chronicle. It was made at the end of the 14th century, and its manuscripts were written in the century that followed.

46 Gawlas, "Pytania o tożsamość", 69 et seq.; cf Tomasz Jurek, *Obce rycerstwo na Śląsku, do połowy XIV wieku* [Foreign knights in Silesia, until the mid-fourteenth century] (Poznań, 1996), 158 et seq.

included the rules for paying tithes and the duration of fasts. They became the subject of prolonged disputes with the native clergy who tried to defend their interests with the help of ecclesiastical censures. The change in collecting the tithes was a result of the adoption of the German law, and fairly soon it included the local population as well. This is why it did not become an indicator of ethnicity – although it was not until the fourteenth century that it was regulated by compromise. In 1248, the settlers were discharged from the obligation of a nine-week-long fast introduced in Poland at the threshold of Christianisation by the papal legate, Jacob of Liège.[47] Regardless of the later fate of this custom, it must have been firmly rooted in popular consciousness for it led to the coining of the term "German fast". It was included in stereotypical descriptions of nations and peoples when they became popular in this region in the fifteenth century.[48] The main features distinguishing Poles in their everyday and religious customs and their clothing are explained in the story of Casimir the Restorer (Kazimierz Odnowiciel), allegedly a monk at Cluny.[49] It was written down not long after 1253 in two slightly different versions of the Life of St. Stanislaus.[50] The pope dispensed the prince's religious vows for the good of the Poles in exchange for symbolic signs of memory about this event in the form of a special haircut, national costumes, and the obligation to pay Peter's Pence.[51] Here we deal with an identity narrative whose importance we can follow in many sources of the late Middle Ages. It was broadly known from

---

47 *Schlesisches Urkundenbuch*, vol. 2: 1231–1259, ed. Winfried Irgang (Wien, 1977), no. 340, 210, § 12: "De esu carnium Theutonicorum et Polonorum."

48 Stanisław Kot, "Pochwały i przygany w dawnych opiniach o narodach," [Praise and exhortations in old opinions about nations] in id., *Polska złotego wieku a Europa. Studia i szkice*, ed. Henryk Barycz (Warszawa, 1987, orig. pub. 1954), 726 et seq.

49 Inga Stembrowicz, "Podanie o Kazimierzu Mnichu w polskim dziejopisarstwie do końca XIV wieku," [A story about Kazimierz Mnich in Polish historiography until the end of the 14th century] in *Symboliczne i realne podstawy*, 220–282.

50 Studies and discussions on the Lives of Saint Stanislaus are summed up in: Drelicharz, *Unifying the Kingdom of Poland*, 113 et seq., 147 et seq.; recently, a significant establishment of facts has been presented by Jacek Banaszkiewicz, "Prolog do Rocznika kapituły krakowskiej, św. Stanisław i czas historyczny," [Prologue to the Annal of the Krakow Chapter, St. Stanislaus and historical time] in *Przeszłość w kulturze średniowiecznej Polski*, vol. 1, 309 et seq.; cf. Agnieszka Rożnowska-Sadraei, *Pater patriae. The cult of Saint Stanislaus and the Patronage of Polish Kings 1200–1455* (Krakow, 2008), 55 et seq.

51 *Vita S. Stanislai episcopi cracoviensis (Vita minor)*, ed. Wojciech Kętrzyński, in MPH 4 (Lwów, 1884), 269–272; *Vita Sancti Stanislai cracoviensis episcopi (Vita maior)*, ibid., 380–382; cf. *Chronicon Polono-Silesiacum – Kronika Polska*, ed. Ludwik Ćwikliński, ibid. 3 (Lwów, 1878), 620/621. cf. Tomasz Jurek, "Fryzura narodowa średniowiecznych Polaków," [National hairstyle of medieval Poles] in *Scriptura custos memoriae. Prace historyczne*, ed. Danuta Zydorek (Poznań, 2001), 635–651.

the oral circulation of stories in other European countries because its elements were mentioned by an anonymous Dominican (from within the milieu of the French court) who was describing Eastern Europe.[52] He set its content over against the actual state of affairs and observed that contemporary Poles had no longer *conuersi cistercieneses*, and some of them had long hair. The latter were also interpreted as an identity symbol or sign of favor since Prince Leszek the Black (supported by the citizens of Cracow) *in favorem Teutonicorum coman nutriebat*.[53] It should be added that in the late Middle Ages, the story of Casimir the Monk was still alive in the popular course of historical knowledge.[54]

It was the concept of restoring the lost kingdom that was better suited to the political reality of the fragmentation in the period, rather than the memory of a lost Slavic empire. It was based on a conviction about the royal status of the Piast dynasty present in the earlier chronicles, and especially in the legend of the splendor of Bolesław the Brave's times and the course of his meeting with the emperor at Gniezno. The existing sources have been minutely analysed in research.[55] The idea of a renewal of the kingdom was formulated soon after the canonisation of Saint Stanislaw. The above-mentioned lives of the saint included a historiosophical construct of the history of Poland built around the obtaining of the crown by Boleslaw the Brave and its loss by his great-grandson Bolesław the Bold (*Bolesław Śmiały*). The glory of the kingdom of the first Bolesław ("magni regis Boleslai corona regni Polonie aucta crevit")[56] was corrupted by the tyrannical rule and wickedness of the other. The punishments for the sin of the murder of the bishop of Cracow were the loss of the crown, the successive rule of many princes, and the numerous calamities that befell the kingdom. God's righteous judgments and the merits of the new saint justified the eschatological prophecy of a future re-unification and re-birth of the kingdom. God would have mercy and forgive the sins of the Poles. In

---

52 *Anonymi Descriptio Europae Orientalis. Imperium Constantinopolitanum, Albania, Serbia, Bulgaria, Ruthenia, Ungaria, Polonia, Bohemia Anno MCCCVIII exarata*, ed. Olgierd Górka, (Cracovia, 1916), 57–58: "Catholici sunt omnes et ob deuotionem, quam habent ad Romanam ecclesiam, quemlibet domus tenetur soluere vnum denarium romane ecclesie et uocatur denarius sancti Petri. Olim omnes Poloni ibant tonsi sicut conuersi cistercienses, sed nunc aliqui incipiunt dimittere crines."

53 *Chronica Dzirsvae*, ed. Krzysztof Pawłowski, MPH, series II-15 (Kraków, 2013), 85.

54 It was the legend of Casimir the Monk that the members of political elite referred to when giving evidence before Cardinal Antonio Zeno regarding the legal dispute with the Teutonic Order in 1422 – Jacek Banaszkiewicz, "Fabularyzacja przestrzeni. Przykład średniowiecznych granic," [Fictionalization of space. An example of medieval borders] in id., *Takie sobie średniowieczne bajeczki* (Kraków, 2012), 119–146.

55 Drelicharz, *Unifying the Kingdom of Poland*, 95 et seq., 427 et seq.

56 *Vita Sancti Stanislai cracoviensis episcopi (Vita maior)*, 391.

the treasury of the Cracow cathedral the royal coronation insignia awaited the ruler when summoned by God.[57] The historiographic structure is based on the scheme: a committed sin, God's wrath and punishment, and hope for forgiveness and a change in the Polish fate, and this becomes then a component of the unification ideology from the very beginning. Later on, its elements were subjected to various modifications,[58] but it remained a permanent feature of the interpretation of the course of events. It should be regarded as a testimony to the formation of a special alliance of Poles with God's providence – the conviction developed later by Jan Długosz in his *Annales*,[59] and willingly updated in various forms all the way through the centuries up to our times. It complemented the ideological alliance with the papacy as mentioned above. Another factor was the creation of Polish lands as the bulwark of Western Christianity – *antemurale Christianitatis*: the country constantly fighting against pagans and being threatened by the aggression of schismatics. This element appeared in the twelfth century and was developed over the next century. In the supplication of Prince Władysław the Elbow-High, quoted in Pope John XXII's permission for his coronation of 1319, it occupied a very prominent place, next to the Peter's Pence.[60] In the fourteenth century, during the disputes over the territorial shape of the re-unified state, the obligation to pay Peter's Pence was readily used as a sign of belonging to the Kingdom of Poland.[61]

---

57 Drelicharz, *Unifying the Kingdom of Poland*, 153 et seq.
58 Cf. Jacek Banaszkiewicz, "Czarna i biała legenda Bolesława Śmiałego," [Black and white legend of Bolesław the Bold] (1981) in id., *Takie sobie średniowieczne bajeczki*, 27–100; Piotr Węcowski, "Strata korony królewskiej po śmierci św. Stanisława w opinii pisarzy późnego średniowiecza," [The loss of the royal crown after the death of St. Stanisław in the opinion of late medieval writers] in *Christianitas Romana. Studia ofiarowane Profesorowi Romanowi Michałowskiemu*, ed. Krzysztof Skwierczyński (Warszawa, 2009), 274–299.
59 Recently: Adam Talarowski, "Dzieje w rękach Opatrzności. Elementy historiozofii Jana Długosza," [History in the hands of Providence. Elements of the historiosophy of Jan Długosz] *Roczniki Historyczne*, 84 (2018), 191–225.
60 Paul Srodecki, *Antemurale Christianitatis. Zur Genese Bollwerksrhetorik im östlichen Mitteleuropa an der Schwelle vom Mittelalter zur Frühen Neuzeit* (Husum, 2015), 73 et seq. According to the author, it was the Teutonic Order that was the first to propagate the rhetoric of being a Christian bulwark in the region.
61 Jan Ptaśnik, *Denar świętego Piotra obrońcą jedności politycznej i kościelnej w Polsce* [Saint Peter's denarius as a defender of political and church unity in Poland] (Kraków, 1908); Maschke, *Der Peterspfennig in Polen*, 61 et seq.; cf. "Wiersz o świętopietrzu" [A poem on Peter's Pence], ed. August Bielowski, in *MPH* 3 (Lwów, 1878), 288–289: "Wrotslav cum Silesia, Nyssa, Swednicz, / Glogovia, Opol, Legnicz, / Ratiborz, Nyemodlin, Olavia, / Pomorania, Chelmensis est Polonia. / Hoc bene probatur, / Census Petri quia datur / Partibus in illis, / Oppidis, castris, quoque villis. / Sicut mater pia / Solvit tota Polonia [...]".

This presented in the most concise way that the impact of the ideological actions of the Polish thirteenth-century political and intellectual elites on the image of the Empire should be supplemented with the issue of the genesis of the Polish community and its place within universal history. In this important area, the history of the Empire encounters the recorded knowledge about the Polish past. The problem arose at the very beginning of annalistic writing, since the first information about Polish lands was added to the compilation of the Annals of Hersfeld and the Annals of Reichenau (Augia), most probably in the version drawn up in Mainz on the occasion of the imperial coronation of Otto I. The time and manner of the reception of the model of Carolingian-Ottonian annalistic writing have been the subject of highly complicated and hypothetical discussions due to the quality of the preserved manuscripts. According to the most recent literature, the process of merging took place in Cracow in the second half of the eleventh century.[62] Regardless of these disputes, it should be emphasized that the oldest layer of Polish annals records suggests the continuation of the registration of events from the history of the Empire until around mid-thirteenth century.[63] The narratives in the first chronicle were devoid of dates and they loosely followed the chronology of events. In the era of great encyclopaedic historical compilations of that century, however, it became necessary to more accurately reconcile the described events with the available knowledge of universal history. The task required filling information gaps and was exceedingly difficult. An important role in this was played by the community of Polish Dominicans and the needs they had related to organizing a biography of Saint Stanislaus according to the patterns established in this hagiographical model.[64] Wincenty of Kielce, the author of *Vita Maior*, intertwined Stanislaus' life with the history of the country and established its basic chronological framework. He also undertook (in 1266–1271) the compilation of a new version of the Annals of the Cracow Chapter. He prefaced the text with an introduction and a chronicle of the world from its creation to the seventh century. It was an extract from the *Etymologies* by Isidore of Seville, and it completed the above-mentioned notes

---

62 I accept the convincing argumentation put forward by Tomasz Jasiński recently in: "Początki rocznikarstwa w Polsce," [The beginnings of Annalistic in Poland] in *Kościół, kultura, polityka pierwszych Piastów*, ed. Waldemar Graczyk *et al.* (Warszawa/Ciechanów, 2016): 169–185. Traditional hypotheses of the Polish source literature in this matter are defended by Drelicharz, *Unifying the Kingdom of Poland*, 28 et seq.

63 In the most important account of the earlier chronicles, the Annals of the Krakow Chapter, the last information is about Wilhelm of Holland's death – *Annales cracovienses priores cum kalendario*, ed. Zofia Kozłowska-Budkowa, MPH, series II-5 (Warszawa, 1978), 86.

64 A thorough analysis was made by Banaszkiewicz, "Prolog do Rocznika," 320 et seq.

taken from the German chronicles. Soon, there was a broad and long-term reception of the *Chronicle of the Popes and Emperors* by Martinus Polonus (Martinus Oppaviensis).[65] It contained only a few references to the Polish lands, but excerpts from it were used in the early fourteenth century as elements of the chronological frame for a new annalistic outline of Polish history emerging at that time.[66] It included information about the emperors from Arnulf for the year 899 to the coronation of Frederick II in 1214 (or 1239).[67] A compilation of Polish history was made in the Franciscan community in Cracow and it included into the records what had probably been written there from the materials from the Cracow chapter. The record of events continued for several dozen years, and successive versions of the annals obliterated its original wording.[68] In fact, during the re-writing, the records of the events from the time before the baptismal conversion of Poland were abandoned. There was another chronicle compiled in the Franciscan community, the Dzierzwa Chronicle from the second decade of the fourteenth century. It is a summary (with minor modifications, but preserving the motif of the Slavic empire) of Master Vincentius' Chronicle, with a concise continuation until 1288 and

---

65 What is known about the author and the text is summed up by Jacek Soszyński: "Wstęp," [Introduction] in Marcin Polak, *Kronika papieży i cesarzy* [Chronicle of Popes and Emperors], the Polish translation and commentary by Agnieszka Fabiańska and Jacek Soszyński (Kęty, 2008), 11–84. Cf. Jacek Soszyński, *Kronika Marcina Polaka i jej średniowieczna tradycja rękopiśmienna w Polsce* [The chronicle of Marcin Polak and its medieval handwriting tradition in Poland], Studia Copernicana 34 (Warszawa, 1995).

66 Jacek Banaszkiewicz, "Rocznik tzw. małopolski (minorycki) z początku XIV wieku – próba dookreślenia zabytku," [The so-called Lesser Poland Annal (of Friar Minor) from the beginning of the 14th century – an attempt to define the monument more precisely] in *Przeszłość w kulturze*, 353–365.

67 *Rocznik małopolski* [The Lesser Poland annal], ed. August Bielowski, MPH 2, (Lwów, 1872), 816–825, here: 818: "Anulfus fuit ultimus imperator quantum ad posteritatem magni Caroli". *Rocznik małopolski* [The Lesser Poland Annal], ed. August Bielowski, MPH 3 (Lwów, 1878), 135–202, here: 164–165: *Fredericus ultimus coronatur Rome et post hunc nullus Romam pervenit, ut coronetur.*

68 The complicated history of the Franciscan compilation is analysed against the background of the whole Little Poland chronicle written by Wojciech Drelicharz, *Annalistyka małopolska XIII–XV wieku. Kierunki rozwoju wielkich roczników kompilowanych*, [The Lesser Poland annalystic of the 13th–15th centuries. Directions of development of large compiled years] Rozprawy Wydziału Historyczno-Filozoficznego PAU 99 (Kraków, 2003). Earlier, the author published a concise outline of his results: id., "Richtungen in der Entwicklung der kleinpolnischen Annalistik im 13.–15. Jh.," in *Die Geschichtsschreibung in Mitteleuropa. Projekte und Forschungsprobleme*, ed. Jaroslaw Wenta (Toruń, 1999), 53–72; cf. id., *Idea zjednoczenia*, 327 et seq. The 19th-century editions of the annals contain many incorrect identifications of the source texts, and it requires a lot of effort to familiarise oneself with the results of the later source studies.

an introduction in which the history of emperors is replaced with a biblical genealogy of the Poles presented as descendants of Iawan (*Iawan quem Poloni vocant Iwan*), Noah's grandson.[69]

The relationship between the creation of a coherent version of Polish history and the evolution of the image of the Empire, amounting in fact to the minimization of its significance, can be further clarified by referring to the development of the situation in Silesia, in a different ideological direction. The members of the local Piast line not only maintained close contacts with the imperial court and princes, but after the mid-thirteenth century they further strengthened these ties by engaging in the election of Richard of Cornwall and in other disputes over the German throne.[70] The coronation plans of Prince Henry IV Probus of Wrocław, which were drawn up around 1280, were initially planned in close cooperation with Emperor Rudolf I.[71] Over the next decade, Engelbert, a Cistercian monk from the monastery at Lubiąż, later on the abbot of the Cistercian monastery at Mogiła near Krakow, and then at the Pomeranian monastery at Byszewo-Koronow, worked on a regional version of Polish history.[72] The *Polish Chronicle* (Polish-Silesian Chronicle) consists of two parts, but was not completed. In the next century, the text was supplemented by the additions from another author. The chronicle was compiled in a German-speaking community. Its author was familiar with Polish historiography and contemporary interpretations of its threads to which he added his own views, in a rather unrestrained manner. Summarising the first book and in part the second book of the Master Vicentius' Chronicle,[73] he accused it of lacking objectivity and of concealing events unfavorable to its people. He

---

69   *Chronica Dzirsvae*, ed. Krzysztof Pawłowski, 1; cf. Jacek Banaszkiewicz, *Kronika Dzierzwy XIV-wieczne kompendium dziejów historii ojczystej* [The Chronicle of Dzierzwa – a 14th-century compendium of the history of Poland] (Wrocław etc., 1979).

70   Jurek, *Obce rycerstwo*, 178 et seq.

71   Tomasz Jurek, "Plany koronacyjne Henryka Probusa," [Henryk Probus's coronation plans] in *Śląsk w czasach Henryka IV Prawego*, ed. Kazimierz Wachowski, Wratislavia antiqua. Studia z dziejów Wrocławia 8 (Wrocław, 2005), 13–29.

72   *Kronika polska* [The Polish Chronicle], ed. Ludwik Ćwikliński, in MPH 3, 578–656; cf. Wojciech Mrozowicz, "Die Polnische Chronik (Polnisch-Schlesische Chronik) und die Chronik der Fürsten Polens (Chronica principum Poloniae) als Mittel zur dynastischen Identitätsstiftung der schlesischen Piasten," in *Legitimation von Fürstendynastien in Polen und dem Reich. Identitätsbildung im Spiegel schriftlicher Quellen (12.–15. Jahrhundert)*, ed. Grischa Vercamer and Ewa Wółkiewicz (Wiesbaden, 2016), 249–262.

73   Wojciech Mrozowicz, "Z problematyki recepcji kroniki Wincentego w średniowiecznym dziejopisarstwie polskim (ze szczególnym uwzględnieniem śląskiej Kroniki polskiej)," [On the reception of the chronicle of Wincenty in medieval Polish historiography (with particular emphasis on the Silesian Polish Chronicle] in *Onus Athlanteum*, 326–336; Banaszkiewicz, *Mistrz Wincenty*, 301 et seq.

almost completely reversed the political meaning of the narrative and, instead of defending Polish sovereignty, he emphasised all the ties with the Empire.[74] There are many such references in his text. The first Polish king was to be Mieszko, who then was visited by Emperor Otto III after he was baptized. The emperor crowned him during the feast and made him his vassal – *coronavit suo dyademate et sic imperio feodalem fecit*. His successor, Bolesław the Brave, received his crown from Emperor Henry I (actually, the second). The chronicler quotes a story about Casimir the Monk, but adds a reference to Casimir's coronation by Emperor Henry II (III) before he returned to Poland. Bolesław the Wry-Mouthed provoked the emperor Henry IV (V) into invading Poland, and during the negotiations near Wrocław he cunningly imprisoned him and forced him *in Kolberg castrum* to serve in the kitchen. In return for releasing him, Bolesław gained his first-born son Władysław's marriage with the emperor's daughter Agnes. It was for this reason that when Boleslaw wanted to be crowned, the angel took the crown from his head and put it on the head of King Michael of Hungary – "cum in regem coronari deberet, angelus coronam de capite illius rapuit ac regi Ungarie Michaeli imposuit". The Poles were calling the Germans dogs – *Teutonicos canes appelantes* – and in hatred for the dead called the emperor's camp: *Psipole* [Dogs' Field], *id est Campus canum*.[75] The author knew the Polish language and was willing to use etymology for historical explanations. He did not spare the Poles his harsh comments, yet he did preserve a sense of belonging to their state (*monarchia Cracovie*). It was subject to the emperors from the moment it received royal dignity. The ones with the strongest claim to the throne were the Silesian Piasts, and Henry the Bearded was seeking the crown for his son, Henry the Pious. The political bias of the *Polish Chronicle* is a testimony to the emergence of a regional version of historical memory and identity in Silesia.[76] Initially, their formation was hampered by the impact of the existing records of Polish historiography and the common origin of the dynasty, while a clear motive for their development was the sense of the civilizational superiority of the German newcomers and the ties with the empire. In the German chronicle writings of the thirteenth

---

74 The discussion about the chronicler's opinions is summarised by Drelicharz, *Unifying the Kingdom of Poland*, 191–229.
75 *Kronika Polska*, 616–617, 620–621, 627–628, 630.
76 Sławomir Gawlas, "Ślązacy w oczach własnych i cudzych. Uwagi o powstaniu i rozwoju regionalnej tożsamości w średniowieczu," [Silesians in the eyes of their own and others. Notes on the emergence and development of regional identity in the Middle Ages] in *Ślązacy w oczach własnych i obcych*, ed. Antoni Barciak (Katowice – Zabrze, 2010), 41–67.

century Poland remained a subordinate country,[77] and the emperors maintained their superiority.[78]

The apogee of the Polish-German conflicts fell on the period when there was an effort to restore the unity of Polish lands and renew the royal dignity, which happened at the turn of the fourteenth century. The friction mainly concerned internal relations, but also conflicts with neighbours, especially with Brandenburg. Stereotypical accusations against the Germans formulated in such circumstances emphasized their deceitfulness, ruthlessness, and the lust for domination. In 1306, these features were exposed in the trial of Bishop Jan Muskata of Cracow, a supporter of Bohemian rule. He was accused of favouring the Germans in the chapter, and of terrorising his opponents with the help of German mercenaries. He wanted to oust the real prince and his patron, Władysław the Elbow-High, and after expelling Polish landowners to the territories of schismatics, he replaces them with foreigners:

> [...] verum heredem et patronum terre et ecclesie Cracovienses videlicet dominum ducem Wladislaum et terigenas Polonos de propriis dominiis ad gentes exteras et scismaticas profligare et alienigenas inducere.[79]
>
> [... the true heir and patron of the land and church of Cracow, of course Władysław the Elbow-High, drove out native Poles from their own estates to external people and schismatics while inviting foreigners.]

A few years later, in the continuation of the Annals of the Cracow Chapter, equally violent accusations were made about the attitude of Cracow burghers during the rebellion of Mayor Albert. They were compared to Judas for they acted filled with German rage like traitors, enemies of peace and hidden foes – "rabie furoris Germanici perusti, fraudis amici, pacis quoque palleati hostess et occulti".[80] In the nineteenth- and twentieth-century national historiography such expressive statements of this type were readily generalised as testimonies

---

77 Grabski, *Polska w opiniach obcych*, 219 et seq., 256 et seq.
78 In 1290, Emperor Albrecht I granted the domain of Henryk IV Probus to King Wenceslaus II of Bohemia, and in 1300 also Greater Poland as a fief – *Archivum Coronae Regni Bohemiae*, ed. Venceslaus Hrubý, vol. 2 (Pragae, 1928), no. 39, 64–64; no. 71, 110.
79 *Analecta Vaticana*, ed. Johannes Ptaśnik, Monumenta Poloniae Vaticana 3 (Cracoviae, 1914), no. 121, 78; cf. Sławomir Gawlas, "Verus heres. Z badań nad świadomością polityczną obozu Władysława Łokietka w początku XIV wieku," [From research on the political awareness of the Władysław Łokietek's camp in the early 14th century] *Kwartalnik Historyczny*, 95,1 (1988), 77–104.
80 *Rocznik kapituły krakowskiej*, 104.

of legitimate self-defence in the fight against German aggression.[81] It is difficult, however, not to notice an explicit anachronism in such interpretations. Source texts were indeed a reflection of collective emotions, but within a fairly limited social reach, and political stability favoured their suppression.[82]

In the late Middle Ages, the ideological legacy of the period of fragmentation remained generally up to date. The development of literary culture ensured the continuation of the memory of the Polish-German conflicts from the previous era, but it was subject to further modifications. An important testimony is the so-called Greater Poland Chronicle (*Kronika wielkopolska*).[83] The chronology of its compilation is one of the most contentious problems of Polish historiography.[84] In the light of present knowledge, it was to be the first part of a new outline of Polish history, prepared in the third quarter of the fourteenth century, most likely in the last years of the reign of Casimir the Great, by the royal vice-chancellor, Jan of Czarnków, or someone from his circle. It contains the outlines of an ideological programme corresponding to the needs of the times of the last member of the Piast dynasty. The work was not finished, and the narrative of the chronicle breaks down in 1273. Its author used the works of his predecessors, but he based himself mainly on the Dzierzwa Chronicle and the Annals of the Poznań Chapter. He introduced many significant modifications, many of which were accepted by his successors. To fill in the gaps in his knowledge, he used arguments based on dozens of risky and complicated etymologies. With their help, he constructed a relatively extensive and difficult to succinctly summarize historical and geographical reasoning that was to supplement the image of Polish origins.[85] Slavs came from Slaw (*Slauo*), and his descendant was named Nemrod – "Nemroch enim in slawonico dicitur

---

81   Roman Grodecki, *Powstanie polskiej świadomosci narodowej* [The rise of Polish national consciousness] (Katowice, 1946).
82   Benedykt Zientara, "Cudzoziemcy w Polsce X–XV wieku: ich rola w zwierciadle polskiej opinii średniowiecznej," [Foreigners in Poland in the 10th–15th centuries: their role in the mirror of Polish medieval opinion] in *Swojskość i cudzoziemskość w dziejach kultury polskiej*, ed. Zofia Stefanowska (Warszawa, 1973), 9–37.
83   *Chronica Poloniae Maioris*, ed. Brygida Kürbis, MPH, series 11-8 (Warszawa, 1970).
84   The most recent state of the discussions of source studies: Drelicharz, *Unifying the Kingdom of Poland*, 338–63.
85   The description was subjected to a critical and literary analysis by Brygida Kürbis, *Studia nad Kroniką Wielkopolską* [Studies on the Chronicle of Greater Poland] (Poznań, 1952), 115 et seq.; ead., *Dziejopisarstwo wielkopolskie XIII i XIV* [History of Greater Poland XIII and XIV] (Warszawa, 1959), 189 et seq. The researcher sought to prove that the description is an interpolation made in the 14th century added to the main text of the chronicle compiled at the end of the previous century. The author's etymological comments need to be revised in the broader context. Cf. the comments to the critical edition and Paweł Migdalski, *Słowiańszczyzna północno-zachodnia w historiografii polskiej*,

Nemerza quod in slawonico interpretatur non pax seu non mensurans pacem". The fatherland of the Slavs was Pannonia. Its name was derived from Pan, because in Greek and Slavic, the term means a nobleman (*totum habens*). Pan lived in Pannonia and from whence three of his sons migrated: "primogenitus Lech, alter Rus, tertius Czech". They founded their own kingdoms, but it was the Lechites, or Poles, who retained superiority and supremacy. Later, other Slavic kingdoms were created, whose names are also explained. It turned out that the Slavs and Germans came from two brothers: Jan and Kuss, descendants of Japheth – "Slawi et Theutunici a duobus germanis Japhet nepotibus Jano et Kuss". This was evidenced by the geographical descriptions of Germania in Isidore of Seville and Martinus Polonus. Its territory was described with the aid of rivers. The chronicler decided that the Rhine and Danube belonged to the Germans (*gens Theutonica*), and the Elbe, Oder and Vistula Rivers to the Poles and Czechs. The vast lands located between, reaching the North Sea (that is the Baltic Sea) had been recently occupied by Saxons (*Saxones*) who, expanding their area, established permanent settlements there. All Slavic countries except Pannonia paid tribute to the Poles until the times of Casimir the Monk. The common origin of Slavs and Germans is testified to by the etymology of their name, which means blood brotherhood (*fraternitas consanguinitate*). It derives from the yoke (*germo*) which binds two oxen in a harness. Like oxen, the Slavs and Germans were bound by the mutual neighbourhood that gave rise to a sense of brotherhood: "nec ulla gens in mundo est sibi tam communis et familiaris velut Slavi et Theutonici".[86]

Emphasizing neighborly cohabitation, lack of open hostility, and expressions of sympathy did not mean, however, recognition of any kind of subjugation to the Empire or retreat from emphasizing Poland's sovereignty. The chronicler, presenting the fabulous history of the Poles, completes the story of Wanda with information that before she jumped into the Vistula, she received an oath of loyalty and tribute from the Alemans – "dextris Almanorum fidelitatis et omagii".[87] Describing the rule of Lestek III that occurred at the time of Christ's birth, he listed the names of Lestek's twenty sons whom he had begotten with concubines. The ruler ordered the crowning of his firstborn, Pompilius, the son of Julius Caesar's sister, and gave the half-brothers their own duchies reaching from the North Sea to Westphalia, Saxony, Bavaria and Thuringia. The chronicler pointed out that some of them gave their names to the cities they

niemieckiej i duńskiej [North-Western Slavdom in Polish, German and Danish historiography] (Wodzisław Śląski, 2019), 43 et seq.
86 *Chronica Poloniae Maioris*, "Prolog", 4–7.
87 Ibid., 1, 9.

founded. Further on, he presented a more detailed description of them, mentioning over twenty cities and castles from Mecklenburg and its neighbors. Their belonging to the area occupied by the sons of Lestek was indicated by real or often only fictional etymology. The list goes beyond the region inhabited by the Polabian Slavs. To cite only a few examples, we can mention Bremen, which was supposed to carry the "burden" of battles with the Westphalians and Friesians during their invasions by the Slavs – "Bremon dictum de pondere, quia pondus inimicorum, ut puta Vestualium et Frisonum et aliarum nacionum Slavis ipsos invadendo, eisque reistendo sufferebat". Similarly, the name Schleswig was said to derive from the Slavic herring – "Sleswyk, a sledz quo slawonice allec dicitur". At least some of the explanations were not made up by the chronicler and were based on direct contacts with this still mixed-language region, in the circle of people who knew Latin, and therefore the clergy.[88] It is possible to notice (in some of the mentionings) distorted references to the oral memory of real events. This is especially true of the fate of Prince Niklot of the Obodrites who lost Schwerin when defeated by an emperor – "quidam imperator devicto rege Slavorum nomine Mykkel". His sons kept Mecklenburg.[89]

In the further part of his narrative the chronicler modifies slightly the meaning of the meeting with Otto III at Gniezno. The emperor, received with honors, puts the crown on Bolesław's head as a sign of the covenant and gifts are exchanged, but immediately afterward the symbolism of the victorious sword of the Polish ruler is exposed. The sword is called "Szczerbiec" (the Jagged Sword) and is given to Bolesław directly by an angel.[90] The ruler, moreover, was to restore the boundaries of the old Polish "empire" also in the west. The tributary superiority over the Polabian Slavs was lost by the exiled Casimir the Monk who maintained cordial contact with Saxony and his mother's family. In the description of the invasion of Emperor Henry V, Bolesław the Wry-Mouthed is still called the king, and in the new version one finds an opinion about German envy of his successes. The ruler evoked hostile feelings among the imperial court dignitaries because he not only dared to wage war

---

88   Ibid., 8, 14–15; the chronicler returned to the etymology of Bremen when describing the rule of Bolesław the Brave to whom he attributed its construction and explained that: *Bremø enim onus sive pondus dicitur in wlgari* – ibid., 10, 17.

89   Ibid., 15. Niklot's fate was described in great detail by Helmold von Bosau in his 12th century chronicle. A direct contact with it is unlikely. In 1378 a free translation of the chronicle was made: *Mecklembургische Reimchronik des Ernst von Kirchberg*, ed. Christa Cordshagen and Roderich Schmidt (Köln/Weimar/Wien, 1997). In the part describing later events there are episodes evidencing verbal contacts with Polish lands. The problem requires further study.

90   Cf. Marcin Biborski and Janusz Stępiński, "Szczerbiec (the Jagged Sword) – the Coronation Sword of the Kings of Poland," *Gladius* 31 (2011), 93–147.

with the Holy Roman Empire, but he elevated the kingdoms subordinated to him at his own discretion – "non solum sacro imperio bella indicere presumpsisset sed eciam regna Romano subiecta Imperio proprio arbitrio quibus mallet excellenter sublimando donaret".[91] The feelings of equality with and (at the same time) of interest in the Empire is testified to by the inclusion in the narrative, in the description of the history of Wiślica, of stories about the fate of Walter and Helgunda, and Prince Wisław. Helgunda, the daughter of the king of the Franks and fiancée of the King of the Alemans' son, chose Walter, who defeated his opponent in a duel, but himself became a victim of feminine infidelity. The plot is an adaptation of the threads of the German *Heldenepik* (heroic epic). It became popular in later historiography and was subject to further editing.[92] There is also a colorful description of the actions of Władysław II's wife, referred to as a relative of the Emperor Henry, together with her contempt for Polish knights and deceitful intrigues. On the other hand, contacts with Emperor Conrad III, who allegedly visited Prince Bolesław IV the Curly (Bolesław Kędzierzawy) during his trip to Jerusalem in 1147, met with some sympathy from the chronicler. When describing events of the thirteenth century, the author uses mainly the information from the Greater Poland Annals about conflicts with Brandenburg and the participation in fights with the Germans. He is quite restrained in repeating the political tendency of the sources, but he introduces some of his own comments. He expands, presumably after Martinus Polonus, an account of the conflict between Pope Gregory IX and Emperor Frederick II, and the papal excommunication of the emperor. When describing the unsuccessful siege of the borough of Lebus by the archbishop of Magdeburg, the chronicler adds his own (otherwise unknown) justification for the archbishop's claims. In the time of an unspecified Bolesław, the city was to be conquered by Emperor Henry and given to Magdeburg – "asserens illud per Henricum, tempore imperator Boleslai, expugnatam fuisse et ecclesie Maydeburgensi donatum". A little further, he develops a description of the circumstances in which Bolesław the Horned (Bolesław Rogatka) transfers Lebus to the archbishop of Magdeburg in exchange for help against his brothers. This prince was the first to bring the Germans to Poland and separated out from Silesia the cities of Zittau, Görlitz, and other towns and castles. He finishes with an ironic comment: "who cannot see that Germans are brave and courageous men" – "quisne vidit Theutonicos viros strenuos et animosos esse".[93]

---

91   *Chronica Poloniae Maioris*, 26, 38.
92   Banaszkiewicz, "Rudiger von Bechelaren," 391–406.
93   *Chronica Poloniae Maioris*, 67, 86, 88, 94.

In an almost contemporaneous chronicle and perhaps one with the same authorship, royal Vice-Chancellor Jan of Czarnków describes in detail the internal events in Poland of 1370–1384 in which he had participated.[94] For this reason, he devotes considerable space to border conflicts with Brandenburg, whose inhabitants are referred to as Saxons (*Saxones*). Earlier, they appear in this sense in the *Greater Poland Chronicle*. Due to its personal character, Jan's narrative is similar to a diary. The author was an educated priest who was very well versed in the political realities of his time.[95] Several times he mentions activities of the emperors in a substantive way, leaving off any unfriendly epithets. He therefore believed that they did not threaten Polish interests. He accurately calls Charles IV the Roman emperor and the king of Bohemia – *Emperor Romanorum et Rex Bohemie*. He dedicates a comprehensive and respectful posthumous memory to him. The emperor, given the epithet of *praeclarus*, died in Prague *plenum bonis operibus*. The chronicler describes his marriages and family descent from Henry VII's election *per electores imperii* as emperor after Albrecht's death, and the bestowing of the kingdom of Bohemia upon his son John. He presents his rule in black colors. The king preferred *Rhinenses et Suevos* to the Bohemians, so he was banished for a time, but with the help of the Germans (*Theutonici* or *Almani*) he does not stop doing harm to the Czechs – "non tamen doli machinamenta Bohemis inferre neglexit". As a king, he was brave and generous, but also hypocritical and mendacious – "valde streuus et liberalis sed fallax et mendacii non ignarus". With his lies, deception and money ("per mendacia, dolum et pecunias"), he first took Kłodzko, and then he harassed Prince Henryk VI of Wroclaw in such a manner that the latter handed over his duchy to him.[96]

Collective stereotypes of the Germans refer not to the Empire but its inhabitants. One can only guess that they served to strengthen the national way of understanding its territorial foundations. This does not mean, however, that the very idea of the Empire was questioned. The interdependence of the development of Polish identity and the way of presenting the prerogatives

---

94   *Kronika Jana z Czarnkowa* [Chronicle of Jan from Czarnków], ed. Jan Szlachtowski, MPH 2, 601–756.

95   The chronicler's views have been analysed recently by Arkadiusz Borek, "Tożsamość czternastowiecznego prałata na przykładzie Janka z Czarnkowa" [The identity of a fourteenth-century prelate on the example of Janek from Czarnków], in *Symboliczne i realne*, 333–376.

96   *Kronika Jana z Czarnkowa*, 685–688. Henryk of Wrocław was so oppressed that he had to hand over his principality to Władysław the Elbow-High, but the latter under the influence of bad councillors gave it back, then the prince handed it over to the king of Bohemia.

of both universal powers, emphasised in the observations made thus far, was highly dependent on the reception of political thought in the Latin world. The development of the idea of royal sovereignty in the fourteenth century,[97] the collapse of the material foundations of the emperor's power as king of Rome (that is as German king), and the dynastic rules of political rivalry did not provide any impetus for the active participation of the Polish lands in discussions regarding the imperial *dominium mundi*, and incidental claims to sovereignty were ignored as well.[98] It was the long-lasting conflict with the Teutonic Order, on the other hand, that exerted a great influence on the ways of thinking of the Polish elites and led to the formulation of legal and public constructs. However, it was not interpreted in terms of a Polish-German dispute. The conflict with the Order as a Church institution renovated the papal authority and became the basis for the provisions of the canonical penal process.[99] In the record of court materials of the 1320/1321, 1339 and 1422 trials, the most important problem was the affiliation of Pomerania and other lands to the Kingdom of Poland and the violation of the will of the Piast founders. While presenting the course of the war in 1409–1411, the concept of a just war was referred to. The defeat of the Order is presented in terms of the struggle between good and evil, and is explained by the Order's exorbitant and unrestrained pride, and contrasted with the arch-Christian humility and piety of the Polish King Władysław II Jagiello for propaganda purposes.[100] Sigismund of Luxembourg

---

97   Jan Baszkiewicz, *Państwo suwerenne w feudalnej doktrynie politycznej do początku XIV w.* [Sovereign state in feudal political doctrine until the beginning of the 14th century] (Warszawa, 1964), 303 et seq.; *The Cambridge History of Medieval Political Thought c. 350–c. 1450*, ed. J.H. Burns (Cambridge, 1988), 341 et seq.; Bernard Guenée, *L'Occident aux XIVe et XVe siècles. Les états*, 4. ed., Nouvelle clio 22 (Paris, 1991).

98   Cf. Grabski, *Polska w opiniach Europy*, 137 et seq.

99   The dispute with the Teutonic Order has left a very extensive documentation and literature, but of fundamental importance still is: Andrzej Wojtkowski, "Tezy i argumenty polskie w sporach terytorialnych z Krzyżakami. Część pierwsza (1310–1454)," [Polish theses and arguments in territorial disputes with the Teutonic Knights. Part one (1310–1454)] *Komunikaty Mazursko-Warmińskie. Kwartalnik* 1, 91 (1966), 3–98; id., "Tezy i argumenty polskie w sporach terytorialnych z Krzyżakami. Część druga (1454–1525)," [Polish theses and arguments in territorial disputes with the Teutonic Knights. Part two (1310–1454)] ibid., 1–2, 95–96 (1967), 3–84; id., "Procesy polsko-krzyżackie przed procesem z lat 1320–1321", ibid., 1, 115 (1972), 3–101. Cf. *Arguments and Counter-Arguments. The Political Thought of the 14th – and 15th Centuries during the Polish-Teutonic Order Trials and Disputes*, ed. Wieslaw Sieradzan (Toruń, 2012).

100 Sven Ekdahl, *Die Schlacht bei Tannenberg 1410. Quellenkritische Untersuchungen, Band I: Einführung und Quellenlage* (Berlin, 1982), 108 et seq., 156 et seq.; Marek Janicki, "Grunwald w tradycji polskiej od wieku XV do XVII," [Grunwald in the Polish tradition from the 15th to the 17th century] in *Na znak świetnego zwycięstwa. W sześćsetletnią rocznicę bitwy pod Grunwaldem. Katalog wystawy 15 lipca–30 września 2010, vol. 1: Studia*, ed. Dariusz Nowacki,

is only an amicable arbitrator of this dispute in 1412–1420.[101] The Roman king, acting in the role of a superarbitrator, sought to strengthen his imperial authority. The Polish representatives played a diplomatic game which boiled down to an attempt to use him against the Order, and after the verdict announced in Wrocław, which they viewed as unfavourable, they appealed to Pope Martin V.

In the propaganda and diplomatic struggle at the international forum after the Polish-Lithuanian Union, and especially after the victory at Grunwald (Tannenberg) in 1410, the Polish side engaged a group of learned theologians and lawyers. It turned out then that the contemporary legal constructions and theoretical justifications for the authority of both universal powers were very well-known in Cracow. The problem is broad in scope and has been well-researched,[102] and there is no possibility here to develop it further. The argumentation presented in public sought to effectively prove its points. Territorial claims against the Order were based on the principle of the inviolability and inalienability of the rights of the Polish crown.[103] According to

---

(Kraków, 2010), 89–154; recently: Adam Talarowski, "Od poganina do króla arcychrześcijańskiego. Wizerunek Władysława Jagiełły w Rocznikach Jana Długosza," [From a pagan to an arch-Christian king. The image of Władysław Jagiełło in the Annals of Jan Długosz] in *Średniowiecze Polskie i Powszechne*, ed. Jerzy Sperka and Bożena Czwojdrak 9 (13), 2017. 127–152.

101 Zenon Hubert Nowak, "Internationale Schiedsprozesse als ein Werkzeug der Politik König Sigismunds in Ostmittel- und Nordeuropa 1411–1425," *Blätter für deutsche Landesgeschichte* 111 (1975), 172–188; id., *Międzynarodowe procesy polubowne jako narzędzie polityki Zygmunta Luksemburskiego w północnej i środkowowschodniej Europie (1412–1424)*, [International Amicable Processes as a Tool of Sigismund of Luxembourg's Policy in Northern and Central-Eastern Europe (1412–1424)] (Toruń, 1981).

102 Krzysztof Ożóg, *Uczeni w monarchii Jadwigi Andegaweńskiej i Władysława Jagiełły (1384–1434)* [Scholars in the monarchy of Jadwiga Andegaweńska and Władysław Jagiełło (1384–1434)], Polska Akademia Umiejętności, Rozprawy Wydziału Historyczno-Filozoficznego 105 (Kraków, 2004); Krzysztof Ożóg, *The Role of Poland in the Intellectual Development of Europe in the Middle Ages* (Kraków, 2009), 94 et seq., 111 et seq.; cf. id., "Intellektuelle im Dienste des Staates – Das Beispiel Polens im späten Mittelalter," in *Das Reich und Polen. Parallelen, Interaktionen und Formen der Akkulturation im Hohen und Späten Mittelalter*, ed. Alexander Patschovsky and Thomas Wünsch, Vorträge und Forschungen 59 (Ostfildern, 2003), 301–321.

103 To illustrate we may quote Paweł Włodkowic's treatise: "Ad videndum. Scriptum magistra Pauli ad impugnandum privilegia Cruciferorum" (1421), in Ludwik Ehrlich, *Pisma wybrane Pawła Włodkowica*, [Selected writings by Paweł Włodkowic] vol. 1–3, (Warszawa, 1968–1969), here: vol. 3 (Warszawa, 1969), 91–195. The author questions the legality of donations to the Order since the Polish king and his kingdom *subsunt pape*, and the latter did not confirm them. The ruler could not act to the detriment of the kingdom "quia Rex non est dominus bonorum et iurium Regni sed administrator" – ibid., 141; Cf. Henryk Litwin, "W poszukiwaniu rodowodu demokracji szlacheckiej. Polska myśl polityczna w piśmiennictwie XV i początków XVI wieku" [Searching the genealogy of noble democracy. Polish political thought in the literature of the 15th and early 16th centuries],

it, no previous concessions made by Polish rulers could have lasting consequences. The justification corresponded to the realities of the Polish elective monarchy of the first Jagiellon, but could have been incorporated into more universal constructs. At the same time, references are made to the natural law (*ius gentium*) and the concept of a just war supporting military actions against the spiritual institution. In this context, the full sovereignty of royal power was emphasised. Even before the expedition against the Teutonic Order, the professor of canon law, Stanisław of Skalbmierz, prepared a sermon *De bellis iustis*, in which he specified the conditions for waging war. He argued, among other things, that both the king and the emperor acted upon their own powers – "sive sit rex sive imperator auctoritate propria". Thus, they had equal rights – "cum neuter habeat super se superiorem".[104] During the trial before King Sigismund of Luxemburg in Buda in 1412, the Polish prosecutor Andrzej Łaskarzyc wanted to prove "quod omnia privilegia Cruciferorum, per summos pontifices et imperatores concessa, sunt surrepticia, eo, quod obtinuerunt ius patronatus domini regis et principum Polonie".[105] In the next phase of the dispute at the forum of the Council of Constance in 1415, when the emperor asked the Polish and Teutonic legations whether they recognised his supremacy: "ab si irkennen unseren gnedigen herren Romischen koning etc. und das heilige reych vor eren obirsten" – he received a negative response from the Polish side: "si das reich nicht irkennen, sunder ir konig von Polan sei ein freier konig".[106]

The participation of a large and well-prepared Polish delegation at the Council of Constance made it possible to attempt a challenging of the ideological foundations of the Teutonic State in Prussia.[107] To discredit it, the

---

in *Między monarchią a demokracją. Studia z dziejów Polski XV–XVIII wieku*, ed. Anna Sucheni-Grabowska and Małgorzata Żaryn (Warszawa, 1994), 13–53.

104 Ludwik Ehrlich, *Polski wykład prawa wojny XV wieku. Kazanie Stanisława ze Skalbmierza De bellis iustis* [Polish lecture on the law of war in the 15th century. Sermon by Stanisław from Skalbmierz De bellis iustis] (Warszawa, 1955), 100–102, § 11; cf. id., *Paweł Włodkowic i Stanisław ze Skarbimierza* (1954), 2 ed. (Warszawa, 2017), 29 et seq.; Hartmut Boockmann, *Johannes Falkenberg, der Deutsche Orden und die polnische Politik. Untersuchungen zur politischen Theorie des späteren Mittelalters* (Göttingen, 1975), 171 et seq.

105 *Lites ac res gestae inter Polonos Ordinemque Cruciferorum*, 2nd ed., ed. Ignacy Zakrzewski, vol. 2 (Posnaniae, 1892), 60, § 53; here: § 51: "Cruciferi sunt de iure patronatus dominorum regis et principum Polonie, quia ipsi dominus rex et principes fundaverunt predictum Ordinem". The accusations of the Polish side were formulated in 81 articles known to us from the summary of the emperor's verdict, cf. Ożóg, *Uczeni w monarchii*, 190 et seq.; Wiesław Sieradzan, *Misja Benedykta Makraia w latach 1412–1413* (Malbork, 2009).

106 *Codex epistolaris Vitoldi magni ducis Lithuaniae 1376–1430*, ed. Antoni Prochaska (Cracoviae, 1882), no. 641, 322–325, quot. on 323; cf. Boockmann, *Johannes Falkenberg*, 202 et seq.

107 Stefan Kwiatkowski, *Zakon Niemiecki w Prusach a umysłowość średniowieczna. Scholastyczne rozumienie prawa natury a etyczna i religijna świadomość Krzyżaków do około 1420 roku* [The German Order in Prussia and the medieval mind. Scholastic

Poles used a scandal caused by a treatise of the Dominican friar, Johannes Falkenberg, entitled *Satira contra haereses et cetera nephanda Polonorum et eorum regis Jaghel*.[108] Ultimately, the author's views were not considered heretical, but the Polish side managed to take the dispute with the Order to the level of doctrinal principles. This was necessary because the opponents had at their disposal documents and evidence perfectly consistent with the principles of international law at that time. The main figure was the Cracow professor of canon law, Paweł Włodkowic. He prepared a number of treaties questioning the foundations of the Order's power in Prussia.[109] Referring to the discussion on the *bellum iustum* and superiority of *ius naturale*,[110] with the help of various authorities he questioned the emperor's power over peacefully living pagans. Reflecting upon the importance of imperial privileges, he argued that: "Imperium dependet a potestate pape nam ad ipsum spectat examinacio, approbacio et reieccio electi ad Imperium".[111] In opposition to the opinion separating the ecclesiastical and secular powers – "potestatem pape in spiritualibus and the potestatem imperatoris in temporalibus",[112] he stated that the pope had both swords – "papa habet utrumque gladium".[113] On the other hand, "execucionem gladij temporalis transtulit Ecclesia in imperatorem et ceteros reges".[114] He stressed, however, that "nomen imperatoris novum est respectu regum qui fuerunt omni tempore".[115] These statements belonged to a popular set of anti-imperial arguments and the fact that they were included into the argumentation against the Order was updating the tactical ideological alliance between Poland and the papacy after the Great Schism.

In 1429, at the congress of Lutsk, Emperor Sigismund made an attempt to break the Polish-Lithuanian union by offering the crown to Great Prince

---

understanding of the law of nature and the ethical and religious awareness of the Teutonic Knights until around 1420] (Toruń, 1998).

108 Boockmann, *Johannes Falkenberg*; Sophie Wlodek, "La 'Satire' de Jean Falkenberg. Texte inédit avec introduction," *Mediaevalia Philosophia Polonorum*, 18 (1973), 51–120; cf. Johannes Falkenberg, *De monarchia mundi*, ed. Władysław Seńko, Materiały do Historii Filozofii Średniowiecznej w Polsce, 9 (20) (Wrocław/ Warszawa/Kraków/Gdańsk, 1975).

109 Ehrlich, *Pisma wybrane*, vols. 1–3; most important are the treatises: "Saevientibus olim Prutenis" (1415), vol. 1, 2–98; "Opinio Ostiensis" (1415), 1, 113–137; "Ad aperiendam" (1416), 1, 144–259 and 2, 2–167; "Ad videndum" (1421), 3, 91–194.

110 Cf. Kwiatkowski, *Zakon Niemiecki*, 132 et seq.; Stanisław Wielgus, *The Medieval Polish Doctrine of the Law of Nations: ius gentium* (Lublin, 1998).

111 Ad videndum, 163, cf. Ad aperiandam 126, 130.

112 Ehrlich, *Pisma*: Ad aperiendam, 121.

113 Ibid.: Ad aperiendam, 130; Opinio Ostiensis 126.

114 Ibid.: Ad aperiendam, 129.

115 Ibid.: Ad aperiendam, 143.

Vytautas (Pol. Witold) of Lithuania.[116] When he accepted the offer, a political conflict broke out. The Polish side invoked that this was a violation of the Polish Crown's rights and argued that through the union Władysław Jagiello incorporated his lands into Poland as the highest prince of Lithuania. The Poles intervened with Pope Martin V and received his support.[117] The imperial delegation carrying the relevant documents was detained, but an escalation of tensions was prevented by Vytautas' death in the autumn of 1430. To strengthen the diplomatic argument, opinions of five Cracow professors were ordered in this matter. In their *Consilium*,[118] they considered whether, according to the law, the elected *Rex Romanorum* needed papal approval and could appoint kings before the imperial coronation.[119] The answer was, of course, negative: "nec licet propter vetustam consuetudinem, nec poterit propter defectus imperialis plenitudinis, ut talis electus in regem sine pape speciali licencia eligat vel coronet".[120] The arguments referred to the authority of Church law,[121] and omitted Roman law.[122] The making of kings was the prerogative of the Apostolic See: "cum igitur creatio in regem denuo tam de consuetudine quam

---

116   Grzegorz Błaszczyk, *Burza koronacyjna. Dramatyczny fragment stosunków polsko-litewskich w XV wieku* [Coronation storm. A dramatic fragment of Polish-Lithuanian relations in the 15th century] (Poznań, 1998).

117   *Codex epistolaris saeculi decimi quinti, vol. 2: 1382–1445*, ed. Anatol Lewicki, Monumenta Medii Aevi Historica res gestas Poloniae illustrantia 12 (Cracovia, 1891), no. 186, 253. Pope Martin V, accepting the Polish argumentation: "Carissimus in Christo filius noster Sigismundus Romanorum rex illustris illa [i.e. ducatus Lithuanie et terre Russie] seiungere et liberare a dicto regno Polonie et erigere in novum regnum" in his letter to the bishop of Chełm [Culm] called on him not to support in any way a coronation of Vytautas.

118   Stanisław Zachorowski, "Consilia w sprawie koronacyi Witolda," [Conferences on the coronation of Witold] in id., *Studya z historyi prawa kościelnego i polskiego* (Kraków, 1917), 149–201, as an appendix (pp. 186–201) the author published the text of *Consilium* and the answers of professors from the University in Vienna which were prepared upon Sigismund's order.

119   "Ad questionem, quia queritur, an in regem Romanorum electus canonice, cuius electio a papa est aprobata, cum nondum sit imperator aut per Ecclesiam iuxta ritum ab antiquo tantum in impetratorem consecratus, poterit denuo aliquem impetratorem in regem eligere et creare" – ibid., 187.

120   "Isto premisso ponitur igitur ista conclusio. Non potest electus in imperatorem aliquem in regem denuo creare, licet eleccio ipsius sit ab ecclesia approbata, non tamen consecracio vel coronacio facta" – ibid., 187–188.

121   "Item imperator debet habere, ut notat glossa magna in decreto Romani tres coronas: ferream, que notat fortitudinem, argenteam, que notat puritatem, auream, que notat excellenciam. Sed hac excellencia caret electus, poterit ergo ferream de facto dare, non auream, quia nihil dat, qui non habet, de iure patronatus Quod autem cum multis similibus" – ibid., 188.

122   Ibid., 156 et seq., 167 et seq.; the empire pleaded Roman law.

ex preeminencia dignitatis est Sedis apostolice".[123] The whole interpretation of the historical development of the Union of Poland and Lithuania was meticulously presented by the Polish delegation to the Reichstag at Nuremberg.[124]

The positions presented as to the emperor's power were formulated to solve specific political and legal conflicts. In the above observations it was necessary to deprive them of their complex and diverse context of philosophical and ideological conditions. The emphasising of the pope's authority was only of tactical significance.[125] At the time of the Great Schism and general councils, the University of Cracow and the Polish intellectual elites were very active in discussing the reform of the Church and in developing the idea of conciliarism.[126] The fact that Poland joined the papal camp did not mean that these ideas

---

123   Ibid., 190.
124   *Codex epistolaris*, no. 179, 237–241. Vytautas' coronation violated the rights of *corone regni Polonie*. The desire to make it *apud illustrissimum principem dominum Sigismundu regem Ungarorum, ut dicitur, electum in regem Romanorum* is the violation of King Władysław's will and his subjects. Cf. Błaszczyk, *Burza koronacyjna*, 117 et seq. Referring to Sigismund as king of Hungary was a deliberate sting. At the council of Basil in 1434, the emperor's stance was commented upon by Mikołaj Lasocki who as a Polish representative had prepared a comprehensive and most interesting memorial for the envoys from Castile. He described the geographical position of Poland, the circumstances of its union with Lithuania, its conflict with the Teutonic Order, and the role of the emperor (*imperator, qui semper fuit inimicissimus illi regno*) together with the latter's intrigues for Vytautas' coronation. Cf. Kurt Forstreuter, "Eine polnische Denkschrift auf dem Konzil in Basel," *Zeitschrift für Ostforschung* 21 (1972), 684–696; Stephen C. Rowell, "Du Europos pakraščiai: Lietuvos Didžiosios Kunigaikštytės ir ispanų karalysčių ryšiai 1411–1412 m. ir 1434 n. tekstuose," [Two Frontiers of Europe: Relations between the Grand Duchy of Lithuania and the Spanish Kingdoms in 1411–1412. and 1434 n. in the texts] *Lietuvos Istorios Metraštis* 1 (2003), 149–188, here no. 10a, 173–185; also Karolina Grodziska, "Mikołaja Lasockiego obrona pamięci króla Władysława Jagiełły na soborze bazylejskim," [Mikołaj Lasocki, defending the memory of King Władysław Jagiełło at the Council of Basel] in *Cracovia, Polonia, Europa. Studia z dziejów średniowiecza ofiarowane Jerzemu Wyrozumskiemu w sześćdziesiątą piątą rocznicę urodzin i czterdziestolecie pracy naukowej*, ed. Waldemar Bukowski, Krzysztof Ożóg, Franciszek Sikora, and Stanisław Szczur (Kraków, 1995), 345–353.
125   Tomasz Graf, *Episkopat monarchii jagiellońskiej w dobie soborów powszechnych XV wieku* [Episcopate of the Jagiellonian monarchy in the era of general councils of the 15th century] (Kraków, 2008), 151 et seq. In 15th century Poland it was the king who decided on appointments of Polish bishops, and this was the source of friction in relations with the pope. For example, Pope Martin V was surprised to find that Władysław Jagiello wanted him to wait for the king's decision in this matter.
126   Thomas Wünsch, *Konziliarismus und Polen. Personen, Politik und Programme aus Polen zur Verfassungsfrage der Kirche in der Zeit der mittelalterlichen Reformkonzilien* (Paderborn/München/Wien/Zürich, 1998) (Konziliengeschichte, Reihe B: Untersuchungen), esp. 285 et seq.; cf. Krzysztof Ożóg, "La réforme de L'Eglise et de conciliarisme en Pologne au XVe siècle: bilan des recherches," *Quaestiones Medii Aevi Novae* 6 (2001), 261–276; id., *Die Role of Poland*, 119 et seq.

were automatically abandoned. In the second half of the century, the popes, who were engaged in strengthening control over the Papal States and in fighting against the heritage of conciliarism, had to sanction in concordats the increasing dependence of national episcopates on secular monarchs.[127] The greater autonomy of temporal power and a growing sense of state sovereignty is evident in the treatise *Monumentum pro rei publice ordinacione* by Stanisław Ostroróg. It contains a programme to improve the functioning of the state and probably was drawn up in the 1470s.[128] The author was a doctor of both civil and canonical law, carried out diplomatic missions, held the highest offices, and was a member of the royal council. He strongly emphasises the total sovereignty of the Polish king and his submission to God's will alone – "Poloniae rex asserit (quod et verum est, nemini enim subiacet) nullum superiorem se praeter Deum recognoscere". Ostroróg's remarks are directed against the supremacy of both the emperor and the pope. Notarial officers authorised by them should be replaced by the ones appointed by the Polish king vested with imperial rights – "iura omnia imperialia habet rex, quicumque non recognoscit

---

127 Stefan Świeżawski, *Eklezjologia późnośredniowieczna na rozdrożu* [Late medieval ecclesiology at a crossroads], Studia res gestas Facultatis Theologicae Universitatis Jagellonicae illustrantia, 1 (Kraków, 1990), 71 et seq.

128 The treatise has survived in two slightly different versions. In the second quarter of the 16th century, when the movement of the nobility to reform the state (called the executionist movement) gathered strength, it was copied, prefaced, and prepared for edition. Cf. the edition with a Polish translation: Adolf Pawiński, *Jana Ostroroga żywot i pismo O naprawie Rzeczypospolitej. Studium z literatury politycznej XV wieku* [Jan Ostroróg's life and the work 'On the repair of the Republic'. A Study in Political Literature of the 15th century] (Warszawa, 1894). This more popular version did not correspond to the demands of that time and was quickly forgotten. In the literature on the subject, the 17th century handwritten copy, preserved in the library of the Jesuit College at Lublin, is regarded as more faithful to the original. Yet, it contains a large number of defects made during the process of copying. Cf. Joannis Ostrorog, *Monumentum pro Reipublicae utilitate congestum*, ed. Theodorus Wierzbowski (Varsoviae, 1891). Because of groundless doubts as to its authenticity, there has been no critical edition of the treatise, which currently is being prepared by Adam Talarowski under my leadership. Below, I agree to the oral opinion of Marek Janicki and refer to the version of the 16th century as more faithful to the original. Cf. Juliusz Domański, Zbigniew Ogonowski, and Lech Szczucki, *Zarys dziejów filozofii w Polsce; wieki XIII–XVII* [An outline of the history of philosophy in Poland; 13th–17th centuries] (Warszawa, 1989), 83 et seq.; Andrzej Wyczański, "Memoriał Jana Ostroroga a postulaty egzekucyjne XVI wieku," [The Memorial of Jan Ostroróg and the enforcement postulates of the 16th century] in *Ludzie, Kościół, Wierzenia. Studia z dziejów kultury i społeczeństwa Europy Środkowej (średniowiecze – wczesna epoka nowożytna)*, ed. Wojciech Iwańczak and Stefan K. Kuczyński (Warszawa, 2001), 483–487; the Polish translation with commentaries in *700 lat myśli polskiej. Filozofia i myśl społeczna XIII–XV wieku*, ed. Juliusz Domański (Warszawa, 1978), 236–261.

superiorem". The pope should be treated with respect, but not obedience. Bishops should be appointed by the king alone. Financial benefits paid to the pope do not serve to fight the opponents of Christianity, they are collected under the pretence of piety (*sub specie pietatis*), but they are appropriated by "cunning and deceitful Italians" – *astuti et callidi ... Itali*.[129] This observation corresponds to the contemporary reality of the Papal States and papal nepotism. The demands that the German language (*lingua Theutona*) in public life should be replaced by Polish are justified by the natural and perpetual aversion between these languages – "inter has duas linguas natura veluti quandam perpetuam discordiam odiumque inseruit naturale". Whoever wants to live in Poland should speak Polish – "discant polone loqui, si qui Poloniam habitare contendunt". This is what the dignity of the Poles demands, because they should know that the *Almani* treat their Polish language in the same way.[130] An effort should be made to unify the law in Poland by imposing it from above. The Roman law created by senators (*centum patres*) and emperors (*dignissimeque imperatores*) should be followed. The author was aware that it was considered to be imperial law. Its use, however, would not be a sign of subordination to the German empire, because it is used by others who do not recognise any supremacy – *non recognoscunt superiorem*.[131]

The most complete image of the Holy Roman Empire in the Polish Middle Ages was outlined in Jan Długosz's work.[132] The exhaustive use of this material encounters a barrier given its size. The present analysis will focus on his main work, *Annals or Chronicles of the Famous Kingdom of Poland*.[133] The chronicle covers the entire history of Poland – from the genealogy of the peoples after the Flood to contemporary events, reported almost until the chronicler's death in 1480.[134] The author was an outstanding figure: a canon of Cracow and a close

---

129 In both versions the arrangement of articles differs considerably, therefore I refer to: Pawiński, *Jana Ostroroga*, 128, 130, 136; cf. Ostroróg, *Monumentum*, 4, 6, 8.
130 Pawiński, *Jana Ostroroga*, 148; Ostroróg, *Monumentum*, 15.
131 Pawiński, *Jana Ostroroga*, 158; Ostroróg, *Monumentum*, 20.
132 The problem has been presented in a most comprehensive way by: Jadwiga Krzyżaniakowa, "Niemcy w opinii Jana Długosza," in Krzyżaniakowa, *Nie ma historii bez człowieka*, 225–240.
133 Ioannis Dlugosii, *Annales seu cronicae incliti Regni Poloniae, liber I–XII*, ed. Jan Dąbrowski et al. (Varsaviae – Cracoviae, 1964–2005). A new critical edition in 11 volumes totals 3900 pages (without commentaries); cf. Krzysztof Ożóg, "Nowa edycja Roczników Jana Długosza. Próba bilansu," [New edition of Annals of Jan Długosz. Balance sheet attempt] in *Jan Długosz (1415–1480). Życie i dzieło*, ed. Lidia Korczak, Marek Daniel Kowalski, and Piotr Węcowski (Kraków, 2016); the volume also contains the selected bibliography.
134 To facilitate the reference to older editions, when citing the *Annales*, I give: the year, book, and page; in the case of book one, with no dates, I give only the book number and page.

associate of Bishop Zbigniew Oleśnicki; he maintained contacts with the circle of professors of Cracow University, held diplomatic missions, and was the tutor of King Casimir IV Jagiellon's sons.[135] When he was working on Polish history, he had at his disposal existing collections of various historiographic texts.[136] Their use made it possible to take into account almost all the historical heritage preserved to his day.[137] The chronicler was often biased by the tendencies of his sources, and added his own interpretations to the information he provided. The existence of the so-called autograph of the first part of *Annales* to 1406 allows us to follow subsequent comments which generally sharpen the meaning of the narrative. For the fifteenth century, chronicle accounts ceased to play such a significant role. The author relied heavily on information obtained from his protector Zbigniew Oleśnicki, took into account the documents of the Polish-Teutonic disputes, and took over the patterns of Polish propaganda as had developed in international arguments.[138] Długosz worked on the annals beginning around 1450. When reporting current events, he relies mainly on his knowledge as an active participant in them.[139] In his preface he says that he will present not only the history of the Poles, but also their neighbours and that of the papacy and Empire – "Bohemorum, Hungarorum, Ruthenorum, Pruthenorum, Saxonum, Lythwanorum, Romanorum insuper pontificumatque imperatorum".[140] Despite his extensive research and great

---

135 There is neither a current biography of the writer nor a satisfactory bibliography; the publications accompanying the celebration of the 600th anniversary of his birth are discussed by Hanna Rajfura, "Nowe badania nad życiem i twórczością Jana Długosza. Osiągnięcia i potrzeby," [New research on the life and work of Jan Długosz. Achievements and needs] *Studia Źródłoznawcze* 56 (2018), 193–199.

136 Jacek Wiesiołowski, *Kolekcje historyczne w Polsce średniowiecznej XIV–XV wieku* [Historical collections in medieval Poland, 14th–15th centuries] (Wrocław, 1967).

137 On lost sources see: Tomasz Nowakowski, *Źródła do dziejów Mazowsza w XI–XIV wieku. W poszukiwaniu rocznika płockiego* [Sources for the history of Mazovia in the 11th–14th centuries. In search of the Płock vintage] (Bydgoszcz, 2012).

138 Wojciech Polak, *Aprobata i spór. Zakon krzyżacki jako instytucja kościelna* [Approval and dispute. The Teutonic Order as a church institution] (Lublin, 1999); cf. Adam Talarowski, "Od poganina do króla arcychrześcijańskiego".

139 Recently Wojciech Drelicharz, "Miejsce 'Excerpta ex fontibus incertis' w warsztacie historiograficznym Jana Długosza," [The place of 'Excerpta ex fontibus incertis' in the historiographic workshop of Jan Długosz] in *Jan Długosz (1415–1480)*, 71–86; cf. Sławomir Gawlas, "Astrolog przyjacielem historyka? Diariusz Zbigniewa Oleśnickiego w genezie Roczników Jana Długosza," [An astrologer friend of a historian? Diary of Zbigniew Oleśnicki in the genesis of Annals of Jan Długosz] in *Kultura średniowieczna i staropolska. Studia ofiarowane Aleksandrowi Gieysztorowi w pięćdziesięciolecie pracy naukowej*, ed. Danuta Gawinowa et al. (Warszawa, 1991): 455–469.

140 *Annales*, 62.

erudite effort,[141] the task was only partially completed[142] and the *Annals* were not transformed into a universal chronicle. Nevertheless, the chronicler devotes a lot of space and attention to events in the Empire, especially regarding contemporaneous times, but he is consistent in presenting them from the perspective of Polish interests.

As it was in Polish chronicle writings starting with Gallus Anonymus, when describing the inhabitants of the Empire, Jan Długosz most often uses the term: *Almami*, much less often *Theutoni*, and only exceptionally *Germani*. Presenting a new, broader biblical genealogy of Slavs and Poles, he combines it with an extensive geographical description called *Chorographia*. In this context, he mentions the destruction of Troy and the escape of Priam and Antenor on ships to Venice, later Padua (where Antenor was buried). It was from this place that he sets off to conquer Germany. The chronicler explains in this place the origin of its name and lists its provinces:

> Priamus cum comitibus Germaniam occupavit, et ab ipso et germano Anthenore Germania fuit dicta, que nunc a Teutos (qui est Mercurius) Teutonia vocatur, a Latinis autem Lemania dicitur, a Lemano fluvio; que has continet regiones: Lotharingiam, seu Brabanciam, Vistfaliam, Phrisiam, Thuringiam, Saxoniam, Sveviam, Bavariam Franconiam.
>
> [Priamus occupied with his companions Germany, and from himself and his brother Anthenor it was called *Germania*, which nowadays from

---

141 Długosz was drawing information from a very extensive set of ancient and medieval works and used every occasion to get new materials; still relevant to this is Aleksander Semkowicz, *Krytyczny rozbiór Dziejów Polski Jana Długosza (do roku 1384)* [Critical analysis of the history of Poland by Jan Długosz (until 1384)] (Kraków, 1887); cf. Sławomir Zonenberg, *Źródła do dziejów Pomorza Gdańskiego, Prus i Zakonu krzyżackiego w Rocznikach Jana Długosza (do 1299 roku)* [Sources for the history of Gdańsk Pomerania, Prussia and the Teutonic Order in Annals of Jan Długosz (until 1299)] (Toruń, 2000); recently Agnieszka Januszek-Sieradzka, "Wątki francuskie w *Rocznikach* Jana Długosza," [French themes in Annals of Jan Długosz] in *Jan Długosz – 600-lecie urodzin. Region – Polska – Europa w jego twórczości*, ed. Jacek Maciejewski, Piotr Oliński, Waldemar Rozynkowski, and Sławomir Zonenberg (Toruń – Bydgoszcz, 2016), 61–83.

142 Stanisław Solicki, "Metoda pracy nad dziejami obcymi w Annales Poloniae Jana Długosza," [The method of working on foreign history in Jan Długosz's Annales Poloniae] *Studia Źródłoznawcze*, 22 (1977), 105–109; the author established that from among circa 3600 references, as many as 1400 concern the history of other countries, including: Germany (empire) – 143, Bohemia – 378, Hungary – 264, the Teutonic Order – 235, the Papacy – 140, Lithuania – 136, and Ruthenia (Rus') – 135. It should be added that the calculation might be inaccurate, and after a volume of references is taken into account, the disproportion of foreign history diminishes significantly.

Teutos (which is Mercury) is called *Teutonia*, by the Latins it is called *Lemania*, from the *Leman* river; it comprises these regions: Lotharingia, Brabant, Westphalia, Friesland, Thuringia, Saxony, Swabia, Bavaria, Franconia.]

The invaders then attacked Gaul, which is called France because of its wildness. Brutus escapes on the same ship and gave the name to England.[143]

These regions mirrored the contemporary diversity of the Empire, which was transferred to ancient times. It can be added in this matter that Długosz presents the described events in national categories, but in accordance with the realities of his own time.[144] He regards the inhabitants of the German Reich as a community of origin and language, and at the same time a political entity in which they participated during conventions or Reichstags (*generalis dieta*): the emperor, electors and princes. Other entities are also exceptionally mentioned, such as at the convention called by Sigismund of Luxembourg in 1431 to Nuremberg – "in Nuremberga omnium electorum imperii et omnium principium et communitatum Almanie conventus".[145] Generally speaking, however, the internal structure of the Empire was of little interest to the chronicler. He had too little information about the events of the past and only occasionally mentions the princes who participate in raids against Poland. He notices the existence of regional communities (usually referred to as *nacio*) when he wants to particularly emphasize the strength of the invaders, as in 1158 when describing the expedition of Frederick Barbarossa: "omnes enim viri imperii et omnem Alamanicam nacionem, Francos, Swewos, Rinenses, Baworos, Saxones, Lothoringos, Misznenses".[146] In such cases, the list of participants is justified by rhetorics. The situation does not change when he is constructing the narrative of his contemporary times. The chronicler's attention focuses on the emperor's policy, and only exceptionally on conflicts with the German principalities.

Initially, the eastern border of Germany was marked by the Elbe River. Długosz mentions this several times when constructing arguments to show the

---

143 *Annales*, I.68; cf. Krystyna Pieradzka, "Genealogia biblijna i pochodzenie Słowian w pierwszej księdze 'Annales' Jana Długosza," [Biblical genealogy and the origin of the Slavs in the first book of 'Annales' by Jan Długosz] *Nasza Przeszłość*, 8, 1958, 83–116; the chronicler constructed his reasoning on the basis of Isidore of Seville, the chronicle of Peter the Franciscan called Puteolanus, and some unrecognised sources – ibid., 105–106.

144 Sławomir Gawlas, "Świadomość narodowa Jana Długosza," [National awareness of Jan Długosz] *Studia Źródłoznawcze* 27 (1983), 3–66, esp. juxtapositions in the form of tables 20–27.

145 *Annales*, 1431.XI.45.

146 *Annales*, 1158.V.62; cf. 1410.XI.124–125; 1412.XI.141; 1438.XII.183.

priority of Poles among the Slavs.[147] He tries to compile a comprehensive set of different plots and eagerly refers to the etymology of names. Slavs, just like Germans, came from Japheth. His descendant Lech, traveling from Pannonia, gave his younger brother Czech his land. Rus was not a brother but only a descendant of Lech. When defining the borders of his country, the chronicler took into account knowledge based on the reception of Ptolemy's *Geography*[148] and identified ancient Sarmatians with Poles – *Sarmate sive Poloni*. He opposed the assumptions that the Vistula River was part of the border between Scythia and Germania, because Poles had always lived on the Vistula (*nulla gens quam Polonica*). The proper border of European Sarmatia was the Elbe River – "Alba seu Labya ex montibus, qui Bohemiem Morawiamque disterminant, oriens mediam provinciam prelabitur, qui Polonie sive Sarmacie Europie et Germanie limitem facit".[149]

The adopted Sarmatian identification becomes a component of the political ideology of the Polish nobility in the early modern era.[150] At the same time, Długosz refers to the concept of "imperial" borders of the state of the Poles developed in Polish historiography and included the Polabian Slavs "usque ad Almaniam, que nunc Myszna dicitur". Depending on the circumstances, he interprets the meaning of the term "Slavic language" in different ways and is eager to identify it with the Polish language. The western border he sets as far out as possible, encompassing eminent cities: "Bukowyecz, que nunc Lubyk, Ham, quo nunc Hamburg, Breme, Slesnyk, Czesznya" [?]. The past of these lands is testified to by the names "in Polonico seu Slavonico" – although many of them had been distorted by "Theotonicis Saxonibus, qui eorum terras occuparunt".[151] In a version more elaborated than those of his predecessors, he describes Wanda's rule, and her suitor is said to be the "princeps Almanorum

---

147 Cf. Andrzej Janeczek, "Świadomość wspólnoty słowiańskiej w pełnym i późnym średniowieczu," [Awareness of the Slavic community in the full and late Middle Ages] in *Słowianie – idea i rzeczywistość. Zbiór studiów*, ed. Krzysztof A. Makowski and Monika Saczyńska (Poznań, 2013), 19–70.

148 Jadwiga Bzinkowska, *Od Sarmacji do Polonii. Studia nad początkami obrazu kartograficznego Polski* [From Sarmatia to the Polish community. Studies on the beginnings of the cartographic image of Poland] (Kraków, 1994).

149 *Annales*, I.67, I.88–89, cf. I.100.

150 Tadeusz Ulewicz, *Sarmacja. Studium z problematyki słowiańskiej* [Sarmatia. A study of Slavic issues] (Kraków, 1950).

151 *Annales*, I.117; I.142 et seq.; cf. Monika Saczyńska, "Czy istnieli Słowianie w późnym średniowieczu. Uwagi na podstawie lektury *Roczników* Jana Długosza," [Whether there were Slavs in the late Middle Ages. Notes on the basis of the Annals of Jan Długosz] in *Słowianie – idea i rzeczywistość*, 71–105.

Rythogarus".[152] The whole area on this side of the Elbe River was severed from Poland as a result of the crimes of Pompilius II, who was inspired by his German wife – *ex principibus Almanorum*. Consequently, the "regiones Polonicas sive Slavicas" located between Westphalia, Meissen and the Baltic is occupied by the *nacio Theutonica*.[153] These historic borders were only temporarily restored by Bolesław I the Brave.[154]

The story of the border on the Elbe and of how the territory inhabited by the Polabian Slavs belonged to Poland should not be interpreted as a justification of territorial claims against the Empire. To remember the glorious past meant to emphasise the prestige of the Slavs and among them the preeminence of the Poles. Długosz respected the authority of the emperor and the pope, but he gave a higher position to the latter. This, however, did not mean political dependence. Real or alleged interventions by the popes in the past he regarded as justified when they were in line with Polish interests. As the head of the Church, popes should not overcommit their authority to secular life and political goals. The chronicler was hard on the behaviour of many such popes. He particularly criticized the situation during the Great Schism. He did not show much sympathy for contemporary popes and strongly defended the sovereignty of the Polish Church against the pontifs appointing bishops.[155] It was not only an expression of the increasing secularization of temporal power, but above all it shows Długosz's conviction of God's omnipotence, which did not need any mediation to act.[156] He took an even more explicit attitude towards the universal prerogatives of the emperors. He repeatedly mentions the respect due to them, but in specific cases a lot depended on the context. In confrontation with the Hussites, Sigismund of Luxembourg is described as: "Romanorum imperator, quem omnis Europa venerata est".[157] The emperors' powers were so important that their authority was used to emphasize Poland's sovereignty when drawing up a new version of the description of the congress in Gniezno.

For spreading the Christian faith, Prince Mieszko I was supposed to receive a crown from the pope just before his death, but the latter withdrew his decision

---

152 *Annales*, I.129 et seq.; cf. Banaszkiewicz, "Rüdiger von Bechelaren".
153 *Annales*, I.142 et seq.
154 Cf. *Annales*, 1012.II. 270 et seq.; 1013.II.271 et seq.; 1031.II.304 et seq.
155 The problem has been thoroughly analysed by Urszula Borkowska, *Treści ideowe w działach Jana Długosza. Kościół i świat poza Kościołem* [Ideological content in the sections of Jan Długosz. The Church and the world outside the Church] (Lublin, 1983), esp. 47 et seq., 60 et seq.
156 Cf. Talarowski, Dzieje w rękach Opatrzności.
157 *Annales*, 1424.XI.205; cf. Ibid., 1109.IV.253: "orbis terrarum imperator".

under the influence of a vision showing him the sins of Poles. Emperor Otto III, cured of his illness through the intercession of Saint Adalbert, went to his gravesite at Gniezno in 1001. After a great reception, he ordered the royal anointing of Bolesław I the Brave. He distinguished his kingdom with the sign of a white eagle. The black imperial eagle was a sign of sovereignty over "naciones omnes Teutonice", and the White Eagle was to subordinate "singulos Slaworum et barbarorum naciones". At the same time, the emperor recognised the new king and his successors as

> [...] imperii Romanorum socium et amicum, subiciens sibi et regno suo omnes Polonorum regiones nacionesque donans vero singulos principatus, terras et districtus (...) sub barbaris infidelibus et scismaticis nacionis acquisitos et in posterum munere et suffragio divino acquirendos.
>
> [as companion and friend of the Holy Roman Empire, he put him and his realm in charge of all Polish regions and nations by giving him every single principality, county and district (...) which had been acquired from the barbarian pagans and schismatics and will be acquired in future by divine gift and choice.]

The imperial will now sanction a special position for the Poles. Otto confirmed his decisions by imperial privilege with a golden bull in which he freed the *reges Regnumque Polonie* from obedience and subordination – "a sua suorumque successorum imperatorum Romanorum obediencia et subieccione perpetuo remittens et absolvens".[158] The decisions were sealed by the marriage of the son and successor of Mieszko II to the emperor's niece Richeza. It was supposed to add splendour to the royal dignity of *claritate imperiali sanguinis*. Marriage was therefore a complement to equal status.[159] According to the chronicler, Bolesław the Brave actually subordinated neighboring peoples to himself. After his death, it turned out that his widowed daughter-in-law Richeza listened only to the advice of the Germans (*Almanis*) and appointed only them to offices. So, she was expelled and with her son, Casimir I, went to Saxony, to which she took the royal crowns and the entire treasury.[160] The son, sent to study in Paris, became a monk in Cluny. At the request of the Polish

---

158 Ibid., 1001.II. 228–240.
159 Cf.: Duke Mieszko III the Old of Greater Poland, when his son was born: "nomenque filio in baptismate Ottho imposuit ne cezarum Otthonum, ex quibus ipse materno sanguine satus erat, nomen obliterari posset" – *Annales*, 1156.V. 57.
160 Ibid., 1036.II.313–316.

delegation, the pope dispensed his religious vows in exchange for eternal rent (*tribulum perpetuum*). Returning to the country, Casimir visited his mother in Salzwedel and met with Emperor Henry III who at his request was willing to return the crowns.[161]

In the following years, according to the sources he used (mainly Martinus Polonus and Ptolemy of Lucca), the chronicler mentions the emperors' expeditions to Bohemia and Hungary, Henry IV's disputes with the pope, his fight with his son (with chronological errors), the concordat at Worms, and the succession of Lothar of Supplinburg. He continues to note in detail subsequent changes on the German throne.[162] The first conflict between Poland and the emperor which he describes is the invasion of Henry V in 1109, presented according to earlier chronicles as the triumphant victory of Bolesław III the Wry-Mouthed. Although Długosz notes the name of the battlefield (*Caninus Campus – Pszepole*), he weakens its meaning by emphasising the honorary treatment of numerous German prisoners. According to the conditions of the peace concluded at Bamberg, the emperor was to recognize Bolesław's independence and his status as *empire amicum*. The reconciliation was confirmed by the marriage of Władysław II's son with the sister of the emperor, Christina, and the release of *omnes captivos Alamanorum*.[163] The defeated emperor was clearly the best partner. In line with the tendency of this narrative, Emperor Lothar had to admit in 1136 that Pomerania and Rugia (Ger. Rügen) belonged to the Polish prince and were *Polonorum terras naturales*, so he resigned from demanding homage and tribute.[164] It should be added here that the marriage with the sister of the emperor brought bad results because under the influence of her ambitions and intrigues a civil war broke out between Władysław II and his younger brothers. The defeated prince fled *ad Conradum imperatorem*.[165] Długosz was the first Polish chronicler to describe under the year 1158 the victorious intervention of Frederick I Barbarossa in the Polish ruler's defence. He tries to mitigate the effects of the defeat by emphasising the difficult military situation of the emperor, his readiness for peace, and some completely fictitious information about bonding with opponents through the marriage of the imperial relative Adelaide with the prince of Greater Poland, Mieszko III. The chronicler stresses that the Piasts had not complied with the terms of the

---

161 Ibid., 1041.III.30–33.
162 Długosz' opinions on conflicts between the Hohenstaufen and popes could not have been positive, but Rudolf of Habsburg was: "homo inter Almanos humilis sortis et generis, sed animi magni et celebris" – *Annales*, 1274.VII.188; cf. 1291.VII.264.
163 Ibid., 1109.IV.253–254; 1110.IV.256–257.
164 Ibid., 1136.IV.328.
165 Ibid., 1146.V.35.

settlement.¹⁶⁶ It was not until 1163 that (at the emperor's request and under the threat of his wrath) Władysław's sons could return to Silesia. Then the hostility between the Polish princes and the emperor and Germany disappeared – "hostili respectu, qui a cesare Almanisque (...) sublato".¹⁶⁷

Długosz is quite consistent in softening the image of the empire as a power that was threatening Poland, but he uses every opportunity to emphasise its sovereignty. According to the sources he uses, the role of the enemy was taken over by Poland's immediate neighbors, that is, the margraves of Brandenburg, called by the chronicler the Saxon (*Saxones*). He noted the unjust takeover by them for a small sum of money of the Lebus borough – "a Polonorum Regno iniuste alienatus ad marchionatum Brandenburgenesem transit". He particularly condemns the margraves' participation in the assassination of King Premislaus II in 1296. This hideous crime would not have happened had it not been for the hatred of the Germans toward the Poles and their desire to damage the glory of the Polish kingdom:

> [...] etsi Theutonicorum erga Polonos malignus invidusque perspici possit animus, qui orientem gloriam Regni Polonie, quantum in ipsis erat, extinguere pessumque dare conati sunt.¹⁶⁸

> [... although the evil and envious character of the Germans towards the Poles could be seen, who tried to extinguish and destroy the glory of the Polish realm, as far as they could.]

In the fourteenth century, after the occupation of Pomerelia (Danzig Pomerania), it is the Teutonic Order which becomes the opponent condemned by the chronicler. Długosz accuses the Teutonic Knights of pride, greed, hypocrisy, cruelty, failure to keep agreements, and the fight against Christians. He mentions that their food came from the Empire, and that they spoke German. However, he does not use these circumstances as an important argument directed against all the residents of the Empire.¹⁶⁹

---

166 Ibid., 1158.V.63–65; cf. Kazimierz Jasiński, *Rodowód pierwszych Piastów* [The genealogy of the first Piasts] (Warszawa/Wrocław, 1992), 235f.
167 *Annales*, 1163.V.74–76, 1164.V.76.
168 Ibid., 1250.VII.72–73; 1296.VIII.289–292.
169 Jadwiga Krzyżaniakowa, "Poglądy Jana Długosza na zakon Krzyżacki i jego stosunki z Polską," [Jan Długosz's views on the Teutonic Order and its relations with Poland] in *Studia Grunwaldzkie*, vol. 2, ed. Marian Biskup et al. (Olsztyn,1992), 7–37; cf. Gawlas, *Świadomość Jana Dlugosza*, 50 et seq.

When describing the history of the Kingdom of Poland under the rule of the last Piasts, Długosz did not have abundant sources for a universal history. Yet, he notes the elections of subsequent emperors and is particularly interested in their Roman coronations.[170] In this context it is the description of the Emperor Charles IV's trip to Cracow in 1364 that deserves special attention. The free presentation of the course of events is made possible thanks to the fact that Długosz bases his description largely on the oral legend of the congress of rulers. According to the chronicler, Charles, (at that point referred to as the Roman and Bohemian king), upon news of the approaching kings of Poland, Hungary, Denmark, and Cyprus as well as numerous princes, dismounts from his horse along with his entire retinue of princes and barons. In this situation, the rulers who welcome him do the same. During the feast organised by the Cracow councillor Wierzynek, he assigns the highest place to the Polish king, Casimir III, the second to Charles, and the following to other rulers:

> Kazimirum Polonie regem primum et superiorem locum, secundum Karolum Romanorum et Bohemie regem, tercium Hungarie, quartum Cipri et ultimam Dacie accipere iussit.

> [He ordered to give Casimir the Polish king the first and highest place, the second to Charles the king of the Empire and Bohemia, the third to Hungary, the forth to Cyprus and the last do Denmark.]

The chronicler, who in other passages calls Charles 'Roman emperor' (*Romanorum imperator*), puts in the mouth of the councillor the justification for his special obligations towards his king – "quod nulli magis quam domino suo Kazimiro Polonie regi (…) ad favendum de amplissimo honore obligaretur".[171] This distinction of the Polish king's position goes clearly against the unquestionable prestige of the Roman emperor.

The most recent information about the perception of the Empire is brought up by the narrative of Długosz's contemporary times. The text is so comprehensive that its analysis can only be documented by reference to examples. According to the reality of that time, there was a far-reaching separation of two entities: the emperor and the German Empire, the latter represented by its

---

170   *Annales*, 1313.IX.87–88 – Henry VII's coronation; 1324.IX.128–129 – Louis of Bavaria (the chronicler calls him only the Roman king); 1355.IX.273 – Charles IV.
171   Ibid., 1363.IX.319–321 (1363); cf. Roman Grodecki, *Kongres Krakowski w roku 1364* [Krakow' congress in 1346], ed. Jerzy Wyrozumski (Kraków, 1995); Stanisław Szczur, "Krakowski zjazd monarchów z roku 1364," [Krakow convention of monarchs from 1364] *Studia Historyczne*, 75 (2009), 35–58.

electors and princes. The most important decisions were made with the participation of princes, sometimes at a *generalis dieta*, most often in Nuremberg, in which "electores imperii et principes Almanie" participated.[172] Exceptionally, in 1473, the chronicler comments on the engagement of the emperor's son, Maximilian I, to Maria, daughter of Charles the Bold. Emperor Frederick III was then to promise to the prince of Burgundy the royal coronation during the negotiations at Trier: "[...] non sine preiudicio et iactura principum Almanie et totius nacionis Germanice Carolum Burgundiae ducem Romanorum regem creari, eligi et in Aquisgrano coronari promittit." Conditions that pursued private interest are described by Długosz as ignoble – "titulum Romanorum regni et auctoritatem ex Germanis in Gallos ob privatum questum translatum esse et catholicis orbis Cesarem, quasi nihil melius successori suo Romanorum regi prestari posset." The contract violated the order set by God himself and was not implemented because it was against the divine will.[173]

The chronicler follows carefully the policies of subsequent emperors. He pays much attention to their status and to their coronations in Rome. He describes the course of the imperial coronation of Sigismund of Luxembourg in 1433 and, particularly extensively, that of Frederick III in 1452.[174] They bring about a change in the titles he uses in the narrative:

"Sigismundus rex Romanorum et Hungarie was later referred to as Sigismundus imperator et Hungarie rex. Similarly, Fridericus Romanorum rex et Austrie dux was later on referred to as imperator (sometimes cesar) et Austrie dux". Długosz regards each of the emperors in a different individual way. In his opinion, Sigismund of Luxemburg was a deceitful and lying enemy who was thinking one thing and promising another – "rex caliditatis vafre permistum ingenium aliud clausum gestans pectore aliud depromens, lingua adeo in promittendo blandus".[175] He therefore enjoys Sigismund's troubles and failures. His successor, Albrecht II, was "princeps mitis et modestus et religionis

---

172 *Annales*, 1428.XI.231; cf. 1431.XI. 45; 1466.XII.173; 1471.XII.283; 1473.XII.307; 1473.XII.314–316.
173 Ibid., 1473.XII.315.
174 Ibid., 1433.XI.104–106; 1452.XII.140–143. The chronicler described the accompanying ceremonies and pointed out that contrary to the old custom, Frederick passed by Milan in order not to recognise the rule of Francisco Sforza. Pope Nicholas V was to say to the Milanese envoys that: "sicut poterat transferre imperium de Grecie ad Almanos ita et forcius illam coronacionem de Mediolano ad Romam".
175 Ibid., 1419.XI.99; cf. Jarosław Nikodem, "Wróg Królestwa Polskiego. Zygmunt Luksemburski w opinii Jana Długosza," [An enemy of the Kingdom of Poland. Zygmunt Luksemburski in the opinion of Jan Długosz] in *Cor hominis. Wielkie namiętności w dziejach, źródłach i studiach nad przeszłością*, ed. Stanisław Rosik and Przemysław Wiszewski (Wrocław, 2007), 183–199.

christiane amator ferventissimus", but he ruled for a very short time.[176] He was the father of Elisabeth, who was the wife of Casimir IV Jagiellon and the mother of his sons, and their dynastic rights were derived from him, which the chronicler repeatedly emphasizes. The positive characteristics of the emperor are therefore not accidental. In addition, his successor on the Hungarian throne was the Polish King Władysław III of Varna. The picture of his reign in Hungary as presented in the *Annales* contains very few elements of reality because it was constructed as a consistent polemic using the allegations of Habsburg propaganda.[177] The character of Frederick III is presented in an ambiguous way. In general, he does not pose a direct threat to Polish interests, but extensive descriptions of his constant troubles, defeats and humiliations depreciate the majesty of an emperor. On the other hand, he was a political partner in the efforts to push the hereditary rights of Władysław's son, Casimir Jagiellon, to the Bohemian throne. In 1470, the chronicler describes the proposal of Frederick III to arrange a double marriage for his and Casimir Jagiellon's daughters with their respective sons, Maximilian and Władysław, as "sub equis conditionis fedus cum Friderico imperatore".[178] Ultimately, in 1473, the emperor and electors recognise Władysław Jagiellon as a natural heir to the Kingdom of Bohemia – "naturalem et legitimum Bohemie regem".[179]

Throughout his whole chronicle, Długosz constantly refers to the set of negative stereotypes defining all the Polish neighbors. He is particularly unfriendly to Bohemians, infected as they were with Hussitism, and who are greedy, haughty, hateful of Poles and always eager to cooperate with the emperor against them. The Hungarians are cowards, quarrelsome, capricious, and willing to break their allegiance to their rulers. The Wallachians in turn are cunning, cruel and lead a predatory life. Ruthenians, on the other hand, are treacherous and prone to sodomy, and are people who hate Poles and willingly cooperate with Tatars. The chronicler treats the Lithuanians with a certain arrogance and believes that they are "inter septentrionales populos obscurissimi". He thinks them to be quarrelsome, deceitful, prone to plunder

---

176 *Annales*, 1439.XII.209; the author also presents a reliable description of his physical appearance.
177 Władysław of Varna accepted the Hungarian throne only in the name of the defence of Christianity. As king, he cared only for the achievement of all ideals of a knightly king and crusader who was killed for his faith. On the polemic between the chronicler and Habsburg propaganda: Patrycja Szwedo, "*Sub banderio cruciatae* – Władysław III Jagiellończyk jako średniowieczny rycerz idealny. Wizerunek władcy na podstawie *Roczników* Jana Długosza," *Średniowiecze Polskie i Powszechne* 9, 13 (2017), 186–210.
178 *Annales*, 1470.XII.252–253.
179 Ibid., 1473.XII.316–317; cf. 1477.XII.400: in Vienna, the emperor *confert regalia* to Władysław Jagiellon *tradendo vexilia Bohemica*.

and atrocities, allying with the Teutonic Knights, and sending Tatars against the Poles. Even more explicit are the characteristics of the pagan Turks and Tatars.[180] Negative attitudes towards neighbors can be seen already in the first Polish chronicles. In the late Middle Ages, the stereotypical characteristics of national and regional societies became very popular in communities of literary culture.[181] Against this background, the characteristics of the Germans in the *Annals* are not particularly negative. The main objection was the German sense of superiority, contempt for Poles, and constant envy of all their successes. The chronicler mentions this several times,[182] but does not expose in any special way the thread of mutual dislike.

The image of the Holy Roman Empire in the Polish Middle Ages was created in the conditions of an immediate vicinity. It was composed with the use of little real knowledge and was closely related to the growth of collective memory. It was selective because only certain events were subject to written record in chronicle narratives. Their set was constantly supplemented and adapted to the needs of changing times, but at the same time kept the overarching continuity of the ideological message. The universal Empire was a great challenge, and difficult to solve for the developing Polish identity. It evoked admiration and respect, and at the same time the need to defend Polish sovereignty. Arguments were provided from the memory of the glorious past. Poles had never paid tribute and had never surrendered. The more they made sure of it, the more willing they were to see the advantages of their great neighbour.

180 Gawlas, "Świadomość narodowa," 47 et seq.; cf. Borkowska, *Treści ideowe*, 145 et seq.; Jarosław Nikodem, "Jan Długosz o stosunkach polsko-czeskich w czasach husyckich," [Jan Długosz on Polish-Czech relations in the Hussite times] in *Jan Długosz (1415–1480)*, 169–182; Robert Urbański, *Tartarorum gens brutalis. Trzynastowieczne najazdy mongolskie w literaturze polskiego średniowiecza na porównawczym tle piśmiennictwa łacińskiego antyku i wieków średnich* [The thirteenth-century Mongol invasions in the Polish literature of the Middle Ages against the comparative background of Latin antiquity and the Middle Ages] (Warszawa, 2007), 261 et seq.

181 Kot, *Pochwały i przygany*; cf. Sławomir Gawlas, "Marność świata i narodowe stereotypy. Uwagi o wielokulturowości na Śląsku w XV w.," [Vanity of the world and national stereotypes. Notes on multiculturalism in Silesia in the 15th century] in *Korzenie wielokulturowości Śląska ze szczególnym uwzględnieniem Śląska Górnego*, ed. Antoni Barciak (Katowice/Zabrze, 2009), 29–53.

182 The 1466 peace with the Teutonic Order was so advantageous that "plerique Almanie et cometanei principes super tam magnifica Regni Polonici sublimacione singularis torquerentur invidia et pacis calumnialiter condiciones" – *Annales*, 1466.XII.161; cf. 1439.XII.201; 1458.XII.313.

CHAPTER 8

Polish Hagiographic Sources and Their View of the Germans in the Middle Ages

Roman Michałowski

The hagiographic literature of the Polish Middle Ages is scarce.[1] There are two reasons. First, it should be noted that in medieval Poland writing as such was poorly developed; it was much weaker than in the West. This was an important reason, but the question is whether it was the most important one. The other reason lies in the nature of the cults of saints. Until as late as the mid-13th century they played but an insignificant role in Poland.[2] It is, therefore, not surprising that the demand for literature devoted to saints was limited. In later centuries, although its role grew, it never became as significant as it was in the

---

1   The research was funded by the National Science Centre, Poland as part of the grant No. 2015/17/B/HS3/00502. For more on Polish medieval hagiography, see Jerzy Starnawski, *Drogi rozwojowe hagiografii polskiej i łacińskiej w wiekach średnich* [Development paths of Polish and Latin hagiography in the Middle Ages], Pontificia Academia Theologica Cracoviensis. Facultas Historica, 5 (Kraków, 1993); Teresa Dunin-Wąsowicz, "Hagiographie polonaise entre XIe et XVIe siècle," *Hagiographies. Histoire internationale de la littérature hagiographique latine et vernaculaire des origines à 1550*, ed. Guy Philippart, Corpus Christianorum. Hagiographies 3 (Turnhout, 2001), 179–202; Aleksandra Witkowska, "Polska twórczość hagiograficzna. Próba bilansu, [Polish hagiographic works. Balance sheet attempt]" in ead., *Sancti Miracula Peregrinationes. Wybór tekstów z lat 1974–2008* (Lublin, 2009, 1st ed. 2005), 13–29; Halina Manikowska and Dorota Gacka, "Hagiografia a historyczność, czyli o historii w hagiografii i hagiografia w służbie historii, [Hagiography and historicity, or about history in hagiography and hagiography in the service of history]" in *Przeszłość w kulturze średniowiecznej Polski* 1, eds. Jacek Banaszkiewicz, Andrzej Dąbrówka, and Piotr Węcowski (Warszawa, 2018), 657–748. For more on Polish descriptions of miracles, see first of all: Aleksandra Witkowska, "Miracula małopolskie z XIII i XIV wieku – Studium źródłoznawcze, [Miracula of Lesser Poland from the 13th and 14th centuries – A source study]" *Roczniki Humanistyczne* 19/2 (1971), 29–161. On medieval Polish hagiography as compared to European hagiography *Les saints et leur culte en Europe centrale au Moyen Age (XIe–début du XVIe siècle)*, eds. Marie-Madeleine de Cevins and Olivier Marin, Hagiologia. Etudes sur la sainteté et l'hagiographie – Studies on Sanctity and Hagiography 13 (Turnhout, 2017).

2   Roman Michałowski, "Le culte des saints du Haut Moyen Age en Pologne et en Europe Occidentale," in *La Pologne et l'Europe Occidentale du Moyen Age à nos jours. Actes du colloque organisé par l'Université Paris VII-Denis Diderot. Paris, les 28 et 29 octobre 1999*, eds. Marie-Louise Pelus-Kaplan and Daniel Tollet, Publikacje Instytutu Historii UAM 58 (Poznań-Paris, 2004), 29–41.

West. True, in the 13th century, St. Stanislaus became not only a patron of the kingdom but also a miracle-worker whose tomb attracted crowds of the faithful. In addition to St. Stanislaus, there were also other miracle working saints. On the other hand, the number of Polish canonisations was minimal. In the late Middle Ages the only other canonization, apart from Stanislaus', was that of Hedwig of Silesia.

Of the modest number of hagiographic texts originating in Poland only some will be of use in the present study. If they are to reflect the Polish view of Germans, we need to exclude texts which, although originating in Poland or commissioned in Poland, were written by foreigners. This means omitting the works of Bruno of Querfurt, even if we agree with the hypothesis that the great missionary wrote them at the court of Boleslaus the Brave. For the same reason we will have to leave aside the two oldest surviving *vitae* of St. Hedwig,[3] since their author – according to the most likely hypothesis – was a Franciscan from Wrocław, i.e., most certainly a German.[4] A Wrocław Franciscan may have written the *Vita of Anne*, wife of Henry the Pious, so drawing on the same premise, we will have to leave aside this source as well.[5]

The application of the principle formulated above will reduce even further the corpus of texts available for the present study. Yet, there is another difficulty. With some exceptions, the authors of Polish hagiographic sources are unknown, which is why attributing a text to a Pole is in most cases not always obvious, and so is a matter of guesswork. There were many foreigners among the local clergy, not only in 13th century Silesia. Thus, we have to realise that including a work in our source base will in many cases be a decision based on a hypothesis.

The oldest hagiographic source meeting these criteria is the *Vita of St. Adalbert*, known from its incipit as *Tempore illo*.[6] It originated most likely in Gniezno and is dated broadly between the first half of the 12th century and the year 1248. To a large extent its author used the earlier *vitae* of St. Adalbert (*Vita I* and the *Vita* by Bruno of Querfurt), and also introduced some additional

---

3   *Vita sanctae Hedwigis*, ed. Aleksander Semkowicz, MPH 4 (Lwów, 1884), 501–655.
4   Maciej Michalski, *Kobiety i świętość w żywotach trzynastowiecznych księżnych polskich* [Women and holiness in the lives of 13th-century Polish princesses] (Poznań, 2004), 38–48.
5   *Vita Annae ducussae Silesiae*, ed. Aleksander Semkowicz, MPH 4, 656–661. Michalski, *Kobiety i świętość*, 56–60; pp. 311–317 feature the Latin text and the Polish translation of this particular vita.
6   *De sancto Adalberto episcopo*, ed. Wojciech Kętrzyński, MPH 4, 206–221. Gerard Labuda, "Nad legendą o św. Wojciechu 'Tempore illo'. Analiza źródłoznawcza, [Above the legend of St. Wojciech 'Tempore illo'. Source analysis]" *Ecclesia Posnanensis*. in *Opuscula Mariano Banaszak Septuagenario dedicata*, ed. Feliks Lenort, Konrad Lutyński (Poznań, 1998), 11–31.

material associated with the martyr's activity in Poland during his mission there. This material may have been written by an interpolator. What matters from our point of view is the fact that the words "German" or "Germany" do not appear in the text. When describing the Bishop of Prague's school years and career in the church, the author does mention Magdeburg and Mainz, but he does not give the name of the country. The word "Saxony" or any other word of the kind is not used. In the part concerning Poland the hagiographer presents St. Adalbert as its evangeliser and founder of the Polish nation.[7] The author's national self-identification is beyond doubt in this case. On the other hand, he shows absolutely no interest in the Germans.

A characteristic feature of medieval Polish hagiography is its political dimension, referring to the history of the Polish nation and state. An example here is the *Tempore illo* legend. Another, even more vivid one is the hagiography concerning St. Stanislaus.

A corpus of texts devoted to this martyr emerged in the mid-13th century. Our point of reference will be the most extensive of these works, *Vita maior s. Stanislai*.[8] Its author was Wincenty of Kielcza, a Dominican from the monastery of the Holy Trinity in Cracow and prior to that he had been a cathedral canon from Cracow, a man from a family of knights who had settled in the Opole region. In his work he draws extensively on the *Vita minor s. Stanislai*, copying entire chapters from it.[9] *Vita minor* may have, in fact, been written by him as well.

The Polish roots of the hagiographer are beyond doubt, and when it comes to *Vita maior*, it conveys a strong expression of Polish national consciousness, as cultivated among the clerical elites of Cracow. Suffice it to say that the work in question formulates for the first time – and so emphatically – the ideology of unification. That is, the author expresses his hope that Poland, divided into separate principalities, would become united again and regain the crown it had lost following the murder of St. Stanislaus by Boleslaus the Generous. Wincenty of Kielcza not only expresses such a view, but also justifies it, citing

---

7   My remarks can be found in Roman Michałowski, "The Nine-Week Lent in Boleslaus the Brave's Poland. A Study of the First Piasts' Religious Policy," *APH* 89 (2004), 5–50, here 46–47.
8   *Vita sancti Stanislai Cracoviensis episcopi* (*Vita maior*), ed. Wojciech Kętrzyński, MPH 4, 319–439 (hereafter cited as VSMaior). For more on the *Vita minor* and *Vita maior* of St. Stanislaus, see Wojciech Drelicharz, *Unifying the Kingdom of Poland*, 113–128, 147–190 including the literature on the subject.
9   *Vita s. Stanislai episcopi Cracoviensis* (*Vita minor*), ed. Wojciech Kętrzyński, MPH 4, 238–285 (hereafter cited as VSMinor).

a theological argument and an elaborate historical disquisition.[10] As a result, the work, hagiographic in its nature, acquired distinct historiographic features.

What is the attitude towards the Germans against this background of intensely experienced Polishness? There are very few references to them. Drawing on Gallus Anonymous' chronicle, Wincenty describes Otto III's visit to Poland.[11] He emphasizes the role played by the emperor in raising Boleslaus the Brave to the rank of king: Otto places his crown on the Polish ruler's head, thus consecrating him as king, and offers him, in addition to the crown, other royal insignia as well. Wincenty was fully aware of the fact that Otto was a Roman Emperor – this is how he explicitly refers to him. He also claims that during the events in question Boleslaus became an imperial associate and friend. The hagiographer took the Roman references from Gallus, adding that after visiting Boleslaus, Otto returned to Germany. Thus, the author knew that the emperor should be linked to Germany and this knowledge by no means diminished his positive attitude towards him. Significantly, the word used at this point of the narrative in *Vita minor sancti Stanislai* is not *Alemania* but *patria*.[12] This suggests a positive attitude of the author towards Germany.

There are positive overtones also in other details given by Wincenty in the *Vita maior*: it is precisely in Germany that Casimir the Restorer received his high-quality education and when he returns to Poland from exile, he receives military support from the emperor, who was residing in Germany at the time. While the second piece of information is partly supported by Gallus, the first is the hagiographer's own invention.[13] It should be noted that Casimir the Restorer occupied an important and by all accounts positive place in Polish historical memory, and became a figure of legend in the 13th century at the latest.[14] Without him it would be impossible to understand Poland's history. In

---

10   In addition to W. Drelicharz's study quoted above, see also Paweł Żmudzki, "Liber de passione i Vita maior s. Stanislai. Na marginesie książki Wojciecha Drelicharza o idei zjednoczenia Królestwa," *Kwartalnik Historyczny* 122 (2015), 855–875; Zbigniew Dalewski, "Przeszłość zrytualizowana: tradycja królewskich koronacji," *Przeszłość w kulturze średniowiecznej Polski* 2, ed. Halina Manikowska (Warszawa, 2018), 29–57, here 30–31.
11   VSMaior I, chap. 3, 365–366.
12   VSMinor, chap. 20, 269.
13   VSMaior II, chap. 9, 380; chap. 12, 382.
14   Pierre David, *Casimir le Moine et Boleslas le Pénitent*, Études historiques *et* littéraires *sur la* Pologne médiévale 5 (Paris, 1932); Inga Stembrowicz, "Podanie o Kazimierzu Mnichu w polskim dziejopisarstwie do końca XIV wieku, [A story about Kazimierz Mnich in Polish historiography until the end of the 14th centur]" *Symboliczne i realne podstawy tożsamości społecznej w średniowieczu*, eds. Sławomir Gawlas and Paweł Żmudzki (Warszawa, 2017), 222–282.

such circumstances, positive references to Germany and the Germans in the context of this ruler appear especially telling.

References to the Germans can also be found in the third part of the *Vita*, which contains descriptions of miracles worked by St. Stanislaus after his death. The accounts are taken and adapted from one or two reports. In 1250 a papal commission was established, featuring Archbishop Pełka of Gniezno, Bishop Thomas of Wrocław, and Abbot Henry of Lubiąż. The aim of the commission was to compile the necessary documentation for the canonization of St. Stanislaus, specifically, to collect accounts of miracles attributed to him. The commission's report was lost, yet we can get some idea about its contents on the basis of another report, drawn up in 1252 by the Franciscan James of Velletri, whose task was to verify the work of the commission.[15]

Thus, the third part of the *Vita* mentions a German woman named Adelaide, "good and pious". She twice had a vision in which she was told to order the cathedral custodian to elevate the body of St. Stanislaus. She was rewarded with a miraculous healing. It should be noted that in one of these visions, the woman saw the holy bishop himself and he spoke to her in German.[16] The elevation was an important act in the development of the cult of Stanislaus, of which the hagiographer was, of course, well aware.[17] As we can read elsewhere, a German priest regains his sight thank to St. Stanislaus.[18] Wincenty of Kielcza writes about a girl of the same nationality. She was punished at the tomb of the saint for misleading the faithful by pretending with her garments to be a virgin.[19] Guided by the spirit of penance, she confesses her guilt in public. Finally, the hagiographer describes the miracle of the healing of the German Wiker's two sons. This was St. Stanislaus' response to Wiker's prayer and votive offering.[20] In all the cases in question the hagiographer mentions the nationality of the protagonist of the miracle. However, the people described in the

---

15   *Miracula sancti Stanislai*, Wojciech Kętrzyński, MPH 4, 285–318; more recent edition: *Cuda świętego Stanisława* [Miracles of Saint Stanislaus], ed. Zbigniew Perzanowski, trans. J. Pleziowa, Analecta Cracoviensia 11 (1979), 47–141. On the oldest collections of the miracles of St. Stanislaus, see Aleksandra Witkowska, "Trzynastowieczne miracula św. Stanisława biskupa krakowskiego, [The thirteenth-century miracula of St. Stanisław, the bishop of Krakow]" ead., *Sancti Miracula Peregrinationes*, 212–225.
16   VSMaior III, chap. 5, 397–398.
17   Maria Starnawska, "Dominikanie, św. Jacek i elewacja szczątków św. Stanisława przez biskupa Prandotę, [Dominicans, St. Jacek and the elevation of the remains of St. Stanisław by Bishop Prandota]" in *Mendykanci w średniowiecznym Krakowie*, eds. Krzysztof Ożóg, Tomasz Gałuszka, Anna Zajchowska (Kraków, 2008), 407–424.
18   VSMaior III, chap. 9, 412–414.
19   VSMaior III, chap. 46, 423–424.
20   VSMaior III, chap. 30, 414.

Third Book of the *Vita* include individuals whose nationality is not mentioned, but who have German names. A name alone is not enough to draw conclusions about ethnicity. Poles did sometimes assume German names, for example through family ties; and the other way around – Germans assumed Polish names, although this may have been rarer in the beginning.

In the 13th–14th centuries, as well as in later periods, there were many Germans living in Cracow and other Polish cities and who played a significant role in the economy and politics.[21] The cities also had a Polish population. In Cracow itself the Poles were a minority, but in the environs of the city they were a dominant force, both politically and in terms of numbers. This ethnic mosaic is reflected in descriptions of miracles by St. Stanislaus from the *Vita maior*.[22] In addition to the Germans, there are Poles presented as both the people who experience the miracles and as members of their families and witnesses. There are significantly more Poles. Yet what matters the most for us is the fact that the hagiographer is as positive about the Germans as he is about his compatriots.

Around 1320 the *Vita maior* of St. Stanislaus was rewritten in Cracow and became known from its first words as *Tradunt*.[23] What is important from our point of view is the fact that the positive information about Germans and Germany from the *Vita maior* is transferred unchanged into the rewritten version. Its author mentions Otto III's role at the Congress of Gniezno and the name of the country to which the emperor returns after the congress.[24] And he writes about everything that links Casimir the Restorer to that country.[25] Listing Stanislaus' miracles, the hagiographer mentions the German woman Adelaide and cites the scene in which the saint spoke to her in her mother

---

21 Jerzy Rajman, *Kraków. Zespół osadniczy. Proces lokacji. Mieszczanie do roku 1333* [Cracow. Settlement complex. Location process. Townsmen until 1333], Akademia Pedagogiczna im. Komisji Edukacji Narodowej w Krakowie. Prace Monograficzne 375 (Kraków, 2004), 344–350 and passim.

22 On the question of ethnicity in 13th century collections of miracles in Lesser Poland, see Grzegorz Pac, "Niemcy w trzynastowiecznych miraculach krakowskich, [Germans in the 13th-century Krakow miracula]" *Monarchia, społeczeństwo, tożsamość. Studia z dziejów średniowiecza*, eds. K. Gołąbek *et alii*], Warszawa, 2020, s. 431–451).

23 [Vita Tradunt] *Vita s. Stanislai*, Martini Galli Chronicon [...], ed. Joannes Vincentius Brandtkie (Varsaviae, 1824), 319–380. For more on this work, see Krzysztof Ożóg, *Kultura umysłowa w Krakowie w XIV wieku. Środowisko duchowieństwa świeckiego* [Intelectual Culture in Krakow in the 14th Century. The environment of secular clergy], Prace Komisji Historycznej. Polska Akademia Nauk. Oddział w Krakowie 49 (Wrocław, 1987), 97–99; Drelicharz, *Idea zjednoczenia królestwa*, 316–326; Węcowski, *Początki Polski w pamięci*, 88–91. I support the dating of the piece proposed by W. Drelicharz.

24 [Vita Tradunt] *Vita s. Stanislai*, 322–323.

25 [Vita Tradunt] *Vita s. Stanislai*, 323–324, 336.

tongue.[26] We need to bear in mind that although the hagiographer copied entire pages from the original, he does introduce some thoughtful changes. Some stemmed from his desire to improve the composition of the work, others are an expression of very clear ideological views. We should, therefore, conclude that if the author introduced elements into the original which shed positive light on the Germans, he did not find these elements disturbing. This is the least that can be said.

It is also worth looking at what is called the *Miracula s. Adalberti*, a collection that presents the saint's posthumous story.[27] It is part of a larger whole, never published and comprising the *Vita*, *Miracula*, and *Translatio* (*In partibus Germaniae*, BHL 43). The work originated just a few years before 1295, most likely in Gniezno.[28] It is part of a series of Polish hagiographic works with clear ideological-political connotations.[29] What is striking in it is the description of the events accompanying Otto III's arrival at the tomb of St. Adalbert.[30] In this description the anonymous author used Gallus Anonymous' chronicle, *Vita s. Stanislai minor* and *Vita s. Stanislai maior*, but he provides his own ideological interpretation of the Congress of Gniezno, featuring a thesis that St. Adalbert was the originator of the Polish crown. What is important from our point of view is the hagiographer's opinion that as a result of Boleslaus the Brave's coronation by Otto III, Polish dukes became independent from Roman kings. We can see in this a polemic with tendencies present at the time in Silesia, where political support was sought from the Roman king (Henry Probus' homage to Rudolf I)[31] and where political thought was developing accordingly (*Chronica Polonorum* also referred to as *Chronicon Polono-Silesiacum*).[32] The main reason why I have chosen this particular work is the following: the hagiographer states that after leaving Gniezno, the emperor returned home, thus leaving out the precise phrase "to Germany" found in the *Vita maior* of St. Stanislaus. If this omission had been deliberate, it would testify to the author's distancing

---

26 [Vita Tradunt] *Vita s. Stanislai*, chap. 24–25, 362–363.
27 *Miracula sancti Adalberti*, ed. Wojciech Kętrzyński, MPH 4, 221–238.
28 Drelicharz, *Idea zjednoczenia królestwa*, 249.
29 Przemysław Wiszewski, "Wokół wyobrażeń i propagandy władzy królewskiej Piastów, [Around the images and propaganda of the royal power of the Piast dynasty]" in *Proměna středovýchodní a vrcholného středověku*, eds. Martin Wihoda and Lukáš Reitinger (Brno, 2010), 416–483, here 458–460; Drelicharz, *Idea zjednoczenia królestwa*, 247–258.
30 *Miracula sancti Adalberti*, chap. 9, 235–237.
31 Jurek, "Plany koronacyjne Henryka Probusa," 16–17.
32 *Kronika polska*, 604–656. On the ideology expressed in the work, see Drelicharz, *Idea zjednoczenia królestwa*, 199–240; my point of view, Roman Michałowski, *Princeps fundator. Studium z dziejów kultury politycznej w Polsce X–XIII wieku*, [A study of the history of political culture in Poland in the 10th–13th centuries] 2nd ed. (Warszawa, 1993), 115–127.

himself from Germany. On the other hand – and this has to be very clearly pointed out – the *Miracula sancti Adalberti* lacks any other traces of aversion to the Germans, something so strong in those days among the Gniezno clergy, and emphatically evidenced by a 1285 letter from Archbishop Jakub Świnka to three Roman Curial cardinals.[33] Therefore, the omission in question may be of no significance.

Let us now focus on 13th–15th centuries hagiography from Lesser Poland. It makes up a substantial – given the conditions in the Middle Ages in Poland – corpus of texts, containing both *vitae* and *miracula*.

The protagonist of the *Life of St. Kinga*[34] (Kunigunda) – a work written in the 1320s following a commission from the Poor Clares of Stary Sącz – is a Hungarian princess who marries Boleslaus the Chaste, Duke of Sandomierz and later also of Cracow.[35] At the time he was undoubtedly the most powerful among the Polish dukes, ruling a province that made him the honorary leader of the Piasts. The anonymous author of the *Vita*, perhaps a Franciscan, of course was aware of the saint's foreign origins and her international family connections; moreover, he strongly emphasizes them. At the very beginning of his work he presents, with great panache, Kinga's genealogy,[36] beginning with her grandfather, King Andrew of Hungary, who married St. Hedwig's stepsister. His children from the marriage included a son Béla and a daughter St. Elizabeth. Béla, also King of Hungary, was the father of Kinga, whose mother was Mary, daughter of the Greek Emperor. The emperor came from the family of Emperor Nero, while Mary's mother came from the family of Catherine, the great saint, virgin and martyr. Apart from Kinga, Béla and Mary had many other children: Anna married the Duke of Croatia, Margaret became a Dominican nun, Constance married a Ruthenian prince and in those days many miracles happened through her intercession. Elizabeth was given in marriage to the Duke of Bavaria, while Yolanda – to the Duke of Greater Poland. The hagiographer adds that Béla and Mary's son Stephen had a daughter named Mary. She married King Charles of Sicily and their son was St. Louis. Another

---

33 *Codex diplomaticus Majoris Poloniae* 1 (Poznaniae, 1877), no. 616, 574–575. On Jakub Świnka's anti-German views, see Nowacki, "Arcybiskup Jakub Świnka,", 107–120.

34 *Vita sanctae Kyngae*, ed. Wojciech Kętrzyński, MPH 4, 682–731 (hereafter cited as VK). On this source, see Maria Helena Witkowska, "Vita sanctae Kyngae ducissae Cracoviensis jako źródło hagiograficzne, [Vita sanct. K. duc. as historicla source]" *Roczniki Humanistyczne* 10 (1961) no. 2, 41–162; Michalski, *Kobiety i świętość*, 48–53.

35 On Kinga, see Barbara Kowalskia, *Święta Kinga. Rzeczywistość i legenda. Studium źródłoznawcze* [Saint Kinga. Reality and legend. A source study] (Kraków, 2008).

36 VK, chap. 1, 683–685.

son, Coloman, Duke of Ruthenia, married Salomea, daughter of Leszek, Duke of Cracow.[37]

The author presents a very broad geographical panorama of his protagonist's family connections stretching from Sicily to Poland and from Bavaria to Ruthenia, and his description contains the names of rulers of various countries and peoples. The reasons why the hagiographer decided to compile such a list are clear: it was about explaining the sources of Kinga's sainthood. He saw them in the excellence of her family, manifested in holiness and secular power and dignity.[38] Hence the presence of such an abundance of saints as well as rulers, including Emperor Nero, as found in the genealogy. The very subject matter of the work or, to be more precise, the way of understanding it, prompted the author to think in terms of nationality.

A question arises: what place in this panorama of countries and nationalities is occupied by the Germans? The hagiographer is somewhat reticent to refer to this country. The name of Bavaria is mentioned, but there is no information about the origins of St. Hedwig and about the husband of St. Elizabeth. It is difficult to say whether these omissions hide the author's negative attitude towards the Germans, but this reticence should, nevertheless, be noted.

How is the question of nationality presented in the remaining chapters of the work? The pages of the *Vita* feature the names of nuns from the Stary Sącz convent. In addition to Polish names there are also German names, but whether there were German nuns in the convent remains unclear.[39] The author does not refer to nor does he comment on this. Elsewhere we find a reference to a sister named Elizabeth Hungara, who is most certainly a Hungarian.[40] In this case the context would indicate the hagiographer's positive attitude toward this nationality. The same opinion emerges from a cry of a demon which possessed

---

37   Not all genealogical facts given by the author of the *Vita* are true, see Witkowska, "Vita sanctae Kyngae," 119 with footnote 264 on pp. 119–120.

38   On the holy dynasties in Central Europe in the 13th–14th centuries, see Gábor Klaniczay, *Holy Rulers and Blessed Princesses. Dynastic Cults in Medieval Central Europe*, trans. Éva Pálmei (Cambridge, 2002), 195–294; Michalski, *Kobiety i świętość*, 164–180 (both also mention Saint Kinga). The question of holy dynasties in the high and late Middle Ages was tackled by André Vauchez, "'Beata stirps'. Sainteté et lignage en Occident aux XIIIᵉ et XIVᵉ siècles," *Famille et parenté dans l'Occident médiéval. Actes du Colloque de Paris (6–8 juin 1974) organisé par l'Ecole Pratique des Hautes Etudes (VIe Section) en collaboration avec le Collège de France et l'Ecole Française de Rome*, eds. Georges Duby and Jacques Le Goff, Collection de l'Ecole Française de Rome 30 (Roma,1977), 397–407; idem, *La sainteté en Occident aux derniers siècles du Moyen Age*, Bibliothèque des Ecoles françaises d'Athènes et de Rome 241, (Roma, 1981), 204–215, 256–272.

39   VK, chap. 20, 704.

40   VK, chap. 64, 730.

some poor wretch. When Kinga was approaching, the demon moaned: woe is me, the Hungarian is coming![41]

The subject matter of this paper leads inevitably to the question as to whether the author refers to Germans, calling them explicitly by this name. Indeed, he does, and – this has to be noted straightaway – the references are accompanied by a negative tone. At some point the hagiographer says that after the death of Leszek the Black, the Germans *hostiliter* seize the region of Sącz and with the help of some magnates build a burg. The princess goes there to restore peace and a knight named Peter shoots at her with a bow, nearly hitting her. The godmother of Peter – a Pole, as the context suggests – was Kinga.[42] Thus, the Germans not only are invaders but also try to corrupt the Poles. We know from other sources that these were troops of Henry Probus, a Piast duke, but for Kinga's hagiographer they were simply Germans (of course, the army of the ruler in question did include knights of this nationality).[43]

Worthy of note is also Chapter 59, which begins with the following statement: "One day, when the war waged by the godless was on the rise and when the Germans sought to create a rift in the monastery ..."[44] We do not know what 'the rift' in the Stary Sącz monastery intends to indicate, but there is no doubt that the hagiographer is offering a negative testimony about the Germans, whom, on the one hand, he accuses of trying to do great harm to the Poor Clares' convent and on the other he compares to some godless warmongers. In the course of his account, the author makes his intention more specific: the citizens – of the town of Stary Sącz, as we can imagine – thus Germans[45] invite in robbers who attacked the monastery and who only are forced to flee thanks to the saint's prayers.

The *Miracula of St. Kinga*,[46] which, as is often assumed, was written by an author other than that of the *Vita*, comes from 1329 and is based on earlier reports. A large majority of the individuals mentioned in the collection were

---

41   VK, chap. 37, 712.
42   VK, chap. 42, 717.
43   *Rocznik Traski*, [The Traska annal] ed. August Bielowski, MPH 2 (Lwów, 1872), 852; cf. Marek Barański, *Dominium sądeckie. Od książęcego okręgu grodowego do majątku klasztoru klarysek sądeckich* [The dominion of the Sącz region. From the princely castle district to the property of the convent of Poor Clares in Nowy Sącz] (Warsaw, 1992), 106.
44   VK, cap. 59, 724: "Quadam vice guerra impiorum increscente et Teutonis discidium claustro ordinare cupientibus".
45   On the ethnic relations in Stary Sącz, soon after the foundation, see Feliks Kiryk, "Dzieje miasta w okresie staropolskim," [The history of the town in the Old Polish period] in *Historia Starego Sącza od czasów najdawniejszych do 1939 roku*, ed. Henryk Barycz (Kraków, 1979), 45–113, at 49.
46   *Miracula sanctae Kyngae*, ed. Wojciech Kętrzyński, MPH 4, 732–744.

certainly Poles. This is evidenced by the names as well as other information about them. However, there are two entries almost certainly referring to Germans.[47] Both concern people living in Nowy Sącz – a town inhabited primarily by Germans.[48] But there are other arguments as well. Although several of the miraculously healed individuals have the Christian name of Margaret, the Margaret from Chapter 13 has a father with a German name, and in both cases the witnesses include people with German and Christian names, but no people with Polish names.

Regardless of their nationality, people presented in the analyzed source act more or less in the same manner and therefore it is impossible to draw on this basis any conclusions about the hagiographer's national stereotypes. What can be said for certain is that in the hagiographer's view, Kinga's miraculous powers affected people regardless of their nationality – Poles, Germans and Hungarians. There is an interesting piece of information in Chapter 9, according to which acknowledging that St. Kinga came from the royal family of the Hungarian nation was a prerequisite for experiencing a miracle from her.[49] We can see in this the author's highly positive attitude to the nation in question. However, elsewhere the hagiographer cites an anecdote which does not show the Hungarians in a good light.[50]

The *Life of St. Salomea* in its present form is a kind of palimpsest.[51] The *vita* written in the second half of the 13th century was mixed with a 14th-century hagiographic legend. It is not always easy to separate the earlier text from the later one. However, it is assumed that the *miracula* forming part of the *Vita* were written down in their original form in the 13th century (beginning in 1269), as is evidenced by the dates of the various miracles. From the entire

---

47   *Miracula sanctae Kyngae*, chap. 9, 734–735; chap. 13, 736.
48   *Dzieje miasta Nowego Sącza* 1 [History of the town Nowy Sącz], ed. Feliks Kiryk (Warszawa-Kraków, 1992), 91–92.
49   *Miracula sanctae Kyngae*, chap. 9, 734. I comment on this fragment in an article, Roman Michałowski, "Wizja Kingi, księżnej krakowskiej. Przyczynek do historii świętych rodzin w średniowieczu," [The vision of Kinga, Duchess of Krakow. Contribution to the history of holy families in the Middle Ages] in *Księga. Teksty o świecie średniowiecznym ofiarowane Hannie Zaremskiej*, ed. Halina Manikowska (Warszawa, 2018), 201–216.
50   *Miracula sanctae Kyngae*, chap. 20, 741–742.
51   *Vita sanctae Salomeae reginae Haliciensis*, ed. Wojciech Kętrzyński, MPH 4, 770–796, *post mortem* miracles 784–796. On this *vita*, see Brygida Kürbisówna, "Żywot bł. Salomei jako źródło historyczne," [Life of Bl. Salomea as a historical source] in *Studia historica. W 35-lecie pracy naukowej Henryka Łowmiańskiego*, ed. Aleksander Gieysztor et al. (Warszawa, 1958), 145–165. St. Salomea and her early cult have been discussed recently by Elżbieta Sander, *Błogosławiona Salomea i klasztory klarysek w Zawichoście, Skale i Krakowie do końca XV wieku* [Blessed Salome and the convents of the Poor Clares in Zawichost, Skala and Kraków until the end of the 15th century] (Kraków, 2015), 41–68.

work it is only those miracles which attract our attention. The description of the miracles mentions primarily Poles. In some cases, however, we are right to assume that the individuals in question – for example, Gertrude and her husband Herman, (the latter being a citizen of Cracow) – are German.[52] This is suggested by the German names of both spouses and the fact that they live in a city that was predominantly German. In one case we can be certain of this nationality: a woman who experiences a miracle is referred to by the hagiographer as German.[53] These people behave – let us put it this way – normally, and are not different from the more numerous Poles found in the *miracula* of St. Salomea.

From the point of view of source studies, we are dealing with a quite similar situation in the case of the *Life of St. Hyacinth*.[54] In its present form the work comes from the mid-14th century, but it contains a list of miracles written down in the second half of the previous century. The *Vita* was written by Stanisław, a Polish Dominican from the Cracow monastery. Polishness has a great significance for the hagiographer. He begins his work by saying that through St. Hyacinth the Light of God came to the Poles, and elsewhere says emphatically that the saint was a Pole and that, sent by St. Dominic, he had brought the Dominican Order to his homeland. Others sent with St. Hyacinth were Blessed Ceslaus and a German named Herman, who, however, did not reach Poland, but remained in Friesach. Herman, like his two companions, a member of the entourage of Bishop Ivo of Cracow, is presented in a positive context and the fact that he stayed in Germany does not seem to be a moral charge against him. That he wanted to concentrate on working in his homeland was understandable.

There are no more explicit references to the Germans in the work. The descriptions of miracles feature German names as well as Cracow burghers. However, these facts are not sufficient for us to be able to say definitely that a given individual was a German.[55] Worthy of note is the following point. The *vita* was written by a Pole from a Polish monastery located in a German city,

---

52 *Vita sanctae Salomeae*, chap. 7, art. 32, 794–795.
53 *Vita sanctae Salomeae*, chap. 7, art. 20, 791.
54 *De Vita et miraculis sancti Iacchonis (Hyacinthi) ordinis fratrum praedicatorum*, ed. L. Ćwikliński, MPH 4, 818–903. On St. Hyacinth, his early cult and sources for these topics, see Raymond J. "La vie de s. Hyacinthe du lecteur Stanislas envisagée comme source historique," *Archivum Fratrum Praedicatorum* 27 (1957), 5–38; *Święty Jacek Odrowąż. Studia i źródła*, [Saint Jacek Odrowaz. Studies and Sources] ed. Marek Zdanek, Studia Dominikańskiego Instytutu Historycznego w Krakowie 2 (Kraków, 2007); Anna Zajchowska, "Medieval Hagiography of St Hyacinth," *Les saints et leur culte*, 195–209.
55 Pac, "Niemcy w trzynastowiecznych miraculach krakowskich".

indeed in its very heart, just one hundred meters from the Main Market Square. It contains no trace of aversion to Germans.

Let us look at the collections of miracles compiled in 15th century Cracow.[56] As we read them, we come to the same conclusions as when we read the 13th–14th centuries texts mentioned earlier. Germans are rarely mentioned there as those who experience miracles. They appear in the same context as Poles, with the hagiographers treating both with the same sympathy.[57] It is difficult to speak of any national stereotypes emerging from the analyzed descriptions of miracles. The hagiographer described the Germans and the Poles in the same fashion – as pious people turning trustingly to the saint for help.

What deserves a separate discussion are the miracles of St. Hyacinth from the late 15th century.[58] Two out of the seven entries mention Germans.[59] We do not have to make guesses as to their nationality; the authors of the entries mention it explicitly. In both cases the question is about liberating the persons in question from fetters, with one of them being described as a fratricide. A question arises as to whether the fact that the two Germans – or at least one of them – being presented as criminals should not be regarded as a manifestation of negative national stereotypes. Such a conclusion would be wrong. First of all, the analyzed entries provide an account of events that did indeed take place. Germans in fetters are not a product of human imagination; such people were present in Cracow at that time, and in this case, they came to the local Dominican monastery to provide an account of the miracle. Incidentally, the author of the first entry was German himself, as is suggested by a note in the margin commenting on the entry. It was written by the author of the subsequent entries.

The 15th century brought two lives of saints that were significant for the Poles of that time. The author of both was Jan Długosz. The great historiographer

---

56 Aleksandra Witkowska, "Zbiory krakowskich miracula z XV i początku XVI wieku," [Collections of Krakow miracula from the 15th and early 16th centuries] (1st ed., 1984), in ead., *Sancti Miracula Peregrinationes*, 226–240; ead., *Kulty pątnicze piętnastowiecznego Krakowa* [Pilgrimage cults of 15th-century Krakow], Towarzystwo Naukowe Katolickiego Uniwersytetu Lubelskiego. Instytut Geografii Historycznej Kościoła w Polsce. Biblioteka Historii Społeczno-Religijnej 3 (Lublin, 1984).

57 E.g. *Miracula venerabilis patris Prandothe, episcopi Cracoviensis*, ed. Wojciech Kętrzyński, MPH 4, chap. 32, 476; *Miracula s. Iohannis Cantii*, ed. Wojciech Kętrzyński, MPH 6 (Kraków, 1893), chap. 16, 487.

58 Anna Zajchowska and Maciej Zdanek, "Mirakula świętego Jacka z lat 1488–1500. Edycja krytyczna, [Miracle of Saint Jack from 1488–1500. Critical edition]" *Studia Źródłoznawcze* 46 (2009), 95–105.

59 Ibid., chap. 3 and 5; 102, 103.

wrote a *Life of St. Stanislaus*⁶⁰ and a *Life of St. Kinga*.⁶¹ These texts contribute little, if anything at all, to the present analysis. They are literary adaptations of earlier works. There is some factographic amplification, but it is of no significance to us, as it almost never concerns Germany and the Germans. At most, we can point to a fragment in the *Life of St. Kinga*, where its author writes about the misfortunes that befell Poland after the murder of St. Stanislaus. The country fell victim to raids by the Bohemians, Saxons, Teutonic Knights and Germans.⁶² It is difficult to say whether any anti-German prejudice emerges from this sentence or whether it is simply an account of the historical reality. Długosz took the anti-German fragments from a 14th century *Vita s. Kingae*, without changing their meaning, as was the case with the meaning of the descriptions of miracles which have Germans as their protagonists.

Let us try to draw some conclusions from the material presented here. The Germans and Germanness appear in Polish hagiographic sources in three roles: as rulers, as a country, and as people living in Poland. Some of the works tackle key questions from Poland's history, so it is not surprising that Otto III occupies such a prominent place in them, so closely linked was he with Poland's history and so highly regarded in the Polish tradition. Germany as a country appears mainly in a historical aspect, with regard to the emperor in question and, above all, to Casimir the Restorer. References to the past were also an opportunity to formulate political theses concerning the present and this is the context in which Roman kings appear and the kingdom they symbolize. Finally, Germans as ordinary people were, first of all, settlers living in Poland.

All in all, however, the Germans and Germanness occupy limited space in Polish medieval hagiography. This is by no means obvious, considering the fact that in the second half of the 13th and first half of the following century the relations between a part of the Polish population and settlers from the West were sometimes tense.⁶³ A classic example here is Archbishop Jakub Świnka's 1285 letter to three Roman Curial cardinals – extensively commented on in the literature on the subject – in which the archbishop presents the Germans as

---

60   *Vita sanctissimi Stanislai episcopi Cracoviensis*, eds. Ignatius Polkowski and Żegota Pauli, *Joannis Dlugossii senioris canonici Cacoviensis Opera* 1 (Cracoviae, 1887), 1–181.
61   *Vita beatae Kunegundis*, Joannis Dlugossii senioris canonici Cacoviensis Opera, 183–342.
62   *Vita beatae Kunegundis*, chap. 11, 228.
63   Benedykt Zientara, "Konflikty narodowościowe na pograniczu niemiecko-słowiańskim w XIII–XIV wieku i ich zasięg społeczny," [National conflicts on the German-Slavic border in the 13th–14th centuries and their social scope] *Przegląd Historyczny* 59 (1968), 197–212; Tomasz Jurek, "Polska droga do korony królewskiej 1295–1300–1320," [Polish road to the royal crown 1295–1300–1320] *Proměna středovýchodní a vrcholného středověku*, 139–191, here 151–152; toning this down: Gawlas, "'Verus heres'. Z badań," 77–104.

dangerous to Poland and Polishness.[64] We can, of course, argue that the source in question represents the point of view of the clergy or, to be more precise, its elite, but hagiographic works were written precisely by clergymen and by no means rank-and-file clergymen at that. On the other hand, we know that Jakub Świnka's letter is not the only such testimony. We cannot fail to mention the *Annals of the Poznań Chapter*, which, under the year 1309, contain an accusation that the Germans want to exterminate the entire Polish nation.[65] The list of examples is extensive.

Another conclusion is as follows: sometimes a negative opinion about the Germans is not present although it could be expected. I mean here, especially, the *Miracula s. Adalberti*. After all, it is a work written in Gniezno at the same time as Jakub Świnka's letter. And yet the *Miracula s. Adalberti* contains no unequivocal traces of resentment towards the Germans. On the contrary – the author refers to the figure of Otto III and presents him in a very positive light. He attributes to the emperor a great role as someone who glorified Boleslaus the Brave and with him Poland as well. It was not only the view of this particular hagiographer, but also that of Wincenty of Kielcza, not to mention the classic of medieval Polish historiography, Gallus Anonymous. Jakub Świnka's letter provides evidence – if evidence is needed at all – that the empire was unequivocally associated with Germany. This, however, did not affect the opinion of the author of the *Miracula s. Adalberti* about the emperor. Of course, as we remember that his thesis was that Poland was independent of the Roman kings, but this was a political view and not a national stereotype.

Despite the relative scarcity of the available source material, we can say something about the attitude of hagiographers to the German state and the German country as well as the Germans. I have just mentioned the positive opinion about Otto III; let me also add that in the context of Casimir the Restorer's case, we see Wincenty of Kielcza's approval of Germany and of its ruler. "Ordinary" Germans mentioned in the descriptions of miracles are presented sympathetically, as pious people who trust in God.

As a matter of fact, there is only one work in which a negative opinion seems to prevail. I mean here the *Life of St. Kinga*. It is not difficult to explain why. We are dealing here with a Polish dynastic monastery, which, just like the entire region of Sącz, supported Ladislaus the Elbow-High in his fight to take control of Lesser Poland, first in his conflict with the Premyslids and then with

---

64   *Codex diplomaticus Majoris Poloniae* 1, no. 616, 574–575.
65   *Rocznik kapituły poznańskiej* [The Annals oft he Poznan chapter], ed. Brygida Kürbis, Roczniki wielkopolskie. MPH. series nova 6 (Warsaw, 1962), 55.

Cracow.[66] At the time when the analysed work was written, the conflict with the Cracow townsmen, the apogee of which came with the rebellion of *Vogt* (*advocatus*) Albert, was still fresh and painful in people's memory.[67] Even if initially social and not national,[68] the conflict was soon defined as national by Ladislaus' supporters, with the ruler representing the Polish, and Cracow the German side. However, there was no automatism here. In *Tradunt*, the *Life of St. Stanislaus*, which originated in the same atmosphere, the hagiographer sided with Ladislaus' cause and yet there are no anti-German elements in the work.

A question arises as to the reasons behind the discrepancy between the anti-German attitude of some part of the Polish elites, including ecclesiastical elites, and the usually positive attitude of Polish hagiographers about Germans and Germanness. This contradiction can be explained as follows: the Germans in Polish hagiography are either protagonists of events from a distant past, protagonists who played a positive role in Poland's history, or the faithful gathering around the tombs of Polish saints, piously asking for their intercession. The authors of the works in question could feel nothing but sympathy for both groups.

I have pointed out that in medieval Poland the significance of the cult of saints and, consequently, of hagiographic writing was markedly smaller than in other countries of Europe – at least Western Europe – at the time. It could be described as a Polish specificity. The question is: was Polish hagiography's positive attitude to an otherwise hated nationality also uniquely Polish? I will explore this in the future.

66 Barański, *Dominium sądeckie*, 122–123.
67 An overview of the literature concerning the rebellion of Vogt Albert is provided by Anna Grabowska, "Bunt wójta Alberta w historiografii polskiej," [The rebellion of mayor Albert in Polish historiography] in *Bunt wójta Alberta: Kraków i Opole we wzajemnych związkach w XIV wieku*, ed. Jerzy Rajman, Annales Universitatis Paedagogicae Cracoviensis. Studia Historica 13 (Kraków, 2013), 19–31.
68 Sławomir Gawlas, *O kształt zjednoczonego Królestwa. Niemieckie władztwo terytorialne a geneza społeczno-ustrojowej Polski* [For the shape of a united kingdom. German territorial sovereignty and the genesis of Poland's social and political system], Res humanae. Studia 1, 2nd ed. (Warsaw, 2000), 94.

PART 3

German Views Regarding Poles in the Middle Ages – Hagiographical, Historiographical and Medieval German Literature Sources

CHAPTER 9

Poland and the Poles in Early and High Medieval German Historiography

Volker Scior

Questions concerning the perceptions of neighbors have been studied multiple times in recent years. Moreover, for the Early and High Middle Ages (the era which is the focus in this paper), there are already some studies at hand. They have varying topics, of course. As far as the Frankish or German realm is concerned, the focus has mainly been on the perceptions of northern Europe like Denmark, Norway and Sweden,[1] as well as on the western Frankish kingdom and France in the West[2] or the Slavs in the East.[3] When in the following what we call "Poland" and "the Poles" are put in the centre of our focus, then this refers more to the volume's title than it can be reasonably derived from a general meaning of Poland and its inhabitants in contemporary historiography. Regarding the sources, it can be said here at the beginning that terms like *Polani* or *Polonia* are seldomly found in the sources.[4] It can be said as well that Slavs in general are the focus in some texts, but in the end only a very few sources tell us about what we call Poland or the Poles in later times. This paper's topic thus lacks a significant base of sources. That is why in the following only a very few representations in historiography can be sketched. Thus, the paper is limited to a few texts from the 11th and 12th centuries in which Slavs and especially 'Poles' are described at all. The main focus is on Thietmar of Merseburg, who wrote his chronicle in 1018, Adam of Bremen (1075/80), and Helmold of Bosau (1168/1172). Before turning to these sources, it is necessary to make some general theoretical and methodological statements.

---

1 Cf. Volker Scior, *Das Eigene und das Fremde. Identität und Fremdheit in den Chroniken Adams von Bremen, Helmolds von Bosau und Arnolds von Lübeck* (Berlin, 2002); David Fraesdorff, *Der barbarische Norden. Vorstellungen und Fremdheitskategorien bei Rimbert, Thietmar von Merseburg, Adam von Bremen und Helmold von Bosau* (Berlin, 2004).
2 For the Late Middle Ages cf. e.g. Martin Kintzinger, *Westbindungen im spätmittelalterlichen Europa. Auswärtige Politik zwischen dem Reich, Frankreich, Burgund und England in der Regierungszeit Kaiser Sigmunds* (Stuttgart, 2000).
3 Cf. e.g. Thomas Wünsch, *Deutsche und Slawen im Mittelalter. Beziehungen zu Tschechen, Polen, Südslawen und Russen* (München, 2008).
4 This becomes clear very quickly when one searches the digital MGH (www.dmgh.de).

The history of perceptions as a field of historical science deals to a great extent with images of foreigners as present in past historical periods. After the theoretical and methodological foundation within medieval studies, which began in 1980s, the perspective on medieval texts shifted in a general way. By today, it can be regarded as undisputed that the so-called value of a historical source not only depends on its realistic content, which derives from the possibility of reconstructing the 'reality' behind the text, but also from the author's images and ideas as expressed in a medieval text. The effect has been a shift of the historians' focus from the descriptions to the describers, from the representations to the authors and the conditions of text production.[5] It is especially historiographic texts which are suitable for this approach. After the national-historical approaches of earlier times, the interdisciplinary research of clichés, stereotypes, and contemporary knowledge has shown clearly how strong the perspectives on foreign people were defined by old images and traditional knowledge in the sense of prejudices, and how slowly such 'knowledge' about other people could be changed. Also aside from imagological studies, the research by medievalists about 'the other(ness)' is closely related to the aforementioned approaches of a history of images, ideas, and perceptions.[6]

---

5   Cf. Hans-Werner Goetz, *Vorstellungsgeschichte. Gesammelte Schriften zu Wahrnehmungen, Deutungen und Vorstellungen im Mittelalter*, eds. Anna Aurast, Simon Elling, and Bele Freudenberg (Bochum, 2007); cf. earlier and basic for later reflections: Michael Harbsmeier, "Reisebeschreibungen als mentalitätsgeschichtliche Quellen: Überlegungen zu einer historisch-anthropologischen Untersuchung frühneuzeitlicher deutscher Reisebeschreibungen," in *Reiseberichte als Quellen europäischer Kulturgeschichte. Aufgaben und Möglichkeiten der historischen Reiseforschung*, eds. Antoni Mączak and Hans Jürgen Teuteberg, Wolfenbütteler Forschungen 21 (Wolfenbüttel, 1982), 1–31; Bernd Thum, "Frühformen des Umgangs mit 'Fremdem' und 'Fremden' in der Literatur des Hochmittelalters. Der 'Parzival' Wolframs von Eschenbach als Beispiel," in *Das Mittelalter – Unsere Fremde Vergangenheit*, eds. Joachim Kuolt, Harald Kleinschmidt and Peter Dinzelbacher (Stuttgart, 1990), 315–352, here 317: "Die Definition des 'Fremden' beinhaltet also immer auch eine offene oder verschwiegene Definition des 'Eigenen'".

6   Cf. besides the literature in note 5 (above): Christian Lübke, *Fremde im östlichen Europa. Von Gesellschaften ohne Staat zu verstaatlichten Gesellschaften (9.–11. Jahrhundert)*, Ostmitteleuropa in Vergangenheit und Gegenwart 23 (Köln-Weimar-Wien, 2001); Hans-Henning Kortüm, "Advena sum apud te et peregrinus. Fremdheit als Strukturelement mittelalterlicher conditio humana," in *Exil, Fremdheit und Ausgrenzung in Mittelalter und früher Neuzeit*, eds. Andreas Bihrer, Sven Limbeck and Paul Gerhard Schmidt, Identitäten u. Alteritäten 4 (Würzburg, 2000), 115–135; Marina Münkler, *Erfahrung des Fremden. Die Beschreibung Ostasiens in den Augenzeugenberichten des 13. und 14. Jahrhunderts* (Berlin, 2000); Marina Münkler/Werner Röcke, "Der ordo-Gedanke und die Hermeneutik der Fremde im Mittelalter: Die Auseinandersetzung mit den monströsen Völkern des Erdrandes," in *Die Herausforderung durch das Fremde*, ed. Herfried Münkler (Berlin, 1998), 701–766; *The Stranger in Medieval Society*, eds. F.R.P. Akehurst and Stephanie Cain Van D'Elden, Medieval

Already the interests of a medieval author as revealed in his descriptions determine his representations, for example, of the characteristics or the 'typical' behavior of neighbors. Furthermore, the medieval author's knowledge about foreign neighbors, coming from written sources, oral accounts, or sometimes as an eyewitness himself, form his descriptions. Besides, his ideas of certain values determine his perspective on foreigners or other people. From these criteria which determine the perception, one can reconstruct the author's ideas or imagined images of neighbors – not, of course, their factual behavior. Thus, studies in the field of the history of perception show that texts about others and foreigners often tell us less about these people than about the author and his own ideas. The significant number of studies in the history of mentalities in medieval travel literature has shown that as well. Specific occasions for writing, the *causae scribendi* and *legendi*, the historic-political situations at the time of the writing time, the the principal of a text – all these elements influence the works.[7] One effect is that research has come to the understanding that there is a need for detailed case studies in order to examine all the elements which are characteristic of an author and his work. This is, of course, not possible in a very short paper such as this.

With reference to early and high medieval perspectives on Poland and the Poles in Frankish-German historiography, the chronicle of bishop Thietmar of Merseburg is essential. Thietmar has been called one of the most interesting figures of the German High Middle Ages.[8] His work is very special in different ways, and he cannot be categorized easily in the long row of historiographers in this époque, nor can his chronicle, which was written between 1012 and 1018 and in great part seems to fit the genre of medieval chronicles.[9] His ideas of the

---

Cultures 12 (Minneapolis, 1998); *Fremdheit und Reisen im Mittelalter*, eds. Irene Erfen and Karl-Heinz Spieß (Stuttgart, 1997); Felicitas Schmieder, *Europa und die Fremden. Die Mongolen im Urteil des Abendlandes vom 13. bis in das 15. Jahrhundert* (Sigmaringen, 1994); *Der Umgang mit dem Fremden in der Vormoderne. Studien zur Akkulturation in Bildungshistorischer Sicht*, eds. Christoph Lüth, Rudolf W. Keck, and Erhard Wiersing, Beiträge zur Historischen Bildungsforschung 17 (Köln-Weimar-Wien, 1997), 155–193.

7   For a theoretical and methodological reason see Scior, *Das Eigene und das Fremde*.
8   Hans-Werner Goetz, "Die Slawen in der Wahrnehmung Thietmars von Merseburg zu Beginn des 11. Jahrhunderts," *Letopis. Zeitschrift für sorbische Sprache, Geschichte und Kultur* 2 (2015), 103–118, here 103.
9   Thietmar von Merseburg, *Chronicon*, ed. Robert Holtzmann, MGH SSrG N.S. 9 (Berlin, 1955); in German: ed. Werner Trillmich, FSGA 9 (Darmstadt, 1957). On the manuscripts, cf. Klaus Nass, *Die Reichschronik des Annalista Saxo und die sächsische Geschichtsschreibung im 12. Jahrhundert*, Schriften der MGH 41 (Hannover, 1996), 143–178. Cf. now also Volker Scior, "Der menschliche Körper und seine Grenzen. Die Chronik Thietmars von Merseburg in körpergeschichtlicher Perspektive," in *Historiographie der Grenzwelten. Thietmar von Merseburg (975/6–01.12.1018)*, ed. Dirk Jäckel (Studien zur Vormoderne 3), (Berlin, 2021–forthcoming).

Slavi have already been studied by others.[10] Often in focus have been especially the relations and military conflicts between German, Polish, and Bohemian kings. There are several reasons for the fact that Slavs play an important role in Thietmar's ideas. One of the most important is that Thietmar himself had personal contacts with Slavs.[11] On his father's as well as on his mother's side, he was of a high noble lineage and became bishop of Merseburg in 1009 – which was the smallest diocese in the whole Ottonian realm. Its inhabitants were mainly Slavs who had not yet been entirely Christianized. That was, briefly put, the situation in Thietmar's episcopal see when he was consecrated bishop.[12] He did not, like other medieval historiographers, write about foreign people he only knew from oral stories or from literature. Instead we know that he had several personal contacts with Slavs. The seat of Thietmar's family, the counts of Walbeck, was only some 50 kilometers away from the river Elbe, the border with the Slavs.[13] Thietmar had contacts with Slavs very early in his life. When he was only eight years old, the Slavs east of the river rejected Christianity and returned to their old polytheistic religion.[14] Thietmar and his family witnessed these events, and even if one must not psychologize these facts from a modern point of view, it is still hard to believe that the chronicler would have stayed completely unimpressed by these experiences. His father, who had married a daughter of the well regarded house of the counts of Stade, was one of the most important people in the entourage of king Otto II until his death in 991 (when Thietmar himself was sixteen), and he had participated in several military actions against the Slavs in 'Poland'.[15] By that time, Thietmar had been educated in the famous cathedral school in Magdeburg which was also attended by nobles from Slavic regions.[16] Here, Thietmar must have gained a

---

10 Cf. David Fraesdorff, *Der barbarische Norden*; Goetz, "Die Slawen in der Wahrnehmung Thietmars"; Karlheinz Hengst, "Thietmar und die Slawen," in *Thietmars Welt. Ein Merseburger Bischof schreibt Geschichte, Ausstellungskatalog*, eds. Axel v. Campenhausen, H. Kunde et al. (Petersberg/Fulda, 2018), 287–305; cf. upcoming: Volker Scior, Thietmar von Merseburg und die Slawen, in *Thietmar von Merseburg zwischen Pfalzen, Burgen und Federkiel. Palatium. Studien zur Pfalzenforschung in Sachsen-Anhalt*, ed. Stephan Freund (Regensburg, 2020).

11 To these aspects see the introduction of the chronicle in the FSGA (note 9, above) as well as Goetz, "Die Slawen in der Wahrnehmung Thietmars," 103–108 with further literature, and Hengst, "Thietmar und die Slawen," esp. 289–291.

12 Hengst, "Thietmar und die Slawen," 287–288; Goetz, "Die Slawen in der Wahrnehmung Thietmars," 103.

13 Hengst, "Thietmar und die Slawen," 289.

14 Goetz, "Die Slawen in der Wahrnehmung Thietmars," 108.

15 Hengst, "Thietmar und die Slawen," 289.

16 Ibid.

certain familiarity with the *lingua Slavica missionarica*. Even if it is uncertain how far knowledge of the Slavic languages reached, it is striking that Thietmar used many Slavic names and expressions in his chronicle even though he did not have to. At the very least he must have had a basic conversancy with the language.

Regarding the chronicle, one can say that Thietmar uses the term "Slavi" as a general term for the inhabitants of those regions between the Elbe and Oder that were claimed by the German kings.[17] The term *Slavi* does not mean 'Slavic speaking people'.[18] Still, in Thietmar's eyes the Slavic regions were united by a common language.[19] He often explains the meaning of Slavic names.[20] The name *Dobrawa* of the Bohemian wife of Duke Mieszko of Poland, for example, meant *Slavonice* 'the good' – and Thietmar emphasises that her character was as good as her name since she influenced her husband to be baptized.[21] Concerning the Slavic language, Thietmar regards the whole area inhabited by Slavs as a unified whole.[22] It is, however, striking that this unifying characteristic is bound to the language. If one regards the (few) passages in which Thietmar explicitly writes '*Slavi*' and does not mention the language, he is always dealing with the regions and people between the Elbe and Oder.[23] Bohemians, Poles and Russians are not once called *Slavi* explicitly. Thus, for Thietmar, there is no political-ethnical unity of the Slavic people. Russia and the Russians, but also Poland and Bohemia and their inhabitants are always called *Ruzzi*, *Polani* oder *Bohemi*, not once *Slavi*.

Thietmar's reports are concentrated on the neighbors' noble classes. The non-noble people are not referred to at all. His historiographic view is concentrated only on the nobles and elites of Poland, and he does not attend to the other groups in the society. His view of the nobles is mostly, but not always, negative. He describes the Polish nobility as being able to enter into a contract or military alliance with the German kings.[24] But he reproves Duke Mieszko I, since his wedding was not approved by church authorities;[25] and he criticizes Mieszko's successor, Boleslaw I Chobry, for many reasons.[26] He says he is sly

---

17 Goetz, "Die Slawen in der Wahrnehmung Thietmars," 109.
18 Ibid.
19 Ibid.
20 Hengst, "Thietmar und die Slawen," 289.
21 Goetz, "Die Slawen in der Wahrnehmung Thietmars," 109.
22 Ibid., 108–110 with a discussion of further examples from the text.
23 Ibid., 109.
24 Hengst, "Thietmar und die Slawen," 293–296.
25 Ibid., 293.
26 Fraesdorff, *Der barbarische Norden*, 248–249, with examples.

like a fox and characterizes him very negatively with stereotypes.[27] It can be assumed that the reason for this negative judgment of Boleslaw lies in the fact that he was successful in avoiding a political fragmentation of the Polish realm, a unity which then led to conflicts with the Frankish-German kingdom.[28] Thietmar felt quite closely connected to this kingdom. His closeness to the emperors can be read from his text, allowing us to recognize his identification with the German *regnum*.[29] This is one point where we can see that the historiographer's own identity with certain communities and groups determined what he valued positively or negatively. In Thietmar's eyes, Boleslaw was an all-time betrayer.

While Thietmar always thinks in religious terms and judges the Slavic heathens very negatively, this is not the case in the passages about the Poles, since their nobles had become Christian – in the author's view 'already Christianized', since it was only a question of time until the whole world would be Christianized. To the Christian author it seemed to be the worst of cases; heathens, who in earlier times had been under the influence of the Frankish-German kingdom, now fought in the army of Henry II against the Christian Polish army.[30] On the one hand, those passages show that Thietmar regrets the loss of the emperor's influence over these people; on the other hand they show that a Christian ruler should not have heathen allies.[31] As much as Thietmar defends the military campaigns of Henry II against the (Christian) duke of Poland, Boleslaw, he does not endorse at all the alliance of the emperor with the heathen *Liutici*.[32] The political reasons that make the alliance with the heathens advantageous do not overrule his religious objections to this.

Compared to historiographical accounts from others, Thietmar's reports about the Polish dukes and nobility, about alliances and wedding policies, are quite comprehensive. In this point, he is an exception. Particularly Boleslaw I Chrobry and Mieszko are mentioned in other sources,[33] but not in detail. Other

27   Cf. Thietmar of Merseburg, IV, 58.
28   Hengst, "Thietmar und die Slawen," 293–296.
29   Cf. on this topic: Wolfgang Eggert and Barbara Pätzold, *Wir-Gefühl und regnum Saxonum bei frühmittelalterlichen Geschichtsschreibern*, Forschungen zur mittelalterlichen Geschichte 31 (Weimar, 1984), 98–119, 273–275.
30   Goetz, "Die Slawen in der Wahrnehmung Thietmars," 116.
31   Goetz, "Die Slawen in der Wahrnehmung Thietmars," 116; Fraesdorff, *Der barbarische Norden*, 248–250.
32   Goetz, "Die Slawen in der Wahrnehmung Thietmars," 116.
33   *Annales Quedlinburgenses*, ed. Martina Giese, MGH SSrG 72 (Hannover, 2004), 518: Boleslaw als *dux Poloniae*. Cf. Also *Annales Magdeburgenses a. 1148*, ed. Georg Heinrich Pertz, MGH SS 16 (Hannover, 1859), 190: "Magdeburgensis archiepiscopus Fridericus et quidam alii principes Saxoniae Polonicis ducibus Bolizlavo et Meseconi in epiphania

texts from the 11th and 12th centuries report about single local events or settlements, for example the small grouping of houses at Usch, which was *in extremis Poloniorum finibus* and which is mentioned only because Bishop Otto I of Bamberg passed through it on his way to Gnesen.[34] In other texts in a very general manner Poles and Bohemians are counted among the Slavic inhabitants of certain regions.[35] In most cases, these 'reports' are no more than a short reference or a specific statement. Still, they prove that other historiographers had at least some idea of the Poles and Poland.[36] Generally one can say that Poland and the Poles are mentioned only when they play some role for other people or events which in fact were of interest for the Frankish or German historiographers, for example when St. Adalbert performed baptisms there.[37] Actually, there is no further information about Poland from contemporary sources. 'Poland' and the 'Polish peoples' hardly come to the minds of Frankish-German historiographers.

That is the reason why only a very few other texts tell us something about these regions. One of them is what is called 'the church history' of Hamburg which was written by the cathedral scholaster Adam of Bremen in the last quarter of the 11th century.[38] Adam, whose geographical and ethnographical passages are very famous and who reports in detail about the North of Europe,[39] also mentions the Poles in some sentences. He counts them among the Slavs close to

---

Domini occurrentes in Crusawice fedus amicicie cum eis inierunt. Ibi etiam marchio Otto, filius marchionis Adalberti, sororem Polonicorum principum sibi in legitimum matrimonium copulandam suscepit". Cf. also Wipo: *Wiponis Opera*, in MGH SSrG 61, ed. Harry Bresslau, (Hannover, 1915), cc. 9 and 29; pp. 31sq and 48; and Hermann of Reichenau: *Herimanni Augiensis chronicon a. 1–1054* in MGH SS 5, ed. Georg Heinrich Pertz, ad a. 1004 and 1032, 118 and 121.

34 *Vita of Bishop Otto I. of Bamberg*, ed. Jürgen Petersohn, MGH SSrG 71 (Hannover, 1999), 112 with note 10.

35 *Vita Heinrici regis*, ed. Marcus Stumpf, MGH SSrG 69 (Hannover, 1999), 234: "universis in id ipsum consentientibus Poloniam et Boemiam ceterasque Sclavorum adiacentes regiones".

36 Cf. e.g. *Annalista Saxo ad anno 1021*, ed. Georg Waitz, MGH SS 6 (Hannover, 1844), 675.

37 *Miracula s. Adalberti*, ed. MGH SS 4 (Hannover, 1841), 614: "sanctus Adalbertus in Polonia baptizaverat, cum illuc advenisset pro filia ducis Polonie".

38 Adam of Bremen, *Gesta Hammaburgensis Ecclesiae Pontificum*, ed. Bernhard Schmeidler, MGH SSrG 2 (Hannover-Leipzig, 1917; repr. 1993); Adam of Bremen, *Gesta Hammaburgensis Ecclesiae Pontificum*, ed. Werner Trillmich, FSGA 11, 7th ed. (Darmstadt, 2000), 137–499 (with an epilogue by Volker Scior, 758–764). On Adam see also Scior, *Das Eigene und das Fremde*, 29–37.

39 Scior, *Das Eigene und das Fremde*. Cf. e.g.: Ove Jørgensen and Tore Nyberg, *Sejlruter i Adam af Bremens danske øverden*, Kungl. Vitterhets Historie och Antikvitets Akademien, Antikvariskt arkiv 74 (Stockholm, 1992); G.A. van der Toorn-Piebenga, "Friese ontdekkingsreizigers in de elfde eeuw," *It beaken. Tydskrift fan de Fryske Akademy* 48/2 (1986), 114–126.

the Baltic Sea, having geographical borders with the Prussians, the Bohemians and the Russians.[40] In spite of a divergent use of terms it is clear that the *Sclavi* form a unity in Adam's eyes, and the chronicler lays open the aspects which form this unity as far as he sees it. When discussing the question whether the *Bohemi* and the *Polani* belonged to the Slavs or not, he argues that they would, since they had the same *habitus* and the same *lingua* as other Slavs.[41] These characteristics, *habitus* and *lingua*, can be regarded as very traditional aspects for the attribution of ethnical identity.[42] For this attribution of identity it does not matter if the identity really exists. What is important, however, is that the aspects *habitus* and *lingua* constitute the identity in Adam's mind. The passage shows that Adam looks at the Slavs as an ethnic group that is distinguished from other communities. The *lingua* is a quite traditional aspect of identity, although it has importance in the actual contexts of the missionary activity as well, since knowledge of the 'Slavonic language' was a crucial condition for a successful Christianization of the North. Adam of Bremen knows of the Swedish-Polish alliances under Boleslaw[43] and of the suppression of the Poles and their duke Mieszko II by Emperor Konrad in the 1030s.[44] By acknowledging only those missionaries who were dispatched to the North specifically by the archbishop of Hamburg himself, he writes his chronicle in opposition to other missionary efforts. He strictly refuses to recognize the influence of other episcopal sees in the Christianization of the North and he criticizes, for example, bishop Osmund who had been consecrated by a Polish archbishop.[45]

To understand these judgments in Adam's chronicle concerning the Slavs in general and the Poles in particular, one has to be aware of the purpose of the work and its audience. Since it is not the main topic of this paper, I will note but briefly two crucial facts that should be considered.[46] Firstly, there is the emphasizing of Hamburg's supremacy over the Nordic regions, which forms a constant feature in the work; secondly, the chronicle is addressed to Liemar (*praef.* and *epil.*), archbishop since 1072. Brought together with the time of writing, 1072/75–81, one can, without exaggeration, speak of a situation in

---

40   Adam of Bremen, scholion 14; IV, 13.
41   Adam of Bremen, *Gesta Hammaburgensis*, II, 21: "si Boemiam et eos, qui trans Oddaram sunt, Polanos, quia nec habitu nec lingua descrepant, in partem adieceris Sclavaniae".
42   Cf. already Isidor of Sevilla.
43   Adam of Bremen, scholion 24.
44   Adam of Bremen, *Gesta Hammaburgensis*, II, 56.
45   Adam of Bremen, *Gesta Hammaburgensis*, III, 15.
46   To the following cf. Volker Scior, "Adam of Bremen," in *Handbook of Medieval Nordic Literature in Latin*, eds. Stephan Borgehammar, Karsten Friis-Jensen, and Lars Boje Mortensen (Turnhout: forthcoming) (Online-Version https://wikihost.uib.no/medieval/index.php/Adam_Bremensis).

which it was almost necessary for propagating the archbishopric's rights and supremacy, and to emphasize its successes in the Nordic mission. The work reflects an actual historical-political crisis of the episcopal see with the need to defend its own claims against persons and institutions disputing them. The Nordic kings had tried to gain independence from the archbishopric – and thereby from the German kings – striving for their own church organization: Svend Estrithson of Denmark, Harald Hardrade of Norway, and Emund of Sweden. Adam's negative views on everyone opposing the rights of his see – be it kings, missionaries, or bishops sent out or consecrated by others than by Hamburg's own archbishops – become a delicate issue when focusing on the pontificate of Liemar, since Pope Gregory VII then supported the efforts for independence of the Nordic reigns. Liemar was siding with Henry IV in the investiture controversy. Liemar also attacked the papal policy towards the episcopacy. In 1074/5, when he wrote his chronicle, Adam called Gregory a *periculosus homo*, and was excommunicated in 1075. In two letters from 1075, Gregory tried to pull the Danish king onto his side in the conflict against Henry IV, and in a letter from 1080 to the Swedish king, the pope legalized the influential activities of bishops not sent out by Hamburg. From Adam's point of view, the archbishopric threatened to lose the *legatio gentium* and at the same time its *honor*. Archbishop Liemar, who had only recently been appointed and without approval of Bremen's cathedral chapter, was to be informed and prepared for the diocese's ambitious and disputed tasks. Adam proverbially sketched out what had been achieved in the past and what was reachable in the future, with regard to range of the missionary activity. The work defends the existential rights and interests of a diocese already in decline. The foundation of the first Danish episcopal see in Lund in 1104 made real the loss of Hamburg's legation and influence; at that point its supremacy was history. It is very possible that these developments were already foreseen in 1075. All these aspects are important when we try to figure out Adam's ideas about the missionaries or priests dispatched or ordained by Polish bishops. Without regarding these briefly sketched aspects, the objections raised about of Polish bishops could be interpreted as an anti-Polish attitude. But they are not. They are the effect of Adam's own identification with his archbishop.

What is called the *Chronica Slavorum* of Helmold of Bosau, which was written sometime in the years 1186/1172, mainly focuses on the Slavs who lived close to the river Elbe.[47] Still, in some cases Helmold mentions the Poles. To him,

---

47 Helmold of Bosau, *Chronica Slavorum*, ed. Bernhard Schmeidler, MGH SSrG 32 (Hannover, 1937), 1–218; Helmold of Bosau, *Chronica Slavorum*, ed. Heinz Stoob, FSGA 19 (Darmstadt, 1990). On the author and his identifications cf. Scior, *Das Eigene und das Fremde*.

they belong to the *Slavania* like the Russians, Prussians, Bohemi, Mahari, and Sorbs.[48] Of course, Helmold is passing on an older conception of a heathen and the barbaric North – as for other authors, the Slavs belong to the North, the *aquilo*, a cold region held by heathen enemies and quite barbaric in relation to the writers' own circumstances.[49] The geographical aspects go hand in hand with religious values, which are also expressed for the readers of the time.[50] Helmold often calls the Slavs very cruel, *crudelissimi*, and the Poles so as well.[51] Whereas Helmold often describes other Slavs, he gives hardly any further information about the Poles. Poland was too far away from his interests.

All in all, it can be summed up quite briefly that Frankish-German historiographers in the Early and High Middle Ages clearly had an idea of their Eastern neighbor, but 'Poland' and 'the Poles' did not play an important role for them. It is especially Thietmar of Merseburg, who wrote his chronicle in the East of the German kingdom and who mentions the Poles. Personally involved, due to the bonds of his father and family, he focused on 'the Poles'. Still, in reality he had an eye only on the nobility, the dukes, their weddings or their military actions. What came into the minds of Western authors were at last two aspects. At first, there was the political state. Depending on how the Polish nobility acted in alliances with or against the German King and Roman Emperor, they were either favored by the historiographers or not. Secondly, there was the religion of the Slavs. Before their Christianization, it was above all the heathen polytheistic religion that characterized the Slavs; afterwards it was the Christian creed, and again it was whether or not they were Christian which determined how they were judged. 'The Poles' thus were seen as a political and religious community; the attribution of qualities depended on the knowledge, interest, and values of the Western historiographers. In the end, after reading the references to 'Poland' and 'the Poles' in early and high medieval historiography, it is hard to believe that any of the authors were interested in their Eastern neighbors in today's sense.

48 Helmold of Bosau, *Chronica Slavorum*, 1.
49 Fraesdorff, *Der barbarische Norden*, 157–168.
50 Fraesdorff, *Der barbarische Norden*, 319–333.
51 Helmold of Bosau, *Chronica Slavorum*, 1.

CHAPTER 10

Poland and the Polish People in Late Medieval German Historiography

Norbert Kersken

The historiography in the late medieval Roman-German Empire, (the time period from the end of the Staufers and what is called the Great Interregnum up to the middle of the 15th century), exhibits a number of characteristics that deserve consideration in a comprehensive discussion of this topic. While previously there had been an older tradition going back to the Carolingian times of chronicles being written in close association with the royal court, in the Late Middle Ages there was neither a practice of historiography closely associated with the court, nor were there other specific places or social centers that had become centers of a historiographical tradition. The historiography in the second half of the Middle Ages as cultivated at various locations and regional centers is remarkably abundant and diverse. Yet, this diversity, despite numerous individual studies about it in more recent times,[1] even 150 years after Ottokar Lorenz's[2] synthesis, has in reality received comparatively little consideration.[3] In contrast to the time period from the 10th through the early 13th centuries, there has hitherto been little attention devoted to the history of how the Empire perceived[4] its eastern neighbors, especially Poland, during the Late Middle Ages.[5] In the following survey of late medieval historiography in the Empire as it relates to comments about Poland and its inhabitants, the

---

1   The turn in the 1980s toward the researching of late medieval historiography is marked by the volume of articles entitled *Geschichtsschreibung und Geschichtsbewußtsein im späten Mittelalter*, ed. Hans Patze, Vorträge und Forschungen 31 (Sigmaringen, 1987).
2   Ottokar Lorenz, *Deutschlands Geschichtsquellen im Mittelalter seit der Mitte des 13. Jahrhunderts*, 3., revised edition (Berlin, 1886/1887, repr. Graz, 1966).
3   The most important synthetic study in recent years is surely Rolf Sprandel, "Geschichtsschreiber in Deutschland 1347–1517," in *Mentalitäten im Mittelalter. Methodische und inhaltliche Probleme*, ed. František Graus, Vorträge und Forschungen 35 (Sigmaringen, 1987), 289–316.
4   As to this concept, see: Hans-Werner Goetz, *Vorstellungsgeschichte. Gesammelte Schriften zu Wahrnehmungen, Deutungen und Vorstellungen im Mittelalter*, eds. Anna Aurast, Simon Elling, Bele Freudenberg, Anja Lutz, and Steffen Patzold (Bochum, 2007).
5   Consequently the studies remain important from Andrzej Feliks Grabski, *Polska w opiniach obcych X–XIII w.* [Poland in the opinion of foreigners X–XIII centuries], Warszawa, 1964;

first step will be to present the representative texts in a structured way. Then I will inquire into their core descriptive themes. To conclude, I will address the patterns in the perceptions as revealed in the chronicles. The period of history under discussion runs from the last quarter of the 13th century to the close of the 15th century.

1 Chroniclers and Texts

To start with, it is important to underscore that there were no texts in late medieval German historiography that were specifically oriented towards depicting the relationships of the Empire with its eastern neighbors. In fact, this distinguishes the historiography of the 14th–15th centuries from that of the 11th century, when Saxon chronicles actually did pay special attention to their Slavic neighbors and also the emerging rule of the Piasts (one thinks say of Thietmar of Merseburg, Adam of Bremen, or Helmold of Bosau, or the annals from Quedlinburg, Magdeburg or Niederaltaich).[6] The reason for this lies in the fact that the importance of the political relationships of the Empire to its eastern neighbors (especially to Poland) had diminished significantly since the later period of the Staufers.

In view of this progressive breakdown in an awareness of the history of relations from the viewpoint of the main political power, namely the kingdom, two alternative viewpoints for perceptions of the eastern neighbors came to guide the historiography: one perspective turned its attention to the regional neighborhood and another took a universal history point of view

The local perspective can be found in the German regional historiography of the late medieval period. This historiographic interest in political developments among the eastern neighbors (and localized in Saxony in the 10th and 11th centuries) also manifested itself in the late 13th and the 14th centuries in the southeast of the Empire, primarily in Austria. The most important of these

---

idem, *Polska w opiniach Europy zachodniej XIV–XV w.* [Poland in the opinion of Western Europe 14th–15th century], Warszawa, 1968.

6 To this, Erich Donnert, "Studien zur Slawenkunde des deutschen Frühmittelalters," *Wissenschaftliche Zeitschrift der Friedrich-Schiller-Universität Jena GSR* 12 (1963) 189–224; Stanisław Rosik, "Die sächsischen Chronisten Widukind von Corvey und Thietmar von Merseburg über Anfänge Polens und Schlesiens," in *Niedersachsen – Niederschlesien. Der Weg beider in die Geschichte*, eds. Wojciech Mrozowicz and Leszek Zygner (Göttingen, 2005), 19–35; Knut Görich, "Die deutsch-polnischen Beziehungen im 10. Jahrhundert aus der Sicht sächsischer Quellen," *Frühmittelalterliche Studien* 43 (2009) 315–325; Andrzej Pleszczyński, *Przekazy niemieckie o Polsce*.

texts is offered through the eyes of the detailed *Steierische Reimchronik* by Ottokar of Styria (=Otacher ouz der Geul), who takes up in detail the topic of the Polish connections during the period of the second half of the 13th century, namely the time of Ottokar II Přemysl and the last Přemyslids.

For texts with a universal history perspective, one can name those which have a place in the tradition of the great universal history chronicles. Texts such as these originated in various regions of the Empire, especially in the southwest, in northern Germany, in the southeast, and in Bavaria, Austria, and Bohemia as well.

The southwest region of the Empire (the cities on the middle and upper Rhine) show a long historiographical tradition of observing and commenting on imperial history. In earlier periods these perspectives were associated with the great monasteries (St. Gallen, Reichenau); however, in the 14th century what emerged was an urban perspective, from Lindau, Strasbourg,[7] and Mainz. In the post-Staufen period, primarily in the second half of the 14th century, several lengthy works were written which presented the imperial history and drew (in part) on the universal chronicles of the late 13th century. This view now also included giving attention to various developments in eastern Europe. Of these chroniclers the first one to mention is the work of the Franciscan, Johannes of Winterthur, which he composed in the 1340s in Lindau on Lake Constance, and which covered the time period from 1198 until 1348.[8] It contains several reports about Polish history for the years 1326 to 1345 which deal with more than just facets in the history of German-Polish relations. In Straßburg, the chronicle of the academically trained jurist Matthias of Neuenburg in the middle of the 14th century followed the papal-imperial chronicle of Martin of Troppau, in which the relations with Poland had to do primarily with the genealogy of the Piasts.[9] Similarly the cleric Reinbold Slecht (at the beginning of the 15th century) resumed the account of the Swabian *Flores temporum* for the period 1366–1422; he took notice of the confrontation between the Teutonic Order and Poland.[10] Dietrich of Nieheim (Niem), a jurist at the papal curia (who was active in the conciliar movement at the beginning of the 15th century), also touched upon Polish matters in his history of the

---

7   Norbert Warken, *Mittelalterliche Geschichtsschreibung in Strassburg. Studien zu ihrer Funktion und Rezeption bis zur frühen Neuzeit* (Saarbrücken, 1995).
8   *Die Chronik Johanns von Winterthur*, ed. Friedrich Baethgen, MGH SS rer. Germ. N.S. 3 (Berlin 1924).
9   *Die Chronik des Mathias von Neuenburg*, ed. Adolf Hofmeister, MGH SS rer. Germ. N.S. 4 (Berlin, 1924/40).
10   Richard Fester, "Die Fortsetzung der Flores Temporum von Reinbold Slecht," *Zeitschrift für die Geschichte des Oberrheins* 48 (1894), 87–143.

Great Schism and in his history of the Roman emperors.[11] In Mainz, a general chronicle appeared at the beginning of the 15th century (handed down bearing the name of Johannes Kungstein) and it contains some reports about Poland for the years 1352 to 1410.[12] Of great value as contemporaneous reports are the logs of the Mainz businessman Eberhard Windeck, who for ten years (from 1415 to 1424) lingered in the orbit of Sigismund of Luxembourg and for the time period from 1412 to 1438 reports on a series of events that were related to Poland (with the relations to the Teutonic Order and the Hussite wars being in the foreground). He also inserts a series of documents in his account.[13] One sees this characteristic as well in the Speier chronicle, which provides several reports covering Polish connections for the period of the 1450/1460s.[14]

The northern reaches of the Empire, beginning in the 11th century, relayed important contributions to what was known about the Slavic neighbors, and these included references to Poland and the Poles. Adam of Bremen began things, followed later by Helmold of Bosau and (in the middle of the 13th century) by Albert of Stade. The late medieval historiography that built upon this had a clear primary emphasis in view of the fact that it originated in Lübeck; it underscored the city's political and cultural importance in the context of the Hanseatic League.[15] The chroniclers came without exception from the milieu of the mendicant orders. At the beginning of the 14th century a conventual Franciscan from Lübeck continued the Annals of Stade up to 1324, which of course provided reports about Poland only up to the coronation of Władysław

---

11 *Theoderici de Nyem de scismate libri tres*, ed. Georg Erler (Lipsiae, 1890); idem, "Historie de gestis Romanorum imperatorum," in *Historisch-politische Schriften des Dietrich von Nieheim*, eds. Katharina Colberg and Joachim Leuschner, Vol. 2, MGH Staatsschriften 5, 2 (Stuttgart, 1980), 3–142.

12 *Chronicon Moguntinum*, ed. Carl Hegel, MGH SSrG. 20 (Hannoverae, 1885).

13 Eberhart Windecke, *Denkwürdigkeiten zur Geschichte des Zeitalters Kaiser Sigismunds*, ed. Wilhelm Altmann (Berlin, 1893); overview of the inserted documents, ibid., 523–526; to this lately Joachim Schneider, *Eberhard Windeck and his "Buch von Kaiser Sigmund" Studien zu Entstehung, Funktion und Verbreitung einer Königschronik im 15. Jahrhundert*, Geschichtliche Landeskunde 73 (Stuttgart, 2018).

14 *Speierische Chronik*, ed. Franz Jospeh Mone, *Quellensammlung der badischen Landesgeschichte* 1, (Karlsruhe, 1848), 371–520.

15 To this: Johannes Bernhard Menke, "Geschichtsschreibung und Politik in den deutschen Städten des Spätmittelalters," *Jahrbuch des Kölnischen Geschichtsvereins* 34/35 (1960), 85–194, here: 85–126; Klaus Wriedt, "Geschichtsschreibung in den wendischen Hansestädten," in *Geschichtsschreibung* 401–426; Barbara Hoen, *Deutsches Eigenbewußtsein in Lübeck. Zu Fragen spätmittelalterlicher Nationsbildung*, Historische Forschungen 19 (Sigmaringen, 1994).

Łokietek.[16] Detmar, a *lector* at the Lübeck monastery of St. Katherine's, was engaged by the Lübeck council during the years 1368–1395 to write a chronicle in middle low German and in it he also frequently reports about Polish affairs.[17] And to conclude this list, in the second decade of the 15th century a Lübeck Dominican, Hermann Korner, composed a universal chronicle (initially in Latin) which, in the contemporaneous part, frequently reports news related to Poland,[18] and what was called the Rufus Chronicle from around 1430 did this as well.[19] In the old Saxon part of the Empire, in Minden in eastern Westphalia, around 1355–1370 a Dominican, Heinrich of Herford, incorporated into his universal chronicle a few reports related to Poland from a Brandenburg point of view.[20] The second place in the Saxon north of the Empire where reports about Poland came together was Magdeburg. The *Gesta archiepiscoporum Magdeburgensium*[21] and the Magdeburg *Schöppenchronik* (Chronicle of the Magdeburg Lay Judges)[22] offer for the first half of the 15th century a series of entries relevant to this topic, primarily related to the conflicts of the Teutonic Order with Poland. In the annals of the Cistercian monastery of Riddagshausen near Braunschweig[23] there are only two small notes and also the important Erfurt chronicles pay little attention to Poland at the end of the 13th and the beginning of the 15th century.[24]

Most of the reports dealing with Poland are found in entries by chroniclers in the region of Bavaria-Austria-Bohemia. For the most part this can be explained

16 *Annales Lubicenses*, ed. Johann Martin Lappenberg, MGH ss 16 (Hannoverae, 1859), 411–429.
17 *Detmar Chronik*, ed. Karl Koppmann, Die Chroniken der niedersächsischen Städte. Lübeck, vols. 1–2, Die Chroniken der deutschen Städte 19, 26 (Leipzig, 1884, 1899).
18 *Die Chronica novella des Hermann Korner*, ed. Jakob Schwalm (Göttingen, 1895).
19 *Rufus-Chronik*, ed. Karl Koppmann, Die Chroniken der niedersächsischen Städte. Lübeck; ibid., vol. 3, Die Chroniken der deutschen Städte 28 (Leipzig, 1902), 197–276.
20 Henricus de Hervordia, *Liber de rebus memorabilioribus sive chronicon*, ed. August Potthast (Gottingae, 1859); the universal chronicle by Gobelin Person in Paderborn has only one relevant entry, for 1410: *Cosmidromius Gobelini Person*, ed. Max Jansen, Veröffentlichungen der Provinz Westfalen 7 (Münster, 1900), 1–227.
21 *Gesta archiepiscoporum Magdeburgensium*, ed. Wilhelm Schum, MGH ss 14 (Hannoverae, 1883), 361–484.
22 *Die Magdeburger Schöppenchronik*, ed. Karl Janicke, Die Chroniken der niedersächsischen Städte. Magdeburg Vol. 1, Chroniken der deutschen Städte 7 (Leipzig, 1869, repr. 1962).
23 *Annales Riddagshusani*, ed. Gottfried Wilhelm Leibniz, Scriptores rerum Brunsvicensium 2, (Hanoverae, 1710), 68–84.
24 "Cronica s. Petri Erfordensis moderna," in *Monumenta Erphesfurtensia saec. XII, XIII, XIV*, ed. Oswald Holder-Egger, MGH SSrG. 42 (Hannover-Leipzig, 1899), 117–398; *Chronicon Theodorici Engelhusii continens res Ecclesiae et Reipublicae ab o.c. usque ad a. 1421*, ed. Gottfried Wilhelm Leibniz, Scriptores rerum Brunsvicensium 2, 978–1143.

by the fact that Poland was a neighboring region to Bohemia and Hungary, and consequently there were more extensive interactions with Poland that arose through this proximity. This is especially clear in Ottokar's Styrian rhymed chronicle from the first decade of the 14th century.[25] Occasionally in Austrian annals some attention is given to events in Poland out of an interest in the history of foreign relation, e.g., in the annals from Salzburg, Klosterneuburg, and Melk;[26] this also applies to the short annalistic notes from the monastery Fürstenfeld (near Munich) and to the Lower Bavarian biography of Emperor Louis IV.[27] In his regional history *Liber certarum historiarum* (with its Habsburg orientation) Johann of Viktring in the 1340s pays some attention to Polish points of view as well;[28] that was the case primarily with regard to the various marriages between the Piast dukes and Bavarian and Austrian dukes. From this same time period comes the papal-imperial chronicle by Heinrich Taube of Selbach in Eichstätt written as a continuation of *Flores temporum*.[29] Augsburg chronicles, primarily for the middle of the 15th century, provide some information that is related to Poland.[30] At the end of the 15th century it was then the large works of Bavarian regional historiography (the works of Ulrich

---

25 *Ottokars österreichische Reimchronik*, ed. Joseph Seemüller, MGH Dt. Chroniken 5, 1–2 (Hannover, 1890–1893, repr. Zürich-Dublin, 1974).

26 *Annales sancti Rudberti Salisburgenses*, ed. Wilhelm Wattenbach, MGH SS 9 (Hannoverae, 1851) 757–810; *Annales Claustroneoburgenses*, ed. Wilhelm Wattenbach, ibid., 607–613 (I), 614–624 (II), 628–637 (III), 742–746 (IV), 735–742 (V), 755–757 (VII); *Annales Mellicenses*, ed. Wilhelm Wattenbach, ibid., 480–535.

27 *Notae Fuerstenfeldenses de ducibus Bavariae a. 1211–1304*, ed. Georg Waitz, MGH SS 24 (Hannoverae, 1879) 74–75. – *Chronica Ludovici imperatoris quarti*, ed. Georg Leidinger, MGH SS rer Germ. 19 (Hannover/Leipzig, 1918) 105–138.

28 *Iohannis abbas Victoriensis Liber certarum historiarum*, ed. Fedor Schneider, MGH SS rer. Germ. 36 (Hannoverae/Lipsiae, 1909/ 1910).

29 *Die Chronik Heinrich Taubes von Selbach mit den von ihm verfaßten Biographien Eichstätter Bischöfe*, ed. Harry Bresslau, MGH SS rer. Germ. N.S. 1 (Berlin, 1922).

30 "Chronik der Stadt Augsburg," in *Die Chroniken der schwäbischen Städte* 1, ed. Ferdinand Frensdorff, Chroniken der deutschen Städte 4 (Leipzig, 1865) 3–198; *Chronik der Stadt Augsburg von der Gründung bis zum Jahre 1469*, ibid., 267–333; Burkhard Zink, *Chronik*, Die Chroniken der schwäbischen Städte. Vol. 2, eds. Ferdinand Frensdorff and Mathias Lexer, Chroniken der deutschen Städte 5 (Leipzig, 1866); Hector Mülich, *Chronik*, eds. Friedrich Roth and Mathias Lexer, Die Chroniken der schwäbischen Städte 3, Chroniken der deutschen Städte 22 (Leipzig, 1892); *Anonyme Chronik von 991–1483*, Die Chroniken der Stadt Augsburg 6. Chroniken der deutschen Städte 22, 445–529.

Füetrer in Munich[31] and of Hans Ebran of Wildenberg[32] and Veit Arnpeck[33] in Landshut) which –although not systematically and only occasionally – take some account of events in Poland. Likewise, in the anonymously passed down (so-called) 'Austrian Chronicle of the 95 Rulers' from 1390[34] and in the Austrian chronicle by Jakob Unrest (which deals with the time of Emperor Frederick III) multiple references to Poland are made.[35] During this time period once again the tradition of papal-imperial chronicles was taken up, and in the sections on contemporaneous events, references to Poland are time and again made and laid out. Andreas of Regensburg, who wrote in the 1420s while a canon in Regensburg,[36] and Thomas Ebendorfer, who was active in Vienna around 1450, should be mentioned here.[37] Both men wrote presentations of regional histories as well as outlines of universal histories. In the world chronicle written in the first decade of the 16th century by Johann Staindel of Passau, the sections on contemporaneous events contain only a few entries that relate to Poland.[38] Of special importance are the reports with regard to Poland in the large contemporaneous Bohemian chronicles of the 14th century, specifically the *Chronicon*

---

31   Ulrich Füetrer, *Bayerische Chronik*, ed. Reinhold Spiller, Quellen und Erörterungen zur Bayerischen und Deutschen Geschichte NF II, 2 (München, 1909).

32   *Des Ritters Hans Ebran von Wildenberg Chronik von den Fürsten aus Bayern*, ed. Friedrich Roth, Quellen und Erörterungen zur Bayerischen und Deutschen Geschichte NF 1 (München, 1905).

33   Veit Arnpeck, "Chronica Baioariorum," in idem, *Sämtliche Chroniken*, ed. Georg Leidinger, Quellen und Erörterungen zur bayerischen und deutschen Geschichte NF 3 (München, 1915) 1–443; idem, "Bayerische Chronik," ibid., 447–705; idem, "Chronicon Austriacum," likewise, 709–845.

34   *Österreichische Chronik von den 95 Herrschaften*, ed. Josef Seemüller, MGH Dt. Chr. 6 (Hannover, 1906/09).

35   Jakob Unrest, *Österreichische Chronik*, ed. Karl Großmann, MGH SSrG. N.S. 11 (Weimar, 1957).

36   Andreas von Regensburg, "Chronica summorum pontificum et imperatorum Romanorum," in idem, *Sämtliche Werke*, ed. Georg Leidinger, Quellen und Erörterungen zur bayerischen und deutschen Geschichte N.F. 1 (München, 1903), 1–158, 704–707, 710 et seq.; idem, "Diarium sexennale," ibid., 301–342; to this Krzysztof Ożóg, "'Bawarski Liwiusz'. Andrzej z Ratyzbony i jego zainteresowania Polską w pierwszej połowie XV wieku," ['Bavarian Livius'. Andreas of Regensburg and his interest in Poland in the first half of the 15th century] in *Świat średniowiecza. Studia ofiarowane Profesorowi Henrykowi Samsonowiczowi*, eds. Agnieszka Bartoszewicz, Grzegorz Myśliwski, Jerzy Pysiak, and Paweł Żmudzki, (Warszawa, 2010), 745–760.

37   Thomas Ebendorfer, *Chronica regum Romanorum*, ed. Harald Zimmermann, MGH SSrG. N.S. 18 (Hannover, 2003).

38   Johannes Staindel, *Chronicon generale*, ed. Andreas Felix von Oefele. Rerum Boicarum Scriptores 1, (Augustae Vindelicorum, 1763), 417–542.

Aulae Regiae by Peter of Zittau,[39] as well as in the chronicles that build upon it: one by Francis of Prague from the middle of the 14th century,[40] another by Beneš Krabice of Weitmühl from the years 1372–1374,[41] and one that came a bit later by Přibík Pulkava[42] as well as in the autobiography of Charles IV from 1346–1350.[43] These texts provide detailed information for the first half of the 14th century about developments in Poland since they were written against the background of the close relationships between the Bohemian and the Polish kingdoms and the problem of the political ties of the Silesian principalities. The information, however, is essentially limited to Polish-Bohemian relations. In Silesia itself there are reports that relate to Poland[44] in a few annals from Breslau,[45] Heinrichau,[46] and Ratibor.[47] Reports are more abundant in the historical work from the Augustinian monastery in Sagan, the *Catalogus abbatum Saganensium*, composed at the end of the 14th century by Abbot Ludolf and continued in the first years of the 16th century by Prior Peter Weynknecht,[48] as well as the contemporaneous accounts from the Breslau cathedral's canon Sigismund Rosicz[49] and from the Glogau monastery's vicar, Caspar Borgeni, for the years 1472–1493.[50]

---

39 *Petra Žitavského Kronika*, 3–337.
40 *Chronicon Francisci Pragensis*, ed. Jana Zachová, FRB S.N. 1 (Praga, 1997).
41 Benessius de Weitmil, "Chronicon," ed. Josef Emler, FRB 4 (Praha, 1884), 457–548.
42 *Cronica Boemorum*, ed. Josef Emler, FRB 5 (Praha, 1893), 3–207.
43 *Karoli IV imperatoris Romanorum Vita ab eo ipso conscripta = Autobiography of emperor Charles IV*, eds. Balázs Nagy and Frank Schaer, Central European Medieval Texts (Budapest, 2001).
44 What are not considered are the chronicles from Leubus and Brieg, what is called *Chronicon Polono-Silesiacum* from the 1280s and the *Chronica principum Poloniae* from the 1380s; here to Wojciech Mrozowicz, "Die Polnische Chronik (Polnisch-Schlesische Chronik) und die Chronik der Fürsten Polens (Chronica principum Poloniae) als Mittel zur dynastischen Identitätsstiftung der schlesischen Piasten," in: *Legitimation von Fürstendynastien in Polen und dem Reich. Identitätsbildung im Spiegel schriftlicher Quellen (12.–15. Jahrhundert)*, eds. Grischa Vercamer and Ewa Wółkiewicz, Deutsches Historisches Institut Warschau. Quellen und Studien 31 (Wiesbaden, 2016), 249–262.
45 *Annales Wratislavienses maiores* sowie *Annales civitatis Wratislaviensis*, ed. Wilhelm Arndt, MGH SS 19 (Hannoverae, 1866) 531–533, 527–531.
46 *Annales Cisterciensium Henricoviensium*, ed. Wilhelm Arndt, MGH SS 19 (Hannoverae, 1866) 544–547.
47 "Chronicon Ratiboriense," ed. Augustin Weltzel, *Zeitschrift des Vereins für Geschichte und Alterthum Schlesiens* 4/1 (1862) 114–126.
48 *Catalogus abbatum Saganensium*, ed. Gustav Adolph Stenzel, Scriptores rerum Silesiacarum 1 (Breslau, 1835), 173–528.
49 Sigismund Rosicz, *Gesta diversa transactis temporibus facta in Silesia et alibi*, ed. Franz Wachter, Scriptores rerum Silesiacarum 12 (Breslau, 1883), 37–86.
50 *Annales Glogovienses bis zum J. 1493 nebst urkundlichen Beilagen*, ed. Hermann Markgraf. SRS 10 (Breslau, 1877); about the author: Paul Knötel, "Der Verfasser der 'annales

2 Politics and Events

Now the intention is to examine all the chronicle texts mentioned here with regard to their interests in and comments on Poland and Polish relations, however this will be limited to those comments about the events from the mid-13th century onward. The texts can also serve a supplemental role in evaluating all information about the Polish history of the period; one can gain through them important insights into an overall understanding of Poland and its history.

As to the method on how best to proceed, that is significantly problematic; one surely may not assume that the whole of the late medieval chronicles from the Empire have at their core a shared mindset, intention or conception of history. For making well-founded assertions, it would be better to evaluate each chronicle individually regarding its comments about Poland, but that is not possible in this context. Instead the effort will be to outline at a minimum the tendencies found in the chronicles presented here, and through this reveal the perceptions and estimations of Poland conveyed in them.

The chroniclers from the late 13th to the end of the 15th centuries basically attend to three domains: *first* of all, actual events in Polish history; *secondly*, information about Polish foreign relations; *thirdly*, references to familial and marital relations.

I

Ranking first are the topics and reports that can be designated as genuinely "Polish". These address essentially three moments from the history of the constitutional development of Poland during the late medieval period. The first of these is the coronation of Władysław Łokieteks as king of Poland in January 1320. This is one of the most reported events overall. The *Chronicon Aulae Regiae* from Prague and the *Annales Lubicenses* offer reports and are both temporally and geographically proximate to the event. Later on, in Lübeck Detmar also mentions this event, as well as chroniclers at a greater distance, for example, Johann of Viktring in Carinthia and Johannes of Winterthur at Lake Constance. All of the chroniclers underscore the role of the pope, who had given his approval to the coronation.[51] Several times it is highlighted that

---

Glogovienses'," in: Zeitschrift des Vereins für Geschichte und Altertum Schlesiens 22 (1888) 94–108; annotated Polish translation: Kaspar Borgeni, *Rocznik głogowski do roku 1493 (Annales Glogovienses bis z.J. 1493)*, ed. Wojciech Mrozowicz (Głogów, 2013).

51 "Hoc anno Lokotko, dux Sandomerie, a sede apostolica obtinuit coronam regalem Polonie, ..." (*Chron. Aulae Regiae*, II, 9: 256); "Qui [Johannes XXII.] post modicum ducem Kracoviae, cognomento Locket, imposita corona capiti suo, regem fecit ordinari Kracoviae et Poloniae ..." (*Ann. Lubic.*, 425); "Hic eciam papa regnum Polonie relevavit,

the papal approval was gained through a pledge of a monetary remittance and the regular payment of Peter's Pence: *dicto papae infinitam dedit pecuniam, nec non omnes homines sui regni fecit aeternaliter censuales*.[52] Only the Ratibor annals mention Łokietek's death in the middle of the 15th century.[53]

The second moment mentioned is the royal succession after the death of Casimir III. Understandably, this situation received remarkably little attention, with only two comments at the beginning of the 15th century, firstly in the Breslau annals[54] and secondly by Johannes Kungstein in Mainz. According to the latter, a *magna dissension* arose between the emperor and the king of Hungary about the vacancy on the throne of Poland.[55] It reports that Skirgaila assumed the kingship,[56] but for one thing it leaves unmentioned the rule of Louis of Hungary (1370–1382) and for another it incorrectly construes Skirgailas' intermediary role in 1385.

Significantly more attention is given, by contrast, to the happenings in the years 1385–86, namely, the crowning of Hedwig of Anjou and the Polish-Lithuanian personal union.[57] A brief accurate presentation is provided by Hermann Korner in Lübeck. He knows about the two daughters of Louis of

---

quod olim defecit, missa corona et titulo regalis nominis Lottoni duci Kracovie, ..." (*Iohannis Victoriensis Liber*, 110); "Quidam aiunt papam hec demandasse regi Gragogie et, quia sibi in hoc paruit, regem eum fecit, qui ante dux unus Polonie fuit." – Johannes von Winterthur, *Chronica*, ed. Friedrich Baetgen, MGH SS rer. Germ. N.S., Berlin, 1924, 102; "He let hertoghen Lokede van Cracowe wyen to koninghe der Polene." (*Detmar-Chronik*, cap. 498: 428).

52   *Ann. Lubic.*, 425; this context is also emphasized by Peter of Zittau: "Incepitque statim denarium sancti Petri de uno quoque capite humano sedi apostolice decimaliter solvere, qui antea longo tempore denegatus fuerat, ..." (*Chron. Aulae Regiae*, II, 9: 256); further on Johann of Viktring: "... auctoritate et censu beati Petri illud roborans confirmavit." (*Iohannis Victoriensis Liber*, V, 3: II, 110) and Detmar of Lübeck: "Des makede he sin rike eweliken tinsachtich, also dat in deme rike jewelk minsche mot deme stole to Rome gheven alle jar enen penning, de is gheheten sunte Peters penning." *Detmar-Chronik*, cap. 428, 498.

53   *Chronicon Ratiboriense*, 115.

54   "Anno Domini 1370. septem diebus ante festum sancti Martini Casymirus rex Polonie ultimus Polonus obiit sine herede. Et Lodowicus rex Ungarie factus est rex Polonie pro eo, cuius pater fuit Gallicus de dono regis Francorum provisus per papam, et sic filius eius habuit duo regna." (*Ann. civitatis Wratislav.*, 530).

55   "Eo tempore magna terrarum dissensio vertebatur inter imperatorem et regem Ungarie pro regno Polonie, quod propter obitum regis Cracoviensis defuncti nuper vacare videbatur." (*Chron. Mogunt.*, 28).

56   Ibid.: "Hoc regnum postea Schirial scismaticus rex Liteanorum est adeptus."

57   To the historiographic perception of these events, Andrzej Feliks Grabski, "Jadwiga – Wilhelm – Jagiełło w opiniach europejskich," [Jadwiga-Wilhelm-Jagiełło in European opinions] *Nasza przeszłość* 23 (1966) 117–166, esp. 133–152.

Hungary, about the thwarted marital union of William of Austria with Hedwig *propter avariciam Polonorum*, and her subsequent marriage to the Grand Duke of Lithuania Jagiełło as well as his and his retinue's baptism at Cracow.[58] The Heinrichau annals reveal an accent that comes from a Lithuanian view of matters: it mentions the acceptance of Christianity, the baptismal name of the Lithuanian "king"; his marriage to the daughter of the Hungarian king, and the commencement of his reign (*optinuit regnum eiusdem provincie*).[59] These goings-on are described in detail in Bavarian chronicles, by Andreas of Regensburg, Thomas Ebendorfer, and Hans Ebran of Wildenberg. Thomas Ebendorfer reports on the two daughters of Louis of Hungary and the switching around of the original wedding arrangements for Maria and Hedwig; Thomas' interest lay with the marriage of Maria to Sigismund.[60] But in contrast, Hans Ebran of Wildenberg, with a joy in storytelling, circulated *ein ware und schöne histori* about the christianization of Lithuania, writing that after the death of the *konig von Bolon* (meaning Louis of Hungary), the Polish nobility could not come to agreement over a successor, so they elected Meschbot, the oldest of three princely brothers from Lithuania, and he was given the baptismal name "Ladislaus".[61] There are several details in this story that deserve highlighting: knowledge about several pretenders to the throne (among them the duke of Masovia, Siemowit IV), the mediating role taken on by the governor of Cracow, and providing the names of the three Lithuanian grand dukes: 'Meschbot', (which is Jogaila), Witold and 'Schwiderbal', (which is Švitrigaila). Of note is the substitution of the name Meschbo or Meschbot for Jogaila, for which there is no other such instance. Possibly the author used as his starting point the name of the first known Polish ruler, Mieszko. Jogaila's efforts toward christianizing Lithuania are recognized, but at the same time criticized for being superficial.[62] The surprising fact that the person who was the instigator of all these developments, Hedwig of Anjou, is simply passed over in silence

---

58   "[Lodowicus] genuit duas filias, scilicet Mariam … et Hedewigem, quam desponsaverat pater eius Wilhelmo, filio Lippoldi ducis Austrie postea a Sweytzer interfecti, sed ipsam non obtinuit propter avariciam Polonorum, quia Polonia fuit Hadewigi a patre assignata, sed tradiderunt eam cum regno Vergel duci Lithuanorum, qui baptizatus est cum multis Lithuanis in castro Krakoviensi." (Korner, *Chron. novella*, cap. 627: 76); idem, cap. 155, 312.

59   "Litwani et rex eorum ad fidem convertuntur Cristi, qui rex … sub fide conversionis duxit filiam regis Ungarie et ab episcopo Cracoviensi in Cracovia baptizatur; qui eciam optinuit regnum eiusdem provincie, qui fuit selator fidei et cleri multum, et vocatus est Vladislaus." (*Ann. Cisterciensium Henricov.*, 547).

60   Thomas Ebendorfer, *Chronica*, 565.

61   Ebran von Wildenberg, *Chronik*, 143.

62   Ebran von Wildenberg notes in the margin of his personal copy: "aber sein sun, kvng Kasmi, pavt stift, kloster- und pfarkiren. aber das gemain folch ist noch grob, vnd so ain

by the chronicler can be explained as follows: the story is being told from a markedly Lithuanian perspective. Andreas of Regensburg incorporated all these events into his report of information which had been communicated to him in 1423 by Andrzej Łaskarz, bishop of Posen, whom he met when the latter paused in Regensburg on his way to Italy. He briefly describes the particulars regarding the successors of Casimir III and Louis of Hungary, and the marriage of Hedwig of Anjou with Jogaila was among them.[63] The Austrian chroniclers present these events from the point of view of the Habsburg William the Courteous, Hedwig's intended spouse. Particularly detailed is the report in the Salzburg annals for the year 1386[64] and in the Austrian chronicle, whose author ascribes the dissolution of Hedwig's marriage to William to the mother of Hedwig and spouse of Louis of Anjou, Elisabeth of Bosnia.[65] The sequence of events are briefly mentioned in the Melk annals[66] and retrospectively under the year 1403 in the Klosterneuburg annals.[67] Both the Klosterneuburg and

    pavr gefragt birt: "bas gelavbst?" so ist sein antbort: 'ich gelavb, bas der kvnig gelavbt'." (ibid., 144).

63 "Filias autem suas idem Ludwicus rex Polonie et Ungarie postea locavit Hedvigem tamquam heredem in Cracovia. Mariam autem in Ungaria. Hedvigis duxit maritum dictum prius Gegelo Litwanum genere, qui accepto baptismo vocatus et Wlatislaus, iam regem Polonorum in Cracovia Hedvige mortua cum prole sua." (Andreas von Regensburg, "Chronica", 307f.); see also below, note 166.

64 "Item filius ducis Austrie Leupoldi, Wilhelmus nomine, de Cracovia est expulsus, et regina Cracovie, filia regis Ungarie, cum qua dictus dux Wilhelmus matrimonium contraxerat, post ipsius expulsionem regi Lituanie, predicto matrimonio non obstante, matrimonialiter est sociata, ex dispensatione domini Urbani pape sexti. Qui rex occasione eiusdem matrimonii ad fidem katholicam conversus sacrum baptisma suscepit, et in Cracovia potenter regnavit." (*Ann. s. Rudberti Salisburg.*, ad a. 1386: 840).

65 "Zu der zeit herczog Wilhalm, herczog Leupolts sun von Österreich, ward mit seiner prawt in das künigreich gen Krakaw gefüret, und do ward zwischen in die chanschaft volfüret, wan er bey ir offt ain nacht hat gelegen. Nu schündet der veint alles menschleichs hailes die alte küniginn von Ungeren, künig Ludweigs wittiben, und von rat wegen des grossen grafes sant si zu aim haiden in die Littaw und verhies im ir tochter, ob er si wolt nemen zu ainem weibe. Derselb | haiden cham gen Krakaw mit grosser macht und liez sich da tauffen, allain durch des künigreichs willen, alz etleich wellent. Der nam die frawn über irs herczen willen wider got und daz rechte mit dem willen irr vaigen muter, an der got daz grozz unrecht, alz hernach geschriben stet, scheinperleich hat gerochen." (*Österreichische Chronik*, V, 408: 204f.

66 "Eodem anno filius eius [Leopoldus III.] Wilhelmus dux expulsus est a Krakovia, ubi tunc rex habebatur." *Annales Mellicenses*, ed. Wilhem Wattenbach, MGH ss 9 (Hannover, 1851) 484–535, at 514.

67 "Regina de Apulia venit ad Austriam, et duxit in maritum ducem Wilhelmum, qui quondam fuit rex Polonie: quia barones et potentiores, sicut debuit dormire cum regina in prima nocte, tunc maiores domini voluerunt ipsum iugulare, et regina ammonuit ipsum, et sic furtive evasit, et amplius non redibat; et domini de Polonia redderunt ipsam contra

Melk annals identify William explicitly as *rex Polonie*. Ludolf of Sagan also reports this series of events with special attention to the planned marriage of Hedwig and William,[68] which Dietrich of Nieheim suggests had already been consummated and who portrays William as king.[69]

II

The second thematic block deals with Polish foreign relations. These primarily are related to Silesian matters, for example, the account about the youngest son of Henry II the Pious, Władysław of Silesia, who in 1267 was named archbishop of Salzburg, which Otto of Steiermark (briefly), Johann of Viktring, and the Austrian chronicles report.[70] As to the confrontations between Bolko II of Schweidnitz, *potentissimus in regno Polonie*, and Charles IV, this is reported by Hermann Korner for the year 1351.[71] Polish relations throughout the struggles of Ottokar II Přemysl are reported by neighboring observers: Ottokar of Steiermark, Johann of Viktring and Thomas Ebendorfer.[72] Polish-Brandenburg relations were initially addressed under the year 1285 in relation to the issue of the succession in Pomerelia[73] and the assassination of Przemysł II in Rogasen (*Rogoźno*) in 1296.[74] When writing about the double election in October 1314 of Friedrich the Fair and Louis of Bavaria as Roman-German king, a Bavarian chronicle speaks of the Brandenburg Prince-elector as representing *Polonia cum Pranburga*.[75] The invasion of Brandenburg by Władysław Łokietek with

---

voluntatem eius cuidam pagano, quem coronaverunt in regem." (*Ann. Claustroneoburg.*, ad a. 1403: 736).

68   *Catalogus abbatum Sagan.*, 218.
69   "Et illo temporе Vilhelmus filius Leopoldi ducis Austriae, maritus Haduigis filiae Ludouici regis Hungariae, cui Ludouicus rex Hungariae dedit in dotem Haduigae regnum Poloniae. Et cum Cracouiae resideret, quidam nobiles Poloni eundem iuuenem inuita dicta regina eius uxore inde fugarunt, et dominum Ladislaum modernum regem Poloniae tunc ducem Litphanorum ac idolatram seu paganum sub conditione quod se faceret baptisari eidem reginae matrimonii copularunt, qui factus Christianus cum regina diu in matrimonio stetit, …" (Theodoricus, *De scismate*, I, 58, 26).
70   Ottokar, *Reimchronik*, cap. 71, v. 8660–8672, 8713–8836, 114f.; *Iohannis Victoriensis Liber* 100, 170; *Österreichische Chronik* III, 265, 121f.
71   Korner, *Chron. Novella*, cap. 56 ad a. 1351, 59.
72   Ottokar, *Reimchronik*, cap. 140, v. 152001–15228, 201; *Iohannis Victoriensis Liber*, 231, 233f.; Thomas Ebendorfer, *Cronica*, 490f.
73   Staindel, *Chronicon*, 512a.
74   According *Detmar-Chronik*, cap. 393, 378: he was murdered by his own people – "By der tiid [1297] wart ghedodet de koning van Polonien to Rogozna van sinen eghenen ridderen."
75   "Nam Ungaria, Styria, Moravia et Suevia, Colonia, Alsatia cum Austria: hii astabant Fridrico. Sed omnibus hoc dico: Bohemia cum Saxonia, Polonia cum Pranburga, Michsnia

the aid of Lithuanian auxiliary troops in early 1326 is given major attention in the contemporary chronicles. Initially in the north it is mentioned in the annals of the Kolbatz monastery,[76] and then in the great contemporaneous Bohemian histories, the *Chronicon Aulae Regiae*[77] and later the chronicle of Francis of Prague,[78] the chronicles of Beneš Krabice of Weitmühl,[79] and Pulkava,[80] the annals from Heinrichau in Silesian,[81] as well as the universal history chron-

cum Tŭringia, Treveris cum Maguncia, Renus cum utraque Bawaria: hii astabant Ludwico preclarissimo regi magno." (*Chron. Ludovici quarti*, ad a. 1314: 126).

[76] "Eodem anno ... pagani sabbato ante Oculi I: iro curante hoc Lokyst, rege Polonotum ueneruut usque Frankenvorde et innumerabiles homiries precipue juuenss fortes et mulieres et virgines abduxerunt in terram captiuitatis, cum quibus et nephanda et miserabilia commiserunt; sed et infantes et antiquiores et rebelles interfecerunt, quorum tamen circa L in quadam ecclesia cujusdam ville, prope Wrankenuorde per sequentibus eos ciuibus dicte ciuitatis incendio perierunt." – *Annales Colbazenses*, ed. Rodgero Prümers. Pommersches Urkundenbuch 1/2 (Stettin, 1877), 465–496, here 487.

[77] "Hoc anno ex permissione Johannis pape inter Cruciferos domus Deutonice in Prusia et saracenos dictos Lythoanos sunt amicabiles per triennium facte treuge, ita san, quod infra istud triennium se mutuo inpedire non debeant aliqualiter vel turbare, quod heu in magnum detrimentum Christianorum devenit et ecclesie. Nam inveteratus dierum Lokotko, rex Polonie, volens sedi apostolice et pape complacere, ut asseruit, contra marchionem Brandinburgensem iuvenculum, Lodowici de Bawaria regis Romanorum, filium innumerabiles Lythowanorum turbas pugnaturus sibi assumit, marchionatumque Brandenburgensem invadit ac iuxta civitatem Frankinfurd et in universo ipsius confinio plagam in christianos exercuit et tyrannidem nimis magnam. Per paganos enim Lythowanos Christianam sanguinem effundere sicientes et oportunitatem habentes ville et oppida comburuntur, monasteria quoque plurima monachorum, quam sanctimonialium confringuutur, Christi famuli et famule trucidantur et violantur, et vulgares homines velut pecudes innumerabiles ad paganorum patriam deducuntur. Tanta mala ibi per paganos tunc perpetrata sunt, quod sine gemitu cordis narrari non possunt." (*Chron. Aulae Regiae*, II, 17: 278 et seq.).

[78] "Eodem anno [1326] dux Crakovie dictus Loketko, magnas turbas Lytwanorum sibi associans marchionatum Bramburgensem invadit et iuxta civitatem Frankenwrd in confinio ipsius universe plagam in christianos exercuit et tyrannidem nimis magnam. Monasteria plurima destruuntur, oppida et ville cremantur et homines velud pecudes innumerabiles ad paganorum patriam deducuntur." (*Chron. Francisci Pragensis*, II, 15: 115).

[79] "Eodem anno dux Lokethko congregata Lytwanorum magna multitudine terram Brandeburgensem hostiliter devastavit, viros et mulieres captivos abduxit." (Benessius, "Chronicon," 480).

[80] "Anno vero Domini MCCCXXVI Wladislaus alias Loketko, rex Cracovie, multos infideles Litwanos, Ruthenos paganos ad partes marchie Brandemburgensis destinavit et pluribus innuinem dampna fecit." (Pulkava, *Cronica Boemorum*, cap. 100, 203).

[81] "Litwanorum exercitus, de terra sua egressus, cum conductu regis Cracovie Vlodezlai, qui appellatus est Loketh, intraverunt dyocesim Lubuczensem, in qua magnam multitudinem hominum christianorum captivam duxerunt et ipsos miserabiliter tractaverunt; ..." (*Ann. Cisterciensium Henricov.*, 546).

icles of Johannes of Winterthur,[82] Heinrich of Herford,[83] Heinrich Taube of Selbach,[84] and Detmar of Lübeck.[85] Peter of Zittau, Johannes of Winterthur and Heinrich of Herford name Pope John XXII as the instigator of the military campaign. Johann of Winterthur links the military action with the earlier papal approval of the royal coronation of Władysław, while Heinrich of Herford explains the event as a reaction to the occupation of Pomerelia by the Teutonic Order in 1309.[86]

The agreements of Trentschin and Visegrád from 1335 (in which the Bohemian claims to the Polish crown were relinquished) are addressed only in Bohemian chronicles.[87] Using this opportunity and given the failed marriage arrangements between Margarethe of Luxembourg and Casimir III in 1341, they

---

82 "Nam in quibusdam christianitatis, ut fertur, extremitatibus Teutonicis cruciferis diffuse dominantibus, paganorum truculentam rabiem eos contingencium cohercentibus et refrenantibus, ne per suas invasiones et incursiones pestiferas fidelium terris quantum gliscunt nocere possint, dominus papa in mandatis districtissime dedit, quatenus ipsos per terram suam liberum transitum habere sinerent, ut in vindictam et iniuriam imperatoris ad terram filii sui demoliendam vocatam Brandenburg aceessum habere possent. Qui iussioni papali contraire pertimescentes inviti cum eiulatu, ut ita dicam, amarissimo paganis transitum pro suo libitu indulserunt. Quidam aiunt papam hec demandasse regi Gragogie et, quia sibi in hoc paruit, regem eum fecit, qui ante dux unus Polonie fuit." (Johann von Winterthur, *Chronik*, 102).

83 Henricus de Hervordia, *Liber*, cap. 94: 211.

84 "Rex Lichphonie cum multitudine paganorum marchionatum Brandenburgensem crudeliter depopulat. Hic marchionatus modico tempore ante absque naturali herede vacavit per obitum Waldemari marchionis ibidem supra nominatus." (Heinrich Taube, *Chronica*, 39).

85 "In deme sulven jare [1326] Lockede, de koning van Krakowe, do he sine dochter hadde gheven deme koninghen van Ungheren unde sineme sone hadde gheven des koninghes dochter van Lettowen, do sammelde he ute den lande des heydeschen dedes also vele; de toghen in des marcgreven lant di Prinzslawe. De lantde vorhereden unde dreven dar uth vele ghuder lude, vrowen unde man. Do weren bi deme koninghe van Kracowe des paves boden. De beden de Dudeschen brodere, dat se in ereme lande de heydene scholden nicht hinderen. Also was dat lut. Over in deme weghe, dar de Lettowen toghen to lande, dar volghede na van Polene en helt vormeten." (Detmar-*Chronik*, cap. 544: 454).

86 "Injuriam hanc antiquam rex Polonorum temporibus nostris corde revolvens, Letwinis paganis, consilio et placito pape Johannis, ut dicbatur, qui marchionem Lodwicum propter patrem suum Lodewicum imperatorem odivit, amicitia, fide, federibusque sociatur, sperans per eos de Marcomannos se posse vindicare." – Henricus de Hervordia, *Liber*, cap. 94: 211.

87 *Chron. Aulae Regiae* III, 11: 331: "Qualiter Johannes, rex Boemie, alienavit regnum Polonie." – *Chron. Francisci Pragensis*, III, (3) 8: 159f., quotation see note 141.

address the abandoned (that is to say, unrealized) political union of Poland and Bohemia.[88]

Casimir III's politics towards the east against Halych in the 1340s and 1350s receives significant attention in imperial chronicles of the late 14th century. The incursion of the Tartars into Lesser Poland in the wake of the battles over the successor to the prince of Halych, Bolesław George II, in the winter of 1340/1341 is reported by Johann of Viktring,[89] Francis of Prague,[90] Beneš of Weitmühl[91] and in particular detail by Johannes of Winterthur.[92] The latter, as did briefly

---

[88] "Hoc itaque regnum Polonie, quod triginta septem annis in persona piissimi Wenceslai regis fuerat regno Boemie unitum, ab ipso modo quibusdam adiectis condicionibus est divisum." (*Chron. Aulae Regiae*, III, 11: 331); verbatim as well *Chron. Francisci Pragensis*, III, (III) VIII: 160. Ad 1341: "... et per ipsam [Margaretham] regnum Polonie unitum fuisset regno Boemie, quod prius per paternam avariciam extiterat separatum." (*Chron. Francisci Pragensis*, III (VI) XIV: 176).

[89] "Hoc anno rex Ruthenorum moritur, et rex Krakovie racione consortis, que filia regis Livonie fuerat, terram apprehendere festinavit, et abductis inde spoliis pluribus, quibusdam civitatibus depredatis ad propria est reversus. Rex Tartarorum hoc audiens regnum asserit esse suum, tamquam sibi et suis progenitoribus censuale, cum infinita multitudine Tartarorum ad metas Krakovie venit. Et depopulatis atque vastatis finibus illis compulit regem Krakovie metuentem auxilium Ungarorum, Teutonicorum, ut abigerentur, ne ulterius diffunderentur, nunciis et litteris implorare. Novissime tamen angariati per prohibicionem obsistencium fluviorum interpositorum ac armatorum occurrencium ad propria redierunt." (*Iohannis Victoriensis Liber*, 218).

[90] "Anno Domini MCCCXLI Tartari Poloniam intraverunt et maximam partem terre devastaverunt, vindictam sumentes in christianis propter terram Rutenorum, quam pridem debellaverat dux Polonie propter ducem terre prefate, qui exstitit ei in linea consanguinitatis astrictus, quam intoxicatum nobiles dicte terre morti tradiderunt." (*Chron. Francisci Pragensis*, III, (6) 14: 173).

[91] "Anno Domini MCCCXLI Kazymirus, rex Polonie, habuit gwerram cum Ruthenis et Lytwanis infidelibus, qui venerant ad occupandum regnum et terras Polonie et Deo propicio recesserunt post tempus breve." (Benessius, "Chronicon," 490); see for context: Grzegorz Błaszczyk, *Dzieje stosunków polsko-litewskich od czasów najdawniejszych do współczesności. T. 1: Trudne początki.* [The history of Polish-Lithuanian relations from the earliest times to the present day. T. 1: Difficult beginnings.] Seria Historia 191 (Poznań, 1998), 62f.

[92] "Anno dominice incarnacionis MCCCXLI. in quadragesima tanta multitudo Tartarorum et aliorum paganorum famis inedia conpulsa terram regis Gragowie et Ungarie ingressa est, quod quantum ad longitudinem in XX miliaribus et quantum ad latitudinem in V vel IX, ut fertur, terre spacium occupavit. [...] Quod audiens rex Kragowie, cuius consors soror uxoris regis Ruthenorum iam intoxicati fuerat, illuc cum exercitu properavit et immensam peccuniam ab eo relictam rapiens reversus est. Propter quod imperator Tartarorum hec intelligens nimio furore agitatus paganos memoratos ad devastandam regionem regis Kragowie et alias finitimas regiones principum fidelium emisit. Qui inter cetera facta sua civitatem unam regalem pertinentem regi Kraggowie obsederunt. Quod videns rex sepedictus exercitum congregavit et in eos irruens in obsidione constitutos occidit ex ipsis

the annalist of Ratibor, also writes about the Bohemian-Polish conflict of 1345, including the besieging of Cracow.[93] Detmar of Lübeck mentions Casimir's campaign against Ruthenia in 1349.[94] Mathias of Neuenburg,[95] Heinrich Taube,[96] and Johannes Kungstein in Mainz[97] mention the Polish-Lithuanian conflicts of 1352.

Andreas of Regensburg[98] gives a contemporaneous report on the political settlement between Władysław II Jagiełło and Sigismund of Luxembourg in 1423 in Kežmarok. He also knew details about the plans for Witold's coronation.[99] As to the campaign of the Polish-Hungarian crusader army against the Ottomans and the defeat at Varna in 1444, both the Magdeburg annalist[100] and Peter Weynknecht in Sagan address it, and the latter especially

---

VI milia et civitatem viriliter defendit. Reges paganos plures et alios maiores natu, qui se peccunia redimere poterant, illesos abire permisit. In illo conflictu duces Polonie fortiter egerunt." (Johannes von Winterthur, *Chronik*, 181, 184).

93 Johannes von Winterthur, *Chronik*, 257; *Chronicon Ratiboriense*, 115.

94 "In deme jare Cristi 1350 do toch de konink van Polen Casemer in Rutzenland na twelften, unde vorherede dar vele mit brande unde mit rove." (*Detmar-Chronik*, cap. 680: 521).

95 "Item eodem anno LII. rex Lytovie [Kenstut] cum auxilio Tartarorum cum exercitu innumerabili per Russyam, quam quasi destruxit, transiens animo destruendi Cracovum, cum rehabuisset fratrem suum [Lubart] captivum dudum et cum omnes vicine terre ad eius resistenciam properarent, recessit in Prussiam, in perfidia perseverans." (Mathias von Neuenburg, *Chronica*, cap. 148: 465)

96 "Anno Domini MCCCLII. de mense Marcii Tarthari et Rutheni pagani cum multis legionibus armatorum || contra regem Cracovie intrant Poloniam et unam civitatem vicerunt et terram et homines devastant. Tandem armatorum multi sunt occisi, et reversi sunt ad terram suam." (Heinrich Taube, *Chronica*, 102f.).

97 "Anno D. 1352. Tartari pagani cum maximo exercitu invaserunt terminos christianorum et Rutenorum et regionem regis Crackoviensis, terras predictas et habitantes in eis devastantes." (*Chron. Mogunt.*, 4).

98 "Item hie ist ze merkchen, daz unser herr der kunig und der kunig von Polan und herczog Witolt und der dispot [309] und dez kaysers räte von Kriechen sind gewest pey einander zu dem Kassmarkcht und sind mit einander veraint." (Andreas von Regensburg, "Diarium sexennale," 301–342, here 308f.; idem. 571).

99 "Exinde venit Nürbergam, ubi Johannem episcopum Zagrabinesem et Ernestum ducem Bavarie misit in Litwaniam ad coronadum ducem Witoldum in regem. Qui impediti per Wladislaum regem Polonie, patruum eiusdem ducis Witoldi alias Alexandri nominati, qui noluit, ut ductaus ille Litwanie mutaretur in regnum, vacui sunt reversi. Interea prefatus dux Litwanie Alexander, qui in paganismo dictus fuerat Witoldus, est defunctus." (id., "Fortsetzung der Chronica de principibus terrae Bavarorum," in *Sämtliche Werke*, 565–587, here 571); plan for coronation also noted by Eberhard Windeck on the occassion of the death of Witold: "Witolt der groß fürste in der Littouwem den der konig Sigemiontt zü eime konige gemacht haben wolt, als ein Romscher konig danne macht hett, und wolt im rich cleinöter darzu geben haben." (Windecke, *Denkwürdigkeiten*, cap. 332: 314).

100 *Gesta archiepiscoporum Magdeburg.*, 468; short reference in *Ann. Riddagshusani*, 83.

acknowledges Władysław III.[101] The meeting in Glogau between George of Podiebrad and Casimir IV in May of 1462 is only reported by contemporaneous observers, Peter Weynknecht and Caspar Borgeni.[102] And finally, Caspar Borgeni and Jacob Unrest report on the Polish-Hungarian conflicts over Podiebrad's successor in the years 1471/1474.[103]

The reports about confrontations between Poland and the Teutonic Order can be grouped together as a separate thematic sector. What is striking is the special attention that the Lübeck chroniclers Detmar und Hermann Korner give to the conflicts in the years 1330/1331,[104] the Peace of Kalisch in 1343,[105] the so-called Golubian war in the summer of 1422 (which ended with the Peace of Lake Melno in 1423)[106] and the campaign of Polish and Hussite troops against the Teutonic Knights in Neumark in June 1433.[107]

'The great clash', the battle of Tannenberg (Grunwald) of 1410, understandably attracted major attention among numerous chroniclers in the Empire. For a few chroniclers, this confrontation was the sole occasion on which they provide descriptive accounts of Poland.[108] The event garnered the special attention of observers in the north-German area, as was the case in Lübeck in what is called the Rufus Chronicle and in Magdeburg in the Magdeburg *Schöppenchronik*. A detailed and contemporaneous narration is also offered by Jakob Twinger of Königshofen in Strasbourg[109] and (relying on this) the Bern

---

101 "In qua pugna ipse eciam rex Polonie Wladislaus cecidit, adolescens spectabilis, fama ac opere pre ceteris Polonie regibus commendabilis. Thewtonicam nacionem valde dilexit ac promovit, in civitatibusque Polonie hanc viis omnibus, quibus valuit, plantare et exaltare sathagebat." (*Catalogus abbatum Sagan.*, 313).
102 *Catalogus abbatum Sagan.*, 344; Borgeni, *Annales*, 15.
103 Borgeni, *Annales*, 17, 30 et seq.; Unrest, *Österreichische Chronik*, 21 et seq.
104 *Detmar-Chronik*, cap. 567f.: 462–468.
105 "In deme sulven jare [1343] in sunte Jacobes daghe do makede de meyster van Prutzen, broder Luder, enen guden vrede mit deme koninghe van Krakowe unde Polenen uppe deme slotte Moryn; he gaf weder deme koninghe, wat he hadde des sines, dat to deme rike horde, also dat land Coyave, Doborin unde dat slot, dat dar het Braburch.", ibid., cap. 633: 497.
106 The context is explicated thoroughly by Korner, *Chron. Novella*, cap. 1379: 450f.
107 Id., cap. 1559: 518, 521.
108 That applies to Gobelin Person, Jakob Twinger von Königshofen, the so-called Königshofen-Justinger-Chronik from Bern, Conrad Justinger.
109 Jakob Twinger von Königshofen, *Chronik. Die Chroniken der oberrheinischen Städte. Straßburg*. Vol. 1–2. ed. Karl Hegel. Die Chroniken der deutschen Städte 8, 9 (Leipzig, 1870/1871), here vol. 2, 913–915.

city chronicles[110] as well, then later Eberhard Windeck in Mainz as well as Peter Weynknecht in Sagan.[111]

Shorter reports are found in Saxony written by Hermann Korner,[112] in the *Gesta archiepisoporum Magdeburgensium*,[113] in the universal chronicle by Gobelin Person[114] and Dietrich Engelhus,[115] in an Augsburg chronicle,[116] and in the Oldenburg chronicle by Johann Schiphower,[117] while a few chroniclers from Saxony,[118] Austria,[119] Silesia,[120] and Bohemia[121] provide only brief annalistic notations. It is not how these texts represent the battle,[122] but rather what knowledge they reveal of particulars from the Polish side.

Only a portion of the chroniclers call the Polish king by name, those being some writers from the Saxon[123] and the Austrian-Silesian regions.[124] In the Lübeck chronicle the king is erroneously referred to as Boleslaus,[125] otherwise he is called Wladislaus,[126] whereas Ludolf of Sagan writes *Vladislaus vel Wolislaus*. The Magdeburg *Schöppenchronik* calls him by his Lithuanian name Jagiello,[127] whereas Andreas of Regensburg uses both names.[128] On the other

110 *Die Berner Chronik des Conrad Justinger*, ed. Gottlieb Studer, Bern, 1871.
111 *Catalogus abbatum Sagan.*, 256.
112 Korner, *Chron. Novella*, cap. 814: 109.
113 *Gesta archiepiscoporum Magdeburg.*, 456.
114 Gobelin Person, *Cosmidromius*, 186f.
115 Engelhus, *Chronicon*, 1139.
116 *Chronik der Stadt Augsburg*, 116.
117 Johann Schiphower, *Chronicon Archicomitum Oldenburgensium*, ed. Heinrich Meibom, SSrG 2, (Helmaestadii, 1688), 123–194, here 167.
118 *Ann. Riddagshusani*, 82; *Annales Vetero-Cellenses*, ed. Georg Heinrich Pertz, MGH SS 16 (Hannoverae, 1859), 41–47, here 46.
119 *Ann. Mellicenses*, 515.
120 *Ann. civitatis Wratislav.*, 530; *Annales Cisterciensium Henricov.*, 547; *Chronicon Ratiboriense*, 117.
121 *Chronicon Palatinum 1348–1438. Geschichtsschreiber der hussitischen Bewegung in Böhmen 1*, ed. Konstantin Höfler, Fontes rerum Austriacarum I, 2, 1 (Wien, 1856), 47–50, here 47; *Chronicon capituli Metropolitani Pragensis*, ibidem, 65–66, 66.
122 See Grabski, *Polska w opiniach Europy*, 253–276 Sven Ekdahl, *Die Schlacht bei Tannenberg 1410. Quellenkritische Untersuchungen. Vol. 1: Einführung und Quellenlage*, Berliner historische Studien 8; Einzelstudien 1 (Berlin, 1982) 188, 230–233.
123 *Gesta archiepiscoporum Magdeburgensium* and Hermann Korner in Lübeck and the referring to that so-called *Rufus-Chronik*.
124 Thomas Ebendorfer, Sigismund Rosicz und Peter Weynknecht in Sagan.
125 "... Boleslaus, de konynk van Polen, ..." (*Rufus-Chronik*, cap. 1379: 175).
126 Thomas Ebendorfer; Sigismund Rosicz; *Catalogus abbatum Saganensium*; in the *Gesta archiepiscoprum Magdeburgensium* he is named Waldislaus.
127 "... an sinem namen geheiten Jagel ..." (*Magdeburger Schöppenchronik*, 329).
128 "Prefatus Wladislaus rex Polonorum, ... in paganismo Gegelo vocatus" (Andreas von Regensburg, "Chronica," 254).

hand, most all of the chronicles give the name of the Lithuanian grand duke, Vytautas, but of course in its Polish form, Witold.[129] Veit Arnpeck in Landshut points out that Duke Henry XVI of Bavaria-Landshut twice undertook military campaigns into Prussia to support the Teutonic Knights against the king of Poland and the grand dukes of Lithuania.[130]

Events in the years after the battle at Tannenberg-Grunwald are only mentioned by a few chroniclers. These were: the Breslau arbitration decision of Sigismund in 1420;[131] the so-called Gollubian war that followed upon the Polish-Lithuanian incursion into Prussia in the summer of 1422, (and ended with the Treaty of Lake Melno);[132] the meeting in Kežmarok between Władysław Jagiełło and Sigismund;[133] the plans for the royal coronation of Witold in 1430;[134] and the campaign of the Polish and Hussite troops against the Teutonic Order in the Neumark in the summer of 1433.[135] The confrontations between the Prussian estates and the Order (in the Thirteen-Years-War) are reported in the annals of Klosterneuburg, the Magdeburg annals, and by Sigismund Rosicz and later by Jakob Unrest und Peter Weynknecht in Sagan,[136] with the battle near Konitz in 1454 between the Order's army and the combined troops of the Prussian Confederation and Poland receiving significant attention.[137] The handing over of Marienburg in 1456 to the Polish king is

---

129 Gobelin Person, *Cosmidromius*, 186, 187 (*Vitoldus, Witoldus*); *Magdeburger Schöppenchronik*, 329 (*Wytolde*); Korner, *Chron. Novella*, cap. 814: 109 (*Witoldus*); *Detmar-Chronik*, cap. 1138: 150 (*Witolt*); Twinger, *Chronik*, 914 (*Witolde*); Engelhus, *Chronicon*, 1139 (*Witoldus, alias Alexander*); Andreas von Regensburg, "Chronica," 152 (*Bitoldus*); Windecke, *Denkwürdigkeiten*, cap. 38: 22 (*Witolt*); Ebendorfer, *Cronica*, 560 (*Witoldus*); Staindel, *Chronicon*, 528b (*Witoldus*); Rosicz, *Gesta diversa*, 43 (*Wytoldus*).

130 "Hic Hainricus duas expediciones in Prusiam in favorem fidei nostre et cruciferorum de domo Teutonicorum contra Wladislaum regem Polonie et fratrum eius Bitoldum ducem Littuovie et Schiderbalem fecit, qui duo aduc pagani erant, eo tempore, quo fratres teutonici bellum perdiderunt et magister ordinis nacione de Junging cum 600 cruciferis interfecti sunt." (Arnpeck, *Chron. Baioar.*, cap. 64: 360); respectively Arnpeck, *Bayer. Chron.*, 613.

131 Windecke, *Denkwürdigkeiten*, 29; *Magdeburger Schöppenchronik*, 349; *Gesta archiepiscoporum Magdeburg.*, 458; to this Holtzmann, Robert: "Der Breslauer Reichstag von 1420," in *Schlesische Geschichtsblätter* (1920) 1–9, here 6.

132 Korner, *Chron. Novella*, 450: cap. 1379; a reference to that as well: Andreas von Regensburg, "Chronica," 307; to this William Urban, *Tannenberg and After* (Chicago, 2003), 279–281.

133 Andreas von Regensburg, "Chronica," 308f.

134 Ibid., 571.

135 Korner, *Chron. Novella*, 518, 521; Windecke, *Denkwürdigkeiten*, 346: cap. 379.

136 *Ann. Claustroneoburg.*, 742; *Gesta archiepiscoporum Magdeburg.*, 470; Rosicz, *Gesta diversa*, 65; Speier, *Chronik*, cap. 51: 393; Unrest, *Österreichische Chronik*, 12.

137 *Gesta archiepiscoporum Magdeburg.*, 470; Ebendorfer, *Cronica*, 848; *Catalogus abatum Sagan.*, 330; Rosicz, *Gesta diversa*, 67.

reported at length in the Speier chronicle and more briefly in several Augsburg chronicles.[138] As to the Second Treaty of Thorn in 1466, it was written about contemporaneously in Silesia by Sigismund Rosicz in Breslau, and later by Weynknecht in Sagan and Hector Mülich in Augsburg.[139]

III

The third thematic field in which Poland and Polish-German relations are addressed deals with political marriages. These chronical notations from a Polish point of view relate to the marital unions of members of the royal house on the one hand, and on the other to members of the Silesian Piasts marrying members of the imperial aristocracy. Most of the unions are mentioned only in individual chronicles.

The marriages of Polish princes with imperial princes came about at the end of the 13th century with the last representatives of the Přemyslids. The marriage of Wenzel II's sister, Kunigunde, to Boleslaw II of Masovia in 1291 (as a safeguard for Wenzel's ambitions to the Polish crown) is reported by the Austrian chronicle.[140]

As to the unions of members of the Polish royal house, the first one to be mentioned is the marriage plan of the daughter of Przemysł II, Elisabeth Richza. Her betrothal to Otto of Brandenburg (who died before the marriage took place in 1299) is known to Peter of Zittau;[141] her marriage to Wenzel II in 1303 is reported by him in his the *Chronicon Aulae Regiae*,[142] and her brief marriage (1306/1307) to Rudolf von Habsburg, the son of Albrecht I, is reported in the Zbraslav Chronicle, the chronicle of the Erfurt monastery of St. Peter, as well as by Matthias of Neuenburg in Straßburg.[143] The betrothal in 1335 of Elisabeth, the daughter of Casimir III, to Johann the Child, the son of Henry XIV of Bavaria and Margarethe of Luxembourg (thus the grandson of Johann of Bohemia), is reported by Francis of Prague in the wake of the Visegrád agreements between

---

138　Speier. *Chronik*, cap. 112: 418; *Chronik der Stadt Augsburg*, 327; Mülich, *Chronik*, 127; *Anonyme Chronik*, 505.

139　Rosicz, *Gesta diversa*, 82; *Catalogus abbatum Sagan.*, 333of.; Mülich, *Chronik*, 207.

140　"Die aine [Tochter Ottokars II.] ward geben ze Prag in sand Claren orden; doch wie si darnach darinne lebt, daz waiz man ze Prag wol. Darnach ward sy gegeben herczog Woleslaen von Polan." (*Österreichische Chronik*, III, 293: 136.

141　*Chron. Aulae Regiae*, I, 69: 85. *Chronica Marchionum Brandenburgensium. Nach einer Handschrift der Trierer Stadtbibliothek und den Excerpten des Pulkawa*, ed. Georg Sello, *Forschungen zur brandenburgischen und preußischen Geschichte* 1 (Leipzig/Berlin 1888), 111–180, here cap. XIV, 128, does not mention the marriage plan.

142　*Chron. Aulae Regiae*, I, 67: 81f.; I, 69: 85–87.

143　*Chron. Aulae Regiae*, I, 85: 110; "Cronica s. Petri Erfordensis moderna," 329; Mathias von Neuenburg, *Chronica*, cap. 35: 337.

Casimir and Johann.[144] Also, the subsequently planned Luxembourg-Piast marital union (between the aforementioned Margarethe, now widowed, and Casimir III himself) never came about, since Margarethe died in July 1341 right before the actual ceremony, something about which Francis of Prague and Heinrich Taube of Selbach provide contemporaneous reports.[145] The marriage of Louis IV's son, Louis VI the Roman, to Kunigunde, the daughter of Casimir III in the summer of 1345 is contemporaneously reported by Johann of Winterthur[146] and Heinrich of Herford, who then right away speaks about the Wittelsbach as the future king of Poland.[147] In the 15th century there were many genealogically significant Jagiellonian-Habsburg unions.[148] The importance of the marriage of Cimburgis of Masovia (a daughter of Alexandra of Lithuania, who in turn was a sister to Władysław Jagiełło) to Duke Ernst the Iron of Austria at the beginning of 1412 lay in that fact that through her son Friedrich III she became the female ancestor of the later Habsburgs. Only Jakob Unrest mentions the union.[149] For the Jagiellonian dynasty, the marriage in 1454 of Casimir IV to Elisabeth of Austria (who is referred to as the "mother of all Jagiellons") had a comparable importance. The marriage is reported by Sigismund Rosicz in Breslau, Veit Arnpeck in Landshut and Jakob Unrest in Carinthia.[150] Veit Arnpeck, who however confuses Elisabeth with her sister Anna, takes this opportunity to name a few of the progeny of this union, in particular Hedwig, the spouse of George the Rich, Vladislav II, Johann Albert

---

144 *Inter cetera amicie federa est promissum, quod Iohannes, puer quingennis, filius Henrici, ducis Bavarie, qui gener regis Boemie extitit, ducere debeat future tempore filiam regis Polonie pro uxore.* (*Chron. Francisci Pragensis*, III, (3) 8: 159f.)
145 *Chron. Francisci Pragensis*, III, (3) 8, 175; Heinrich Taube, *Chronica*, 51.
146 Johannes von Winterthur, *Chronica*, 256.
147 "Tandem Marchie majorem partem germano suo Romulo, qui filiam regis Poloniorum uxorem habuit, donavit, rege Romanorum hoc ipsum approbante.... Lodewicus sane Marchiam totam germano suo Romulo, futuro sicut credebatur regi Polonie, contradidit hereditarie et perpetuo possidendam, Karolo rege Romanorum adnitente ..." (Henricus de Hervordia, *Liber*, 272, 278).
148 Uwe Tresp, "Eine 'famose und grenzenlos mächtige Generation': Dynastie und Heiratspolitik der Jagiellonen im 15. und zu Beginn des 16. Jahrhunderts," *Jahrbuch für europäische Geschichte* 8 (2007), 3–28.
149 "[Ernst] nam zu weyb frawn Czimburg, hertzog Allexander tochter aus der Massa von Polan." (Unrest, *Österreichische Chronik*, wie Anm. 35, 4); to this: Eva Bruckner, *Formen der Herrschaftsrepräsentation und Selbstdarstellung habsburgischer Fürsten im Spätmittelalter* (PhD., Wien, 2009), 191 et seq.
150 "Nuptie regis Polonie. Anno ut supra die dominica ante septuagesimam Casimirus rex Polonie celebravit nuptias cum sorore Ladislai regis Bohemie Cracovie." (Rosicz, *Gesta diversa*, 65); "Die ain tochter [Albrechts] ward zu weyb geben dem kunig von Polan, kunig Casmero, ..." (Unrest, *Österreichische Chronik*, 1).

(who had just succeeded his father), Cardinal Friedrich Jagiełło, Sigismund, and Christof, whom in fact he is mixing up with Alexander the Jagiellon.[151] The third Jagiellonian-Habsburg marital union, the Vienna double wedding of 1515, had an incomparably stronger historiographic echo.[152] No less historiographical attention was given to the wedding of George the Rich from Bavaria with Hedwig, the daughter of Casimir IV in Landshut in November 1475, since it (because of the circumstances and perception at the time) was seen as an event that had more than regional historical importance. Attention was given it in Bavarian chronicles of the later 14th century, namely, by Veit Arnpeck and Ulrich Füetrer.[153]

A second group of historiographical passages about German-Polish marriage agreements deals with contacts among the nobility at regional levels. For the Empire this was primarily about Brandenburg and Bavaria; on the other side it regarded the marriage unions of the Silesian Piasts. The marriage of Konstanze, the daughter of Przemysł I of Greater Poland, to Konrad I of Brandenburg in 1260 is only reported in Brandenburg chronicles.[154] The marital unions of the Silesian Piasts with members of noble families in the neighboring regions of

---

151 "Predicta domina regina Elizabet ex Alberto marito quatuor liberos procreavit, ... Elizabet ... et Annam, que Casimiro regi Polonie desponsata fuit, qui magnifica gaudens prole quinque filios et quinque filias ex ea procreavit aduc superstites, Hedwigem ducissam Bavarie, que es duce Georgio duas suscepit filias, ..., item Wladislaum regem Hungarie et Bohemie, virum utique virtuosissimum, Albertum, qui defuncto genitore paterno potitus est regno, Fridericum cardinalem sedis apostolice legatum per Poloniam etc., archiepsicopum in Tartaria et episcopum Cracoviensem dignissimum, Sigismundum que et Christoferum duces Littovie ac Albe Russie, viros preclarissimos atque omni laude dignissimos,...." (Arnpeck, *Chron. Austr.*, 798f.)

152 Krzysztof Baczkowski, *Kongres wiedeński 1515 roku* [Congress in Vienna 1515] (Oświęcim, 2015).

153 Sebastian Hiereth, "Zeitgenössische Quellen zur Landshuter Fürstenhochzeit 1475," in *Verhandlungen des Historischen Vereins für Niederbayern* 85 (1959) 1–64; Thomas Alexander Bauer, *Feiern unter den Augen der Chronisten. Die Quellentexte zur Landshuter Fürstenhochzeit von 1475*, Sprach- und Literaturwissenschaften 26 (München, 2008); Walter Ziegler, "Die Geschichtsschreibung zur Landshuter Hochzeit 1475: Bericht und Überlegungen," in *Studien zur bayerischen Landesgeschichtsschreibung in Mittelalter und Neuzeit: Festgabe für Andreas Kraus zum 90. Geburtstag*, ed. Alois Schmid, Zeitschrift für bayerische Landesgeschichte. Beiheft 41 (München, 2012), 193–243, here: 194 et seq.; Thomas Alexander Bauer, "Die Darstellung der Landshuter Fürstenhochzeit von 1475 und des Landshuter Erbfolgekriegs (1504–1505) in zeitgenössischen Quellentexten," in *Handbuch Chroniken des Mittelalters*, eds. Gerhard Wolf and Norbert H. Ott (Berlin, 2016), 483–519, here: 485–514.

154 "Iohannes duxit uxorem Sophiam ... et genuit ... Conradum qui duxit uxorem Constanciam, filiam Primizlai ducis, cum magna parte terre iuxta Wartam." (*Chron. marchionum Brandenburg.*, cap. IX: 123).

Bohemia, Austria, and Bavaria are reported almost exclusively just by the chroniclers who came from these local regions. So the Zbraslav Chronicle and Beneš Krabice of Weitmühl note the marriage of Viola Elisabeth of Cieszyn to the last Přemyslid, Wenzel III, in October 1305[155] and the wedding of her half-sister Agnes to Heinrich of Schweidnitz.[156] Silesian marital unions with Bavaria and Austria are mentioned primarily in texts from the monastery Fürstenfeld written by Ulrich Füetrer and by Veit Arnpeck, in Carinthia by Johann of Viktring, and by Matthias of Neuenburg (located in the Habsburg territory on the upper Rhine). The wedding in the summer of 1260 between Louis II of Bavaria and Anna of Glogau, who is referred to as *filia ducis Polonie, ducissa de Polonia* or *aine von Polandt*, is reported by the Fürstenfeld chronicler.[157] The marriage of Otto III of Carinthia and Euphemia of Liegnitz, who likewise is referred to as *filia ducis Polonie*, is reported in 1297 by Johann of Viktring.[158] The wedding of Stephen I of Bavaria to Judith of Schweidnitz in 1299 is noted by (among others)

155 "[...] contraxit matrimonium cum Viola, filia Mesche, ducis de Theschin; hec puella nomine mutato Elizabeth est vocata." (*Chron. Aulae Regiae*, I, 84: 106); "Wenceslaus Vngarie, Boemie et Polonie rex, duxit in coniugem Fyolam, virginem speciosam, filiam ducis Tessnensis." (Benessius, "Chronicon", 464); as to that: Karel Maráz, *Václav III. (1289–1306). Poslední Přemyslovec na českém trůně* [Wenceslas III. (1289–1306). The last Přemyslid on the Czech throne] (České Budějovice, 2007), 50.
156 "Dominus Heinricus, filius domini Bolconis, ducis Silesie de Sweidenitz, duxit legitime sub matrimoniali federe Agnetem virginem, domini Wenceslai regis, ... filiam, ..." (*Chron. Aulae Regiae*, I, 129: 234); "Domicellam Agnetem, regine sororem, nolente regina duci Henrico Polono coniugio tradidit, ..." (ibid. II, 1: 243). "Eodem anno regina Grecensis sic dicta filiam suam Agnetem, quam genuit ex rege Wenceslao seniore, absque consensu et consilio regine Elizabeth, sororis dicte puelle, tradidit et copulavit matrimoniali federe Henrico, filio Bolkonis, ducis Slesie." (Benessius, "Chronicon," 472).
157 "Post quam accepit in coniugem filiam ducis Polonie dominam Annam; ex qua habuit filiam Agnetem et Ludovicum, egregie indolis virum; sed inmatura, proh dolor! morte preventus est." (*Notae Fuerstenfeld.*, 74); "essetque ibi etiam dominus Ludwicus illustris dux Bawarie et filius suus iunior dux Ludwicus, quem genuit per dominam Annam serenissimam ducissam de Polonia, ..." – "Chronica de gestis principum," in *Bayerische Chroniken des 14. Jahrhunderts Chronicae Bavaricae saec. XIV*, ed. Georg Leidinger. (Hannover 1918), ad 1290: 42; "Nach dem nam er [Louis II the Strict of Bavaria] aine von Polandt, genant fraw Anna [von Glogau]; die gepar im ainen sun, genant Ludwig, und ain tochter, genant Agnes." (Füetrer, *Bayerische Chronik*, cap. 240: 169); "Eodem anno [1260] dominam Annam filiam Conradi ducis Polonie in uxorem duxit von der mass." (Arnpeck, *Chron. Baioar.*, cap. 21: 235); the homeland of Anna is given as "Mass"; one could suppose that bases on the name and not the landscape-name Masovia; *in dem jar nam herzog Ludbig di ander hausfrauen Anna, herzog Conrad von Poland tochter.* (Arnpeck, *Bayer. Chron.*: 517).
158 "Meinhardus comes ... quatuor habuit filios ...; tercium Ottonem, qui filiam ducis Polonie habuit, et ex ea quatuor filias progenuit." (*Iohannis Victoriensis Liber*, 256).

the chronicler in Niederaltaich, the abbot of Viktring, and Veit Arnpeck.[159] The Zbraslav and the Carinthian chroniclers report the marriage of Bolesław III, later the duke of Brieg, and Johann of Viktring refers to him solely as *quidam dux Polonorum*; this union was arranged for him when he was a child by his guardian, Wenzel II to the latter's daughter.[160] The union of Agnes, the daughter of Henry III of Glogau, to the Bavarian duke, Otto III (who had stayed at Henry's court after his failed attempt to assert himself as King of Hungary), is described by Ottokar of Styria quite vividly and in detail: from the couple's first meeting up through the wedding in Landshut.[161] The marital union of Beatrix, the daughter of Bolko I of Schweidnitz, to the Bavarian Duke Louis in October 1308 (prior to his election as king) is reported by almost all the Bavarian chronicles, with the texts consistently identifying Beatrix as

---

159   "Stephanus dux Bavarie, …, duxit filiam Pulkonis de Polan in uxorem, celebratis ibidem nupciis." – *Hermanni Altah. Annales*, ed. Georg Waitz., MGH SS, 24, (Hannoverae, 1879), 53–57, here: 55; "… dominus Stephanus dux inferioris Wabarie duxit sororem eius [Betaricis], videlicet dominam Gaeyttam." (*Chron. Ludovici quarti*, 120); "Der konig Ludwig und herzog Steffan von Beiern, sin vetter, heten zwo swestere, herzogen Pulken tochtere von der Swidenitz von Polan. Di konigin hiez Beatrix, di herzogin hiez Jutta." – *Sächsische Weltchronik. Dritte Bairische Fortsetzung*, ed. Ludwig Weiland, MGH Dt. Chron. 2 (Hannoverae, 1877), 340–348, here 344); "Stephanus dux Bawarie, …, duxit u[xorem] filiam Polkonis ducis Pol[onie]." (*Iohannis Victoriensis Liber*, 375); "Hic dux Steffanus Geuttam filiam ducis Polonie de Swidnücz in uxorem duxit." (Arnpeck, *Chron. Baioar.*, 247); "Herzog Steffan nam zu der ee Geutta, ains herzogen tochter von Swidnücz." (Arnpeck, *Bayer. Chron.*, 524).

160   "Tercia [filia Wenceslai] est et filia domina Margaretha, qui duci Wratislaviensi Bouslao est matrimonialiter sociata." (*Chron Aulae Regiae* I, 90: 123; "filiarum … altera duci cuidam Polonorum est sociata, …" (*Iohannis Victoriensis Liber*, II, 13); see Libor Jan, *Václav II.: král na stříbrném trunu: 1283–1305* [Wenceslas II.: King on the Silver Thorn: 1283–1305] (Praha, 2015), 214.

161   Ottokar, *Reimchronik*, 88720–89049: 1155–1158; earlier and contemporaneously: "Domnus Otto rex Ungarie et dux Bawarie mirabiliter a captivitate Ungarica liberatus, per Prusciam et Rusciam ad terram suam rediens, in ipsa via filiam ducis Gloavie nomine Elyzabet desponsat, quam postea breviter ducit uxorem." – *Annales Osterhovenses*, ed. Wilhelm Wattenbach, MGH SS 17 (Hannoverae, 1861) 537–558, here ad a. 1308: 555; *Chronica de ducibus Bavariae*, ed. Georg Leidinger, MGH SSrG. 19 (Hannover/Leipzig, 1918) 151–175, here 152. From Oberaltaich the writer labeled Heinrich of Glogau at this occasion as *dux Polonie*; from that as well Andreas von Regensburg, "Chronica," 547; The Salzburgerian Annales (*Ann. s. Rudberti Salisburg.*, 819) mention the marriage in Straubing on Pentecost 1309 and the *uxor sua de Glogawe*; furthermore in chronicles of the late 15th century: Füetrer, *Bayerische Chronik*, cap. 237: 167 named Agnes *Machthild*, there might be a confusion with the name of her mother, Mechthild von Braunschweig; Ebran von Wildenberg, *Chronik*, 141: Heinrich von Glogau is here *ein hertzog in Bolon*; Arnpeck, *Chron. Baioar.*, 244: *dux Polonie*; Arnpeck, *Bayer. Chron.*, 523: *von ainem herzogen von Eyffn in Palant*.

a daughter of a Polish duke.[162] The second "Polish" marriage for Anna, the oldest daughter of King Albrecht I, to Henry VI of Breslau is mentioned by Matthias of Neuenburg and Veit Arnpeck.[163] The union of Agnes, the daughter of Leopold I of Austria, to Bolko II from Scheidnitz, *in Poloniam*, is mentioned by Johann of Viktring, Matthias of Neuenburg, and the Austrian chronicle.[164] And finally, Veit Arnpeck reports the marital union of Margarethe, the daughter of Louis I of Brieg, with Albrecht of Bavaria in 1353.[165] These mentionings of marital unions of Silesian dukes or the daughters of Silesian dukes deserve attention in that although in some cases reference is made to the respective residence towns (Breslau, Schweidnitz, Brieg), Silesia itself is never mentioned. Much more so the talk is of a *dux Polonie* or his daughter.

---

162 "[Ludowicus] accepta coniuge ducis Polonie filia Beatrice ..." (*Notae Fuerstenfeld.*, 75); "ipse inclitus dux [Ludovicus] in uxorem duxit dominam Beatricem filiam illustris ducis Polonie Pulkonis, [...]" (*Chron. Ludovici quarti*, 120); *Sächsische Weltchronik. Dritte Bairische Fortsetzung* (159); "Lůdewicus ducis Polonie duxit filiam." (*Iohannis Victoriensis Liber*, 350); "Ex Ludwico imperatore descenderunt ex Polana Lúdwicus et Stephanus filii et marchionissa in Missen." (Mathias von Neuenburg, *Chronica*, cap. 24a: 297); "Nu wonte der kaiser [Louis IV.] zu Rom mit grosser und reichlicher zerung und kostung, und die kaiserin, was aine von Poland" (Füetrer, *Bayerische Chronik*, cap. 240: 169); "Ludovicus dux Bavarie superioris ... duas uxores habuit. Prima dicta fuit Beatrix filia ducis Polonie,...." (Arnpeck, *Chron. Baioar.*, cap. 45: 282); "Ludbig, herzog in Oberbyren, hat gehabt zbo hausfrauen. di erst bas frau Beatrix, ains herzogen tochter von Polan,...." (Arnpeck, *Bayer. Chron.*, 568); "Er lie 6 sün, Ludbig, Stefan, Albrecht, Wilhalm, Ludbig den Römer und Otto, bey zbain elichen hausfrauen, der küngin von Polan und ain gräfin von Holand ..." (ibid.: 582); The confusion with the both wifes: *Ludbig der Römer, ... und sein jünger bruder Otto, der paider muter was von Polan, den was in der ersten tailung di march zu Brandenburg.* (ibid., 584).
163 "Unam [Anna von Habsburg] dedit Goldemaro marchioni [in] Brandenburg. Quo mortuo sine liberis ipsam dedit duci [Henrico VI.] in Presla Polonie." (Mathias von Neuenburg, *Chronica*, cap. 35: 58); ohne Erwähnung des Ehegatten: "Reliquit [rex Albertus] adhuc decem liberos, ... videlicet ... Annam ducissam Polonie, ..." (Arnpeck, *Chron. Austr.*, 778).
164 "Quarum [...] alteram in Poloniam dux Albertus Lůpoldi filias honorifice maritavit." (*Iohannis Victoriensis Liber*, II, 96; II, 128); "Item dux Lúpoldus strennuissimus, qui relictis duabus filiabus ex filia comitis Sabaudie, quarum una postea data est duci [de] Swidnicz Polonie." (Mathias von Neuenburg, *Chronica*, cap. 24: 294); "Die ander tochter herczog Leupoltz ward fraw ‖ Agnes genennet und ward aim herczogen von Polan gemëhelt zen Slezien, Herren zu Swidenicz." (*Österreichische Chronik*, IV, 371: 179f.
165 "Albertus ... duxit Margaretam filiam ducis Ludovici, ducis Polonie de Briga, in uxorem." (Arnpeck, *Chron. Baioar.*, cap. 52: 319); Arnpeck, *Bayer. Chron.*, 585; "im [Albrecht] ward verheirat frau Margreth aus Polant, herzog Ludbig von Briga tochter." (Arnpeck, *Bayer. Chron.*, 585).

3 Perceptions and Valuations

As in the earlier Middle Ages, Poland appears in the chronicles of the Empire primarily with respect to the history of the relations between the two. This really needs no further explanation or justification. What is new in the post-Staufen period is that Poland seems to be more distant from the Empire. Differently than in the 11th century, there are no texts that take up the topic of a direct German-Polish relationship. The perceptions from the history of the mutual relations are now conveyed primarily by way of Silesian-Bohemian points of view and the history of the Teutonic Order. Only a few observations extend beyond this confine or show any awareness of the important events in Polish history in the years 1320, 1370, or 1385. How marginal the level of knowledge was is something seen in the background report about the developments in Poland from decades before, which Andreas of Regensburg records. He got this information on the occasion of the Posen bishop's, Andrzej Łaskarz's, journey to the Council of Pavia when the bishop passed through Regensburg while travelling south. The bishop's chaplain, also named Andreas, shared with the chronicler the genealogical connections in the Polish history of the previous 100 years, which the Bavarian Andreas added to his chronicle of the Hussite movement.[166]

Overall there are hardly any references to specific stereotypes about Poland in the late medieval German chronicles. Yet, a few observations and constellations of information do attract some attention.

The title of the Polish kings is not presented solely as *rex Poloniae*. What was widely used by the chroniclers of the 14th and 15th centuries is the appellation *rex Cracoviae*.[167] One finds it among north German and upper German historiographers, but less markedly so in Bavarian and Bohemian chronicles. On the occasion of the coronation of Władysław Łokietek, the *Annales Lubicenses* denotes him as *rex Kracoviae*;[168] the continuations of the Lübeck Detmar chronicle and the Magdeburg *Schöppenchronik* refer in their reports of 1410 to the "King of Cracow or Poland".[169] Johannes of Winthertur and Matthias of Neuenburg in the 1340s, when writing about contemporaneous

---

166   Andreas von Regensburg, "Diarium sexennale," 307f.; see id., *Chronica Husitarum*, in id., Sämtliche Werke, 343–459, here 409f.; see for that: Ożóg, "Bawarski Liwiusz," 747, 750.
167   To this Grabski, *Polska w opiniach Europy*, 141.
168   *Ann. Lubic.*, ad a. 1316: 425.
169   "De konnigh van Krackowe eder van Polenen" (*Detmar-Chronik*, cap. 1138: 151); "der koning van Krakowe, ok geheiten de koning van Polen" (*Magdeburger Schöppenchronik*, III: 329).

events, use *rex Cracovie* exclusively[170] (or sometimes *Kragowie* or *Kragogie*).[171] In the 15th century one finds the appellation *künig von Krackowe* being used by Jakob Twinger of Königshofen;[172] *rex Crackoviensis* und *konig von Krakauw* by Johannes Kungstein,[173] *rex Cracovie* by Dietrich of Nieheim;[174] Reinhold Slecht writes for 1410 about the *rex Kracko seu Polonie*,[175] the Augsburg chronicle speaks of the *kung von Kragkaw*[176] and in Eberhard Windeck one finds *konig von Krakouwe* alongside the appellation *konig von Polant*.[177] Heinrich Taube of Selbach, after the middle of the 14th century, likewise speaks solely of *rex Cracovie*,[178] and in passing one may mention that Wigand of Marburg at the court of the Grand Master in Prussia at the end of the 14th century likewise speaks solely of *rex Cracovie*.[179] In Bohemia, Charles IV uses only the expression *rex Cracovie*[180] in his autobiography; Beneš Krabice of Weitmühl alongside his usual *rex Polonie* only once uses the appellation *rex Krakouie*[181] and Přibík Pulkava and the annals from Heinrichau use the form *rex Cracovie* in the report for 1326.[182] It is Andreas of Regensburg who alone gives an explanation of this use of the title, linking it to the place of residence of the Polish king: *Prefatus Wladislaus rex Polonorum, qui est rex Cracovie in volgo vocatur, eo quod Cracovie regni sui sedem teneat*.[183] Some chroniclers formed from this title a designation for the Kingdom of Poland. Peter of Zittau, in the Zbraslav chronicle, speaks of *Cracouia ac Polonie regnum*[184] and Beneš Krabice of *Cracouia et totum Polonie regnum*.[185] More explicitly, Jakob Twinger speaks of the *künigrich zu Krackowe*,[186] a Viennese chronicler refers to *chünichreich von Krakaw*,[187]

---

170   Matthias von Neuenburg, *Chronica*, 135, 143, 159, 372, 376, 382.
171   Johannes von Winterthur, *Chronica*, 102, 181, 184, 203, 256, 257.
172   Twinger, *Chronik*, 913f.
173   *Chron. Mogunt.*, 4, 88.
174   Dietrich von Nieheim, *Historie*, 129.
175   Slecht, *Chronicon*, 125.
176   *Chronik der Stadt Augsburg*, 116.
177   Windecke, *Denkwürdigkeiten*, cap. 37: 21; cap. 38: 21f.
178   Heinrich Taube, *Chronica*, 51, 103.
179   *Die Chronik Wigands von Marburg*, ed. Theodor Hirsch. Scriptores rerum Prussicarum 2 (Leipzig, 1863), 429–662, here 436, 492, 525, 556, 648.
180   Charles IV, *Vita*, cap. 8: 80; cap. 14: 146; cap. 17: 159; cap. 18: 160; cap. 18: 162; cap. 18: 164; cap. 18: 168.
181   Benessius, "Chronicon", ad a. 1338: 505.
182   Pulkava, *Cronica Boemorum*, cap. 100: 203; *Ann. Cisterciensium Henricov.*, 546.
183   Andreas von Regensburg, "Chronica," 265.4, 12, 18.
184   *Chron. Aulae Regiae*, I, 71: 88.
185   Benessius, *Chronicon*, ad a. 1300: 463.
186   Twinger, *Chronik*, 913.
187   *Österreichische Chronik*, III, 297: 138.

and Johannes Kungstein to the *regio regis Crackoviensis* and to the *regnum Krakaw*.[188] This forming of a title could also be applied to the feminine form. So, Hedwig, daughter of Louis of Anjou and consort of Władysław Jagiełło, is spoken of by the Salzburg annalist as *regina Cracovie*.[189] Yet this terminology could also lead to some misleading notions: so, according to the Lübeck annalist, Władysław Łokietek was crowned *rex Kracoviae et Poloniae*[190] und Jakob Twinger of Königshofen writes about Louis of Anjou as *künig Ludewig van Ungern ... hette drü künigreiche Ungern, Krackowe und Polonien ...*[191] Karl Hegel, the publisher, related that to Lesser Poland and Greater Poland. In this context it is worthy of note that differently than the Bohemian chronicler mentioned above, Charles IV in his autobiography refers to Przemysł II explicitly as king of Lesser Poland (*rex inferioris Polonie*) and to Władysław Łokietek and his son Casimir as *reges Cracovie seu inferioris Polonie*.[192] And finally, what is unique is Peter of Zittau's rendering of the monarchical title for Przemysł II based on his Greater Poland center of power as duke, referring to him then as the king of Kalisch (*rex Kalisiensis*).[193]

While *Polonia* as a reference point is not used exclusively for the royal title, it is almost without exception the basis of the appellation for the Silesian dukes primarily when they are referring to Silesian marriages. So, Anna of Glogau

188   *Chron. Mogunt.*, 4, 12.
189   *Ann. s. Rudberti Salisburg.*, ad a. 1386: 840.
190   "Qui [Johannes XXII.] ... ducem Kracoviae, cognomento Locket ... regem fecit ordinari Kracoviae et Poloniae, ..." (*Ann. Lubic.*, 425).
191   Twinger, *Chronik*, 913.
192   "Wenceslaus secundus, rex Boemie, possederat inferiorem Poloniam predictam cum ducatibus Cracovie et Sandomerie racione unice filie Przemisl, regis inferioris Polonie, ducis Cracoviae et Sandomerie, quam acceperat in uxorem.... et dicebat se ius habere in regno Polonie inferioris, asserendo quod femina non posset hereditare in regno. Et sic guerra a longis temporibus duraverta inter reges Boemie et Kazomirum ac patrem suum quondam, Wladislaum nomine, reges Cracovie seu inferioris Polonie." (Charles IV, *Vita*, cap. 8: 82).
193   *Chron. Aulae Regiae*, I, 67: 81f.; before though: "Quomodo dux Calisiensis in regno Poloniae coronatus fuerit et quomodo fuerit interemptus." (ibid. I. 50: 60); similiar: Benessius, "Chronicon", 461 et seq.; see: Grabski, *Polska w opiniach obcych*, 252–254; idem, *Polska w opiniach Europy*, 140. – It is remarkable that the Erfurt chronicler expresses himself similarly when he reports that Rudolf of Habsburg had married Elisabeth Richza, the daughter of the Duke of Kalisch: "Cui rex pater suus filiam ducis Kalisie uxorem dedit, que ante fuerat in matrimonio regis Wenezlai, quam sorore regis Romanorum mortua duxerat in uxorem." – "Cronica s. Petri", 329.

is *filia ducis Polonie*,[194] Bolko I of Schweidnitz *dux Polko de Polonia*,[195] Judith of Schweidnitz *filia ducis Polonie*,[196] Maria of Beuthen *filia ducis Polonie*,[197] Beatrix of Schweidnitz *ducis Polonie filia*,[198] Agnes of Glogau *filia ducis Polonie*,[199] Boleslaw III of Brieg *dux Polonorum*,[200] Henry VI of Breslau is *dux Vratizlavie in Poloniam*,[201] whose consort Anna, the daughter of Albrecht I, is *ducissa Polonie*,[202] Bolko II of Schweidnitz is *dux [de] Swidnicz Polonie*,[203] Margarethe of Troppau *filia ducis Polonie*,[204] Margarethe of Brieg *filia ducis Polonie*,[205] and finally Paul of Jägerndorf, Bishop of Freising, receives the gloss: *Hic fuit de Polonia*.[206]

Now and then the late medieval chroniclers provide what is factually false information. Very seldom is the name of the Polish king ever given incorrectly. Nevertheless, there are examples of this in the Lübeck chronicles. So Detmar of Lübeck calls Przemysł II, Bolesław[207] and Hermann Korner and the

---

194 *Notae Fuerstenfeld.*, 75; "ducissa de Polonia – Cronica des gestis principum", 42; "aine von Polandt, genant fraw Anna" – Füetrer, *Bayerische Chronik*, cap. 240: 169; "Anna, herzog Conrad von Poland tochter" – Arnpeck, *Bayerische Chronik*, 517.

195 *Cronica s. Petri Erfordensis moderna*, 315; "Pulcho dux Polonie" – Heinrich Taube, *Chronica*, 3; "Pulko dux Polonie" – Ebendorfer, *Cronica*, 501.

196 *Iohannis Victoriensis Liber*, 375; Arnpeck, *Chronica Baioariorum*, cap. 25: 247; idem, *Bayerische Chronik*, 524.

197 Dietrich von Nieheim, *Historie*, 129.

198 *Notae Fuerstenfeld.*, 75; *Iohannis Victoriensis Liber*, 66; *Chronica Ludovici*, 120; Füetrer, *Bayerische Chronik*, cap. 251: 174; Ebendorfer, *Cronica*, 814; "eins konigs tochter von Bolon" – Ebran von Wildenberg, *Chronik*, 113; Arnpeck, *Chronica Baioariorum*, cap. 45: 282; "ains herzogen tochter von Polan" – idem, Bayerische Chronik, 568.

199 "[Otto III.] est a duce Polonie captivatus. Cuius filia in uxorem recepta ..." (Andreas von Regensburg, "Chronica," 547); "des hertzogen [von Polandt] tochter" (Füetrer, *Bayerische Chronik*, cap. 237: 167); "[...] von einem hertzogen in Bolon; desselben tochter [...]" (Ebran von Wildenberg, *Chronik*, 141); "[Otto III.] a duce Polonie secundo captus. Qui Agnetem filiam suam sibi desponsavit ..." (Arnpeck, *Chronica Baioariorum*, cap. 24: 244); Arnpeck, *Bayerische Chronik*, 523.

200 *Iohannis Victoriensis Liber*, II, 1: "altera [Margarethe, filia Wenceslai II.] duci cuidam Polonorum est sociata."

201 *Iohannis Victoriensis Liber*, 366;

202 Arnpeck, *Chronicon Austriacum*, 778.

203 Matthias von Neuenburg, *Chronica*, cap. 24: 294; *Iohannis Victoriensis Liber*, II, 96, 128 talks about a mariage *in Poloniam*.

204 Matthias von Neuenburg, *Chronica*, cap.: 135, 444.

205 Arnpeck, *Chronica Baioariorum*, cap. 52, 319.

206 *Gesta episcoporum Frisingensium*, 326.

207 "den hertoghen Bolizlawen van Kalys, de koning wart der Polene" – *Detmar-Chronik*, cap. 420, 390.

Rufus chronicle speak about Władysław Jagiełło as Bolesław,[208] while Ebran of Wildenberg refers to him, Jogaila, as Meschbo.[209] It is only among the north German and Upper Rhine chroniclers that one finds (infrequently) an incorrect identification of the grand duke as being the king of Lithuania, as when Skirgaila, the brother of Jogail, is misidentified by Johannes Kungstein[210] and Detmar of Lübeck,[211] and when the *Schöppenchronik*[212] and Twinger of Königshofen[213] speak about Vytautas in the report for 1410.

Remarkably seldom is incorrect information given about Polish political marriages. Matthias of Neuenburg writes of Ottokar II's consort, Kunigunda of Halych, as *uxor sua, que Polonica extitit*.[214] Ulrich Füetrer writes about Margarethe of Holland or Hennegau, the second spouse of Emperor Louis IV and mother of Louis the Roman, as *die kaiserin, was aine von Polandt* and he calls her *fraw(en) Margaretha(m) von Poland*,[215] whom he is certainly confusing with Louis' first wife, Beatrix of Schweidnitz. Veit Arnpeck, when naming the children of Elisabeth of Luxembourg and Albrecht II von Habsburg, confuses the daughter Elisabeth, whom Casimir IV married, with the older Anna.[216] Jakob Unrest refers to the second wife of Henry VI of Gorizia as *Kathrein, aine auss der Massa von Polan*, so from Masovia,[217] but that should actually be Katharina of Gara, daughter of the Hungarian palatine Nikolaus of Gara. The Austrian Rhymed Chronicle presents the spouse of the last Árpád, Fenena, the daughter of Siemomysł of Kujawien, as the daughter of the duke of Glogau[218] and includes in the report about Henry IV of Breslau an account

---

208 "Bolezlaus rex Polonie ... intravit terram Prutzie" (Korner, *Chron. novella*, cap. 814: 109); "Boleslaus Polonorum rex ... Prutziam intravit" (ibd., cap. 1379: 450); afterwards: "in deme sulven jare toch Boleslaus, de konynk van Polen, ... in Prutzen" (*Rufus-Chronik*, cap. 1379: 175).
209 See note 56 above.
210 Here Skirgaila wrongly described as successor in Poland: "Hoc regnum [Polonie] postea Schirial [Skirgaila] scismaticus rex Liteanorum est adeptus." (*Chron. Mogunt.*, 28).
211 "... weren de konnigh van Krackowe eder van Polenen unde de konnigh van Lettowen." (*Detmar-Chronik*, cap. 1138: 150).
212 "... Wytolde sinen broder den koning van Littowen, ..." (*Magdeburger Schöppenchr.*, III: 329).
213 "... der künig von Krackowe ... mit künig Witolde, ..." (Twinger, *Chronik*, 914).
214 Matthias von Neuenburg, *Chronica*, 26, 322.
215 Füetrer, *Bayerische Chronik*, 174, 184.
216 "Predicta domina regina Elizabet ex Alberto marito quatuor liberos procreavit, ... Georgium, ... Elizabet, ... et Annam, que Casimiro regi Polonie desponsata fuit, qui magnifica gaudens prole quinque filios et quinque filias ex ea procreavit ..." (Arnpeck, *Chronicon*, 798).
217 Unrest, *Österreichische Chronik*, 11.
218 Ottokar, *Reimchronik*, cap. 533, v. 41089–41145: 1, 533f.; *Österreichische Chronik*, IV, 333: 158.

of the murder of Bishop Stanisław of Krakau;[219] however, in two manuscripts of the Rhymed Chronicle and in the Austrian Chronicle of the 95 Rulers, the name of the bishop is given as Wenzel of Cracow.[220] Another piece of mistaken information concerns the murder of the provost of Bernau in front of St. Mary's church in Berlin in August 1324, which Heinrich of Herford links to the Polish-Lithuanian incursion into Brandenburg in 1326.[221]

A historiographical mode of expression (used in various ways) employs a transposing of asserted current political positions into either the far distant past or into divine visions or promises. Ulrich Füetrer, around 1480, describes a dream of Charlemagne in which an angel of God promises him: *Dir wirt auch undertan Sicilia, Schottenlandt, Arragun, Engellandt, Tennenmarck, Polandt, die fraissamen Rewssen, Hungern, Behaim, die starcken Sachsen, das künigkreich Marsilia; und mit gar grosser arbait und müe wirstu bezwingen Hyspania*. With this, the Munich poet and historian is describing an idea of Empire which would have been unthinkable in the time of Charlemagne and in the 15th century had no relation to reality. Be that as it may, Poland in this instance has a place in the field of vision of a Bavarian chronicler.

These observations come to an end around the year 1500; in the second half of the 15th century new practices and ways of perceiving things developed in historiography. The transition to humanistic forms of historiography that emerged with the reception of the geographical works of Ptolemy, the reception of Tacitus' *Germania*, and the *Antiquitates* of Annius of Viterbo provided a basis in succeeding years for a new niveau in the perception and description of the eastern neighbors of the Empire.

Translated by Philip Jacobs (English-Exactly)

---

219 Ottokar, *Reimchronik*, cap. 223, v. 21464–21510: 284.
220 Ottokar, *Reimchronik*, cap. 223: 284; *Österreichische Chronik*, III, 297: 138: "sand Wenczla, der bischoff ze Krakaw."
221 "Prepositus de Bernov, hominem corpore grossum et pinguem, vinciunt, caput inter crura detorquentes, dorsum ejus gladiis aperiunt, profluvium sanguinis attendunt, de exitu belli per ipsum divinare cupientes." (Henricus de Hervordia, *Liber*, cap. 94: 211; the report was copied later by Hermann Korner, to this Dietrich Kurze, "Der Propstmord zu Berlin 1324," in *Jahrbuch für Berlin-Brandenburgische Kirchengeschichte* 60 (1995) 92–136, here 97 [repr.: idem, *Berlin-Brandenburgische Kirchengeschichte im Mittelalter. Neun ausgewählte Beiträge*, eds. Marie-Luise Heckmann, Susanne Jenks, and Stuart Jenks, Bibliothek der brandenburgischen und preußischen Geschichte 9 (Berlin, 2002) 207–250, here 212f.]

CHAPTER 11

Poland, Silesia, Pomerania and Prussia in the Empire's Hagiographic Sources

Stephan Flemmig

1   Introduction

The pursuit of hagiographic texts may initially be motivated by theological or historiographic interests. The theological approach is based upon a normative dogmatic assertion that there is a higher measure of truth purported in the lives of saints. The saintly life, as a rule linearly-biographically structured, becomes like a vessel which holds the visible evidence of God whose divine spiritual power and action are present in our world. A historiographic study, on the other hand, asks questions more so about the facts in the life of a saint, and about the trustworthiness of historical witnesses. Such a pursuit is frequently anachronistic. Often the intended theological truth character of the hagiographic legend lies above the historical factuality. Any given hagiographic text could be disappointing when viewed with regard to the evidential value of the witnesses' testimony. A third way to approach the texts would be to consider hagiographic texts as a form of mediation among quite different cultural practices, understood through images or stereotypes. This approach is often connected to literary studies, but is not limited to that discipline alone.[1]

Certainly, any such a separation according to theological, historiographic or any other kind of motivation is artificial. No modern theologian would totally disregard the historiographic or literary dimensions; similarly, no historians or literary theorists would ignore the insights from adjoining disciplines. Notwithstanding this, the practical differentiation into theological, historiographic, or any other variant motivation can be a starting point for the following search for stereotypes in hagiographic sources.

---

1   *Die Legende der heiligen Hedwig. In der Übersetzung des Kilian von Meiningen* [*The Legend of St. Hedwig. In the translation by Kilian von Meiningen*], ed. Sabine Seelbach (Münster, 2016), 253–54. Current literary dispositions, verbally to be understood as images, aimed to a particular social group in the Middle Ages, which could be used as a basis for stereotypes: Langner, *Annäherung ans Fremde*, here especially 15–25.

2 The Tradition

First of all, the question is about the material itself. Looking at this issue, what one notices is that Poland, Silesia, Pomerania or Prussia find no prominent presence in the hagiography of the Empire. In researching the available lives of saints (*Vitae*) and accounts of their miracles or passions (*Passiones* and *Miraculae*), only a handful of texts reveal respective points of contact. Specifically, this refers to hagiographic texts about Adalbert of Prague, Otto of Bamberg, and Hedwig of Silesia. References along these lines appear as well in the description of the lives of the Five Brothers, and also the hermits and martyrs in Poland. As a result, we are dealing with various periods of time, which has consequences for the respective hagiographic texts and the statements (with stereotypes) about Poland, Silesia, Pomerania and Prussia contained in them.

Turning first to Adalbert of Prague, he suffered his martyrdom in the year 997 among the Baltic old Prussians. The Five Brothers died shortly afterwards, in 1003. Otto of Bamberg was chaplain in Poland at the beginning of the 12th century; his two missionary journeys to Pomerania are dated to 1124/25 and 1128. Hedwig of Silesia died in 1243. There is little to add to the lives and influence of these persons and the same is true with regard to their cults and veneration in the Empire, in Poland or beyond. What alone would be of interest would be the hagiographic texts – and the representations of Poland, Silesia, Pomerania and Prussia found in them.[2]

1. There are two extant hagiographic works about Adalbert – in addition to fragmentary traces in other sources. One is concerned with the *Vita Sancti Adalberti*, and the other with the *Passio Sancti Adalberti*. The authorship of this first Vita is still under debate. Presumably the *Vita* was written soon after Adalbert's death, say in 998 or 999. According to Heinrich George Pertz, publisher of the *Scriptores Serie* of the *Monumenta Germaniae Historica*, the *Vita*

---

2   Compare to the persons mentioned here: Gerard Labuda, "Adalbert Vojtěch (hl.) [Adalbert Vojtěch (St)]," in *Lexikon des Mittelalters I* (München, 1980), 101–02; Alexander Gieysztor, "Johannes u. Gefährten [John and Companions]," in *Lexikon für Theologie und Kirche* 2 (Freiburg/Basel/Rom/Wien, 1994), 210–11; Norbert Kersken, "Otto von Bamberg [Otto of Bamberg]," in *Religiöse Erinnerungsorte in Ostmitteleuropa. Konstitution und Konkurrenz im nationen- und epochenübergreifenden Zugriff*, ed. Joachim Bahlcke, Stefan Rohdewald, and Thomas Wünsch (Berlin, 2013), 561–73; Jürgen Petersohn, "Otto, hl. [Otto, St.]," in *Lexikon des Mittelalters VI [Medieval Lexicon VI]* (München, 1993), 1580–81; Benigna Suchoniówna, "Jadwiga," in *Polski Słownik Biograficzny, Tom X* (Wrocław/Warsaw/Krakow, 1962–1964), 297–99; Teresa Dunin-Wąsowicz, "Hedwig v. Schlesien [Hedwig of Silesia]," in *Lexikon des Mittelalters IV* (München, 1989), 1985–86.

appeared in Rome in the milieu of the Aventine monastery of St. Bonifatius and Alexius. Pertz considers a later abbot, Johannes Camparius, to have been the author. Subsequent research has generally acknowledged Pertz's thesis, however it was based on some uncertain suppositions. In 2000, Johannes Fried called into question this old thesis. Based on a long-neglected and scarcely considered manuscript from Aachen, and additionally supported by other circumstantial evidence, Fried supposed that the oldest centre of any veneration of Adalbert lay in Lüttich-Aachen. Fried considers Bishop Notker of Lüttich, a close and trusted member of the court of Otto III, as the actual author of the Adalbert's *Vita*.[3] Yet, Notker's authorship is in turn considered dubious, for example, by Peter Kubin, who assumes that a student of the Lüttich bishop was the author.[4]

Regardless of the uncertain provenance of the saint's legend, one can hold that the *Vita Sancti Alberti* was popular in medieval times, especially in the Empire. Jadwiga Karwasińska has identified 37 manuscripts, 29 of them being complete texts.[5] In fact, one may suppose that even additional manuscripts exist.[6] The *Vita Sancti Alberti* was handed down in three independent editions, each one different in extent and contents. The most extensive is edition A.[7] Presumably this edition was inspired by Emperor Otto III, so it is

---

3 Johannes Fried, "Gnesen-Aachen-Rom. Otto III. und der Kult des hl. Adalbert. Beobachtungen zum älteren Adalbertsleben [Gnesen-Aachen-Rome, Otto III and the cult of St. Adalbert. Observations to the older life of Adalbert]," in *Polen und Deutschland vor 1000 Jahren. Die Berliner Tagung über den "Akt von Gnesen"*, ed. Michael Borgolte (Berlin, 2002), 235–279; Jerzy Strzelczyk, "Einleitung [Introduction]," in *Heiligenleben zur deutsch-slawischen Geschichte. Adalbert von Prag und Otto von Bamberg*, ed. Lorenz Weinrich (Darmstadt, 2005), 3–19, here 12–13.

4 Petr Kubín, "Die Bemühungen Ottos III. um die Einsetzung eines Heiligenkultes für Bischof Adalbert von Prag (†997) [The endeavour of Otto III to establish a cult of Saintliness for Bishop Adalbert of Prague (+ 997)]," in *Böhmen und seine Nachbarn in der Přemyslidenzeit*, ed. Ivan Hlaváček and Alexander Patschovsky (Ostfildern, 2011), 317–40, here 323–24.

5 Jadwiga Karwasinska, "Wstęp," in *Sancti Alberti episcopi Pragensis et martyris Vita prior*, ed. Jadwiga Karwasinska, V–XLVII, here VIII–XXII.

6 Michałowski emphasizes that the Adalbert cult reached its highest point towards the end of the millenium, after the death of Otto III except in Bohemia. However, it rapidly diminished in importance. Nevertheless, this does not apply to the popularity of the life of Adalbert. Roman Michałowski, "Die Heiligenkulte sowie die staatlichen und ethnischen Grenzen: Polen und die Nachbarländer vom 10. bis zum 14. Jahrhundert [Cult of Saints, its state and ethnic limits: Poland and its neighbour countries from 10th to 14th centuries]," in *Grenzräume und Grenzüberschreitungen im Vergleich. Der Osten und der Westen des mittelalterlichen Lateineuropa*, ed. Klaus Herber and Nikolaus Jaspert (Berlin, 2007), 339–360, here 341–344.

7 *Sancti Adalberti episcopi Pragensis et Martyris Vita prior. A. Redactio Imperialis vel Ottoniana*, ed. Jadwiga Karwasińska (Warszawa, 1962), 1–47 (hereafter cited as *Vita sancti Adalberti*).

accordingly designated as the Ottonic or emperor's edition. Just after Emperor Otto's death, another edition, shorter particularly in its middle part, was written in the Aventin Monastery.[8] Finally there is the last one, called edition C, which was composed in the Benedictine monastery of Monte Casino.[9] The following discussion will be based upon edition A, because both editions B and C were circulated only in Italian areas (with the exception of a single Austrian Manuscript).[10]

The author of *Passio Sancti Alberti* was Brun (Bruno) of Querfurt. He likely also suffered a martyr's death in the Polish-Rus'-Prussian border area in early 1009. Contrary to the *Vita*, the *Passio* has been handed down in two editions, 1004 and 1008,[11] with considerably fewer copies, that is, in only seven manuscripts and in one print version from an unknown manuscript.[12]

2. Shortly before his martyrdom, Brun of Querfurt also wrote another hagiographic report – the aforementioned story of the lives of the Five Brothers, settlers and martyrs in Poland. This Life of the Five Brothers, however, survives in only one manuscript – a clear statement of the limited circulation of narrations of lives and passions of the saints.[13]

There are three narrations existent about Bishop Otto of Bamberg, who even today is venerated as a missionary to Pomerania. The oldest *Vita* appeared presumably between 1140 and 1146 in the Prüfening monastery near Regensburg, which Bishop Otto himself had founded.[14] However, Jürgen Petersohn has

---

8   *Sancti Adalberti episcopi Pragensis et Martyris Vita prior. B. Redactio Aventinensis altera*, ed. Jadwiga Karwasińska (Warszawa, 1962), 49–67.

9   *Sancti Adalberti episcopi Pragensis et Martyris Vita prior. C. Redactio Cassinensis*, ed. Jadwiga Karwasińska (Warszawa, 1962), 69–84.

10 Strzelczyk, "Einleitung," 12–15; Kubín, "Die Bemühungen Ottos III.," herep. 323–325.

11 *S. Adalberti Pragensis Episcopi et Martyris Vita altera auctore Brunone Querfurtensi. Redactio longior*, ed. Jadwiga Karwasińska (Warszawa, 1969), 1–41 (hereafter cited as *Passio Adalberti. Redactio longior*, to the redaction, which appeared 1004). Ibid., 43–69, the *Redactio brevior* (hereafter cited as *Passio Adalberti. Redactio brevior*, to the redaction, which appeared 1008).

12 Jadwiga Karwasińska, "Wstęp," *S. Adalberti Pragensis episcopi et martyrs Vita altera auctore Brunone Querfurtensi*, ed. ead. (Warszawa, 1969), V–XXXI, here especially VII–XII; Strzelczyk, "Einleitung," 15–16.

13 *Vita quinque fratrum eremitarum* [seu] *Vita uel Passio Benedicti et Iohannis sociorumque suorum*, ed. Jadwiga Karwasińska (Warszawa, 1973), 27–84 (hereafter cited as *Vita quinque fratrum*). As delivered tradition of the Five Brothers *Vita* comp. Jadwiga Karwasińska, *Wstęp*, ibid., 9–21, here 13–15.

14 *S. Ottonis episcopi Babenbergensis Vita Prieflingensis*, ed. Jan Wikarjak and Kazimierz Liman (Warszawa, 1966), 1–74, (hereafter cited as *Vita Prieflingensis*). As delivered

doubts as to whether Monk Wolfberg could be its author.[15] Two further *Vitae* about Otto of Bamberg appeared during the 50's of the 12th century in the Michelsberg monastery near Bamberg. Ebo wrote one *Vita* between 1151 and 1159;[16] and in 1159 Herbord produced his *Dialogus*, a Vita about Otto in dialogue form.[17] Both *Vitae*, by Ebo and by Herbord, were consulted in the canonization process of Otto, which came to a successful conclusion at a *Hoftag* in 1189 in Würzburg.[18]

As had been done before with the Adalbert's *Vita*, the Ottonian *Vitae* were recast into legends. However, as mentioned previously, the observations that follow here are limited to the hagiographic representation of Otto and not such liturgical handling of the material.

3. The basis for all legends about Hedwig is the *Legenda maior* (from around 1300) by an anonymous author of ecclesiastical origin.[19] The legend unites a *Vita* of the saint with a detailed listing of the miracles performed by Hedwig. The *Legenda* is often passed down in what is called the *Genealogia*, an enumeration of Hedwig's ancestors, as well as with the canonization documents and the sermon of Pope Clemens IV on the occasion of the canonization ceremony. Likewise, the *Legenda minor*, often handed down together with the *Legenda maior*, summarizes the previously mentioned detailed description of her life.

In the late 14th and in the 15th centuries, the *Legenda maior* was translated a total of four times into German. There is proof that all those who ordered

---

tradition compare to Jan Wikarjak/Kazimierz Liman, "Wstęp," in ibid., VII–XXII, here XIX–XXII.

15 Jürgen Petersohn, "Einleitung [Introduction]," in *Die Prüfeninger Vita Bischof Ottos I. von Bamberg nach der Fassung des Großen Österreichischen Legendars*, ed. Jürgen Petersohn (Hannover, 1999), 1–35, here 17–20.

16 *Ebonis vita sancti Ottonis episcopi Babenbergensis*, ed. Jan Wikarjak and Kazimierz Liman (Warszawa, 1969),1–146 (hereafter cited as *Ebonis vita Ottonis*). As delivered tradition compare Jan Wikarjak/Kazimierz Liman, *Wstęp*, in ibid., V–XXIV, here XXII–XXIV.

17 *Herbordi dialogus de Vita S. Ottonis episcopi Babenbergensis*, ed. Jan Wikarjak and Kazimierz Liman (Warszawa, 1974), 1–212 (hereafter cited as *Herbordi dialogus*). As delivered tradition comp. Jan Wikarjak/Kazimierz Liman, "Wstęp," in ibid., V–XXVII, here XXIV–XXVII. Summary of Ottos three narrations Strzelczyk, "Einleitung," 18–19 as well as Kersken, "Otto von Bamberg," 562.

18 Kersken, "Otto von Bamberg," 562.

19 *Vita sanctae Hedwigis*, ed. Aleksander Semkowicz, MPH 4 (Lwów, 1884; repr. Warsaw, 1961), 510–642 (hereafter cited as *Vita sanctae Hedwigis*]. Ibid., 642–51 the *Genealogia*.

the manuscripts as well as those who came to own them had a specific relationship to Hedwig. However, Hedwig's *Vita* did not find its way into a set of legends. Outside of the geographic center of Hedwig veneration– in spite of her popularity as a saint– there was only a limited interest in Hedwig.[20]

3 Stereotypes in the Hagiographic Sources

Regarding the representations of Poland, Silesia, Pomerania and Prussia using stereotypes, there are four thematic fields to consider which are mentioned in the sources. Firstly, there are geographic and ethnic descriptions of these countries and their inhabitants. The second essential motive is the conversion of the heathen population. Thirdly, in the different sources certain prominent Polish, Pomeranian or Silesian persons are mentioned and are characterized. Finally – fourthly – the relation of Poland, Silesia, Pomerania and Prussia to the Empire and its problems are discussed.

In what follows, I offer a very brief discussion of these respective thematic fields. This will reveal that often there is only fragmentary information presented, from which only roughly sketched images emerge.

3.1 *Geographic and Ethnographic Descriptions:*

In the *Vita* of Adalbert of Prague, initially there is mention of a place in the Germanic area, which the natives call 'Land of the Slavs'.[21] In another place in the *Vita*, it recognizes as part of that 'Land of the Slavs' the Dukedom of Poland, an extensive realm.[22] After that, Danzig is mentioned as a border town between Poland and the sea.[23] The *Vita* contains no other geographic or ethnographic information about Poland. With regards to (old) Prussia, the results are even skimpier. There is only a statement saying that the god of the Prussians is to be found in their bellies, therefore "avarice is united with death".[24]

---

20   Werner Williams-Krapp, "Hedwig von Schlesien [Hedwig of Silesia]," in *Die deutsche Literatur des Mittelalters. Verfasserlexikon 3* (Berlin/New York, 1981), 566–69, here 566–68; Seelbach, *Legende [Legends]*, 260–61.
21   *Vita sancti Adalberti*, chap. 1, 3–4, here 3: "Est locus in partibus Germanie, diues opibus, prepotens armis ferocibusque uiris, quem incole Sclauoniam cognomine dicunt".
22   *Vita sancti Adalberti*, chap. 25, 37–38, here 38 mention of a Polish Duke as well as chap. 27, 40–41, here 40 to the extensive realm.
23   *Vita sancti Adalberti*, chap. 27, 40–41, here 40.
24   Ibid.: "[…] an Pruzzorum fines adiret, quorum deus uenter est et auaricia iuncta cum morte".

Adalbert's *Passio* delivers, as well, only marginal information. Poland is referred to as a dukedom;[25] interestingly a part of the text mentions that a big city, Gnesne, (Gniezno/Gnesen) is to be found in the country.[26] The Prussians are unfavorably presented; according to Brun of Querfurt, they are barbarians, dogs and wolves.[27]

Also, several times it stresses the strangeness of the Polish language, and that it takes an inordinate amount of effort to learn it.[28]

The three *Vitae* about Otto of Bamberg show an unevenness of detail in their geographic and ethnographic descriptions. Poland is referred to as a dukedom.[29] Herbord refers to Breslau and Posen as episcopal sees and erroneously refers to Kalisch as such.[30] Further on, Gnesen is mentioned as the capital city and the residence of the archbishop.[31] According to the *Vita* by Prüfening, Polish is viewed as a barbarian language.[32]

Pomerania, the central backdrop of the Vitae, is separated from Poland by wild border areas and frightful forests.[33] The *Vitae* show two possible ways of traveling from Bamberg to Pomerania from Franconian territory, either by way of Bohemia and Poland, or through Saxony and Lutizenland.[34]

In the Dialog by Herbord, Pomerania is characterized in a detailed manner. The name of this land "situated by the sea" comes from the Slavic language.

---

25 *Passio Adalberti. Redactio longior*, chap. 21, 26–28, here 26–27 and *Passio Adalberti. Redactio brevior*, chap. 21, 22, 59–61 refer to Polish Duke Boleslaus.

26 *Passio Adalberti. Redactio longior*, chap. 24, 29–31, here 29: "Est in parte regni magna Gnezne, [...]". cf. *Passio Adalberti. Redactio brevior*, chap. 24, 62: "Est in parte regni ciuitas magna Gnezden, [...]".

27 *Passio Adalberti. Redactio longior*, chap. 25, 31–32, and *Passio Adalberti. Redactio brevior*, chap. 25, 62–63.

28 *Vita quinque fratrum*, chap. 6, 41–42, here 41; chap. 10, 50–54, here 54; chap. 13, 58–68, here 59: "[...] Sclauonice lingue idioma superfluo sudore parauimus, [...]".

29 For example, *Vita Prieflingensis* II, chap. 2, 29–31, here 30 (Speech of Polish Duke); *Ebonis vita Ottonis*, II, chap. 4, 62–64 (also speech of Polish Duke); *Herbordi dialogus* II, chap. 2, 62 (speech of dukedom Poland).

30 *Ebonis vita Ottonis* II, chap. 3, 56–61, here 61; *Herbordi dialogus*, II, chap. 8, 75–77, here 76.

31 *Ebonis vita Ottonis* II, chap. 3, 56–61, here 61; *Herbordi dialogus* II, chap. 8–9, 75–79, here 76–77.

32 *Vita Prieflingensis* I, chap. 2, 6–7, here 7.

33 *Vita Prieflingensis* III, chap. 1, 56–57, here 56: "[...] versus Poloniam iter tetendit, quam a confinio Pomeranorum horrenda quedam ac vasta admodum solitudo distingit". *Herbordi dialogus* II, chap. 10, 79–80, here 79: "Taliter a duce Polonie dimissi per Uzdam castrum in extremis Polonie finibus transeuntes nemus horrendum et vastum, quod Pomeraniam Poloniamque dividit intravimus".

34 *Vita Prieflingensis* II, chap. 1–2, 28–31; ibid., III, chap. 4, 59–61; *Ebonis vita Ottonis* II, chap. 3, 56–61, here 60–61.

The land itself is shaped like a triangle; its neighbors beyond the sea are Denmark and Rügen, and then Saxony and Lutizenland, Prussia, Russia and Poland as well. Pomerania itself is described as a productive land, rich in meat and fish, different cereals, nuts and seeds. Honey is in great supply, and there are numerous meadows and pasturelands. The Pomeranian beer is also very much praised. Unfortunately there is no wine, because the inhabitants do not cultivate the grape. However, in another place there is mention that bishop Otto did introduce viticulture. Those who live there, the Pomeranians, were (in Herbord's opinion) experienced warriors; they lived from plundering and robbery and had a natural savagery. Yet in another place, they are described as a mild, noble, honest people.[35]

In different Ottonian *Vitae* there are several Pomeranian towns mentioned and to some extent depicted e. g. Stettin, as capital of Pomerania,[36] Wollin,[37] Pyritz,[38] Kammin,[39] Demmin,[40] Kolberg and Belgard,[41] Stargard[42] and Wolgast.[43] The name of the city Wollin, according the author, came from Julin, derived from Julius Caesar;[44] the name of the city Belgard [Slavic: the white/beautiful Borough] from its beautiful location.[45] In the *Vitae* by Ebo and Herbord, Kammin is presented as a dukedom.[46] Also Rügen[47] and Usedom[48]

---

35   *Herbordi dialogus* II, chap. 1, 59–62. Ibid., chap. 41, 141–44.
36   For example, the *Vita Prieflingensis* II, chap. 7, 36–37, here 37; *Ebonis vita Ottonis* III, chap. 1, 91–94, here 93–94; *Herbordi dialogus* II, chap. 5, 68–71, here 69.
37   *Vita Prieflingensis* II, chap. 5, 34–35; *Ebonis vita Ottonis* II, chap. 7, 66–67; *Herbordi dialogus* II, chap. 24, 104–10, here 104–05.
38   *Vita Prieflingensis* II, chap. 4, 32–34, here 32–33; *Ebonis vita Ottonis* II, chap. 5, 64–65, here 64; *Herbordi dialogus* II, chap 12, 82–83, here 83.
39   *Vita Prieflingensis* II, chap. 4, 32–34, here 33; *Ebonis vita Ottonis* II, chap. 5, 64–65, here 65; *Herbordi dialogus* II, chap. 19, 96–97, here 96.
40   *Ebonis vita Ottonis* III, chap. 5, 102–04, here 102.
41   *Vita Prieflingensis* II, chap. 20, 50–51, here 50 (Kolberg); *Ebonis Vita Ottonis* II, chap. 18, 86–89, here 87 Kolberg and Belgard; *Herbordi dialogus* II, chap. 39, 137–39, Kolberg and Belgard.
42   *Ebonis vita Ottonis* II, chap. 4, 62–64, here 63.
43   *Vita Prieflingensis* III, chap. 4, 59–61, here 61; *Herbordi dialogus* II, chap. 39, 137–39, here 139.
44   *Vita Prieflingensis* II, chap. 5, 34–35, here 34.
45   Ibid., chap. 20, 50–51, here 51.
46   *Ebonis vita Ottonis* II, chap. 5, 64–65, here 65; *Herbordi dialogus* II, chap. 19, 96–97, here 96.
47   *Ebonis vita Ottonis* III, chap. 23, 133–36; *Herbordi dialogus* II, chap. 1, 59–62, here 60.
48   *Vita Prieflingensis* III, chap. 4, 59–61, here 61; *Herbordi dialogus* III, chap. 5, 102–04, here 104; *Herbordi dialogus* III, chap. 2, 150–52, here 151.

as well as the navigable river Oder[49] are mentioned there. Concerning the church organization, there is a report on an effort by Otto to establish an episcopal see in Wollin.[50]

The legend of St. Hedwig does not contain any detailed geographic or ethnographic information. There is just general mention of the principality of Poland, and the dukedom of Silesia. Nevertheless, a good number of places in Silesia and Poland are mentioned, mostly to indicate the origin of persons to whom the holy miracle happened.[51]

3.2   The Conversion of the Formerly Heathen Population

The fundamental object of hagiographic texts is, as mentioned in the introduction, not to mediate factual knowledge – such as geographic or ethnographic references. The subject of the missionary effects of a certain saint is in hagiographic texts much more significant. The *Vitae* and *Passiones* narrations of interest to us here, those of Adalbert of Prague and Otto of Bamberg, follow a typical pattern. The description of paganism and its heathen practices often leads to a very detailed report about the endeavors of the saints in their missionary efforts. The mission can be successful in one instance, but then other times it can fail. When the efforts of a mission fail, that might possibly end in the martyrdom of the missionary, but it could also end in apostasy, in the abandoning of the faith by only superficially converted peoples. In those cases when the mission is successful and endures, the faith of those converted is expressed in the worship of the saints – another typical motive in hagiographic texts.

The *Vita of St Adalbert* is focused on the failure of the mission to the Prussians. They rejected Adalbert and his companions, Benedict and Gaudencius, beat them and chased the saint away before he eventually suffered martyrdom.[52] The report of his sufferings follows this pattern.[53] However, the passion not only gives information about the mission among the Baltic Prussians, but also among the Poles. Actually, it narrates the journey of

---

49   *Vita Prieflingensis* II, chap. 5, 7, 14, 34–35, here 34; 36–37, here 37; 45; *Ebonis vita Ottonis* II, chap. 7, 66–67, here 66; *Herbordi dialogus* II, chap. 37, 132–135, here 134.
50   *Ebonis vita Ottonis* II, chap. 15, 78–79. Indirect, without naming the place, *Vita Prieflingensis* III, chap. 15, 73–74 and *Herbordi dialogus* II, chap. 42, 144–45, here 145.
51   *Vita sanctae Hedwigis*, 583–628.
52   *Vita sancti Adalberti*, chap. 27–30, 40–47.
53   *Passio Adalberti. Redactio longior*, chap. 24–34, 29–41 and *Passio Adalberti. Redactio brevior*, chap. 24–34, 62–69.

Adalbert through Poland towards the Baltic area. According to the passion, Adalbert baptized many people in Gnesen.[54]

In the case of the Five Brothers, to whom Brun of Querfurt devotes a life and passion account, they actually died as victims of a robbery[55] – so it is only conditionally that one would consider their deaths as martyrdom.

In the *Vitae* of Otto of Bamberg, a large part of them concerns the paganism of the Pomeranians, their conversion and then their repeated desertion of their new faith. Certain elements – fully stereotypes – are prominent because of their frequent presentation.

Different practices are mentioned as characteristic of paganism: The description of idol worship is very detailed. Among those mentioned, Triglaw, a statue with three heads, was worshipped in Stettin.[56] The people used to dedicate a beautiful horse to him which then acted as oracle for this deity.[57] In another place, a spring was worshipped[58] and there is also mention of a walnut-tree as an idol.[59] As further elements of heathen faith and pagan practices, the *Vitae* of Otto tell of the alleged killing of (new born) girls, the practice of polygamy, the consuming of human flesh and blood, and the burying of their dead in forests or fields.[60]

Prior to Otto, there seems to have been a Spaniard by the name of Bernhard, who tried to Christianize the Pomeranians, but did not succeed.[61] This Bernhard, and afterwards the Polish duke Boleslaus III (Wrymouth), urged Otto to become a missionary.[62] Otto of Bamberg prepared for his missionary work very thoroughly, selected companions, and looked for interpreters.[63]

The *Vitae* report that Otto was repeatedly met with hostility in Pomerania, and he was several times threatened and even encountered violence.[64] The

---

54 *Passio Adalberti. Redactio longior*, chap. 24, 29–31, here 30; *Passio Adalberti. Redactio brevior*, chap. 24, 62.
55 Cf. *Vita quinque fratrum*, chap. 13, 58–68, here especially. 61–68.
56 *Vita Prieflingensis* II, chap. 11, 42–43; *Ebonis vita Ottonis* III, chap. 1, 91–94, here 93–94; *Herbordi dialogus* II, chap. 32, 122–25, here 124.
57 *Vita Prieflingensis* II, chap. 11, 42–43; *Herbordi dialogus* II, chap. 33, 125–26.
58 *Herbordi dialogus* II, chap. 32, 122–25, here 124–25.
59 *Vita Prieflingensis* III, chap. 11, 70–71.
60 Ibid. II, chap. 21, 51–53; *Herbordi dialogus* II, chap. 18, 92–95. Ibid., chap. 22, 99–100 explicit to Polygamy.
61 *Ebonis vita Ottonis* II, chap. 1, 49–54.
62 Ibid., chap. 2, 54–56; *Herbordi dialogus* II, chap. 6, 72–73.
63 *Ebonis vita Ottonis* II, chap. 3, 56–61, *Herbordi dialogus* II, chap. 7, 73–74.
64 For examples of the enemies and threats of violence against Otto, cf: *Vita Prieflingensis* III, chap. 7–8, 12, 64–67, 71–72; *Ebonis vita Ottonis* II, chap. 4, 62–64, here 63–64; *Ebonis vita Ottonis* III, chap. 20, 129–30; *Herbordi dialogus* II, chap. 24, 104–10.

missionary work of Otto focused its endeavors initially on individuals – who are actually named persons, a prince, two young men, a group of children, etc.[65] Mainly it was the baptism of the prominent people or groups of people which influenced the baptism of other circles in the population.[66]

In the next phase, mass baptisms took place as well as general catechism instructions for the population and mass preaching to the Pomeranians.[67] In this regard, the concept of mass baptisms is fully justified – there are were baptisms which seem utopic, such as 22,165 or also 25,156 persons baptized in a single ceremony.[68] Later, Otto had the heathen temples demolished and erected Christian churches.[69]

The different *Vitae* repeat that after Otto's first mission journey, the Pomeranians deserted the faith again. They once again started worshipping their idols (alongside Christ), and destroyed churches and built temples again.[70] They also worked on Sundays and on holy days.[71] But Otto succeeded in the re-Christianization of Pomerania. The miracles he was able to perform as well as the threat of possible force from outside of Pomerania helped him in his efforts.[72]

---

65 *Vita Prieflingensis* II, chap. 9, 39–41, as well as *Ebonis vita Ottonis* II, chap. 9, 69–71 to the conversion of Domuslaw (Domazlaus) inhabitant of Stettin. In the *Vita Prieflingensis* III, chap. 9, 68 the strict prohibition from the Bishop to Christian children not to play with heathen children: "Monet episcopus eos, qui baptizatos se esse meminerint, ab his, qui baptizati non fuerant, separari et nulla deinceps cum infidelibus communione misceri. Ad hanc vocem pueri Christiani pueros paganos abicere atque procul repellere episcopo inspiciente ceperunt ita, ut nullum eorum in medio sui stare permitterent". *Herbordi dialogus* III, chap. 9, 163–66 to Conversion of Mizlauzs, Prince of Gützkow.

66 Explicit *Ebonis vita Ottonis* II, chap. 5, 64–65, here 64: "Tercia die ad Piritscum castrum primum Pomeranie venit, ubi cives eius ad fidem exhortans quatuordecim diebus sedit, eis nimirum abnuentibus et servum Dei ad alia migrare loca facientibus seque novam hanc legem sine primatum et maiorum suorum consilio aggredi non posse testantibus". Further on *Ebonis vita Ottonis* II, chap. 11, 72: "Nos, inquint, pater honorande, antiquam patrum et maiorum nostrorum legem sine consensu primatum, quos in hac Stetinensi nostra metropoli reveremur, infringere non presumpsimus […]".

67 *Vita Prieflingensis* II, chap. 13, 15, 19, 20, 21, 43–46, 48–53; *Ebonis vita Ottonis* II, chap 5, 11, 15, 64–65, 72, 78–79; *Herbordi dialogus* II, chap. 15–21, 30, 36, 87–99, 118–21, 131–32.

68 *Vita Prieflingensis* II, chap. 20, 50–51, here 51 tells about 22.165 baptized; *Ebonis vita Ottonis* II, chap. 11, 72 tells about 22.156 baptized.

69 *Herbordi dialogus* II, chap. 22, 99–100, here 100; ibid., chap. 31, 121–22; *Herbordi dialogus* III, chap. 7–8, 161–63.

70 Explicitly the *Vita Prieflingensis* III, chap. 5, 62; *Ebonis vita Ottonis* II, chap. 18, 86–89, here 89; *Ebonis vita Ottonis* III, chap. 1, 91–94; *Herbordi dialogus* III, chap. 16, 176–177.

71 *Herbordi dialogus* III, chap. 29, 190–91.

72 *Ebonis vita Ottonis* III, chap. 13, 115–18. Ibid., chap. 30, 118–21. *Herbordi dialogus* III, chap. 10, 166–69.

To a certain extent, the Poles are shown in the *Vitae* of Otto in a positive image over against the Pomeranians who are heathens or apostates from the faith. There is no doubting the Poles' Christian faith. As a young man, the later missionary, Herman, stayed at the court of the Polish duke, Ladislaus I.[73] According to Herbord, Otto learned the local Polish language while in Poland, and opened a boys school there, presumably because "there is a lack of educated people".[74] Ladislaus' successor, Boleslaus III Wrymouth, is then characterized as a pious Christian.[75] The *Vita* reports that it was this Duke Boleslaus who threatened Pomeranians with war if they would not accept the Christian missionaries.[76]

This last piece – the willingness of the Polish duke (if necessary, with force) to coerce his pagan neighbors to accept the mission – can be taken as segue to the Hedwig legend.

The legend repeatedly mentions the events of the year 1241 – the death of Hedwig's son, Henry the Pious, in a battle against the pagan Mongols.[77] The Silesian prince is presented as the defender of Christianity. Otherwise there is no other mention of the problems with missionary efforts in the Hedwig legend. Clearly, Poland and Silesia appear as Christian countries. So, the numerous reports of her miracles in the *Legenda maior* that Silesia, Poland and also Pomerania had requested the help of Saint Hedwig, are quite consistent with this.[78]

3.3 *Reference to Polish, Pomeranian and Silesian Personalities*

It has already been noted that in the *Vitae* of Adalbert, Otto and Hedwig, alongside the saints, other historic people are mentioned. Boleslaus the Brave is only briefly referred to in the *Adalbert vita*,[79] whereas he is more explicitly appreciated in the *Passio of St Adalbert*.[80] According to the *Passio*, the Polish duke,

---

73 *Vita Prieflingensis*, chap. 4, 8–10.
74 *Herbordi dialogus* III, chap. 32, 196–98, here 197: "Itaque in Poloniam peregre vadens, ubi sciebat litteratorum esse penuriam, scolam puerorum accepit et alios docendo seque ipsum instruendo brevi tempore ditatus atque honori habitus est. Linguam quoque terre illius apprehendit".
75 Cf. below.
76 *Ebonis vita Ottonis* III, chap. 13, 115–18. Ibid., chap. 30, 118–21. *Herbordi dialogus* III, chap. 10, 166–69.
77 *Vita sanctae Hedwigis*, 515, 525–26, 559–70.
78 Cf. ibid., 583–628; here 598–99, to the Believers in Pomerania.
79 *Vita sancti Adalberti*, chap. 25, 37–38, here 38 and chap. 27, 40–41, here 40.
80 *Passio Adalberti. Redactio longior*, chap. 21, 26–28, here 26 and chap. 25, 31–32, here 32. cf. *Passio Adalberti. Redactio brevior*, chap. 21, 59–60, here 59 and also chap. 25, 62–63, here 63.

"Father of the servants of God" loved Adalbert. Brun recounts that Adalbert, during his martyrdom, called Boleslaus "the most Christian of all Christian lords".[81] Besides Boleslaus I, the *Passio of St Adalbert* acknowledges also his father Mieszko I, and briefly mentions the battles of Margrave Hodo against the Polish Prince.[82]

In the *Five Brothers Vita* of Brun, Boleslaus I the Brave is mentioned again – his name Boleslaus is translated as "greater in glory".[83]

In den *Vitae* of Otto of Bamberg, the positive description of Boleslaus III Wrymouth is amplified. The duke is described as diligent and wise, of noble descent. Completely devoted to the Church of Christ, he is a friend to the poor, comforter of those in need, amiable and humble.[84] He has waged war successfully against Bohemia, Moravia, Hungary, Rus', nomadic Cumans, pagan Prussia, and Pomerania.[85] He secured the dynasty, at least temporarily, through a peace treaty with the Great Principality of Kiev.[86] Finally, the Polish duke invited Otto to do missionary work in Pomerania, and received him with honors everywhere, supported his missionary travels and, as already underscored, threatened Pomerania with war if they would further rebuff a renewal of the mission.[87]

Duke Wartislaw I. is another historical Pomeranian ruling figure mentioned in the *Vitae* of Otto. Wartislaw is positively characterized; he became Christian before his subjects did and supported Otto in his Christianization efforts.[88]

Naturally, the legend of Hedwig alludes to her husband, Duke Heinrich I the Bearded, as well as to her son, Duke Heinrich II, the Pious. The legend says that Heinrich I was a splendid duke, who because of the virtuous example of

---

81 *Passio Adalberti. Redactio longior*, chap. 25, 31–32, here 32; *Passio Adalberti. Redactio brevior*, chap. 25, 62–63, here 63.
82 *Passio Adalberti. Redacti longior*, chap. 10, 8–10, here 8–9. cf. *Passio Adalberti. Redacti brevior*, chap. 10, 49–50, here 50.
83 *Vita quinque fratrum*, chap. 6, 41–42, here 41.
84 *Vita Prieflingensis* II, chap. 2, 29–31, here especially 30: "Tandem confecto itinere a duce Polonie Bolezlao receptus honorifice est, cum quidem ille non secus in adventu tanti tunc hospitis letaretur, quam si ipsum recepisset hospicio Salvatorem". cf. also *Vita Prieflingensis* III, chap. 1–2, 56–58. Further on *Ebonis vita Ottonis* II, here especially chap. 4, 62–64, here 62: "Erat enim dux ipse magne in Christi ecclesia reverentie, amator pauperum et piisimus inopum consolator, humilitatis et caritatis virtute omnibus amabilis, congregationibus fidelium et domiciliis sanctorum magis quam urbibus exstruendis operam dare solitus". cf. *Herbordi dialogus* II, chap. 2, 62.
85 *Herbordi dialogus* II, chap. 3, 62–63.
86 Ibid., chap. 4, 64–68, here 64–65.
87 Cf. above.
88 *Vita Prieflingensis* II, chap. 3, 32.

his saintly wife was able to rule all the better his dukedom, Poland.[89] Their son, Heinrich II, is characterized as a faithful, brave knight of Christ, who shed his blood for the sake of Christianity.[90]

Over against these figures, Duke Conrad of Mazovia and Duke Boleslaus II the Bald, are negatively portrayed in the Hedwig legend. Duke Conrad, a cruel minded man, took Hedwig's husband as a prisoner. Then, the God-fearing woman went personally to Conrad, who, feeling the angelic presence of Hedwig, let her husband free.[91]

All the more negatively presented is the image of Boleslaus II, Duke of Liegnitz-Brieg, grandson of Hedwig. He caused much damage to his land; was responsible for extreme material losses and the death of several hundred persons.[92]

3.4 The Relation of Poland, Silesia, Pomerania and Prussia to the Empire

With reference to the relation of Poland, Silesia, Pomerania and Prussia to the Empire, there are three points to be mentioned in a discussion of these hagiographic texts. It has already been indirectly indicated that the missions were initiated from within the Empire; and they were was essentially carried out by individual personalities: Adalbert of Prague's mission to Prussia and Otto of Bamberg's to Pomerania. Of the Five Brothers, who died before they could start their mission, two of them, as well as Benedict and John, came from Italy.[93]

In addition, there were marriage alliances between the Empire and Poland, which are also mentioned in the hagiography. The first one mentioned is the wedding of the Polish duke, Ladislaus I Herman, to Judith, daughter of Emperor Heinrich III. In the *Vita* of Otto of Bamberg from Prüfening, it is commented that this alliance was one encouraged by him.[94] Also there is mention of the wedding of Hedwig of Andechs (St. Hedwig) to the Silesian duke, Henry I.[95]

Finally, the hagiographic texts also indicate active commercial relations. In Herbord's *Dialog* there is mention of cloth-trade from the Empire to Pomerania.[96]

---

89 *Vita sanctae Hedwigis*, 514, 519.
90 Ibid., 515, 525–26, 559–70.
91 Ibid., 524.
92 Ibid., 570–72.
93 Michałowski, *Heiligenkulte* [Cult of the Saints], 354; Gieysztor, *Johannes u. Gefährten* [*John and companions*], 210–11.
94 *Vita Prieflingensis* I, chap. 4, 8–10.
95 *Vita sanctae Hedwigis*, 514.
96 *Herbordi dialogus* I, chap. 36, 39–40, here 39.

4   Conclusion

Thomas Wünsch is able to name the cults of at least 29 saints in the time period from the 10th to the 15th centuries; they were at first only regionally significant, and later they expanded to Poland. Conversely, there are only a few examples of one or the other saint's cult in Poland which extended further to the West. These few examples are Adalbert, Stanislaus of Krakow, and Hedwig of Silesia. Their spread to the West, especially into the Empire, was due essentially to the transfer of relics, iconographic materials, as well as being named in liturgical documents.[97]

The limited spread of the cults of Polish saints to the West (from the Polish viewpoint) was due to a relatively low regard of Poland in the hagiography of the Empire. One has to consider a time period extending through three centuries in order to identify the *Vitae, Passiones* and *Miraculae*, of a total of just three individuals from medieval times who were honored as saints. Only by considering such a lengthy period was it possible to gather sufficient evidence from Poland, Silesia, Pomerania and Prussia and the inhabitants of these lands. Even with the inclusion of the Five Brothers' *Vita*, the results do not change that much.

This evaluation of the hagiographic texts indicates that the texts discussed here did not intend to hand down any geographic, ethnographic or historical facts about Poland or its neighboring lands. The foreground intention of these texts is theological, aimed essentially at the idea of the missionary efforts. At the same time, these statements sketch out a certain image of Poland, Pomerania and Silesia. Prussia, however, is hardly present in the texts – except as the place of martyrdom for St. Adalbert.

The original context of these texts indicates a very positive image of Poland; it was taken to be a Christian land with Christian inhabitants. The Polish nobility was interested in spreading and defending their Christian faith. The same result applies to Silesia as well. There were dynastic unions with the Empire.

It was different with Pomerania. There were difficulties spreading the faith until it finally succeeded, as confirmed in the youngest hagiographic text, Hedwig's *Vita* from 1300. Finally, on the threshold of the 14th century, pious

---

97   Thomas Wünsch, "Kultbeziehungen zwischen dem Reich und Polen im Mittelalter [Cult relations between the Empire and Poland in medieval age]," in *Das Reich und Polen: Parallelen, Interaktionen und Formen der Akkulturation im Hohen und Späten Mittelalter*, ed. Alexander Patschovsky and Thomas Wünsch (Stuttgart, 2003), 357–400, here 391, 398–99.

Pomeranians as well were willing to ask for assistance through the cult of St. Hedwig. Commercial contacts started quite early between Pomerania and the Empire.

Thus, the stereotypes in Poland and its neighboring lands – both positive and negative– were also presented, but not at a deep enough level. An analysis of other kinds of sources would, in this regard, deliver definitely clearer results.

Translated by Philip Jacobs (English-Exactly)

CHAPTER 12

Perception of Poland in Peter Suchenwirt's Heraldic Poems: Reflections on Dependence between Assessments and Genres

Paul Martin Langner

I

This paper describes a sector of communication inside the community of European nobles in the late Middle Ages. It will give some information on the self-consciousness and reciprocal perceptions within this social group. This aspect becomes important through a comparison of texts that belong to different genres that were read within aristocratic circles. By comparing texts belonging to diverse genres, contradictory valuations of the status of Polish knights become perceptible. In addition to that, we also come to understand more about the geographical knowledge of that time. The focus in this paper will be on the heraldic poems ("rêden")[1] of Peter Suchenwirt, who lived in Vienna at the end of the 14th century. In order to be able to discuss the intended train of thought, it is first necessary to give some thought to the different understandings of "genre" in historical studies and in German literary studies. These differences are significant for understanding the historiographical works and is the basis for this paper. The heraldic poems ("rêden") produced by Peter Suchenwirt were written for Austrian nobles. It is worth considering whether the Suchenwirt's poems should be counted among historical texts. This classification makes it possible both to interpret the assessments of Polish nobles and knights in German-language poems of the High and Late Middle Ages and to add a feature to the paradigm of the description of these genres as well. However, it must be borne in mind that historical research understands the term "genre" differently than does German literary studies. The decisive difference is that in the perspective of medieval historiography, intentional categories become tangible in different genres. According to Schmale, the view of medieval authors is that different genres emerge on the basis of diverging

---

1   For this term see: Karina Kellermann, *Abschied vom 'historischen Volkslied'. Studien zur Funktion, Ästhetik und Publizität der Gattung historisch-politische Ereignisdichtung* (Tübingen, 2000), 49–65.

strategies, which then structure and influence statements in different ways.[2] However, it must also be assumed that a strict classification of genres did not exist in the Middle Ages; instead a variety of "hybrid forms" can be observed. In contrast to this notion, which focuses on the intentional orientation of genres, German literary studies ascribe specific textual features to each genre,[3] and from these relations develops a "system" of genres. These characteristics separate the genres from each other.

This relation can be shown through this figure:

$$Genre_1 <== features_{\alpha,\ \beta}.$$
$$Genre_2 <== features_{\gamma,\ \zeta}.$$
$$Genre_3 <== features_{\mu,\ \varphi,\ \omega}.$$
$$...$$
$$Genre_n <== features_{m,\ n}$$

There are more options for the foundations of genres, as Hempfer has shown in his study[4] of literary genres. Hempfer's results cannot be summarized in this paper. The pragmatic description given by textual features to a genre is enough in the present discussion for understanding the position of German literary studies. Historical research, on the other hand, does not propose characteristics for, but recognizes intentional matters in the emergence of genres, which then leads to different ways to record real events. A part of the argumentation about intentional orientation, to which Schmale refers, can be sketched as follows: In his opinion, remembered history should not be understood as a recorded reality, but rather as a content of memory that is subject to intentional imprints and also to intentional or unintentional modifications. This intentional interpretation of genres results from the relation of the writer to the content of the memory.[5] The recording of history indicates that there is a "before" for both the writer and his consumer, followed by an "after".[6] This temporal and conditional relationship of the two periods has a causal connection.

---

2   Franz-Josef Schmale, *Funktion und Formen mittelalterlicher Geschichtsschreibung. Eine Einführung. Mit einem Beitrag von Hans-Werner Goetz* (Darmstadt, 1993), 105–107.

3   See for the various definitions of genres, for example: Dieter Lamping, Sandra Poppe, and Sascha Seiler, *Handbuch der literarischen Gattungen* (Stuttgart, 2009); Klaus W. Hempfer, "Gattung," *Reallexikon der Literaturwissenschaft* 1, ed. Klaus Weimar et al. (Berlin/Boston, 2003), 651–655.

4   Klaus Hempfer, *Gattungstheorie* (München, 1973).

5   Schmale, *Funktion*, 19f.

6   Ibid., 20.

> Erinnerung und Absicht zur Erinnerung, zumal schriftlicher Erinnerung, sind aber im Grunde nicht nur auf die Vergangenheit gerichtet, sondern von der Sprache her auch auf die Zukunft und auf Kommunikation.[7]

Accordingly, Schmale continues to argue:

> Weil Erinnerung sprachliche, begriffliche Vergegenwärtigung ist, bringt sie Gedächtnisinhalte in eine ganz bestimmte und eindeutige Form, die in sprachlicher Form allein sichtbar und vermittelbar ist. Der Geschichtsschreiber muss sich daher auf eine bestimmte sprachliche Gestalt festlegen. Diese ist selbstverständlich von den Strukturen und den Begriffen der Sprache, in der geschrieben wird, abhängig.[8]

The transcriptionalization of the content of memory always requires genres. The written and therefore remembered past is adopted in a social group. The sense of a written memory of historical moments is only important in this social context. The social groups are grounded in institutions or understand that such institutions make them a uniquely singular group. "Die erinnerte Vergangenheit ist damit konstitutiv für das Bestehen von Gruppen, für die der Historiograph die Rolle des überindividuellen Subjekts [Erzählers] übernimmt."[9]

It should also be borne in mind that the evidence of the past constitutes the existence of the group in the future.

> Wenn eine Standortbestimmung gegenüber einer Vergangenheit und durch diese erfolgt, dann erfolgt auch das zukünftige Handeln und Verhalten in Ablehnung oder Zustimmung zur gesamten Vergangenheit oder zu Teilen derselben, entweder durch Identifikation oder durch Emanzipation.[10]

---

7   Ibid., 21. Translation by ML: "Memory and the intention of remembrance, especially written memory, are basically not just centered on the past, but with the support of language also adjusted on the future and on communication."
8   Ibid., 22: Translation by ML: "Because memory is a linguistic and conceptual recall of the past, it brings contents of memory in a specific and unambiguous form that is only tangible and communicable in language. This is depending on the structures of and concepts in language, in which it is written." The relation to the reality is different in Latin and German language, but it cannot be discussed here.
9   Ibid., 21. Translation by ML: "The remembered past is constitutive for the existence of groups for which the Historian takes on the role of a supra-individual subject [narrator]."
10 Ibid. Translation by ML: "When taking a position on the past and occurs through this, then actions will also take place in future and behavior in rejection or consent to all or to a part of the past, either through identification or through emancipation."

The historiographical texts gain importance for a group and the view of their self-consciousness for the future. Several points are added by Schmale:
- Evidence of history as revealing the actions of God;
- Exemplary proof of good or bad deeds, which can be role models for one's own actions;
- Legitimization of certain relationships through the past;
- Report on the reputation of a famous person.

The written history is an intentional way of using the contents of memory. In order to inscribe these intentions in a text, specific textual properties are necessary, which make the genres distinguishable from one another.

Accordingly, another paradigm is formed for the understanding of historiographical genres:

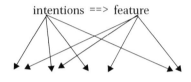

genre$_1$, genre$_2$, genre$_3$, … genre$_n$

Schmale divides the intentional interest, on the one hand, into procedural depictions in chronicles and, on the other hand, into more personal representations in the genres of what are called historia.[11] Schmale is guided by the writing of the English chronicler Gervasius of Canterbury (* ~ 1145–† ~ 1210).[12] Gervasius saw in chronicles[13] and annals[14] the tendency to an ordering of its material and account using time – years, months and days. However, in historiographical writings the focus is on a special interest in processes.[15]

---

11 This classification of historiographical writings does not seem compelling and is rarely realized by medieval historians, yet this classification was – as Gervasius has shown – discussed, although many documents of medieval writings mix the characteristics of both genres. Cf. Gerhard Wolf et. al., "Einleitung," in *Handbuch der Chroniken des Mittelalters*, eds. idem and Norbert N. Ott (Berlin/Boston, 2016), 13–19.
12 Lexikon des Mittelalters IV, col. 1360f.
13 Elsewhere Schmale, *Funktion*, 111 counts the chronicles also among the "historical writings".
14 Schmale, *Funktion*, 109.
15 Cf. Schmale, *Funktion*, 109.

According to Gervasius,[16] the historiae,[17] which include also the vitae of saints and hagiographic writings, place emphasis on the description of the deeds, attitudes and lifestyles of important persons. However, in his discussion of the historiographical genres, Schmale emphasizes that the persons to whom chronicles or narrative accounts are dedicated do not resonate in medieval historiography because of their personal moral characters, so they are not intended to be exemplars of individuals, but instead the attention that is given them stems from the fact that they are officials of some medieval institution.[18]

The narrative texts are interpretive and substantive, and describe – with the exception of the vitae of saints – the actions of one person towards other people.[19] In the vitae of saints what appears is the intervention of divine actions. The appearance of the transcendent world can also be found in hagiographic genres as part of the medieval understanding of history and divine order.[20]

To summarize this, there is no definite genre system in the Middle Ages, but there are specific features regarding the plan and intention of the various forms of historical records.

The chronicles and also the historiographical texts in the form of historia were written as commissioned text for the nobility. This means that the intentions of the nobles must be found in the text as well as the corresponding intentions of the authors.

After this explanation of how historiographical genres ought to be understood, we can proceed to describing some observations as found in various texts of the Middle Ages, with special attention to the poems by Peter Suchenwirt. These observations arise through a comparing of the images and assessments of Polish knights and nobles in different genres.

In descriptions of Polish knights or noblemen in chronicles of the High Middle Ages as found in several texts, one can detect that there is an ambivalent relationship in them. Two examples in two different chronicles show positive assessments.

1) "The emperor celebrated the feast of the chain of St. Peter in Nienburg, but in Merseburg the feast of St. Lawrence and the Ascension of St. Mary. The

---

16   "historicus diffuse et eligenter incredit, cronicus vero simpliciter graditus et breviter." Quotes after: *The historical works of Gervase of Canterbury* 1, ed. Wilhelm Stubbs, 2 vols. RBMS. 73,1–2 (London, 1879–1880), 87f.
17   Schmale points out that this terminus "genre" is understood in other contexts as "narrative" see Schmale, *Funktion*, 111.
18   Ibid., 117, 109.
19   Ibid., 110.
20   Ibid., 113–116.

dukes of Poland and Bohemia came along with the principals of the Empire with splendid gifts, and also with the representatives of the emperor of the Greeks, who asked the Roman emperor for peace and friendship and for support against the tyrant Rokker, who was making trouble in some parts of the Roman Empire and the land of the Greeks. On this holy day, Duke Boleslaus of Poland submitted to the emperor with a handshake and wore the sword ceremoniously before the ruler when he entered the church."[21]

2) "At the time when my Lord was the Bishop of the Church of Babenberg, Prince Boleslaus ruled Poland, a strong and prudent man, of noble and old descent. Since he acted bravely and cautiously, he managed to pacify all the borders of his territory, which had been attacked and oppressed in the time of his predecessors by enemy forces, and the castles and cities that had been seized from his empire were recaptured by his strong hand."[22]

In texts that record the chronological sequence of events, there are other assessments of Polish knights and nobles. For the year 1030, we find a note in the Annalista Saxo:

> Mieszko, the prince of Poland, who demanded the title of king against will of the Roman Empire, when he learned of the death of Margrave Thietmar, led an army of pagans into the holy church after secretly conspiracy with the devil's ally, Siegfried and other lawbreakers....
>
> Between the Elbe and Saale, Mieszko devastated more than a hundred villages with fire and killing, he captured 1965 Christian men and women brutally, and the venerable Bishop of Brandenburg, Liuzo, he

---

21 *Annalista Saxo*, ed. Georg Waitz, MGH SSrG 6 (Hannover, 1844), 542–777, here 769 (a. 1135). – "Imperator conmemorationem sancti Petri ad vincula Nienburch, festivitatem vero sancti Laurentii et assumptionem sancte Marie Mersburh celebravit. Illuc confluebant cum primariis regni Polonie et Boemie duces, et legati Grecorum imperatoris, honorifica secum munera ferentes, pacem ab imperatore et amiciciam ac auxilium contra Rokkerum tirannum poscentes, qui partem Romani imperii et terram Grecorum nimis vexaverat. [...] Dux autem Polonie Bolizlaus in die sancto manibus applicatis miles eius efficitur, et ad eclesiam processuro gladium eius ante ipsum portavit."

22 *Herbordi Dialogus de Vita Ottonis Babenbergensis*, ed. Rudolf Köpke, MGH SSrG 33 (Hannover, 1868), 53. – "Tempore quo dominus meus episcopus Babenbergensem regebat ecclesiam, Bolezlaus, vir strennuus et prudens, et ingenuae atque avitae nobilitatis decore illustris, ducatum Poloniae administrabat. Qui dum se gnaviter et provide gereret, omnes terrae suae terminos sub praedecessoribus suis hostium violentia invasos et perturbatos, et castra urbesque a sua potestate alienatas manu robusta recuperare praevaluit."

took to prison as a worthless slave, and did not spare the holy altars, but stained everything with death and blood and seized noble women with violence.[23]

And: After the king's withdrawal, the duke of Poland broke his promises, did not take part in the military procession, nor did he observe the other commitments that he had affirmed under oath, thereby drawing the king's ire again.[24]

Otto von St. Blasius (~ early 12th century) wrote this information for the year 1147. However, in medieval chronicles, when the breaking of a promise by the Polish aristocracy is spelled out or reference made to their aggressiveness, it usually happens from the perspective of a German ruler or one of his allies who have taken military action against Polish nobles or knights to enforce their own claims to power, with the hope of subduing the Polish knights.

Accordingly, the chronicle of St. Blaise of Otto tells how King Friedrich I approached Poland. The chronicle says that the king believed he had swiftly conquered the Polish knights and surrounding regions, but soon found out he had been cheated since the Polish peers had not fulfill the concessions, they had promised him under the threat of violence. The quotation shows the prerogative of the German ruler in that he did not tolerate another view of the situation.

This is not the moment to pause to speak about the whole stock of medieval chronicles; the texts quoted here are examples of the ambivalent views of Polish knights and noblemen in the chronicles of the High Middle Ages. Turning to the German-language poetry from the same period, it becomes apparent that these latter texts contain almost totally positive descriptions of Polish noblemen and knights as well as the region of Poland. The German-speaking aristocratic literature (which includes chronicles and poetry) thus proves the ambivalent attitude of the German historians in the Middle Ages towards knights and peers from the region of Poland. The German poetry of this period describes the Polish fighters as trustworthy, helpful, and courageous knights.[25]

In the Nibelungenlied (22. Aventiure) the Polish knights are described as faithful and valiant followers of king Etzel and they like to sing. Several times

---

23   *Annalista Saxo*, ed. Georg Waitz, MGH SSrG 6 (Hannover, 1844), 542–777, here 678.
24   *Ottonis de Sancto Blasio Chronica*, ed. Adolf Hofmeister, MGH ss. rer. Ger. 47 (Hannover, 1912), 7. – "Nam post regressum regis periurus [polonorum] effectus nec expedicioni interfuit nec cetera, que sacramentis firmaverant, custodiens iram denuo regis promeruit."
25   Martin Langner, *Annäherung ans Fremde durch sprachliche Bilder. Die Region Polen und ihre Ritter in Dichtungen des Hochmittelalters* (Berlin, 2018), 108.

the poet takes up again his view of the Polish knights, and every time he adds another positive feature to his image of them.[26]

The fragment "Dietrich and Wenezlan" emphasizes the combative power of the prince and his excellent attitude. He really demonstrates a well-developed courtly culture.[27] In the epic poem "Rabenschlacht" there is a duke, Hornborge, who is a rich and helpful noble.[28]

In the poem "Dietrichs Flucht" there is a duke, Bertram, who is also a Polish knight and noble; he fetched gold from his headquarters with fifty donkeys to pay for Dietrich's war against Ermenrich.[29] These and other moments verify the positive images of Polish knights in the German-language epic poems of the late 12th century and on into the 13th century.

The only exception is the anonymous text "Biterolf and Dietleib", which expresses a claim to power over the Polish knights, which the Polish knights oppose.[30]

Looking at both the chronicles and the poetry, the attitude among the German noblemen seems ambivalent toward knights from other regions of Europe, like Poland. But it is noticeable that the positive assessments about Polish knights are found mainly in the German poetic texts. From this observation arises the question as to the extent to which the affiliation of a text to a genre predisposes it in its evaluation of foreign knights?

Do the intentional or structural conditions of a genre influence the description of Polish knights? Is there a link between the assessment and the genre with regard to medieval historiography?

II

In order to discuss this question, the genre of the heraldic poem of Peter Suchenwirt can be briefly described.

Suchenwirt is a good example for discussing how Polish knights are assessed in German texts. His texts were commissioned by the nobility and were intended for them. Since he was not a member of the aristocracy, Suchenwirt

---

26   Martin Langner, "Eingeschriebene Performanz: Narratologische Strukturen zur Darstellung von Bewegung in mittelalterlichen Texten," in *Anwendungsorientierte Darstellungen zur Germanistik. Modelle und Strukturen*, ed. Aleksandra Bednarowska et al., Perspektivenwechsel 3 (Berlin, 2013), 223–241.
27   Langner, *Annäherung*, 65–74.
28   Ibid., 84.
29   Ibid., 84–85.
30   Ibid., 74–81.

as a contractor put himself entirely at the service of the nobility. For, despite a bourgeois background, Peter Suchenwirt belonged to the group of so-called *Wappendichter*, which means "heraldic crest poets". As a result, Suchenwirt stood between two social strata: the nobility on the one hand, and the bourgeoisie on the other. His personality and his values may well have been influenced by his city-born origin as well as his noble patrons. Thus, this poet would appear to be a good example for testing whether the results presented for the High Middle Ages will still hold for a later epoch.

The term of "genre of heraldic poems" is not used consistently in research, and this genre seems to be among the historiographic "hybrids" that Schmale mentions. One way of specifying the genre is to refer to the texts generally as "poems of a (family) crest" ("Wappendichtung").[31] This description stresses that the feature of this genre is a narrative of a coat of arms.[32] Of course, "calling out" is an important feature of the heraldic rêde, but at the same time in the poems of Suchenwirt examined here this element does not occur, or it does so only peripherally. This shows that this criterion cannot be the decisive element for a definition of the genre.

The *argumentum a gestis* seems to also be a significant element that marks the genre. The texts of the "Wappendichtung" were addressed either to a living person or more often to the survivors of the deceased, so the texts can be a laudatory poem or, above all, an obituary. Other formal criteria of this genre have not been sufficiently researched: couplets or cross-pair rhyming verses characterize the texts, yet are not a very significant element. The rhyming forms are used very often and also occur in other genres. Therefore, it seems to be practical to use the medieval term "rêde" to refer to the genre. But this term also needs a more detailed description.

Primisser used the term "laudation" (*Ehrenrede*) in his edition (1827).[33] A "rêde" is a narrative text with verses and a close link to reality, which could mean that in this genre, historical events are appropriately and realistically described. Thus, the term *Ehrenrede* underlines the character of a dedication, in which the

---

31 The genus name *Wappendichtung* appears in its generality hardly suitable to capture the various subtypes (H. Kuhn). Compare to this: Ludger Lieb, "Wappendichtung," *Reallexikon der deutschen Literaturwissenschaft* 3, ed. Klaus Weimar et al. (Berlin/New York, 2007), 816–817, who lists although the book of Brinker von der Heyde in his bibliography, but apparently has not evaluated it.

32 This genre appears in the mid-13th century, for example in Konrad von Würzburg's Tournament of Nantes. Poems of the Flemish poet Gelre, also Lupold Homburg, and later John of Holland show developments of this genre, accomplished by Peter Suchenwirt. To Lupold Homburg see Karina Kellermann, "Eine kurtze rede wore. Die vier politischen Reimreden des Lupold Homburg," in *Wolfram-Studien* 24 (2017), 199–219.

33 Alois Primisser, *Peter Suchenwirts Werke aus dem 14. Jahrhundert* (Wien, 1827).

text highlights the praise of the nobleman and makes a claim to be a realistic depiction. Nonetheless, the term *Ehrenrede* does not adequately describe the functional character of this genre, which the term *Wappendichtung* does.

Brinker von der Heyde[34] puts the functional context more clearly in the foreground during her investigation of this genre. She differentiates the term "Speech of Honor" into the terms "heraldic laudation" (*heraldische Preisrede*) and "heraldic funeral oration" (*heraldische Totenklage*).[35] On one hand the reference to the heraldic proclamation is made by the respective epithets; on the other hand, the "laudation" is directed toward a living honoree, while the "heraldic obituary" clearly takes over the task of a memorial. This is the concept followed in this paper.

Suchenwirt has left 52 poems, most of which are "heraldic obituaries", but there are also some "heraldic laudations". In addition, the corpus of his texts contains critical or parodying speeches.

Peter Suchenwirt was born around 1330 not as a noble man. After his education as a heraldic poet he lived at the court of King Ludwig I of Hungary for some time, and was a colleague of Heinrich von Mügeln and Heinrich der Teichner, and he dedicated a funeral oration to the latter. (Primisser XIX). Some years later he was member of the elector's court of the Wittelsbachs in Mark Brandenburg. The lordly prince may have been Ludwig the Elder (1315–1361), or Albrecht of Nürnberg († 1361). It seems that Suchenwirt returned to Vienna after the death of Ludwig the Roman (Reg. 1351–1365). At the end of his life, Suchenwirt was a rich citizen of Vienna in close contact to the court of Austrian dukes. A document from the sale of his house in Vienna confirmed that he was a permanent resident of the town. The date of his death is unknown, but it seems that he died in the first decade of the 15th century.

Since the poems of Suchenwirt follow a specific schema of honoring a person, they contain many historical or geographical details. Often, he added a detailed praise of the person's virtue and in this way he presents the person to whom the poem was dedicated as morally distinguished.[36]

---

34   Claudia Brinker von der Heyde, *Von manigen helden gute tat. Geschichte als Exempel bei Peter Suchenwirt* (Frankfurt/M., Bern, 1987).

35   Claudia Brinker von der Heyde, "Peter Suchenwirt," in *Die deutsche Literatur des Mittelalters. Verfasserlexikon* 9, ed. Kurt Ruh et. al. (Berlin, New York, 1995), 481–488.

36   *Geschichte der deutschen Literatur von den Anfängen bis zur Gegenwart. Die deutsche Literatur vom späten Mittelalter bis zum Barock* 4/1: *Das ausgehende Mittelalter. Humanismus und Renaissance 1370–1520* eds. Hans Rupprich and Hedwig Heger (München, 1994), 208.

The elaboration of the middle part of the "rêde", recounting the deeds,[37] leads to a more or less chronological depiction or additive sequences of occurrences. This *argumentum a gestis* has a connection to Schmale's view. He had marked, on the one hand, the historical writings by focusing on the description of the "deeds, attitudes, and ways of life" of a person. On the other hand, the narrative texts should be "pointed, interpretive and reasoning" and should describe the actions of the respective historical person towards other people.[38] The listed characteristics correspond to the "heraldic rêden", which is why it seems justified to count them among the genre of the *historia*, as pointed out above.

The extensive and sometimes verbose descriptions of the actions led many poems (as we now understand them) to become overly long, yet Suchenwirt was a poet who created perfect texts in this genre, intended for an aristocratic public. These poems made Suchenwirt famous.

Since Suchenwirt lived in Vienna and knew the conditions in the medieval Austrian duchy, the "heraldic rêden" approximate quite well the real living conditions of the Austrian nobility. But it is interesting to look at the texts in which he describes princes who passed through East Central Europe and met with the princes of Poland. In the following I will investigate the perspective and the contextualization of remarks on Poland in the Suchenwirt's texts.

Unfortunately, there is no current edition of the texts of Peter Suchenwirt, however his poems are still available in the first edition by Alois Primisser from 1827. This edition is reasonably good with regard to the quality of the text, but the comments are related to the time period of its editing. Consequently, some corrections have to be made.

In his texts, one can read a series of data or allusions in which references are made to cities or nobles of the region that fell within the borders of what is today Poland.

In the poem "Of the Five Princes who died in 1386" (Primisser XX) he reports on a historical series of events. The youthful duke Wilhelm of Austria (1370–1406) was formally married to one of the daughters of King Ludwig I of Hungary, Hedwig (1373–1399). But the nobility of Poland refused to accept Hungarian hegemony, created by the personal union of Ludwig I, because it was disappointing to them that Ludwig had not returned some areas to Poland, as they had hoped. Hedwig's young groom, Wilhelm, was fooled in 1384. After his coronation, he was hindered from consummating his marriage to Hedwig by being lured under false pretenses from the city.

---

37 What is referred to as an *argumentum a gestis*.
38 Schmale, *Funktion*, 110.

> Then a lot of unfaithfulness was 121
> committed in the Land of Cracow:
> a duke, named Wilhelm,
> who was born to Austria,
> whose youth and strong body 125
> had to suffer many injuries through betrayal
> he had to leave his wife in Cracow
> in that country.[39]

Sometime later he disguises himself as a dealer and once again returns to Cracow with the hope of still marrying Hedwig. However, the young duke was betrayed and only through the intervention of Hedwig did he manage to escape the city alive.

> They gave him haul,
> and he was driven from there 130
> [...]
> gold, silver, beautiful robes 135
> horses and many fabrics
> were given to the gentleman as a pledge
> which brought him back to Cracow
> just as Judas betrayed God.[40]

Later on, Hedwig had to marry the Lithuanian prince Władysław II. Jagiełło (* prior to 1362–† 1434) who established the Jagiellonian dynasty in Poland, which created the basis for the Golden Age in Poland.

> His wife was given a pagan man 131
> who had been baptized insincerely
> rather because of the people and the land
> than about the Christian faith.[41]

---

39 "Danach in Krakawer lant // vil untrew wart erchoren: // ein hertzog Wilhalm ist genant // zu Osterreich geporen, // des jugent und vil werder leib // veratnůss tet vil ande, // der must lazzen dort sein weib // zu Krakaw in dem lande."

40 "[...] wenn er mit valsches gutes hab // wart van dannen verchauffet; // [...] // Gold, silber, reich gewant, // pferd und manig schawben // gab man den herren da zu miet, // die in gen Krakaw prachten // recht als Judas Got verriet."

41 "[...] ein haiden man sein frawen gab, // der falschlich was getauffet // mehr umb die leut und umb daz lant // denn umb den christen glaubenx [...]."

The remark that the "falsely baptized" Jagiełło was the successor to the throne shows that Suchenwirt understood the political reason why Wilhelm had been prevented from becoming king. But the poet does not specify the reason in his heraldic rêde. Since he mentions that Jagiełło accepted baptism merely because of the subjects of the country but not out of Christian faith, that says as much that pragmatism in politics was pursued and no legitimate Christian purpose. The aristocracy and many merchants in Cracow took the view that Poland was a state and no longer Hungary. The marriage and rule of duke Wilhelm of Austria had failed because of the completely different conception on the part of the Polish nobility and the citizenry of Cracow. Suchenwirt refers to political pragmatism and the real reason remains concealed.

In the poem by Suchenwirt this process is hinted at. For example, the reader of the poem will not understand that Wilhelm was in Cracow twice; only someone who is familiar with the historical events would know this. Conspicuous, however, is the type of description by Suchenwirt. He talks in this poem only about "Krakawer lant". He explicitly does not refer to the Polish sphere of domination, as he does in other texts, with the name "Poland", but concentrates the process solely in the royal city of Cracow with its inhabitants. It should be noted that he does not assign blame to the Polish nobility. Suchenwirt uses the general term "they" (for example, see v. 137), that is, a nonspecific group that was not assigned a social class.

> Their loyalty deviated from honour,   143
> they did not consider that a disgrace[42]

So, anyone who hides behind this "they" cannot be discovered by reading Suchenwirt's text. Rather, he is telling a more or less romantic story of a cheated groom, without pronouncing blame or making a critical remark. The ascription of cause remains allegorical when he draws a comparison between the betrayal of Christ and the treachery of duke Wilhelm von Habsburg.

> [...] those who brought him back to Krakow,   138
> rightly than as Judas betrayed God.[43]

Additionally, Suchenwirt actually shifts the time period of the process, which took place between 1384 and 1386, and focuses it only on the year 1386, the year in which Jagiełło moved to Cracow to become king and marry Hedwig.

---

42   "[...] ir trew von eren nam den sprungk, // az dauchte si chain schande."
43   "[...] die in gen Krakaw prachten [...] recht als Judas Got verriet [...]."

Previously, in 1383, Jagiełło had accepted baptism, one year before Wilhelm was betrayed. However, Suchenwirt brings the process close to 1386, because after the coronation of Jagiełło and his marriage to Hedwig, the Polish throne was no longer legally accessible for Wilhelm.

The different notion of the process causes it to be tightly timed, thereby endorsing a stronger rejection of Jagiełło.

It was not just Suchenwirt's reticence to call out the "true traitors" and the real reason, allowing then the Polish nobility to remain without fault. Rather, one hears in the text that a reluctance prevailed about a "pagan" heir to the throne. As a criterion of Suchenwirt, the Christian faith is invoked and he raises no criticism against the Polish nobility. This proves that within the circle of the aristocracy one would not accuse each other of being a traitor, keeping in mind that the Suchenwirt's poem was commissioned by the Austrian nobility.

At the same time, Wilhelm encountered another difficult development in Austria.

Suchenwirt interweaves the story of the unfortunate groom into the report of the death of his father, Leopold III, who died on 9 July 1386 at the battle of Sempach. Although Wilhelm was Leopold's eldest son, at the age of 16 he was too young to succeed over a group of the higher nobility in Austria. Suchenwirt stresses in this "rêde" the youthfulness of the duke when he writes in line 125: "des jugent und vil werder leib / veratnůss tet vil ande".[44] Wilhelm was not able to assert himself, but instead of him his cousin, Albrecht IV. (1371–1411), was appointed as duke of Austria, and the latter was also supported by the citizenry of Vienna. Wilhelm seems to have failed twice in succeeding to power in both imperial cities, Cracow and Vienna, because he lacked support from the economically strong middle-class. Nine years later, in 1395, Albrecht III died, and so his territories became vacant. An agreement made Wilhelm duke of a part of Austria, which included Styria, Carinthia, Carniola, and the coastal states.[45]

In 1386 Suchenwirt could not protect the young prince in his poetry, because to have eulogized him would have compromised him with other members of the Habsburgs.

The poem of Suchenwirt, in which he earned the good graces of Leopold III of Austria (1351–1386) and mentions the sad story of his son Wilhelm in the succession to the throne of Poland, all fell into a time in which several political

---

44   "His youthful and strong body // had to suffer much betrayal."
45   Eva Bruckner, *Formen der Herrschaftsrepräsentation und Selbstdarstellung habsburgischer Fürsten im Spätmittelalter*. (Wien, 2009), 152–164; Alois Niederstätter, *Österreichische Geschichte 1278–1411. Die Herrschaft Österreich. Fürst und Land im Spätmittelalter* (Wien, 2001), 194–198.

processes were taking place simultaneously. Since Searchwirt had to rely on the nobility, he remained silent.

He knew rather well the regions that were involved in military action in Poland. In the heraldic obituary for Friedrich von Kreuzpeckh († 1360) he is very well aware of the geographic divisions in Poland. From Tatra,[46] the army moved through the country to the north against the pagan Lithuanians. Suchenwirt knew the sequence of the regions, noting the progression through Tatra, Poland and Masuria, the way the army marched. (Primisser XIV–vv. 218–220)

In the heraldic obituary for Leuthold von Stedeck (Primisser XV) Suchenwirt tells us about the same war and remarks that king Kazimierz Wielki (1310–1370) took part in this campaign.

In the heraldic obituaries XIV und XX, Suchenwirt takes note of the quarrel with king John of Bohemia when in 1331/2 John tried to gain influence in the upper part of Italy, but an alliance of Austrian, Hungarian and Polish troops foiled this plan. Also, his claim to Poland was suppressed. In this context king John besieged Cracow in 1345, but without success.

In this brief notice we see the Polish knights among the other powerful armies in the fight against the European nobles over hegemonic claims.

But there is more cultural information in the heraldic poems of Suchenwirt.

When Duke Albrecht III of Austria moved against the pagan Lithuanian princes in 1375, he took the route from Vienna via Wroclaw, Torun and Malbork and there he turned to east, along the coast of the Baltic sea. Two times there were great celebrations for him. In Breslau and also in Torun, the duke and his knights are festively celebrated by the women. It should be clear that the celebrations were not actually pulled off by the German citizens, because the "Chronical of Silesia" does not note this celebration.[47] So the organizer of this meeting must have been the (Polish) nobles.

> so many people were never seen before
> so well-armed and so well on horseback
> "save the money rather", has been avoided
> at horses and rich garment
> the army moved with any with no plundering and violence

---

[46] Primisser assumes in this geographical name of a city in the Crimea, the reading as an indication of the Tatra seems more plausible.

[47] *Chronicon silesiae ab anno Christi 1052 usque in annum 1573 ultra quinque saecula. Chronik Schlesiens über fünf Jahrhunderte vom Jahre Christi 1052 bis zum Jahre 1573*, eds. Lars-Arne Dannenberg and Mario Müller, Görlitzer Handschrift, G V 52, 2nd rev. ed. (Görlitz-Zittau, 2013).

with great honor without any shame
through the towns and through the countries,
till to the town Breslau.⁴⁸

    PRIMISSER V: VV 46–53

To honor the Austrian duke, the women put on fine robes and exquisite jewelry, came with excellent, but modest attire and there was a short time for exuberant cheerfulness.

tender and lovely women
adorned their proud bodies
for many lovely views
right as the bright may, who
let the meadows and the wood blossom
you see many joyful moments
with jokes, dance and laugh.⁴⁹

    VV 55–6the

So, the ladies and gentlemen in Poland knew of courtliness and followed similar customs to all other nobles in Europe.

The same situation is sketched for Torun:

There you saw the reflections
from small mouths and cheeks
with pearls, ribbons, clips
the women embellished
and decorated for the pleasure
crowns, hats and chaplets
were seen and many dances
with custom and with honour.⁵⁰

    VV 72–79

---

48 "So vil volk man nie gesach // o wol gewapent und geriten; spar daz gelt waz da vermiten an rozzen und an reicher wat. / Hin tzog daz her an mizzetat / mit grozzen ern sunder schant/ durch di stet und durch di lant / piz gen Prezzla in di stat."

49 "[…] die zarten minichleichen weip, // di tzierten iren stoltzen leib // tzu vrawden maniglaye // recht als der chule maye // blůmet anger und den walt. // man sach da frewde manikvalt // mit schimphen, tantzen, lachen."

50 "[…] da sach man widerglaste // von mundelein und von wangen; // mit perlen, porten, spangen // di vrawen sich da tzierten // und gen der lust vlorirten; // chron, schapel, und chrentze // sach man und vil der tentze // mit tzuchten und mit eren."

This is how the heraldic poet Peter Suchenwirt describes the courtly conventions in Poland. And it would be the same as if he was talking about other countries. Furthermore, his texts draw similar pictures in comparison to those found of noble writers about a hundred years before. Therefore, it can be proposed that the literature of the European nobility accepted other noble families in a similar way. One difference, however, is remarkable. Suchenwirt does not describe the kind of real combats between the knights that we can read in "Dietrich and Wenezlan" or in "Die Klage". That is the only difference from the poems from a hundred years earlier. But in sum the findings are the same. Polish knights were seen by the German poets in positive images in the Middle Ages.

In the heraldic poems of Peter Suchenwirt, the mentioning of Polish knights and the regions all in all present positive images and assessments. This makes clear that at the end of the 14th century, aristocratic society looked upon itself as an European community, intermarried and valuing each other, as had been the case in the 12th and 13th centuries. Thus, if a bourgeois author, such as Peter Suchenwirt, working in the service of nobles, wrote poetic obituaries whose readers were noblemen from another European region, the texts reveal only images that would be expected in an aristocratic society. In this way Suchenwirt concealed in one poem some facts and makes only a general comment there, but he did not disappoint the expectations of the nobles. This observation refers to the substantive aspect of these texts.

The consideration on the connection between genre and assessment touches on the formal aspects of the poems. All the pictures of Polish knights and related regions are from texts that were not addressed to Polish readers or listeners. There is therefore no connection between the clients and the positive images of Polish knights of the late 14th century in the texts of Suchenwirt. The question of the connection between assessment and the genre allows itself to be answered after this investigation of these poems: the genre is placed in the field of tension between intention and the expectation of the audience. As, on the one hand, the characteristics of the text emerge from the intention, which results from the relationship of the author to the history; on the other hand, the texts are determined by the expectation of the audience. This result concretizes the observations of Schmale, who had seen the intention as an important influence on the assessments in text.[51]

---

51   Schmale, *Funktion*, 144.

Intentions ==> Features

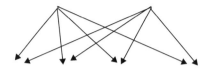

Genre$_1$, Genre$_2$, Genre$_3$ ... Genre$_n$

Performative disposition

Expectation of the audience

Both poles – intention and expectation – are performatively executed in the oral presentation. Medieval texts were intended for oral arrangement. It can be said that the genre is realized in the performance – and not in the written or printed tradition, which is secondary. In this way, the intentions correspond to the expectations. In the tension between intention and expectation, the genre emerges as the form of the text during the presentation. Thus, in the text of the performance, the assessments that correspond to the intention and expectation are realized. The genres formulate the assessments attributed to them through intentions and expectations.

CHAPTER 13

Constructions of Identities and Processes of Othering. Images of Polish Characters, Polishness and Poland and Their Roles in Medieval German Literature

Florian M. Schmid

1 Construction of Identities and Processes of Othering

In the current cultural and social theoretical debate there is a multitude of divergent conceptualizations of the term *identity*.[1] It is often postulated that the determination of identity as one's 'self' happens through a relational confrontation with the 'other'. A mental demarcation between the *self* and the *other* via attributions can be made through the use of stereotypes, especially when the engagement takes place not with other individuals, but with groups. Research has recognized various forms of identity,[2] two of which are of particular relevance for the following reflections on images of Polish characters, their Polishness, Poland, and their roles in medieval German literature: the *personal* and the *collective identity*.

---

[1] The interdisciplinary, far-reaching and often diverging research on *identity*, *otherness* and *stereotypes* cannot be reviewed in this article. The cited individual studies provide references to further studies. Current research in English usually uses the term *otherness* as a hypernym for further terms like *strangeness*, *foreignness* or *alienness*. German research literature often distinguishes between *das Eigene* (one's 'own') and *das Fremde* (the 'alien') which is not directly reflected in the English differentiation between the 'self' and the 'other'. In German there is a semantic difference between the concept of one's 'own' (related to both individual and group concepts of identity) and the 'self' (more related to individual forms of identity) or the 'alien' (something difficult to understand with peculiar qualities) and the 'other' (the difference can, but must not be highly distinct). In this article, I will speak of the *other*, translate the German research accordingly, and only differentiate when problems of terminology are directly addressed, for instance, in regard to question as to in which circumstances the *other* becomes the *strange* or the *strange* becomes *familiar*.

[2] For a research overview on postmodern concepts of identity and stereotype, also with regard to space, see Antje Schönwald, *Identitäten und Stereotype in grenzüberschreitenden Verflechtungsräumen. Das Beispiel der Großregion*, RaumFragen. Stadt – Region – Landschaft (Wiesbaden, 2012), 45–84.

The sociologist Thomas Luckmann understands (in the framework of an anthropological and societal theoretic clarification of the concept of identity) the personal identity "als Daseinsform des Menschen"[3] [as man's way of being], which constitutes man as such, or as "eine allgemeine gesellschaftliche Gegebenheit menschlichen Lebens"[4] [a general social givenness of human life]. From this timeless concept, he delimits a second form of personal identity, which is to be understood as a subjective problem, historically dependent on very specific social structures and which thus plays a role in the Western modern period, but not in the European Middle Ages.[5] According to Luckmann, the form of personal identity, which also existed in pre-modern times, is located at the intersection of *Leib* [body], *Bewusstsein* [consciousness] and *Gesellschaft* [society]:[6] one can directly experience only the environment; one experiences his/her fellow human beings in social relationships, whereby the body is grasped as a field of expression for the processes of consciousness; one experiences himself/herself as a detour via his/her fellow human beings, because the experiences of the 'other' are directed back to himself/herself.[7] Luckmann calls this "wechselseitige" [reciprocal], "intersubjektive"[8] [intersubjective] or "mitmenschliche" "*Spiegelung*"[9] [co-human mirroring]. The basic structures of the social formation of personal identity described in this way,[10] which are thus based on socialization and social interaction, clarify the historical conditionality and, at the same time, the historical changeability of the formation (processes) of identity.

Every human being is socialized in a historically specific society, characterized, inter alia, by a socially mediated worldview, language and culture,[11] which influences his/her perceptions, attitudes and actions. On the basis of these assumptions, Luckmann develops the thesis that personal human identity does not develop from *inside to out* but from *outside to in*.[12] The formation

---

3   Thomas Luckmann, "Persönliche Identität, soziale Rolle und Rollendistanz," in *Identität. Kolloquium vom 5.–11.09.1976 in Bad Homburg*, eds. Odo Marquard and Karlheinz Stierle, Poetik und Hermeneutik: Arbeitsergebnisse einer Forschungsgruppe 8 (Munich, 1979), 293–313, at 293.
4   Luckmann, "Persönliche Identität, soziale," 295.
5   Ibid.
6   Ibid., 297.
7   Ibid., 299.
8   Ibid.
9   Ibid., 300.
10 Ibid., 298.
11 Ibid.
12 Ibid., 299.

of identity is therefore to be understood as a permanent and interminable, situational and often even affective process; identity must always, e.g. often ad hoc, be renegotiated, drafted, and constantly updated in concrete historical situations.[13] To sum up, identity is thus a product of social and dynamic construction processes.[14]

For the Middle Ages, research identifies in particular the relevance of a collective identity.[15] According to the Egyptologist Jan Assmann, collective identity is to be thought of as the individual's identification with social groups and thus does not exist in itself, but only to the degree that certain individuals profess it.[16] Thus, collective identity is created through the *kulturelle Gedächtnis* [cultural memory], which is to be understood as the memorial culture of a group, through which the group defines itself.[17] The historian Volker Scior summarizes the research on foreignness to the effect that for medieval authors the relevance of different collective partial identities has to be assumed.[18] He refers among others to national, gentile, regional, Christian, and institutional identities.[19]

The question of the interrelation, interdependence and interpenetration between 'self' and 'other' is fundamental, especially in intercultural contexts. When in the following the images of Poles, Polishness and Poland in German

13 Carla Meyer/Christoph Dartmann, "Einleitung," in *Identität und Krise? Zur Deutung vormoderner Selbst-, Welt- und Fremderfahrungen*, eds. iidem, Symbolische Kommunikation und gesellschaftliche Wertesysteme. Schriftenreihe des Sonderforschungsbereichs 496 17 (Münster, 2007), 9–22, at 19.

14 Cf. Meyer/Dartmann, "Einleitung," 17.

15 In particular, Niethammer has pointed out the problem that supposed collective identities can be ideologically instrumentalized in order to call up stereotypical images of the 'self' and the 'other' and to enable simple demarcations between inside and outside; Lutz Niethammer, *Kollektive Identität. Heimliche Quellen einer unheimlichen Konjunktur* (Reinbek, 2000). For thoughts on an interaction of personal and collective identity see, for example, Jürgen Straub, "Personale und kollektive Identität. Zur Analyse eines theoretischen Begriffs," *Identitäten Erinnerung, Geschichte, Identität* 3, 2nd ed., eds. Aleida Assmann and Heidrun Friese (Frankfurt/M., 1999), 73–104.

16 Jan Assmann, *Das kulturelle Gedächtnis. Schrift, Erinnerung und politische Identität in frühen Hochkulturen* (Munich, 1992), 130–60, esp. 130–33.

17 Assmann, 48–56 distinguishes between *kulturelles Gedächtnis* [cultural memory] and *kommunikatives Gedächtnis* [communicative memory]. The latter is strongly personal, and includes recent memories that people share with their contemporaries and is therefore very transient; ibid., 50.

18 Volker Scior, *Das Eigene und das Fremde. Identität und Fremdheit in den Chroniken Adams von Bremen, Helmolds von Bosau und Arnolds von Lübeck*, Orbis mediaevalis, Vorstellungswelten des Mittelalters 4 (Berlin, 2002), 26.

19 Ibid., 23–25.

medieval literature are investigated, it must be clarified if and to what extent these are constructed within the text and thus indirectly also having the effect for the text-external recipient of being 'other' or 'alien'. Already from Luckmann's argument it has become clear that otherness, alienness or strangeness are relational concepts. The educationalist Ortfried Schäffter defined alienness as a mode of relationship in which we encounter external phenomena, but not as a property of things or persons: "Fremdheit ist [...] keine Eigenschaft von Dingen oder Personen, sondern ein Beziehungsmodus, in dem wir externen Phänomenen begegnen."[20] This means that the evaluator is not just an observer, but one is always involved and affected himself/herself. Accordingly, alienness is something we ascribe to something or somebody else from our own perspective and in our own positionality. Consequently, the cultural scholar Christian Holtorf states that anyone who talks about other people, says something about him- or herself: "Wer [...] über Fremde spricht, sagt damit etwas über sich selbst."[21] Statements about alienness are thus attributions with mutual potential for knowledge – for both those who are being assessed and those who are judging.[22] In regard to the Middle Ages, however, the investigation of the construction of otherness or alienness does not necessarily promise

---

20 Ortfried Schäffter, "Modi des Fremderlebens. Deutungsmuster im Umgang mit Fremdheit," *Das Fremde. Erfahrungsmöglichkeiten zwischen Faszination und Bedrohung*, ed. id. (Opladen, 1991), 11–42, at 12. Schäffter, at 15 distinguishes possible interpretive patterns of otherness on the basis of four elementary order schemata of system-specific inside/outside relationships: "Ordnungen transzendenter Ganzheit: Das Fremde als tragender Grund und Resonanzboden von Eigenheit. Ordnungen perfekter Vollkommenheit: Das Fremde als Negation von Eigenheit. Ordnungskonzepte dynamischer Selbstveränderung: Fremdheit als Chance zur Ergänzung und Vervollständigung. Konzeption komplementärer Ordnung: Eigenheit und Fremdheit als Zusammenspiel sich wechselseitig hervorrufender Kontrastierungen." [Orders of transcendent wholeness: the stranger as a supporting ground and sounding board of ownness. Orders of perfect completeness: the stranger as a negation of ownness. Order concepts of dynamic self-change: strangeness as an opportunity for completing and rounding out the 'self'. Conception of complementary order: ownness and strangeness as an interaction of mutually generated contrasts.]
21 Christian Holtorf, "Spielräume einer Geschichte des *Fremden*," in *"Fremde". Zum Umgang mit Fremden in der Geschichte und Gegenwart*, ed. Presse- und Informationsstelle der Freien Universität Berlin, Dokumentationsreihe der Freien Universität Berlin 21 (Berlin, 1993), 15–18, at 15.
22 Edith Feistner, "Selbstbild, Feindbild, Metabild: Spiegelungen des Mittelalters," in *Forschungen zur deutschen Literatur des Spätmittelalters. Festschrift für Johannes Janota*, eds. Horst Brunner and Werner Williams-Krapp (Tübingen, 2003), 141–58, at 141 has extended this dialogical or mutual dependence of self-image and alien image with the "*Metabild*" [*meta image*]. The meta image is composed of both the image of the 'self' and the 'other' and is to be understood as the self-image in the eyes of the 'other'.

far-reaching insights into persons, cultures, countries, and objects constructed as 'alien', but nevertheless about the viewer's self-perception and construction of one's own identity.

In the field of historical science, Scior (for example) has worked out a finding for the medieval chronicles by Adam of Bremen, Helmold of Bosau, and Arnold of Lübeck, which may possibly also be valid for literary works in the narrower sense: Scior could not identify any attempt within the chronicles to objectively portray the stranger or the foreign land as such.[23] As a consequence, medieval representations of alienness cannot be measured by their realistic content or be used for the reconstruction of facts.[24] According to Scior, attribution of alienness happens across all chronicles, especially via religious, ethnic, legal, cultural-*civilizational* criteria, "aber auch nach solchen, die sich auf das Aussehen und Verhalten oder auf Eigenschaften beziehen"[25] [but also on those that relate to appearance and behavior or to characteristics]. The description of 'others', according to Scior, was often used primarily to highlight the achievements of a community within which an author or the community's representatives were located.[26] While Scior sharply distinguishes between one's 'own' and the 'alien' and concentrates on the question of how the self-interpretation by individual high medieval authors determines their patterns of perception of the stranger, he does not emphasize how the representation of the 'other' rebounds on the construction of their own identities. For a while now, research has not only been interested in borders, but has had a special interest in hybridity, "also für individuelle oder kollektive Bedeutungsmuster, die sich auf der vermeintlichen Grenze zwischen mehreren Kulturen entwickeln und die die Grenze neu als Zone des Übergangs und des Austauschs definieren"[27] [that is, for individual or collective patterns of meaning that develop on the supposed boundary between multiple cultures and that redefine the boundary as a zone of transition and exchange]. By investigating the literary constructions of images and processes of othering, not only the construction of differences and boundaries, but also signs of the construction of something new or hybrid shall be considered.

The 'other', 'alien', or stranger is thus determined in its relationality, but it requires a further differentiation. The historian Hans-Werner Goetz has

---

23 Scior, *Das Eigene und das Fremde*, 332.
24 Ibid., 332.
25 Ibid., 334.
26 Ibid., 337.
27 Meyer/Dartmann, "Einleitung," 10.

specified that strangeness is not primarily a social, but a mental concept: it exists initially in the imagination due to sensations and attributions, and only secondarily becomes a social phenomenon only in the case of widespread, similar notions.[28] For the early Middle Ages, Goetz defines a broad spectrum for the stranger, ranging from the non-resident to the completely 'alien' as in the medieval notions of monsters; strangeness is delineated as a consistent concept of one's 'own'.[29] He states that in the early Middle Ages, the foreigner appeared to be quite integrated into society; he was not just the 'other' and rarely the enemy or the unwanted guest: "Der *Fremde* schien im frühen Mittelalter durchaus in die Gesellschaft integriert, er war nicht einfach der *andere* und nur selten der Feind oder der ungeliebte Gast."[30] Goetz also addresses the graduality of the transition from the 'other' to the stranger; the historian Karin Hitzbleck sets the difference sharply. Both the 'other' and the stranger are initially neutral categories, but can be distinguished from each other: While the 'other' connects the perception of the fundamentally unfamiliar with an act of understanding, the stranger initially implies a lack of understanding.[31] Identity, the 'self', the 'own', the 'other', the 'alien', the 'foreign', and the stranger are determined situationally, dynamically, and in some cases gradually. This basic consensus of interdisciplinary identity and otherness research, that identity, sameness, otherness, and alienness are constructs, that there is a relational connection between the 'self' and the 'other', and that the construction of identity is the result of self attributions and ascriptions within social interaction, is the starting point for the following reflections on German literary works of the Middle Ages.[32]

---

28   Hans-Werner Goetz, "Fremdheit im früheren Mittelalter," in *Herrschaftspraxis und soziale Ordnungen im Mittelalter und in der frühen Neuzeit. Ernst Schubert zum Gedenken*, eds. Peter Aufgebauer and Christine van den Heuvel, Veröffentlichungen der Historischen Kommission für Niedersachsen und Bremen 232 (Hannover, 2006), 245–65, at 249.

29   Idem, 248. Goetz, 263, points out that the quite consistent early medieval concept of otherness in the sense of a delimitation from the 'self' (which expresses itself in corresponding terms and in the ideas conveyed by it), only partially coincides with the presupposed concept of otherness in modern research.

30   Idem, 265 (emphasis in the original).

31   Kerstin Hitzbleck, "Einleitung: Transformationen des Fremden im Spätmittelalter und in der Frühen Neuzeit," in *Die Erweiterung des "globalen" Raumes und die Wahrnehmung des Fremden vom Mittelalter bis zur frühen Neuzeit/L'extension de l'espace "global" et la perception de l'Autre du Moyen Âge jusqu'à l'époque moderne*, eds. Kerstin Hitzbleck and Thomas Schwitter, Itinera 38 (Basel, 2015), 5–31, at 6.

32   Cf. Scior, *Das Eigene und das Fremde*, 10, 332.

The question is whether and, if so, how these findings are reflected and/or negotiated within literary works of the Middle Ages; what interest, what knowledge, and what evaluations of the 'other' are to be deduced.[33] The German philologist Horst Wenzel points out that the German courtly literature from the twelfth and thirteenth centuries is not so much about identity, but rather about identifiability and non-identifiability in different contexts, for example in regard to participation and non-participation in the clan, at court, in church, and in their associated systems of order.[34] It is noticeable that in a variety of literary works the 'other' is indeed often constructed in contrast to the 'selves' of the protagonists and the intended extra-textual audience. However, often there appears to be no firm interest in depicting the 'other's' otherness. The German philologist Bernd Thum concludes that the 'other' was ever again understood as having a material quality of its own, but not as a spiritual-cultural program with its particular existential quality: "Offenbar sah man das Andere, *Fremde* immer wieder als etwas Dingliches, nicht aber als geistig-kulturelles Programm mit eigener existentieller Qualität."[35] Such a hypothesis seems to imply a linear

---

33 In regard to the construction of otherness and processes of othering in medieval German literature, research has mainly been executed on the depiction of the Orient. Even though knowledge about the empirical reality greatly expanded in the late Middle Ages, in epics as well as in prose romances almost exclusively written transmitted *topos knowledge* is narrated. For a summary of research of otherness from a point of view of German philology see Florian Kragl, *Die Weisheit des Fremden. Studien zur mittelalterlichen Alexandertradition. Mit einem allgemeinen Teil zur Fremdheitswahrnehmung* (Bern, 2005), esp. 45–154.

34 Horst Wenzel, "Der unfeste Held. Wechselnde oder mehrfache Identitäten," in *Unverwechselbarkeit. Persönliche Identität und Identifikation in der vormodernen Gesellschaft*, ed. Peter von Moos, Norm und Struktur 23 (Köln, 2004), 163–83, here 163.

35 Bernd Thum, "Frühformen des Umgangs mit 'Fremdem' und 'Fremde' in der Literatur des Hochmittelalters. Der Parzival Wolframs von Eschenbach als Beispiel," in *Das Mittelalter – unsere fremde Vergangenheit. Beiträge der Stuttgarter Tagung vom 17.–19.09.1987*, eds. Joachim Kuolt, Harald Kleinschmidt, and Peter Dinzelbacher, Flugschriften der Volkshochschule Stuttgart 6 (Stuttgart, 1990), 315–52, at 325 (emphasis in the original). Thum basically separates an external from an internal other. For the former, he distinguishes six criteria by which others are perceived as such: (1) phenomenological observation (customs, rituals, clothes etc.); (2) forms of domination and representation; (3) foreign languages and names; (4) the relation between the sexes; (5) the phenomenology of the external, physical (skin color etc.); (6) foreign religions; ibid., 330–35. In regard to the *internal* stranger Thum differentiates between (1) "das *Archaische*, zu verstehen als das Affektgetriebene, Grobe, Undifferenzierte und nicht Differenzierende, Gnadenlos-Gewalttätige, *lügenhaft* in die Irre Führende und Deviante" [the archaic, to be understood as the affect-driven, gross, undifferentiated and non-differentiating, merciless-violent, lying misleading and deviant]; (2) *Äußerlichkeit* und *Scheinhaftigkeit*.

development in dealing with the 'other' and was therefore correctly criticized by Scior, because it is often still today the case that otherness is viewed as having no existential quality of its own.[36] Striking is, however, that in German medieval literature the 'other' is mostly constructed analogously to one's 'own' and thus can be interpreted accordingly.[37] The concept or identity of a character tends to be largely independent of such a category like ethnicity, but is essentially constituted by qualities that can be used to identify a character in a text. The German philologist Armin Schulz catalogues above all nobleness, virtue, heroism, and kinship, as well as suitability as a ruler, lover, marriage and reproductive partner.[38] Taking these findings of literary studies into account, it becomes evident that they are very similar to the ones Scior found in relation to medieval chronicles as mentioned above. Consequently, it would be surprising if the medieval literary works differ much from these findings in their depiction of Poles, Polishness and Poland. However, it does seem worthwhile to investigate which images are created in which way and for what purpose.

By applying the adduced assumptions and principles of identity construction and othering to Middle High German literature, this study shall focus on identities that are constructed by the narrator via the creation of the specific and connoted relations of a narrated character to itself and to other characters through interaction as well as to areas of reference known to the intended, extra-textual audience. Taking this point of view as a prerequisite, attributions by a character to itself or to its own group(s) as well as to other characters or groups – and also those by the narrator – position those being assessed as well as the evaluators in a system of specific norms and values such as *êre, sterke, muot, kuonheit, triuwe, minne, vreude, tugent* [honor, strength, courage, daring, loyalty, courtly love, courtly joy, virtue] etc. which are implicitly or

---

   Interne Fremde erfahren die Helden der höfischen Epik auch in der höfischen Zivilisation selbst, dort nämlich, wo sie sich als bloß rituell, veräußerlicht, scheinhaft erweist, wo die großen sozial-ethischen Fragen verdeckt bleiben und nicht einmal symbolisch gelöst sind" [externality and appearance: *internal otherness* is experienced by the heroes of courtly epics also within courtly civilization, where it proves to be merely ritualistic, externalized, apparent, where the great social-ethical questions are concealed and not even solved symbolically]; (3) "Die *interne Fremde*, die Gegenwelt, Stimulans der Identität des *Eigenen* kann auch *Gott* sein" [the *internal other*, the counterworld, also *God* can be the stimulant of the identity of one's '*own*']; ibid., 342–43 (emphasis in the original).

36 Scior, *Das Eigene und das Fremde*, 14 n. 19.
37 Thum, "Frühformen des Umgangs mit 'Fremdem' und 'Fremde,'" 320–21, 346–47.
38 Armin Schulz, *Schwieriges Erkennen. Personenidentifizierung in der mittelhochdeutschen Epik*, Münchener Texte und Untersuchungen zur deutschen Literatur des Mittelalters 135 (Tübingen, 2008), 3–4.

explicitly effective in a literary work. A distinction has to be made between the self-presentations and the external perceptions of otherness at the level of the characters, as constructed by the narrator, and the images that are supposed to have an effect on the extra-textual recipients.

It is well known that the construction and perception of the 'other' are often shaped and framed by stereotypes, i.e., by their implicit possibilities and limitations, their including and excluding effects such as enabling, categorizing, and simplifying perceptions and interactions as well as the uptaking and the wittingly or unwittingly upholding of traditional, political and other perspectives.[39] The term *stereotype* stands in sociology and psychology for modes of imagination and perception of whole groups or classes that reduces given objects in terms of their semantic features and, for the most part, arbitrarily categorizes them in order to allow faster cognitive orientations.[40] The contribution that literature can make in forming, forging, transmiting, confirming, and dissolving stereotypes has been widely discussed; likewise, the relationship between literature and reality has often been addressed.[41] At least gradually, literature has its own ways of perceiving, interpreting and shaping a world. A transfer of a literary representation to reality appears to be in various ways highly problematic. For instance, it is not possible to infer directly or indirectly from textual findings the semantically corresponding attitudes of their

---

39 Stereotypes serve orientation in a diverse world, have an economizing function, by making the management of the surrounding world more efficient, at the same time they can also have an ideologizing function; cf. Magda Telus, "Gruppenspezifische Stereotype und Identität," in *Nachbarn im Ostseeraum über einander. Wandel der Bilder, Vorurteile und Stereotypen?*, eds. Frank-Michael Kirsch, Christine Frisch, and Helmut Müssener (Huddinge, 2001), 113–24, at 113.

40 Although the basic concept of stereotypes claims timeless validity, the term originating from the printers' language was, adopted from French, in today's understanding coined by Walter Lippmann's book *Public Opinion* (New York, 1922; repr. 1954). For the history and semantics of the term see Martin Reisigl, "Stereotyp," in *Historisches Wörterbuch der Rhetorik*, ed. Gert Ueding, 12 vols. (Darmstadt, 1992–2015), 8: 1368–89.

41 For instance, Hermann Meyer, "Das Bild des Holländers in der deutschen Literatur," in *Forschungsprobleme der Vergleichenden Literaturgeschichte*, ed. Kurt Wais (Tübingen, 1951), 171–88, at 172–73, clearly differentiates the task of a sociologist from that of a literary scholar. The former is interested in the social phenomenon of stereotypical images in themselves, while the literary scholar asks whether and, if so, to what extent an image created in literature relates to the extra-literary content of consciousness which is described by sociologists, whether it differs or assimilates, whether literature is rather receptive or productive; cf. Ruth Florack, *Bekannte Fremde. Zu Herkunft und Funktion nationaler Stereotype in der Literatur*, Studien und Texte zur Sozialgeschichte der Literatur 114 (Tübingen, 2007), esp. 7–58.

producers and recipients.[42] Daniel Fulda points out, for example, that stereotypes invoked by a literary work essentially depend on those that a recipient has mentally stored, that is, they are framed and minted by reading methods and presettings ["Welche Stereotype ein Text aufruft, hängt wesentlich von den mental gespeicherten Stereotypen der Rezipienten ab"].[43] This, however, can hardly be verified with regard to the Middle Ages due to a lack of data.

With regard to medieval literary studies, the term stereotype refers to a lesser extent to negative or positive prejudices, but rather to a reduction of qualities that are assigned to a character and are typical of single characters and/or groups as well as for a genre, an individual work of literature, or even a specific version of a text. Stereotypes in both understandings can be included in images and can be relevant for their constitution, but an image must not necessarily be stereotypical.[44] In this context, an image is understood as a constructed depiction of characters and topography by narration that is not per se a negative or positive one. When looking at the narrative constructions and reflections of attributions and the points of view from which they take place, a distinction has to be made between the level of the narrator and the level of the characters, as well as between their explicit and implicit judgements and markings.[45] Furthermore, the dynamic shifting with regard to weighting the different attributions has to be considered. In contrast to a modern concept of

---

42   Cf. Katrin Berwanger, "Einleitung," in *Stereotyp und Geschichtsmythos in Kunst und Sprache. Die Kultur Ostmitteleuropas in Beiträgen zur Potsdamer Tagung, 16.–18.01.2003*, eds. Katrin Berwanger and Peter Kosta, Vergleichende Studien zu den slavischen Sprachen und Literaturen 11 (Frankfurt/M., 2005), XIII–XXX; Daniel Fulda, "'Wiedererkennen von Bekanntem'. Literarische und soziale Stereotype in der frühneuzeitlichen Komödie," in *Frühneuzeitliche Stereotype. Zur Produktivität und Restriktivität sozialer Vorstellungsmuster V. Jahrestag der Internationalen Andreas Gryphius Gesellschaft. Wrocław, 8.–11.10.2008*, eds. Mirosława Czarnecka, Thomas Borgstedt, and Tomasz Jabłecki (Bern, 2010), 169–84, esp. 169–72; Konstanze Jung, *Stereotypisierungen und Hybridisierungen in ausgewählten deutschen Romanen nach 1945 unter Berücksichtigung der deutsch-polnischen Beziehungen. Interkulturelle Perspektiven für das Fach Deutsch und den historisch-politischen Unterricht* (Hamburg, 2016), 25–28.

43   Fulda, "'Wiedererkennen von Bekanntem'," 169.

44   For the demarcation of stereotypical research from imagology see Veruschka Wagner, *Imagologie der Fremde. Das Londonbild eines osmanischen Reisenden Mitte des 19. Jahrhunderts. Mit 3 Abbildungen*, Ottoman Studies/Osmanistische Studien 3 (Göttingen, 2016), 201–16.

45   Cf. Elke Platz-Waury, "Figur$_3$," in *Reallexikon der deutschen Literaturwissenschaft. Neubearbeitung des Reallexikons der deutschen Literaturgeschichte*, eds. Klaus Weimar et al., 3rd ed. (Berlin, 1997–2003), 1: 587–89, at 587.

characters as mental models of persons, Elisabeth Lienert sums up the typical aspects of characters in Middle High German narrative works as follows:

> Figuren in vormodernem Erzählen, Figuren vor allem in der als *archaischer* geltenden Heldenepik, sind konstituiert durch Name und Herkunft, Eigenschaften und Affektäußerungen, Handlungsfunktionen und Interaktionen mit anderen, bisweilen durch ihre Geschichte (nur selten in biographischer Anlage), gelegentlich ihre Fama und/oder tradierte Rollenvorgaben; nur ausnahmsweise durch ihre Innenwelt oder durch Ansätze zu Veränderung oder gar Entwicklung.[46]

Accordingly, categories such as name, origin, characteristics, expressions of affects, action functions, interactions with others, the history of a character, its *fama* and traditional role(s), inner world and dispositions to change or development will be discussed in regard to the construction and depiction of the 'other'. Of particular interest will be the analysis of the representation of a character's inner world, since it may feature character-specific views, perceptions and emotions which might also be conveyed to the intended extra-textual recipient but not to further characters in the text. It is also important to investigate which character receives its own voice by means of direct speech (to what extend and with what quality) and which character is narrated only by the narrator. The use of the literary technique of direct speech is traditionally regarded as a means through which the intended recipients' sympathies can be directed.[47] Furthermore, it seems to be important to research the ways

---

46 Elisabeth Lienert, "Aspekte der Figurenkonstitution in mittelhochdeutscher Heldenepik," *Beiträge zur Geschichte der deutschen Sprache und Literatur* 138 (2016), 51–75, at 52 (emphasis in the original).

47 The essential functions for the use of a character's direct speech are, for example, the approximation of the time of action to reading time, the perspectivation and relativization of statements, and the reduction of the narrative distance to the recipient; Henri Mitterand, "Dialogue et littérarité Romanesque," in *Le Dialogue*, eds. Pierre R. Léon and Paul Perron (Montréal, 1985), 141–54, at 150–51. Furthermore, it might support focusing on the importance of the positioning of dialogues with regard to the negotiation of relationships between figures and their characterization, the dialogue structure, and its content; Hans-Gert Roloff, *Stilstudien zur Prosa des 15. Jahrhunderts: die Melusine des Thüring von Ringoltingen*, Literatur und Leben 12 (Cologne, 1970), 187. In addition, direct speech can be effective in contrast to the narrator's speech and serve the illustration; Catherine Drittenbass, *Aspekte des Erzählens in der "Melusine" Thürings von Ringoltingen. Dialoge, Zeitstruktur und Medialität des Romans*, Beiträge zur älteren Literaturgeschichte (Heidelberg, 2011), 29. For possible ways of direction sympathy in the

of creating and describing both characters and topography via correspondence relations and contrast relations. The following analysis is not an effort to research in general the medieval images of Poles, Polishness and Poland, but primarily aims to gain the images created and presented within Middle High German literature.

2 Literary Reflections on and Constructions of Poles, Polishness and/or Poland

In Middle High German literature there are different expressions to denote the stranger or the foreign land.[48] Of greater importance are the lexical fields *gast*, *ellende*, and *vremde*.[49] The male substantive *gast* is used with the meanings (1) "gast" [guest], (2) "der fremde" [the stranger/foreigner/'alien'] and (3) "fremder krieger, krieger überhaupt verwendet" [foreign warrior, warrior in general]; the adjective *gastlich* has the meaning "nach weise eines gastes, eines fremden" [according to the way of a guest, a stranger], the adverb *gastlîche* (1) "nach weise eines gastes, wie es sich für einen gast schickt" [according to

---

extra-textual recipients see Anica Schumann, "Der sympathische Gegner: Mechanismen der Sympathiesteuerung im *Laurin*," *Zeitschrift für Deutsche Philologie* 136 (2017), 39–62.

48 Goetz, "Fremdheit im früheren Mittelalter," 252–63 has analyzed various Latin words that potentially contained implications of the 'other' and were used in the early and high Middle Ages: he lists *exter(n)us* as an opposite to *intern*, *peregrinus* as a "not fully incorporated into the law stranger and traveler," *advena* as a newcomer from outside, *extraneus* as opposed to *proprium*, to one's 'own', and *alienus* as a collective term for all the 'non-own' belonging to somebody else. Other words (such as *ignotus*) do not primarily emphasize otherness. This also applies to *barbarus* which is the only more examined word that clearly – with negative connotations – expresses the demarcation of one's 'own' (cultural or religious) community. *Barbarus* refers to others, but emphasizes not the otherness per se, but the wildness, savagery and non-Christianity, which delimits someone or something from the own group.

49 Less advanced, however, is the semantics of the Middle High German word for *other*. In the context of these considerations, only the central substantive, adjectives and possibly adverbs are adduced, while compounds, derivatives and verbs will not be listed. The basis is the BMZ, when no other source is indicated; *Mittelhochdeutsches Wörterbuch*. Mit Benutzung des Nachlasses von Georg Friedrich Benecke, eds. Wilhelm Müller and Friedrich Zarncke, 4 vols. (Leipzig, 1854–66; repr. Stuttgart, 1990). The newer *Mittelhochdeutsches Wörterbuch*, eds. Mainzer Akademie der Wissenschaften und der Literatur and Akademie der Wissenschaften zu Göttingen (*MWB Online*; last update: 7-15-2018) lists lemmata online only up to and including the letter H.

the way of a guest, as it is proper for a guest] and (2) "geschmückt" [decorated].[50] The neutral substantive *ellende* stands for (1) "das fremde land, abwesenheit von der heimat" [the foreign land, absence from home(land)], but also for (2) "elend" [misery]. Similarly, the semantic spectrum of the adjective *ellende* is employed in the meaning of (1) "von der heimat fern" [far away from home], (2) "in weiterer ausdehnung des begriffes fremd, geschieden von etwas" [in a further extension of the term alien, separated from something], (3) "armselig, elend" [miserable, pathetic].[51] The semantic field *vremde* including different word derivations and word classes is much more extensive. The male substantive *vremde* is used with the meaning "der fremde" [the stranger], the female substantive with (1) "die fremde, der heimat entgegengesetzt" [the foreign land, opposite to the homeland] or (2) "das fremd oder auch fern sein" [being foreign or even far away]. The adjective *vremede* is used in the sense of (1) "gegensatz von einheimisch, nicht zu unserm lande oder hause gehörig" [opposite of domestic, not belonging to our country or home], (2) "nicht eigen" [not one's/their 'own'], (3a) "nicht bekannt oder vertraut" [not known or familiar], (3b) "von einem fern" [remote from one] or 4) "ungewöhnlich, seltsam, wunderbar" [unusual, strange, wonderful], the adjective *vremdeclich* as "fremd, fremdartig" [foreign, alien]; the adjective *vremdeclîche* as "auf fremde weise" [in a strange way]. Among the word class, the adjective *wilde*

---

50   The semantics are similarly described in the *MWB Online*: *gast* (1) "Fremder" [stranger], (2) "(fremder) Held, Krieger, Feind" [(foreign) hero, warrior, foe], (3) "Hausgast" [house guest]; *gastlich* respectively *gastlichlîche(n)*: (1.1 adjective) "fremd, feindlich" [foreign, hostile], (1.2 adverb) "auf die Art eines Fremden" [in the manner of a stranger], (2) "wie es einem Fremden zukommt, fremden Gästen angemessen ist; gastlich, gastfreundlich" [as befits a stranger, is appropriate for foreign guests; hospitable, hospitable], (3) "geschmückt, schmuck" [decorated, spruce] (http://www.mhdwb-online.de/wb.php?-buchstabe=G&portion=280 [2-20-2019]).

51   The *MWB Online* differentiates in regard to semantics in a similar way: The substantive *ellende* has the meanings (1) "Fremde, Fremdheit an einem Ort (oft im Hinblick auf Herkunft oder Folge von Verbannung)" [stranger, strangeness in one place (often in terms of origin or consequence of exile)] or (2) "rechtl. 'Elendeneid', der Reinigungseid eines Beklagten ohne genügend Eideshelfer" [juridical *oath of a foreigner*, the oath of purgation of a defendant without sufficient compugators]; the adjective *ellende*, which often appears substantivized, is used with the meanings (1) "fremd (etwa als 'nicht heimisch' oder 'fern' (einer Sache, Person/ von etw., jmdm.)" [foreign (such as non-local or distant (an object, a person from something/somebody)], (2) "armselig, einsam, elend, beklagenswert" [miserable, lonely, pathetic, lamentable], the adjective *ellendec* with (1) "fremd" [foreign] or (2) "jämmerlich, arm" [miserable, poor], the adjective or adverb *ellendeclich* with (1) "fremd, verbannt" [foreign, banished] or (2) as adverb "jämmerlich, bedauernswert" [miserable, deplorable] (http://www.mhdwb-online.de/wb.php?buchstabe=E&portion=760 [2-20-2019]).

should also be mentioned, which is often stereotypically and essentially used with four meanings, the third of which is important for these considerations: (1) "dem zahmen entgegengesetzt" [contrary to tame], (2) "mehr ethisch: irre, unstät, untreu" [more ethical: mad, unsteady, disloyal], (3) "fremd, fremdartig; seltsam, wunderbar, unbegreiflich" [foreign, alien; strange, wonderful, incomprehensible] and (4) "unangebaut, wüste" [uncultivated, desert]. Possible, but less pertinent, is the adjective *wunderbære* [wonderful, miraculous]. Naturally, otherness, alienness, foreignness, or strangeness are often expressed by combinations of an adjective and a substantive, for instance to refer to foreign languages, customs, countries and/or persons. The adduced word fields with their diverse possibilities of combinations demonstrate a medieval need for a differentiated vocabulary for dealing with the 'other', and at the same time they show both similarities and differences to today's use of individual words. As a consequence, it has to be examined if and how these expressions were used in the literary reflection and construction of Poles, Polishness and/or Poland. In this article, Pole, Polish, Poland respectively (and accordingly all analogous expressions like German, Russian, Hun and so on) shall be understood as that which in the medieval literary works is addressed by the adjective *pôlânisch* (or Middle German *pôlênisch*), the substantive *Pôlân(e)* (or Middle German *Pôlêne*) (referring to persons and territory), *Pôle* or *Pôlônîer* (referring to persons), and *Pôlônlant* (referring to territory).

In a variety of narrative, lyrical and dramatic texts of different genres Polish characters, Polishness and/or Poland are mentioned.[52] Polish characters

---

52 Most of the works discussed in this article are also treated in regard to Poles and Poland by George T. Gillespie, *A Catalogue of Persons Named in German Heroic Literature (700–1600). Including named animals and objects and ethnic names* (Oxford, 1973) (only listed), Danielle Buschinger, "Deutsch-polnische Wechselbeziehungen im Mittelalter," *Germanica Wratislaviensia* XCII (1991), 45–53, Otfrid Ehrisman[n], "Die Fürsten ûzer Polan. Polen in der deutschen Heldendichtung des Mittelalters," *Germanica Wratislaviensia* XCII (1991), 33–44 and, published after the conference on which this volume is based, Paul Martin Langner, *Annäherung ans Fremde durch sprachliche Bilder: die Region Polen und ihre Ritter in Dichtungen des Hochmittelalters* (Berlin, 2018). Buschinger offers little more than an enumeration and brief descriptions. She presents some convincing interpretations; partly the argumentation is not stringent, however. For instance, when it is stated that heroic epics do not depict a contemporary image of Poland. This appears to be an anachronistic perspective, because works of this genre usually tell about people and events of an (indefinite) past. With much more detail Langner deals with the texts in a small monographic study and often comes to convincing interpretations, but the work is sometimes imprecise. For example, the *Klage* is dated about a 100 years too late and is not formally described correctly, and he mistakenly considers the character *Berhtram von Bôle* from the heroic epics *Dietrichs Flucht* and *Rabenschlacht* as a Pole; Langner, 53, 85. Gillespie,

appear usually as warriors and/or as members of the nobility, and Poland can be part of a list depicting a number of peoples and/or their territories. Some examples may be sufficient to illustrate this phenomenon. Poland is often mentioned together with Bohemia, but also along with Russia or Hungary. For instance, Bohemia and Poland (together with Austria, v. 4868) are given as fiefs in the anonymously transmitted verse narrative *König Rother* [*King Rother*] (presumably between 1152 and 1180;[53] v. 4870: *Behein unde Polen*) by the protagonist to the lord of Tengelingen as an acknowledgement for helping him win a bride.[54] Poland and Russia are mentioned as defeated countries in a list with several other countries in the *Rolandslied* (c.1172; v. 1772: *Rûzzen unde*

---

11 and Lienert/Wolter, however, identify him as Bertram of Pola (Istria); *Rabenschlacht. Textgeschichtliche Ausgabe*, eds. Elisabeth Lienert and Dorit Wolter, Texte und Studien zur mittelhochdeutschen Heldenepik 2 (Tübingen, 2005), 236, cf. 240. Therefore, a more precise look, especially based on Ehrismann, as well as a different view on the works with regard to the construction of otherness and processes of othering, is worthwhile. This article deals with literature in a narrower sense and therefore does not address German historiography of the early and high Middle Ages. These chronicles sometimes contain other information, weightings and perspectives; cf. Buschinger, "Deutsch-polnische Wechselbeziehungen," 45, 50–51; Ehrismann, "Die Fürsten ûzer Polan," 34; Gerard Koziełek, "Aus der Frühzeit der deutsch-polnischen Wechselbeziehungen. Chronikale Überlieferungen," *Germanica Wratislaviensia* XCII (1991), 21–31; Ursula Liebertz-Grün, "Pôlân und Brezlâ in der Reimchronik des Ottokar von Steiermark," *Germanica Wratislaviensia* XCII (1991), 55–60; Wolfgang Spiewok, "Das Polenbild in Hartmann Schedels Weltchronik," *Germanica Wratislaviensia* XCII (1991), 61–73; Gerhard Kosellek, *Reformen, Revolutionen und Reisen. Deutsche Polenliteratur* (Wiesbaden, 2000), 21–31. Formally relevant texts, whose statements about Poles and Poland are hardly verifiable and also hardly new in terms of content, are not considered here such as the uniquely handed down *Kudrun*; to a possible reference to Poland see stanza 288 and the explanation in the commentary; text edition: *Kudrun. Mittelhochdeutsch/Neuhochdeutsch*, ed., trans. and annotated Uta Störmer-Caysa, Reclams Universal-Bibliothek 18639 (Stuttgart, 2010). German-language literature originating in Poland and Bohemia also are not considered here, since the place of origin hardly allows a differentiation of texts that were composed on German territory; these works have to be understood as German literature. For an overview on literary relations between Poles, Germans and also Czechs see Thomas Wünsch, *Deutsche und Slawen im Mittelalter. Beziehungen zu Tschechen, Polen, Südslawen und Russen* (Munich, 2008), esp. 70–73.

53 Joachim Bumke, *Mäzene im Mittelalter. Die Gönner und Auftraggeber der höfischen Literatur in Deutschland 1150–1300* (Munich, 1979), 92.

54 The *König Rother* is transmitted in one manuscript and four fragments; http://www.handschriftencensus.de/werke/200 [2-20-2019]. Text edition: *König Rother. Mittelhochdeutscher Text und neuhochdeutsche Übersetzung von Peter K. Stein*, ed. Ingrid Bennewitz in collaboration with Beatrix Koll and Ruth Weichselbaumer, Reclams Universal-Bibliothek 18047 (Stuttgart, 2000).

Boelan) of the priest Konrad;⁵⁵ Poland and Hungary are listed as Christianized territories, for example in the romance *Lohengrin* (some time between 1283 and 1289;⁵⁶ lines 7551–53: *Alsus bî keiser Heinrîch wart / Ungern, Pôlân zuo der kristen ê geschart, / die von got und von im sich alle touften*),⁵⁷ or representatives are part of a list of (mean) rulers such as in a text by the poet Boppe (second half of the thirteenth century)⁵⁸ (I 20,13: *der Beheîn und der Pôlân* [...]). Some of the enumerations refer to the time period in which the text was written; others, as in the case of the *Lohengrin*, reflect knowledge handed down about the past, for instance, when Poles were viewed as pagans, whereas at the time of the writing they were already largely Christianized. Depending on text and genre, it is therefore necessary to differentiate between a possible diagnostic value between the time of action within the text and the time at which the text was written. Danielle Buschinger has proposed the hypothesis that these lists are primarily supposed to indicate the author's broad geographic knowledge.⁵⁹

55   Eberhard Nellmann, "Pfaffe Konrad," in *Die deutsche Literatur des Mittelalters. Verfasserlexikon*, 2nd, completely new revised ed., eds. Kurt Ruh et al., 14 vols. (Berlin, 1978–2008), 5: 115–31, at 120. The *Rolandslied* is transmitted in one manuscript and six fragments; http://www.handschriftencensus.de/werke/202 [2-20-2019]. Text edition: *Das Rolandslied des Pfaffen Konrad*, ed. Carl Wesle, Altdeutsche Textbibliothek 69, 3rd rev. ed. by Peter Wapnewski (Tübingen, 1985; repr. Berlin, 2012). Poland is also mentioned in a list of defeated adversaries in v. 6848 (*Behaim unt Polân*) by Roland for Charlemagne. In the *Karl der Große* by the Stricker (different datings between 1215 and c.1233), which is largely based on the *Rolandslied*, Poland (v. 339: *Beheim unde Pôlan*) is also mentioned in a similar context which shows the transmission of a certain kind of knowledge; Karl-Ernst Geith/Elke Ukena-Best/Hans-Joachim Ziegeler, "Der Stricker," in *Verfasserlexikon*, 9:417–49, at 423. The *Karl der Große* is remarkably transmitted in 23 more or less complete manuscripts and 19 fragments; http://www.handschriftencensus.de/werke/366 [2-20-2019]. Text edition: Strickers Karl der Große, ed. Johannes Singer, Deutsche Texte des Mittelalters 96 (Berlin, 2016).
56   Friedrich Panzer, *Lohengrinstudien* (Halle/Saale, 1894), 58–59; *Lohengrin. Edition und Untersuchungen*, ed. Thomas Cramer (Munich, 1971), 156–63.
57   The *Lohengrin* is transmitted in three more or less complete manuscripts and one fragment; http://www.handschriftencensus.de/werke/232 [2-20-2019]. Text edition: *Lohengrin*, ed. Cramer. Mentioned is also Pomzyla, a duke of Poland (lines 2757–58: *Ein herzog von Pôlân rîch was Pomyzlâ genennet, / den sluoc der keiser mit der hant.*) and a genealogical connection between Hungarian and Polish nobility (line 7547: *Des küniges Steffâns [of Hungary] swester sun der Pôlân künic was wesende*).
58   Gisela Kornrumpf, "Boppe," in *Verfasserlexikon*, 1:953–57, at 953. Boppe's oeuvre is transmitted in three manuscripts and one fragment; http://www.handschriftencensus.de/werke/1764 [2-20-2019]. Text edition: *Der Spruchdichter Boppe. Edition – Übersetzung – Kommentar*, ed. Heidrun Alex, Hermaea: Germanistische Forschungen, Neue Folge 82 (Tübingen, 1998).
59   Buschinger "Deutsch-polnische Wechselbeziehungen," 45–46.

Certainly this may be true, as it can be seen explicitly in a late example, the uniquely transmitted *Erlauer Osterspiel* (first part of the fifteenth century; manuscript written between 1400 and 1440).[60] In this Easter Play, the character Rubin emphasizes his alleged well travel experiences in a comic way to a doctor and mentions among others places Poland, Bohemia, Moravia and Austria: *ze Polan, Pehaim, Meichsen / da la*ᵉ*rt ich die peutelein, / und das unerber Osterlant, / das ist mi*ᵉ*r alles vor erchant* (Erlau III, vv. 180–83).[61] Thus the text plays in a literary manner with the widespread use of lists of peoples and/or territories. Martin Langner adds with regard to *König Rother* and the *Rolandslied* that the mentioning of Poland within enumerations presents it as a European region and as part of a large reach of power; the effects would thus be that such lists bolster its prominence as well as add emphasis regarding the power of the respective characters.[62] In further cases there are more details depicted, but mainly en passant. For instance, this is the case with the Arthurian romance *Erec* (late twelfth century, possibly written before or c.1180/85) by Hartmann of Aue. In this work the clothing of five kings attending the wedding of Erec and Enite is described: their furs are made of the best gray sable, and Russia and Poland are viewed as being known for the best ones (vv. 1988–91/2980–83: *die geville waren gra, / daz niemand anderswa / kain pessern mochte han, / ze Reussen noch ze polan.*).[63] This is not only a reference to what was actually the case (furs had been imported from the areas of today's Scandinavian countries in addition to Russia and Poland since the eighth century), but Russia and Poland are also depicted as high-quality production sites, so that even kings wear their products. In general, however, German chivalric romances, which are largely base on French literary works, do not depict Poles, Polishness and/or Poland to any great extent, probably because of the geographical separation between 'France' and 'Poland'.

In some works, images of Poles and Poland are featured more prominently. This is the case in several heroic epics, which were written for a noble audience

60 Bernd Neumann, "*Erlauer Spiele*," in *Verfasserlexikon*, 2: 592–99, at 593.
61 http://www.handschriftencensus.de/werke/1191 [2-20-2019]. Text edition: "Erlauer Osterspiel," in *Erlauer Spiele. Sechs altdeutsche Mysterien nach einer Handschrift des XV. Jahrhunderts*, ed. Karl Ferd. Kummer (Wien, 1882; repr. Hildesheim, 1977), 31–89 (No. III).
62 Langner, *Annäherung ans Fremde*, 40, 42, 44.
63 The *Erec* is transmitted in one manuscript and three fragments; http://www.handschriftencensus.de/werke/148 [2-20-2019]. Text edition: Hartmann von Aue, *Ereck*. Textgeschichtliche Ausgabe mit Abdruck sämtlicher Fragmente und der Bruchstücke des mitteldeutschen Erek, eds. Andreas Hammer, Victor Millet and Timo Reuvekamp-Felber in collaboration with Lydia Merten, Katharina Münstermann and Hannah Rieger (Berlin, 2017). There are two counts of verses – including and excluding a pre-story.

and feature noble protagonists. In them both confrontations and exchanges between German and Polish characters appear and their Polishness and/or Poland are addressed.[64] Heroic epics seem to lend themselves to an investigation of the constructing of intercultural images and processes of othering, because they tell on the one hand about contacts between different cultures or their individuals, and on the other hand about groups that were comprised of members of different peoples. Heroic epics were written in the 12th, but mainly in the 13th century, and were based on a centuries-long and still vivid and ongoing oral narrative tradition.[65] The Middle High German heroic epics originated in the geographical area of today's central and upper Germany and Austria. In its early medieval origins, these heroic sagas are regarded as a mode and form of historical memory for the illiterate warrior nobility.[66] Historically verifiable events from the Migration Period (375–568) are interconnected via the formal procedures of reduction, assimilation, personalization, and synchronization or integration. Reduction means the simplification of a complex historical context; assimilation is the procedure of organizing storytelling through traditional narrative schemata; the term personalization aims at the construction of kinship conflicts instead of political acts; synchronization or integration refers to the procedure of merging persons and events of different times into one world of heroes.[67] Heroic epics are characterized by a specific claim to historic truth in comparison to other narrative genres and thus take a special position with regard to the constitution of characters and the construction of space.[68] While they have a relation to real persons and actual geography, these reflexes of extra-textual reality often remain vague. Similar to historiographical works, there is a cross-textual reference point, in clear contrast to today's novels. Dietrich of Bern is considered the most prominent character of the Germanic heroic saga and epics, in which the memory of the Ostrogoth king

---

64   This is not the case for *Dietrichs erste Ausfahrt* [*Dietrich's First Adventure*], in which *Polant* (841) is only mentioned when Dietrich sends wedding messengers all over the world. Text edition: *Dietrichs erste Ausfahrt*, ed. Franz Stark, Bibliothek des Litterarischen Vereins in Stuttgart 52 (Stuttgart, 1860).

65   Cf. Florian M. Schmid, *Die Fassung *C des "Nibelungenlieds" und der "Klage". Strategien der Retextualisierung*, Hermaea: Germanistische Forschungen. Neue Folge 147 (Berlin, 2018), 11–16.

66   Elisabeth Lienert, *Mittelhochdeutsche Heldenepik. Eine Einführung*, Grundlagen der Germanistik 58 (Berlin, 2015), 11.

67   Cf. Lienert, *Heldenepik*, 9–13.

68   Schmid, *Fassung *C*, 337–53.

Theodoric the Great († 526) lived on.[69] The literary characters of heroic epics may not be arbitrarily manipulated because of both the historic origins as well as the oral tradition. On the one hand, the narrated characters are part of the cross-textual material, the *materia* or *histoire*; on the other hand, they are part of the *artificium* or *discours* in regard to their specific characterization in each individually transmitted text.[70] In the following, the works will be discussed chronologically according to their presumed date of creation. This does not demonstrate a development of the genre or of the images of Poles, Polishness and/or Poland, but clarifies certain characteristics of the genre.

2.1 *Nibelungenlied* and *Klage*

The *Nibelungenlied* [*Song of the Nibelungs*] and the *Klage* [*Lament*] were composed around the year 1200. They have been handed down together in this particular sequence in almost all complete manuscripts. The *Nibelungenlied* handed down in an abundance of copies (37 manuscripts and fragments) tells of the murder of the dragon slayer Siegfried by his wife's, Kriemhild's, brothers, who were the kings of Burgundy, and of a battle to the death at the court of Kriemhild's second husband, the Hun king Etzel, referring to Attila (reigned 434–53), which Kriemhild initiates as revenge for Siegfried's murder.[71]

---

69 For the extensive and varied testimonies for and allusions to Dietrich of Bern and Theodoric the Great up to the seventeenth century see *Dietrich-Testimonien des 6. bis 16. Jahrhunderts*, ed. Elisabeth Lienert in collaboration with Esther Vollmer-Eicken and Dorit Wolter, *Texte und Studien zur mittelhochdeutschen Heldenepik* 4 (Tübingen, 2008). For modes of remembering and ways of shifting in the portrayal of the historic person see David McLintock, "Dietrich und Theoderich – Sage und Geschichte," in *Geistliche und weltliche Epik des Mittelalters in Österreich*, eds. David McLintock, Adrian Stevens, and Fred Wagner, Publications of the Institute of Germanic Studies 37/Göppinger Arbeiten zur Germanistik 446 (Göppingen, 1987), 99–106; Edith Marold, "Wandel und Konstanz in der Darstellung der Figur des Dietrich von Bern," in *Heldensage und Heldendichtung im Germanischen*, ed. Heinrich Beck, Ergänzungsbände zum Reallexikon der germanischen Altertumskunde 2 (Berlin, 1988), 149–82.

70 Cf. Markus Stock, "Figur. Zu einem Kernproblem historischer Narratologie," in *Historische Narratologie. Mediävistische Perspektiven*, eds. Harald Haferland and Matthias Meyer in collaboration with Carmen Stange and Markus Greulich, Trends in Medieval Philology 19 (Berlin, 2010), 187–203, at 191. For a historical exploration of the literary character within the framework of historical narratology, "textuelle und kulturelle Anthropologien, generisches Wissen über Figuren, intertextuelle Sinnkonstitutionen" [textual and cultural anthropologies, generic knowledge of figures, intertextual constitutions of meaning] are to be included; ibid. 192.

71 The *Nibelungenlied* is transmitted in 13 more or less complete manuscripts and 24 fragments; http://www.handschriftencensus.de/werke/271 [2-20-2019]. Text edition version B: Das *Nibelungenlied* nach der St. Galler Handschrift, ed. and annotated Hermann

As Kriemhild travels to her second husband-to-be, she stops for four days in Traismauer (C 1359.3, 1363.1),[72] a small site situated at the Danube river and close to Vienna. Shortly before arriving at this place, her uncle, the bishop of Passau, takes leave of Kriemhild because his sphere of influence ends there. This locality belongs to Etzel's territory, so she is entering into the protection of her future husband.[73] Polish characters are part of Etzel's entourage, which consists of both members from various ethnicities, who speak different languages, as well as being Christians and Non-Christians:

> *Von vil maniger sprâche   sach man ûf den wegen*
> *vor Ezelen rîten   vil manigen küenen degen,*
> *kristen unde heiden,   vil manic wîtiu schar.*
> *Dâ si ir frouwen funden,   si fuoren vrœlîchen dar.*

[People of various languages were seen on the roads, a lot of brave knights from Etzel, Christians and pagans alike, a broad group, They found their lady and were pleased by that.]
Nibelungenlied, C 1365; cf. B 1335 [1337]

Although it is Kriemhild who travels far and abroad and the meeting takes places in a territory unknown to her, the narrator does not depict her as the recently arrived stranger, but instead does this to the ones who are at home in their territory and only alien to her and to the intended audience's point of view. The encounter is characterized by a countermovement (Kriemhild's journey and the arrival of Etzel and his entourage) and thus dynamically viewed, as well as marked by a resting point, since Kriemhild crosses a border into a new area of power and waits four days for Etzel's arrival. From a structural

---

Reichert, de Gruyter Texte (Berlin, 2005); text edition version C: *Das Nibelungenlied nach der Handschrift C*, ed. Ursula Hennig, Altdeutsche Textbibliothek 83 (Tübingen, 1977). The *Nibelungenlied* is cited according to C. In research, B is often quoted on the basis of the edition of Bartsch/de Boor; *Das Nibelungenlied. Mittelhochdeutsch/Neuhochdeutsch. Nach dem Text von Karl Bartsch und Helmut de Boor ins Neuhochdeutsche übersetzt und kommentiert by Siegfried Grosse*, reviewed and improved ed. (Stuttgart, 2002; repr. 2006). I will add the count of the passages after Bartsch/de Boor in square brackets to ensure comparability with other studies.

72 In *Nibelungenlied* B (1329.3a [1332.3a], 1333.1a [1336.1a]) it says *Zeizenmûre* which is geographically incorrect.
73 *Das Nibelungenlied und die Klage. Nach der Handschrift 857 der Stiftsbibliothek St. Gallen. Mittelhochdeutscher Text, Übersetzung und Kommentar*, ed. Joachim Heinzle, Bibliothek deutscher Klassiker 196 (Berlin, 2013), 1326.

point of view, a new beginning is marked; yet at the same time, even though by location she is now the alien, from her point of view (as well as that of the external recipients of the text), the unknown people who come to meet her are perceived as strangers even in their own territory; a territory that is supposed to be Kriemhild's new home. She is a filter figure in this account, since the 'strangers' are seen through her (and the recipient's) shared lens. When Etzel is riding towards his future wife, his dust-raising entourage undergoes an internal differentiation. First come Russians, Greeks, Poles and Wallachians.[74] They are followed by the warriors from the Kiev country and the *Pescenære*; only the members of the latter group are explicitly othered, since they are characterized as *wilde* (C 1367.2a; cf. B 1337.2a [1340.2a]).[75] Then Danes, Thuringians, and finally the Huns come, and they announce the arrival of the ruler.

Von Riuzen und von Kriechen   reit dâ vil manic man:
Pôlânen unde Vlâchen   den sach man ebene gân
ir pferit und ros diu guoten,   dâ si mit kreften riten.
swaz si site habeten,   der wart vil wênic iht vermiten.

[There rode many people from Russia and Greece. One could see the Poles and the Wallachians riding quickly on their excellent horses, which they rode in an exceptional manner. They did not hide their customs at all.][76]

Nibelungenlied, C 1366; cf. B 1336 [1339]

As a (stereo-)typical characteristic of Polish fighters, their excellent riding skills and the value put on riding first class horses are featured by the narrator. These qualities are presented in a way that gives the Poles an agency, for their skills are displayed by themselves and as their own marker. On an intra-textual level, they create their own image – even when this is, of course, a positioning of the characters by the narrator. Other people demonstrate different abilities, such as the *Pescenære* with their archery skills (C 1367.2–4; cf. B 1337.2–4 [1340.2–4]). In the following stanza it says:

---

74 *Vlâchen* probably refers vaguely to roman tribes, in this case most likely to South Slavs; *Nibelungenlied*, ed. Grosse, 863.
75 This tribe can most likely either be identified as a Finno-Ugrian; *Nibelungenlied*, ed. Grosse, 863, or as the Pechenegs, a semi-nomadic Turkic people from Central Asia; Hansgerd Göckenjan, "Pecenegen," in *Lexikon des Mittelalters*, ed. Robert Auty et al., 10 vols. (Munich, 1980–99), 6: 1845–46.
76 All translations by Florian M. Schmid.

> *Ein stât bî Tuonouwe   lît in Ôsterlant,*
> *diu ist geheizen Tulme: dâ wart ir* [scil. Kriemhild] *sît bekant*
> *vil manic site vremde,   den si nie dâ vor gesach.*
> *si enpfiengen dâ genuoge,   den leide sît von ir geschach.*
>
> [There is a city on the Danube in Austria called Tulln. There, Kriemhild got to know numerous foreign customs, which she had never seen before. Many people greeted her there, who later had to suffer because of her.]
>
> *Nibelungenlied,* C 1368; cf. B 1338 [1341]

In this stanza the customs of Etzel's entourage are explicitly marked as being foreign (*vremde*) and previously unknown to Kriemhild. What is being described is a cultural strangeness, not a social one.[77] The 'other' is hardly narrated as the 'other', rather what is being addressed is the encounter with it. Even though the recognition of the 'other' implies an awareness of one's 'own', the text does not recount on an intra-textual level how Kriemhild feels about, evaluates, and reacts to these peoples, customs, self-presentations and/or images, and how her mental horizons might have been altered. Even though the text addresses the process of getting to know one another (*bekant werden*), it does not address the extent to which the 'other' is unknown to the intended recipients of the text. The literarily coded process of differentiation with regard to the depiction of Etzel's entourage illustrates a preceding integration process of the individual members of the entourage, even though at this point there is no indication of the way that happened, and yet at the same time it bears witness to the current one, namely the integration of Kriemhild. Although cultural differences (languages, customs, ethnic groups, armaments, abilities, values) are narrated, no communication problems resulting from them are discussed. The main goal of this depiction is to demonstrate the exceptionality of the diverse entourage and in so doing also show Etzel's power. The description of the arrival of Etzel's vassals and followers evokes an image of an Eastern world empire[78] and marks the geographical dimension of Etzel's domain.[79] The text thus mirrors

---

77   For the differentiation between cultural strangeness in contrast to social strangeness as non-belonging, see Herfried Münkler/Bernd Ladwig, "Vorwort," in *Furcht und Faszination. Facetten der Fremdheit,* ed. Herfried Münkler, Studien und Materialien der Interdisziplinären Arbeitsgruppe Die Herausforderung durch das Fremde der Berlin-Brandenburgischen Akademie der Wissenschaften (Berlin, 1997), 7–9, at 8.

78   Ehrismann, "Die Fürsten ûzer Polan," 35–36. When the strongest peoples around the Huns' empire (located in Hungary) are mentioned, the historic situation from about the tenth century is reflected; ibid.

79   Langner, *Annäherung ans Fremde,* 52.

a traditional policy of strengthening royal power by the admittance of various groups; their loyalty, military service, and revenue had long been seen as a buttress of royal power. The text's way of presenting this can also be interpreted as a "wohlüberlegte Empfangschoreographie" [carefully considered, choreographed welcoming scene]:[80] first the members of the distant frontier peoples arrive, then the Germanic tribes, followed by Etzel's brother, and finally Etzel himself appears. According to this choreography, there is an implicit hierarchy among the representatives of the individual ethnic groups according to their significance for both the text's characters, especially for Etzel and Kriemhild, as well as for the text's intended audience. The Poles evidently belong to the borderland. Thus, this reflects a typical negotiation process between core and periphery:[81] The own center, being a fief to the dominion of the feudal lord, becomes periphery by the proximity of its representatives to the ruler; nevertheless, these peripheries remain part of the center. At the same time, the formerly peripheral territory of the Huns becomes a new action center for Kriemhild. As could be observed, the Poles constitute themselves as a group, as a social association within a larger one; no individual person is named. In one of the following stanzas a character is mentioned who is called Hornboge, however, without any indication of his origin being supplied. In the heroic epics the attributions of origin to a specific character might differ from work to work, but in the epics mentioned below, namely, *Biterolf und Dietleib, Dietrichs Flucht* and *Rabenschlacht* Hornboge is considered to be a Polish compatriot, so he might well be considered as being a Pole in the *Nibelungenlied*, too:

> *Hornboge der snelle wol mit tûsint man*
> *kêrte vonme künige gein sîner frouwen dan.*
> *vil lût wart geschallet nâch des landes siten.*
> *von den Hiunin mâgen wart ouch dâ sêre geriten.*

[The brave Hornboge rode in front of the king towards his queen with a good thousand men. A great noise was made[82] according to the country's

---

80   *Nibelungenlied*, ed. Grosse, 864.
81   The concept of an unequal relationship between *core* and *periphery* was articulated forcefully by Wallerstein in regard to the early modern world economy; Immanuel Wallerstein, *The Modern World-System*, 2 vols. (New York, 1974–80), 1: "Capitalist Agriculture and the Origins of the European World-Economy in the Sixteenth Century".
82   Langner, *Annäherung ans Fremde*, 49, translates *geschallet* as sung, which is possible according to its semantics, but not explicitly expressed. Schulze translates as "erhob sich ein lautes Getöse" [a loud roar arose] which appears to be more likely; Das *Nibelungenlied*.

custom. The relatives and friends of the Huns showed their excellent riding skills.]

Nibelungenlied, C 1371; cf. B 1341 [1344]

Hornboge gets assigned a stereotypical heroic attribute (*snelle* [brave, agile]). His 1,000 warriors signalize the extent of his wealth and at the same time imply the far greater power of Etzel.[83] The making of a great noise is possibly another feature that could refer to a Polish custom in a specific situation, but it does not refer to Poles uniquely. The main aims of the entourage's members are to impress, to demonstrate strength and power, to welcome and to express joy; all this in culturally specific ways. Hornboge is mentioned in another stanza (C 1925; cf. B 1877 [1880]) when a friendly jousting between the Burgundians and the Huns is narrated. All participants including Hornboge are described as outstanding, honorable fighters; a special characteristic referring to Poles, Polishness and/or Poland is not given. Instead, Hornboge and the hero Ramung position themselves *nâch hiunischen siten* (C 1925.2b; cf. B 1877.2b [1880.2b]) [according to customs of the Huns] in the bohort.

In contrast to the *Nibelungenlied*, in the *Klage* (transmitted in 16 manuscripts and fragments) there is an explicit individuation: [*d*]*er herzoge Herman, / ein vürste ûzer Pôlân* [the Duke Herman, a prince from Poland] (*B 345–46/*C 321–22).[84] The text (*B 345–72/*C 321–50) provides hardly any further information except that he, together with *Sigehêr von Vlâchen* (*B 347/*C 323), leads 2,000 knights (*B 350/*C 326), and together with *ûz Türkîe Walber* (*B355–56/*C 331–32), willingly avenges Kriemhild's sorrow, but the text also makes clear that all the warriors are going to die (*B 367/*C 343). Featured is a trio of Eastern European princes in Etzel's service who also can be found in the heroic epic *Biterolf und Dietleib*, so that one could speak of a cross-textual motif.[85] The Polish Duke Herman and his 1,000 knights are positively marked

---

    Nach der Handschrift C der Badischen Landesbibliothek Karlsruhe. Mittelhochdeutsch und Neuhochdeutsch, ed. and trans. Ursula Schulze (Düsseldorf, 2005), 441.

83 Langner, *Annäherung ans Fremde*, 49.

84 The *Klage* is transmitted in nine more or less complete manuscripts and seven fragments; http://www.handschriftencensus.de/werke/195 [2-20-2019]. Text edition for versions *B and *C: Die Nibelungenklage. Synoptische Ausgabe aller vier Fassungen, ed. Joachim Bumke (Berlin, 1999). The *Klage* is cited according to *C.

85 Cf. Joachim Bumke, *Die vier Fassungen der "Nibelungenklage". Untersuchungen zur Überlieferungsgeschichte und Textkritik der höfischen Epik im 13. Jahrhundert*, Quellen und Forschungen zur Literatur- und Kulturgeschichte 8/242 (Berlin, 1996), 487.

as good fighters who readily comply with their vassalage.[86] Functionally, the insertion of such literary figures probably serves little in providing contour for the individual ethnic groups or characters. According to Lienert, the additions of names of persons and countries are supposed to produce a kind of *historical* aura of the happenings.[87]

2.2 *Biterolf und Dietleib*

Biterolf und Dietleib [*Biterolf and Dietleib*] was probably written around the year 1250,[88] but is handed down in a single manuscript from the very beginning of the sixteenth century (*Ambraser Heldenbuch*, 1504–16/17).[89] It contains heroic as well as novelistic elements and thus is not a heroic epic in a narrower or traditional sense, but is called instead a heroic romance. It features a search for a parent: the hero Dietleib looks for his father Biterolf, who left the family in order to serve Etzel when his son was still a toddler. Yet it includes revenge campaigns as well, among which are those of Etzel against the *fuᵃrsten aus Polan* [the princes from Poland] (v. 3422, 3517).

When Etzel is waging a war against the king of Prussia, the latter finally is captured (vv. 1518–1663). Afterwards, as a vassal in the service of Etzel, he is ordered to go to war against his neighbor Poland. The text explicitly addresses his emotions, marking a distinction between deeds one chooses and those one

---

86   Lienert interprets this text passage about the fate of Etzel's allies structurally: "dem Sterben der Großen geht das Ende der weniger bedeutenden Krieger voraus" [the death of the great warriors is preceded by the demise of the lesser warriors]; *"Die Nibelungenklage."* Mittelhochdeutscher Text nach der Ausgabe von Karl Bartsch. Einführung, neuhochdeutsche Übersetzung und Kommentar, ed. Elisabeth Lienert, Schöninghs mediävistische Editionen 5 (Paderborn, 2000), 372–73.

87   *Nibelungenklage*, 373. The *Klage* and/or the *Biterolf* were probably mediators for the fact that Duke Herman from Poland found entry into the Viennese Piarist manuscript (k) of the *Nibelungenlied* (fifteenth century); Ehrismann, "Die Fürsten ûzer Polan," 37. There, Herman is not mentioned at Etzel's welcoming of Kriemhild (but the Poles are in k 1353.2a), but only later in three additional stanzas in the context of an army campaign against the Burgundians (k 2127–29); text edition: Die *"Nibelungenlied"*-Bearbeitung der Wiener Piaristenhandschrift (Lienhart Scheubels Heldenbuch: Hs. k). Transkription und Untersuchungen, ed. Margarete Springeth, Göppinger Arbeiten zur Germanistik 660 (Göppingen, 2007).

88   Michael Curschmann, "Biterolf und Dietleib (Biterolf)," in *Verfasserlexikon*, 1: 879–83, at 879.

89   http://www.handschriftencensus.de/werke/757 [2-20-2019]. Text edition: *Biterolf und Dietleib*, newly ed. and introduced by André Schnyder, Sprache und Dichtung: Forschungen zur deutschen Sprache, Literatur und Volkskunde, Neue Folge 31 (Bern, 1980).

has to do. He fights against the Poles only reluctantly but is bound by his oath to do so:

> *der Preussen kůnig do gelassen ward, / daz er trůge mit jm hasz. / ein tail tet er vngern das, / wann er ir nachgepaur hiess. / der kunig jns nicht darumbe erliess, / daz er jm hette geswarn: / er mŭst auf seine veinde varn* (vv. 3440–46).

> [The king of the Prussians was left there carrying hatred with him. A part of him did so reluctantly, for he was his neighbor. The king [Etzel] did not let him off because he had sworn to him: he had to go against his enemies.]

Thus, this work features a close connection between the neighboring Prussians and Poles, a relation, however, which remains subordinate in vassalage to a more powerful king and thereby receives no agency of its own. This special connection between neighbors, who do not want to make war against each other, reflects a time in the past, but certainly not the actual time of the work's writing when there were indeed conflicts between the two peoples.[90]

The first Polish character mentioned is *Hornboge*, (most likely) called *von Polan der hertzoge* [duke of Poland] (vv. 1231–32).[91] He stays as a hostage at Etzel's court and, among others, welcomes Biterolf and his men as Etzel's guests. In what follows, he repeatedly receives the (stereo-)typical attribute 'the young' (*vnd Hornpoge der helt jung*; v. 4940; cf. vv. 3451–52, 11614). On all occasions, he is featured as an outstanding warrior who fights on Etzel's side. Etzel orders Hornboge to fight against the Poles and he slays a huge number of young Polish fighters: *Hornboge und Ramůnch, / die felleten manigen helt iunc* (vv. 3723–24). In contrast to the king of Prussia, an internal tension in Hornboge over fighting against the Poles is not mentioned at all – possibly in order to portray him as a positive character from Etzel's (as well as from the extra-textual recipient's) point of view. In any case, it reveals the primacy of vassalage over all other relations. Despite their fighting strength, the Polish characters repeatedly suffer great distress. From the Polish army itself only one

---

90 Cf. Zitzewitz, *Das deutsche Polenbild*, 15.
91 The syntax is not clear; possibly, the text differentiates between Hornboge and a captive Polish duke. However, at this point, the war against the Poles is yet to come, so that in terms of chronology it is more likely that Hornboge actually is the mentioned duke of Poland.

character is named: *der hertzoge Herman* [Herman, Duke of Poland] (v. 3583). He defends himself against Biterolf, who cuts a swath through the Polish army (vv. 3578–3617). Biterolf himself is called *gast* (v. 3586) by the narrator; even though he is fighting for Etzel, he is still marked as an 'other', evidently only temporally connected to and not completely integrated into Etzel's entourage. The Polish characters and members of the army are portrayed as excellent fighters, but eventually they are defeated by outstanding heroes such as Biterolf. Apparently, the Polish characters are described as being in the end no match for the fighting strength of Etzel's heroes. The Polish duke is finally defeated by Etzel's heroes and imprisoned: *da muest auch volgen mit jn dan / der hertzoge aus Polan, / wann er den sig het da verlorn* (vv. 3747–48). It is noticeable that Poles and Russians are perceived together as common enemies, for example, when Ramung complains about the at least 3,000 dead (v. 3767): "'die wir hewte han verloren / durch der küenen Reussen zorn / vnd auch von den Polan.'" (vv. 3769–71). When the captured Duke Herman, who in v. 3845 is also called *füst aus Polan* [prince of Poland] and in v. 3866 *den Polan vogt* [the Polish lord protector], is brought to Etzel, it is again emphasized that the Prussians have fulfilled their vassal duty to the best of their ability:

> *Do sy nun fueren vber lanndt / vnd man in vånusse vant / den herzogen von Polan, / die Preüssen hetten auch getan / das peste, daz sy künden* (vv. 3801–05).
>
> [When they crossed the country and the Duke of Poland was found in captivity, the Prussians had also done the best they could].
> vv. 3801–05

The angry King of the Huns would have had Duke Herman killed, if his wife Helche had not put in a word for him (v. 3890–92).[92] The enemies are designated as such by the narrator, but in most cases the word *gast* is used, as in the *inquit*-formula, when the captive Herman declares himself to Etzel: *da sprach der gast, es were recht*: (v. 3885). This may not only be due to a meaning of this word such as stranger but may also depend on courtly communication that retains certain manners despite being angry. This is the only encounter with a short direct speech (four verses) by Herman, in which he officially surrenders

---

92 The *Nibelungenlied* is the first written heroic epic. In terms of content, however, this does not correspond to the chronology, since later epics in part report temporally earlier actions. For example, Helche was Etzel's first wife.

and accept the status of a hostage: *'es sey ritter oder knecht, / was jr ligt erschlagñ tot, / die sol ich puessen mit der not, / als ich darumbe geysel bin.'* (vv. 3886–89). It can be concluded that the work shows very little interest in portraying the inner world of this character, his Polishness, or to evoke any sympathy in the extra-textual recipient for this figure, even though Herman is evidently an excellent fighter. Finally, Herman receives his country as a fief, is released with his surviving fighters to return to Poland, and he will serve Etzel in the future as a vassal supporting him in battles (vv. 3992–97). We can learn from this text passage as well as from the battle that several different characters label the Polish characters as enemies. It is striking that Herman has no stereotypically assigned attribute such as 'the strong', 'the bold' etc. as heroes often have. Although Polish characters are described as very good fighters, the text makes it quite clear that the Polish characters are viewed as the counterparty that has to be overcome and are eventually no match for Etzel's heroes who are defined by their outstanding fighting skills and mindset.[93] There is hardly any reflection on interior motives or thoughts; the text focuses on the fighting performances of Etzel's heroes. In this way, the text constructs a hierarchy between the most amazing heroes and the excellent Poles, who bear a distinct image of being a strong enemy.

Hornboge and Ramung are the ones who organize putting the fallen and their weapons on wagons and taking care of their funeral (vv. 3787–91). Hornboge appears another time. When Etzel's army moves to Worms against the Burgundians, he too is there (v. 4940). Together with Ramung he leads 3,000 warriors from *Vlachen lannde* [Wallachia] (vv. 9722–25) whose weapons are horn bows (vv. 10188–89: *die Vlachen kamen ingeriten / mit manigem hůrnen pogen, / [...]*). Otfrid Ehrismann proposed that their army commander could have been given the aptronym 'Hornboge' because of this special weapon; this would be a fictional appelation then.[94] Afterwards he is briefly mentioned together with Ramung as a willing fighter (v. 11614, vv. 12086–87).

There is one more noticeable text passage, when the high frequency and quality of the tournaments by the Burgundians in Worms are discussed by Etzel's brother Blödelin with Rüdiger, who has just urged caution when approaching Worms. Blödelin says to Rüdiger:

---

93 Cf. Langner, *Annäherung ans Fremde*, 79.
94 Ehrismann, "Die Fürsten ûzer Polan," 38.

Nu reite, edler Rudeger, / wir Hûnen gesahen d</i>och nie mer, / wie turnieren sey getan; / die Preüssen vnd die Polan / haben sein selten icht gephlegen.

[Now, ride off, noble Rüdiger, we Huns have never seen how tournaments can be extraordinarily orchestrated. The Prussians and the Poles hardly ever organize tournaments.]
vv. 8275–79.

As above, when the reluctant battle of the Prussian king against the Poles was addressed, Prussians and Poles are viewed as being very close to each other in regard to territory (neighbors) and a certain aspect of culture (the organizing of tournaments). Furthermore, a west-eastern cultural gradient is imagined as seen in the statement that both people are not familiar with the finesses of properly organized tournaments. Interestingly enough, this characterization takes place in the direct speech of a character who represents himself as being culturally inferior from a courtly point of view, since Blödelin is a Hun himself and not familiar with the excellent organization of a tournament, perhaps, even less so than Prussians and Poles. The latter two people thus form a cultural transition area in regard to the knowledge and/or exercise of fine courtly tournaments.

2.3 *Dietrich und Wenezlan*

Dietrich und Wenezlan [*Dietrich and Wenezlan*] was written shortly after 1250, perhaps still in the first part of the thirteenth century and is handed down in a single fragment.[95] The special feature of this heroic epic is that a Polish character is not only presented as an antagonist of Dietrich of Bern, but that the adversary is also one of the main characters. This is Wenezlan, *vurste von Bolan* [prince of Poland] (v. 63, 221 et al.). He is often called only *der Bolan* [the Pole] (such as in v. 114, 252, 324, 401, 408 et al.).

The action begins when one of Dietrich's warriors, Wolfhard, delivers a battle challenge from Wenezlan back to Dietrich. Apparently, Wolfhard (and Hildebrand) had earlier been captured by Wenezlan, held as hostages and one of them is now acting as a messenger. The challenge demonstrates Wenezlan's

---

95 Joachim Heinzle, "*Dietrich und Wenezlan*," in *Verfasserlexikon*, 2: 149–51, at 149. http://www.handschriftencensus.de/werke/88 [2-20-2019]. Text edition: *Alpharts Tod. Dietrich und Wenezlan*, eds. Elisabeth Lienert and Viola Meyer, Texte und Studien zur mittelhochdeutschen Heldenepik 3 (Tübingen, 2007).

great self-confidence as a fighter[96] as well as his high status, since Dietrich is the warrior with the greatest reputation. It is discussed between the characters whether Wenezlan is a worthy opponent for Dietrich, so that Dietrich could gain honor in the fight – but his opponent could do so as well. Dietrich asks Wolfhard for advice, who then praises Wenezlan explicitly as being the boldest man he has ever seen: 'So chunen man ich nie gesah / in allen minen ziten, / weder nahen noh witen. / [...]' (vv. 28–30). This laudation by the opposing party characterizes Wenezlan as an extraordinary warrior, but it is a formulaic one. Battle challenges are typical for this genre and Wolfhard himself is traditionally portrayed as a hothead and someone who seeks fights, so that he might also present the possible adversary in an excellent way for the reason of promoting combat. Dietrich must first be persuaded to fight, and a known motif of hesitation (Zaudermotiv) is employed, but then he accepts the challenge of the <rîche[n]> vurste von Bolan [the powerful prince of Poland] (v. 67). Dietrich's courtesy shows in the appreciative calling of Wenezlan 'hohe[r] chunge rich' ['noble and powerful king'] (v. 104) and a 'vurste[] uzerchorn' ['chosen prince'] (v. 131) during an interaction with his followers. Indirectly, Wenezlan's fighting spirit is also marked by Dietrich's self-descriptions. The fight is a public one and Etzel, who usually does not make the journey to the place of such a contest,[97] travels with Dietrich, which marks the exceptionality of the event. They travel towards their enemy, and the fight will take place on Wenezlan's territory, showing that the text clearly distinguishes between Etzel's kingdom and territories outside of it. Topographically, the battlefield is described with barely any detail: Si quamen an di Salza <dan>. / Uber brukken man beg<an> / zu den vinde an ir lant. [Then they arrived at the Salza. They crossed bridges to enter the enemy's land.] (vv. 183–85). The river Salza has been identified differently in research; mainly as a feeder river to the Enns in today's Austria or as a feeder river to Bega northeast of Soest in North Rhine-Westphalia.[98] None of the possible locations, however, refers to a Slavic territory. The fight between

---

96 Cf. Langner, Annäherung ans Fremde, 68.
97 Dietrich und Wenezlan, eds. Lienert/Meyer, 98–99.
98 Justus Lunzer, "Dietrich und Wenezlan," Zeitschrift für deutsches Altertum 55 (1917), 1–40, at 16–23; Gerhard Eis, "Zu Dietrichs Slawenkämpfen," Zeitschrift für deutsches Altertum 84 (1952/53), 70–84, at 75. In total, Salza could be a reference to one of the following rivers: Salza, a feeder river to the Enns, Styria; Salzabach, a feeder river to the Enns in the Salzkammergut, Liezen district, Styria; Salza, a feeder river to the Helme, Thuringia; Salza, a feeder river to the Saale, Saxony-Anhalt; Salzabach (Teichl), a stream from the Sengsengebirge near Windischgarsten, Upper Austria; Salza, a feeder river to the Unstrut, Thuringia; Salzach, in the Salzburger Land, a tributary river of the Inn which was called Salza until the eighteenth century.

Dietrich and Wenezlan is presented as a combat of individuals between two armies. Shortly before the fight the narrator refers to Wenezlan as *liehtgemal* [the shining handsome] as well as *unverzaget* [fearless] (v. 265), which he had similarly called Dietrich shortly before (v. 250), so that Wolfhard, Dietrich, and the narrator present Wenezlan in the same exceptionally positive and knightly manner. The fight itself is genre-typically described as an outstanding event, which everyone wants to attend; in addition to the armies, Etzel along with Wenezlan's wife and her entourage are in attendance: *von zwein recken wart niemer / ein sô herter strît gestriten* (vv. 358–59). In the long battle description, it is striking that Dietrich and Wenezlan are on an equal footing. The narrator always speaks of both of them by using pronouns such as they, their, both and so on, for instance, when both physical (v. 381: *Vil sere mům̊te si der sweiz* [The sweat affected them severely]; cf. vv. 350–51, 472–74 et al.) und mental aspects (such as in v. 332: *Si heten grimmigen mut* [They had great fighting spirit.]) are described.[99] There is no differentiation between them in terms of fighting abilities, skills and determination. When they push each other off their horses in a joust and lie on the ground as if they were dead (vv. 315–21), it is the Pole who first stands on his feet again (vv. 324–25) and thus seems to be slightly stronger than Dietrich. In the following sword fight, however, no one is superior to the 'other'. On the level of the characters, the attending women wish for victory for both opponents: *Man sah da michel schowen / und ouch wunschen von den frouwen / hailes vunt in beiden* (vv. 391–93). Interior views (thoughts and intentions) are hardly conveyed within the long fight description. There is one introspection in both characters which features the service to women, followed by one that Wenezlan has:

> *Nun daz si dahten an diu wip, / si wæren bedesamt gelegen / von mům̊de und ouch von herten slegen. / Doh sah der starche Bolan / dem vogt von Berne [scil. Dietrich] daz wol an, / daz im diu chraft ab gie.*

> [Then they thought of the women. Both of them were marked by tiredness and also because of the firm strikes. However, the strong Pole clearly saw that Dietrich's strength was weakening.]
> vv. 398–403.

The equilibrium of the combat is also expressed dynamically by the to-and-fro movement: At first, Wenezlan holds the upper hand and battles Dietrich

---

99   Cf. Langner, *Annährung ans Fremde*, 70–71.

backwards through his own army, which leads to a groaning from the Huns (vv. 417–19). Shortly before a victory for Wenezlan seems likely, Dietrich remembers his extraordinary strength, but only after an exhortation by Wolfhard in direct speech (vv. 429–55), and then he in turn drives Wenezlan back through his own army (vv. 462–63). The fight is not decided before the evening. The fragment ends with a speech by Dietrich featuring an internal reflection on his condition and situation, typically indicated with the verb *denken* [to think], in which his exhaustion is clearly marked: *Her Ditrich gedahte doh: / 'Ja herre, wi lange sol ditze sin? / Ez mŭz iezu das leben min / <...>'*] (vv. 508–10). Who in the end will be victorious is not certain, but the text clearly demonstrates a reciprocal mirroring of the protagonists. In epics about Dietrich, it is mainly he who wins the fights, but in some works there are also reconciliations between Dietrich and his opponents and – rarely – a probable defeat is prevented by stopping the fight as in the *Walberan*-extension of the *Laurin*. A small detail has to be added: When Dietrich drives Wenezlan back through his army, at that point it is referred to as being Russian (v. 478: [...] *der Riuzen her* [...]). This is not highly problematic though, since a close connection of both people can be observed in several works; for instance, and as mentioned above in the discussion about *Biterolf und Dietleib*, Poles and Russians were viewed as the common enemies of Etzel's heroes. Unlike in *Biterolf und Dietleib*, there is no evidence of any negative characterization of Wenezlan by other characters or the narrator. It is clear that the fragment is not based on a negative image of an enemy, even though the corresponding word *vînt* is repeatedly used to describe the counterparty. In regard to topography, the few details given cannot be associated with a Polish or Russian territory. As far as the fragment status permits, the work is about a great Polish character – without telling or constructing specifics about Poles, Polishness or Poland. Rather, a positive social identity negotiated by combat is at the center of the literary work.

2.4 *Dietrichs Flucht* and *Rabenschlacht*

Dietrichs Flucht [*Dietrich's Flight*] and *Rabenschlacht* [*The Battle of Ravenna*] form a double epic which were written in the fourth quarter of the thirteenth century and are transmitted in four more or less complete manuscripts and one fragment.[100] In both heroic epics, a reference to Polish characters, Polishness

---

100   *Dietrichs Flucht* was possibly written in 1275 (perhaps earlier) or 1295/96; Hugo Kuhn, "Dietrichs Flucht und Rabenschlacht," in *Verfasserlexikon*, 2: 116–27, at 119. Transmission of *Dietrichs Flucht*: http://www.handschriftencensus.de/werke/87 [2-20-2019]. Text edition: *Dietrichs Flucht. Textgeschichtliche Ausgabe*, eds. Elisabeth Lienert and Gertrud Beck,

and/or Poland is made exclusively via the character Hornboge. In *Dietrichs Flucht* it recounts several attempts by Dietrich of Bern to return to his inherited land, struggling against the forces of his uncle Ermenrich, but always he must return again to his exile at Etzel's court. In a direct speech by the hero Baltram of Pola (Istria), 17 fighters are listed who have been sent with armies by Etzel's wife Helche to support Dietrich. This includes Hornboge who is presented by Baltram as a Pole: '*und chumt von Bolan ouz der marche / Hornborge der mære*' (vv. 5903–04). The word *marche* explicitly reminds both the characters and the intended audience that Poland had been a borderland to Etzel's sphere of power and thus demonstrates both the power as well as the extension of Etzel's territory and its borders. In addition to this mention of his origin, the stereotyped attribute *mære* [the known/famous/glorious/tremendous] is ascribed to Hornboge. He is characterized as an outstanding fighter, but not further individualized within the group of warriors. When he is mentioned a second time by the narrator in a list of 18 heroes, he is once again called *Hornpog von Polan* [Hornboge of Poland] (v. 8576). With the exception of two other characters, Dietleib (*von Stier*, v. 8568) and Herman (*von Ostervranchen*, v. 8581) there are no other indications of origin for any of the other heroes. This finding is different in Baltram's list, in which the origins of more heroes are stated. This can be interpreted in different ways: Perhaps, and what is the more likely interpretation, the author intended to highlight these heroes, or they were fairly unknown and the additional information was needed, for Hornboge hardly plays a role in this heroic epic – but this is also true for other heroes. The group of heroes is praised by the narrator for their excellence, strength and courage (vv. 8586–91):

Swaz ich iu der helt genant han, / fur war ist mir daz chunt getan, / si waren in allen landen / die tiuristen zů ir handen, / die můter ie getruch. / Si waren starch und chůn genůch.

[Whatever heroes I have mentioned to you, truly, I had been told myself. They were in all the lands the most excellent that any mother ever carried. They were exceedingly strong and courageous.]
  Dietrichs Flucht, vv. 8586–91

Texte und Studien zur mittelhochdeutschen Heldenepik 1 (Tübingen, 2003). Transmission of the *Rabenschlacht*: http://www.handschriftencensus.de/werke/305 [20.02.2019]. Text edition: *Rabenschlacht*, eds. Lienert/Wolter. The fragment of each text does not belong to the same codex, so that there is a total of six transmitted manuscripts.

Ehrismann convincingly interprets the mentioning of Hornboge (who helps Dietrich against Ermenrich) for the purpose of demonstrating Dietrich's power.[101]

In the *Rabenschlacht*, in which Dietrich also tries in vain to regain his position of rule, Hornboge is explicitly assigned his place of origin when he is first mentioned:

> *Hornboge von Bolan*
> *sprach ze dem Bernære:*
> *'Fumf tousent rekchen ich hie han,*
> *daz sint alles degne mære.*
> *Die wil ich', sprach der starche,*
> *'iu ze helfe furen ouf romisch marche.'*
>
> [The strong Hornboge of Poland said to Dietrich: 'I have 5,000 warriors, all of them are strong fighters. I will lead them to your aid towards the Roman borderland.']
>
> *Rabenschlacht*, 46

Hornboge's offer of help is part of a series of pledges to support Dietrich by different heroes in direct speech before the battle between Dietrich and Ermenrich, so that it does not stand out. His 5,000 men exceeds the numbers of his warriors in the other epics discussed above and are a handsome offer by Hornboge compared to the other ones, the offers ranging from 800 up to 12,000 fighters. His offer is placed in the middle of the pledges and is the highest to that point. The number of fighters draws a powerful picture of Hornboge. The assigned stereotypical attribute *starche* [the strong] (46.5) refers to his own fighting ability but is a stereotypical attribute of a hero. The Polish prince is integrated within a larger group of European knights and he is viewed as both powerful and supportive.[102] All of them intend their offers to help in positioning themselves highly in the court society.[103] Hornboge is mentioned by the narrator only one more time in the text when he leads three divisions (615.6: *Horbogen volgten scho^ener schare drie.*) against Ermenrich and proves to be a strong leader and fighter:

---

101   Ehrismann, "Die Fürsten ûzer Polan" 42.
102   Cf. Langner, *Annäherung ans Fremde*, 84.
103   Cf. ibid.

> *Welt ir nu horen gerne,*
> *mit wem der da was:*
> *Er dient dem von Berne,*
> *als uns das bůch las.*
> *Er frumte Ermriche*
> *grozen schaden, daz wizzet sicherliche.*

[Would you like to hear now whom he was with: he served the one of Bern, as the book tells us. He inflicted great damage on Ermenrich, you may be assured.]
Rabenschlacht, 616

As before, Hornboge is associated with Dietrich as a positively viewed character. With these two mentions – offer of support to Dietrich and his successes in battle – Hornboge's role in the *Rabenschlacht* is a very small one. His role is primarily functional to demonstrate the power of a great military commander. His deeds do not develop their own dynamics.[104] Being part of Etzel's intercultural entourage, Hornboge is not othered neither in *Dietrichs Flucht* nor in the *Rabenschlacht*.

3   Discussion

Polish characters, Polishness and/or Poland are mentioned in numerous German literary works of the Middle Ages. This is done with varying degrees of detail and with different interests and resulting functions. When the epistemological interest focuses on the constructions of the 'other', then the corpus is relatively manageable. The quite varied Middle High German vocabulary employed to designate an 'other' is a prerequisite of the discussed works, because often the difference between the 'self' and the 'other' is explicitly distinguished and named, as in the *Nibelungenlied* (such as C 1397,1a; cf. B 1367,1a [1370,1a]: *Die kunden und die geste* [the locals and the foreigners]). The 'other' is not only marked by words of the lexical fields *gast*, *ellende* and *vremde*, but also by further expressions (such as *bekant werden*). However, the 'other' is basically hardly designed as such. Even though a distinction has to be made between different genres in terms of the degree of a reflection of reality or a reference to reality, in the field of heroic poetry no change or development can

---

104   Ehrismann, "Die Fürsten ûzer Polan," 40.

be observed in the course of the twelfth and thirteenth centuries. From the narrated intercultural criteria for differentiation such as origin, language, culture (ways of life, traditions, customs), religion, and status group, with regard to Poles, Polishness, and/or Poland, only origin and culture (and the latter solely in the *Nibelungenlied*) are kept current.[105] In all the discussed works, Polish characters are featured as outstanding fighters; only the *Nibelungenlied* refers to a kind of Polishness by mentioning specific customs such as riding skills, the value put on excellent horses, and possibly the making of a noise to impress and welcome their future queen, Kriemhild. This finding is not striking, because other groups are also not portrayed in an any more detailed way. Although the *Nibelungenlied* is transmitted in a large number of manuscripts and fragments and thereby presumably was widely known, it had in this respect but little impact on the further history of its genre. It is mainly the similarities between heroes of different origins which are highlighted, for example, in terms of combat abilities and skills, even when the works feature a downward gradient between the protagonists and their opponents, the latter often including the Polish characters. The necessary strength of the opponent, which must be exceeded for the confirmation of self and/or increase of status, hardly allows a disqualification of the adversaries in this regard.[106] It illustrates, though, a reciprocal mirroring happening between and among heroes. Even in the case when the action takes place abroad, this is hardly arranged with any detail except for a designation. However, this is only partly due to the genre, but rather mostly to the fundamental interest of Middle High German narrative literature in dealing with status and power negotiations within a courtly, quite intercultural society.[107] The heroic epics show that rule and power are

---

105   The category *gender* plays an important role in heroic epics by determining spaces of action and, as a result, often concrete ways of action and behavior, but it does not do so in the construction of a cultural *other*. Depending on the situation, male figures show norm-led, pragmatic, and heroic behavior; behavioral changes of female figures mostly result from changes of action, especially due to experiences of violence and injustice; cf. Lienert, "Figurenkonstitution," 69, 74.

106   Certainly, a distinction between different combat abilities and skills is also made within heroic epics. A relevant example is *Alpharts Tod* [*Alphart's Death*], in which the overpowering Alphart can only be overcome by two opponents when they disregard the rules of knightly combats and approach him together at the same time.

107   Cf. Florian M. Schmid, Anita Sauckel, "Verhandlung und Demonstration von Macht. Germanistische und Skandinavistische Perspektiven," in *Verhandlung und Demonstration von Macht. Mittel, Muster und Modelle in Texten deutschsprachiger und skandinavischer Kulturräume des Mittelalters*, eds. Florian M. Schmid and Anita Sauckel, Zeitschrift für deutsches Altertum – Beiheft 32 (Stuttgart, 2020), 1–27.

more important than a unity of the subordinates, which in reality often was not even possible to achieve. Some of the literary works show the ongoing fights for power and some even an endeavor to enlarge their dominions, which was common in reality as well. In heroic epics, nobility, virtue and heroism are evidently prerequisites. With the action taking place in an indefinite past, the real possible experience of otherness hardly plays a role, the 'other' is usually determined from the characters' perspectives. Whether this reflects the knowledge of the intended recipients can hardly be determined. The 'other' is presented in a simplistic way on the basis of a few characteristics that might have been particularly noticeable from the point of view of one's 'own', but which by no means must be representative or essential,[108] such as the excellent riding skills of the Poles in the *Nibelungenlied*. Even though the characterization of the figures is often stereotypic, the views on Poles and Poland are not. Heroic epics are based on historical persons and events. These historical starting points or occasions of storytelling include the invasion by the Huns into Eastern Europe, which then triggered Slavic migratory movements. The different Slavic tribes, which since the tenth century had probably come together under the leadership of the Polans and eventually became the Poles,[109] find their way into the storytelling about Germanic heroes. Little is known about the history of these collective tribes and their culture;[110] the German heroic epics provide practically no respective reflections amplifying other sources.

The discussed works address Polishness on different levels as referring to an individual character, groups (fighters, armies), region, and people. There is hardly any evidence for identifying historic persons as the actual reference points of the Polish literary characters. This can be explained, inter alia, with the above-mentioned narrative methods, i.e., to connect persons and events of different times with each other. The literary characters, whose origin is called (or might be presumably) Poland within the discussed epics, are named in the case of individual agents and mostly ascribed a stereotypical attribute of a hero (with the exception of Herman in *Biterolf und Dietleib*). The works show little interest in describing individual characteristics, expressions of affects, a history of a narrated figure, or even trying to individuate it. The depiction of Wenezlan

---

108   Stanzel rates this differently. He assumes a reduction in the essential traits of the new in depictions of other peoples; Franz K. Stanzel, "Der literarische Aspekt unserer Vorstellungen vom Charakter fremder Völker," *Anzeiger der Österreichischen Akademie der Wissenschaften. Philosophisch-Historische Klasse III* (1974), 63–80, at 66.
109   Cf. Zitzewitz, *Polenbild*, 11; Jörg Schwarz, *Das europäische Mittelalter 2: Herrschaftsbildungen und Reiche 900–1500*, Grundkurs Geschichte (Stuttgart, 2006), 157.
110   See Zitzewitz, *Polenbild*, 12.

in *Dietrich und Wenezlan* features facets of his *fama* and is constructed implicitly by deeds (capturing the two warriors of Dietrich, his fighting skills, mindset) and explicitly by the praise of his enemies, as well as aspects of an inner world via the means of introspection. The works do not address dispositions to change and very rarely does a Polish character receive his own voice by means of direct speech (such as Herman in *Biterolf und Dietleib*, Wenezlan in *Dietrich und Wenezlan*, Hornboge in the *Rabenschlacht*), even though speeches are quite frequently used within the works. Wenezlan is the one Polish figure who stands out in regard to action function. As can be expected from heroic epics, the Polish characters think highly of themselves and are viewed in the same way by their opponents, at least in regard to – cross-textually presented and cross-culturally valid – values such as *êre, sterke, muot, kuonheit* and *triuwe*. In the discussed works not only nobleness, virtue, heroism, and kinship but also suitability as a ruler (Herman, Wenezlan) are viewed as prerequisites among the male fighters according to their position in society. The relation between the sexes in regard to Polish characters plays a minor role, for instance, when in the case of the intercessional Helche in *Biterolf und Dietleib* she speaks in favor of Herman, or when Wenezlan's wife in *Dietrich und Wenezlan* attends the combat, in which also the service to women is addressed. These kinds of passages might reflect the negotiation of the men's suitability as a ruler, marriage and reproductive partner from a women's perspective. The works show different ways of integrating a *gast* into the own society. Some integrations happened before the narrated action takes place, some are mentioned as being in process, others (also) with their result, mostly in regard to vassalage (with the exception of *Biterolf*). Out of the collective partial identities mentioned above, primarily the gentile one plays a role in regard to Polish characters. All works illustrate the intersection of *Leib* [body], *Bewusstsein* [consciousness] and *Gesellschaft* [society] described by Luckmann, when the exterior is perceived as a sign of expressing the interior. In general, a noble human body in German medieval literature is not just seen as a simple body, but as a handsome and strong one with which social status can be and is demonstrated. The indivualized Polish characters might be stratified from top to bottom into a three-level model as Ehrismann suggests:[111] Wenezlan, who takes on Dietrich and is the protagonist of his own epic, if this statement can be made because of the fragmentary character of the text, is at the top. Julius Lunzer had interpreted Wenezlan as a reflection of a real Wenzel, such as King Wenceslaus II

---

111   Cf. Ehrismann, "Die Fürsten ûzer Polan" 44.

of Bohemia (1278–1305), since in the year 1300 he was also King of Poland.[112] This hypothesis however does not match with the dating of the fragment to the middle of the thirteenth century. Roswitha Wisniewski has suggested it is his grandfather Wenceslaus I (1230–53), son of Premysl Ottokar I;[113] however, he was not king of Poland. Another possible historic person is St. Wenceslaus of Bohemia († 929/35), who would be the most likely person in regard to chronology. Wenzel might also be just a signifier, since it was a typical Bohemian name. The general problem is not only chronology, but also the content, as when Wenezlan's warriors are called Russians. This, however, might be a misunderstanding or a writing error by the manuscript's scribe, or it is not problematic at all, because Poles and Russians were often linked together, even though viewed as different people. In any case, Wenezlan's army is characterized as that of a hostile and other power, and this is important for the text. Due to the mentioned problematic identification, Gerhard Eis refrains from bringing into play any historical person and suggests that in *Dietrich und Wenezlan*, Dietrich is featured as the one fighting against the Slavs.[114] A level below Wenezlan, there is Herman of Poland, who is at Etzel's court according to the *Klage*, defeated by Etzel in the later *Biterolf und Dietleib*, when he then becomes Etzel's vassal. Friedrich Vogt considers identifying him as Ladislaus Herman of Poland (1081–1102).[115] Joachim Bumke however says there is a need for further investigation[116] and dismisses these kinds of speculations about possible historical backgrounds and role models as unfounded and hardly credible.[117] Hornboge, on a third level, mainly plays a role of representation for Etzel. In *Biterolf und Dietleib* he lives as a hostage at Etzel's court, in *Dietrichs Flucht* and the *Rabenschlacht* he supports Dietrich in the fight against Dietrich's uncle Ermenrich. His name may be fictional, referring originally to the weapons of the Wallachians in *Biterolf und Dietleib*. This narrated character is one of those who appear in several works; evidently, it is part of the cross-textual material. How Hornboge is characterized varies only in minor nuances from work

---

112   Lunzer, "Dietrich und Wenezlan".
113   Roswitha Wisniewski, *Mittelalterliche Dietrichdichtung*, Sammlung Metzler 205 (Stuttgart, 1986), 144.
114   Gerard Eis, "Zu Dietrichs Slawenkämpfen." *Zeitschrift für deutsches Altertum und deutsche Literatur* 84 (1953), 7–84, here: 74.
115   Friedrich Vogt, "Zur Geschichte der Nibelungenklage," in *Rektoratsprogramm der Universität Marburg* (1913), 137–67, at 162–63; cf. Friedrich Panzer, *Das Nibelungenlied. Entstehung und Gestalt* (Stuttgart, 1955), 80; Ehrismann, "Die Fürsten ûzer Polan," 43.
116   Bumke, *Fassungen*, 477 n. 54.
117   Id., 487.

to work, for instance when his origin is stated or omitted, he leads different numbers of warriors (*Nibelungenlied*: 1,000; *Klage*: 2,000; *Biterolf und Dietleib*: 3,000; *Rabenschlacht*: 5,000),[118] or he is linked to different persons as in the case of the above-mentioned Eastern European trio.

In general, Polish characters are presented as either a part of Etzel's representative entourage or as demonstration objects for the power of the Germanic heroes.[119] The positive conception of Polish heroes is epically necessary.[120] Ehrismann argues in regard to content as well as history that both Polish characters and Poland play a relatively small role in the German heroic epic, because the Germanic-German heroic saga was usually set in other places for historical reasons.[121] The country of Poland is mentioned across genres in a variety of literary works, but is practically and genre-typically not described in any detail. In the genre of the heroic epic such as the *Nibelungenlied* and *Biterolf and Dietleib*, Poland is subject to Etzel's power. In all works, a realistic narrative framework is created by naming places that largely refer to real places and territories, but their descriptions remain vague. Almost all hypotheses regarding the identification of real persons have been rejected in research with regard to chronological or content counterarguments. Although literarily depicted names and events show parallels with the agents and actions of historical reality, the origin of the texts is usually set earlier than the times in which the persons lived. As mentioned above, this finding is related to the genre of heroic epics. In further genres such as songs and *Sangspruchdichtung*, it is highly likely that the textual information can be assigned to specific persons or customs, because they refer to contemporary realities. Only two examples may be quoted to illustrate this. The *lai*, song, and Sangspruch poet Tannhäuser (mid-thirteenth century)[122] wrote between 1256 and 1266 the so called lai VI *ich muos clagen* [I have to lament], which both laments the present time, yet also offers praise of the princes.[123] The poet also refers to numerous contem-

---

118   These numbers cannot be compared adequately because they are related to different situations, but they demonstrate a variation between the works.
119   Ehrismann, "Die Fürsten ûzer Polan" 43.
120   Ibid., 39, 43.
121   Ibid., 33.
122   Burghart Wachinger, "Der Tannhäuser," in *Verfasserlexikon*, 9: 600–10, at 600.
123   Tannhäuser's poems are transmitted in two manuscripts; http://www.handschriftencensus.de/werke/5725 [2-20-2019]. Text edition: *Tannhäuser. Die Gedichte der Manessischen Handschrift. Mittelhochdeutsch/Neuhochdeutsch. Einleitung, Edition, Textkommentar* by Maria Grazia Cammarota, Übersetzungen by Jürgen Kühnel, Göppinger Arbeiten zur Germanistik 749 (Göppingen, 2009), 174; cf. Johannes Siebert, *Der Dichter Tannhäuser: Leben – Gedichte – Sage* (Halle/Saale, 1934), 159–71; Bumke, *Mäzene*, 176–230.

poraneous rulers from the immediate past in the context of praising generous patrons, including a Polish prince (versicle 20–23). The following passages may be cited as an extract:

ûs Bôlônlande ein fürste wert · | des wil ich niht vergessen · | vrô Êre sîn zallen zîten gert · | diu hât in wol besessen ·

[I must not forget also the noble prince of Poland; Lady Honor always wished for him and possessed him completely:]
    versicle 20/vv. 74–77

herzogen Heinrîch êren rîch · | von Pressela genennet · | den wil ich loben sicherlîch · | mîn zunge in wol erkennet

[Duke Henry who is called the honorary of Wroclaw; I really want to praise him, my singing knows how to judge him adequately]
    versicle 21/vv. 78–81.

The duke referred to can probably be identified as Duke Henry III, the White, from Silesia-Wroclaw (* 1227/30, † 3 December 1266).[124] The Polish custom of a short hairstyle is referred to in the poem III (1292–94) by Seifried Helbling (* c.1240, † after 1300).[125] The reference takes place together with a valuation of this custom as being different (III,225–28): *waz wil dû Pôlân hôchbeschorn? | den Ungern wære daz vil zorn, | der ir langem hâr erkür | die hôhen pôlânischen schüer* [What do you want high-sheared Pole? The Hungarians would be very angry if someone preferred the high Polish shear to their long hair]. Embedded in this stereotyped statement about a culture-specific feature of Poles is a lamentation that foreign customs and costumes of other peoples are imitated.[126]

---

124 Buschinger, "Deutsch-polnische Wechselbeziehungen im Mittelalter," 48, identifies two persons, which is hard to verify by the syntax: "ûs Bôlônlande ein fürste wert" would refer to Duke Boleslaw II of Silesia (Bolesław II Rogatka; * c.1217; † 1278). For further examples see Buschinger, 48–50, 52–53.

125 In the poem XIII a fictional letter writer and minstrel *Sifrit Helblinc* is mentioned, which is however not the real name of the unknown author or a reference point of a collection of 15 poems; Ingeborg Glier, "Helbling, Seifried," in *Verfasserlexikon*, 3: 943–47, at 943–44. Poems by Seifried Helbling are transmitted in http://www.handschriftencensus.de/werke/601 [2-20-2019]. Text edition: Seifried Helbling, *Der kleine Lucidarius*, ed. and annotated Joseph Seemüller (Halle/Saale, 1886; repr. Hildesheim, 1987).

126 In poem VIII,763–67 within a discussion of the dress code at the court the manner of clothing is presented as a regional feature, and this also in regard to Poland. But the clothing

The *causa scribendi* of the different authors of the discussed literary works usually is not a description of cultural differences of any people. Consequently, the depiction of Poles, Polishness, and/or Poland is not very detailed. The aim of the works is obviously not to fathom the 'other' as being foreign in its nature. It is clear that in most of the works, the 'other' is designed largely analogously to one's 'self'.[127] Described are encounters with cultural, not social strangeness. This analogy is in the end a hybrid construction by transforming the 'other' into an othered 'self'. Otherness is thus not defined as a polar opposite of sameness and/or selfhood. The interpretive pattern can be identified as a secular-courtly one which coins the depiction of all characters regardless of their place of origin. Othering happens mainly in the parts narrated by the narrator, less in the direct speech of characters. In all discussed works it could be observed that the confrontation with the 'other' takes place via different narrated forms of verbal and nonverbal interaction, and that both the literary constructed 'self' as well as the 'other' is the result of a combination of attributions, ascriptions, and positionings – even though they are ascribed, filtered, and viewed through the lenses of medieval poets and scribes depending on time, place, audience, and genre.

> is not described in any detail: *die Bêheim tragent ir gewant, / als sit ist in Bêheimlant, / die Sahsen und die Pôlân / tragent ouch gewant an / dâ bî man sie erkennet* [The Bohemians wear their clothes, as is customary in Bohemia, the Saxons and the Poles also wear clothes from which they can be identified]. Shortly after, the short hairstyle of the Poles is also addressed (VIII,793–96): *und swer in dem lande snit / gewant nâch der Pôlân sit, / daz dem sîn hâr wær geschorn / hôch ûf für diu ôrn: / daz sold im nimer wahsen* [and whoever wears a garment in the style of the country of Polish custom, and whose hair would be cut like that, above the ears all away: it shall never grow for him again].

127   Cf. Thum, "Frühformen des Umgangs mit 'Fremdem' und 'Fremde'," 320–21, 346–47.

PART 4

Regional Zones of Contact between Germans and Poles in the Middle Ages

CHAPTER 14

Between Real Experience and Stereotypes: The Silesian People in the Middle Ages with Respect to Their Neighbors (in Historiographic Sources)

Wojciech Mrozowicz

In reference to the conference's central issue indicated in its title, namely, the mutual perception of Germans and Poles in the Middle Ages, it is important to emphasize that the situation in the region of Silesia in this historical period was in many ways incomparable to other parts of Poland. Contrary to other historical provinces of the country, the region had loosened its ties with the Polish state relatively early, i.e. during the 13th century. Moreover, in the first decades of the 14th century Silesia had already become a fiefdom of the Bohemian Crown, constituting thereafter one of its dependencies. The political changes were accompanied by settlement activity and ethnic transformations and, as a result, in the late Middle Ages the ethnic structure of the Silesian population had been completely modified. Originally Slavic, and in the majority Polish, inhabitants of the region had come to be dominated by people who had arrived from the West, mainly from various German lands. Even though the indigenous and immigrant communities were often separate from one another, because direct interactions were necessary, they eventually merged and thus the inhabitants of Silesia frequently came to have a problem defining their own identity. A typical example here is a famous Silesian scholar, Witelon (died ca. 1270–1314), whose father was probably a German from Thuringia and his mother Polish, who therefore called himself *"filius Thuringorum et Polonorum"* [a son of Thuringians and Poles].[1] This reality also affects the way in which the issue in question will be presented in this article since it is frequently difficult to determine the ethnic origins of the authors of the quoted works; additionally, their affiliation does not always correspond to their national and political sympathies.

---

1   Jerzy Burchardt, *Witelo filosofo della natura del XIII sec. Una biografia* [Witelo Philosopher of Nature of the Thirteenth Century. A biography] (Wrocław, 1984); Benedykt Zientara, "Nationality conflicts in the German-Slavic borderland in the 13th–14th centuries and their social scope", *APH* 22 (1970), 207–225, at 222.

Until the 13th–14th centuries Silesian historiography was strongly dependent on Polish chronicles and annals; thus the oldest Silesian annals – the *Kamieniec Annals I* – made generous use of the annals from Lesser Poland[2] and – possibly – from Gallus Anonymus'[3] chronicle, as well as the *Hungarian-Polish Chronicle*.[4] The anonymous author of the Silesian *Chronicon Polonorum* drew copiously from the famous *Polish Chronicle* written by the master Wincenty Kadłubek.[5] As a result these (and many other) works presented the history of Silesia as wholly "Polish". They perceived Silesia as part of Poland, governed from the very beginning by Polish rulers. After Poland was fragmented into provinces by Duke Bolesław III Wrymouth in 1138, his son, Vladislaus II the Exile, succeeded him. The *Chronicon Polonorum* emphasises the fact that he came from the Polish dynasty of the Piasts and that he ruled in Silesia and in the capital city of Cracow.[6] When the chronicle mentions the death of Duke Henry II the Pious during the Battle of Legnica in 1241, it immediately goes on to criticise one of his direct successors, Bolesław II the Horned, because he "Poloniam perdidit" [he had lost Poland].[7] Many more examples of this historiographic tendency can be quoted.

The neighbours of Silesia were then also the neighbours of Poland. Silesian historiographers devoted a lot of attention to them, emphasising, e.g., the common origins of the inhabitants of Bohemia and Poland. Still in the 1380s, Piotr of Byczyna, the author of the *Chronicle of Polish Dukes* (*Chronica principum Poloniae*), the most important historiographic work of the Silesian Middle

---

2 *Rocznik kamieniecki* [Kamieniec Annals I], ed. August Bielowski, MPH 2 (Lviv, 1872), 776–778; about the sources of this annals see: Wacław Korta, *Średniowieczna annalistyka śląska* [The medieval annals of Silesia] (Wrocław, 1966), 43–85.
3 *Galli Anonymi, Cronicae et Gesta ducum sive principum Poloniae* ed. Karol Maleczyński. MPH. Series nova 2 (Cracow, 1952).
4 Martin Homza, *Uhorsko-pol'ská kronika. Nedocenený prameň k dejinám strednej Európy* [The Hungarian-Polish Chronicle. An underestimated source related to the history of Central Europe] (Bratislava, 2009).
5 *Kronika polska* [The Polish Chronicle], ed. Ludwik Ćwikliński, MPH 3 (Lviv, 1878), 578–656. *Magistri Vincentii dicti Kadłubek, Chronica Polonorum*, ed. Marianus Plezia, MPH. Series nova 11 (Cracow, 1994). About the sources of the Silesian *Chronicon Polonorum* see: Wojciech Mrozowicz, "Z problematyki recepcji kroniki Wincentego w średniowiecznym dziejopisarstwie polskim (ze szczególnym uwzględnieniem śląskiej 'Kroniki polskiej')" [On the issue of the reception of the Vincentius chronicle in Polish medieval historiography (with particular emphasis on the Silesian *Polish Chronicle*)], in: *Onus Athlanteum. Studia nad kroniką biskupa Wincentego*, ed. Andrzej Dąbrówka and Witold Wojtowicz. Studia Staropolskie. Series nova (Warsaw, 2009), 326–336.
6 *Kronika polska*, 629, 644.
7 *Kronika polska*, 643–652.

Ages,[8] presents the origins of the Bohemian and Polish nations (and thus the states) in the following way:

> When the languages were confounded after the deluge, as we read about it in the Book of Genesis, all the peoples were scattered around the world.[9] Of them, two Slavic brothers were looking for a place to live and occupy lands. One of the them was called Czech and the other Lech.[10] In the end the one called Czech came to Bohemia and decided to stay there, while Lech settled in what is now Poland. Thus Bohemians [Czechs] come from Czech and Poles from Lech. That is why they were then called Lechites or Lechs.[11]

This resorting to Biblical *topoi* and a Bohemian chronicle by Přibík Pulkava of Radenín to describe and illustrate the common origins of both nations is a way to emphasize the significance of the stereotype of Slavic solidarity, which is sometimes mentioned by Bohemian and Polish chroniclers and historians.[12]

---

8   *Kronika książąt polskich* [*The Chronicle of Polish Dukes*], ed. Zygmunt Węclewski, MPH 3 (Lviv, 1878), 423–578.

9   Cf. Gen 10 5, 20, 31. Of course, Slavs being among the descendants of Jafet, Cham and Sem in the Book of Genesis are not mentioned.

10 Rus, the third of three brothers, is not mentioned in the *Chronicle of Polish Dukes*. The *Chronicle of Greater Poland* from the end of 13th (or beginning of the 14th) century provides information about him, see *Chronica Poloniae Maioris*, ed. Brygida Kürbis, MPH. Series nova 8 (Warsaw, 1970), 4. Cf. Norbert Kersken, *Geschichtsschreibung im Europa der nationes. Nationalgeschichtliche Gesamtdarstellungen im Mittelalter*, Münstersche Historische Forschungen 8, Köln-Weimar-Wien, 1995, 530–532; Edward Skibiński, "Kronika wielkopolska" [*Chronicle of Greater Poland*], in: *Vademecum historyka mediewisty*, ed. Jarosław Nikodem, Dariusz Andrzej Sikorski (Warsaw, 2012), 260–265.

11 *Kronika książąt*, 430: "post divisionem linguarum factam post diluvium, ut in Genesi legitur, disperse sunt omnes gentes per varia loca, de quibus duo fratres Slavi successu temporum pro possessionibus capiendis hinc inde habitacula quesierunt, quorum unus Czech, alter Lech appellati. Horum tandem unus, qui Czech dicitur, Bohemiam perveniens ibi mansionem elegit. Lech vero, ubi nunc est Polonia, constituisse dicitur sedem suam. De Czech itaque Bohemi, de Lech autem processerunt Poloni, propter quod et Lechite seu Lechi sunt tunc temporis nominati", see also: Jan Malicki, *Laury, togi, pastorały. Szkice o kulturze literackiej renesansowego Śląska* [Laurels, gowns, crosiers. Sketches of Renaissance literary culture of Silesia] (Katowice, 1983), 16; Jan Malicki, *Mity narodowe – Lechiada* [National myths – Lechiada] (Wrocław, 1982), 104; Sławomir Gawlas, "Ślązacy w oczach własnych i cudzych. Uwagi o powstaniu i rozwoju regionalnej tożsamości w średniowieczu" [The Silesian people in their own eyes and in the eyes of others. Remarks on the beginnings and development of regional identity in the Middle Ages], in *Ślązacy w oczach własnych i obcych*, ed. Antoni Barciak (Katowice-Zabrze, 2010), 65.

12 Jaroslav Pánek, "Slezsko a české země v polských kronikách XIV. století (Příspěvek k dějinám česko-polských vztahů)" [Silesia and Bohemian lands in the Polish chronicles

Possibly because of this approach, further on in the *Chronicle of Polish Dukes*, Piotr of Byczyna does not make any judgments about Bohemians even though the relations with them were sometimes strained. However, he is critical of Bohemian rulers, especially Wenceslas II of Bohemia and John of Bohemia, whose politics resulted in a conflict with the Silesian Piasts and the ultimate subjugation of the Silesian duchies to the Bohemian Crown.[13] In contrast, one of the Silesian Piasts, Louis I of Brzeg and Legnica, who commissioned the *Chronicle of Polish Dukes*, saw his future not in the union with Bohemia but with Poland, claiming the throne in Cracow.[14]

A different historiographic concept, to an extent reflecting the way of thinking of the incoming Germans, may be seen in the works written within the community of Silesian Cistercians, where historiographic writing was at its most active in the 13th–14th centuries.[15] A short rhyming work (47 verses altogether) entitled *Versus Lubenses*[16] by an anonymous author, widely commented on in historiography, was written shortly after 1371 in the order's oldest monastery in Lubiąż (founded in 1175).[17] Its content is worth quoting here

---

of 14th century (A contribution to the history of Czech-Polish relations)], *Slezský sborník* 71/3 (1973), 218–232, at 227; Wojciech Mrozowicz, *"Regno Bohemie in perpetuum applicavit.* Śląsk a Czechy w śląskiej historiografii średniowiecznej" [*Regno Bohemie in perpetuum applicavit*. Silesia and Bohemia in Silesian medieval historiography], *Śląski Kwartalnik Historyczny Sobótka* 66/3 (2011), 27–36, at 28; Marie Bláhová, "Představy o společném původu Čechů a Poláků ve středověké historiografii" [Images about the common origin of Bohemian people and Poles in medieval historiography], *Historia Slavorum Occidentis* 2 (3) (2012), 234–254, at 239.

13 *Kronika książąt*, 518, 537; Pánek, "Slezsko", 229–231; Jaroslav Pánek, "La conception de l'histoire tchéque et de relations tchéco-polonaises dans les plus anciennes chroniques polonaises", *Mediaevalia Bohemica* 4 (1974), 5–124, at 73–75; Roman Heck, "Główne linie rozwoju średniowiecznego dziejopisarstwa śląskiego" [The main lines of development in Silesian medieval historiography], *Studia Źródłoznawcze* 22 (1977), 61–75, at 67; Mrozowicz, *"Regno Bohemie"*, 27–28. See, as well, below, note 44.

14 Wojciech Mrozowicz, "Die Polnische Chronik (Polnisch-Schlesische Chronik) und die Chronik der Fürsten Polens (*Chronica principum Poloniae*) als Mittel zur dynastischen Identitätsstiftung der schlesischen Piasten", in *Legitimation von Fürstendynastien in Polen und dem Reich. Identitätsbildung im Spiegel schriftlicher Quellen (12.–15. Jahrhundert)*, ed. Grischa Vercamer and Ewa Wółkiewicz, Deutsches Historisches Institut Warschau. Quellen und Studien 31, (Wiesbaden, 2016), 249–262, at 260–262.

15 Heck, "Główne linie," 64; Wojciech Mrozowicz, "Średniowieczne śląskie dziejopisarstwo klasztorne" [The medieval cloister historiography of Silesia], in *Tysiącletnie dziedzictwo kulturowe diecezji wrocławskiej*, ed. Antoni Barciak (Katowice, 2000), 141–159, at 144–148.

16 *Monumenta Lubensia*, ed. Wilhelm Wattenbach, (Breslau, 1861), 14–15; *Wiersz o pierwszych zakonnikach Lubiąża* [A poem about first monks in Lubiąż], ed. August Bielowski, MPH 3 (Lviv, 1878), 708–710.

17 The *Versus Lubenses* are discussed, above all by: Siegfried Epperlein, Gründungsmythos deutscher Zisterzienserklöster westlich und östlich der Elbe im hohen Mittelalter und der

because it presents the motifs of national stereotypes quite distinctly. In the beginning it tells the story of founding of the Cistercian abbey, replacing a former Benedictine monastery. Duke Bolesław I the Tall summoned the friars from their monastery in Pforta to Lubiąż, where the founder's loved ones were buried – his wife, mother and son Jan. Upon arriving at Lubiąż, the Cistercians threw statues of Mars and Julius into the cesspool and arranged "habitacula pacis" [spaces of peace] in which to worship to Christ and his saints. All the information concerning the Cistercian beginnings in Lubiąż is fully credible. Only the mention of their struggle with the pagan idols raises doubts: why had the Benedictines not dealt with them earlier? In the context of the information provided further on in *Versus Lubenses*, the author may have wanted to emphasize the Cistercian achievement in this area as well.

As a matter of fact, this text could well conclude at this stage. This initial part, as discussed, may well constitute an independent whole and in this reduced form it has so functioned in modern times.[18] Because it is mainly devoted to a description of the history of the founding of the Cistercian

Bericht des Leubuser Mönches im 14. Jahrhundert," *Jahrbuch für Wirtschaftsgeschichte* 8 (1967), 303–335; hereafter the Polish translation is cited: "*Mit fundacyjny* niemieckich klasztorów cysterskich a relacja mnicha lubiąskiego z XIV wieku," trans. Edward Potkowski, *Przegląd Historyczny* 58/4 (1967), 587–604; Konstanty Jażdżewski, *Lubiąż. Losy i kultura umysłowa śląskiego opactwa cystersów (1163–1642)* [Lubiąż. The history and intellectual culture of the Silesian Cistercian abbey], (Wrocław, 1992), 111–115; Wojciech Mrozowicz, "Z dyskusji nad początkami klasztorów w średniowiecznej historiografii śląskiej," [From discussions on the beginnings of monasteries in the Silesian medieval historiography] in *Origines mundi, gentium et civitatum*, ed. Stanisław Rosik and Przemysław Wiszewski. Acta Universitatis Wratislaviensis 2339. Historia 153 (Wrocław, 2001), 171–178; id., *Średniowieczne śląskie*, 146–147; id., "Versus Lubenses", in *The Encyclopedia of the Medieval Chronicle*, ed. Graeme Dunphy (Leiden-Boston, 2010), 1476–1477; Robert Bartlett, *The Making of Europe. Conquest, colonization and cultural change 950–1350* (London, 1993); hereafter the Polish translation is cited: *Tworzenie Europy. Podbój, kolonizacja i przemiany kulturowe 950–1350*, trans. Grażyna Waluga, (Poznań, 2003), 236; Waldemar Könighaus, *Die Zisterziernserabtei Leubus in Schlesien von ihrer Gründung bis zum Ende des 15. Jahrhunderts*, Deutsches Historisches Institut Warschau. Quellen und Studien 15 (Wiesbaden, 2004), 11, 15–16, 27–28; Andrzej Pleszczyński, *Przekazy niemieckie o Polsce i jej mieszkańcach w okresie panowania Piastów* [German accounts about Poland and its inhabitants during the Piasts rule] (Lublin, 2016), 180–187; Andrzej Pleszczyński, Joanna Sobiesiak, Karol Szejgiec, Michał Tomaszek, and Przemysław Tyszka, *Historia communitatem facit. Struktura narracji tworzących tożsamości grupowe w średniowieczu* [Historia communitatem facit. The structure of narratives forming group identities in the Middle Age] (Wrocław, 2016), 41–64.

18   Cf. the fragmentary copy (from the turn of the 16th and 17th centuries) of the *Versus Lubenses*, preserved in the collection of Silesian sepulchral inscriptions copied by Simon Grunaeus (d. 1628) in the manuscript of the University Library in Wrocław, call number Akc. 1950/781 (fol. 186r).

monastery in Lubiąż, it may as such be considered a rhyming *fundatio*, i.e. one of the genres functioning in monastic historiography.[19]

Yet a more extensive continuation was added – and it is not clear exactly when. The extension presents the first years of the history of the monastery in Lubiąż – the period of the first two abbots. To emphasize the immensity of the effort the Cistercians undertook to civilize the area, the anonymous author describes the disastrous conditions in Silesia before they arrived. Thus, this part of *Versus Lubenses* is merely a development of the most important theme of the preceding part. The method of narration employed here lends itself to presenting the views of the situation in Silesia for approximately 200 years before the piece was written, i.e. the time of the founding of the monastery. A relatively extensive fragment describing the land where the Cistercians had settled is written in an ironic and mocking tone. The delights (*delicie*) which the first monks encountered on their arrival were lands devoid of farmers and covered with forests. There were no towns ("civitas aut oppidium [...] non fuit ullum"), while in the vicinity of any strongholds there were markets, uncultivated fields and chapels. The inhabitants of the land, the *Polish people* ("gens Polonie"), were impoverished and lazy. They ploughed sandy soil with wooden ploughshares, harnessing cows or oxen, which they also grazed. They lacked salt, iron, money, good clothes and shoes. The situation in the land changed with the arrival of the Cistercians from Germany, which is presented in the next fragment of *Versus Lubenses*. They transformed this land ("terra per eos tota hiis referta") and their effort and sweat created a life that was free of hardships. "Nunquam credamus – wrote an anonymous Cistercian – hec quod per nos habeamus, / Vel sint optata per eos sic elaborata" (We will never believe that what we owned or what we desired was not achieved through their hard work).[20] A point of reference here was the situation in the German lands, which were much better developed in terms of their economy and civilization, and which was well known to the Cistercians. From this perspective Silesia and

---

19 About this historiographic kind see: Volker Honemann, "Klostergründungsgeschichten," in: *Die deutsche Literatur des Mittelalters. Verfasserlexikon* 4, 2. Edition, (Berlin-New York, 1983), 1239–1247; Jörg Kastner, *"Historiae fundationum monasteriorum". Frühformen monastischer Institutionsgeschichtsschreibung im Mittelalter*, Münchener Beiträge zur Mediävistik und Renaissance-Forschung 18, (Munich, 1974), especially 53–54; Wojciech Mrozowicz, "Z dyskusji nad początkami klasztorów w średniowiecznej historiografii śląskiej," [From discussions on the beginnings of monasteries in Silesian medieval historiography] in *Origines mundi, gentium et civitatum*, ed. Stanisław Rosik and Przemysław Wiszewski, Acta Universitatis Wratislaviensis 2339. Historia 153, (Wrocław, 2001), 171–178, at 171–172. The *Versus Lubenses* as *fundatio* consider: Mrozowicz, *Średniowieczne śląskie*, 147; Könighaus, *Die Zisterziernserabtei Leubus*, 11.

20 *Wiersz o pierwszych zakonnikach*, 710.

its Polish inhabitants failed to gain a favorable appraisal in the eye of the anonymous Cistercian from Lubiąż, even though he and his brethren were aware that they owed their presence and estates to local dukes. It is plausible to think that such views were not rare in Silesia in the late Middle Ages.

Abbot Peter II, a putative author of the second part of the chronicle of the monastery in Henryków, known as the *Book of Henryków*,[21] speaks in the same vein about the achievements of Silesian Cistercians, referring to the same stereotypes as seen above (albeit avoiding such explicit judgments about the indigenous inhabitants of Silesia). He wrote in circa 1310 about the first monks who arrived in Henryków:

> [they] departed from the Holy Eden of the monastery of Lubiąż for this place – then quite savage and covered with many forests – and not only did they furrow the earth here by hoe and ploughshare, and sustain themselves by eating bread [they had baked] by the sweat of their brow, but, because they were worthy of it, and thanks to them, the flower of the Cistercian Order [...] might be planted in this place.[22]

However, the authors of the *Book of Henryków*, both Abbot Peter II and his predecessor, Peter I, quite often remark that the history of the actual lands which were incorporated by the Cistercian estate had begun before the monks and German settlers arrived. This view is missing in *Versus Lubenses*. Indigenous inhabitants of Silesia differed from the Germans – according to the *Book of Henryków* – with their customs and legal culture. The Cistercian monks' comprehension and knowledge of said culture in the context of their expanding estate, was important in case their rights to it were ever in dispute; this was

---

21   *Liber fundationis claustri sancte Marie Virginis in Heinrichow czyli Księga henrykowska* [Liber fundationis claustri sancte Marie Virginis in Heinrichow or the Book of Henryków], ed. and trans. Roman Grodecki (Wrocław, 1991); the English translation: Piotr Górecki, *A local society in transition. The "Henryków Book" and related documents*. Studies and texts 155 (Toronto, 2007), 91–202. About this work see, above all: Józef Matuszewski, *Najstarsze polskie zdanie prozaiczne. Zdanie henrykowskie i jego tło historyczne* [The oldest Polish prose sentence. The sentence of Henryków and its historical background] (Wrocław, 1981); Piotr Górecki, *The Text and the world: The* Henryków Book, *its authors, and their region, 1160–1310* (New York, 2015) – here further literature, 261–274.

22   *Liber fundationis*, 155: "egressi de sacro Lubensis cenobii paradyso ad hunc locum, tunc satis horridum et multis nemoribus obsitum, non solum hic terram rastro sulcantes et vomere panem in sudore wltus pro nature sustentaculo comederunt, sed et pre gaudio spiritus, quia digni habiti sunt, ut per eos huic loco flos ordinis Cisterciensis insereretur"; translation: Górecki, *A local society*, 147.

the main motive for writing the work. The first of the authors of the *Book of Henryków*, Abbot Peter I, declared that it would be:

> [...] to record the events that followed, that is, the accounts of the gifts of inheritances to the cloister, so that the servants of Christ who shall long hence do battle for the true God in this place may know the reason for the gift of each inheritance from this booklet; and in order that if someone from among men should raise a claim against them for any cause, after perusing the present [writings] they may be able to answer correctly and reasonably.[23]

At the same time it was an account of the expansion of the German settlement and its law in Silesia, and thus the *Book of Henryków* is sometimes treated in German literature as "the most German testimony of the Middle Ages";[24] on the other hand Polish historiography, paradoxically to a certain extent, emphasizes its great significance for the Polish history of Silesia and – because it features the oldest sentence recorded in Polish – for the history of the Polish language.[25]

It is worth noting that the life of Saint Hedwig, the patron saint of Silesia, written before 1300 possibly in Cistercian circles, avoids any mention of national stereotypes, even though Hedwig's German origins and the German origins of the author seem to offer an opportunity for such references. One cannot escape an impression that the text intentionally avoids mentioning the ethnic background of any of the pilgrims to Saint Hedwig's grave in Trzebnica, the people miraculously cured or the participants in the celebrations accompanying the announcement of her canonization, because their places of origin (diocese, locality) very often were situated outside Silesia.[26]

Historiographic discussion of the conditions in Silesia and a judgement about its inhabitants in the times preceding German settlement, which began with the opinions expressed in *Versus Lubenses* and (to a lesser degree) the

---

23 "ea que secuntur, id est raciones donacionum hereditatum huius claustri scribere incipiamus, quatinus famuli Christi in hoc loco longe postmodum vero Deo militaturi ex presenti libello reciones donacionis uniuscuiusque hereditatis cognoscant, ut si quis hominum eos quacunque de causa inpetierit, convenienter et racionabiliter ex consideracione presentium valeant respondere"; translation: Górecki, *A local society*, 99–100.

24 See e.g., *Das Gründungsbuch des Klosters Heinrichau. Aus dem Lateinischen übertragen und mit Einführung und Erläuterungen versehen von Paul Bretschneider*, Darstellungen und Quellen zur schlesischen Geschichte 29, (Breslau, 1927), 1.

25 See, above all: *Liber fundationis*, XL–XLIV; Matuszewski, *Najstarsze polskie*; generally about other problems raised in the *Book of Henryków* see: Górecki, *A local society*, 1–13; id., *The text and the world*.

26 Zob. *Vita sanctae Hedwigis*, ed. Aleksander Semkowicz, MPH, 4 (Lviv, 1884), 501–655.

Book of Henryków, developed in two directions in the 19th and 20th centuries. In his comments on *Versus Lubenses*, which Wilhelm Wattenbach (d. 1897) published in 1866, he emphasized the pertinence of the characteristics of Silesian lands before the arrival of the Cistercians. According to him, it gave a perfect description of the conditions in Silesia and even included direct [!] recollections of the situation of that time. The efforts made by the Cistercians, who had invited German colonists to Silesia, pulled the land out of its backwardness.[27] This image perfectly met the needs of Wattenbach's times when modern nations, and – consequently nationalisms – were being born. It was then that the idea of historiographic justification of the supremacy of German civilization over Slavs emerged. In Silesia it was formulated and implemented most distinctly by Gustav Adolf Harald Stenzel (d. 1854) and developed further by Wattenbach (mentioned above) and Colmar Grünhagen (d. 1911); the latter directly equated the history of Silesia with its Germanisation.[28]

On the other hand, there were historians who doubted the credibility of such sources, perceiving them as stereotypical. In 1913 Olgierd Górka spoke of "the characteristics [...] tinged with exaggeration".[29] Siegfried Epperlein provides further examples of similar opinions voiced by such historians as Heinrich F. Schmid, Zygmunt Wojciechowski, Karol Maleczyński, and Joseph Gottschalk.[30] Epperlein himself interpreted the work in terms of a Cistercian "foundation myth", emphasizing the effort undertaken by the monks leading to the economic and civilizational development of the region. *Versus Lubenses* reflects the way the Cistercians perceived themselves and the greatness of their endeavor. Additionally, in the context of intensifying German eastwards expansion in the 12th–13th centuries, this pattern acquires a new meaning – the

---

27 *Monumenta Lubensia*, 6–7; see also: Epperlein, *Mit fundacyjny*, 598.
28 See, e.g.: Colmar Grünhagen, *Geschichte Schlesiens*, 1: *Bis zum Eintritt des habsburgischen Herrschaft 1527* (Gotha, 1884), IX. also: Hermann Markgraf, "Die Entwicklung der schlesischen Geschichtsschreibung", *Zeitschrift des Vereins für Geschichte und Alterthum Schlesiens* 22 (1888), 1–29, at 21–23; or: Marek Cetwiński, "Dorobek i potrzeby z zakresu wydawnictw źródłowych do dziejów Śląska – średniowiecze (akta i dokumenty)" [Achievements and needs in the field of source publications to the history of Silesia – the Middle Ages (acts and documents)], in: *Stan i potrzeby śląskoznawczych badań humanistycznych*, ed. Kazimierz Bobowski, Ryszard Gładkiewicz, and Wojciech Wrzesiński, (Wrocław-Warsaw, 1990), 215–226, at 225; *Encyklopedia Wrocławia* [Encyclopedia of Wrocław], ed. Jan Harasimowicz (Wrocław, 2001), 242, 785, 883. On the later followers of this approach to the history of Silesia see Epperlein, *Mit fundacyjny*, 598–599.
29 Olgierd Górka, *Studya na dziejami Śląska. Najstarsza tradycja opactwa cystersów w Lubiążu* [Studies on the history of Silesia. The oldest tradition of the Cistercian abbey in Lubiąż] (Lviv, 1911), 54.
30 Epperlein, *Mit fundacyjny*, 599.

work by the Cistercian from Lubiąż points "also to the arrogance of some of the feudal lords who [...] often had a negative opinion of the indigenous Slavic people".[31] Appreciating these aspects, Roman Heck drew different conclusions about *Versus Lubenses*, considering their tone as "moderate", stating that they actually reflected "primarily the monks' pride in their civilizational achievements, which they claimed for themselves, and a certain feeling of superiority towards indigenous Polish people".[32]

In his view of *Versus Lubenses* Robert Bartlett adopted similar assumptions, and he considered this work, and especially the discussed fragment which he quoted in full in his work on the making Europe, as "part of their [the Cistercians'] self-presentation".[33] However, despite its attractiveness, the analogy which he presented, comparing civilizational missions carried out by the Cistercians in Silesia and the Spanish in the New World in the 16th century, seems methodologically unsound as it does not observe the rules of the comparative method. It is also worth noting that another shortcoming of Bartlett's approach (*nota bene* allowing for the perspective of "Europeanisation" to be viewed as a one-directional transmission of cultural patterns) is that he completely ignores the peculiar nature of Silesia.[34]

The conventional view of the Bohemians as viewed in Silesian historiography was totally transformed in the 15th century under the influence of Hussitism, which was unequivocally always condemned by the Catholic Silesian chroniclers and annalists.[35] The new stereotype saw the Bohemians as the nation of heretics. For example, Ludolf of Żagań (d. 1422), the chronicler of the Augustinian monastery of Canons Regular in Żagań, a Saxon educated in Prague, wrote that the Bohemians, who used to be "O nacio preclara! O gens inclita! O populus quondam Deo peculiaris!" (A famous nation! An illustrious tribe! A people once especially chosen by God), once a religious

---

31   Epperlein, *Mit fundacyjny*, 599–603, quotations 601.
32   Roman Heck, "Uwagi o średniowiecznym dziejopisarstwie śląskim," [Remarks on the Silesian medieval historiography] in *Średniowieczna kultura na Śląsku*, ed. Roman Heck (Wrocław, 1977), 7–19, at 14; see also: Heck, "Główne linie," 66. Konstanty Jażdżewski was indignant at such wording, see Jażdżewski, *Lubiąż*, 112.
33   Bartlett, *Tworzenie Europy*, 234–236, at 236.
34   Piotr Górecki, "'Tworzenie Europy' Roberta Bartletta w kontekście anglosaskich badań historycznych nad początkami i kształtowaniem się Europy" [Robert Bartletts 'The Making of Europe' in the context of Anglo-Saxon historical research on the origins and shaping of Europe], in: Bartlett, *Tworzenie Europy*, 505–515, at 514.
35   Wojciech Mrozowicz, "*Constancie flammis adiectus*. Johannes Hus und der Hussitismus in den Augen schlesischer Chronisten" [DOI: http://dx.doi.org/10.12775/BPMH.2016.004], *Biuletyn Polskiej Misji Historycznej / Bulletin der Polnischen Historischen Mission* 11 (2016), 121–146.

leader of nearly all Christian nations, now turning their back on the truth and becoming "inverecunda meretrix" (a shameless harlot).[36] The same attitude towards the Bohemians is seen in other works of the 15th century Silesian historiographers. However, they did not judge the Bohemians in the same way as Ludolf of Żagań, who was only aware of the developments from the first stage of the Hussite movement; they viewed them from the perspective of the whole period of the Hussite wars and the incidents from the reign of King George of Poděbrady. Following the already fully-developed stereotype, the latter could only be referred to as a "ketczerisscher konig" (heretic king), "venenosus draco" (poisonous snake), "venenosus hereticus" (venomous heretic), or "occupator regni Bohemie" (occupier of the Kingdom of Bohemia) etc.[37] Among the king's adamant critics was, e.g., the city preacher from Wrocław, Nikolaus Tempelfeld (d. 1474), a Silesian educated at the University of Cracow and even its chancellor.[38] In his sermons and treatises he was decidedly critical of King George, claiming that a heretic cannot be considered a king of Catholics. He wrote in one of the treatises that "such a coronation of an usurper is as if a crown were put on a tree or stone [...] or if a horse, ox or donkey were crowned, no-one with any sense would ever recognize them as a king or lord."[39]

---

36 *Catalogus abbatum Saganensium*, Scriptores rerum Silesiacarum 1, ed. Gustav Adolf Stenzel (Breslau, 1835), 173–426, at 285.

37 Wojciech Mrozowicz, "Jak hrabiowie kłodzcy, potomkowie króla Jerzego z Podiebradów, zostali książętami śląskimi" [How the counts of Kłodzko, the descendant of King George of Poděbrady, became Silesian princes], in: *Kultura Ziemi Kłodzkiej. Tradycje i współczesność*, ed. Edward Białek, Wojciech Browarny, Małgorzata Ruchniewicz. Orbis Linguarum – Wydanie Specjalne 116 (Wrocław, 2016), 36–51, at 36; Halina Manikowska, "Świadomość regionalna na Śląsku w późnym średniowieczu" [Regional consciousness in Silesia during the late Middle Ages], in *Państwo, naród, stany w świadomości wieków średnich. Pamięci Benedykta Zientary*, ed. Aleksander Gieysztor and Sławomir Gawlas (Warszawa, 1990), 253–267, at 263.

38 Jan Drabina, "Mikołaj Tempelfeld z Brzegu" [Nikolaus Tempelfeld of Brzeg], *Colloquium Salutis. Wrocławskie Studia Teologiczne* 2 (1970), 83–102; Martin Čapský, *Město pod vládou kazatelů. Charismatičtí náboženští vůdci ve střetu s městskou radou v pozdně středověkých českých korunních zemích* [City under preachers. Charismatic religious leaders clash with the city council in the lands of the Bohemian Crown in the late Middle Ages] (Každodenní život, 63, Prague, 2015), 89–91, 101–103.

39 "Tractatus Magistri Nicolai Tympelfelt doctoris theologiae Universitatis Kracoviensis et Canonici Wratislaviensis contra Georgium Podibrat assertum regem Bohemiae," in *Das Königthum Georg's von Poděbrad. Ein Beitrag zur Geschichte der Entwickelung des Staates gegenüber der kathollschen Kirche* (Leipzig, 1861), 372–388, at 377: "si ligno vel lapidi supponeretur haec corona nihil sibi conferret dignitatis [...] sic et si equus, bos vel asinus esset coronatus a nullo penitus sanae mentis pro rege vel domino foret cognescendus"; see also: Drabina, *Mikołaj Tempelfeld*, 92.

A curate of the collegiate church in Głogów and the author of the *Głogów Annals*, Kaspar Borgeni (d. before 1495),[40] speaks about King George of Poděbrad in the same vein. The chronicler also transfers his negative feelings onto the much criticized king's descendants – the dukes of Ziębice and the counts of Kłodzko, Henry I the Elder and his three sons, George, Henry and Albrecht, who in 1488 married three daughters of the duke of Żagań and Głogów, Jan II the Mad.[41] Kaspar Borgeni also criticises the Bohemians themselves, who destroyed and desecrated holy Christian symbols during the wars in Silesia and thus behaved like heretics.[42] Johannes Froben (d. 1510), the author of the *Annales Namslavienses* written on the eve of the modern period, also does not conceal his negative opinion of King George of Poděbrad and the heretical Bohemians.[43]

A wholly new phenomenon may be observed in the attitude of Silesian historiography towards the Bohemians in the transition from the Middle Ages to modern times – a century and a half of the functioning of Silesia within the Bohemian Crown finally began to bear fruit. A fundamental change in the pattern of presenting the earlier history of the land on the river Oder is seen in some historiographic works. Admittedly, references to the Polish beginnings of the history of Silesia known from earlier historiographic works may still be encountered, such as in the *Shortened Silesian Chronicle*, whose anonymous author, undoubtedly of Polish origin, laments that Silesia "a dominis naturalibus ad exteros devolvitur, [...] filii quoque Polonici regni eiecti sunt foras, regnant pro eis exterae gentes et nationes" (from natural lords passed to the foreigners [...], the sons of the Polish Kingdom were thrown out and in their place foreign peoples and nations rule).[44]

However, a wholly new perspective emerges as seen in the *Bohemian Chronicle* by Benedikt Johnsdorff, a Canon Regular from the Monastery on the Sand in Wrocław. To explain the historical and political context in which his monastery functioned, he decided to present its history in the context of the

---

40   *Annales Glogovienses bis z. J. 1493. Nebst urkundlichen Beilagen*, ed. Hermann Markgraf, Scriptores rerum Silesiacarum, 10, (Breslau, 1877); *Rocznik głogowski do roku 1493 (Annales Glogovienses bis z. J. 1493)*, trans. and ed. Wojciech Mrozowicz (Głogów, 2013), 61, 73, 79.
41   Ibid., 125–127.
42   Ibid., 13, 130.
43   The work has not yet been published. About it, see: Roland Czarnecki, *Kronika Namysłowa autorstwa Johannesa Frobena jako utwór dziejopisarstwa miejskiego* [The chronicle of Namysłów by Johannes Froben as a work of urban historiography] (Warsaw, 2015). About the opinion on the Bohemian people, see: ibid., 158–161, 164.
44   *Kronika szląska skrócona (Cronica Silesiae abbreviata)*, ed. Aleksander Semkowicz, MPH 3 (Lviv, 1878), 728–729. This motif had already appeared earlier in *Kronika książąt*, 518: "terra Wratislaviensis et ducatus a dominis naturalibus sic ad exteros devolvitur et perdita est libertas principum Polonorum".

history of Bohemia from its legendary beginnings.⁴⁵ In his view Silesia and Bohemia had always been one political body. Another work of annalistic character from the same period, known in the Silesian manuscript tradition as the *Historia Bohemica, Polonica et Silesiaca*,⁴⁶ presents a similar view. The work probably originally focused just on the history of Bohemia and only later were local themes added in Silesia. In this way it presents the idea of a common history of Silesia and Bohemia since the dawn of time. It is interesting that the annals show the legendary eponym of the Poles, Lech, as the founder of Silesian Legnica. This is a symbolic parting with the stereotype of Slavic solidarity as mentioned above.

At the same time, in the late Middle Ages, the view on Poland changed. Following the period of fragmentation of the country into provinces, Poland rebuilt its statehood during the 14th century, albeit without Silesia, thus becoming one of the latter's neighbors. A new stereotype appeared in the historiography of the region – a Polish troublemaker making life miserable for the Silesians. Kaspar Borgeni, the aforementioned chronicler from Głogów, consistently adopted an anti-Polish attitude in his annals, emphasizing it with corresponding rhetoric. Poles are consistently presented as invaders, sometimes

---

45   First part: *Česká kronika Benedikta Johnsdorfa* [The Bohemian chronicle of Benedikt Johnsdorf], ed. Jaromír Mikulka (Ostrava, 1959); second part: *Die böhmische Chronik des Benedict Johnsdorf*, ed. Franz Wachter, Scriptores rerum Silesiacarum 12, (Breslau, 1883), XIX–XX, 109–124. See also: Wojciech Mrozowicz, "Jonsdorff, Benedikt," in *The Encyclopedia of the Medieval*, 945; Blanka Zilynská, "Die Böhmische Chronik Benedikt Johnsdorfs über die Böhmische Krone im Rahmen der Kronländer," in *Geschichte – Erinnerung–Selbstidentifikation.DieschriftlicheKulturindenLänderndrBöhmischenKroneim 14.–18. Jahrhundert*, ed. Lenka Bobková and Jan Zdichynec, (Prague, 2011), 82–108.

46   For a partial edition of this text, see: *Chronica Bohemorum ab initio gentis ad annum 1438*, Monumenta historica Bohemiae, ed. Gelasius Dobner, 3 (Pragae, 1774), 43–59. In this edition the manuscript of the University Library in Wrocław (call number IV F 104, fol. 2ʳ–10ᵛ) was not considered, in which the text of the *Historia Bohemica, Polonica et Silesiaca* is more extensive. On this work see: Wojciech Mrozowicz, "Die *Acta quedam notatu digna* im Lichte einer neuentdeckten Handschrift. Plädoyer für die Neuausgabe des Werkes," in *Editionswissenschaftliche Kolloquien 2003/2004. Historiographie, Briefe und Korrespondenzen. Editorische Methoden*, ed. Matthias Thumser, Janusz Tandecki and Antje Thumser, Publikationen des deutsch-polnischen Gesprächskreises für Quelleneditionen, 3 (Toruń, 2005), 85–98, at 96; Marie Bláhová, "Společné dějiny? Slezská redakce anonymní 'České kroniky' 15. století" [Common history? Silesian version of the anonymous 'Bohemian chronicle'], in: *Slezsko – země Koruny české. Historie a kultura 1300–1740*, ed. Helena Dáňová, Jan Klípa, and Lenka Stolárová (Prague, 2008), 233–243; eadem, "Vliv české středověké historiografie na historickou kulturu Slezska v pozdním středověku" [Influence of Czech medieval historiography on Silesian historical culture in the late Middle Ages], in: *Korzenie wielokulturowości Śląska ze szczególnym uwzględnieniem Śląska Górnego*, ed. Antoni Barciak (Katowice-Zabrze, 2009), 54–66.

described with such epithets as "impiissimi" (ultimately godless), acting in a perfidious, cruel and avaricious way.[47] The descriptions of their forays always end with words such as "multa damna fecerunt" (they caused a lot of damage) or "ecclesias spoliaverunt" (they plundered churches).[48] Such conduct by the Poles in war was always condemned by Kaspar Borgeni. The Bohemian king, Vladislaus II, who came from the Polish Jagiellonian dynasty, is the occupier of the Kingdom of Bohemia ("occupator regni Bohemiae" – referred to in the same manner as king Georg of Poděbrad) or an *intrusus* (interloper).[49] The annalist notes with satisfaction the loses which Casimir IV Jagiellon suffered at the battle of Chojnice in September 1454 and in other armed clashes.[50] When in 1474 Vladislaus II, accompanied by his father Casimir IV Jagiellon, invades Silesia, it was Satan who inspired them: "Intravitque Sathan in regem Poloniae, scilicet Kazimirum et in Wladislaum, [...] qui intraverunt Slesiam et multa et irrecomparabilia damna fecerunt" (Satan got into the Polish king, Casimir and Vladislaus, who invaded Silesia and caused a lot of irreperable damage), while Matthias Corvinus was "miseratus de simplicitate regis Polonie et filii sui" (surprised with the stupidity of the Polish king and his son).[51]

Borgeni's anti-Polish attitude was intensified by yet another aspect of the politics practiced by the Jagiellons, who assumed power in the Duchy of Głogów in 1491. The first of them, the king's son, Jan Olbracht, nominated as his governor Jan Karnkowski – a notoriously litigious man and tax oppressor. The annalist refers to him with a Polish word *pan* (his lordship), the only Polish word featured in the annals written in Latin and German.[52] The use of the word is clearly ironic. Also, Johannes Froben's *Annales Namslavienses* (mentioned above) feature negative opinions about Poles.[53]

During the passage from the Middle Ages to modern times, the ethnic situation in Silesia was characterized in a different vein by a German from Brzeg, Barthel Stein (d. ca. 1521–1523). In his description of the region he claims that the whole land was divided into two parts, one inhabited by immigrant Germans and the other by Poles, who had lived in Silesia forever. The border between the two was the Oder river.[54] Stein wrote about both in the following way:

47   *Annales Glogovienses*, e.g., 31, 32.
48   Ibid., e.g., 31, 42.
49   Ibid., 31.
50   Ibid., 17–18.
51   Ibid., 17.
52   Ibid., 64.
53   Czarnecki, *Kronika Namysłowa*, 161–164.
54   Bartholomeus Stenus, *Descripcio tocius Silesie et civitatis regie Vratislaviensis* / Barthel Steins *Beschreibung von Schlesien und seiner Hauptstadt Breslau*, ed. Hermann Markgraf, Scriptores rerum Silesiacarum 17 (Breslau, 1902), 10. See also: Anna Skowrońska, "Z szesnastowiecznych polemik o polskość Śląska" [From sixteenth-century polemics about

There is a huge difference between the two peoples. One [the Poles] is a rural people, austere, with no crafts and no talents; they live in villages and hamlets in shoddy huts made from wood and clay patched together; rarely do they live in walled towns. Our people [the Germans] on the contrary, as if civilization came from the West, they live decently in a more developed way; they are more talented; they live in fortified towns; their houses are usually built from fired bricks. They are better at establishing trade relations and they know about commerce, and thanks to this they have expanded their towns and embellished them. Our people, who speak the German language and own half of the lands, came and took the land or came gradually to make profit from trading with the neighbors, who had plenty of expensive furs, hides, cattle, wax, honey, tar and lead, [...] especially since they were invited by the dukes.[55]

Presenting the ethnic situation in Silesia, Barthel Stein was probably inspired by Aeneas Silvius Piccolomini's *Historia Bohemica*. In his views, reflecting German national identity, Stein undoubtedly is referring to the earlier stereotypes, while in his – independently written it seems – characterisation of the situation in the lands on the Oder before the arrival of the Germans, he departs to an extent from the Cistercian stereotype known from earlier works.[56] What seems important is that he emphasizes the assets of Silesia before the arrival of the Germans and recognizes the fact that they came to Silesia at the invitation of local dukes.

Polishness of Silesia], *Śląski Kwartalnik Historyczny Sobótka* 10/3 (1955), 433–445, at 435–436; Matthias Weber, "Zur Konzeption protonationaler Geschichtsbilder. Pommern und Schlesien in geschichtlichen Darstellungen des 16. Jahrhunderts," *Die Konstruktion der Vergangenheit. Geschichtsdenken, Traditionsbildung und Selbstdarstellung im frühneuzeitlichen Ostmitteleuropa*, ed. Joachim Bahlcke and Arno Strohmeyer, Zeitschrift für Historische Forschung. Beiheft 29, (Berlin, 2002), 55–79, at 63–65.

55 Stenus, *Descripcio tocius Silesie*, 8, 10: "Videas maximam utriusque populi differenciam, ut hii [Poloni] agrestes, rudes, nullius industrie, nullius ingenii, habeant in pagis ac vicis tuguria ligno lutoque sine arte compacta, raras menibus incinctas urbes; nostri [Germani] contra, tanquam ab occasu serpat humanitas, culciores vita, moribus industrii, prompciores ingenio, munitas habitant urbes, edificia plurimum coctili laterculo structa; comerciorum periciores et mercature gnari, quo civitates suas simul auxerunt, simul ornaverunt. Gentem ergo nostram, quam lingwa diximus uti Teutona, et que hujus terre dimidium tenet, advenam credimus et hujus partis occupatorem, vel que paulatim huc confluxerit, ut que lucrum de finitimorum commerciis fuerit secuta, unde pretiose pelles, boum coria, denique pecorum, cere, mellis, sepi, plumbi vis ingens. Hac re plures in dies illecti sedes hic positas excoluerunt: invitantibus eciam ultro principibus." Cf. Bartłomiej Stein, "Zwięzły opis ziemi śląskiej" [A brief description of the Silesian Land], trans. Franciszek Ilków-Gołąb, *Rocznik Teologiczny Śląska Opolskiego* 1 (1968), 11–60, at 29.

56 Skowrońska, *Z szesnastowiecznych polemik*, 435.

I would like to end this short review of medieval Silesian historiography and its use of various stereotypes with a reference to the work published by Wilhelm Wattenbach together with the *Versus Lubenses* mentioned here.[57] This rhyming piece survives in only one manuscript from Lubiąż, known as the diary of Johannes Bartpha (of Bardejov, d. after 1480), featuring an interesting collection of historiographic texts connected with Silesia and especially Lubiąż. The publisher entitled it *De provinciis Germanie*. The characterizing of individual German lands begins with a poem about Swabia: "Swevia promissa percepto munere frangit" (Swabia breaks promises when it is bribed).[58] The work from Johannes Bartpha's diary is one of the rhymes presenting the characteristics of various nations, which were popular not just in the Middle Ages. They were important sources for the stereotypes that gave form to popular images of individual nations.[59] The rhyme from Lubiąż is probably a local adaptation of a more widely-known work.[60] As a Hungarian who had arrived to Silesia, Johannes Bartpha wrote that his adopted homeland, which in accordance with the custom of that time he called Poland, fosters people from various parts of the world ("Diversi generis homines Polonia nutrit"). He presents a view of Silesia and Silesians that is so very different from what historiographic sources of the time offered.[61]

Translated by Bartłomiej Madejski

---

57 See above, note 16.

58 *Monumenta Lubensia*, 33–34: "Swevia promissa percepto munere frangit". Cf. Wojciech Mrozowicz, "Sachsen im Bewußtsein der Schlesier im Mittelalter", in *Niedersachsen – Niederschlesien. Der Weg beider in die Geschichte*, ed. Wojciech Mrozowicz and Leszek Zygner (Göttingen-Wrocław, 2005), 83–94; Sławomir Gawlas, "Marność świata i narodowe stereotypy. Uwagi o wielokulturowości na Śląsku w XV wieku" [Vanity of the world and national stereotypes. Remarks on multiculturalism in Silesia in the 15th century], in: *Korzenie wielokulturowości*, 29–53, at 49.

59 See, e.g.: Stanisław Kot, "Old international insults and praises," *Harvard Slavic Studies* 2 (1954), 181–209; id., "Nationum Proprietates," *Oxford Slavonic Papers* 6 (1955): 1–43, and 7 (1957), 99–117.

60 Cf. [Franz Joseph] M[one], "Städte- und Völkerspiegel", *Anzeiger für Kunde der deutschen Vorzeit* 7 (1838), 507–508; Wilhelm Wackernagel, "Die Spottnamen der Völker", *Zeitschrift für deutsches Alterthum* 6 (1848): 254–261, at 259.

61 On the other hand Gawlas, *Marność świata*, 48.

CHAPTER 15

Prussia I: '... *und das her konng mochte werdin czu Polan, und nicht von cristinlicher libe* ...' Historians within the Teutonic Order (Ordensgeschichtsschreibung) in Prussia in the Middle Ages with Regard to Poland

Grischa Vercamer

The historiography in Prussia up to the 16th century has repeatedly been the subject of German and Polish research in recent decades.[1] Academics like Udo Arnold, Hartmut Boockmann, Odilo Engels, Edith Feistner, Krzysztof Kwiatkowski, Arno Mentzel-Reuters, Gisela Vollmann-Profe, and Jarosław Wenta have published on the topic.[2] However, none of these works has

---

1 The research for that article has been supported by the National Science Centre, Poland, under Polonez fellowship reg. no 2016/21/P/HS3/04107, funded by the European Union's Horizon 2020 research and innovation programme under the Marie Skłodowska-Curie grant agreement No 665778.
    As to the quote in the title: The continuator of the chronicler Johannes Posilge emphasised that Jagiello agreed to be baptized because he only wanted to become king. – *Forts. Posilge* a. 1409, SRP 3, S. 306. The following abbreviations will be used in the text: SRP = Scriptores rerum Prussicarum. Die Geschichtsquellen der preußischen Vorzeit bis zum Untergange der Ordensherrschaft, 5 Bde. (1–5), ed. Theodor Hirsch (Leipzig 1861–74, repr. Frankfurt 1965); ZfO = Zeitschrift für Ostmitteleuropaforschung.
2 There are some research surveys on the topic: Arno Mentzel-Reuters, "Deutschordenshistoriographie," in *Handbuch Chroniken des Mittelalters*, ed. Gerhard Wolf and Norbert H. Ott (Berlin-Boston: De Gruyter, 2016), 328–330; Udo Arnold, "Geschichtsschreibung im Preussenland bis zum Ausgang des 16. Jahrhunderts," *Jahrbuch für die Geschichte Mittel- und Ostdeutschlands* 19 (1970), 74–126; Udo Arnold, *Studien zur preußischen Historiographie des 16. Jahrhunderts* (Bonn, 1967); Hartmut Boockmann, "Geschichtsschreibung des Deutschen Ordens. Gattungsfragen und Gebrauchssituationen," in *Geschichtsschreibung und Geschichtsbewußtsein im Spätmittelalter*, ed. Hans Patze, Sigmaringen, 1987, 447–469; Edith Feistner, Michael Neecke, Gisela Vollmann-Profe, *Krieg im Visier. Bibelepik und Chronistik im Deutschen Orden als Modell korporativer Identitätsbildung* (Tübingen, 2007); Jarosław Wenta, *Studien über die Ordensgeschichtsschreibung am Beispiel Preussens* (Toruń, 2000), Ernst Opgenoorth, "Stationen der Geschichtsschreibung des Preußenlandes von Peter von Dusburg bis zu Hartmut Boockmann," in *75 Jahre Historische Kommission für Ost- und Westpreußische Landesforschung*, ed. Bernhart Jähnig (Lüneburg, 1999), 114–137; Krzysztof Kwiatkowski, "Die 'Eroberung Preußens' durch den Deutschen Orden – ihr Bild und ihre Wahrnehmung in

addressed the perception of Poland within the Prussian historiography.[3] That makes the task easier, because one can both build on an established research field, yet by pursuing this focused interest, some new territory will be explored.

A characteristic of this particular historiography is that the term *Ordensgeschichtschreibung* (i.e. Historiography of the Teutonic Order) in its function[4] as the 'official' historiography of the Order can only be applied to the first chronicles in the 14th and early 15th centuries. The later works would be better categorized as 'Landeschroniken' ('regional chronicles'), since the Order as sovereign was no longer the only focus of consideration. Adam Szweda addresses the later 'Landeschroniken' in this volume, so the task of this contribution will be the reflection on Poland and its people in the earlier period until around 1400. After reviewing the earlier chronicles (see table 1) I have selected three chronicles as being appropriate for the task at hand. These are the chronicles of Peter of Dusburg (1326), Wigand of Marburg (1394) and Johann of Posilge (until 1405, with continuation to 1419).

Before taking a closer look at these three chronicles, I would like to offer a brief methodological introduction as to how I approach the sources in this article: There are, of course, various hermeneutic methods for examining the view of the 'other'. Andrzej F. Grabski, for example, in his work 'Poland in the opinion of Western Europe in the 14th/15th centuries' ("Polska w opiniach Europy Zachodniej XIV–XV") chose on the one hand a group-specific perspective (how did merchants and craftsmen, or intellectuals and writers, or diplomats and travelers, or knights, or clergy view Poland?) and on the other hand a discourse-specific perspective (the perception of the Polish-Lithuanian Union, the battle of Tannenberg-Grunwald, the Polish conflicts with the Teutonic

---

    der Literatur des Deutschen Ordens im 14. Jahrhundert," in Kryžiaus karų epocha Baltujos regionu tautų istorinėje sąmonėje. Mokslinių straipsnių rinkinys, eds. Rita R. Trimonienė and Robertas Jurgaitis (Saulės, 2007), 131–168, looks similarly at the 'constructed' space in Dusburg's text as a poetic and rhetorical dimension just as I did it with the imagination of 'time' within the text of Dusburg: Grischa Vercamer, "Zeit in Peters von Dusburg 'Chronica Terrae Prussiae' (1326). Chronologische Ordnung oder Mittel zum Zweck?," *Zapiski historyczne* 76, 4 (2011), 7–25.

3 Only seldomly do we find surveys on special historical events like battles or peace treaties and their depiction in the Prussian historiography: Gisela Vollmann-Profe, "Vom historiographischen Umgang mit Niederlagen: die Schlacht von Tannenberg in preußischen Chroniken des 15. Jahrhunderts," in *Vom vielfachen Schriftsinn im Mittelalter: Festschrift für Dietrich Schmidtke*, eds. Freimut Löser and Ralf G. Päsler (Hamburg, 2005), 607–622; Slawomir Zonenberg, "The Second Peace of Torun of 19 October 1466 in the Polish, Prussian and Teutonic historiography of the 15th–16th centuries," *Zapiski historyczne* 81,4 (2016), 47–68.

4 Franz-Josef Schmale, *Funktionen und Formen Mittelalterlicher Geschichtsschreibung*, (Darmstadt, 1985); Boockmann, "Geschichtschreibung," 448; Arno Mentzel-Reuters, "Deutschordenshistoriographie," 301–308.

TABLE 15.1   Prussian Chronicles and Annales mainly 13th/14th cen.

Narratio de primordiis ordinis Theutonici (anonym)	around 1204–1250; Reporting period: 1190–1199
Hartmann of Heldrung, Bericht über die Vereinigung des Schwertbrüderordens mit dem Deutschen Orden	1250–1282; 1209–1252
Heinrich of Lettland, Chronicon Livoniae	1208–1259; Reporting period: 1186–1227
Livländische Reimchronik (anonym)	ca. 1300; Reporting period: 1180–1290
B. Hoeneke, Jüngere livländische Reimchronik	1346/48; Reporting period: 1315–1348
Peter of Dusburg, Chronica Terrae Prussiae	1326; Reporting period: 1190–1326
Nikolaus of Jeroschin	1331–1341; Reporting period: 1190–1331
Epitome gestorum Prussiae	1338–1352; Reporting period: World chronicle-1352
Hermann of Wartberge, Chronicon Livoniae	1378–1380; Reporting period: 1186–1378
Ältere Hochmeisterchronik (anonym)	1433–1440; Reporting period: 1190–1433
Wigand of Marburg, Preussische Reimchronik	1393–94; Reporting period: 1294–1394
Johann of Posilge, Chronike des Landes Prussin	1360–1415; Reporting period: um 1200–1419
Annales Thorunenses (Franciscan)	throughout; Reporting period: 941–1410, 1428–1540
Fontes Olivenses; Chronica Olivensis, Annales Olivenses	1201–1500; Reporting period: 1201–1500

Knights[5] within the great church councils of the 15th century, the danger of the Turks, etc.). Jarochna Dąbrowska (she has a contribution in this volume as well) chose a different approach by addressing in her dissertation "Stereotypes

---

5   Grabski, Andrzej Feliks, *Polska w opiniach Europy zachodniej XIV–XV w.* [Poland in the opinion of Western Europe 14th–15th century], Warszawa 1968. He describes well (e.g., 185–193) how the Prussian crusader looked at Lithuania as a still pagan country even after 1385 and how the European knighthood loved the annual events in Königsberg and the crusades into Lithuania.

and their linguistic expression in the Polish image of the German press" (1999), modern topic stereotypes ('patriotism', 'strict Catholicism', 'rebelliousness etc.), which are considered in Germany as typical for Poles and Poland.

For the Middle Ages, such national stereotypes are more difficult to define and to verify, but here too research efforts have been made especially for the Franco-German area. Jean-Marie Moeglin published in 2010 a history of French and German relations in the Late Middle Ages[6] and wrote one chapter on the perception of the 'other' ("Die Sicht des anderen und die Beziehung zum anderen"), which is also quite instructive for the history of the German-Polish relationship. He shows first of all that the French and Germans demonstrated a long-lasting mutual indifference towards the neighbor caused by a lack of language skills. The opposite was the case in the French relationship with England (which was stronger and more intensive) given that the noble class of England spoke French and thus there was a common basis for communication.[7] True enough, returning to the French-German case, certain social groups, such as merchants, maintained steady contacts with the neighbor, but in their language skills they were limited to their specific domains (i.e. economic interests).[8] Furthermore, many chroniclers assumed (probably correctly) that detailed information about the neighbor would bore their readers. Georg Jostkleigrewe speaks of the authors' 'covered knowledge' ('verdeckte Kenntnis') about their national neighbor, which pops up only now and again in their texts. Obviously, they avoided providing further information in order not to bore the readers or to compromise the neighbor's society.[9]

Moeglin testifies that at least major events in the neighbor's country were of some interest and classifies them in three key areas: (1) enthronement, (2) war, marriage, international alliances, (3) regional news from the border areas. Very few, mostly clichéd, national stereotypes were already noticeable in the high medieval chronicles of France, for example, the *superbia* of the Germans was apparently already a commonplace in the French chronicle.[10] But real national confrontations can only be found at the end of the Middle Ages by the 15th/16th centuries (Jakob of Wimpfeling with his *Germania 1501* is such an example).

An old wise insight is that the view of the 'other' always locates the 'own' as well.[11] However, especially when the research focus lies on the historical

---

6   Jean-Marie Moeglin, *Deutsch-Französische Geschichte. 1214 bis 1500* (Darmstadt, 2010).
7   Id., *Deutsch-Französische Geschichte*, 283.
8   Id., *Deutsch-Französische Geschichte*, 287.
9   Jostkleigrewe, *Das Bild des Anderen*, 84–104.
10 Moeglin, *Deutsch-Französische Geschichte*, 294.
11 Jostkleigrewe, *Das Bild des Anderen*, 36, Scior, *Das Eigene und das Fremde*, 9.

view from outside of one nation / country / people, the 'other' is in most of the cases for the medieval studies of German-Polish affairs unfortunately construed in an all-encompassing and generally superficial manner.[12] In fact, one sometimes finds statements by Polish chroniclers such as: the Germans are 'brave and arrogant' (as in the French cases cited above). It reminds one on the famous phrase of John of Salisbury: "Quis Teutonicos constituit iudices nationum" ('Who set up the Germans as judges over the peoples of the earth?').[13] But most of the time one detects in the medieval historiographical material assessments of individuals (e.g. kings, bishops) or social groups (e.g. counsellors, knights, merchants etc.) or regions (e.g., Silesia) – and not so much the whole nation. The perceptions of these subcategories, of course, strongly influence the over-all perception of the 'other's nation'. If nowadays a representative of a nation, e.g. the German President or the German Chancellor, visits another nation, e.g. Poland, his/her actions in the visiting country are at least subconsciously compared to existing cliché images of 'Germans' – sometimes shaping or modifying the image in a positive or negative way. Surely, this was already true as well for medieval representatives of the other 'nation'. For instance, when the Polish King Casimir III in 1365 visited the main castle of the Teutonic Order, the Marienburg, and stayed there with his entourage for three days, the members of the Order in the castle certainly gained a fuller impression of the king, which then influenced their over-all image of 'Poland'. Therefore, for the discourse 'Otherness'-'Self' – especially if we use the genre of historiographical texts – we should necessarily consider the analytical distinctions: nation / people – region, specific groups – individuals, otherwise we get a rather distorted image. What does it mean, for instance, for the general 'Poland picture' in the late Middle Ages, when in most Prussia chronicles the Polish king Casimir III is viewed positively, while his later successor, king Władysław-Jagiello, is viewed rather negatively?

Finally, it goes without saying that the 'Sitz im Leben' (Hermann Gunkel) of a given text, the author and the addressees must all be taken into account. Every particular text-passage in question must be assessed in its context.[14]

---

12 This is in slight contrast to František Graus, *Die Nationenbildung der Westslawen im Mittelalter* (Sigmaringen, 1980), 27, who opines that the 'We'-group does not necessarily have to be taken as 'national'.

13 *The Letters of John of Salisbury*, ed. W.J. Millor and H.E. Butler, rev. by C.N.L. Brooke, 1 (London, 1955; repr. Oxford, 1986), no. 124, 206. Cf. Horst Fuhrmann, "'Quis Teutonicos constituit iudices nationum?' The Trouble with Henry" *Speculum* 69 (1994), 344–358.

14 Krzyżaniakowa, Jadwiga, "Poglądy polskich kronikarzy średniowiecznych na Niemcy i stosunki polsko-niemieckie [Views of Polish medieval chroniclers on Germany and Polish-German relations]," in *Wokół stereotypów Niemców i Polaków*, ed. Wojciech

With that methodological set-up in mind, we can access the three texts mentioned above.

1 Peter of Dusburg[15]

Peter of Dusburg refers to himself in the dedicatory letter he wrote to the Grand Master Werner von Orseln as *frater Petrus de Dusburgk eiusdem sacre professionis sacerdos* ('Peter of Dusburg a priest by holy profession'). He probably came from Doesburg / Ijssel in today's Netherlands (east of Arnhem)[16] – definitely he was not born in Prussia. Unfortunately, no exact life data can be pinpointed for him. The only constant is the year 1326, in which he wrote the chronicle.[17] Was he later on in Prussia a Sambian canon in Königsberg (today Kaliningrad), as the recent research suggests, or rather based in Marienburg (today's Malbork)?[18] It is at least very probable that he spent a longer time in Königsberg.[19] On the other hand, it must be noted that the chronicler enjoyed

---

Wrzesiński (Wrocław, 1993) 15–72 (repr. *Nie ma historii bez człowieka. Studia z dziejów średniowiecza*, ed. IH UAM (Wrocław, 2010), 241–291), 243, emphasizes this.

15   Four different editions were taken into account for this article: *Chronicon terrae Prussiae von Peter von Dusburg*, ed. Max Toeppen. Scriptores rerum Prussicarum 1, Leipzig, 1861, 21–219; Peter von Dusburg, *Chronik des Preussenlandes*, ed. Klaus Scholz and Dieter Wojtecki, FSGA 25 (Darmstadt, 1984); Piotr z Dusburga, *Kronika ziemi pruskiej*, eds. Sławomir Wyszomirski and Jarosław Wenta (Toruń, 2004); Petrus de Dusburgk, *Chronica Terrae Prussiae*, eds. Jarosław Wenta and Sławomir Wyszomirski, MPH NS XIII (Krakow, 2007).

16   The old research opinion that favors 'Duisburg/Rhein' is rather not probable, because the Order had no possessions in that area. Cf. Scholz/Wojtecki, "Einleitung," in *Petri de Dusburg, Chronica Terre Prussie*, 7; rather Duisburg in the area of Utrecht, cf. Wenta, "Introduction," in *Kronika ziemi pruskiej*, XVI–XVII. The Teutonic Order had since 1286/87 some estate there, which was slowly developed and eventually became the bailiwick Utrecht.

17   Wenta, in *Kronika ziemi pruskiej*, XVII–XVIII, saw an official Petrus (1318), later dean (1331), later 'custos' (1334) and eventually again official (as he appears in the charters – this person would have spent 38 years (since 1356 we cannot identify him anymore) in the Sambian chapter. The name Petrus was common and there should be some caution in identifying our chronicler with all these Peters. The identification of Peter with the author of the *Epitome* (ibid.) seems to make more sense.

18   Jarosław Wenta, *Studien über die Ordensgeschichtsschreibung am Beispiel Preußen* (Toruń, 2000), 210. – There is a canon with the same name who can be traced in Marienburg to 1313.

19   The detailed description of the convent in Königsberg and of the Prussian family Candein (in the region of Königsberg) supports the idea of Königsberg. There is a small problem, up until now not recognised by research: the otherwise well-documented conflict between the Sambian bishop and the Order beginning in 1321 is not mentioned within the

the confidence of the Grand Master and had access to the religious archives at the Marienburg.[20] It should be added that he was a well-educated clergyman[21] and not, as the older research had assumed because of his writing style, only a cleric with a rudimentary education. The chronicle's text comprises 250 pages, and is divided into four books.[22] The first book tells about the beginnings of the Order in the Holy Land, the second book about the arrival in Prussia, and the third book about the battles with the Prussian tribes (the Pomeranians and the Lithuanians) up to the time of the author. The fourth, rather short, book *de incidentibus* ('about events') was written to give a set of data (in an annalistic style) within a wider framework of world-history in order to compensate for the limited geographic range of the first three books, which were confined to the Holy Land and Prussia/Lithuania.[23] As it is, the third book, about the conquest of Prussia, is the most comprehensive as well as the most important part of the complete work. The author was in this part of his work able to report from his own experience and also from direct testimonies, as he himself makes clear in the beginning of the book.[24] In general, the region of Prussia in the 13th century (i.e. the conquest of Prussia by the Teutonic Order) is the center of interest. The addressees are to be found both outside of Prussia (the Curia in Rome) and inside of Prussia (the Teutonic knights and friars). It is essential to remember the knight friars as being readers – although the text is in Latin, surely, the Order's priests were able to translate or pick out individual examples. The chronicle was written very anecdotally, so it was suitable for being used in this way.[25]

---

chronicle. For the conflict cf. Radosław Biskup, *Das Domkapitel von Samland (1285–1525)* (Toruń, 2007), 197 et seq.

20 He cited the text of the Kruschwitzer contract (1230) directly (*Chronicon terrae Prussiae* II, 5, 36–37); cf. as well Marzena Pollakówna, *Kronika Piotra z Dusburga* (Wrocław, 1968), 203–207. Would he possess such confidence and access as a canon from Königsberg who was involved in the conflict with the Order? This issue cannot be discussed here.

21 Stefan Kwiatkowski, "Scotistische Einflüsse in der Chronik von Peter Dusburg," in *Die Geschichtsschreibung in Mitteleuropa*, ed. Jarosław Wenta (Toruń, 1999), 135–7, at 136; Jarosław Wenta, "Peter von Dusburg," in *Verfasserlexikon* 11 (2004), col. 1188.

22 Survey on further reading: Mentzel-Reuters, "Deutschordenshistoriographie," 310–313.

23 The fourth book might be treated like a chronological grid/survey similar to those often seen in modern historiographical works. Dusburg's sources for that part are Tolomeo of Lucca and Martin of Troppau, cf. Scholz/Wojtecki, "Einleitung," in *Petri de Dusburg Chronica Terre Prussie*, 16. Wenta, "Introduction," in *Kronika ziemi pruskiej*, XXIV–XXV.

24 *Chronicon terrae Prussiae*, De modo agendi libri huius, 24: "pauca, que vidi [self-experienced], alia, que audivi ab his, qui viderunt et interfuerunt [report from eye-witnesses], cetera, que relacione veridica intellexi [old, trustworthy reports]."

25 Cf. Vercamer, "Zeit in Peters von Dusburg Chronica," 522.

By the time of the writing of the text, the conflict with the Polish king, Władysław I the Elbow-high (1306–1333), and the announced baptism of the Lithuanian Grand Duke Gediminas (1316–1341) had become very threatening factors impacting the very legitimacy of the Teutonic Order presence in Prussia. The Holy Roman Empire played hardly any role in this conflict,[26] so the Order sought instead support especially from the Curia.[27] These aspects are strongly reflected in the text of the chronicle.

Speaking of the manuscripts: All in all, only six copies of the chronicle survive and they all date from the 16th/17th centuries.[28] However, with the translation of the Dusburg text by Nicholas of Jeroschin into German, which was made between 1331–1341 and handed down from manuscripts of the 14th century, we possess a quite good point of comparison,[29] which shows us clearly that the surviving manuscripts of the Dusburgian text from the 16th/17th centuries had not changed too much from the version in the 14th century.[30]

2   Peter of Dusburg's Attitude towards Poland/the Poles

Peter describes primarily the exemplary struggle and enthusiasm of the Teutonic Knights in the 13th century as they fought against the pagans (first the Prussians and then the Lithuanians). The Poles appear in that struggle often only marginally (cf. table 2). In view of the extensive reach of his chronicle, the 25 passages are almost negligible. From that number he mostly refers to individuals (16 instances), while the people of Poland are mentioned five times and the region/social groups only four times. Judging it in terms of narratology, we can only spot four passages (of the 25 mentioned above) as being important ones – they have a high-ranking narrative status in the chronicle.

---

26   Cf. Klaus Conrad, "Werner von Orseln," in *Die Hochmeister des Deutschen Ordens 1190–1994*, ed. Udo Arnold (Marburg, 1998), 60–65; Klaus Militzer, *Die Geschichte des Deutschen Ordens* (Stuttgart, 2005), 112–113.

27   The general support of the German emperor Frederick II for the Grand Master Hermann of Salza and the Teutonic Order and especially the famous Golden Bull (1326/35) for the Order by the emperor are not mentioned at all by Peter of Dusburg, while the Papal acceptance is broadly depicted. (*Chronicon terrae Prussie* II, 6, pp. 38–39). Cf. Marcus Wüst, "Zu Entstehung und Rezeption der 'Chronik des Preußenlandes' Peters von Dusburg," in *Neue Studien zur Literatur im Deutschen Orden*, ed. Arno Mentzel-Reuters and Bernhart Jähnig, (Stuttgart, 2014), 197–210.

28   Wenta, *Studien*, 206; Scholz/Wojtecki, "Einleitung," in *Petri de Dusburg Chronica Terre Prussie*, 18 et seq.

29   Cf. http://www.handschriftencensus.de/werke/487. Wenta, *Studien*, 221–23.

30   Cf. Feistner et al., *Krieg im Visier*, 155–156.

TABLE 15.2 Peter of Dusburg and number of text-passages mentioning Poland

Peter of Dusburg	Poland – number of all text-passages[a]	People mentioned	Region/ groups mentioned	Individuals mentioned	Number of important passages
	25	5	4	16	4

a   Peter von Dusburg, *Chronik des Preussenlandes* II,1, 54; II, 2–3, pp. 56–59; II, 5, 63; II, 10, pp. 90–93; II, 11, pp. 92–95; III, 1, 96; III, 10, pp. 110–113; III, 46 and 55, pp. 158–161; III, 61, pp. 176–179; III, 166, 285; III, 167, 286–287; III, 195/96, pp. 314–315; III, 241, pp. 356–357; III, 248, pp. 362–365; III, 250, pp. 366–367; III, 258 and 262; pp. 372, 378–380; III, 277, pp. 390–391; III, 340, pp. 446–449; III, 346, pp. 452–453; III, 357, pp. 462–463; III, 361, pp. 464–467; Supplement 10, pp. 544–545; Supplement 12, pp. 546–547; Supplement 13, pp. 548–549; Supplement 17, pp. 550–551.

Looking first at these text-passages in a general way, certain tendencies of the author become clear:

1. Poland/the Poles as a country and people are not introduced specifically (as was the case with earlier chronicles from within the Holy Roman Empire) – they are presumed by the author to be a known entity for the readers. Very importantly: At no point is the reputation of the Poles in general blackened or seen in a bad way; it is always only about Polish individuals.

2. The Poles themselves are unable to defeat or even fend off the pagans from Prussia and Lithuania. The Polish dukes are helpless against the Lithuanian invasions of Polish territory. Peter's meta information: They were basically dependent on the help of the Order.

3. The Teutonic Knights fought more bravely than did the Polish troops; the latter often fled from the pagan armies. That is, of course, a form of legitimization for the presence of the Teutonic Order in Prussia.

4. Although some Polish regions are mentioned here and there in the chronicle (particularly the neighboring ones: Mazovia, Kuyavia, Dobriner county), they are not regionally specific and all of them are collectively regarded by Peter as the 'Polish' neighbors. He does not differentiate among the regions. This is interesting, because de facto there had been a lot of internal conflicts among the different Polish regions ruled by the Piasts, which Peter seems to ignore.

5. The individual Polish rulers (all Piasts) are usually mentioned only briefly and are not specially introduced – actually Peter does not differentiate in any way the Piast princes from princes of other countries like the Empire,

England or France, which he often mentions. It is crucial that the Polish princes are in principle positively perceived, such as Konrad of Mazovia, Casmir of Kujawy, Leszek the Black of Kraukau, and Bernhard II of Schweidnitz. Only the prince Bolesław II of Mazovia (1251–1313), and the king Władysław Łokietek (1260/61–1330) are rebuked for their cooperation with the pagan Lithuanians. It is striking that Peter does not use personal invectives (such as liar, coward etc.), even toward the contemporary Polish ruler, Władysław Łokietek. Rather, Peter argues factually (by looking analytically at specific deeds of the Polish king and arguing that the Polish king was not a defender of the faith, that he acted to the detriment of the Teutonic Order, etc.). In the eyes of Peter, Władysław Łokietek is undoubtedly an intriguer and an opponent of the Order: The Polish king allies himself with the Lithuanian Grand Prince Gediminas; he even uses the military support of Gediminas to invade the Kulmer country (part of Prussia). – Nevertheless, the chronicler deals with these actions of the king very factually and objectively. One might see this calm style as additional evidence that a greater circle of readers, like the Roman Curia, were the addressees of this work.

We can add a small side observation to these general points: Contrary to the previous one, it is striking that only one Piast Silesian prince (Bernhard II von Schweidnitz) is mentioned as a Prussian crusader (Preußenreisender), whereas foreign princes from the Empire, France, England appear much more frequently as crusaders supporting the Teutonic Knights. This might be read as a hint at a fundamental distance between the Polish nobility and the majority of the German-speaking Teutonic Knights, which was not even consciously intended by the author.

How does Peter narrate this general picture? How does he concretely construct his examples? We will have a brief look at this: For instance, we can take the above-mentioned bravery of the knights of the Order compared to the Poles. Already in 1228, at the very beginning of the Teutonic Knights' presence in Prussia, when Hermann von Salza had sent two knight-brothers to assess the situation in Mazovia, all of a sudden, a military conflict with the Prussians broke out. While most of the Poles fled, the brothers and their retinue remained on the battlefield until they were all seriously injured ("fugientibus Polonis in primo congressu ... fratres semivives").[31] This is the normal style of Peter directly juxtaposing the Poles and the Teutonic Knights: At the end of the 1230s the Poles were still being attacked by the Prussians and it only slowly occurs to the Prussians that now they would have to deal with really tough

---

31   Peter von Dusburg, *Chronik des Preussenlandes*, II, 5, p. 62.

fighters in the form of Teutonic Knights. There is a fine example of this: As the Prussian pagans started another invasion into Polish lands and took many Poles as hostages, they saw the Teutonic Knights from a distance and asked one Polish hostage about them. He answered:

> [...] these men were pious and brave knights in arms, who had been sent from Germany by the pope in order to fight against them, until they [the Prussians] would have subjected themselves to the Roman see. When the Prussians heard that, they laughed sneeringly and left.[32]

Obviously, in using such a narration style Peter wants to mythologize the Order. Another example: When the Lithuanian prince *Pucuwerus* was about to invade Poland with a big army, the Polish dukes, Casimir and Władysław Łokietek, pleaded with the Prussian 'Landmeister' Meinhard to help them. The Landmeister generously fulfilled their wish and assisted with a large number of Teutonic Knights. But shortly before the fight began, the two Polish dukes took flight from the battlefield ("prefati duces cum omnibus suis Polonis terga verterunt") and left the Teutonic Knights on their own. While ignoring the negative circumstances, the knights continued to fight bravely although outnumbered. They themselves had to retreat slowly; a lot of them were seriously injured by the pagan opponent.[33]

Is there a depiction of the Poles as a people or country as a whole? Unfortunately not. We have to figure that out by using individual examples. For instance, a treacherous Polish knight (named *Nineric*) came to the city of

---

32 Peter von Dusburg, *Chronik des Preussenlandes* II, 11, p. 94, the whole sequence: "In quo castro dum fratres habitarent, Prutheni intraverunt Poloniam hostiliter, et dum viderent fratres in armis sequentes eos, ammirati sunt ultra modum, unde essent et ad quod venissent. Quibus responsum fuit a quodam Polono, qui captus ab eis ducebatur, quod essent viri religiosi et strenui milites in armis, de Alemania per dominum papam missi ad bellandum contra eos, quousque duram eorum cervicem et indomitam sacrosancte Romane ecclesie subiugarent. Quo audito subridentes recesserunt." ("While the Teutonic knights lived in this castle, the Prussians invaded Poland with a hostile attitude. As they became aware of the armed brethren-knights, who followed them, they were quite puzzled about where the knights had come from and why they came. They received an answer from a Pole, whom they had captured before, that these men were pious and brave knights in arms, who had been sent from Germany by the pope in order to fight against them, until they [the Prussians] would have subjected themselves to the Roman see. When the Prussians heard that, they laughed sneeringly and left").

33 Peter von Dusburg, *Chronik des Preussenlandes* III, 248, pp. 362–364: "Quo viso [the Polish flight] fratres perterriti non habentes potenciam resistendi tante multiudini recesserunt eciam, sed non sine magno periculo suorum, quia multi frratres et alii Christifideles fuerunt graviter vulnerati, antequam honeste possent a dicto certamine declinare."

Kulmsee within the territory of the Teutonic Knights to hand this town over to *Scumand*, the leader of the pagan Jadwiger, who were lying in wait for a sign from Nineric. However, the citizens of Kulmsee discovered the betrayal and hanged the Polish traitor together with his son and servant.[34] On another occasion, the Teutonic Knights conquered the castle of Nakel in Greater Poland, where a Polish knight named Henryk had his seat and hence he constantly robbed travelers passing by the castle. When asked why he made all the raids, he replied, "Because no one has forbidden me to do so."[35] The chronicler comments, "Look at how not punishing crimes helps the instinct to sin."[36] – That might be read as open criticism directed at the Polish prince (later king) Władysław Łokietek, who was in charge.

But, interestingly enough – and this is important – Peter von Dusburg in both cases declines to use the opportunity to move from individual cases to a judgment about the nature of the Poles in general (for example, he did not say: 'This is how Poles typically behave').

We can take a closer look at the depictions of some Polish dukes: Konrad of Masovia (1187/88–1247) is described as a supporter of the Teutonic Order and is introduced as a "vir totus Deo devotus et fidei zelator".[37] Casimir of Kuyavia (1211–1267), the son of Konrad, is depicted as extraordinarily brave when fighting against the Pomeranian duke, Swatopolk, while almost all the other Polish knights had fled.[38] Leszek II the Black of Krakow (1241–48) is as well a "vir Deo devotus", who tried to gather men in Krakow in order to fight back against 800 ransacking Lithuanian warriors within the Polish territory. Only 300 Poles answered the ducal call, nonetheless Leszek rushed with them against the Lithuanian and killed all the enemy.[39]

A negative light though is cast on Bolesław II of Masovia (1253/58–1313): He negotiated a truce with the pagan Lithuanians in Płock while Casimir II of Łęczyca chased the same pagans for their robbing and plundering in Polish territories in the year 1292. As a consequence of the truce, Casimir lost 1800 Polish warriors who were ambushed by the pagans.[40] Later on, Peter points out

---

34   Peter von Dusburg, *Chronik des Preussenlandes* III, 166, p. 284.
35   Peter von Dusburg, *Chronik des Preussenlandes*, Supplement 13, p. 548: "Hic captus fuit a fratribus, et cum quererent ab eo, cur tot et tanta mala perpetrasset, respondit: 'Quia mihi nullus prohibuit aut defendit.'"
36   Ibid.: "Ecce quomodo impunitas scelerum intencionem tribuit delinquendi."
37   Peter von Dusburg, *Chronik des Preussenlandes* II, 10, p. 92.
38   Id., III, 55, p. 170: "[...] quos videntes Poloni perterriti omnes fugerunt preter quendam militem Martinum de Cruezewiez vexilliferum et ducem Casimirum."
39   Id., III, 196, p. 314.
40   Id., III, 250, p. 366.

that Bolesław continued cooperating anyway with the pagans.[41] The Teutonic Order even had to destroy one castle of Bolesław's (named Wiśnia), because the Polish duke protected pagans there.[42]

Władysław Łokietek (1260–1333) is viewed negatively as well, although Peter uses very careful arguments – the king was still ruling at the time Peter was writing. Here is an example:

> In the year 1326 Łokietek, king of the Poles, asked Gediminas, the prince of Lithuania, to whose daughter the son of Łokietek had only shortly before been married, if Gediminas could send him some Lithuanian warriors to assist him. Gediminas dispatched 1200 riders. After uniting them together with his own troops, Łokietek gave orders to invade the country of the margraves of Brandenburg close to Frankfurt and he destroyed the whole area, with more than 140 villages, along with parish churches and three monasteries [the abominations are described in detail by Peter, GV]. The army was followed by a Pole, who felt pity for all the murdered Christians. He pretended to be a friend of the pagans, and then chose the right moment and location to kill the castellan of Garten David [a Lithuanian] in public and in front of many people. David was considered to be the leader of that conflict, who did all these wicked things to the Christian faith in general and to all the Christians in particular.[43]

Peter formulates, thus, his criticism toward the Polish king very skillfully: Even a Polish nobleman was so ashamed by the policy of his own king and the alliance with the pagans that he literally committed suicide by killing the Lithuanian leader in public, just to end the murdering.

---

41   Id., III, 258/262, p. 372, p. 378.
42   Id., III, 258, p. 372.
43   Id. III, 361, pp. 464–466: "Anno Domini MCCCXXVI Loteko rex Polonie rogavit Gedeminum regem Lethowinorum, cuius filiam filius eius noviter duxerat in uxorem, ut ei aliquos armigeros de gente sua mitteret. Qui precibus eius acquiescens MCC equites destinavit ei. Hii de mandato dicti Lotekonis adiuncti populo suo armata manu hostiliter intraverunt terram marchionis de Brandenburgk circa civitatem Frankenvurdam et totam illam contractam, que continebat ultra centum et XL villas, ecclesias parochiales totidem, cenobia monachorum ordinis Cisterciensis tria [...]. Hunc exercitum quidam Polonus dolens de tanta strage Cristianorum secutus fuit simulans se amicum infidelium, et dum locus et tempus advenerat opportunum, David castellanum de Gartha et capitaneum huius belli, qui infinita mala, ut premissum est, intulit fidei et fidelibus, in conspectu plurium interfecit."

At the high point and again at the very end of the chronicle, King Łokietek is rebuked for his attack and the devastation of the 'Kulmerland' (a region within Prussia on the border to Poland) in the year 1329:

> How outrageous and incredible is this wicked deed: This king, formerly a duke, was raised not long ago by the apostolic see to be a king, in order to become an even more faithful, eager and humble defender of the holy church, the faith and the faithful. But now he is not up to this task anymore, but even fights against other defenders of the faithful.[44]

In other places the narration scheme is more or less the same: Poles are very skillfully reduced to a position of extras in assisting the Teutonic Order in its actions. While building the castle of Marienwerder on the Vistula, a big group of Polish dukes appears there: the duke of Masovia, the duke of Kuyavia, the duke of Krakow, the duke from Wrocław, the duke of Gniezno, along with Swantopolk, the duke of Pomerania, and his brother, Sambor. This most illustrious circle came to support the Teutonic Knights.[45]

3   Johann of Posilge: Chronik des landes von Pruszin

Johann, who probably studied in Prague before 1367, was born in Prussia (Posilge, today Żuławka, close to Marienburg). He was at first a priest in Deutsch-Eylau (1372–74) and then later an official in Riesenburg (as an ecclesiastical judge serving the Bishop of Pomesania, from 1376).[46] His year of death is assumed to be 1405. His chronicle was originally written in Latin prose, but survives only in a German translation (five copies have survived).[47] – some

---

44   Id., Suppl. 10, p. 544: "Ecce stupendum et exsecrabile nefas: Iste rex antea fuit dux et noviter a sede apostolica in regem institutus, ut esset sancte ecclesie, fidei et fidelium eo diligencior et fidelior et magis strenuus propugnator. Nunc autem non solum non defendit cetum fidelium, sed eos, qui defendunt, crudeliter impugnat."

45   Id. II, 10, p. 92.

46   Kurt Forstreuter, "Johann von Posilge," in *Neue Deutsche Biographie* 10 (1974), 566 [Online-Version]; URL: https://www.deutsche-biographie.de/pnd101426259.html#ndbcontent <15.9.2018>; Gisela Vollmann-Profe, "Iohannes de Posilge, Chronike des Landes von Prussin," in *The Encyclopedia of the Medieval Chronicle*, ed. Graeme Dunphy (Leiden, 2010), 922; http://www.geschichtsquellen.de/repOpus_03036.html <2018-05-10>; Bernhart Jähnig, "Innenpolitik und Verwaltung des Deutschen Ordens in Johann von Posilges Chronik des Landes Preußen," in *Vom vielfachen Schriftsinn im Mittelalter. Festschrift für Dietrich Schmidtke*, ed. Freimut Löser and Ralf G. Päsler (Hamburg, 2005), 205–236.

47   http://www.handschriftencensus.de/werke/1168 <17.5.2018>.

TABLE 15.3 Johann of Posilge and the number of text-passages mentioning Poland

Johann of Posilge	Poland – number of all text-passages[a]	People mentioned	Region/groups mentioned	Individuals mentioned	Total Number of all the *important* passages
	51	14	11	36	7

a Johann von Posilge: Chronik des Landes Preussen, pp. 85,87, 98, 101, 141–142, 144–45, 150–151, 159 (twice), 163, 166, 168, 174–175, 186, 187, 196, 205, 206, 213–214, 219–220, 223–224, 227, 228, 229–30, 244–45, 247, 248, 267–269, 271–272, 277, 287, 288, 289, 291, 301–303, 306, 312–313, 313–314, 315, 316–318, 327, 340 (twice), 343–348, 370, 372, 374, 376, 379–80, 381–382, 382.

additional sequels, the most important in 1419,[48] were made by continuators so that it is an important source for the time before and after the battle of Tannenberg. It comprises 300 pages in the edition (pp. 79–388), so the chronicle is a quite comprehensive source. As a native of Prussia, Posilge is not only interested in the Order, but also in the regional history – so the Chronicle stands on the cusp of the transition from *Ordensgeschichtsschreibung* to *Landeschronistik*. However, I must emphasize – after a thorough reading of the chronicle – that I cannot follow the generally accepted research thesis that Posilge, as a Prussian native, looked critically at the Teutonic Knights as being foreigners in Prussia. From my point of view, Johann of Posilge is faithful to the Order and expresses no discernible criticism towards the Teutonic Knights. In addition to Peter of Dusburg and Nicolas Jeroschin, Johann relies heavily on sources like the '*Annales Torunenses*' which were edited in the *Scriptores Rerum Prussicarum* by Ernst Strehlke alongside of Johann of Posilge.

4 Johann of Posilge's Attitude towards Poland/the Poles

In general, it can be stated that Johann Posilge and his continuators (until 1419) have basically no negative intentions towards the Poles. Frequently, friendly situations are in fact described where the diplomats of the Order and Poland meet in a friendly and peaceful manner and show mutual respect at convened

48 The thesis by Jarosław Wenta that the author is Johannes von Redden (an official after 1416 in Pomesania, † between 1419 and 1422) is rejected by Ralf Päsler because it cannot be proven. See Ralf G. Päsler *Deutschsprachige Sachliteratur im Preußenland bis 1500. Untersuchungen zu ihrer Überlieferung* (Köln 2003), 284–290.

diets or occasions for negotiations. Overall one can say that the Poles are significantly more present in this chronicle than in Peter of Dusburg's or Wigand's works (see table 3) – dominated by text-passages where individuals are described (out of a total of 51 in 36 places), mostly the Polish king. In particular, the contemporaneous Polish king, Władysław-Jagiello (1362–1434), however, is viewed critically and often in the later phase of 1410–1419 is depicted as a liar, as a violator of other Christians (because of the participation of pagans in his army) and as being arrogant. Here seems to be a distinguishing difference between the text of Johann and the text of his continuator – the latter has a very fierce attitude towards the Polish king. Yet conversely, Hedwig/Jadwiga, the Polish queen and his wife, is presented extremely positively as being peace-loving and positively disposed toward the Order.

When Posilge and his continuator describe individual groups, then it is normally the Polish elites. Their contact with the Order occurs either in warlike actions or as part of negotiations. Especially the Council of Constance plays an important part in this. Two traits dominate the description of these Polish elites: they act hypocritically and arrogantly. For instance, they lie outrageously in public at the Council of Constance and react angrily when they were caught in it. They send letters with lies to German princes in order to discredit the Order; but the letters fail to have their intended effect, since the German princes are well-informed about the Teutonic Order. Sometimes, Johann of Posilge seems even to blame and mock the Polish councilors and negotiators for their stupidity, as they maneuver themselves into hopeless situations in international negotiations.

Now and again greed is highlighted as an additional characteristic: Polish military leaders constantly try during the years of conflict with the Teutonic Order (1410–1419) to make money from their positions of power. However, in general, one can note that the time immediately before 1410 (perhaps the last 10 years before) was accompanied by mutual conflicts and military campaigns between the Order and Poland and this is reflected by Posilge in a rather objective and non-judgmental way – these seem simply to belong to everyday-life.

The Polish people in general, on the other hand, are mentioned only a few times and are normally even treated by Posilge with caution: the Mazovian population (Poles!) for instance, like the Prussian population, suffered from the atrocities in 1410–1414 at the hands of the Polish army, which was comprised also of pagan troops. By the way, the Poles are fully accepted as neighbors by Posilge; nowhere does one find any prejudice that judges them as being wicked *per se*. Posilge draws clear differences between individuals (king, representatives of elites) and the Polish people. His narrative style is to be described as sober/objective. His critical remarks refer mostly to situations and not over-all personal characteristics. That means that the Polish king in one particular situation could be depicted as lying and brazen and in another situation as nice and open-minded.

I would like to illustrate these general observations with a few examples:[49] Johann of Posilge reflects in one text-passage on the state of Poland in 1385. Ludwig of Hungary had died, but before he did, he had arranged the marriages of his daughters Maria and Hedwig to princes within the Holy Roman Empire. Wilhelm of Austria, as husband, had already consummated the marital union with Hedwig by sharing the marriage bed with her. But the Poles drove the young Austrian duke out of Poland, and forced Hedwig (who loved her husband), to accept Jagiello, the pagan prince of Lithuania, as her spouse. The Poles acted wickedly, serving only their own advantage.

> After Wilhelm of Austria had slept with Jadwiga and they both loved each other, the Poles behaved very badly as they drove Wilhelm out of the country and invited instead Jagiello, the king of Lithuania, to come along. They named him king of Poland, while forcing Jadwiga to renounce Wilhelm and accept Jagiello as her husband. The mean Poles enjoyed themselves during their evil deed, as they were quite talented in doing such bad things towards their own wives.[50]

---

49   Appropriate positions on the topic can be found throughout the Edition: Johann von Posilge, *Chronik des Landes Preussen* (henceforth: Posilge), ed. Ernst Strehlke, Scriptores Rerum Prussicarum 3 (1866) 79–388; pp. 141–142; 159, 168, 186, 205/206, 213–14, 248, 267–269, 277, 287, 306, 316–318 (battle of Tannenberg), 340, 343–348, 372, 374–376 (Council of Constance); 381–382.

50   Posilge, 141–142: "Und als herczog Wilhelm von Osterrich alreit hatte beslofen Hedewig, und sie sich lip hatten mitenander, des worin die Polan von ihrer bosheit, und vortrebin herczogen Wilhelm us deme lande und ludin Jagil, den koning von Littowin, czu yn, und worffen yn uf vor eynen koning czu Polan, und twungen die edele vrowin Hedwig, das sie iren rechtin heren vorkysen muste und Jagil nehmen czu manne. Und die snoden [Lexer: 'ärmlichen', 'schlechten' – 'schnöden'] Polan trebin dese sachin umb eres bosen genyses willen, wend sie obirgeben wordin mit gobe, das sie die snodekeit totin an irer eygenen vrowen." This was, however, a typical position from within the Order, since the union Poland-Lithuania was seen as a great risk for the Order, cf. Grabski. *Polska w opiniach Europy zachodniej*, 197–198. Official complaints from the Order to the pope call Jagiello 'a usurper'.

Here, Johann of Posilge expresses his quite critical view of the Krakow nobility. It is interesting, especially because the story is most probably not true: Hedwig was in reality at the time of the death of her father just 9 years old and was only engaged to Wilhelm of Austria (there had been no marriage ceremony yet and no consummation).[51] At the age of 11 (10 days after her eleventh birthday) she was crowned 'King' of Poland on 15 Oct. 1384 (due to the Kaschauer privilege of 1374) – the engagement with Wilhelm was broken off – with the consent of Pope Boniface IX after paying him 200,000 florins – and nobody from the Habsburgian side complained.[52] Here Posilge is clearly in step with the Teutonic Order's propaganda.

Another anecdote is interesting: A Polish servant of an official, the Karwensherr (master of the stables), in Marienburg ("Is was eyn torecht Polnisch knecht, der dinthe dem karwenshern"), one night climbed through a window into the parish church of Malbork and dug up the body of the priest Johann of Myndin ("meister Johannem von Myndin" – a pastor who had died 3 years previously). The Polish servant did not manage to drag the body out of the church because the doors were locked. In the morning he was found sleeping when early Mass began. Those who found him fled (apparently out of fear), and the offender himself did the same ("und der thore wart ouch fluchtig"). Later, he was found at work and was arrested. What is so intriguing about this anecdote apart from being humorous? Posilge does not at all try to generalize or derive from that one foolish Pole a broader judgement such as: this is another example of the foolishness of the Polish people. On the contrary, he refers purely to this one Polish servant.

In one last example in that chronicle, the death of the Polish queen is commented upon: The author writes that the 'blessed lady Hedwig loved the Teutonic Order and was very partial to it. During her lifetime there was peace between the Order and Poland.' She is very even quoted by Posilge, while talking to the commander of Thorn (Toruń), as saying:

> The blessed lady Jadwiga was very fond of the Teutonic Order and felt much tenderness for the knights. As long as she lived, there was peace between Poland and the Teutonic Order. Once she spoke with the the

---

51 Contemporary or nearly contemporaneous records of the completion of the marriage between William and Jadwiga are quite contradictory. Some 80 years later, Długosz stated that William was in the year 1385 driven from Krakow castle after he had entered the Queen's bedchamber in order to officially consume the marriage. But on the other hand this chronicler wrote, that many people knew about Duke William and the queen having already shared the bed for a fortnight before.

52 Robert Frost, *The Oxford History of Poland-Lithuania. Vol I: The Making of the Polish-Lithuanian Union, 1385–1569* (Oxford, 2015), 34–35.

count of Sayn, the commander in Thorn: 'The Order should not worry as long as I live. But when I die, you will surely have war with Poland'. It happened precisely like that.[53]

Another time Johann of Posilge describes in a neutral and unembellished way how Władysław-Jagiello blocked the trade routes to Prussia – and opened them again, because he realized how he had harmed his own country with the blockade:

> [...] so the king of Poland blocked the street[s] and nobody was able to travel from Prussia through his country; this policy was kept until the tenth year; the country and the customs were so much ruined, that he [the king] himself after that let pass whoever wanted to.[54]

5 Wigand of Marburg[55]

Wigand was himself not a friar. He came from the Holy Roman Empire (either from Marburg in Hesse or from Styria in Austria) and arrived in 1390 in Prussia, where he immediately became the herald of Grand Master Konrad von Wallenrode.[56] He wrote his rhymed chronicle up until 1394 while he was in

---

53 Posilge, 370: "Dy selige vwowe Hedwig hatte den ordin gar lib und was ym gar eyn genedige vrowe, unde by erim lebin bleib is vruntlich zcwoschin den Polen stehen und dem ordin. Sy sagite off eyn zcit dem graffen von Seyn, dem kompthur was zcu Thorun:»Dy wile wir lebin, bedarf sich der ordin nicht besorgin, sunder wenne wir tot sin, so habit ir gewislichin kryk mit den Polen.« Also hat sichs ouch irfolgit."

54 Posilge, 168: "[...] do legete der koning von Polan die strosze nedir, das nymant von Pruszin durch sin lant mochte czin; und stunt alzo bis in das X jar; do vortorbin sine lant und czolle, das her do von eygin willen durch lis czin, wer do wolde."

55 The principal edition: *Die Chronik Wigands von Marburg. Lateinische Übersetzung und sonstige Überreste* (henceforth: Wigand), ed. Th. Hirsch, SRP 2 (Leipzig, 1863), 453–662. Further literature on the author: Sławomir Zonenberg, *Kronika Wiganda z Marburga* (Toruń, 1994); Hartmut Boockman, "Die Geschichtschreibung des Deutschen Ordens. Gattungsfragen und 'Gebrauchssituationen'" in *Geschichtsschreibung und Geschichtsbewußtsein im späten Mittelalter*, ed. Hans Patze (Sigmaringen, 1987), 449–454, Wenta, *Studien*, 200; Krzysztof Kwiatkowski, "Die Selbstdarstellung des Deutschen Ordens in der 'Chronik' Wigands von Marburg," in *Selbstbild und Selbstverständnis der geistlichen Ritterorden*, ed. Roman Czaja and Jürgen Sarnowsky (Toruń, 2005), 127–138; Udo Arnold, "Wigand von Marburg," in Verfasserlexikon III, 2nd ed., 1981, 20–22; Gisela Vollmann-Profe, "Gesselen, Konrad," in *The Encyclopedia of the Medieval Chronicle*, 1506.

56 In the *Tresslerbuch* (financial register) of the Teutonic Order one finds the note for the year 1409: "Item 1,5 marc wygant von Marcburg eym herolde gegeben von des meisters und groskompthurs geheyse, der huskompthur his". Cf. Das Marienburger Tresslerbuch (MTB) der Jahre 1399–1409, ed. Ernst Joachim, (Königsberg, 1896, repr. 1973), 524.

service; unfortunately, the work survived only in a very superficial and hastily translated Latin prose version (carried out in just 20 days) during the middle of the 15th century (1464). It was done by Konrad Gesselen, who came from the Hessian Geismar, and who later became priest in Thorn. He had been commissioned by Jan Dlugosz.[57] The chronicle covers the events from 1311 to 1394 and the edition covers about 200 pages. It focuses mostly on the struggle and conflict between the Order and Lithuania – other aspects can be found only sporadically.[58] In contrast to Peter Dusburg and Johann of Posilge, the depiction is strongly influenced by Wigand's heraldry profession and his identification with Western European knighthood.[59] Wigand understood neither the historical phenomena nor the political processes behind individual and specific events in a broader context and barely reported them.[60] He valued and portrayed characters who showed robust magnanimity – even among the opponents. He addressed a lay public – first of all normal knights who took part in the Lithuanian crusades ('Litauerreisen').[61] His sources are surprisingly neither Peter of Dusburg nor Nikolaus of Jeroschin – he wrote completely differently. He copied rather from the Cronicon Olivense, Hermann of Wartberg, Canonicus Sambiensis, Annales Thorunenses, Johann of Posilge (and even from smaller collections, such as the Lithuanian 'Wegeberichte').[62]

6 Wigand's Attitude towards Poland/the Poles

The table below (tab. 4) shows that Wigand almost always casually mentions the Poles (there are no lengthier narrative text-passages). The comments on individuals (9 times) stand out against comments on collective groups or the Poles as a whole. Almost always these individuals are Polish kings (Władysław Łokietek/Elbow-high, Kasimir, Władysław-Jagiello).

---

57 Długosz examined, as well, the German version and made corrections in his own work (Annales) from that original, cf. Hirsch "Einleitung," in *Die Chronik Wigands von Marburg*, 431. The Latin copy of Wigand was apparently kept in Toruń, cf. id., 439.
58 Like shown ibid., 446.
59 Kwiatkowski, "Selbstdarstellung," 130.
60 Arnold, "Geschichtsschreibung," 83.
61 Boockmann, "Geschichtsschreibung," 457; Sławomir Zonenberg, "Pochodzenie kronikarza Wiganda z Marburga," [Origin of the chronicler Wigand of Marburg] in *Zapiski Historyczne* 59, 1 (1994), 96–107, 107; Kwiatkowski, "Selbstdarstellung," 131.
62 Theodor Hirsch "Einleitung," in *Die Chronik Wigands von Marburg*, 443–445.

TABLE 15.4 Wigand of Marburg and the number of text-passages mentioning Poland

Wigand of Marburg	Poland – number of all text-passages[a]	People mentioned	Region/ groups mentioned	Individuals mentioned	Number of all *important* passages
	21	3	5	9	0

a Die Chronik Wigands von Marburg, pp. 458, 459–462, 463, 467, 471, 473, 474, 481–82, 486, 498, 499–500, 525, 556, 604, 646, 547–48, 648, 653, 653–654, 656, 658, 680.

Overall, Wigand does not show any interest in portraying the Poles in a wholly negative way. Only at the very end, in the battle in 1394 at Ritterswerder, a castle on a Memel island close to Vilna, does he criticize the support by certain Poles in fighting for the pagan Lithuanian Grand Duke Witowt. "These Poles and their descendants should regret their boldness and arrogance" ("Multi quoque Polonorum erant presentes cum Wytaudo contra christianos bellantes, de quo posteo possent penitere aut sui successores propter presumpcionem et superbiam eorum").[63] But it should be noted that he is only referring to those Poles who actually fought at Ritterswerder and betrayed thus their Christian ideals, not to Poles in general. Otherwise, the author does not get carried away in making harsh personal accusations. For instance, in a similar situation, during the siege of Grodno/Lithuania in the year 1391, Poles fought there alongside the Lithuanian pagan garrison. The author describes that when the Marshal of the Order was able to seize one of the garrisons, he had them executed without regard to whether they were Poles or Lithuanians ("Marschalcus tamen omnes suscepit captivos, interquos forunt poloni, qui fuerunt decollate").[64] He tells the story though without any vicious comments about the Poles as before. Almost at the end of the chronicle (this coming from the pen of the continuator) there appears a text-passage describing the siege of Vilna in 1394, when four French knights, who were traveling and fighting for the army of the Teutonic Knights (so-called 'Preußenreisende'), challenged four Polish knights to a duel. The accepted duel though never came to pass because the Grand Master and the Order's Marshall were of the opinion that it was dishonourable to duel with 'those who impugn the Christian faith':

63 Wigand, 656: "There were a lot of Poles with Witowt fighting against the Christians, and their successors had to pay for their presumption and arrogance."
64 Wigand, 646 (a. 1391): "The Marshall took all prisoners, among them as well Poles, who were [later] beheaded."

> The French wanted to fight in a tournament with the Poles for their arms and horses, but the Grand Master [of the Teutonic Order] interdicted that and Marshal Werner von Tettingen said: Whoever fights with them cannot find any honour for they are warriors against the faith.[65]

It seems that Wigand's over-all perception of the Poles is very pointedly expressed: He had absolutely nothing against them, but as soon as they make common cause with the pagans, they forfeit their *honor* and should not be treated with respect anymore.

Taking a brief look at the places where individuals are mentioned: Władysław I the Elbow-high is blamed for allying himself with pagans and breaking contracts, but nonetheless he is nowhere seriously insulted by the author.[66] For the sake of authenticity (and drama) the chronicler often uses direct speech: Gediminas or a Hungarian envoy express negative opinions towards the behavior of Władysław. The Lithuanian duke e.g. mistrusts the Polish king and feels betrayed by him; the Hungarian king resents the Polish king for his deals with the pagans:

> Afterwards Władysław I the Elbow-high asked Gediminas, if he could come with him to Prussia. Gediminas responded: I arranged with you that we would meet on the birth of Mary exactly there, I came, but you did not; if I had not been protected by my gods, I would have been captured by treason, after I became aware of the traitors. Duke Wilhelm said, after realizing how Władysław wanted to lead the pagans against Christians: If you want to fight against Christians together with pagans, allow us to pass to Hungary, but if you want us to come with you, send the pagans to their homes and we will fight with you with delight. Therefore, the king of the pagans together with his followers were very upset about the fact that he had been called for nothing; in anger he forced the Polish king to pay them their salary, everyone regarding his merits, in gold, silver, cloth or horses. Afterwards they left for their homes.[67]

---

65 Wigand, 660: "Francigine volebant cum Polonis equitare pro armis et equis; sed magister intercepit propter melius, et marschalcus Wernherus Tetinger ait: neminem honorem contingere, qui cum eis equitaret, cum sint fidei impugnatores."
66 Wigand, 467, 471.
67 Wigand, 471, a.1329: "Post hec rex Lokut Polonie regem Gedemynum petiit, ut cum eo in Prusziam transiret. Qui respondit: ego una vice condixi tecum, ut in die nativitatis Marie [8. Sept.] ibidem constitueremur, et ego veni, tu vero non; unde nisi a diis meis protectus fuissem, captivatus fuissem tradimento, cum noverim traditores. Dux Wilhelmus videns, quomodo rex Lokut paganos ducere voluit contra christianos, dixit: Si tu utique vis cum

In other places Władysław did not act properly again: In 1331 he ordered his troops to rob and kill 56 outnumbered knight friars ("Rex querit, qui essent, et ayunt: sunt de Teutonorum exercitu, et rex dixit: exspoliate eos et transfigite omnes; et sic 56 fuerunt interfecti.")[68] – Christian and knightly ethics would have stipulated that the king take the Teutonic Knights hostage. Another person, the son of Władysław, King Casimir III., even though his reign lasted for almost 40 years (1333–1370), is mentioned only briefly, but nonetheless extremely positively. Here we even have access to an original fragment from the German poetical chronicle: Casimir is described as peaceful and inclined towards the Teutonic Order:

> After him his son Casmir was made king of Cracow, who did not put on weapons against the Teutonic Knights and their men, he [the Polish king] kept peace for the royal side until the time of [Grand Master] Winrich, then God finished his life.[69]

Outstanding and often cited is the place where Casimir in 1365 comes as guest to the main castle of the Order, Marienburg, and asks the Grand Master if he might visit the whole castle and not only the guest apartments. The Grand Master generously grants him the wish and after the tour Casimir admits that he had been totally mistaken in his notion of the defensiveness of the Marienburg, but now it is clear to him. With his new impressions of the fortification, he would never want to quarrel with the Order:

> After this had been seen [the Malbork castle], he [the Polish king] said seriously to the Grand Master: Lord, I was really betrayed and in accordance to what the traitors told me, I should have fought you, because you do not have so many victuals; but now I see the opposite, that you live in abundance of everything here etc. and now I do not want to fight with

---

paganis christianos impugnare, permitte, nos transire in Ungariam, sed si debeamus tecum transire, dimitte paganos ad sua et tecum pugnabimus voluntarie. Quare rex paganorum commovetur cum suis, quod gratis vocatus fuisset, et irati coegerunt regem Polonie, sibi salaria in auro, argento, panno et equis largiri, cuilibet secundum sua merita, et sic reversi sunt in patriam."

68 Wigand, 481; a. 1331: "The king asked who the men were, and they said that these were men from the army of the Teutonic Order. The king said: rob and stab them; so 56 knights were killed."

69 Wigand, 486 a. 1333: "Post que filius eius Kazimirus, factus rex Cracovie [still from the Latin version, but followed by the German:], der keine wâpen nie tet an; ûf di brûder und ir man, und den vride hât gehalten, von koniglîchen gewalten, bis an meister Winrichs zît; dô machte in got des lebens quît."

you, and I cannot believe the voices of my followers, because I saw in this castle nothing else than a real abundance of food.[70]

After that, as the author writes, the Polish king departed in friendship and kept this *amicitia* all the way until his death ("[...] et amicitiam ordinis obtinuit, donec vixit").[71] The passage is not only interesting for its content but also exemplifies well how medieval historiographers and – through their eyes – we modern historians – often look at such mutual relationships and perceptions (here in this case of the Order and Poland). Casimir III is mentioned in Wigand's chronicle only three times (!), although Casimir's reign covers more or less half of the period about which Wigand writes (1311–1394). The fragments where Casimir is mentioned, albeit short, are always positive in tone. This means, and so it is confirmed by other sources, that over four decades of Casimir's reign, peace indeed prevailed between the Order and Poland, and the relations must have been extremely good between the two countries. This is not at all discussed by Wigand, he is mainly interested in conflict and war – here we have a clue as to why peaceful Casimir is mentioned in only a few places. Therefore, it is so important for modern historians to look apart from the content *strictu sensu* as well at the gaps in the text and the overall context of the narration in a chronicle.

By the way: the contemporary Polish ruler of the time when Wigand wrote, Władysław-Jagiello (in contrast to the chronicler Johann of Posilge) is not negatively described at all – after all, he is hardly mentioned. It is rather the Lithuanian duke, Witowt, the cousin of Jagiello, who (as a pagan) receives a negative image as seen in the following and last example:

The bishop of Plock (the brother of Duke Semovit of Masovia) headed towards Lithuania and passed by Balga and Christburg (castles of the Teutonic Order). He was generously and hospitably received by the commanders of the castles, who sent him further (probably with an escort) to Ritterswerder, where Duke Witowt was staying at the time. The bishop pretended to negotiate with Witowt on a peace treaty between the Lithuanian and the Order, but in reality helped prepare Witowt's ultimate treason against the Order. The bishop asked for the sister of Witowt as his wife and the marriage was at once conducted and consummated (Johann of Posilge reported that the bishop resigned from his

---

70   SRP 2, 556, a. 1366: "Quibus visis, seriose dixit magistro: domine, vix traditus fuissem et nosco traditores, debebam vobiscum litigare, dicentes, vos victualibus carere, sed modo video oppositum et habundantiam rerum etc., nec volo vobiscum litigare, nec mei poterant huiusmodi credere, que vidi in hoc castro preter alia, que non vidi, victualibus plena."

71   Ibidem: "[...] and he received the friendship of the order as long as he lived."

office). Wigand comments, outraged: "..., quod ab alio episcopo nunquam est auditum" ('[...], that there is never anything further heard of that bishop.').[72]

7 Conclusion

In conclusion and summing this up, I would like to draw a few general theses from the presented observations:

1. The Poles are in none of the three chronicles introduced specifically as neighbors; they are assumed by the authors to be well known to their readers. Furthermore, at no point in all three chronicles can one decipher or detect any 'national' aspersions towards the Poles as a people or a country.
2. The actions of certain groups – mostly diplomats, knights-warriors or nobles/elites – are the ones often narrated. A positive or negative perception of them is absolutely dependent on the situation: sometimes one dealt respectfully and in a friendly manner with each other and sometimes the opposing side was accused of lying, arrogance, brutality (especially towards one's own population in military campaigns or against prisoners of war) or finally of greed. Considering these descriptions of mostly Polish elite groups, it is important to remember that all three chroniclers in every phase of writing proceeded from the higher moral authority of their 'own' side, that is, of the Teutonic Order. Nevertheless, the military campaigns of the Order against Lithuania and into Polish regions (especially in Wigand's text) are often depicted as having an equally great brutality (robbery, devastation, kidnapping, etc.) as one finds in the campaigns from the Polish side. The modern historian should therefore refrain (or at least be very careful) about judging these campaigns with modern eyes (there were no medieval Geneva conventions, only Christian moral doctrines!).
3. Last but not least: The actions of individuals, mostly Polish kings (Władysław I Łokietek, Casimir III, Władysław-Jagiello), are dependent as well on the situation. Sometimes the king, Jagiello, could be friendly and open-minded when negotiating matters, sometimes he would be a

---

72 "Episcopus Dobrinensis [...] venit ad commendatorem de Balga et de Cristburg a quibus honoratur multo, et mittunt eum in Ritterswerder ad Wytaudum; pretendens facere unionem inter Polonos et ordinem, se tradicionem querebat; sic et Wytaud qui ab ordine ad paganos se convertit; stetitque tribus septimanis in Ritterswerder petens in conjugem sororem Wytaudi, et dedit eam ei ibidem nupciis celebratis, quod ab alio episcopo nunquam est auditum." – Wigand, 547–48.

liar and a false Christian. None of the authors, though, tried to draw from the background of one king's action a judgment on how the Poles in general should be perceived. The criticism is always *ad personam* and most of the time very objective and factual; the authors restrain themselves from unnecessary invectives or accusations.

4. As a brief side-observation, it is interesting that the often mentioned Władysław-Jagiello, the contemporaneous king of Poland for Wigand of Marburg and Johann of Posilge, is very often mentioned in Posilge's chronicle but hardly plays a role in Wigand's text. This shows strikingly how the focus of one author is totally different from a second one, although both wrote in the same period and have more or less the same topic.

CHAPTER 16

Prussia II: The Views of Late Medieval Historians in Prussia towards Poland

Adam Szweda

In contrast to the chronicles that have already been discussed in Grischa Vercamer's article, the focus of the subsequent texts relating to this relationship will be on the history of the country and the cities. These texts depict the Teutonic Order mainly as a ruler governing a certain territory – the priority for the historiographs were the problems relating to the Order's rule in Prussia and to its subjects. A particularly significant issue was the conflict growing between the Teutonic Order and the Prussian estates (knights and cities) and an internal crisis (gradual secularization) of the religious corporation.[1] The voices appealing for reform of the Order were becoming increasingly more evident, and this tendency was already present in "Admonishing the Carthusian" (by Heinrich Beringer) which dates back to as early as the 1420s. (This work is known from the 16th century compilation of Bernd Stegmann).[2] The monk

---

1 The most important publications for this topic are: Klaus Eberhard Murawski, *Zwischen Tannenberg und Thorn. Die Geschichte des Deutschen Ordens unter dem Hochmeister Konrad von Erlichshausen 1441–1449* (Göttingen, 1953), 57–119; Tomasz Jasiński, "Spory i konflikty miast z komturami krzyżackimi," [Disputes and conflicts between cities and the Teutonic commanders] in *Zakon krzyżacki a społeczeństwo państwa w Prusach*, ed. Zenon H. Nowak (Toruń, 1995), 51–66; Roman Czaja, *Miasta pruskie a zakon krzyżacki. Studia nad stosunkami między miastem a władzą terytorialną w późnym średniowieczu* [Prussian cities and the Teutonic Order. Studies of the relationship between the city and territorial authority in the late Middle Ages] (Toruń, 1999), 208–221; Sławomir Jóźwiak, "Kryzys władzy terytorialnej," [Crisis of territorial authority] in *Państwo zakonu krzyżackiego w Prusach. Władza i społeczeństwo*, ed. Marian Biskup and Roman Czaja (Warszawa, 2008), 332–354; Roman Czaja, "Die Krise des Landesherrschaft. Der Deutsche Orden und die Gesellschaft seines Staates in Preußen in der ersten Hälfte des 15. Jahrhunderts," *Ordines Militares. Colloquia Torunensia Historica* 16 (2011), 159–171; Roman Czaja, "Die Ritterbrüder des Deutschen Ordens und die städtische Gesellschaft in Preußen bis zur Mitte des 15. Jahrhunderts," in *Herrschaft, Netzwerke, Brüder des Deutschen Ordens in Mittelalter und Neuzeit*, ed. Klaus Militzer (Weimar, 2012), 119–132, here especially 128–132; Stefan Kwiatkowski, "A Conflict for Values in the Origins and the Beginning of the Thirteen Year's War," *Zapiski Historyczne* 81/4 (2016), 5–27.
2 Cf. the new edition of this source: *Gdańska kronika Bernta Stegmanna (1528 r.)*, [The Gdańsk chronicle of Bernt Stegmann] ed. Julia Możdżeń, in cooperation with Kristina Stöbener, Marcin Sumowski (Toruń, 2019), 57–85; about the author and the chronology of the chronicles see *Gdańska kronika*, XL–XLI (Polish), C–CI (German); see also Julia Możdżeń, *Przedstawianie*

calls the Grand Master and the entire Teutonic Order to moral renewal. He condemns the drunkenness and ungodliness of the friars. The ruler (therefore, the Grand Master) is responsible for the country and its subjects before God. The Teutonic Knights will retain Prussia only on the condition of their religious and moral renewal.[3]

Here, specifically the important question is whether this new approach for the Prussian historiography can also be detected in how the Poles are perceived by the authors, which implies another question, namely, whether the Poles are noticed at all in the output of the Prussian chroniclers who were active in the Late Middle Ages.

The first texts discussed here were written by authors associated with the Teutonic Knights (directly or indirectly); later ones were written (mostly) by Prussian burghers, and date back to the times following the incorporation of Prussia into Poland.[4]

We should start from the continuation of the chronicle of Peter of Dusburg that was written by the city clerk (head of the city chancellery) from Chełmno (Kulm), Konrad Bitschin.[5] His chronicle covers the period between 1332–1435 and initially is based on the chronicle of Johann Posilge – the Pomesanian judicial vicar (*officialis*). After 1420 the information in the chronicle becomes more accurate due to the fact that it was now contemporaneous to the author.[6] He demonstrates his attitude towards Poles initially in a quite indirect manner; within a number of references we can find the following phrase: "King of the

---

świata przez kronikarzy gdańskich na przełomie XV i XVI wieku [Presentation of the world by Gdańsk chroniclers at the turn of the 15th and 16th centuries] (Toruń, 2016), 44–45.

3   Carthusian demands are discussed by Stefan Kwiatkowski, *Klimat religijny w diecezji pomezańskiej u schyłku XIV i w pierwszych dziesięcioleciach XV wieku* [Religious climate in the Pomesanian diocese at the end of the 14th century and in the first decades of the 15th century] (Toruń, 1990), 178–179; see also Możdżeń, *Przedstawianie świata*, 264.

4   A synthetic review of the chronicles in Prussia has been presented by Udo Arnold, "Geschichtsschreibung im Preussenland bis zum Ausgang des 16. Jahrhunderts," *Jahrbuch für die Geschichte Mittel- und Ostdeutschlands* 19 (1970), 74–126 and by Hartmut Boockmann, "Die Geschichtsschreibung des Deutschen Ordens. Gattungsfragen und »Gebrauchssituationen«," in *Geschichtsschreibung und Geschichtsbewusstsein im späten Mittelalter*, ed. Hans Patze (Sigmaringen, 1987), 447–469; other publications are listed in the relevant footnotes.

5   Udo Arnold, "Bitschin Konrad," *Die deutsche Literatur des Mittelalters – Verfasserlexikon* 1, ed. Kurt Ruh (Berlin-New York, 2010 – repr. of the 1978 issue), 884–887; Boockmann, "Geschichtsschreibung," 461–462; Jarosław Wenta, "Konrad Bitschin," in *Słownik biograficzny Pomorza Nadwiślańskiego* 2, ed. Zbigniew Nowak (Gdańsk, 1994), 439–441. This researcher regards Konrad's authorship as only a hypothesis, but he himself presents the evidence for the support of this hypothesis.

6   Jarosław Wenta, *Studien über die Ordensgeschichtsschreibung am Beispiel Preussens* (Toruń, 2000), 249.

Poles and Vytautas".⁷ This juxtaposition of a nameless Polish king and a specifically named Grand Duke of Lithuania is quite meaningful. Yet, he clearly expresses his opinion on this issue while recounting the death of Vytautas (1430), whom he calls a "very mighty and powerful ruler". After his death the Poles tried to subordinate Lithuania. The Lithuanians, however, "knowing about the perversity of the Poles,"⁸ ruined the latter's plans, and Duke Boleslaw Švitrigaila, whose "power [in Lithuania] resulted from both the hereditary law and the right of election," struggled to be allied with "the lords of Prussia", who he always knew had unwavering confidence in him."⁹ The anti-Polish attitude of Konrad Bitschin was connected with the issue of the very destructive Polish-Hussite invasion of Pomerania in 1433¹⁰ (and the author reveals this attitude quite explicitly). Apart from the chronicle itself, it can also be seen in the text attributed to Bitschin by the publisher, or the text that he must have been familiar with, namely *Epistola ecclesie deplanctoria*. In this text, references are made to the information presented by Helmold in the *Chronica Slavorum* who emphasizes that the Bohemians and Poles fought in a similar manner, i.e., "being most cruel/inhuman in robberies and inflicting death".¹¹ The author of the *Epistola* criticizes the Poles for their alliance with the Hussites. He – among other things – calls Poland "cursed" and Poles "a stupid people", unworthy of the dignity of a kingdom.¹² The invasion of Pomerania in 1433 together with the accompanying destruction and devastation was a recurring theme in the Prussian historiography of the 15th century.

---

7   Conrad Bitschin, "Fortsetzung zu Peter von Dusburg Chronik," ed. Max Toeppen. SRP 3 (Leipzig, 1866), 484, 487.
8   "Polonorum scientes versuciam [...]."
9   Bitschin, *Fortsetzung*, 495–496. Witold's death, the Boleslaw Švitrigaila election, and the dynastic war in Lithuania have been recently discussed by Robert Frost, *The Oxford History of Poland-Lithuania* 1 (Oxford, 2015), 151–181; Sergey Polekhov, *Nasl'edniki Vitovta. Dinasticheskaia voina v Velikom kniažestve Litovskom v 30. gody XV veka* [Witold's heirs. Dynastic war in the Grand Duchy of Lithuania in the 30s of the 15th century] (Moskva, 2015).
10 About this military expedition, see Paweł Karp, *Polsko-husycka wyprawa zbrojna przeciwko zakonowi krzyżackiemu w roku 1433* [A Polish-Hussite armed expedition against the Teutonic Order in 1433] (Zielona Góra, 2018).
11 Conrad Bitschin, *Epistola ecclesie deplanctoria*, ed. Max Toeppen, SRP 3, 513; cf. Helmold von Bosau, *Slawenchronik*, ed. Heinz Stoob (Darmstadt, 1963), 38: "Est autem Polonis atque Boemis eandem armorum facies et bellandi consuetudo. [...] fortes quidem sunt in congressu, sed in rapinis et mortibus crudelissimi; non monasteriis, non ecclesiis aut cimiteriis parcunt."
12 Bitschin, *Epistola*, 513: "O exercanda Polonia, o gens stolida [...]. Quid ammodo tibi corona regalis in capite, quam occasione tuorum actuum perversorum tam turpiter defedasti?"

Another important narrative source – the Older Chronicle of the Grand Masters (Ältere Hochmeisterchronik) was created approximately in 1440 and was written by a member of the Order; it covers the period between 1190–1433. Its text then was continued until the period following the Thirteen Years' War. The author of this continuation after 1455 has been assumed to be Georg Egloffstein, a Teutonic administrator (*advocatus*) of Lipienko (Leipe), although it may well be more probable that the author was an anonymous village clerk.[13]

With regard to the beginnings of the Teutonic Order on the Vistula River, "a good Christian prince Konrad" is mentioned.[14] This positive characteristic refers to the one who invited the Teutonic Knights into the land of Chełmno and Prussia in general – the Duke of Mazovia, Konrad, from the Piast dynasty.[15] Moreover, in the subsequent parts addressing the early history of the Order in Prussia, when discussing the Poles it is always done in the context of evaluating individual dukes; in this particular way, the Duke of Gdansk, Swietopelk (he waged war upon the Teutonic Knights in 1242–1253), became the embodiment of evil – he had allied himself with the Prussians against the Teutonic Knights and thereby exposed his soul to condemnation.[16] Another interesting issue is the message dated in 1361. At that time, during the Dominican Fair, the Germans were said to have killed many Poles in Gdansk who openly shouted: "Krakow, Krakow". The chronicler provides this reference with a commentary: "it was thought they wanted to betray the city",[17] i.e. to hand it over to Poland in the most treacherous of ways; he links this incident with the escape of Kęstutis, Duke of Lithuania, who was then being imprisoned in Malbork. The publisher of the source aptly states that the Polish-German conflict is not unbelievable given the realities of this confusion, yet the presumption of the probability of treacherous behavior demonstrated by the Poles in Gdansk in 1361 is anachronistic and can be attributed to the 15th century author of "The older chronicle".[18] It may seem that this commentary can be treated as

---

13 Wenta, *Studien*, 251–252; cf. Arnold, "Geschichtsschreibung," 87–88; Boockmann, "Geschichtsschreibung," 462–465; Arno Mentzel-Reuters, "Deutschordenshistoriographie," in *Handbuch Chroniken des Mittelalters*, ed. Gerhard Wolf and Norbert H. Ott (Berlin-Boston, 2016), 328–330.

14 *Die aeltere Hochmeisterchronik*, ed. Max Toeppen, SRP 3, 541: "eyn guttir cristin herczog Conrad."

15 Henryk Samsonowicz, *Konrad Mazowiecki* [Konrad the Masovian] (Kraków, 2008).

16 *Die aeltere Hochmeisterchronik*, 547: "In Pomerener land ryt eyn herczog, Swantopolk genant, uf alle boshit hog vormessin [...]. Der herczog waz yn bosheit vorhart. Dorum vorgaz her seyner zele heil [...]". Cf. Marek Smoliński, *Świętopełk Gdański* (Poznań, 2016), 289–323 – Peter von Dusburg already called Svietopelk "the son of wickedness and perdition" ["filius iniquitatis et filius perditionis"].

17 *Die aeltere Hochmeisterchronik*, 594: "man meynte, sy wolden dy stat vorroten."

18 *Die aeltere Hochmeisterchronik*, 594, note 1.

a manifestation of the anti-Polish attitude of the chronicler. Once again, the Poles seemed to deserve the chronicler's harsh words when Hedwig of Anjou broke off her engagement with William, Duke of Austria, and when the Polish nobles decided that the young queen should marry the "wild pagan", "traitor to Christianity" and "the evil dog" Jogaila.[19] Then, again, the Poles are at the forefront during the war that was waged between 1431–1433. Grand Duke Švitrigaila hated them, and he, in turn, was always good to the Order.[20]

The first continuation of the chronicle was mainly devoted to the conflict of the Prussian estates with the Teutonic Order. The "bad" King of Poland – Casimir IV Jagiellon – appears on this occasion as well: He, despite the appeals of the Grand Master, broke the oath sworn by his father (though Wladislaw Jagiello had died in 1434) and by his brother and by he himself in 1435 to keep eternal peace;[21] thus, this was an accusation of perjury. The Poles are also mentioned as treacherous at that time – in contrast to the Lithuanians and Dukes of Mazovia who kept their words.[22] The pride of King Casimir IV Jagiellon was demonstrated when describing the battle of Chojnice (1454 – mercenary troops in the service of the Teutonic Order defeated the Polish knights there), because the treacherous king addressed his armies before the battle with a speech saying that no Germans should be taken as prisoners, and that the Poles' horses would trample the enemy down, and the Poles would not even need to take out their swords. The Polish troops started to attack with "a lot of screaming", while the mercenaries of the Order responded "with glorious [probably pious] singing".[23] Interestingly, other sources (Polish and Czech) described the mood in the Polish camp in an absolutely different way – that panic arose in the Polish army at the sight of the enemy.[24]

In contrast to this, it should be noted that in the third continuation of "The older chronicle of the Grand Masters", the Poles, and above all the Polish king, are depicted in a very neutral way; it is the king's kindness and generosity towards subsequent Grand Masters, who after the second peace of Thorn (1466) were his vassals, which are emphasized. There are no decisive anti-Polish voices even in the description of the alliance concluded by Grand Master

---

19 Die aeltere Hochmeisterchronik, 608. The opinions of contemporary sources on the subject of the marriage of Jadwiga and Jagiełło and the union of Poland with Lithuania are discussed in Grabski, *Polska w opiniach Europy*, 195–216; cf. Frost, *The Oxford History*, 47–57.
20 Die aeltere Hochmeisterchronik, 632.
21 Die aeltere Hochmeisterchronik, 660–661.
22 Die aeltere Hochmeisterchronik, 670.
23 Die aeltere Hochmeisterchronik, 679.
24 Cf. Marian Biskup, *Trzynastoletnia wojna z Zakonem Krzyżackim 1454–1467* [The Thirteen Years' War with the Teutonic Order 1454–1467] (Warszawa, 1967), 262.

Martin Truchsess with the King of Hungary, Matthias Corvinus, although this particular alliance was against King Casimir IV Jagiellon and could be regarded as a sort of a pretext for any such comments.[25]

Another author who should be mentioned here is Laurentius Blumenau, a lawyer, humanist, and adviser to Grand Master Ludwig von Erlichshausen;[26] he relies on the chronicle of Peter of Dusburg, (its translation into German was made by Nicholas von Jeroschin), the chronicle of Johannes Posilge, the Pomesanian judicial vicar (*officialis*), and the older chronicle of the Grand Masters up to the point of the battle of Grunwald (1410). The way these sources were treated gives us an insight into the specificity of Blumenau's narration as he tends to avoid overly exaggerated details.[27] The general approach presented in his work undoubtedly resulted from the fact that Blumenau was a representative of the Order in its dispute with the knights and Prussian cities, which at that point was being adjudicated before the Holy Roman Emperor, Frederick III. King Władysław Jagiełło is for him only "Jagel" (therefore he uses only the pagan name of this ruler).[28] While describing the events of the early 1430s, Laurentius Blumenau follows the tradition that can be observed in the *Epistola ecclesie deplanctoria*.[29] He introduces information about the Polish-Hussite invasion of Pomerania and refers to "the Slavic nation, more restless than brave, impossible to tolerate rather because of their rage than courage".[30] The narration about the events of 1433 is summarized in the statement that "wildness/inhumanity of the Poles, cruel and insatiable with Christian blood", could not be stopped except by undertaking negotiations and making concessions that were unprecedented in the history of Prussia.[31] In his chronicle, Blumenau published fragments of the peace of Brest/Brześć Kujawski of 1435, but, while discussing its provisions, he seems not to have any knowledge of the fact that this was largely a repetition of the conditions of the peace treaty of Lake Mełno

---

25 *Die aeltere Hochmeisterchronik*, 706–709.
26 Hartmut Boockmann, *Laurentius Blumenau. Fürstlicher Rat – Jurist – Humanist (ca. 1415–1484)* (Göttingen, 1965).
27 Arnold, "Geschichtsschreibung," 88–89; Boockmann, *Laurentius Blumenau*, 210; Mentzel-Reuters, "Deutschordenshistoriographie," 326–327.
28 For example, Laurentius Blumenau, *Historia de ordine Theutonicorum Cruciferorum*, ed. Max Toeppen, SRP 4 (Leipzig, 1870), 59.
29 Cf. above note 11.
30 Blumenau, *Historia*, 60: "gens Slava, plus inquieta, quam strennua, et furore pocius quam virtute intollerabilis."
31 Blumenau, *Historia*, 61: "cruenta [...] ac cristiani sanguinis inexplebilis Polonorum inhumanitas."

in 1422.[32] The chronicler focuses on Prussia, hence the account of "heretics from Bohemia" and their Polish context stand out as an exception.[33]

A certain type of involved city-oriented historiography is represented by Johann Lindau's "*Geschichte des Dreizehnjährigen Krieges*"; he had been the highest city clerk of Gdańsk since 1455 (he died between 1480 and 1483). Despite the name "chronicle" as traditionally adopted for this work, it is better to refer to it rather as a "war monograph" since it contains information from personal experiences, and also uses letters, Hanseatic city books, etc.[34] The reasons for writing it down could be, to a certain extent, pragmatic as the chronicle was useful for Lindau in his work as both a city clerk and also as a representative of the Gdansk Council. We in a way expect from the author that he would be in favor of the Poles. Yet, it should be stated that virtually no evaluative references are present, and this would be due to the character of Lindau's work, which was, as already mentioned, a "war monograph". "Our Lord [Polish] King" is always mentioned with utmost respect but without any more personalized comments.[35] Alternatively he uses objective terms: "King's army", "King of Poland".[36] The only moment in which the Gdańsk-based author refers to the Poles (and here in a negative context) comes during the battle of Chojnice in 1454. He emphasizes then that the cause of the defeat of the Poles – according to what was being said – was the arrogance and pride (*hoffart*) of the Poles since they underestimated their enemies.[37] It is not difficult to notice here that this is analogous to the account of the Old Chronicle of the Grand Masters.

For Prussian anti-Teutonic historiography, mostly representing the voices of cities, the priority was the issue of the estates. The conflict with the Order is described from this specific perspective. King Casimir IV Jagiellon and his kingdom appear here as the new territorial ruler, and his right to this role is not laid out. The final part of the Gdańsk historical document "Die Danziger Chronik vom Bunde" is characteristic of this attitude. It cannot be excluded that it may also have been written by Johannes Lindau, although the authorship itself remains uncertain. It used to be attributed to one of the Gdańsk councilors, Peter Brambeck, but what is certain is that it was created in one of the chancelleries in Gdańsk.[38] The object of this chronicle was the conflict between the Prussian estates and the Order between 1444–1466 and, according

---

32   Blumenau, *Historia*, 61.
33   Boockmann, *Laurentius Blumenau*, 216–217.
34   Możdżeń, *Przedstawianie świata*, 29–31.
35   Johann Lindau, *Geschichte des Dreizehnjährigen Krieges*, ed. Theodor Hirsch, SRP 4, 510, 548, 553, 555 and other: *unser her konigk*.
36   For example, Lindau, *Geschichte*, 556: "des hern koniges volck, der her konigk von Polan."
37   Lindau, *Geschichte*, 510.
38   Możdżeń, *Przedstawianie świata*, 44.

to Udo Arnold, "it breathes the spirit of the parties of its time"[39] and it is an expression of the growing political awareness of the members of the Union in their conflict with the Order. The chronicle also describes the circumstances around the conclusion of the treaty of Thorn in 1466 between the Polish king and Grand Master Ludwig von Erlichshausen, and stresses that henceforth subsequent Grand Masters and the Order were to pay homage and take the oath of loyalty to the king and the Crown. The conclusion says: "In this way, the Grand Master in Prussia was deprived of the best part of the country, both because of his pride and because he persecuted his subjects who could not stand this lawlessness and had to become subjects of another ruler."[40] In this fragment we can read the critique of the Order as well as the justification of its Prussian subjects and also the Poles as a formally indispensable element – Prussia had to have some kind of lord.

Hence, it is not surprising that there are virtually no Polish issues, for example, in work of Jakob Lubbe (1430–1501), the author of the text traditionally considered to be a family chronicle, yet in fact it is a remainder of a trading book supplemented with personal comments.[41] Expectations might be higher in the case of the personal notes of a Gdańsk-based skipper, Casper Weinreich, written in the years 1461–1496, and preserved in a sixteenth-century copy made by Stenzel Bornbach with his own added commentaries. Traditionally, it was referred to as a "chronicle"; in reality it was again a trading book with added notes and comments.[42] Weinreich, however, was a sea-trader, hence he was closer to issues concerning the Hansa or England, but certainly not Poland. However, he noted down the Gdańsk visit of King Casimir IV Jagiellon in 1468 accompanied by his magnificent entourage.[43] More passages concerning Poles appear in Weinreich's notes dating back to the 1480s–within the context of Turkish and Tatar affairs, as these two issues were in his special focus. Therefore, he notes that in 1485 the estates in Thorn promised the Polish king military assistance, and "the Turk", (better: the sultan), withdrew his army when he heard about it.[44] However, Weinreich does not describe the context

---

39 Arnold, "Geschichtsschreibung," 92; Boockmann, "Geschichtsschreibung," 467–468.
40 (Peter Brambeck), *Die Danziger Chronik vom Bunde*, ed. Theodor Hirsch, SRP 4, 443.
41 Jacob Lubbe, *Familienchronik*, ed. Theodor Hirsch, in SRP 4, 694–724; Możdżeń, *Przedstawianie świata*, 32.
42 Możdżeń, *Przedstawianie świata*, 38.
43 Caspar Weinreich, *Danziger Chronik*, ed. Theodor Hirsch, SRP 4, 730.
44 Weinreich, *Danziger Chronik*, 755. About the congress of the estates of Royal Prussia, Grand Master and king in Thorn in 1485 see Beata Możejko, "Odległe pogranicze. Stanowisko stanów Prus Królewskich, a zwłaszcza Gdańska, wobec problemu zagrożenia tureckiego w latach 1485–1488," [A distant frontier. The position of the states of Royal Prussia, and especially of Gdańsk, towards the problem of the Turkish threat in the years 1485–1488] *Średniowiecze Polskie i Powszechne* 3 (2011): 151–160; cf. Paul Srodecki,

of this promised help, i.e., he does not mention the grand diet attended by the king, the estates of Royal Prussia, and the Grand Master, during which the Turkish issue was indeed one of the major problems discussed. The battles of the Polish Prince John I Albert with the Tatars in 1487 are also mentioned. The author of the notes clearly identifies himself there with the Christians, and does not mention that with that he means mainly Poles.[45] Weinreich also mentions the general congress of Polish nobility (Sejm) in Piotrków in May 1488, which was also attended by the Turkish delegation; the skipper estimated the number of horses in the entourage as being around 40.[46] However, characteristically, this citizen of Gdańsk respectfully presents the position of the authorities of his home city and other representatives of the Prussian estates in 1489, who conditioned their help for the king against the Turks on the confirmation of their privileges.[47]

As far as other issues are concerned, the Gdansk skipper notes the case of Poles intercepting the letters from Grand Master Martin Truchsess to the King of Hungary, Matthias Corvinus. This scandal was also discussed during the aforementioned Sejm in Piotrków in 1488, where, according to Weinreich, "the king and his advisers were not satisfied."[48]

Poles were also directly mentioned as perpetrators of robberies when the king sent the army to protect the borders in 1489. The Council of Gdańsk was to intervene with the monarch in this matter.[49]

We should mention, as well, the description of the death of Casimir IV Jagiellon and the list of the king's daughters and sons, whose mention explicitly gives clear evidence of Weinrich's good knowledge of Polish court life. The skipper knew of five sons and five daughters of the ruler; he omitted only Prince Casimir (later recognized as a saint) and two daughters, who died in early childhood.[50] The skipper indicated the exact date of the coronation of John I Albert as being Saint Rufus' day (27 August), "about which this poem

---

Antemurale Christianitatis. Zur Genese der Bollwerksrhetorik im östlichen Mitteleuropa an der Schwelle vom Mittelalter zur Frühen Neuzeit, (Husum, 2015), 230–231.

45 Weinreich, *Danziger Chronik*, 766–767.
46 Weinreich, *Danziger Chronik*, 768; Adam Szweda, "Odprawa posłów tureckich (Piotrków, 1488)," [Send-off of Turkish deputies] in *Inter Regnum et Ducatum*, ed. Piotr Guzowski, Marzena Liedke, and Krzysztof Borodo (Białystok, 2018), 567. Cf. Możdżeń, *Przedstawianie świata*, 89, note 492.
47 Weinreich, *Danziger Chronik*, 775–776.
48 Weinreich, *Danziger Chronik*, 761.
49 Weinreich, *Danziger Chronik*, 773–774.
50 Weinreich, *Danziger Chronik*, 791; Zygmunt Wdowiszewski, *Genealogia Jagiellonów i Domu Wazów w Polsce*, [Genealogy of the Jagiellonians and the Vasa House in Poland] 2nd ed. (Kraków, 2005), 97–137 and table IV.

was made": "Rufus chose Albert as the king of Poles" ("Eliget Ruffus Albertum regem Polonorum").

The last example of these sources is "The Prussian Chronicle" ("Preussische Chronik") by the Dominican Simon Grunau, written in 1517–1530. In contrast to the aforementioned texts, this is a really typical chronicle, in fact the first one written from the perspective of the inhabitants of Prussia.[51] Grunau also discusses the perception and presentation of the history of Prussia in the work of Enea Silvio de Piccolomini, at the time the secretary of Holy Roman Emperor Frederick III, and later elected as Pope Pius II. Grunau's chronicle was also dedicated to the Polish king, whom the Dominican believed to be the inherent ruler of Prussia. In his discussion about Piccolomini's pro-Teutonic attitude, he argues that the recognition of the power of king Casimir IV Jagiellon by the estates in Prussia in 1454 was not treason because the king had a better right to Prussia than did the Grand Master and the Teutonic Order. Similarly, if during the conflict that took place between 1519–1521, some cities in Warmia recognized the supremacy of the Order, it was only because their inhabitants did not know about the historical rights of the king. Thus, Grunau represents a pro-Polish attitude in the political sense by representing the interest of the Prussian estates.[52]

Summing up, it should be said that the fifteenth-century Prussian historiography associated with the Teutonic Order is very critical towards the Poles, who, together with their monarch, are treated as perjurers. Another aspect of this unfavorable image of the Poles was the devastation of Pomerania by the Polish-Hussite invasion in 1433.

The historiography of the Thirteen Years' War and of the later years of the 15th century and the early 16th century considers the Polish king to be the ruler of Prussia but it treats his Polish subjects neutrally at best. A reflection of disputes around older Prussian privileges is still present – although implicit. Discussions are mentioned especially concerning the fact that offices and castles in Pomerania were expected to be entrusted only to locals, and not to royal subjects of the Polish Crown – a regulation which Casimir IV Jagiellon used to violate quite frequently. Generally, the relations between Prussia and Poland are not questioned or discussed, which is fully manifested in the chronicle of Simon Grunau.

51 *Simon Grunau's Preussische Chronik* 1–3, ed. Max Perlbach, Richard Philippi, and Paul Wagner (Leipzig, 1876–1896); Arnold, "Geschichtsschreibung," 99–101; Sławomir Zonenberg, *Kronika Szymona Grunaua* (Bydgoszcz, 2009).

52 Zonenberg, *Kronika*, 52–53.

CHAPTER 17

Kraków 1: 'Ethnic' or 'National' Conflict in 14th Century Kraków?

Marcin Starzyński

Up to now, two source documents have influenced the interpretation of the issue of 'ethnic'/'national' conflicts in 14th century Krakow. Both relate to events that took place in 1312, however one is of a relatively late vintage, dating from the 16th century, while the other is contemporaneous to the events. In the later source document, preserved in a 16th century edition of the "Rocznik Krasińskich", an anonymous author, in turn relying on another source called the "Spominki wiślickie",[1] wrote that Albert, the vogt of Krakow, and the burghers surrendered the town to Prince Boleslaus of Opava [*sic*], but erroneously dated the event to 1332. As a consequence, they were deprived of their vogtship, and those who could not pronounce specific Polish words (very difficult to pronounce for the Germans): "soczevycza, koło, myele młyn" were beheaded.[2] The brevity of the entry unfortunately does not permit one to determine by whom or when Krakow's citizens were tested in this way. Could it have been that Ladislaus the Elbow-High's men-at-arms, who penetrated Krakow after the prince of Opole had pulled out, stopped random townspeople and forced them to pronounce these four Polish words? In any case, the information does not appear in any other source. During that same period, after Ladislaus the Elbow-High had retaken Krakow following the rebellion, the town chancellery changed the language of its records from German to Latin, most likely on the Prince's orders. In a parchment manuscript containing court records for the years 1301–1375, there is a significant note from 1312 which reads: "Here begins the Krakow's court notes written in Latin by Rodger, the town's notary".[3] Previously, when the two source documents were compared, it was easy to

---

1 *Spominki wiślickie* [Memories of Wiślica], ed. August Bielowski, MPH 3 (Lwów, 1878), 124.
2 *Rocznik Krasińskich* [The Krasinski' Annal], ed. August Bielowski, MPH 3, 133.
3 *Liber actorum, resignationum nec non ordinationum civitatis Cracoviae 1300–1375*, eds. Franciszek Piekosiński and Józef Szujski, Libri antiquissimi civitatis Cracoviensis 1300–1400 1 (Cracoviae, 1878), 28: "Hic incipiunt acta civitatis Cracouie et resignaciones conpilate in Latino per Rodgerum notarium civitatis"; cf. Bożena Wyrozumska, "Nationalitätenprobleme der mittelalterlichen polnischen Städte in der Historiographie und im Lichte der städtischen Quellen von Krakau," *Zeszyty Naukowe Uniwersytetu Jagiellońskiego. Prace Historyczne* 113

jump to the conclusion that the grounds for the rebellion had a 'national' character with 'German' Krakow burghers rising up against Ladislaus the Elbow-High. This motive appears throughout the literature from the end of the 19th century through works published today, although in recent publications it is not given as the only source of the conflict.[4] What is more, traces of not so much a dislike of 'Germans' but rather of how they were perceived "in Polish society during the period of colonization," as Wojciech Mrozowicz recently put it,[5] can be found in a different source document from the first half of the 14th century. Most probably recorded in Krakow, but not in its entirety in the circle of the burghers, the two-part "Song of Vogt Albert" contains an interesting monologue in which the protagonist admits to the audience that his nature led him to rebel. "Such is the custom of all the Germans, that wherever they live, they always, everywhere they want to lead".[6] Given that the opinion pronounced by Vogt Albert in the text, which would appear to be of some significance in the present discussion, was not composed in the city itself, it cannot be taken as a true reflection of the actual sentiments in Krakow at the time. If one assumes that it was written at Krakow cathedral or possibly in court circles, *Alemani* would not refer to the 'German' burghers of Krakow, but rather to the knights of the Teutonic Order, who had just conquered Gdańsk in Pomerania and who were in conflict with Ladislaus the Elbow-High to the very end of his reign. With this in mind, we should reconsider the issue raised here and try to look at it from a different perspective – not through the prism of the two source documents mentioned above – to see if conflicts in 14th century Krakow really were rooted in issues of 'nationality'. Did the presence, in a relatively small area, of Poles (mainly from Lesser Poland), Silesians, Germans, Bohemians, arrivals from distant Italy, as well as Armenians and Jews, engender internal strife? All of these groups were engaged in major trade and all were represented in the

---

(1994), 25; Anna Adamska, "Away with the Germans and Their Language? Linguistic Conflict and Urban Records in Early Fourteenth-Century Cracow," *Uses of the Written Word in Medieval Towns: Medieval Urban Literacy II*, eds. Marco Mostert and Anna Adamska (Turnhout, 2014), 65–85.

4   Cf. Anna Grabowska, "Bunt wójta Alberta w historiografii," 19–30 (the article contains a summary of the earlier literature); also: Gawlas, *O kształt zjednoczonego królestwa*, 94; Piotr Okniński, *Kształtowanie się miasta komunalnego w Krakowie w XIII w. Struktury ustrojowe, ramy przestrzenne i podstawy gospodarcze* [Formation of the municipal city in Krakow in the 13th century. Systemic structures, spatial framework and economic foundations] (Warszawa, 2019), chap. 5.

5   Mrozowicz, "Pieśń o wójcie krakowskim," 42 (there the older literature discussed).

6   Mrozowicz, "Pieśń o wójcie krakowskim," 42: "Que est Almanorum cura, ut quemque veniunt, semper volunt primi esse".

town council (except for the Armenians and Jews).[7] To arrive at an answer, let it begin with Krakow's political and economic status in the 14th century.

Entering the second half-century of its existence as a center under the German Law, Krakow in the early 14th century was already an important trading and financial center in Lesser Poland; local merchants regularly traveled to the Netherlands to buy precious textiles.[8] Politically, the local ruling elite (headed by a hereditary vogt) backed the Bohemian Přemyslid dynasty. The change on the throne in 1306 had been supported in lieu of a granting two important privileges – one for hereditary mayoralty and the other established the partial staple rights for copper, giving local merchants a monopoly on trade in this valuable commodity, one of Poland's most important exports to Western Europe.[9] Catastrophic in its effects, Vogt Albert's Revolt ended the period of hereditary vogtship in Krakow's history and ushered in the largest political transformation of the Middle Ages in the town. As a result, the town council, essentially the representative body of the local merchants, took over town government. Ladislaus the Elbow-High had pursued a relatively restrained policy toward the town whose ruling elite had risen up against him and who had invited in a foreign prince from Silesia. Ladislaus' son, Kasimir the Great, in contrast, maintained close contacts with a group of Krakow burghers and borrowed large sums of money from them, and was responsible for the flourishing of this leading town of the kingdom.[10] During this period, two new towns were founded – Kazimierz (1335) and Kleparz (1366) – which thereafter were part of the Krakow metropolitan area. Meanwhile, a building boom was underway

---

7   Cf. Sławomir Gawlas, "Pytania o tożsamość średniowiecznych Polaków w świetle współczesnych dyskusji humanistyki," [Questions about the identity of medieval Poles in the light of contemporary discussions in the humanities] in *Symboliczne i realne podstawy tożsamości społecznej w średniowieczu*, eds. Sławomir Gawlas and Paweł Żmudzki (Warszawa, 2017), 15–82 (there the older literature discussed); also: Sławomir Gawlas, "Die mittelalterliche Nationenbildung am Beispiel Polens. Probleme der Nationenbildung in Europa," *Mittelalterliche nationes, neuzeitliche Nationen. Probleme der Nationenbildung in Europa*, eds. Almut Bues, Rex Rexheuser (Wiesbaden, 1995), 121–43; Henryk Samsonowicz, "My Polacy. Czyli o początkach polskiej świadomości narodowej," [We, Poles. That is, about the beginnings of Polish national consciousness] in *Historia vero testis temporum. Księga jubileuszowa poświęcona Profesorowi Krzysztofowi Baczkowskiemu w 70. rocznicę urodzin*, eds. Janusz Smołucha, Anna Waśko, Tomasz Graff, and Paweł F. Nowakowski (Kraków, 2008), 617–28.
8   Marcin Starzyński, *Das mittelalterliche Krakau. Der Stadtrat im Herrschaftsgefüge der polnischen Metropole* (Koln/Weimar/Wien, 2015), 113–28.
9   *Codex diplomaticus civitatis Cracoviensis* 1, ed. Franciszek Piekosiński (Cracoviae, 1879) (hereafter cited as CDCC 1), nos. 3–4.
10 Cf. Marcin Starzyński, "Civitas nostra Cracoviensis. A Sketch of the Town Politics of Kazimierz Wielki (part I)," *Studia Historyczne* 55 (2012), 285–303, (part II) 56 (2013), 3–32.

in the town of Krakow itself. The parish church and town hall were rebuilt in the gothic style. The tall tower next to the town hall symbolized the independence, position, and prestige of the town. Cooperation between the local merchants and the collectors from the Apostolic Camera led to an unprecedented concentration of capital in the city. In 1336 and 1342, the king approved two collections of town statutes (the so-called first Krakow code),[11] and in 1358, under a separate diploma, referred to as the great privilege for Krakow, the king regulated the many issues concerning town government and the judiciary.[12] In terms of trade policy, a document from 1344 was noteworthy for establishing the course of trade routes from the Kingdom of Poland to Ruthenia and Hungary. This privilege guaranteed Krakow merchants partial control over transit trade on the largest trade route in Europe at the time, which linked Flanders and Cologne to Ruthenia and Genoa's colonies on the Black Sea.[13] With the next diploma of 1354, King Kasimir the Great confirmed the Krakow merchants' leading position not just in national trade;[14] the text of the document included the momentous statement that the fame of the town and its inhabitants had spread throughout the world.[15] Under this act, all foreign merchants, that is, those from outside the Kingdom of Poland, were obligated to sell their goods in Krakow to the town's merchants or other merchants subject to Kasimir the Great. This document in fact sanctioned the role of Krakow as the major trading center in the restored Kingdom of Poland. Krakow's burghers not only had the monopoly on trade in Hungarian copper, they were able to obstruct direct contact between Prussian merchants and Ruthenia; moreover, from 1354 on, they took possession of all of the goods coming from the East. It was obvious that by granting Krakow all of these trade privileges, Kasimir the Great was encouraging the town's development. It has often been noted in the literature that Krakow occupied pride of place in the king's policies for metropolitan areas. Kasimir was not only building a trading center, but also a modern royal residence modeled on Charles IV's Prague.[16] For Krakow, the most important event of the twelve-year Angevin rule had been the town's acquisition of

---

11   CDCC 1, no. 21, 25.
12   Ibid., no. 32.
13   *Antiquum registrum privilegiorum et statutorum civitatis Cracoviensis*, ed. Stanisław Estreicher (Kraków: Polska Akademia Umiejętności, 1936), no. 3.
14   CDCC 1, no. 29; Jerzy Wyrozumski, *Kraków do schyłku wieków średnich* [Krakow until the end of the Middle Ages] (Kraków, 1992), 230–1.
15   CDCC 1, no. 29: "civitas nostra Cracouiensis et incole ipsius, quorum longe lateque per orbem fama ubilibet commendabiliter predicatur".
16   Sławomir Gawlas, "Monarchia Kazimierza Wielkiego a społeczeństwo," [Casimir the Great's monarchy and society] in *Genealogia – władza i społeczeństwo w Polsce średniowiecznej*, ed. Jan Wroniszewski (Toruń, 1999), 223–4.

general staple rights in 1372,[17] confirmed at the outset of Ladislaus Jagiello's reign (1387).[18] In a certain sense, this document caused trade conflicts with Toruń and Lwów that lasted for years. In the end, both were resolved in Krakow's favor. We should make note of one more document issued by Jagiello in 1399, which regulated court proceedings in the town.[19] To sum up, the 14th century was unquestionably the period of Krakow's most dynamic growth during the Middle Ages.

Next, we can take a look at the inhabitants of 14th century Krakow, facilitated by a reading of the preserved city documents: the previously mentioned oldest judicial book of 1301–1375, town court books from 1365 to 1397, and a fragment of the town council book from 1392. Though relevant and authoritative, the geography of migration into Krakow that has been reconstructed based on these source documents is encumbered because of an error. Namely, judicial books recorded only those burghers who, either out of need or necessity, had to appear in court.

Fifty years ago, Marian Friedberg, employing names as a criterion, attempted to estimate the size of Krakow's Polish population in the first decade of the 14th century based on court records (he counted barely 80).[20] Years later, Józef Mitkowski corrected these findings, pointing out the pitfalls of interpreting archival documents that not only did not register all of the townspeople, but in which their identity (often a question of how their names were recorded by the chancellery) could not always be determined. Mitkowski thought that the city's entire Polish population before 1257 – about 5,000 people – was permanently settled there. According to his calculations, in the 14th century the number of Polish burghers would have comprised close to 20% of the entire population of Krakow.[21]

Perhaps we should not be so concerned with Krakow's demographics in the period after the adoption of the Magdeburg Law in the broad sense, but rather with the presence among the ruling elites of arrivals from a particular geographic region. The influx of settlers was heavily influenced by the Wrocław origins of two of the settlement entrepreneurs, Gedko Stilvoyt and Diethmar Volk; a third was Jacob, a former judge or vogt of Nyssa, which was under the bishops of Wrocław. These three settlement entrepreneurs were responsible

---

17   CDCC 1, no. 42.
18   Ibid., no. 649.
19   CDCC 1, no. 42.
20   Marian Friedberg, *Kultura polska a niemiecka* [Polish and German culture] 1 (Poznań, 1946), 281–282.
21   Józef Mitkowski, "Nationality Problems and Patterns in Medieval Polish Towns. The Example of Cracow," *Zeszyty Naukowe Uniwersytetu* Jagiellońskiego 59 (1978), 36–42.

for the geographic region from which the settlers came, recruiting them from Silesian towns with which, we must assume, they were intimately familiar. Later, settlers from the towns of the Holy Roman Empire proper, such as Essen, Fulda, Cologne, Lübeck, and Nuremberg began to appear in Krakow. Interestingly, however, not one of them became involved in the town government. Thus, in the 13th and early 14th centuries the Silesians controlled the town government. Their names are recorded in their strictly German form, as well as universal Christian forms. I would not take it so categorically like Jerzy Rajman, who estimates that "the entire population of Krakow after the adoption of Magdeburg Law spoke German."[22] German was above all the administrative language (chancelleries), or to take a more limited view, of court documents. A few rare surviving diplomas were written in Latin.[23]

During the period of Vogt Albert's Rebellion, the town government was headed by Silesians, who had arrived from the former Duchy of Wrocław from Brzeg and Nyssa; but of greater importance were those from the duchy of Opole, which ceased to exist in 1281, and from Śląsk Opawski (Cieszyn, Ketř, Głubczyce, and Racibórz). It is worth mentioning that the residents of Krakow maintained lively contacts with Prague and that the shortest route connecting the two towns led through Racibórz and Opawa.[24] Several influential patrician families came from some of the towns mentioned above, although political differences between them were noticeable. Perhaps the most influential was the Keczer family (whose name originated either from Ketř, which lay in Bohemia, or from a locally derived surname from there). The settlers from there belonged to at least five lines of the family. Wolrad was councilor in the late 13th century. Diethmar (from a different line of the family) was the settlement entrepreneur of Bronowice near Krakow. Henryk of Ketř was a member of the town council. Gottfried, also a council member, was the husband of Cyna, the daughter of the Diethmar mentioned earlier. Hellwig was a juror. These are the members of the first traceable generation of the family that consolidated the Keczers' later position in Krakow, building up a large fortune and influence among the elite, whose ranks they filled for three generations.[25] It is certain that the family did not belong to the 'vogt party' since they kept their offices after 1312, like

---

22 Jerzy Rajman, "Mieszczanie z Górnego Śląska w elicie władzy Krakowa w XIV wieku," [Townsmen from Upper Silesia in the power elite of Kraków in the 14th century] in *Elita władzy miasta Krakowa i jej związki z miastami Europy w średniowieczu i epoce nowożytnej (do połowy XVII wieku). Zbiór studiów*, ed. Zdzisław Noga (Kraków, 2011), 50.

23 E.g., *Kodeks dyplomatyczny miasta Krakowa* 3 [Diplomatic code of the city of Krakow] (henceforth: KDMK), ed. Franciszek Piekosiński (Cracoviae, 1882), no. 368.

24 Rajman, "Mieszczanie," 51.

25 Ibid., 53–61.

Wigand of Głubczyce, the founder of the well-known Wigandi family.[26] For his part, Herman of Racibórz represented a radically different view on town politics. Recorded at the head of the list of town councilors for many years, he was one of the chief instigators of the burghers' rebellion.[27] What was it then that caused the division between Krakow's political leaders at the time? It would appear that, primarily, the split was about the shape and future of town politics, namely between those who favored opportunities guaranteed by Ladislaus the Elbow-High's rule, and those who wished to exploit earlier contacts established during Bohemian rule in Lesser Poland, as well as their own Silesian or Bohemian-Silesian connections. Therefore, I would not assume a conflict along 'ethnic'/'national' lines within the ethnically diverse circle of Krakow burghers as part of the events of what is called 'Vogt Albert's Rebellion' in the literature.

Immigrants from Italy, called Gallici in source documents, also began to settle in 14th century Krakow.[28] They start to appear in the record after 1315. In 1339, the vogt of Wieliczka was Niccolo Mannente, a Genoan who worked closely with the collectors of the Apostolic Camera. As mentioned earlier, cooperation with this body was one of the most lucrative sources of income for Krakow's burghers. Hence the Gallici relatively quickly gained entry to the city's financial and political elites. They were desirable business partners, whose connections could open entirely new trade horizons. Frederik Gallicus was a member of the jury from 1337 and a member of the town council beginning in 1343. From 1357 to 1358, the Genoan Paulinus Cavallo was a member of the town council and Gottfried Fattinante was a councillor in 1372. The last two mentioned merit a closer look. Shortly after their arrival in Poland both of them not only developed businesses in Krakow, but also established dealings with the royal court, taking over the most lucrative of all of the industries in the kingdom – the salt mines.

Paulinus came to Krakow in the 1330s. He is registered as a Genoan and Krakovian burgher. He worked with the Camera collectors and tried to persuade the Bardi banking family to open a branch in Krakow (the event would have been unprecedented had his plans come to fruition). From the mid-1340s he ran the Bochnia salt mine. In 1350, he purchased a house on the Main

---

26   Ibid., 61–4.
27   Ibid., 66–8.
28   Jan Ptaśnik, "Włoski Kraków za Kazimierza Wielkiego i Władysława Jagiełły," [Italian Krakow for Kazimierz the Great and Władysław Jagiełło] *Rocznik Krakowski* 13 (1911), 58–64.

Market Square, the most prestigious area of the city, clearly accentuating his position in the community.

Gottfried, another of the Genoans who appear in source records, was a salt mine administrator during the reigns of Kasimir the Great, Louis I of Hungary, and Ladislaus Jagiello. A very cunning merchant, he gave significant loans to subsequent kings. Among the information that speaks to the scale of his far-ranging trade contacts is, for example, the fact that he maintained a storehouse in distant Ruthenian Kolomyya. Because of his contacts, he was naturally 'invited' to join the town government. However, he had an unpleasant experience there when in 1372 the servant of Krakow's 'magnus procurator' was imprisoned for robbing two peasants. The 'magnus procurator' felt that this was an infringement on his rights, and in response he had two councilmen jailed, one of whom was Gottfried. As his last will and testament shows, his ties to Krakow, "which begrudged him neither fortune not honors,"[29] were very close. He founded an altar at St. Mary's church and transferred patronage rights to the town council. He left the considerable sum of 500 florins and 100 'marcas' to the town hall, admitting that as he himself had once been in charge of the city treasury he did not adequately execute his responsibilities.[30] The presence of Italians in the town itself and among its leadership was not likely to incite conflict. They were very desirable to those in the town hall. They elevated the town's status.

One should not forget about the Jews who had built an organized community in Krakow long before the city adopted Magdeburg Law.[31] In the new town plan, one of the streets leading out from the Main Market Square was called Jewish (it was first mentioned in the archival records in 1304). A synagogue, ritual baths, and a school were erected. The wealthiest members of the community – bankers and money lenders such as Dobry, Lewko, Ossman, and Smerl – had homes there. The Jews were exempt from town jurisdiction. They had a completely different lifestyle. Although they did not dress any differently than the rest of the burghers, they had at least their own cuisine, their own holy days, and their own language. The quarter between Wiślna and Jewish streets was by no means closed off, and Christians lived there alongside the

---

29   Ibid., 63.
30   *Codex diplomaticus cathedralis ad s[anctum] Wenceslaum ecclesiae Cracovienis* 2, ed. Franciszek Piekosiński (Cracoviae, 1883), no. 396: "pretactus Gotfridus quondam distributor peccuniarum civitatis Cracouiensis et legalis consul extiterat, et si ex sua negligencia in consulendo, distribuendo seu exaccionem exsoluendo aliquos errores commisisset, ex quibus ipsi civitati damna aliqua evenissent".
31   Hanna Zaremska, *Żydzi w średniowiecznej Polsce. Gmina krakowska* [Jews in Medieval Poland. Krakow commune] (Warszawa, 2011), 332–41, 344–67.

Jews. There, conflicts could have and probably did occur. One such conflict is described in the chronicle of Wincenty Kadłubek, but in the 14th century this was not a dangerous neighborhood. The Jews' privileged status and their commercial and money-lending businesses engendered a rising tide of aversion, something described in the memorandum presented by the city council to King Kasimir the Great in 1369. Among other things, the burghers complained that the royal city of Krakow was becoming impoverished. They sought the cause in "Jewish domination". They accused the Jews of rapes and other crimes against the burghers, of breaking not only city ordinances, but also the royal privileges that Krakow had received. Perhaps the abovementioned situation in the town was consciously exaggerated by the chancellery clerk who wrote the document, but it is not different from a record of offenses committed by Jews against Krakow burghers. For example, an unnamed Jew forced a certain Niczco Borkhard and his wife to leave the town. He held Niczco's debenture bond and when the debtor was unable to repay the loan, the moneylender took over his property. Another Jew acted similarly against the burgher Merklin, a pursemaker, although in this case the debenture bond was counterfeit. The third burgher, Wilusz Kazimierz, was saved from being turned out of the town by royal intervention. Another Jew held a bond, also counterfeit, on his home. The councilmen did not fail to mention an incident involving the son of Lewko, the king's banker, mint master, and lease-holder of the salt works in Bochnia and Wieliczka, "without a doubt the most prominent of Poland's medieval Jews."[32] The son was lightly wounded while in the town. The actual perpetrator was never apprehended, but Lewko had "another Christian", most likely a random burgher, detained; he was badly wounded in the process and placed under arrest.[33] The magnitude of the growing problem is illustrated in a document drawn up by the councilmen in March 1370, at the special request of Kasimir the Great. It mentions that in the name of the entire town, a guarantee of safety was granted to Lewko, his wife, and their children, including Kasym, who was described as "episcopus Judeorum" [Jewish bishop], and his successors. It is not difficult to explain the king's motive if we take into consideration the fact that the Krakow burghers' accusations against members of the Jewish community also affected the family of the abovementioned Lewko, who had extended numerous cash loans for Kasimir.

To sum up the above reflections, the answer to the question of whether there were nationality-based conflicts in 14th century Krakow, is negative. There was

---

32 Zofia Wenzel-Homecka, "Lewko," in *Polski słownik biograficzny* 17 (Wrocław, 1972), 251–2.
33 *Liber proscriptionum et gravaminum civitatis Cracoviensis 1360–1422*, ed. Bożena Wyrozumska, (Kraków, 2001), 132–3.

no friction between Polish burghers and German burghers, either during Vogt Albert's Rebellion, or later. There were conflicts between the town government and the Jewish community, but they were not significant in the context of this rebellion. From outside, the town itself was viewed as a foreign area, an assemblage of newcomers from all over, who spoke different languages and were subject to a different set of laws. That is certainly how the inhabitants of nearby villages viewed its residents: as outsiders, as 'Theutonici.' The burghers themselves, although they came from various backgrounds, constituted a unified *communitas* and in view of the facts cited here, the news of the murder of Krakow's burghers (noted in "Rocznik Krasińskich") who were not able to pronounce correctly the Polish-language-puzzle is greatly exaggerated.

CHAPTER 18

Kraków II: *'Ad hoc traxit me natura ...'*. Social Stereotypes in Kraków and the Rebellion of Vogt Albert of 1311–1312

Piotr Okniński

The urban landscape of medieval Poland emerged under the influence of Western European cultural patterns. Already in the Early Middle Ages the stages of Polish urbanization had evolved due to the influx of foreign merchants.[1] Their migrations intensified in the period of what was called the German colonization (*Ostsiedlung*) in the 13th century.[2] Besides money and luxury commercial goods, the newcomers also introduced their specific habits, customs, and institutions; it had been also the German settlers who contributed the most to the establishment of the first autonomous municipalities in the Polish lands.[3] Despite the inevitable Polonization, at least until the mid-16th century, the ruling elite of the largest Polish municipal town, the capital city of Kraków, was dominated by the families of German financiers, merchants, and craftsmen.[4] Their cultural distinctiveness was accompanied by a specific set of political and economic goals that were often opposed to the interests of ducal and royal power and the ambitions of the Polish nobility. The so-called

---

[1] Benedykt Zientara, "Foreigners in Poland in the 10th–15th Centuries. Their Role in the Opinion of Polish Medieval Community," *APH* 29 (1974), 5–28; ibid., "Die deutschen Einwanderer in Polen vom 12. bis zum 14. Jahrhundert," *Die deutsche Ostsiedlung des Mittelalters als Problem der europäischen Geschichte. Reichenau Vorträge 1970–1972*, ed. Walter Schlesinger (Sigmaringen, 1975), 333–348; Christian Lübke, *Fremde im östlichen Europa. Von Gesellschaften ohne Staat zu verstaatlichten Gesellschaften (9.–11. Jahrhundert)* (Köln, 2001).

[2] Adrienne Körmendy, *Melioratio terrae. Vergleichende Untersuchungen über die Siedlungsbewegung im östlichen Europa im 13.–14. Jahrhundert* (Poznań, 1995).

[3] Benedykt Zientara, "Socio-economic and spatial transformation of Polish towns during the period of location," *APH* 34 (1976), 57–83.

[4] Józef Mitkowski, "Nationality Problems and Patterns in Medieval Polish Towns: The Example of Cracow," *Zeszyty Naukowe Uniwersytetu Jagiellońskiego. Prace Historyczne* 59 (1978), 31–42; Henryk Samsonowicz, "Gesellschaftliche Pluralität und Interaktion in Krakau," *Prag und Wien. Funktionen von Metropolen im frühmodernen Staat*, ed. Marina Dmitrieva and Karen Lambrecht (Stuttgart, 2000), 117–129; Karin Friedrich: "Cives Cracoviae: Bürgertum im frühneuzeitlichen Krakau zwischen Stadpatriotismus und nationaler Pluralität," ibid., 143–161; Leszek Belzyt, *Krakau und Prag zwischen dem 14. und 17. Jahrhundert. Vergleichende Studien zur Sozial-, Kultur- und Wirtschaftsgeschichte ostmitteleuropäischer Metropolen* (Toruń, 2003).

rebellion of Vogt Albert in 1311–1312 against the rule of Duke Ladislaus the Elbow-High marked the culmination of national animosities in Lesser Poland. The brutal suppression of the rebellion also appears to be a crucial step on the way toward the restoration of the Polish Kingdom, and resulted in a permanent political marginalization of Polish towns.[5] Polish national historiography of the 19th century tended to perceive the rebellion of the Kraków burgers as a modern insurrection driven by pure German nationalism. Such an anachronistic perspective was obviously affected by the national animosities of the time, which for quite a while hindered research into the history of Polish-German relations.[6] Beginning in the 1960s some very prominent Polish and German scholars have distanced themselves from such sentiments by emphasizing the complexity of the socio-economic background of numerous national conflicts in medieval Central Europe.[7] Without going into complex discussions on the definition of medieval *nationes*, I would like instead to demonstrate how the memory of the Kraków rebellion of 1311–1312 shaped the collective political identity of Polish elites.

The eruption of anti-German sentiments during the rebellion is clearly reflected in two contemporary ducal charters. Both diplomas were aimed against the economic interests of insubordinate burgers and provided far-reaching rewards to the ecclesiastical institutions that remained loyal to the ruler. The first charter was issued on 21 Dec. 1311, approximately half a year after the outbreak of the rebellion and was addressed to the Benedictine monastery of Tyniec. According to the duke's view as expressed in the document, it was issued "due to the public guilt, perjuries, treacheries, and commission of *crimen laese maiestatis* performed terribly and in a most disgraceful way against us by the burgers of our city of Kraków, our successors, and the whole Polish nation, by giving the mentioned city to foreign princes, extirpating and exterminating us, their rightful and legitimate rulers and heirs (…)".[8] An almost

---

[5] Janusz Kurtyka, "Die wiedervereinigte Königreich Polen unter Ladislaus Ellenlang (1304/5–1333) und Kasimir dem Großen (1333–1370)," *Die "Blüte" der Staaten des östlichen Europa im 14. Jahrhundert*, ed. Marc Löwener (Warszawa, 2004), 107–142; Sławomir Gawlas, "Polen – eine Ständegesellschaft an der Peripherie des lateinischen Europas," in *Europa in späten Mittelalter. Politik – Gesellschaft – Kultur*, ed. Rainer Ch. Schwinges, Christian Hesse, and Peter Moraw, Historische Zeitschrift. Beiheft 40 (München, 2006), 237–261.

[6] *Deutsche Ostforschung und polnische Westforschung im Spannungsfeld von Wissenschaft und Politik. Disziplinen im Vergleich*, ed. Jörg Hackmann, Rudolf Jaworski, and Jan M. Piskorski (Osnabrück; Poznań, 2002).

[7] Benedykt Zientara, "Nationality Conflicts in the German-Slavic Borderland in the 13th–14th Centuries and their Social Scope," *APH* 22 (1970), 207–225.

[8] *Kodeks dyplomatyczny klasztoru tynieckiego*, [The Diplomatic Code of the Tyniec Abbey] ed. Wojciech Kętrzyński, (Lwów, 1875), nr 41: "propter demerita publica, periuria, tradiciones,

identical clause is contained in the second charter, issued on 17 April 1312, about two months before the collapse of the rebellion; it is addressed to the Poor Clares monastery in Stary Sącz.[9] As it can be seen, the rebellion was officially presented and condemned not only as a threat to the rule of Ladislaus, but also to his legal successors (*heredes nostros*) as well as the whole Polish nation (*gens Polonica*). After the suppression of the rebellion, Ladislaus also ordered the removal of the German language from use in Kraków's urban chancery; thereafter all urban books of records were to be produced in Latin.[10] Not long after that, approximately in the 2nd quarter of the 14th century, an anonymous clergyman wrote an extensive historiographical note about the rebellion in *The Annals of the Kraków Chapter*, offering an interesting, expressive explanation of the burgers' repugnant behavior. He claimed that "(...) the burgers of Kraków, tormented by the madness of German rage, friends of fraud, hidden and secret enemies of the peace, opposed master Ladislaus, the duke of Kraków and Sandomierz, as well as the ruler of the whole Polish Kingdom, kissing him just as Judas kissed Jesus, acting against the provisions in their oath, with no fear of God, and presented for office Boleslaus, prince of Opole (...)".[11] Obviously, the cited passage clearly fits into the rhetorical and ideological framework of both aforementioned ducal charters. These similarities are completely understandable, for the social milieu of the cathedral chapter in Kraków was closely related to the milieu of the medieval Polish ducal and later royal chancery.

---

prodiciones, comisiones criminis illese maiestatis, quas cives civitatis nostre Cracoviensis nephandissime in nos heredesque nostros ac gentem Polonicam atrociter perpetrarunt tradentes civitatem dictam principis peregrinis, evellendo et exterminando nos suos veros et legitimos dominos et heredes (...)."

9   *Kodeks dyplomatyczny Małopolski* 2, [The Diplomatic Code of the Lesser Poland] ed. Franciszek Piekosiński, (Kraków, 1886), nr 557: "[...] propter demerita publica, periuria, tradiciones, producciones civium civitatis nostre Cracoviensis, que in nos, heredes nostros et gentem Polonicam prodicionaliter verbo, factis et operibus commiserunt, exterminando et excludendo nefandisssime a bonis temporalibus et perpetuis hereditariis in opprobrium nostrum, heredum nostrorum et gentis Polonice, sibi alios dominos ausu temerario fovendo, lese maiestatis scelera perpetrando [...]."

10 Anna Adamska, "Away with the Germans and Their Language? Linguistic Conflict and Urban Records in Early Fourteenth-Century Cracow," in *Uses of the Written Word in Medieval Towns*, ed. Marco Mostert, Anna Adamska (Turnhout, 2014), 65–85.

11 *Rocznik kapituły krakowskiej*, [The Annals of the Cracow Chapter] ed. Zofia Kozłowska-Budkowa, MPH. Nova series 5 (Warszawa, 1978), 104: "[...] cives Cracovienses rabie furoris Germanici perusti, fraudis amici, pacis quoque palleati hostes et oculti, domino Wladyzlao duci Cracovie, Sandomirie ac domino tocius regni Polonie quemadmodum Judas Jesu osculum prebentes, vice iuramenti prestantes cautelam, deposito Dei timore contradixerunt et Bolezlaum ducem Opoliensem induxerunt [...]."

A similar social environment was probably also responsible for the composing of what was called the *Song of Kraków Vogt Albert* (*De quondam advocate Cracoviensi Alberto*).[12] This poetic piece is preserved in two manuscripts from the mid-15th century, written by two anonymous copyists associated with the Kraków cathedral clergy. The song has a form of a traditional liturgical sequence and consists of two parts of different authorship. The first one, the older of the two, could have been formulated shortly after the suppression of the rebellion. It offers a moralizing, satirical, and sensational story of Vogt Albert, the leader of the rebellion, while the second part is a vicious anti-German pamphlet. According to the second part, composed much later than the events it describes, the moral responsibility for the Kraków uprising of 1311–1312 rested with the insidious "nature" of all Germans. The Song's protagonist, Albert, claims: "I was brought to this by the nature typical of the Germans".[13] Apparently, the Germans settling down in foreign countries were too proud, greedy, and vain to submit to the local political and social order: "Wherever they go, they always want to be first, never the subordinated ones".[14] According to the next phrases, these wicked, unjustified ambitions of the German newcomers push them to sneaky intrigues against the indigenous people: "These are the habits through which they acquire favors. First, they humble themselves, soon after they take their [the indigenes'] daughters for wives, having earlier given their own daughters to the locals. This is how they become related. But all of this is only a deceit. Thus, when a German becomes a well-known person, he immediately climbs higher. He goes to the owner of the village and offers him a thousand grosses to become a judge. Thereafter he works every day to immediately become the owner of the village by paying lots of money. This way, the one who was brought in a basket becomes a vogt of the village after expelling the heirs".[15] Undeniably, these were not just the personal views of some anonymous poet. It seems significant that in the oldest acknowledged Polish catalogue of national attributes, composed in

---

12 Henryk Kowalewicz, "Pieśń o wójcie krakowskim Albercie," [The Song of Cracow Vogt Albert] *Pamiętnik Literacki* 56/3 (1965), 125–138; Mrozowicz, "Pieśń o wójcie krakowskim," 32–42.

13 Henryk Kowalewicz, "Pieśń o wójcie,",135: "Ad hoc traxit me natura, / que est Almanorum cura".

14 Ibid.: "Ut quocunque veniunt, / semper volunt primi esse / et nulli prorsus subesse."

15 Ibid.: "Illos habent ipsi mores, / per quos aquirant favores: / primo se humiliant, / mox eorum ducunt natas / suas ipsis prius datas / et sic se conciliant. | Sed sub dolo fit hoc totum: / cum se bene facit notum / iam palpat ulterius, / ad patronum vadit ville, / offert sibi grossos mille / ut fiat sudarius. | Mox adhuc sudat diatim, / ut sit heres ville statim / datis nummis pluribus. / Sic ville fit advocatus, / qui in sporta sit portatus, / exclusis heredibus."

the social milieu of Kraków University and conserved in a rhetorical tractate from 1425–1434, "Saxony" was branded as "usurping": "Saxonia usurpatrix".[16] The accusations expressed in the song discussed above sound particularly similar to another anti-German pamphlet, *De Theutunicis bonum dictamen* [*The Good Writing about the Germans*], composed in Bohemia in the 2nd half of the 14th century.[17] Its anonymous author accuses Germans of deceptiveness, fake modesty, and greed. He claims that they come to foreign countries as humble scribes, publicans, and house servants, flattering their patrons in order to take away their wealth and daughters. After being elected to the town council they steal the whole wealth from the country, oppress their neighbors, and rebel against the true rulers; this is how Judas and Pilate behaved ("Judas et Pilatus sic fecere").[18] The unclear relationship between the Bohemian pamphlet and the poem written in Kraków turns out to be even more suggestive in light of the last strophe of the Polish song, dedicated to the situation of deceived Bohemians: "This is how Bohemians were deceived and expelled from their own properties by these Germans. They have almost vanished, sold off their goods, left with only boots and shirts".[19]

The belief in the treacherous nature of the German burgers of Kraków persisted unshaken; it was even supported by further historical examples of their insubordination. Particular attention has been devoted to their behavior during the civil war in Lesser Poland in 1288–1290, when they opposed the political will of the Polish nobles by giving their town to the Silesian duke, Henry IV Probus. This deed, criticized already in medieval sources, was interestingly evoked in the poem by Klemens Janicki (1516–1543) included in *Vitae regum Polonorum* [*The Lives of Polish Kings*]. This poetic collection, finished in 1542 and printed for the first time posthumously in 1563, enjoyed great popularity in the following centuries, subsequently being modified, paraphrased, and translated. Janicki wrote that during the reign of Lestko the Black (1279–1288) the keys to the city of Kraków were given only to Germans, who later insidiously accepted the rule of Silesians, letting them to sneak into their city

---

16   "Libri formulare saeculi XV," in *Starodawne Prawa Polskiego Pomniki* 10, ed. Stanisław Ulanowski (Kraków, 1888), 8; Stanisław Kot, "Old International Insults and Praises," *Harvard Slavic Studies* 2 (1954), 181–209.

17   František Graus, *Die Nationenbildung der Westslawen im Mittelalter* (Sigmaringen, 1980), 103 et seq., 126 (fn. 290), 221–223.

18   "Ein deutschfeindliches Pamphlet aus Böhmen aus dem 14. Jahrhundert," ed. Wilhelm Wostry, *Mitteilungen des Vereines für Geschichte der Deutschen in Böhmen* 53/3–4 (1915), 228–229.

19   "Sic Bohemi sunt delusi, / de bonis suis detrusi / ab ispis Theutunicis / et iam quasi perierunt, / sua bona expenderunt, / in caligis et tunicis."

under the cover of the night. Although "the perfidious party won", Henry's success achieved by trickery did not last long, for the duke was poisoned by his own people. This way, the one who had lived his life by committing frauds, died deservedly by deceit.[20] Vanity, deceptiveness, and greed were widely attributed to the burgers of Kraków even in later writings. Walerian Nekanda-Trepka (approx. 1584–1640) in *Liber generationis plebeanorum* [The Book of the Origin of Plebeans] preserved in a manuscript from 1626, accused many contemporary Kraków patrician families of obtaining false and unjust ennoblement. In the preface to his work he claimed that in Kraków, "where they [the burgers] have German names, they will change [them] to Polish -ski [a suffix typical to a Polish noble name], and then, after abandoning their merchant origins, they will try to imitate the Polish nobility."[21] When criticizing the insidious nature of Kraków inhabitants, Trepka also recalled numerous historical examples of treasons committed by them against their legitimate rulers, adding also an interesting detail to the story of the rebellion of Vogt Albert. He claimed, namely, that the rebels expelled from Kraków and Poland after the collapse of the uprising eventually "returned calmly to their habitats".[22] With such a remark Trepka clearly is suggesting that the contemporary Kraków patricians were not only related to the former rebels, but were also irreversibly stigmatized by their pathetic, treacherous behavior; in this way, Trepka's passionate accusations directed at the Kraków burgers receive a quasi-historical justification.

20 Klemens Janicki, *Vitae regum Polonorum elegacio craminae descriptiae* (Antverpiae, 1563), fol. 10v.: "Teutonibus solis claves permiserat urbis, / quae Regni titulum possidet una, Niger. / Illi Silesium furtim sub nocte silenti / moenibus accipiunt, cui studuere, ducem. (…) / Perfida pars vicit: regnat Probus, exulat haeres. / Sed res parta dolo non diuturna fuit. / Silesii Henricum dubio rapuere veneno, / quod factis alter, nomine et alter erat. / Qui fraudem in vita coluit, rem fraude paravit, / qua periit, dignus fraude perire fuit."
21 Walerian Nekanda-Trepka, "Liber generationis plebeanorum ('Liber chamorum')," in *Biblioteka Pisarzów Polskich* 13, ed. W. Dworzaczek, J. Bartyś, and Z. Kuchowicz (Wrocław, 1963), part I, 17: "a w Krakowie, co po niemiecku teraz zową się, na polskie ski będą transformować, w ten czas, kiedy kupiectwa porzuciwszy, za ślachtę będą się chcieć udawać […]."
22 Ibid., 15: "z lekka wnieśli się do onych swych siedlisk."

PART 5

German-Polish Stereotypes in Modern Times as a Counterpart to the Medieval Period

CHAPTER 19

Contemporary Stereotypes within German-Polish Relations: A Linguistic Approach

Jarochna Dąbrowska-Burkhardt

> It is harder to crack prejudice than an atom.
> ALBERT EINSTEIN

⋮

> The true enemy of man is generalization.
> CZESŁAW MIŁOSZ

⋮

> A Nation? says Bloom. A Nation is the same people living in the same place.
> JAMES JOYCE

⋮

The interest in what somebody thinks about us or how we are perceived by others, but also how we perceive the "other" or "stranger" has always been incredibly fascinating. The proof of this lies in the many studies about stereotypes and prejudices, which describe this phenomenon in various disciplines like sociology, psychology, history, ethnography, anthropology, literature and of course in linguistics. It can be said that the "image" or "images" from one nation to another emerge from different traditions, historical experiences, expectations and often also from wishful thinking.[1] The attribution of specific

---

1 Wolf D. Gruner, "Das Deutschlandbild als zentrales Element der europäischen Dimension der deutschen Frage in Geschichte und Gegenwart," in *Die hässlichen Deutschen? Deutschland im Spiegel der westlichen und östlichen Nachbarn*, ed. Günter Trautmann (Darmstadt, 1991), 29–59, at 30.

characteristics to certain ethnicities seems to be a necessity for many people and has a long tradition. Even the earliest existent written documents in Old High German like "Glossae Cassellanae" from the 9th century provide evidence for this view. One reads in this document:

> Stulti sunt Romani / Sapienti Paioari / Modica est Sapienti / In romana plus habent / Stultitia / Quam sapientia[2]

> [Roman people are stupid. Bavarians are smart; there is little smartness in the Romans; they have more stupidity than smartness].

An anonymous writer from the 18th century is aware of the matter and wrote as follows in 1738:

> Wer als ein vernüfftiger und ehrlicher Mann eine gantze Nation beurtheilen, und von derselben Gemüths-Beschaffenheit eine zuverlässige Nachricht geben will, der muß nicht allein einen gantz ungemeinen Verstand, sondern auch eine mehr als gewöhnliche Aufrichtigkeit besitzen, und so wohl sich selbst, als das gantze menschliche Geschlecht aus dem Grunde kennen. Er muß hiernechst so wohl aus den Geschichten als aus der Erfahrung wissen, wie die berühmtesten Völcker vor langer oder kurtzer Zeit gewesen, was die theils annoch sind, theils zu werden Hoffnung haben.[3]

> [Whoever, as a rational and honest man, judges an entire nation and wants to give reliable news about the selfsame nature of its mind, must not only possess a wholly uncommon intellect, but also a more than ordinary sincerity, and so must know both himself as well as the entire human race from the bottom up. Here he must know things from both the stories and the experience, how the most famous nations actually were long ago or a while ago, how they are now but also who they wish to become in the future.]

---

2   *Die Althochdeutschen Glossen*, eds. Elias Steinmeyer and Eduard Sievers (Dublin/Zürich, 1985, repr. 1969), 2nd edition, vol III, 12, v. 67 and 13, v. 2–11.

3   Anonymous writer, *Die so genannte Moscowitische Brieffe, Oder Die, wider die löbliche Rußische Nation Von einem Aus der andern Welt zurück gekommenen Italiäner ausgesprengte abendtheuerliche Verläumdungen und Tausend Lügen. Aus dem Französischen übersetzt / mit einem zulänglichen Register versehen, Und dem Brieffsteller so wohl, als seinen gleichgesinnten Freunden, mit dienlichen Erinnerungen wieder heimgeschickt Von einem Teutschen* (Frankfurt / Leipzig, 1738), 15.

In light of this, a description of a whole nation or a particular language community is indeed very complicated. It is difficult to find a single individual with the knowledge as well as the experience necessary for an objective and complex account of a respective ethnic group. A dearth of profound knowledge creates a filter that allows a place for prejudice and stereotypes instead of facts. The provenance of the former often results out of interests, traditions, ideas, imaginations, expectations and intentions of an individual. In addition to that, daily news has an enormous impact on the image of the "stranger". On the one hand, the image may be the result of contact with representatives of other nations; on the other hand, it may be gained from intermediate sources, for example from the mass media. Yet, it is difficult for individuals to verify this news in a critical way. Max Frisch notes in his diaries in Florence in 1947:[4]

> Wogegen wir in Begriffen leben, die wir meistens nicht überprüfen können; das Radio überzeugt mich von hundert Dingen, die ich nie sehen werde, oder wenn ich sie dann einmal sehe, kann ich sie nicht mehr sehen, weil ich ja schon eine Überzeugung habe, das heißt: eine Anschauung, ohne geschaut zu haben. Die meisten unserer Begriffe, wenn sie konkret werden, können wir gar nicht ertragen; wir leben über unsere Kraft.
>
> [Whereas we live in concepts that we usually cannot verify; the radio convinces me of a hundred of things even though I will never be able to see them and even if I could, I won't see them because I will already have a conviction about them, which means – a conviction without having seen them. Most of our concepts, when they became concrete, we cannot bear at all; we live beyond our strength.]

Of interest here is primarily the linguistic approach in the context of modern ethnic stereotypes in German-Polish relations. Nevertheless, this linguistic depiction of the concept *stereotype* underscores its interdisciplinary character and takes into consideration scientific research from the areas of psychology, sociology, anthropology and, of course, history.

From the linguistic perspective, stereotypes are elements of meaning, i.e., concepts that can be described semantically and pragmatically. These elements can be expressed in different ways and, consequently, be reconstructed. Stereotypes are initially placed on a mental-cognitive level, however verbal realization of them takes place in concrete speech acts at the communicative level. On the mental-cognitive level communicative knowledge such as

---

4   Max Frisch, *Tagebuch 1946–1949* (Frankfurt am Main, 1958), 193.

stereotypes can exist consciously or unconsciously. Stereotypes can have various forms of textualisation and be investigated in many different ways. In communication, stereotypes appear in a variety of forms, depending among other things on the type of medium used, i.e. spoken or written language.[5]

Walter Lippmann, the father of the concept *stereotype*, characterizes in his book "Public Opinion" (1922) the *stereotype* as a particularly resistant phenomenon: "There is nothing so obdurate to education or to criticism as the stereotype".[6] According to Lippmann, stereotypes provide people with thought patterns that can be used to interpret many things:

> For the most part we do not first see, and then define, we define first and then see. In the great blooming, buzzing confusion of the outer world we pick out what our culture has already defined for us, and we tend to perceive that which we have picked out in the form stereotyped for us by our culture.[7]

Lippmann also distinguishes between the "world outside" and "pictures in our heads".[8] He means that "pictures in our heads" or in our thoughts do not appear on the basis of personal experiences, but are acquired as finished images in the socialization process. In addition, in the phenomenon of stereotyping, Lippmann distinguishes positive and negative aspects of this process. On the one hand, stereotypes induce people to a certain standard of behavior and reduce their perception of the environment, but on the other hand, they influence the fact that we can think more economically.[9] The economic function of the stereotype results from man's desire for simplification, because generalizations are unavoidable to a certain extent in order for man to be able to act.[10] In addition to that, stereotypes perform a defensive function that protect us from the overwhelming complexity of our environment:

> The systems of stereotypes may be the core of our personal tradition, the defenses of our position in society. They are an ordered, more or less

---

5   Jarochna Dąbrowska, *Stereotype und ihr sprachlicher Ausdruck im Polenbild der deutschen Presse. Eine textlinguistische Untersuchung* (Tübingen, 1999), 85.
6   Walter Lippmann, *Public Opinion* (New York, 1997) (Originally published New York, 1922), 65.
7   Lippmann, *Public Opinion*, 54–55.
8   Id., 3.
9   Id., 63.
10 Angelika Wenzel, *Stereotype in gesprochener Sprache. Form, Vorkommen und Kommunikation in Dialogen.* (München, 1978), 20.

consistent picture of the world, to which our habits, our tastes, our capacities, our comforts and our hopes have adjusted themselves. They may not be a complete picture of the world, but they are a picture of a possible world to which we are adapted.[11]

Ethnic stereotypes are also based on simplifications, referring to images passed down from generation to generation. They are particularly widespread in the text type "joke". The story often quoted in this context is an episode of how representatives of different languages communities were commissioned to write an essay about an elephant. The Frenchman titled his text "The erotic life of an elephant", the Englishman "The elephant in our colonies", the Russian states "Russia – the homeland of an elephant", the Bulgarian provides his text with the title "Bulgarian elephant is the younger brother of a Russian elephant", the American asks in the title the question "The elephants – how to make them bigger and better?", the German publishes a ten-volume textbook "Elephantology – the introduction to the essence of an elephant", and the Polish writes the text "Elephant and the Polish matter".[12]

The prerequisite for understanding the above anecdote is knowledge of ethnic stereotypes that contrast nations. Without them, the above-mentioned symbolizations, which are based on the simplification of complex facts, would be enormously difficult to understand. Presuppositions play an important role here. They are not discussed as implicit prerequisites of an utterance, but are nevertheless present and are an integral part of the statement. From a linguistic point of view, in such anecdotes or jokes we usually deal with the use of a generic noun which includes all the representatives of the species, designating a typical representative. Generic use clearly favours the singular number, and in languages with articles it appears with a definite article – so in the German equivalent of the presented anecdote we have accordingly: "der Pole" [the Pole], "der Deutsche" [the German], "der Russe" [the Russian] etc.). According to Quasthoff, this generic use of the noun (Singulare pro plurali) is an indicator of typifying content when a group of people is represented by one

---

11   Lippmann, *Public Opinion*, 63.
12   Dąbrowska, *Stereotype und ihr sprachlicher*, 37; Lisaweta von Zitzewitz, *5 mal Polen. Panoramen der Welt* (München, 1992), 82; Tomasz Torbus, *Polen. Ein Reisebuch* (Hamburg, 1993), 17–18; Jarochna Dąbrowska-Burkhardt, "O języku niemieckim w Polsce. Stereotypy i wyobrażenia na przestrzeni wieków," [About German in Poland. Stereotypes and ideas over the centuries] *Lingwistyka Stosowana* 23/3 (2017), 16, https://portal.uw.edu.pl/de/web/lingwistyka-stosowana/home.

representative, who is somewhat deprived of his own personality.[13] Quasthoff calls this kind of verbalization of a stereotype its basic form. One understands by it an explicit All-statement, which is based in the depth structure of a simple predication[14] like e.g., "The Frenchman is the best lover".

Stereotypes are by no means a peculiarity of recent years. In antiquity and the Middle Ages, several works, such as Herodotus, Tacitus, Isidor of Seville, Jean Bodin or Johannes Böhm, contain a rich fund of attributes that characterize peoples.[15] Extremely interesting examples of stereotyping dating back to the beginning of the 18th century are the so-called "tables of nations", which must be considered as a text-image relationship, as they provide a textual-graphical overview of the attributes purportedly characteristic of different ethnic groups. This most famous "table of nations" comes from Austria, or more precisely from Styria, and is dated to 1720–1730.[16] Ten nations were included on this board. The Greeks and Turks were considered together as inhabitants of the Ottoman Empire. The table depicts a [jealous] *eifersichtig* and [lustful] *geilsichtig* Italian, next to a [conceited] *hochmütig* Spaniard, a [malicious] *boßhaft* Russian, a Frenchman suffering from [syphilis] *an Eigner* and an Englishman suffering from [consumption] i.e. [tuberculosis] *Schwindsucht* but bravely [fighting at sea] *Ein See Held*.[17] Hungarians and Poles are European troublemakers. They are described as [impulsive] *Ungestimt* and [rebellious] *Aufriererisch*. They prefer to spend their time [arguing] and [squabbling] *mit Zanken*. A German, on the other hand, appears to be [a kind person in his customs], i.e. [openhearted] and [honest] *offenherzig*. The characteristics of the German character are described as [quite good] *ganz gut*.[18] Undoubtedly, such characteristics of ethnic groups are extremely superficial. Stereotypes appear here in descriptive terms, and the individual juxtapositions, referring directly to each other and comparing traits from adjacent headings, are often of a multilateral nature. As an example of such a confrontation, specific gradations on this table can be used. One of them concerns vices. A Hungarian is purported to be [treacherous] *Veräther*, a Russian in the column next to the Hungarian [more treacherous] *Gar Verätherisch*, and [even more treacherous]

---

13   Uta Quasthoff, *Soziales Vorurteil und Kommunikation. Eine sprachwissenschaftliche Analyse des Stereotyps* (Frankfurt am Main, 1973), 291.
14   Eadem, *Soziales Vorurteil und Kommunikation*, 240.
15   Franz K. Stanzel, "Zur literarischen Imagologie. Eine Einführung," in *Europäischer Völkerspiegel. Imagologisch-ethnographische Studien zu den Völkertafeln des frühen 18. Jahrhunderts*, ed. id. (Heidelberg, 1999), 13–14.
16   Franz K. Stanzel, *Europäer. Ein imagologischer Essay* (Heidelberg, 1998), 14–15.
17   Stanzel, "Zur literarischen Imagologie. Eine Einführung," 41.
18   Ibid.

noch Verätherischer than a Russian would be a Greek or Turk. Such multilateral juxtapositions can also be found in the context of religiosity. The Frenchman is to be [good] *gut* at the religious services, the Italian [a little better] *Etwas besser*, and the German even [more pious] *Noch Andächtiger*. According to the same scheme there are comparisons in the column [characteristics] *Natur u. Eigenschafft*. The Swede is described as [cruel] *Graussam*, the neighbouring Pole as [even more cruel or wild] *Noch wilder*, and next to him the Hungarian is mentioned as [the cruelest of all] *AllerGraussambst*.[19] The highest degree of the adjective [cruel] *Graussam* i.e. [the cruelest] *AllerGraussambst* suggests that the Hungarian leads the way in terms of cruelty and thus the gradation of this trait has been completed. Even more striking in this context is the innovative character of describing the next figure in the table, i.e. a Russian, which is presented as [truly Hungarian] *Gut Ungerisch*. The use of the adjective *ungarisch* [Hungarian] formed from a specific perspective indicates its metaphorical character. The Russian is identified in this case with Hungarian, and thus the semantics of the adjective "Hungarian" implies in this context the 'greatest cruelty, 'bestiality' or 'barbarity'.

Compositions of this kind are undoubtedly not very substantial. In spite of their superficiality, however, they give us a historical insight into the collective perception of different ethnic groups in the first part of the 18th century with regard to their customs and traditions, their preferences, virtues or vices, religiosity, diseases or clothing and so on. In this sense, these categorizations can become one of the comparative historical sources in ethnic stereotype analysis.

National stereotypes form a permanent component of the systems of valuing cultural groups. They change from ancestors to descendants as part of a society's concentrated knowledge. A problematic category in this context is the concept of "national character". Researchers stress, however, that it works well in briefly determining the identity of nations in their long processes of development.[20] It should be noted, however, that nations are nothing natural, and should be seen as imaginary communities that are permanently in the process of being created and so are not natural. To create them the respective groups need the work of institutions and a unifying ideology about which the homogeneity of a nation can be established. To this end, an ideology that influences the homogeneity of a nation that is constantly being re-created is essential, since people defined in this way often do not have excessively many social or

---

19   Ibid.
20   Edmund Lewandowski, *Charakter narodowy Polaków i innych* [The national character of Poles and others] (Londyn/Warszawa, 1995), 10.

cultural similarities with each other, and their identity is established precisely as a result of separation from another group.[21] This separation is an important aspect of stereotyping and manifests itself in the relationship between auto- and heterosterototypes. An autostereotype is an image that a certain group has about itself, i.e., its self-esteem. Heterostereotype is the perception of a stranger, the image we have about others. The autostereotype feeds on the stereotype of others, and above all on the image of its closest neighbours. This conceptual group is also invariably associated with two opposite affects: sympathy for one's own group and aversion to a foreign group. A very important aspect of the analysis of individual auto- and heterostereotypes is therefore the consideration of their mutual relations because both sizes are dialectically related to each other. Thus, the appreciation of one's own group is observed with simultaneous devaluation of foreign ethnic groups, which as a result emphasizes the strangeness of other persons and leads to a demarcation.[22]

These interrelationships also play a key role in Polish-German relations. Lempp draws attention to an interesting dependence shaping the behavior of Poles with reference to the postulate of Polish 'non-discipline', which, in contrast to German 'discipline' and 'accuracy', was particularly popular in Polish society during the partition of Poland that lasted into the 19th century.[23] Concurrently it should be emphasized that Poles interpret such 'non-discipline' as 'not conforming to government' and 'not being small-minded', 'not being a servant who pedantically executes all orders', and such terms are reserved in Polish culture to describe Germans. Thus, a completely different system of values has shaped the two societies over the centuries on the basis of their separation from each other.

In the context of this study, the polarities of national stereotypes that are deeply rooted in Europe must be emphasized at least briefly: Based on the geographical location of individual ethnic groups, certain stereotypes are attributed to them. The first polarity concerns the east and west. According to these, nations living in the west are perceived as 'elegant', 'refined' and 'sophisticated', while the eastern ones are perceived as 'somewhat backward', 'peasant', 'unspoilt' or rather 'undisturbed'.[24] The second polarity refers to the

---

21   Etienne Balibar and Immanuel Wallerstein, *Rasse – Klasse – Nation: Ambivalente Identitäten*, (Hamburg, 1992).
22   Andreas Winkler, "Ethnische Schimpfwörter und übertragener Gebrauch von Ethnika," *Muttersprache* 4 (1994), 320–37, at 323.
23   Albrecht Lempp, "West-östliche Bilder," *Friedrich-Ebert-Stiftung Gesprächskreis Arbeit und Soziales* 19 (1993), 15.
24   Manfred Koch-Hillebrecht, *Das Deutschenbild: Gegenwart, Geschichte, Psychologie* (München, 1977), 248.

north-south axis. Here, the southern nations are attributed more temperament, but also unreliability and disorder, while the northern neighbours are considered tidy, yet rather boring.[25] It is particularly striking that these observations can already be seen on the 18th century table of nations, mentioned earlier. There is a strong west-east polarization in the typifications in terms of good and bad characteristics. Thus, the Spaniard is at the positive end and the *Muskawith* [Russian] as well as *Tirk oder Griech* [Turk or Greek] at the negative end. They are called *Ein Lung Teüfel* (Ein Lügenteufel) [lying devil], *Ein Falscher Bolliticus* (falscher/betrügerischer Politiker) [fraudulent politician] and *Gar faul* [even lazy].[26]

Historically, Polish-German relations are often treated as a thousand years of hatred. The proverb dating back to the 17th century and the times of the aristocratic republic, and which is still popular in the Polish language today, emphasizes the conflicted relations between the representatives of both language communities: *Jak świat światem nie będzie Niemiec Polakowi bratem* [for as long as the world exists the German will never be a brother to the Pole]. This widespread phrase used mainly in everyday situations emphasizes the bad attitude of both nations towards each other, and its speaker suggests (in a way) that Germany is responsible for such a situation.[27] According to Jerzy Holzer, the term *the German* in Polish *Niemiec* is derived from the adjective [pol. *'niemy'* = dumb] and so already leaves no doubt about the feeling of strangeness or dislike that accompanied Polish-German relations at the time of this appelation's emergence.[28] The negative attitude of the Poles towards the Germans is also reflected in the Polish designations for Germans. In the time of the German colonization in the Middle Ages, many Swabians came into Polish areas and the intially objective designation *szwab* [Swabian], although it was not always true, has become almost the insult name for all Germans.[29] Having a similarly negative character to *szwab* is the name *krzyżak* [Crusader; Teutonic Knight], which goes back to the time of the Teutonic Order in Prussia (today mainly North Poland). The designation *Krzyżak* has a more literary tone and is to this

---

25   Werner Bergmann, "Was sind Vorurteile?," *Informationen zur politischen Bildung* 271 (2005), 6.
26   Stanzel, "Zur literarischen Imagologie. Eine Einführung," 41.
27   Wojciech Wrzesiński, "Nachbar oder Feind. Das Klischee des Deutschen in Polen im 19. und 20. Jahrhundert," in *Vorurteile zwischen Deutschen und Polen. Materialien des deutsch-polnischen wissenschaftlichen Symposiums 9. bis 11. Dezember 1992*, ed. Franciszek Grucza (Warszawa, 1994), 63–75, at 64.
28   Jerzy Holzer, "Der widerliche Schwabe, der brutale Preuße...," in *Die hässlichen Deutschen? Deutschland im Spiegel der westlichen und östlichen Nachbarn*, ed. Günter Trautmann (Darmstadt, 1991), 83–89.
29   Ibid.

day a connotation of 'expansionism', 'brutality' and 'unrestrained hatred of the Poles'.[30] In modern times Poles call a German also a *prusak* [Prussian], which is identical with the name used for insects: cockroach. Jerzy Holzer emphasizes that regardless of whether it was a German or an insect, this word evoked similar associations for Poles.[31]

However, if we look at history, we can also see longer periods of peaceful coexistence between Germans and Poles. Jerzy Topolski notes that the mixed feelings of Poles towards Germans are perfectly illustrated just by the titles of works dealing with Polish-German relations.[32] And so Wojciechowski's volume from 1945 is entitled *"Polska – Niemcy. Dziesięć wieków zmagania"* [Poland – Germany. Ten centuries of struggle].[33] In 1987 the work *"Polska – Niemcy. Dziesięć wieków sąsiedztwa"* [Poland – Germany. Ten Centuries of Neighbourhood] was published[34] and in 1992 Wrzesiński poses the question: 'German': *"Sąsiad czy wróg?"* [Neighbour or Enemy?].[35] The titles of these works clearly show that Polish-German relations are characterized by ambivalence and cannot be unequivocally pigeonholed.

In post-war Poland, the socialist government propagated mainly the image of the German aggressor and fascist. Birgit Sekulski emphasizes that the German language in post-war Poland is mainly linked to expressions like *Raus!* [Get out!], *Hände hoch!* [Hands up] or *Heil Hitler!*[36] The last phrase is even transformed into *Hitler kaput!* [broken Hitler!/ finished Hitler! / exhausted Hitler!]. Such knowledge of the German language finds a huge resonance in Polish literature and cinematography, exerting an incredible influence on the formation of stereotypes of everyday life, when groups in the backyard are divided into good ones (i.e. Poles) and bad ones (i.e. Germans), the latter using this fragmentary German. This superficial German anchored in the Polish society sometimes turns out to be even disasterous, as was the case on Thursday 3th May 2018 in one of the episodes of "Milionerzy" ["Millionaires"], a Polish game show, based on the original British format of "Who wants to be

---

30 Ibid.
31 Ibid.
32 Jerzy Topolski, "Rozwój stosunków polsko-niemieckich a problemy polsko-niemieckiego pogranicza," *Rocznik Lubuski* 18 (1993), 7–8.
33 Zygmunt Wojciechowski, *Polska – Niemcy. Dziesięć wieków zmagania* (Poznań, 1945).
34 Antoni Czubiński, *Polacy i Niemcy: dziesięć wieków sąsiedztwa. Studia ofiarowane profesorowi Januszowi Pajewskiemu w osiemdziesiątą rocznicę urodzin* (Warszawa, 1987).
35 Wojciech, Wrzesiński, *Sąsiad czy wróg? Ze studiów nad kształtowaniem obrazu Niemca w Polsce w latach 1735–1939* (Wrocław, 1992).
36 Birgit, Sekulski, "'Hände hoch, ich liebe dich!' Stereotype Bilder im deutschen Minimalwortschatz. Ergebnisse eines deutsch-polnischen Projektes," *Sprachliche und soziale Stereotype*, ed. Margot Heinemann (Frankfurt a. M., 1998), 155–183.

a Millionaire?" One of the participants, who by the way gave language skills as his strong point, answers the question about the importance of the word group *caput mundi* as meaning 'the end of the world', assuming that the *caput* comes from German *kaputt*, which was immediately picked up by Internet users such as "The Foe", who tweets, e.g. on Twitter:

> w polskiej edycji gostek, co twierdził, że zna kilka języków, na pytanie co oznacza termin "caput mundi" wybrał "koniec świata". Bo przecież "Hitler kaput!;)"[37]

> [In the Polish edition one guy, though he claimed to know several languages, when asked what the term "caput mundi" means, he chose "the end of the world". Because, "Hitler kaput!";)". [Hitler finished]]

This perception of Germans after The Second World War also occupied Polish writers, such as Olga Tokarczuk, who writes in this context that:

> Der Deutsche war ein in gewissem Sinne metaphysischer Feind, der aus der Ferne wirkte, tückisch und zynisch, doch sobald es unseren Soldaten gelang, ihn gefangen zu nehmen, erwies er sich als feige und erbärmlich. Wenn wir draußen Krieg spielten und auf Kinderart mit Stöcken Gewehre imitierten, wollte niemand von uns Deutscher sein. Das wäre eine Art "Wechsel auf die andere Seite der Macht" gewesen, wie es in Star Wars heißt.[38]

> [The German was a metaphysical enemy in a sense, working from afar, treacherous and cynical, but as soon as our soldiers managed to capture him, he proved to be cowardly and miserable. When we played war outside and imitated guns with sticks in a childlike manner, none of us wanted to be a German. That would have been a kind of "change over to the dark side of force", as it says in Star Wars.]

The Polish cinematography of the 21st century presents an updated picture of the German, but still is based on old, already present stereotypical designations.

---

37 The Foe @foe_pl, tweet from 6.05.2018, answer to Adrian @kraw_a @RWesierski https://twitter.com/kraw_a/status/993106260131303424.

38 Olga Tokarczuk, "Grüße aus Niederschlesien. Nach Jahrzenten der Aufarbeitung ihrer Geschichte steht den Deutschen Trauer zu, die unversöhnliche Haltung der polnischen Regierung ist kindisch," *Frankfurter Rundschau* (2.11.2006), 36.

The comedy "Wkręceni" from 2013, among others, refers to many stereotypes about Western neighbours, which are firmly rooted in the Polish mentality. The "mythical investor from Germany" (who is depicted) is treated by Poles as a king in the hope that he will invest his capital in Poland. When one of protagonists says:

> "I myślą, że jesteśmy Niemcami" [And they think, that we are Germans], the other answers: "A dlaczego Niemcami? Ja na przykład nie chcę być Niemcem", [And why Germans? For example, I don't want to be a German!].
> The dialogue continues: "Jak to? Dlaczego Niemcami? Fico! Kurde, debilu! Mówiłem przecież, przyjechaliśmy tu na niemieckich blachach, tak? Wzięli nas za jakichś Szwabów – po prostu" [But how? Why Germans? Fico, cor! You idiot! I have already said, we came here with German plates, right? They simply took us for some Swabians!"]
> "Za jakich Szwabów?"
> [For what Swabians?]
> "Właściwie nie wiadomo za jakich!"
> [Actually, we don't know for what kind of Swabians!]
> "Normalnych, hitlerowskich!
> [Normal, Hitler's/Nazis!][39]

The motif of The Second World War as a part of the common knowledge of Poles manifests itself in many parts of the film, also nonverbally, e.g., in a fragment when one of the protagonists, impersonating a German, raises his hand preparing for a potential welcome, his gesture is suppressed in the bud by a companion sensitive to this subject. The pragmatic aspects of German-Polish communication are also explored in this way, when an instruction for a perfect impersonation of a German is given:

> Chłopy, ogólnie najważniejsze jest właśnie, że: z góry, oko, mina, postawa, to jest klasa właśnie; z góry na kmiotów[40]
>
> [Guys, in general, the most important thing is that: look down on them, eye, mimic, attitude, this is just the flair; down on bumpkins]

---

39 "Wkręceni" a Polish comedy, film director Piotr Wereśniak, production: Tadeusz Lampka. MTL Maxfilm; 33 minutes – 22 seconds.

40 "Wkręceni" a Polish comedy, 42 minutes 50 seconds – 42 minutes 58 seconds.

Thus, the Polish heterostereotype of a German presents him as a wealthy man from the West. The typical German seems to be perceived better than a typical Pole. He is wealthier and makes one feel like a shy inhabitant of the Polish province.

It is noteworthy that the image presented in the comedy "Wkręceni" is equivalent to the result of the corpus of my research on the Polish and German presses and their discourses in both communities at the beginning of the 21st century.[41]

Stereotypes occur both explicitly and implicitly in the analyzed press corpus. In their implicit realization, it is particularly worth investigating the linguistic means such as: collocations, presuppositions, comparisons, metaphors or irony.

The question of collocations is discussed in more detail below. *Collocations* are associations of expressions, which for semantic and pragmatic reasons are presented together.[42] These sequences of words or terms co-occur more often than would be expected by chance. The lexical collocations are first of all independent of the content structure of particular expressions, but with their stereotypical use they significantly influence the connotations arising in a given context. Thus, they participate in the constitution of meanings, suggesting them discreetly to the reader and often conveying ethnic stereotypes. Depending on the degree of this word connection, they may belong to idiomatic phrases or conventionalized syntagmatic compounds. The images of a "Polish butcher", "Polish tile-layers", "Polish plumber" or "Polish caretaker of German seniors" existing in Germany are precisely according to the principle of *pars pro toto*. These figures are a symbol of a 'cheap labor force' from the East of Europe. In this respect, there is a determination of meaning through the constant repetition of certain elements in a similar context, with the result that the presented issues are not checked but accepted as an indicator.

Coming back to the Polish heterostereotype of a German who appears as a rich westerner, inter alia in the comedy "Wkręceni", it may be said that the perception of Western Europe as a synonym of 'wealth' and 'luxury', as opposed to the 'indigent inhabitant of Poland', is the order of the day. This is how the image of both groups is shaped in my analyses of press texts from the year 2000, i.e., before Poland's accession to the European Union. A special role in this respect is played by collocations revealing that both Polish and German

---

41 Jarochna Dąbrowska-Burkhardt, *Die gesamteuropäischen Verfassungsprojekte im transnationalen Diskurs. Eine kontrastive linguistische Analyse der deutschen und polnischen Berichterstattung* (Zielona Góra, 2013).
42 Dąbrowska-Burkhardt, *Die gesamteuropäischen*, 25.

press texts were written on the basis of general knowledge that "rich" means "better" and "poor" means "worse". The keywords *biedny* (pol.)/ *arm* (ger.) ["poor"] and *bogaty* (pol.) / *reich* (ger.) ["rich"] are marked in **bold** below, the collocations of these lexemes *are set in italics*.

This is illustrated by the following sources:

1. W tej chwili [...] zaczęliśmy być dla Unii *kłopotem*, a nie mile widzianym partnerem. Proszących zaś **biedaków** trzyma się w przedpokojach i nie tak chętnie prosi do wspólnego stołu.[43]

[At this moment [...] we have started to be a *problem* for the European Union and not a welcomed partner. It is better to leave the begging **poor people** in the entrance hall and not to invite them to the common table].

2. Sygnał dla publiczności jest jasny: **bogatsi** Europejczycy *nas nie chcą*.[44]

[The sign / the signal to the public is clear: the **richer** Europeans *do not want us*].

3. Kraje '15' [...] boją się, że *kosztowne przyjęcie* do Unii **biedniejszych krajów** Europy Środkowej pogłębi [...] kłopoty.[45]

[The "15" countries [...] are afraid that the *costly accession* of the **poorer** Central European countries to the EU will exacerbate [...] the *problems*].

4. Euroentuzjaści [...] wskazują, że szok cywilizacyjny związany z umacnianiem UE pozwoli włączyć się ***zapóźnionym społeczeństwom*** do tej *'lepszej Europy'*.[46]

[Euro-enthusiasts point out [...] that the civilizational shock of strengthening the EU will allow ***backward societies*** to join the *"better Europe"*].

Referring to demarcation strategies in the context of auto- and heterostereotypes, an important element is the devaluation of a foreign group with simultaneous appreciation of one's own image. Referring to Koselleck's opposing asymmetrical opposites, it should be stated that they are established in such a way as to exclude mutual respect for antagonistic groups.[47] German and Polish reporting in the year 2000 takes place against the background of the division or exclusion of Europeans into "better" and "worse" inhabitants of the

---

43   Trybuna 17.05.2000, 10.
44   Rzeczpospolita 18.05.2000, A10.
45   Rzeczpospolita 21.06.2000, A10.
46   Polityka 1.07.2000, 45.
47   Reinhart Koselleck, *Vergangene Zukunft. Zur Semantik geschichtlicher Zeiten* (Frankfurt a. M., 1985), 212.

continent.[48] This attribution is documented *expressis verbis* several times in the corpus of the investigations.[49] The axiological evaluations are striking in the sense that: 'rich European are better Europeans' vs. 'poor Europeans are worse Europeans'. However, the results of this investigation show something interesting: In the year 2000, a Pole cannot question the prosperity of the West and the indigence of the East, but to determine who is 'better' or 'worse' in Europe still seems to be possible. Thus, the contextualization of the asymmetrical opposites 'rich' and 'poor' in the Polish corpus together with their collocations 'better' and 'worse' allows one to state their transformation on the principle "rich but worse versus poor but better". This topic is explicitly explored in the weekly magazine "Wprost":

> Gazety przyniosły oto obfite relacje o bestialskim mordzie, dokonanym w podparyskiej miejscowości [...] na trzech mężczyznach. Wszyscy trzej zostali zidentyfikowani jako Polacy [...] Okazuje się, że znało ich – co najmniej z widzenia, ale często także z bezpośrednich rozmów – wiele osób [...] Opinie wystawiane przez te osoby mogą się stać powodem do **naszej** *słusznej dumy*. Wszyscy są zgodni [...], że **nasi** *rodacy* "pili dużo, ale byli bardzo grzeczni i uprzejmi." Zajmowali się głównie żebraniem, ale nie wadzili nikomu. Kiedy ktoś im odmówił monety czy papierosa, nie nalegali, tylko życzyli miłego dnia i dodawali "szczęść Boże". Odwieczna *wyższość osobistego wdzięku i kultury nad pękatym portfelem*? I *kto tu kogo chce przyjmować do Europy*? Okoliczni mieszkańcy podkreślali, że Polacy byli zawsze czyści i że widywano ich, jak się golą i piorą ubrania. Czasami przeszkadzali głośnymi wieczornymi rozmowami, ale generalnie zjednali sobie raczej sympatię. Nic dziwnego, że w końcu znaleźli **się tacy**, którzy zaczęli ich szczerze nienawidzić. Bezdomny facet bez papierów powinien wiedzieć, gdzie jego miejsce: w brudzie, smrodzie, chamstwie i pogardzie. Nikt przecież nie lubi *prymusików*, którzy są *lepsi* nawet wtedy, gdy są *gorsi*.[50]

> [The newspapers were just reporting about a bestial murder of three men near Paris [...]. All three were identified as Poles [...]. It turns out

---

48 Dąbrowska-Burkhardt, *Die gesamteuropäischen Verfassungsprojekte im transnationalen Diskurs*, 200–463.
49 Frankfurter Allgemeine Zeitung, 13.05.2000, 2; Frankfurter Allgemeine Zeitung 13.05.2000, 15; Gazeta Wyborcza 24.06.2000, 18; Rzeczpospolita 27.06.2000, A7; Die Welt 26.06.2000, 8; for more cf. Dąbrowska-Burkhardt, *Die gesamteuropäischen Verfassungsprojekte*, 200–463.
50 Wprost 11.06.2000, 128.

that many people knew them – at least by sight, but often also from direct conversations – [...].The judgments given by these persons can be a reason for *our sincere pride*. Everyone agrees that *our fellow countrymen* "drank a lot, but were very well-behaved and polite". They were mainly involved in begging, but they did not stand in anyone's way. When someone refused them a coin or a cigarette, they did not harass him, but wished him a nice day and added "May God bless you!" Here, *the superiority of personal charm over a full purse has been evident for ages*. And *who wants to take whom in Europe*? Neighbourhood residents emphasized that these Poles were always clean and that they were seen shaving or washing clothes. Sometimes they have disturbed neighbours by noisy evening conversations, but generally they garnered sympathy instead. It's no wonder that finally there were **those** who started to hate them sincerely. A homeless guy without papers should know his place: in the dirt, stench, rudeness and contempt. Nobody likes **primus**, which are *better* even when they are *worse*.]

This fragment visualizes asymmetrical opposites of 'better' – 'worse' and 'wealthy' – 'poor'. The possessive pronoun *nasz* [our] plays an important role in this context: *nasza słuszna duma* [our sincere pride], *nasi rodacy* [our fellow countrymen]. The possessive pronoun creates and consolidates national categories here. It is used in a persuasive way, fulfilling the function of solidarity, and even group pressure. Especially personal pronouns and possessive pronouns in the 1st person plural such as *my* (pol.) / *wir* (ger.) [we] and *nasz* (pol.) / *unser* (ger.) [ours] in relation to positively connotated autostereotypes are to induce someone to identify with their own group. They often occur in emotionally charged discourses. It is also noteworthy that the quoted fragment uses the demonstrative pronoun *tacy* [those], which emphasizes the separation of one's own group from a stranger. The use of pronouns referring to one's own group and to a foreign group as an antithesis such as *my / nasz* [we / ours] and *oni / ich* [they / their] automatically activate judgments and rankings.

It can be said that in the context of research on stereotypes, the values of one's own group are treated as the norm, and sometimes they even advance to the rank of an ideal. This view of the world supports solidarity within one's own group and separates it from others. Usually there is a dialectic relationship between the perception of oneself and the stranger. Research shows that especially during periods of crisis, stereotypes are referred to and, consequently, are disseminated. In these cases, media relations are not dominated by an analysis of the reasons for this state of affairs, but by information leading to an even greater separation of one's own group from another, and goes hand in hand with strategies like generalization, simplification and manipulation.

Undoubtedly, today's images of a German in Poland and a Pole in Germany are expressed within the context of a common membership in the European Union, i.e. a sense of community expressed in various contacts between inhabitants of all age groups and social strata. These contacts take place on many levels: political, scientific, economic, touristic and occupational. Germany has a reputation as a European economic engine and the choice of studying "German Philology" is no longer commented on today as it was back in the 1980s: "You have to know the language of the enemy". On the other hand, the image of a Pole in Germany is dominated by the stereotyped image of a Pole – a thief, which is deeply rooted in public opinion, and was constituted especially in the 1990s. The specific supplement to this context are so-called "Polenwitze", a special category of jokes about Poles, in which they appear to be clever and able to outsmart everyone. At the beginning of the 21st century, this image is complemented by a Pole – a "man of work", whom German public opinion treats thoroughly ambivalently. On the one hand, he/she is needed by the German economy, like a Polish butcher, bricklayer, builder, seasonal worker, nurse or caretaker of elderly people, but on the other hand, the image is a source of fear, as it is synonymous with a "cheap labor force".

Coming back to the preliminary considerations in the context of the mass media, it seems to remain a pious wish that the media message should take place in such a way as not to harm others, i.e. strangers, by leaving out national distinctions, stereotypes and prejudices. The use of language becomes dangerous when one does not see diversity, but conforming uniformity. Then it comes to a hypostasis of one type by talking about "the German", "the Pole", "the French", etc. Peter Ustinov addresses this question in a particularly pictorial way:

> Auch das Gerede von **dem** Russen, **dem** Schotten und **dem** Sizilianer ist natürlich blanker Unfug. **Der** Russe – das heißt, man pfercht rund 150 Millionen Menschen in einem Singular zusammen! Nein, das Typische kann immer nur ein Rahmen sein, und jeder Einzelne hat das Recht und die Möglichkeit, diesen zu verlassen. Und er hat einen Anspruch darauf, dass man zuerst **ihn** sieht und dann erst den Rahmen[51]

---

51   Peter Ustinov, *Achtung! Vorurteile: Nach Gesprächen mit Harald Wieser und Jürgen Ritte* (Reinbek bei Hamburg, 2005), 105.

[Also the talk about **the** Russian, **the** Scotsman and **the** Sicilian is of course sheer nonsense. The Russian – that is to say, one crams about 150 million people together in a singular! No, the typical can only ever be a frame, and every individual has the right and the opportunity to leave it. And **he** has a right to be seen in the first place and later then the frame.]

The commonly observed mixing of serious formats with those that provide entertainment carries the danger that the unconscious use of national stereotypes or their ironic application also reveals them again. What the individual recipient will do with such a mediated stereotype, however, defies linguistic investigation. The task of a linguist dealing with national stereotypes is to detect them and describe the mechanisms of their functioning. The main goal is to sensitize public opinion to the careless and manipulative use of language. Such awareness may lead to further reflection on stereotypes and to an attempt to relativize them.

PART 6

Conclusion

∴

CHAPTER 20

Final Remarks: Germans and Poles in the Middle Ages: The Perception of the 'Other' and the Presence of Mutual Ethnic Stereotypes in Medieval Narrative Sources (10th–15th Centuries)

Thomas Wünsch

Mutual perceptions of one another presuppose differences, but also interests. That is true for both individuals as well as collectives; to both one can readily assign similar characteristics. It is no coincidence that many hypotheses offering definitions about peoples, nations, and cultures are based on assumptions which are commonly observed in the interaction of individual people with one another. Valuable support for there being this kind of transfer process can be found in social psychology, specifically in the identity concept George Herbert Mean developed at the beginning of the 20th century. Identity is a phenomenon that is dynamic, changeable over time, and reciprocal; it can be abstracted from the level of the individual and applied to the collective, and thereby becomes productive for social science research. This capacity for dilation to include the group, the community, or a whole society offers both more, as well as less, than what is found in the individual relationships between people. The 'more', without a doubt, includes the reality that groups do not determine their attitude toward other groups in some uniform way; the inevitable divergence and dissonance are captured in the discourse concept as conceived of by Michel Foucault. It means, first of all, there is a loss of definitude and linearity, yet conversely there is an increase in variance and polyphony. Assessments of the 'self' and the 'other', especially at the level of peoples and nations, always possess alternatives, and they resemble more so an open process rather than a once and for all fixation of attitude. At the same time, situational identity, which is granted the individual without hesitation, finds itself at collectives and their perception of the 'other' and multiplies in this way the spectrum of images of the 'self' and the 'other'.

How one sees oneself as a group (or groups), how one judges oneself, and what action-guiding slogans are gained from these perceptions, may appear sometimes as determined by way of the media. But in reality, that is far less so than in the interaction of individual people with one another. It begins with the apparently simple compound question: who are 'we', and who are the 'others'? The first part of the question loses its innocence when it is combined with the second part about the strangers. Beyond the everyday and 'normal' others whom we as people within our local surroundings encounter at every turn, there exists a "structurally" 'other', who stands outside our 'own' ordered life world, and in the end, as the "radically other", stands outside of every (familiar) life world. What is characteristic of this is that both forms, in one case more faintly, in the other more forcefully, call into question one's 'own' sphere of life. The 'other' is a "disturbance" (Yoshiro Nakamura) which happens to the realm of the 'we', and it is simultaneously an "incitement" (Bernhard Waldenfels), to examine the 'other' more closely. From out of this difference grow curiosity and interest because the 'stranger' as a disruptive factor has burst into the realm of the 'own', creating in this space the challenge of understanding this 'stranger' – and thereby making it own's 'own'.

Communication plays a key role here. In this case it is a special form of communication, which can perhaps best be identified by adding the adjective "intercultural". Were one to persist in using the image which Johann Gottfried Herder brought to the discussion, namely, that of cultures as spheres which progress immutably through space and time, then this connection will not be clear at all. However, if one were to modulate Herder's fundamental idea, which nevertheless does proceed from the notion of cultures being equal, and view these spheres as not having the consistency of billiard balls, but rather as changeable and fluid entities which are capable of successfully learning and consequently synthesizing, then the way toward a communicative model of culture becomes apparent. This is a step that the Czech historian Josef Pekař took when he sought to answer the question (hotly discussed since the end of the 19th century) as to the "meaning of Czech history" (1928) by saying that the Czech culture was an amalgam in which foreign as well as primarily German elements (each according to the epoch) had played a significant role. As a result, he was announcing a synthetic theory of culture, which appeared more useful than an understanding of culture that in "national time periods" is otherwise readily cultivated as monolithic (the view of Pekař's rival, František Palacký). The forming of an identity takes place within such a synthetic understanding of culture as an interactive and thoroughly constructive affair, without a *telos* and without basic assumptions of any kind regarding valuations of the different cultures. That which the later ethnological research (following Franz Boas) referred to as "cultural relativism" or "particularism" is something that one finds Pekař has already pointed out and exemplified. Among them one finds primarily a dynamic in the relationships among cultural entities. Initially interdependence and blending produce a distinctiveness that a nationalistically invested opinion would like, right from the start, to view as the essence issuing from a single root.

When it comes to dealing with the blending and interactivity of cultures, those who come into view are the promoters and representatives of what is necessary for the convergence. Granted, historical research (differently than scholarship about present day societies) cannot collect any unmediated impressions about groups and cultures. Everything is transmitted through the medium of (past) reporting, and it takes on a double role: such reporting is both a part as well as a reflex of the past culture. Chroniclers, hagiographers, poets, (among them also the preparer of deeds and other written materials) are agents of a process of cultural mediation. Yet all the while, in the course of this process of describing the 'other', the basis is also being lain for the 'own', which the results of historical research also promise to make attractive for the present day. The interaction accompanying the process of mediation then triggers cultural synthesis and this leads to the hybridity which is present uniquely in each culture. The parameters for the perceptions are developed and sharpened through intercourse with the 'stranger' – which subsequently, however, also intrudes into one's 'own' and can become a part of it. Consequently, it seems rather secondary whether the information about the 'other' in one (however defined) meaning is "correct" or "false", whether it is friendly or unfriendly. The decisive factor is the production of a communication community to which the (possible) opponent, like it or not, also belongs.

A second step would be to inquire as to the quality of the information, and by so doing, see how from what Karl W. Deutsch identified as a "community of communication" a "knowledge society" emerges. But even in this case it would be premature to sweepingly issue bad grades to the stereotypes which are present in droves in the medieval source materials. For one thing, it is worthwhile remembering that stereotypes, as coagulated knowledge, provide an important insight into the collective mental images and thought patterns. Stereotypes actually make life easier; they avoid complexity. But that does not make them necessarily false. Prior to condemning stereotypes to be reservoirs of 'fake news' or 'fictions', what should be addressed is the more probing question about the communicative networks of which the stereotypes make up only a part. What would become quickly clear is that stereotypes are (also) a means for making the radically 'other' comprehensible, and so are a mode for working through cultural strangeness. One could also see them as signs of interest and – in the case of the denigration of the 'other' – as a paradoxical appreciation. How one is to judge the valence of stereotypes is drawn out from a bilateral observational horizon. At this point an intercultural comparison would be helpful; alongside the German-Polish stereotypes being discussed here, one could also include, for example, the German-French or the Polish-Ukrainian ones.

Yet the challenge remains: read the stereotypes as forms of reflection about the culture of another people, even those of neighboring peoples. Geographical proximity along with simultaneously perceived differences may even in the area of hetero-stereotypes still fuel the tendency towards a polarization. Differently than with peoples who are spatially distant, here the motives leading to competition and direct confrontation play an additional role. The 'other', whom I do not see, represents less of a challenge than the 'other' who literally stands right in front of me. Research in current topical fields show that stereotypes which have hardened into clichés have been the subject of strong criticism since the time of the Enlightenment. Nevertheless, the effort to perceive a whole people or a culture remains a hyper-complex endeavor, which (as social linguistics breaks it down) is simplified by way of sematic and linguistic-pragmatic solutions. The economy of thought plays a key role here, and is observable in several areas, from positive auto-stereotypes to the placards depicting charts of the world's peoples that were common in the Middle Ages. To give an example, if one observes simply the series of the Polish stereotypes for Germans, which stretches from '*Niemcy*' to '*Szwaby*' to '*Hitlerowcy*', then two tendencies become quite clear: firstly, the need (stable through the centuries) to give a neighboring people a 'name'; and secondly how this name-giving is drawn from cultural and political constants.

Concentrating on a single epoch – the Middle Ages – entails a limitation, which then brings some advantages. It is not just because it is dealing with a long-past time period, (which again and again still drifts into the focus of current attention – one thinks about the ceremonies commemorating the anniversary of the 1410 battle at Grunwald/Tannenberg and other such events). But it is also because all epochs prior to the time of mass media and massive flows of information and communication do offer a chance (to a certain extent in real time) to examine carefully the 'knowledge society' as it arose specifically between neighboring peoples such as the Germans and the Poles. For the most part, we know the sources which can shed some light on the mutual perceptions, and based on the internationality and interdisciplinarity that have now been achieved, research is presently quite well positioned to describe the perception of the respective 'other', whether it be stereotypically established or spontaneously occurring. Of course, one must protect against direct derivations; the real art is found more so through the path Odo Marquard espouses, "the hermeneutic of multiple ways of interpreting"; the research brings the sources to speak of something which they had not intended to address at all. Hagiographic texts, as an example, have long been recognized as mediators of cultural practices – and yet when one concentrates on the question of the transporting of stereotypes, they also contain something new. When considering the *interpretatio christiana* as a pattern of presentation (as worked out by Stanisław Rosik for important parts of medieval chronicles), then lives of the saints such as those written about Otto of Bamberg or Hedwig of Silesia also become a reservoir of material for the topic of mutual perceptions. Negative images, like those attached to the Baltic Prussians, the Pomeranians, or even the Polish language itself, raise a question about the nature of the information and how it was received by others. Was it the audience, the "implicit reader" (as Wolfgang Iser refers to it), who dictated the text (that is to say the concepts used in it), or are we dealing merely with sketches, which the author hoped would resonate and find acceptance among the readers?

The intensive polemic between the members of the Teutonic Order and Polish academicians in the 15th century shows that the disparaging of the other side always exhibits two poles: the downgrading of the 'other', who is viewed as an opponent, indeed an enemy, and conversely the upgrading of one's 'own', accompanied by the harshest possible vilification of the other side in an attempt to protect against possible criticism. In the battle of Tannenberg in 1410, what were called 'heathen' military units served in both armies (as we know now and which surely could have been known to those living at the time); in their ranks the Teutonic Order as well as Poland-Lithuania employed non-baptized mercenaries, Tatars and Orthodox on the Polish-Lithuanian side, and non-baptized native Prussians served on the side of the Order. Yet, both sides were raising the claim that they were fighting for Christendom. Surely to the extent that the existence of the Teutonic Order as a spiritual institution had its *raison d'être* in the furtherance of 'the true faith', the mercenaries they hired insinuated a doubt that was a direct blow against the integrity of the Order's mission. For its part, Poland could view itself as a secular institution (if nothing else thanks to a nuanced argument from the Krakow canonists Stanislaus of Skalbmierz und Paulus Wladimiri) and so in this case could more easily explain away the entanglement. Since the two sides ended up ideologically in a stalemate, what emerged out of such contradictory protestations from each side about their respective 'true faith', was a form of pragmatic foreign policy – with the papacy itself becoming its primary proponent. Theological foundations for foreign policy obviously had to give way to secular constructions such as "the common good" or "commandment of peace"; "realism" in foreign affairs was born. One can still view the historical depiction of the battle of Grunwald in the painting by Jan Matejko ("Bitwa pod Grunwaldem" 1878). It is strewn with stereotypes which mirror this ideological mélange: the Order's Grand Master is being pierced through by a lance (obviously in the form of one of the imperial insignia, the Mauritius lance), while the Grand Prince of Lithuania, in whose army the incriminating "heathen" troop units were also found, is presented in a dominating central pose as the triumphant winner, and the Polish king as the "mastermind" of the battle strategy, appears like a divinity in the upper right corner of the painting. Perceiving the 'other' in the form of stereotypical representations (which in this case are intended to have an iconic effect) also serve here quite obviously a collective self-identification and self-affirmation.

In this, the border between the identifications of 'self' and 'other' is completely fluid. Especially the chronicles of the Middle Ages expose in many places that the judgment about the 'other' could be part of the collective identification of 'self'. The marking and constructing of the 'own' succeeds here on the basis of a return-affirmation coming from the expectations and prior knowledge of those reading it. Built out of a combination of new and existing 'text', the intertextuality (like an unseen substrate) fashions the semantic horizon of chronicle writings. What part of it is construction and what is conception, answer or reflex, can hardly be distinguished. The result produces not just stereotypes of peoples (as with the chronicler Bartel Stein, who speaks of rustic Poles and civilized Germans), it also creates "benchmark cultures", which come from a hierarchically organized concept of culture. The (kind of) perception of the 'other', time and again, takes on the form of a self-stylization. What is important for the progress of knowledge in the present, and what the medieval sources in the German-Polish relationship by all means provide, is the search for the generators of this self-stylization. These can be rediscovered (and at first sight this may seem surprising) in a few basic human needs. Where a feeling of endangerment reigns, where cravings for association or autonomy dominate, one will search in vain for an "unbiased" perception of the 'other'. Political assessments morph into moral ones if a nation has the impression that it has its back against a wall (as was the case for Poland during the Council of Constance [1414–1418]). There is little wonder that we seldom find during this period any kind of courteous assessments from Polish intellectuals about the Germans.

Here, as in other places, yet specifically in the context of the history of perceptions, it becomes clear that setting up a dichotomy of essentialism (or primordialism) and constructivism in conceiving a nation is misleading. Serving as the "mechanism of semiotic individuation" (Juri Lotman), the existence but (in fact) also the construction of nations or peoples are jointly a supertemporal phenomenon. Certainly, nations in the Middle Ages were also fabricated or 'made' – not just as organizational parameters like national groupings present at councils or universities, but also as providing some orientation for determining a standpoint when a group is part of a (regularly) conflict-filled relationship with the outside world. It is especially because of this that the German-Polish relationships are superbly suited for a case study analysis. The challenge is not to mix up the causes and effects. What specifically do terms like 'language community', 'memory community', or 'ancestral community" mean? One strategy is to assert a shared ancestry (through kinship) as seemingly being the most likely demonstrably 'objective' view, and then after the fact establishing something like linguistic competence or a shared cultural heritage. Even so, is this not actually the weakest argument? Be that as it may, regarding the German-Polish relationship we talk about "cultures at the border". Yet this means that borders also have their own cultures, which as a 'trans-border' form of life (Zbigniew Kurcz – Andrzej Sakson) marks out a special area which is different from the national cultures. Contacts, interactions, multi-cultural life that extend into everyday experience create for the border region its own 'trans-culturality' (Wolfgang Welsch). This way of living strips itself away from the national stencils and attends to the dynamic of cultural contacts and the social learning experiences that grow from them. 'Self-assignment' is thus exposed to fluctuations; it is also able to switch sides and is hardly able to orient itself on biological criteria.

What predominates, more so, and especially in the German-Polish relationship, is the image of quickly changing and contradictory 'images' – of the 'other' and of one's own 'self'. And for this reason, it seems appropriate to recall Theodor Lessing's polemic (laid out in his essay "History as Giving Meaning to the Meaningless" (1919) (*Geschichte als Sinngebung des Sinnlosen*) against "the simplification of historical motivation". Various and even mutually exclusive options for interacting with the 'other' were being weighed simultaneously, without one having been able in historical real time to foresee a solution in advance. Say for example, in Poland near the end of the 13th century, to a certain extent in the aftermath of the main phase of the German (accompanied by German Law) "eastward migration", the Germans were depicted as opponents, yes even the enemies, by the Gniezno Archbishop; yet conversely the Bishop of Breslau preferred the Germans over the Poles. One can hardly claim that behind such differences stood supertemporal or ancestrally based convictions; more plausibly there were very concrete ecclesiastical or state interests, and often social rivalries enough in city communities. The conflict (mentioned in the contemporaneous Old Czech Dalimil chronicle) between the Germans and the Czechs seems to have followed less so a proto-nationalist logic, and instead corresponded to the model (known from many communities of immigrants) of a conflict between locals and newly arrived migrants during periods of economic stagnation. By implication it follows from this as well that the connotations and even the definitions themselves could change if the circumstances changed.

It would seem more helpful to assume a situativity in the production of stereotypes, the longevity of some individual stereotypes notwithstanding. Many modern stereotypes of Poles and Germans have their roots in earlier times, even if it is difficult to decide whether negative images of Poles (as they show up in the 20th century through the media of films or caricatures) stem from the Middle Ages or the time of Bismarck. The perception-theoretical foundation nonetheless remains the same: Lack of knowledge leads to a lack of understanding, which for its part once again finds expression in biased topical images. The encounter with the 'stranger' as a sub-function of the 'other' can basically take place in several ways. Alongside the *relativization* of one's 'own' (in the sense of a maximally neutral basic attitude) stands the *assertion* of the 'own'. In its wake are found the negative associations of 'strangeness', ranging from simply a departing from normalcy, to wrongheadedness, all the way up to malignancy. Epochal events can have an accelerating effect on the production of stereotypes, but complex models of how someone is perceived are less likely to be generated in one fell swoop. They need a longer run up and an extended discursive firing in the kiln in order to become universal and subsequently also a part of the cultural legacy of a people or a nation. As well, one should not a priori exclude the possibility that it would not have been possible for there to have been in the Middle Ages forms of 'orientalism' (Edward Said) and 'occidentalism' (Ian Buruma – Avishai Margalit), even if these rested on other presuppositions than those of the present. The *tertium comparationis* lies in the projection of an ideal society, state, or community which in its inexorability implies the willingness to use force and to wage "war on the 'others'".

The path to a widening of the field of view suggests itself. The difficulty discussed here is not just limited to Germans and Poles, but rather has its parallels in the German-French relationship (to make use of another bilateral variant), but also in the formation of a European identity over against another, which can take on varying forms. In the same period as the Middle Ages, as the "west-European" view of Poland differentiated itself and (for its part) Poland began working on a positive self-stereotype as the *antemurale christianitatis*, what happened for the first time was a European self-definition. One can read it quite clearly in the imperial diet protocols (which were prepared in the wake of what were called the 'the Turkish diets'). What is discernible is the formation of a self-image in the face of a threat to other parts of Europe caused by the expansion of the Ottoman Empire. This self-image was indeed based on a largely negative substrate – being '*not* Ottoman', and so '*not* Muslim' and in addition '*not* Tatar' and '*not* Orthodox'. Nevertheless, it still led to an awareness of a shared threatening situation, even if the political-military conclusions from it once again showed hardly any kind of unified response. Poland-Lithuania, as a neighboring state to the Ottoman Empire, was however also a state that hosted Muslim and Orthodox populations within itself; in an ambivalent way it took part in these processes of self-perception and self-assignment. The solution was found in a self-stylization as the "bulwark of Christian west" (*antemurale chistianitatis*), which hardly had any foreign policy consequences (that is, military actions), yet all the more so became a concept that nurtured internal cohesion. At the moment in which the Moscow Empire, after the fall of Constantinople in 1453, began to reclaim for itself the intellectual and ecclesiastical legacy of the Byzantine Empire, to a certain extent Poland-Lithuania as a result of the pressure from without shifted closer toward western Europe. Here, in this dynamic (which as far as long-lived stereotypes of people go, took place in a relatively short timeframe of about a hundred years, the 15th century) lie also the differences that the Germans had in their history of perceptions with their other neighbors.

It goes without saying that in that moment in which Poland was able to implement successfully its self-image as a (Latin)-Christian avantgarde in opposition to the threats from the direction of the Muslim and Orthodox states, the relative 'otherness' of the relationship to the west had to give way. The ground for this lies in the yet prevailing theological strategy of seeking legitimacy for a state's actions: if one sees oneself as a Latin-Christian body politic, then other states with differing state religions automatically are stamped with the (negative) 'other'. The Muslim states essentially became "heretical" (unbelieving) states; the Greek Orthodox states (first and foremost the Moscow Empire) became "schismatics" – which at the end of the day amounted to the same thing. What was decisive was not a theological differentiation with the goal of a possible conversion (even though diplomats at least were repeatedly sent to Moscow Russia with missionary intentions, and occasionally also into the Muslim Mongolian Empire). The real goal was a maximal distancing. In the case of Poland, this distancing also served as well the only slightly veiled need to finally clear from the table the tiresome discussion repeatedly broached by the Teutonic Order as to the degree to which Polish lands had been Christianized. In view of the fact that the Lithuanian part of the country under the personal union had only officially in 1386 been Christianized, accomplished in the format of a "national baptism", pursuing the tactic of a distancing from states which had been classified as heretical and schismatic offered the best option. The Poles were, or at least it was their claim, (which the Krakow theologians, philosophers, and jurists verbosely reinforced), a part of the European Christian family of peoples and so to a certain extent were related to the Germans. When the Roman-German Emperor Sigismund of Luxemburg also contemplated re-positioning the Teutonic Order to a southern deployment in the Balkans, the frontline of the Ottoman Empire, then it was clear to all that there was no longer a "war against the heathens" to be waged in Prussia.

Moving beyond these larger-scale developments, it is worthwhile looking at regional and local relationships. For even when eloquent intellectuals such as the Krakow rector and royal envoy to the Council of Constance, Paulus Wladimiri, championed the orthodoxy of the Polish faith, that did not have to necessarily be accepted in the territory of the Teutonic Order's state in Prussia. In fact, the historiography in the towns there makes clear that the Poles were capable of not being just neighbors, but at the same moment also enemies. What at first glance looks to be an aggressive, anachronistic argumentation, can turn out on closer inspection to be a rather undramatic form for dealing with 'otherness'. As in other types of sources as well, say in heraldry or poetry, one may speak of a de-ideologized image of the enemy. The 'other' is a role which has a certain interchangeability to it, which means that instead of the Poles, it could just as well be the Hungarians who fall to being adjudged adversaries. What can serve here as a reference point is the feature of specificity: the more imprecise the stereotype advanced about a people is, the closer lies the presumption that it has to do with non-specific opinions, and is related more so to a specific event rather than meant 'in principle' (and for that reason hardly nationalistic.) What "Germanness" is and what "Polishness" is show themselves to be relative, or in other words, they function as *topoi*.

Here there is a fundamental variance from those classifications and stereo-typifications that one encounters in the wake of missionary efforts. The Pomeranians in the region of the Baltic Sea were the focus of High Middle Ages conversion efforts and likewise political subjugation; the stereotyping happened in order to sanctify this aim. That this was the work of Polish authors, just as the missionizing was the work of Polish princes, only attests that in the times of a Christian formation of a state, the demarcating line from the 'others', the 'strangers' can shift around. Similarly, one can observe this when considering how the Orthodox Ruthenians on the Polish and Lithuanian eastern border were handled beginning in the middle of the 14th century. Here as well, the Polish Kings (and Lithuanian Grand Princes) occasionally appeared on the scene as "missionaries" by seeking (through assuming regency privileges) to disadvantage the Orthodox groups in the population of the southeastern mixed region of Red Russia (known otherwise as Galicia and Western Ukraine). Even though in the end pragmatic principles prevailed and (at least from the side of the state) a homogenizing and harmonizing of the mixed confessional region was pursued, the wide-spread hatred of the 'otherness' persisted for a long time. Since ostracizing unleashes forces of group formation that lead to differentiation even long after the expiration of the original impulse, it is not wrong to see some part of the social tensions in this 'periphery' of the Polish Empire, and then later in Austrian Galicia, as going back to this medieval practice of marginalization. *Mutatis mutandis* one can recognize features of the German negative stereotypes about the Poles being mirrored in the attitudes of the Poles toward the Ukrainians. There is therefore something like an "Defamation International", which seems to follow similar cultural isomorphisms and is especially typical for confessional contact zones.

Scholarship is here called upon not to perpetuate the perception-theoretical pathways of the sources or of that which one up to this point has gleaned from them. Together with the problems of understanding contemporary perceptions between Germans and Poles, for example, in large cities such as Krakow, came the problem (not always adequately noted) of long interpretation traditions that were quite dependent on the *Zeitgeist*. Where the primary potential for conflict in a mixed-ethnic medieval town (like Krakow) lay is not to be found by taking a sidelong glance at the city in the 19th century or the present. Even in those places where clearly negative stereotypes about people were in circulation, that does not mean that the conflicts automatically were based in national perspectives. One should rather assume that the factors with the strongest clout would be the classifying of certain communities based on the law they followed (visible in their respective privileges, as Myron Kapral showed in the case of Lviv) and then the social conflicts that were argued out in this setting. The special problems of categorizing the Jews in the city society and likewise the notorious conflicts between the burghers (German) and the nobility (Polish) still do not make local antagonisms into national ones.

But prior to any hermeneutic stand, there are the heuristic questions about the body of the source material. One can avoid here the gravest mistakes in interpretation when one is clear that tracing out reciprocal stereotypes in the German-Polish relationship is a matter of only a handful of instances in the sources and these are bound up with the particular horizons of the individual authors. Consequently, this is a matter of having value because of rarity. What is called for is a targeted search focused on details in order to even in general uncover clues about the mutual perception of Germans and Poles – and also the number of stereotypes themselves do not seem to be particularly large. The research yield increases in the measure to which the focus on the mere *existence* of information about the German-Polish relationship is re-directed and moved toward the *contingency* of the information itself. Differently than when it had the older history of relationships on the radar screen, (even though it had fruitful individual results), today the accent should be placed more so on the question of the originative conditions, the determinations, and the mechanisms of the spread of information with national stereotype content. This shifts the public back (and rightly so) into a place of emphasis in the historical inquiry process. The conditions of perceptions are the basis upon which the *author* of the chronicle, of the life of a saint, of the town history, etc. stands, but at the same time they are also the communicative milieu in which the *addressees* of these works circulated. This does not make the medieval sources less interesting for the present, for what (if not a steady interest) could be the precondition for the formation of stereotypes? If one understands the genesis of stereotypes as a special form of structured perception, then one will always be able to discover (regardless whether it deals with positive or negative (hetero-) stereotypes), a dose of acknowledgement in it. Stereotypes assume a modicum of familiarity and indicate thereby a closeness. Conflict, were there then to be one, becomes a family matter.

Translated by Philip Jacobs (English-Exactly)

Selected Bibliography

Primary Sources

A local society in transition. The "Henryków Book" and related documents, ed. Piotr Górecki Studies and texts 155, (Toronto, 2007), 91–202.

Adam of Bremen, *Gesta Hammaburgensis Ecclesiae Pontificum*, ed. Bernhard Schmeidler, MGH SS rer. Germ. 2 (Hannover-Leipzig, 1917; repr. 1993).

Adam of Bremen, *Gesta Hammaburgensis Ecclesiae Pontificum*, ed. Werner Trillmich, FSGA 11, 7th ed., (Darmstadt, 2000), 137–499.

Andreas von Regensburg, "*Chronica summorum pontificum et imperatorum Romanorum*," in idem, *Sämtliche Werke*, ed. Georg Leidinger, Quellen und Erörterungen zur bayerischen und deutschen Geschichte N.F. 1 (München, 1903), 1–158.

Annales Glogovienses bis z. J. 1493. Nebst urkundlichen Beilagen, ed. Hermann Markgraf, SRS 10, (Breslau, 1877).

Annales Quedlinburgenses, ed. Martina Giese, MGH SSrG 72 (Hannover, 2004).

Bartholomeus Stenus, *Descripcio tocius Silesie et civitatis regie Vratislaviensis /Barthel Steins Beschreibung von Schlesien und seiner Hauptstadt Breslau*, ed. Hermann Markgraf SRS 17 (Breslau, 1902).

Česká kronika Benedikta Johnsdorfa [*The Bohemian chronicle of Benedikt Johnsdorf*], ed. Jaromír Mikulka (Ostrava, 1959).

Chronica Bohemorum ab initio gentis ad annum 1438, Monumenta historica Bohemiae, ed. Gelasius Dobner, 3 (Pragae, 1774), 43–59.

Chronica Poloniae Maioris, ed. Brygida Kürbis, MPH NS 8 (Warsaw, 1970).

Chronicon domus Sarensis Maior, ed. Jindřicc Řezbář, Jaroslav Ludvíkovský, (Brno, 1964).

Chronicon Silesiae ab anno Christi 1052 usque in annum 1573/ Chronik Schlesiens über fünf Jahrhunderte vom Jahre Christi 1052 bis zum Jahre 1573 [Görlitzer Handschrift GV 52] vol. 1–2, ed. Lars-Arne Dannenberg and Mario Müller, Scriptores rerum Lusaticarum. 6 (Görlitz/Zittau 2013).

Chronicon terrae Prussiae von Peter von Dusburg, ed. Max Toeppen, SRP 1, Leipzig, 1861, 21–219.

Cosmas Pragensis, *Chronica Boemorum*, MGH SS rer. Germ. N.S. 2, ed. Bertold Bretholz, (Berlin, 1923).

Di tutsch kronik von Behem lant: die gereimte deutsche Übersetzung der Alttschechischen Dalimil-Chronik [German chronicle of the Czech lands, a rhymed German translation of the Old Bohemian chronicle of Dalimil], ed. Vlastimil Brom (Brno, 2009).

Die böhmische Chronik des Benedict Johnsdorf, ed. Franz Wachter, SRS 12, (Breslau, 1883), 109–124.

Die Chronik Johanns von Winterthur, ed. Friedrich Baethgen, MGH SSrG. N. S. 3 (Berlin 1924)

Die Chronik der Polen des Magisters Vincentius, ed. Eduard Mühle, FSGA 48, (Darmstadt, 2014).

Die Chronica novella des Hermann Korner, ed. Jakob Schwalm (Göttingen, 1895).

Die Legende der heiligen Hedwig in der Übersetzung des Kilian von Meiningen, ed. Sabine Seelbach (Münster, 2016).

Eberhart Windecke, *Denkwürdigkeiten zur Geschichte des Zeitalters Kaiser Sigismunds*, ed. Wilhelm Altmann (Berlin, 1893).

Ebonis vita sancti Ottonis episcopi Babenbergensis, ed. Jan Wikarjak and Kazimierz Liman, MPH NS 7,2 (Warszawa, 1969).

Gervase, the Monk of Canterbury, *The chronicle of the reigns Stephen, Henry II, and Richard I.*, ed. William Stubbs. Vol. 1, RBMS 73, 1–2 (London 1879).

Helmold of Bosau, *Chronica Slavorum*, ed. Bernhard Schmeidler, MGH SS rer. Germ. 32 (Hannover, 1937) 1–218.

Helmold of Bosau, *Chronica Slavorum*, ed. Heinz Stoob, FSGA 19 (Darmstadt, 1990).

Henry the Woodcutter, *Chronicon domus Sarensis Maior*, ed. Jaroslav Ludvíkovský, Chronica domus Sarensis maior et minor (Třebíč, 2003).

Herbordi dialogus de Vita S. Ottonis episcopi Babenbergensis, ed. Jan Wikarjak and Kazimierz Liman, MPH NS 7, 3 (Warszawa, 1974).

Iohannis abbas Victoriensis Liber certarum historiarum, ed. Fedor Schneider, MGH SSrG. 36 (Hannoverae/Lipsiae, 1909/1910).

Jarloch, *Letopisy* [Chronicle], FRB 2, ed. Josef Emler (Praha, 1874), 461–516.

Johann von Posilge, *Chronik des Landes Preussen*, ed. Ernst Strehlke, SRP 3 (1866), 79–388.

John of Salisbury, *Letters 1. The early letters, 1153–1161*, eds. and transl. William J. Millor, and Harold E. Butler, Christopher N.L. Brooke, Oxford Medieval Texts (Oxford, 1979).

Kanovník Vyšehradský, *Letopis/Pokračování Kosmovo* [Canon of Vyšehrad, Chronicle/Continuation Cosmas of Prague], FRB 2, ed. Josef Emler (Praha, 1874), 201–237.

Kowalewicz, Henryk, "Pieśń o wójcie krakowskim Albercie" [A poem about mayor Albert's rebellion], *Pamiętnik Literacki* 56/3 (1965), 125–138.

Kronika książąt polskich [*The Chronicle of Polish Dukes*], ed. Zygmunt Węclewski, MPH 3 (Lviv, 1878), 423–578.

Kronika polska [The Polish Chronicle], ed. Ludwik Ćwikliński, MPH 3 (Lviv, 1878), 578–656.

Kronika szląska skrócona (Cronica Silesiae abbreviata), ed. Aleksander Semkowicz, MPH 3 (Lviv, 1878), 728–729.

Laurentius Blumenau, *Historia de ordine Theutonicorum Cruciferorum*, ed. Max Toeppen, SRP 4 (Leipzig, 1870).

Liber actorum, resignationum nec non ordinationum civitatis Cracoviae 1300–1375, ed. Franciszek Piekosiński, Józef Szujski, Libri antiquissimi civitatis Cracoviensis 1300–1400, vol. 1, (Cracoviae, 1878).

Liber fundationis claustri sancte Marie Virginis in Heinrichow czyli Księga henrykowska [Liber fundationis claustri sancte Marie Virginis in Heinrichow or the Book of Henryków], ed. and trans. Roman Grodecki (Wrocław, 1991).

Liber proscriptionum et gravaminum civitatis Cracoviensis 1360–1422, ed. Bożena Wyrozumska (Kraków, 2001).

Magistri Vincentii dicti Kadłubek Chronica Polonorum, ed. Marian Plezia, MPH N.S. 11, (Kraków, 1994).

Mnich Sázavský, *Letopis/Pokračování Kosmovo* [Chronicle/Continuation Cosmas of Prague], FRB 2, ed. Josef Emler (Praha, 1874), 238–269.

Monumenta Lubensia, ed. Wilhelm Wattenbach, (Breslau, 1861), 14–15.

Österreichische Chronik von den 95 Herrschaften, ed. Josef Seemüller, MGH Dt. Chr. 6 (Hannover, 1906/09).

Petra Žitavského Kronika Zbraslavská [Peter of Žitava, The Chronicle of Zbraslav], ed. Josef Emler, FRB 4, (Praha, 1884).

Přibík Pulkava z Radenína, *Kronika* [Chronicle], ed. Josef Emler, FRB 5 (Praha, 1893).

Rocznik głogowski do roku 1493 (Annales Glogovienses bis z. J. 1493), trans. and ed. Wojciech Mrozowicz (Głogów, 2013).

Rocznik kamieniecki [Kamieniec Annals], ed. August Bielowski, MPH 2 (Lviv, 1872), 776–778.

Rocznik Krasińskich/Annales Krasinsciani [The Krasinski' Annal], ed. August Bielowski, MPH 3, 128–133.

S. Ottonis episcopi Babenbergensis Vita Prieflingensis, ed. Jan Wikarjak and Kazimierz Liman, MPH NS 7,2 (Warszawa, 1966).

Sancti Adalberti episcopi Pragensis et martyris Vita prior. A. Redactio Imperialis vel Ottoniana, ed. Jadwiga Karwasinska MPH N.S. 4, 1 (Warszawa, 1962).

Sancti Adalberti Pragensis episcopi et martyris Vita altera auctore Brunone Querfurtensi, ed. Jadwiga Karwasińska MPH SN 4, 2 (Warszawa, 1969).

Spominki wiślickie [Memories of Wiślica], ed. August Bielowski, MPH 3 (Lwów, 1878), 124–126.

Tak řečený Dalimil, *Kronika* [So-called Dalimil, Chronicle], vol. 1–3, ed. Jiří Daňhelka et alii (Praha, 1988–1995).

Thietmar von Merseburg, *Chronicon*, ed. Robert Holtzmann, MGH SS rer. Germ. N.S. 9 (Berlin, 1955).

Vincencius, *Letopis = Letopis Vincentia, kanovnika kostela Pražského* [Chronicle of Vincent, canon of Prague], FRB, 2, ed. Josef Emler, Praha 1874, 407–460.

Vita of Bishop Otto I. of Bamberg, ed. Jürgen Petersohn, MGH SS rer. Germ. N.S. 71 (Hannover, 1999).

Vita quinque fratrum eremitarum [seu] *Vita uel Passio Benedicti et Iohannis sociorumque suorum auctore Brunone Querfurtensi*, ed. Jadwiga Karwasinska, MPH, N.S. 4, 3 (Warszawa, 1973).

Vita sanctae Hedwigis, ed. Aleksander Semkowicz, MPH 4 (Lwów, 1884; repr. Warsaw, 1961).

[Wigand:] *Die Chronik Wigands von Marburg. Lateinische Übersetzung und sonstige Überreste*, ed. Th. Hirsch, SRP 2 (Leipzig, 1863), 453–662

Wiersz o pierwszych zakonnikach Lubiąża [A poem about first monks in Lubiąż], ed. August Bielowski, MPH 3 (Lviv, 187), 708–710.

Secondary Sources

Adamska, Anna, "Away with the Germans and Their Language? Linguistic Conflict and Urban Records in Early Fourteenth-Century Cracow," In *Uses of the Written Word in Medieval Town*, eds. Marco Mostert, Anna Adamska, Medieval Urban Literacy 2 (Turnhout, 2014), 65–85.

Althoff, Gerd, *Spielregeln der Politik im Mittelalter. Kommunikation in Frieden und Fehde*, (Darmstadt, 1997).

Althoff, Gerd, "Symbolische Kommunikation zwischen Piasten und Ottonen." In *Polen und Deutschland vor 1000 Jahre*, ed. Michael Borgolte (Berlin, 2002), 305–306.

Arnold, Udo, "Geschichtsschreibung im Preussenland bis zum Ausgang des 16. Jahrhunderts." *Jahrbuch für die Geschichte Mittel- und Ostdeutschlands* 19 (1970), 74–126.

Banaszkiewicz, Jacek, *Polskie dzieje bajeczne Mistrza Wincentego Kadłubka* [Polish fairy tales of Master Wincenty Kadłubek] (Wrocław 2002).

Banaszkiewicz, Jacek, "Gall as a Credible Historian, or why the Biography of Boleslav the Brave is as authentic and far from grotesque as Boleslav the Wrymouth's." In *Gallus Anonymous and his chronicle in the context of twelfth-century historiography from the perspective of last research*, ed. Krzysztof Stopka (Cracow 2010), 19–33.

Banaszkiewicz, Jacek, *Takie sobie średniowieczne bajeczki* [As such medieval fairy tales], (Kraków, 2012).

Banaszkiewicz, Jacek, Andrzej Dąbrówka, and Piotr Węcowski (eds.), *Przeszłość w kulturze średniowiecznej Polski* [The past in the culture of medieval Poland], vol. 1, (Warszawa, 2018).

Barciak, Antoni (ed.), *Korzenie wielokulturowości Śląska ze szczególnym uwzględnieniem Śląska Górnego* [The roots of the multiculturalism of Silesia, with particular emphasis on Upper Silesia] (Katowice-Zabrze, 2009).

Bartlett, Robert, *The Making of Europe. Conquest, colonization and cultural change 950–1350* (London, 1993).

Barycz, Henryk (ed.), *Polska złotego wieku a Europa. Studia i szkice* [Poland of the Golden Age and Europe. Studies and sketches] (Warszawa, 1987).

Bates, David, "Robert Torigni and the Historia Anglorum." In *The English and their Legacy, 900–1200. Essays in Honour of Ann Williams*, ed. David Roffe (Woodbridge, 2012), 175–184.

Belzyt, Leszek, *Krakau und Prag zwischen 14. und 17. Jahrhundert. Vergleichende Studien zur Sozial-, Kultur- und Wirtschaftsgeschichte ostmitteleuropäischer Metropolen* (Toruń, 2003).

Bergmann, Werner, "Was sind Vorurteile?" *Informationen zur politischen Bildung* 271 (2005), 4–13.

Berwanger, Katrin, "Einleitung." In *Stereotyp und Geschichtsmythos in Kunst und Sprache. Die Kultur Ostmitteleuropas in Beiträgen zur Potsdamer Tagung, 16.–18.01.2003*, eds. Katrin Berwanger and Peter Kosta, Vergleichende Studien zu den slavischen Sprachen und Literaturen 11 (Frankfurt/M., 2005), XIII–XXX.

Bláhová, Marie, "Vliv české středověké historiografie na historickou kulturu Slezska v pozdním středověku," [Influence of Czech medieval historiography on Silesian historical culture in the late Middle Ages] In Barciak (ed.), *Korzenie wielokulturowości*, 54–66.

Bock, Nils, Georg Jostkleigrewe, and Bastian Walter (eds.), *Faktum und Konstrukt. Politische Grenzen im europäischen Mittelalter: Verdichtung – Symbolisierung – Reflexion*, (Münster, 2011).

Boehm, Laetitia, "Der wissenschaftstheoretische Ort der 'historia' im Mittelalter. Die Geschichte auf dem Wege zur 'Geschichtswissenschaft'," in *Speculum historiale. Geschichte im Spiegel von Geschichtsschreibung und Geschichtsdeutung*, eds. Clemens Bauer, Laetitia Boehm, and Max Müller (Freiburg i. Br., 1965), 663–93.

Boockmann, Hartmut, *Laurentius Blumenau. Fürstlicher Rat – Jurist – Humanist (ca. 1415–1484)* (Göttingen, 1965).

Boockmann, Hartmut, *Johannes Falkenberg, der Deutsche Orden und die polnische Politik. Untersuchungen zur politischen Theorie des späteren Mittelalters*, Veröffentlichungen des Max-Planck-Instituts für Geschichte, 45 (Göttingen, 1975).

Boockmann, Hartmut, "Die Geschichtsschreibung des Deutschen Ordens. Gattungsfragen und Gebrauchssituationen." In *Geschichtsschreibung und Geschichtsbewußtsein im Spätmittelalter*, ed. Hans Patze (Sigmaringen, 1987) 447–469.

Borkowska, Urszula. *Treści ideowe w dziełach Jana Długosza. Kościół i świat poza Kościołem* [Ideological content in the works of Jan Długosz. The Church and the world outside the Church], (Lublin, 1983).

Brett, Martin, "John of Worcester and his contemporaries." In *The Writing of History in the Middle Ages. Essays presented to Richard William Southern*, ed. Ralph H.C. Davis and John M. Wallace Hadrill (Oxford, 1981), 101–126.

Brinker von der Heyde, Claudia, *'von manigen helden gute tat'. Geschichte als Exempel bei Peter Suchenwirt*, (Frankfurt/M., 1987).

Brom, Vlastimil, "The rhymed German translation of the Old Czech chronicle of so-called Dalimil and its specific identification models compared to the original text," in *Narrating Communities between Latin and Vernaculars* (Turnhout, forthcoming).

Buschinger, Danielle, "Deutsch-polnische Wechselbeziehungen im Mittelalter," *Germanica Wratislaviensia* XCII (1991), 45–53.

Byrn, Richard F.M., "National stereotypes reflected in German literature." In *Concepts of National Identity in the Middle Ages*, ed. Simon N. Forde, Leslie Peter Johnson, and Alan V. Murray (Leeds 1995) 137–153.

Chazan, Mireille, *L'Empire et l'histoire universelle de Sigebert de Gembloux à Jean de Saint-Victor (XIIe–XIVe siècle)* (Paris, 1999).

Clarke, Peter D., Duggan, Anne J., eds., *Pope Alexander III (1159–81)* (Aldershot, 2012).

Czarnecki, Roland, *Kronika Namysłowa autorstwa Johannesa Frobena jako utwór dziejopisarstwa miejskiego* [The chronicle of Namysłów by Johannes Froben as a work of urban historiography] (Warsaw, 2015).

Czubiński, Antoni (ed.), *Polacy i Niemcy: dziesięć wieków sąsiedztwa. Studia ofiarowane profesorowi Januszowi Pajewskiemu w osiemdziesiątą rocznicę urodzin* [Poles and Germans: Ten Centuries of Neighborhood. Studies offered to professor Janusz Pajewski on the eighty anniversary of his birth] (Warszawa, 1987).

Dąbrowska, Jarochna, *Stereotype und ihr sprachlicher Ausdruck im Polenbild der deutschen Presse. Eine textlinguistische Untersuchung* (Tübingen, 1999).

Dąbrowska, Jarochna, *Die gesamteuropäischen Verfassungsprojekte im transnationalen Diskurs. Eine kontrastive linguistische Analyse der deutschen und polnischen Berichterstattung* (Zielona Góra, 2013).

Dąbrowska, Jarochna, "O języku niemieckim w Polsce. Stereotypy i wyobrażenia na przestrzeni wieków." [About German in Poland. Stereotypes and ideas over the centuries] *Lingwistyka Stosowana* 23/3 (2017), https://portal.uw.edu.pl/de/web/lingwistyka-stosowana/home.

Dalewski, Zbigniew, *Ritual and Politics. Writing the History of a Dynamic Conflict in Medieval Poland* (Boston-Leiden, 2008).

Dalewski, Zbigniew, "Przeszłość zrytualizowana: tradycja królewskich koronacji." [A ritualized past: the tradition of royal coronations] in *Przeszłość w kulturze średniowiecznej Polski* 2, ed. Halina Manikowska (Warszawa, 2018), 29–57.

Das Reich und Polen: Parallelen, Interaktionen und Formen der Akkulturation im hohen und späten Mittelalter, eds. Alexander Patschovsky and Thomas Wünsch (Ostfildern 2003).

Davis, Kathleen, *Periodization and Sovereignty: How Ideas of Feudalism and Secularization Govern the Politics of Time*. The Middle Ages Series, (Philadelphia, 2008).

Deutsch, Karl W., *Nationalism and Social Communication. An Inquiry into the Foundations of Nationality*, 2nd ed. (Cambridge/London 1962).

Drelicharz, Wojciech, "Richtungen in der Entwicklung der kleinpolnischen Annalistik im 13.–15. Jh.," in *Die Geschichtsschreibung in Mitteleuropa. Projekte und Forschungsprobleme*, ed. Jaroslaw Wenta (Toruń, 1999), 53–72.

Drelicharz, Wojciech, *Idea zjednoczenia królestwa w średniowiecznym dziejopisarstwie polskim* [The idea of uniting the kingdom in medieval Polish historiography] (Kraków, 2012).

Drelicharz, Wojciech, *Unifying the Kingdom of Poland in Medieval Historiographic Thought*, (Kraków, 2019).

Duggan, Anne J., "*Alexander ille meus*: the Papacy of Alexander III" in *Pope Alexander III (1159–81)*, ed. Peter D. Clarke and Anne J. Duggan (Aldershot, 2012), 13–49.

Duggan, Anne J., "Henry II, the English Church and the Papacy, 1154–76." In *Henry II: New Interpretations*, ed. Christopher Harper-Bill and Nicholas Vincent (Woodbridge, 2007), 154–183.

Duggan, Charles and Anne J. Duggan, "Ralph de Diceto, Henry II and Becket with an Appendix on Decretal Letters." In *Authority and power: studies in medieval law and government presented to Walter Ullmann on his seventieth birthday*, ed. Brian Tiernay, Peter Linehan (Cambridge, 1980), 59–81.

Dunin-Wąsowicz, Teresa, "Hagiographie polonaise entre XIe et XVIe siècle." In *Hagiographies. Histoire internationale de la littérature hagiographique latine et vernaculaire des origines à 1550* 3, ed. Guy Philippart, Corpus Christianorum. Hagiographies 3 (Turnhout, 2001), 179–202.

Ehlers, Joachim, "Was sind und wie bilden sich nationes im mittelalterlichen Europa (10.–15. Jahrhundert)? Begriff und allgemeine Konturen." In *Mittelalterliche nationes, neuzeitliche Nationen. Probleme der Nationenbildung in Europa*, eds. Almut Bues and Rex Rexheuser (Wiesbaden 1995), 7–26.

Ehrismann, Otfrid, "Die Fürsten ûzer Polan. Polen in der deutschen Heldendichtung des Mittelalters," *Germanica Wratislaviensia* 92 (1991), 33–44.

Ekdahl, Sven, *Die Schlacht bei Tannenberg 1410. Quellenkritische Untersuchungen, Band I: Einführung und Quellenlage*, (Berlin, 1982).

Espagne, Michel, "Der theoretische Stand der Kulturtransferforschung." In *Kulturtransfer. Kulturelle Praxis im 16. Jahrhundert*, ed. Wolfgang Schmale (Innsbruck 2003) 63–75.

Fischer-Lichte, Erika, *Ästhetik des Performativen*, (Frankfurt/M., 2004).

Flori, Jean, "La caricature de l'Islam dans l'occident médiéval: Origine et signification de quelques stéréotypes concernant l'Islam." *Aevum* 66, Nr. 2 (1992), 245–256.

Fraesdorff, David, *Der barbarische Norden. Vorstellungen und Fremdheitskategorien bei Rimbert, Thietmar von Merseburg, Adam von Bremen und Helmold von Bosau* (Berlin, 2004).

Fried, Johannes, "Gnesen-Aachen-Rom. Otto III. und der Kult des hl. Adalbert. Beobachtungen zum älteren Adalbertsleben." In *Polen und Deutschland vor 1000 Jahren.*

Die Berliner Tagung über den "Akt von Gnesen", ed. Michael Borgolte, Europa im Mittelalter 5 (Berlin, 2002) 235–279.

Friedberg, Marian. *Kultura polska a niemiecka* [The Polish and German culures], vol. 1 (Poznań, 1946).

Friedrich, Karin, "Cives Cracoviae: Bürgertum im frühneuzeitlichen Krakau zwischen Stadtpatriotismus und nationaler Pluralität." In *Krakau, Prag und Wien. Funktionen von Metropolen im frühmodernen Staat*, eds. Marina Dmitrieva and Karen Lambrecht (Stuttgart, 2000) 143–161.

Frost, Robert, *The Oxford History of Poland-Lithuania*, vol. 1: *The Making of the Polish-Lithuanian Union, 1385–1569* (Oxford, 2015).

Geschichtsschreibung und Geschichtsbewußtsein im späten Mittelalter, Vorträge und Forschungen 31, ed. Hans Patze (Sigmaringen 1987).

Ganseforth, Elisabeth, *Das Fremde und das Eigene: Methoden – Methodologie – Diskurse in der soziologischen Forschung* (Aachen 2016).

Gawlas, Sławomir, "Świadomość narodowa Jana Długosza" [National awareness of Jan Długosz], *Studia Źródłoznawcze* 27 (1983), 3–66.

Gawlas, Sławomir, "Die mittelalterliche Nationenbildung am Beispiel Polens. Probleme der Nationenbildung in Europa." In *Mittelalterliche nationes, neuzeitliche Nationen. Probleme der Nationenbildung in Europa*, eds. Almut Bues, Rex Rexheuser (Wiesbaden, 1995) 121–43.

Gawlas, Sławomir, O kształt zjednoczonego Królestwa. Niemieckie władztwo terytorialne a geneza społeczno-ustrojowej Polski [For the shape of a united kingdom. German territorial sovereignty and the genesis of Poland's social and political system], Res humanae. Studia 1, 2nd ed., (Warszawa, 2000).

Gawlas, Sławomir, "Marność świata i narodowe stereotypy. Uwagi o wielokulturowości na Śląsku w XV wieku [Vanity of the world and national stereotypes. Remarks on multiculturalism in Silesia in the 15th century]." In *Korzenie wielokulturowości*, ed. Antoni Barciak (Katowice-Zabrze, 2009), 29–53.

Gawlas, Sławomir, "Ślązacy w oczach własnych i cudzych. Uwagi o powstaniu i rozwoju regionalnej tożsamości w średniowieczu deleatur" [The Silesian people in their own eyes and in the eyes of others. Remarks on the beginnings and development of regional identity in the Middle Ages]." In *Ślązacy w oczach własnych i obcych*, ed. Antoni Barciak (Katowice-Zabrze, 2010), 41–67.

Gawlas, Sławomir, "Pytania o tożsamość średniowiecznych Polaków w świetle współczesnych dyskusji humanistyki [The question of an identity of medieval Poles in the light of contemporary humanistic discussions]." In *Symboliczne i realne podstawy tożsamości społecznej w średniowieczu*, eds. Sławomir Gawlas and Paweł Żmudzki, (Warszawa, 2017), 15–82.

Geary, Patrick J., "Ethnic Identity as a Situational Construct in the Early Middle Ages", *Mitteilungen der Anthropologischen Gesellschaft in Wien* 113 (1983), 15–26.

Gładysz, Mikołaj, *Zapomniani krzyżowcy. Polska wobec ruchu krucjatowego w XII–XIII wieku* [Forgotten Crusaders. Poland and the Crusade Movement in the 12th–13th centuries] (Warszawa, 2002).

Goetz, Hans-Werner, "Fremdheit im früheren Mittelalter." In *Herrschaftspraxis und soziale Ordnungen im Mittelalter und in der frühen Neuzeit. Ernst Schubert zum Gedenken*, eds. Peter Aufgebauer and Christine van den Heuvel, Veröffentlichungen der Historischen Kommission für Niedersachsen und Bremen 232 (Hannover, 2006), 245–65.

Goetz, Hans-Werner, *Vorstellungsgeschichte: gesammelte Schriften zu Wahrnehmungen, Deutungen und Vorstellungen im Mittelalter*, eds. Anja Rathmann-Lutz et alii (Bochum 2007).

Goetz, Hans-Werner, *Geschichtsschreibung und Geschichtsbewusstsein im hohen Mittelalter*, Orbis medievalis 1, (Berlin, ^{2}2008).

Goetz, Hans-Werner, "Die Slawen in der Wahrnehmung Thietmars von Merseburg zu Beginn des 11. Jahrhunderts," *Letopis. Zeitschrift für sorbische Sprache, Geschichte und Kultur* 2 (2015), 103–118.

Görich, Knut, *Friedrich Barbarossa. Eine Biographie* (München, 2011).

Grabowska, Anna. "Bunt wójta Alberta w historiografii polskiej." [The rebellion of the alderman Albert in Polish historiography] In *Bunt wójta Alberta. Kraków i Opole we wzajemnych związkach w XIV wieku*, ed. Jerzy Rajman, (Kraków, 2013) 19–30.

Grabski, Andrzej Feliks, *Polska w opiniach obcych X–XIII w.* [Poland in the opinion of foreigners X–XIII centuries], Warszawa 1964.

Grabski, Andrzej Feliks, *Polska w opiniach Europy zachodniej XIV–XV w.* [Poland in the opinion of Western Europe 14th–15th century], Warszawa 1968.

Graus, František, *Die Nationenbildung der Westslawen im Mittelalter* (Sigmaringen 1980).

Gruner, Wolf D., "Das Deutschlandbild als zentrales Element der europäischen Dimension der deutschen Frage in Geschichte und Gegenwart." In *Die hässlichen Deutschen? Deutschland im Spiegel der westlichen und östlichen Nachbarn*, ed. Günter Trautmann (Darmstadt, 1991), 29–60.

Güttner-Sporzyński, Darius von (ed.), *Writing History in Medieval Poland. Bishop Vincentius of Cracow and the 'Chronica Polonorum'*, Cursor mundi 28 (Turnhout, 2017).

Haferland, Harald and Matthias Meyer (eds.) in collaboration with Carmen Stange and Markus Greulich, *Historische Narratologie. Mediävistische Perspektiven*, deleatur, Trends in Medieval Philology 19 (Berlin, 2010).

Hahn, Hans N. and Eva Hahn, "Nationale Stereotypen. Plädoyer für eine historische Stereotypenforschung." In *Stereotyp, Identität und Geschichte. Die Funktion von Stereotypen in gesellschaftlichen Diskursen*, ed. Hans H. Hahn (Frankfurt/M. 2002), 17–56.

Handbuch der Chroniken des Mittelalters, eds. Gerhard Wolf and Norbert N. Ott (Berlin-Boston, 2016).

Heck, Roman, "Główne linie rozwoju średniowiecznego dziejopisarstwa śląskiego" [The main lines of development in Silesian medieval historiography], *Studia Źródłoznawcze* 22 (1977), 61–75.

Hempfer, Klaus-W., *Gattungstheorie* (München, 1973).

Hengst, Karlheinz, "Thietmar und die Slawen." In *Thietmars Welt. Ein Merseburger Bischof schreibt Geschichte, Ausstellungskatalog*, eds. Axel v. Campenhausen, H. Kunde et al. (Petersberg/Fulda, 2018), 287–305.

Hitzbleck, Kerstin, "Einleitung: Transformationen des Fremden im Spätmittelalter und in der Frühen Neuzeit." In *Die Erweiterung des "globalen" Raumes und die Wahrnehmung des Fremden vom Mittelalter bis zur frühen Neuzeit/L'extension de l'espace "global" et la perception de l'Autre du Moyen Âge jusqu'à l'époque moderne*, eds. Kerstin Hitzbleck and Thomas Schwitter, Itinera 38 (Basel, 2015), 5–31.

Holtorf, Christian, "Spielräume einer Geschichte des Fremden." In *"Fremde". Zum Umgang mit Fremden in der Geschichte und Gegenwart*, ed. Presse- und Informationsstelle der Freien Universität Berlin, Dokumentationsreihe der Freien Universität Berlin 21 (Berlin, 1993), 15–18.

Holzer, Jerzy, "Der widerliche Schwabe, der brutale Preuße…." In *Die hässlichen Deutschen? Deutschland im Spiegel der westlichen und östlichen Nachbarn*, ed. Günter Trautmann (Darmstadt, 1991), 83–89.

Johnson, Greg, *Towards A New Nationalism*, (San Francisco, 2019).

Jones, Chris, *Eclipse of Empire? Perceptions of the Western Empire and its Rulers in Late-Medieval France* (Turnhout, 2007).

Jostkleigrewe, Georg, *Das Bild des Anderen. Entstehung und Wirkung deutschfranzösischer Fremdbilder in der volkssprachlichen Literatur und Historiographie des 12. bis 14. Jahrhunderts* (Berlin, 2008).

Jostkleigrewe, Georg, "'Rex imperator in regno suo' – an ideology of Frenchness? Late medieval France, its political élite, and juridical discourse." In *Imagined Communities: Constructing Collective Identities in Medieval Europe*, ed. Andrzej Pleszczyński et alii (Leiden/Boston, 2018), 46–82.

Jostkleigrewe, Georg, "Terra – populus – rex: La communauté du royaume vue de dehors. Regards allemands sur la France et les Français." In *Communitas regni: la « communauté du royaume » de la fin du xe siècle au début du xive siècle (Angleterre, Écosse, France, Empire, Scandinavie)*, eds. Dominique Barthélem et alii (Paris, 2020), 31–50.

Jurek, Tomasz, "Polska droga do korony królewskiej 1295–1300–1320." [Polish road to the royal crown 1295–1300–1320] In *Proměna středovýchodní a vrcholného středověku*, eds. Martin Wihoda and Lukáš Reitinger (Brno, 2010), 139–191.

Kellermann, Karina, "Eine kurtze rede wore. Die vier politischen Reimreden des Lupold Homburg" *Wolfram-Studien* 24 (2017), 199–219.

Kellermann, Karina, *Abschied vom 'historischen Volkslied'. Studien zur Funktion, Ästhetik und Publizität der Gattung historisch-politische Ereignisdichtung*, (Tübingen, 2000).

Kern, Fritz, *Anfänge der französischen Ausdehnungspolitik bis zum Jahr 1308* (Tübingen, 1910).

Kersken, Norbert, *Geschichtsschreibung im Europa der nationes. Nationalgeschichtliche Gesamtdarstellungen im Mittelalter*, Münstersche Historische Forschungen 8, (Köln-Weimar-Wien, 1995).

Kersken, Norbert, "Otto von Bamberg." In *Religiöse Erinnerungsorte in Ostmitteleuropa. Konstitution und Konkurrenz im nationalen- und epochenübergreifenden Zugriff*, eds. Joachim Bahlcke, Stefan Rohdewald, and Thomas Wünsch (Berlin 2013), 561–573.

Korta, Wacław, *Średniowieczna annalistyka śląska* [The medieval annals of Silesia] (Wrocław, 1966).

Gerard Koziełek (Gerhard Kossellek) (ed.) *Deutsche Polenliteratur* (Wrocław, 1991).

Kot, Stanisław, "Old international insults and praises." *Harvard Slavic Studies* 2 (1954), 181–209.

Kot, Stanisław, "Nationum Proprietates." *Oxford Slavonic Papers* 6 (1955) 1–43, and 7 (1957), 99–117.

Kragl, Florian, *Die Weisheit des Fremden. Studien zur mittelalterlichen Alexandertradition. Mit einem allgemeinen Teil zur Fremdheitswahrnehmung* (Bern, 2005).

Krzyżaniakowa, Jadwiga, "Poglądy polskich kronikarzy średniowiecznych na Niemcy i stosunki polsko-niemieckie [Views of Polish medieval chroniclers on Germany and Polish-German relations]." In *Wokół stereotypów Niemców i Polaków*, ed. Wojciech Wrzesiński (Wrocław, 1993) 15–72 (repr. *Nie ma historii bez człowieka. Studia z dziejów średniowiecza*, ed. IH UAM (Wrocław, 2010), 241–291.)

Krzyżaniakowa, Jadwiga, *'Nie ma historii bez człowieka'. Studia z dziejów średniowiecza* [There is no history without human being. Studies in the history of the Middle Ages], (Wrocław, 2010).

Kubín, Petr, "Die Bemühungen Ottos III. um die Einsetzung eines Heiligenkultes für Bischof Adalbert von Prag (†997)." In *Böhmen und seine Nachbarn in der Přemyslidenzeit*, eds. Ivan Hlaváček and Alexander Patschovsky, Vorträge und Forschungen 74 (Ostfildern, 2011).

Kwiatkowski, Krzysztof, "Die Selbstdarstellung des Deutschen Ordens in der 'Chronik' Wigands von Marburg." In *Selbstbild und Selbstverständnis der geistlichen Ritterorden*, ed. Roman Czaja, Jürgen Sarnowsky (Toruń, 2005), 127–138.

Kwiatkowski, Krzysztof, "Die "Eroberung Preußens" durch den Deutschen Orden – ihr Bild und ihre Wahrnehmung in der Literatur des Deutschen Ordens im 14. Jahrhundert." In *Kryžiaus karų epocha Baltijos regiono tautų istorinėje sąmonėje. Mokslinių straipsnių rinkinys*, eds. Rita R. Trimonienė and Robertas Jurgaitis (Saulės, 2007) 131–168.

Langner, Martin-M., *Annäherung ans Fremde durch sprachliche Bilder. Die Region Polen und ihre Ritter in Dichtungen des Hochmittelalters* (Berlin, 2018).

Laudage, Johannes, *Alexander III. und Friedrich Barbarossa* (Köln, 1997).

Leclercq, Armelle, *Portraits croisés: L'image des Francs et des Musulmans dans les textes sur la Première Croisade*. Chroniques latines et arabes, chansons de geste françaises des XIIe et XIIIe siècles. Nouvelle bibliothèque du Moyen Âge 96 (Paris, 2010).

Legitimation von Fürstendynastien in Polen und dem Reich. Identitätsbildung im Spiegel schriftlicher Quellen (12.–15. Jahrhundert), eds. Grischa Vercamer and Ewa Wółkiewicz, Deutsches Historisches Institut Warschau. Quellen und Studien 31 (Wiesbaden 2016).

Lempp, Albrecht, "West-östliche Bilder." *Friedrich-Ebert-Stiftung Gesprächskreis Arbeit und Soziales* 19 (1993), 11–26.

Lewandowski, Edmund, *Charakter narodowy Polaków i innych* [The national charakter of Poles and others] (London-Warszawa, 1995).

Lippmann, Walter, *Public Opinion* (repr. New York, 1997) (originally published New York, 1922).

Lorenz, Chris, "'The Times They Are a-Changin'. On Time, Space and Periodization in History." in *Palgrave handbook of research in historical culture and education*, eds. Mario Carretero, Stefan Berger, and Maria Christina Rosalia Grever (London, 2017) 109–133.

Lübke, Christian, *Fremde im östlichen Europa. Von Gesellschaften ohne Staat zu verstaatlichten Gesellschaften (9.–11. Jahrhundert)*, Ostmitteleuropa in Vergangenheit und Gegenwart 23 (Köln-Weimar-Wien, 2001).

Luckmann, Thomas, "Persönliche Identität, soziale Rolle und Rollendistanz." In *Identität. Kolloquium vom 5.–11.09.1976 in Bad Homburg*, eds. Odo Marquard and Karlheinz Stierle, Poetik und Hermeneutik: Arbeitsergebnisse einer Forschungsgruppe 8 (Munich, 1979), 293–313.

Maleczek, Werner, "Das Schisma von 1159 bis 1177. Erfolgsstrategie und Misserfolgsgründe." In *Gegenpäpste: ein unerwünschtes mittelalterliches Phänomen*, eds. Harald Müller and Brigitte Hotz (Wien, 2012), 165–204.

Manikowska, Halina and Dorota Gacka, "Hagiografia a historyczność, czyli o historii w hagiografii i hagiografia w służbie historii [Hagiography and historicity, or about history in hagiography and hagiography used by history]." In *Przeszłość w kulturze średniowiecznej Polski* 1, eds. Jacek Banaszkiewicz, Andrzej Dąbrówka and Piotr Węcowski (Warszawa, 2018), 657–748.

Mentzel-Reuters, Arno, "Deutschordenshistoriographie." In *Handbuch Chroniken des Mittelalters*, eds. Gerhard Wolf and Norbert H. Ott (Berlin-Boston, 2016), 328–330.

Mezník, Jaroslav, "Němci a Češi v Kronice tak řečeného Dalimila". [Germans and Czechs in the Chronicle of the so-called Dalimil] *Časopis Matice moravské* 112 (1993), 3–10.

Michałowski, Roman, "Le culte des saints du Haut Moyen Age en Pologne et en Europe Occidentale." In *La Pologne et l'Europe Occidentale du Moyen Age à nos jours. Actes du colloque organisé par l'Université Paris VII-Denis Diderot. Paris, les 28 et 29 octobre 1999*, eds. Marie-Louise Pelus-Kaplan and Daniel Tollet, Publikacje Instytutu Historii UAM 58 (Poznań-Paris, 2004), 29–41.

Michałowski, Roman, "Die Heiligenkulte sowie die staatlichen und ethnischen Grenzen: Polen und die Nachbarländer vom 10. bis zum 14. Jahrhundert." In *Grenzräume und Grenzüberschreitungen im Vergleich. Der Osten und der Westen des mittelalterlichen Lateineuropa*, eds. Klaus Herbers and Nikolaus Jaspert (Berlin, 2007) 339–360.

Michałowski, Roman, *The Gniezno Summit. The Religious Premises of the Founding of the Archbishopric of Gniezno* (Leiden, 2016).

Michalski, Maciej, *Kobiety i świętość w żywotach trzynastowiecznych księżnych polskich* [Women and holiness in the lives of 13th-century Polish princesses] (Poznań, 2004).

Migdalski, Paweł, *Słowiańszczyzna północno-zachodnia w historiografii polskiej, niemieckiej i duńskiej* [North-Western Slavdom in Polish, German and Danish historiography] (Wodzisław Śląski, 2019).

Mitkowski, Józef, "Nationality Problems and Patterns in Medieval Polish Towns: The Example of Cracow." *Zeszyty Naukowe Uniwersytetu Jagiellońskiego. Prace Historyczne* 59 (1978), 31–42.

Morton, Nicholas, *Encountering Islam on the First Crusade* (Cambridge, 2016).

Możdżeń Julia, *Przedstawianie świata przez kronikarzy gdańskich na przełomie XV i XVI wieku* [Presentation of the world by chroniclers from Gdansk at the turn of the 15th and 16th centuries] (Toruń, 2016).

Mrozowicz, Wojciech, "Sachsen im Bewußtsein der Schlesier im Mittelalter." In *Niedersachsen – Niederschlesien. Der Weg beider in die Geschichte*, ed. Wojciech Mrozowicz and Leszek Zygner (Göttingen-Wrocław, 2005), 83–94.

Mrozowicz, Wojciech, "Constancie flammis adiectus. Johannes Hus und der Hussitismus in den Augen schlesischer Chronisten." *Biuletyn Polskiej Misji Historycznej / Bulletin der Polnischen Historischen Mission* 11 (2016), 121–146.

Mrozowicz, Wojciech, "Pieśń o wójcie Albercie – przekaz historyczny w poetyckim sztafażu [A poem about the mayor Albert – a historical message in a poetic staffage]." In *Bunt wójta Alberta. Kraków i Opole we wzajemnych związkach w XIV wieku*, ed. J. Rajman (Kraków, 2013), 32–42.

Mrozowicz, Wojciech, "Z problematyki recepcji kroniki Wincentego w średniowiecznym dziejopisarstwie polskim (ze szczególnym uwzględnieniem śląskiej 'Kroniki polskiej') [On the issue of the reception of the Vincentius chronicle in Polish medieval historiography (with particular emphasis on the Silesian *Polish Chronicle*)]." In

'Onus Athlanteum'. Studia nad kroniką biskupa Wincentego, eds. Andrzej Dąbrówka and Witold Wojtowicz. Studia Staropolskie. Series nova (Warsaw, 2009), 326–336.

Mrozowicz, Wojciech, "Die Polnische Chronik (Polnisch-Schlesische Chronik) und die Chronik der Fürsten Polens (Chronica principum Poloniae) als Mittel zur dynastischen Identitätsstiftung der schlesischen Piasten." In *Legitimation von Fürstendynastien in Polen und dem Reich. Identitätsbildung im Spiegel schriftlicher Quellen (12.–15. Jahrhundert)*, eds. Grischa Vercamer and Ewa Wółkiewicz, Deutsches Historisches Institut Warschau. Quellen und Studien 31 (Wiesbaden, 2016), 249–262.

Müller-Mertens, Eckhardt, *Regnum Teutonicum. Aufkommen und Verbreitung der deutschen Reichs- und Königsauffassung im früheren Mittelalter*. Forschungen zur mittelalterlichen Geschichte 15 (Berlin, 1970).

Münkler, Marina and Werner Röcke, "Der ordo-Gedanke und die Hermeneutik der Fremde im Mittelalter: Die Auseinandersetzung mit den monströsen Völkern des Erdrandes." In *Die Herausforderung durch das Fremde*, ed. Herfried Münkler (Berlin, 1998), 701–766.

Nass, Klaus, *Die Reichschronik des Annalist Saxo und die sächsische Geschichtsschreibung im 12. Jahrhundert*, Schriften der MGH 41 (Hannover, 1996).

Niederstätter, Alois, *Österreichische Geschichte 1278–1411. Die Herrschaft Österreich. Fürst und Land im Spätmittelalter* (Vienna, 2001).

Niethammer, Lutz, *Kollektive Identität. Heimliche Quellen einer unheimlichen Konjunktur* (Reinbek, 2000).

Oexle, Otto Gerhard, "The Middle Ages through Modern Eyes. A Historical Problem: The Prothero Lecture." *Transactions of the Royal Historical Society* 9 (1999) 121–142.

Okniński, Piotr. *Kształtowanie się miasta komunalnego w Krakowie w XIII w. Struktury ustrojowe, ramy przestrzenne i podstawy gospodarcze* [Formation of the municipal city in Kraków in the 13th century. Political structures, spatial framework and economic foundations] (Warszawa, 2019).

'Onus Athlanteum'. Studia nad kroniką biskupa Wincentego [Studies on the chronicle of Bishop Vincent], eds. Andrzej Dąbrówka and Witold Wojtowicz (Warszawa, 2009).

Ożóg, Krzysztof, Uczeni w monarchii Jadwigi Andegaweńskiej i Władysława Jagiełły (1384–1434) [Scholars in the monarchy of Jadwiga of Poland and Władysław Jagiełło (1384–1434)], Polska Akademia Umiejętności, Rozprawy Wydziału Historyczno-Filozoficznego 105 (Kraków, 2004).

Ożóg, Krzysztof, *Die Rolle of Poland in the Intellectual Development of Europe in the Middle Ages* (Kraków, 2009).

Pac, Grzegorz, "Niemcy w trzynastowiecznych miraculach krakowskich." [Germans in the Crakowian Miracula of the 13th century] In *Monarchia, społeczeństwo, tożsamość. Studia z dziejów średniowiecza*, eds. Katarzyna Gołąbek et alii (Warszawa, 2020), 39–50.

Piskorski, Jan M., *Polska – Niemcy. Blaski i cienie tysiącletniego sąsiedztwa* [Poland – Germany. The light and shadow of a thousand-year-old neighborhood] (Warszawa, 2017).

Pleszczyński, Andrzej, *Niemcy wobec pierwszej monarchii piastowskiej (963–1034). Narodziny stereotypu. Postrzeganie i cywilizacyjna klasyfikacja władców Polski i ich kraju* [Germany towards the first Piast monarchy (963–1034). The birth of the stereotype. Perception and civilization classification of the rulers of Poland and their country] (Lublin, 2008).

Pleszczyński, Andrzej, *The birth of a stereotype: Polish rulers and their country in German writings c. 1000 A.D.* (Leiden 2011).

Pleszczyński, Andrzej, *Przekazy niemieckie o Polsce i jej mieszkańcach w okresie panowania Piastów* [German accounts about Poland and its inhabitants during the Piasts rule] (Lublin, 2016).

Pleszczyński, Andrzej et alii (eds.), *Historia communitatem facit. Struktura narracji tworzących tożsamości grupowe w średniowieczu* [*Historia communitatem facit*. The narrative structure forming group identities in the Middle Age] (Wrocław, 2016).

Primisser, Alois, *Peter Suchenwirt's Werke aus dem vierzehnten Jahrhunderte. Ein Beytrag zur Zeit- und Sittengeschichte*, (Wien, 1827).

Ptaśnik, Jan. "Włoski Kraków za Kazimierza Wielkiego i Władysława Jagiełły." *Rocznik Krakowski* 13 (1911): 49–110.

Quasthoff, Uta, *Soziales Vorurteil und Kommunikation. Eine sprachwissenschaftliche Analyse des Stereotyps* (Frankfurt am Main, 1973).

Rajman, Jerzy, *Kraków. Zespół osadniczy. Proces lokacji. Mieszczanie do roku 1333*, Akademia Pedagogiczna im. Komisji Edukacji Narodowej w Krakowie. Prace Monograficzne 375 (Kraków, 2004).

Rajman, Jerzy, "Mieszczanie z Górnego Śląska w elicie władzy Krakowa w XIV wieku." In *Elita władzy miasta Krakowa i jej związki z miastami Europy w średniowieczu i epoce nowożytnej (do połowy XVII wieku). Zbiór studiów*, ed. Zdzisław Noga (Kraków 2011) 49–80.

Rajman, Jerzy (ed.), *Bunt wójta Alberta: Kraków i Opole we wzajemnych związkach w XIV wieku*, Annales Universitatis Paedagogicae Cracoviensis. Studia Historica 13 (Kraków, 2013).

Reuter, Timothy, *The papal schism, the Empire and the West, 1159–1169* (Oxford, 1975).

Rychterová, Pavlína, "The Chronicle of the so-called Dalimil and its concept of Czech identity", in *Narrating Communities between Latin and Vernaculars* (Turnhout, forthcoming).

Rychterová, Pavlíny and David Kalhous (eds.), *Narrating Communities between Latin and Vernaculars: Historiographies in Central and Eastern Central Europe (13th–16th ct.). Historiograhies of Identity*, Narrating Communities 6, (Turnhout, forthcoming).

Said, Edward W., *Orientalism: Western Conceptions of the Orient*, (London, 2012).

Samsonowicz, Henryk, "Gesellschaftliche Pluralität und Interaktion in Krakau." In *Prag und Wien. Funktionen von der Metropolen im frühmodernen Staat*, eds. Marina Dmitrieva and Karen Lambrecht (Stuttgart, 2000), 117–129.

Henryk Samsonowicz, "My Polacy. Czyli o początkach polskiej świadomości narodowej," [We, Poles. That is, about the beginnings of Polish national consciousness] in *Historia vero testis temporum. Księga jubileuszowa poświęcona Profesorowi Krzysztofowi Baczkowskiemu w 70. rocznicę urodzin*, eds. Janusz Smołucha, Anna Waśko, Tomasz Graff, and Paweł F. Nowakowski (Kraków, 2008), 617–28.

Sax, William S., "The Hall of Mirrors: Orientalism, Anthropology, and the Other." *American Anthropologist*. New Series 100, 2 (1998) 292–301.

Schäffter, Ortfried, "Modi des Fremderlebens. Deutungsmuster im Umgang mit Fremdheit." In *Das Fremde. Erfahrungsmöglichkeiten zwischen Faszination und Bedrohung*, ed. Ortfried Schäffter (Opladen, 1991), 11–42.

Schmale, Franz-Josef, *Funktion und Formen mittelalterlicher Geschichtsschreibung. Eine Einführung. Mit einem Beitrag von Hans-Werner Goetz*, (Darmstadt, 1993).

Schmid, Florian M., *Die Fassung *C des "Nibelungenlieds" und der "Klage". Strategien der Retextualisierung*, Hermaea: Germanistische Forschungen. Neue Folge 147 (Berlin, 2018).

Schnell, Rüdiger, "Deutsche Literatur und deutsches Nationalbewußtsein in Spätmittelalter und Früher Neuzeit." In *Ansätze und Diskontinuität deutscher Nationsbildung im Mittelalter*, ed. Joachim Ehlers, Nationes 8 (Sigmaringen, 1989), 247–319.

Scior, Volker, *Das Eigene und das Fremde. Identität und Fremdheit in den Chroniken Adams von Bremen, Helmolds von Bosau und Arnolds von Lübeck*, Orbis mediaevalis, Vorstellungswelten des Mittelalters 4 (Berlin, 2002).

Scior, Volker, "Thietmar von Merseburg und die Slawen." In *Thietmar von Merseburg zwischen Pfalzen, Burgen und Federkiel. Palatium. Studien zur Pfalzenforschung in Sachsen-Anhalt*, ed. Stephan Freund (Regensburg, 2020), *forthcoming*.

Scior, Volker, "Der menschliche Körper und seine Grenzen. Die Chronik Thietmars von Merseburg in körpergeschichtlicher Perspektive." In *Historiographie der Grenzwelten. Thietmar von Merseburg (975/6-01.12.1018)*, ed. Dirk Jäckel, Studien zur Vormoderne 3, (Berlin, 2021), *forthcoming*.

Skottki, Kristin, *Christen, Muslime und der Erste Kreuzzug. Die Macht der Beschreibung in der mittelalterlichen und modernen Historiographie*. Cultural Encounters and the Discourses of Scholarship 7 (Münster, 2015).

Skowrońska, Anna, "Z szesnastowiecznych polemik o polskość Śląska." [From sixteenth-century polemics about Polishness of Silesia] *Śląski Kwartalnik Historyczny Sobótka* 10/3 (1955), 433–445.

Šmahel, František, "The Idea of the 'Nation' in Hussite Bohemia: an Analytical Study of the Ideological and Political Aspects of the National Question in Hussite Bohemia from the End of the 14th Century to the Eighties of the 15th Century." *Historica* 16 (1969), 143–247, 17 (1969), 93–197.

Sochacki, Jarosław, *Stosunki publiczno-prawne między państwem polskim a Cesarstwem Rzymskim w latach 963–1102* [Public-legal relations between the Polish state and the Roman Empire in the years 963–1102], (Słupsk-Gdańsk, 2003).

Sprandel, Rolf, "Geschichtsschreiber in Deutschland 1347–1517." In *Mentalitäten im Mittelalter. Methodische und inhaltliche Probleme*, ed. František Graus, Vorträge und Forschungen 35 (Sigmaringen 1987), 289–316.

Sprandel, Rolf, "Frankreich im Spiegel der spätmittelalterlichen Historiographie Deutschlands." In *Kultureller Austausch und Literaturgeschichte im Mittelalter*, ed. Ingrid Kasten et alii (Sigmaringen, 1998), 35–45.

Srodecki, Paul, *Antemurale Christianitatis. Zur Genese Bollwerksrhetorik im östlichen Mitteleuropa an der Schwelle vom Mittelalter zur Frühen Neuzeit*, Historische Studien 508 (Husum, 2015).

Stanzel, Franz K., "Der literarische Aspekt unserer Vorstellungen vom Charakter fremder Völker." *Anzeiger der Österreichischen Akademie der Wissenschaften. Philosophisch-Historische Klasse* 3 (1974), 63–80.

Stanzel, Franz K., "Zur literarischen Imagologie. Eine Einführung." In *Europäischer Völkerspiegel. Imagologisch-ethnographische Studien zu den Völkertafeln des frühen 18. Jahrhunderts*, ed. Franz K. Stanzel (Heidelberg, 1999), 9–41.

Starzyński, Marcin, *Das mittelalterliche Krakau. Der Stadtrat im Herrschaftsgefüge der polnischen Metropole* (Köln–Weimar–Wien, 2015).

Straub, Jürgen, "Personale und kollektive Identität. Zur Analyse eines theoretischen Begriffs." In *Identitäten Erinnerung, Geschichte, Identität* 3, eds. Aleida Assmann and Heidrun Friese, 2nd ed., (Frankfurt/M., 1999), 73–104.

Strzelczyk, Jerzy, "Deutsch-polnische Schicksalsgemeinschaft in gegenseitigen Meinungen im Mittelalter." In *Mittelalter – eines oder viele?/ Średniowiecze – jedno czy wiele?*, eds. Sławomir Moździoch, Wojciech Mrozowicz, and Stanisław Rosik (Wrocław, 2010), 111–126.

Świderska, Małgorzata, *Studien zur literaturwissenschaftlichen Imagologie. Das literarische Werk F.M. Dostoevskijs aus imagologischer Sicht mit besonderer Berücksichtigung der Darstellung Polens* (München, 2001).

Symboliczne i realne podstawy tożsamości społecznej w średniowieczu [Symbolic and real foundations of social identity in the Middle Ages], eds. Sławomie Gawlas and Paweł Żmudzki (Warszawa, 2017).

Thomas, Heinz, "Nationale Elemente in der ritterlichen Welt des Mittelalters." In *Ansätze und Diskontinuität deutscher Nationsbildung im Mittelalter*, ed. Joachim Ehlers (Sigmaringen, 1988), 345–376.

Thum, Bernd, "Frühformen des Umgangs mit 'Fremdem' und 'Fremde' in der Literatur des Hochmittelalters. Der Parzival Wolframs von Eschenbach als Beispiel." In

Das Mittelalter – unsere fremde Vergangenheit. Beiträge der Stuttgarter Tagung vom 17.–19.09.1987, eds. Joachim Kuolt, Harald Kleinschmidt, and Peter Dinzelbacher, Flugschriften der Volkshochschule Stuttgart 6 (Stuttgart, 1990), 315–52.

Tolan, John V., *Saracens: Islam in the Medieval European Imagination* (New York, 2002).

Tür an Tür. Polen – Deutschland: 1000 Jahre Kunst und Geschichte, eds. Malgorzata Omilanowska and Tomasz Torbus (Köln 2011).

Trautmann, Günter (ed.), *Die hässlichen Deutschen? Deutschland im Spiegel der westlichen und östlichen Nachbarn*, (Darmstadt, 1991).

Tyc, Teodor, "Niemcy w świetle poglądów Polski piastowskiej." [Germany in the light of the views of Piast Poland] *Strażnica Zachodnia* 4, no. 7–12 (1925), 1–23 (repr. id., *Z średniowiecznych dziejów Wielkopolski i Pomorza. Wybór prac*, ed. Jan M. Piskorski (Poznań, 1997): 279–301).

Utz, Richard, "Coming to Terms with Medievalism." *European Journal of English Studies* 15, 2 (2011) 101–114.

Vercamer, Grischa, "Zeit in Peters von Dusburg 'Chronica Terrae Prussiae' (1326). Chronologische Ordnung oder Mittel zum Zweck?" *Zapiski historyczne* 76, 4 (2011), 7–25.

Vercamer, Grischa, "Imperiale Konzepte in der mittelaterlichen Historiographie Polens vom 12 bis zum 15. Jahrhundert." In *Transcultural Approaches to the Concept of Imperial Rule In the Middle Ages*, eds. Christian Scholl, Torben R. Gebhardt, and Jan Clauss (Frankfurt/Main 2017), 321–366.

Vercamer, Grischa, *Hochmittelalterliche Herrschaftspraxis im Spiegel der Geschichtsschreibung. Vorstellungen von »guter« und »schlechter« Herrschaft in England, Polen und dem Reich im 12./13. Jahrhundert* (Wiesbaden 2020).

Völkl, Martin, *Muslime – Märtyrer – Militia Christi: Identität, Feindbild und Fremderfahrung während der ersten Kreuzzüge*, Wege zur Geschichtswissenschaft (Stuttgart, 2011).

Vollmann-Profe, Gisela, "Iohannes de Posilge, Chronike des Landes von Prussin." In *The Encyclopedia of the Medieval Chronicle*, cur. Graeme Dunphy, (Leiden 2010), 922.

Vollrath, Hanna, "Lauter Gerüchte? Canossa aus kommunikationsgeschichtlicher Sicht." In *Päpstliche Herrschaft im Mittelalter. Funktionsweisen – Strategien – Darstellungsformen*, ed. Stefan Weinfurter, Mittelalter-Forschungen 38 (Stuttgart, 2012), 153–198.

Vollrath, Hanna, "Lüge oder Fälschung? Die Überlieferung von Barbarossas Hoftag zu Würzburg im Jahr 1165 und der Becket-Streit." In *Stauferreich im Wandel*, ed. Stefan Weinfurter, Mittelalter-Forschung 9 (Ostfildern, 2002), 149–171.

Vollrath, Hanna, "Sutri 1046 – Canossa 1077 – Rome 1111. Problems of Communication and the Perception of Neighbors." In *European Transformations. The long Twelfth Century*, eds. Thomas F.X. Noble and John van Engen (Notre Dame, IN, 2012), 132–170.

von Zitzewitz, Hasso, *Das deutsche Polenbild in der Geschichte: Entstehung – Einflüsse – Auswirkungen* (Köln, 1991).

Vorstellungsgeschichte: Gesammelte Schriften zu Wahrnehmungen, Deutungen und Vorstellungen im Mittelalter, eds. Anna Aurast, Simon Elling, and Bele Freudenberg (Bochum, 2007).

Wackernagel, Wilhelm, "Die Spottnamen der Völker." *Zeitschrift für deutsches Alterthum* 6 (1848), 254–261.

Weber, Matthias, "Zur Konzeption protonationaler Geschichtsbilder. Pommern und Schlesien in geschichtlichen Darstellungen des 16. Jahrhunderts." In *Die Konstruktion der Vergangenheit. Geschichtsdenken, Traditionsbildung und Selbstdarstellung im frühneuzeitlichen Ostmitteleuropa,* eds. Joachim Bahlcke and Arno Strohmeyer, Zeitschrift für Historische Forschung. Beiheft 29 (Berlin, 2002), 55–79.

Węcowski, Piotr, *Początki Polski w pamięci historycznej polskiego średniowiecza* [The beginnings of Poland in the historical memory of the Polish Middle Ages], (Kraków, 2014).

Wenta Jarosław, *Studien über die Ordensgeschichtsschreibung am Beispiel Preussens* (Toruń, 2000).

Wenzel, Angelika, *Stereotype in gesprochener Sprache. Form, Vorkommen und Kommunikation in Dialogen* (München, 1978).

Wenzel, Horst, "Der unfeste Held. Wechselnde oder mehrfache Identitäten." In *Unverwechselbarkeit. Persönliche Identität und Identifikation in der vormodernen Gesellschaft,* ed. Peter von Moos, Norm und Struktur 23 (Köln, 2004), 163–83.

Wierlacher, Alois, "Mit anderen Augen oder: Fremdheit als Ferment. Überlegungen zur Begründung einer intellektuellen Hermeneutik deutscher Literatur." In *Das Fremde und das Eigene: Prologomena zu einer interkulturellen Germanistik* (München, 1985), 3–28.

Wierlacher, Alois and Corinna Albrecht, "Kulturwissenschaftliche Xenologie." In *Konzepte der Kulturwissenschaften: theoretische Grundlagen – Ansätze – Perspektiven,* eds. Ansgar Nünning and Vera Nünning, 2nd ed., (Stuttgart 2008), 280–306

Winkler, Andreas, "Ethnische Schimpfwörter und übertragener Gebrauch von Ethnika." *Muttersprache* 4 (1994), 320–337.

Wiszewski, Przemysław, *Domus Bolezlai: Values and social identity in dynastic traditions of medieval Poland (c.966–1138)* (Leiden 2010) (trans. of: Domus Bolezlai. W poszukiwaniu tradycji dynastycznej Piastów (do około 1138 roku), Wrocław 2008).

Witkowska, Aleksandra, "Miracula małopolskie z XIII i XIV wieku – Studium źródłoznawcze." *Roczniki Humanistyczne* 19/2 (1971), 29–161.

Wolverton, Lisa, *Cosmas of Prague: Narrative, Classicism, Politics* (Washington, DC, 2015).

Wrzesiński, Wojciech, *Sąsiad czy wróg? Ze studiów nad kształtowaniem obrazu Niemca w Polsce w latach 1735–1939* [Neighbour or enemy? Studies on the formation of the image of the German in Poland in the years 1735–1939] (Wrocław, 1992).

Wünsch, Thomas, "Kultbeziehungen zwischen dem Reich und Polen im Mittelalter." In Das Reich und Polen: Parallelen, Interaktionen und Formen der Akkulturation im Hohen und Späten Mittelalter, eds. Alexander Patschovsky and Thomas Wünsch, Vorträge und Forschungen 59 (Stuttgart, 2003), 357–400.

Wünsch, Thomas, *Deutsche und Slawen im Mittelalter: Beziehungen zu Tschechen, Polen, Südslawen und Russen* (München, 2008).

Wyrozumska, Bożena. "Nationalitätenprobleme der mittelalterlichen polnischen Städte in der Historiographie und im Lichte der städtischen Quellen von Krakau," *Zeszyty Naukowe Uniwersytetu Jagiellońskiego. Prace Historyczne* 113 (1994), 19–28.

Wyrozumski, Jerzy, *Kraków do schyłku wieków średnich* [Krakow until the end of the Middle Ages] (Kraków, 1992).

Zaremska, Hanna, *Żydzi w średniowiecznej Polsce. Gmina krakowska* [The Jewish people in Medieval Poland. Krakow commune] (Warszawa, 2011).

Zientara, Benedykt, "Konflikty narodowościowe na pograniczu niemiecko-słowiańskim w XIII–XIV wieku i ich zasięg społeczny." [Nationality conflicts on the German-Slavic border in the 13th – 14th centuries and their social range] *Przegląd Historyczny* 59 (1968), 197–212.

Zientara, Benedykt, "Nationality Conflicts in the German-Slavic Borderland in the 13th–14th Centuries and their Social Scope." APH 22 (1970), 207–225.

Zientara, Benedykt, "Foreigners in Poland in the 10th–15th Centuries. Their Role in the Opinion of Polish Medieval Community", APH 29 (1974), 5–28.

Zientara, Benedykt, "Die deutschen Einwanderer in Polen vom 12. bis zum 14. Jahrhundert." *In Die deutsche Ostsiedlung des Mittelalters als Problem der europäischen Geschichte. Reichenau Vorträge 1970–1972*, ed. W. Schlesinger (Sigmaringen, 1975), 333–348.

Zientara, Benedykt, "Socio-economic and spatial transformation of Polish towns during the period of location." APH 34 (1976), 57–83.

Zilynská, Blanka, "Die Böhmische Chronik Benedikt Johnsdorfs über die Böhmische Krone im Rahmen der Kronländer." In *Geschichte – Erinnerung – Selbstidentifikation. Die schriftliche Kultur in den Ländern der Böhmischen Krone im 14.–18. Jahrhundert*, eds. Lenka Bobková and Jan Zdichynec, (Prague, 2011), 82–108.

Zonenberg, Sławomir, *Kronika Wiganda z Marburga* [Chronicle of Wigand of Marburg] (Toruń 1994).

Zonenberg, Sławomir, *Kronika Szymona Grunaua* [Chronicle of Simon Grunau] (Bydgoszcz, 2009).

Index of Geographic Names and Historical (also Fictional) Persons

Adalbert, St. Bishop of Prague and Holy Martyr (d.997)   105, 124–125, 127, 160, 168–169, 173, 191, 228–229, 231–233, 235–236, 238–241
Adam of Bremen, chronicler (d.1081/1085)   8, 185, 191–193, 196, 198, 265
Agnes of Babenberg, Polish Duchess (d.1163), wife of Władysław II   114, 127, 140
Albert, advocate (vogt) of Krakow (ca. 1289–1312)   141, 182, 357–359, 362–363, 366–368, 370, 372
Albert (Albrecht) III., duke of Austria (d.1395)   256–257
Albert (Albrecht) IV., duke of Austria (d.1404)   256
Albert of Stade, German monk, historian and poet (d. c. 1260)   198
Alexander III, pope (c.1100/1105–1181)   69–79, 128
Andreas of Ratisbon (Regensburg), historian (15th c.)   201, 205–206, 211, 213, 221–222
Andrzej Łaskarz, bishop of Poznań (d. 1426)   149, 206, 221
Annalista Saxo, chronicler (d.1166)   248
Armenians   30, 358–359
Attila, ruler of the Huns (d.453), see Etzel   279
Augsburg   200, 213, 215, 222

Baltram of Pola, figure of German heroic poetry   293
Bavaria   115, 124, 126, 129, 143, 156–157, 174–175, 197, 199, 207, 214–215, 217–218, 220
Besançon   45, 69
Bishop of Passau, uncle of Kriemhild, figure of German heroic poetry   280
Biterolf, figure of German heroic poetry   250, 285–287, 298
Blödelin, older brother of Etzel (Attila), figure of German heroic poetry   288–289
Blumenau Laurentius, a lawyer, priest of the Teutonic Order, chronicler (d. 1484)   352

Bohemi /Bohemiani   89, 91–92, 96, 146, 189, 192, 194, 307 n. 11, 371 n. 19
Bohemia (Czechia)   13, 69, 82, 85–86, 88, 91–93, 95–96, 103, 130, 141 n. 78, 146, 156 n. 142, 161, 163, 165, 189, 197, 199–200, 207 n. 75, 210, 213, 215, 218, 222, 229 n. 6, 233, 239, 248, 257, 275, 277, 299, 306–308, 315, 317–318, 353, 362, 371
Bohemians   124, 146, 165, 180, 189, 191–192, 307–308, 314–316, 349, 358, 371
Boleslaus the Brave (Chrobry), Polish Duke and King (d.1025)   11, 104–106, 113, 124–125, 127, 129, 135, 140, 144, 159–160, 168, 170, 173, 181, 238–239
Bolesław II, the Genereous, Polish Duke and King (d.c. 1081)   135, 240
Bolesław II, the Genereous, Polish Duke and King (d.c. 1081)   107, 169
Bolesław III Krzywousty (the Wrymouth), Polish Duke (d.1138)   108–110, 113, 125, 130, 140, 144, 161, 236, 238–239, 248, 306
Bolesław IV Kędzierzawy, Polish Duke (d.1173)   114, 145
Bolesław Rogatka, Duke of Silesia (d.1278)   117, 145, 240, 301 n. 124, 306
Boppe, (d. c.1290) German gnomic poet-Meistersinger   276
Breslau – see Wrocław
Brno   87

Casimir I (Kazimir/Kazimierz, Karolus), the Restorer, Polish Duke (d.1058)   106–107, 127, 134–135, 140, 143–144, 160–161, 170, 172, 180–181
Casimir III, the Great (Kazimierz), Polish King (d.1370)   6, 142, 163, 204, 206, 209–211, 215–216, 223, 325, 340, 343–345, 359–360, 364–365
Casimir IV (Kazimierz) Jagiellon, Polish King, Grand Duke of Lithuania (d.1492)   155, 165, 212, 216–217, 225, 318, 351–356

Casper Weinreich, chronicler from Danzig/ Gdańsk (15th c.) 354
Cavallo Paulinus, Genoan merchant and town councilor in Krakow (14th c.) 363
Češi – see Bohemi
Charlemagne (Karl der Große), King of Franks, Roman Emperor 54
Charlemagne (Karl der Große), King of Franks, Roman Emperor (d.814) 54–55, 123 n. 12, 124, 226
Charles I of Anjou, King of Sicily, count of Anjou and Maine, c. of Provence (d.1285) 52, 174
Christians 25, 28–29, 31–35, 38, 118, 132, 162, 280, 333, 336, 341 n. 63, 342, 355, 364
Conrad I, prince of Brno and Znojmo (d.1092) 87
Cosmas of Prague, chronicler (ca. 1050–1125) 82–90, 95
Cracow – see Krakow

Dalimil (so-called), Czech chronicler (d. c. 1314) 83, 91–95
Danes 281
Dania – see Denmark 69, 163, 185, 193, 234
David Scholasticus (Scotigena), German chronicler (12th c.) 63, 65–66, 80
Detmar of Lübeck, German chronicler (d. c. 1395) 199, 203–204 n. 52, 209, 211–212, 221, 224–225
Dietleib, figure of German heroic poetry 250, 285, 293
Dietrich (of Bern), figure of German heroic poetry 250, 259, 278–279 n. 69, 289–295, 298–299
Dietrich of Nieheim, a jurist at the papal curia (15th c.) 197, 207, 222
Dirsva (Dzierzwa), alleged Polish chronicler (14th c.) 138–139 n. 69, 142
Dobrawa (Dąbrówka), Polish Duchess (d. 977), wife of Mieszko I 104, 189

Eberhard Windeck, German-Hungarian merchant a. chronicler (d. 1440/41) 198, 211 n. 99, 213, 222
Erfurt 199, 215, 223 n. 193

Ermenrich, figure of Geman heroic poetry (modelled on Theodoric the Great) 250, 293–294, 299
Etzel, figure of German heroic poetry (modelled on Attila) 249, 279–293, 295, 299–300

Fatimids, the Arab Caliphate dynasty (10th–12th c.) 36
France 9, 12–13, 42–43, 45–48, 50–52, 55, 61 n. 6, 69, 71–72, 82 n. 4, 103, 157, 185, 277, 324, 330
Franks 29–30, 35, 38, 124, 145
Frederick I Barbarossa, German King, Roman Emperor (d. 1190) 68–74, 76–79, 81, 114, 118, 127–128, 157, 161
Frederick II, King of Germany, Sicily, Italy, Jerusalem/ Roman Emperor (d. 1250) 51 n. 23, 138, 145, 328 n. 27
Fulcher of Chartres, French Chronicler (d. c. 1128) 36, 38–40

Gallus Anonymus, Polish chronicler c. 1115 103, 107–108, 111, 113, 123, 156, 170, 173, 181, 306
Gedimin (Gediminas), Grand Duke of Lithuania (d. 1341) 328, 330, 333, 342
Georg (Jiří) of Poděbrad, Bohemian king (d. 1471) 212, 315–316, 318
Georg Egloffstein, German (Teutonic Order) administrator (advocatus), alleged historian (15th c.) 350
Gerlach of Milevsko, Czech chronicler (d. ca. 1210) 83, 89, 96
Germans (Theutoni) 2–4, 7–9, 13, 56, 68, 81, 85–86, 92–95, 99, 101–103, 107, 109, 111, 113, 115–120 n. 3, 126, 128, 130, 133, 140–141, 143–143, 145–146, 158, 160, 162, 166–182, 275 n. 52, 303, 305, 308, 311, 318–319, 324–325, 350–351, 357–358, 370–371, 382–386
Germany (Theutonia) 1, 3, 6, 9–12, 42, 45, 54, 58, 67, 70, 73, 77, 79–80, 82 n. 4, 92–93, 101–102 n. 3, 103–104, 109, 111, 115, 156–157, 162, 169–174, 178, 180–181, 197, 278, 310, 324, 331, 357, 383–384, 386–387, 391

INDEX OF GEOGRAPHIC NAMES AND HISTORICAL PERSONS   429

Gervase of Canterbury, Emglish chronicler
   (d. c. 1210)   70, 75–77
Gniezno   8, 104, 112–113, 116 n. 70, 117–118,
   124–125, 127, 131, 133 n. 45, 135, 144,
   159–160, 168, 171–174, 181, 233, 334
Gottfried Fattinante, Genoan merchant
   and town councilor in Krakow
   (14th c.)   363–364
Greeks   30, 49, 248, 281, 380

Hans Ebran of Wildenberg, German
   (Bavarian) historian (d. c. 1503)   201, 205
Hartmann of Aue (von Ouwe), German
   knight and poet (d. c. 1210–20)   277
Hedwig of Hungary, see
   Jadwiga of Poland   204–207, 223,
   253–256, 336–339 n. 53, 351
Hedwig of Silesia (of Andechs), Duchess of
   Silesia, wife of Henry I the Bearded   168,
   175, 228, 231–232, 235, 238–242, 312–312
Heinrich Beringer, Carthusian monk and
   religious writer (d.1444)   347
Helche, figure of German heroic poetry, wife
   of Etzel   287, 293, 298
Helmold of Bosau, German chronicler
   (d. 1177)   8, 60 n. 4, 144 n. 89, 185, 193–194,
   196, 198, 265, 349
Henry I the Bearded, Polish Duke
   (d. 1238)   140
Henry II, German King, Roman Emperor
   (d. 1024)   104, 113, 140, 190
Henry II, Plantagenet, king of England
   (d. 1189)   71–79
Henry III, the White, Duke of Silesia
   (d. 1266)   301
Henry IV, German King, Holy Roman
   Emperor (d. 1106)   10, 61, 63–68, 81, 85,
   108, 129, 161, 193
Henry IV Probus, Polish Duke (d. 1290)   139,
   141 n. 78, 173, 176, 371–372
Henry the Woodcutter, Czech chronicler
   (12/13th c.)   83, 89, 91
Henry V, German King, Holy Roman Emperor
   (d. 1125)   60–61 n. 6, 62–63, 65–68, 78 n.
   69, 80, 108–110, 113, 124–125, 140,
   144–145, 161
Henryk of Ketř, Krakow's burgher
   (14th c.)   362

Henryków (Heinrichau)   311–313
Herman of Racibórz, Krakow's burgher
   (14th c.)   363
Herman von Ostervranchen, figure of
   German heroic poetry   293
Herman, Duke of Poland, figure of German
   heroic poetry   284–285 n. 87, 287–288,
   299
Hermann Korner, Lübeck Dominican,
   chronicler (15th c.)   199, 204, 207,
   212–213, 224, 226 n. 221
Hermann of Salza, Grand Master of the
   Teutonic Order (d. 1239)   328 n. 27,
   330
Holy Roman Empire   2, 9–10, 13, 57, 66–67,
   69–70, 72, 79–80, 82, 84, 101, 113, 119,
   122, 126, 132, 145, 154, 160, 166, 328–329,
   337, 339, 362
Hornboge (Hornpoge), figure of German
   heroic poetry   283–284, 286, 288,
   293–295, 298–299
Hyacinth, St. (Hyacinth of Poland), Polish
   Dominican priest and missionary
   (d. 1257)   178–179

Isidore of Sevilla, Spanish scholar and cleric
   (d. 636)   116, 137, 143, 157 n. 143

Jadwiga of Poland, the female monarch of
   Poland, wife of Władysław Jagiellon
   (d. 1399)   174, 336–338, 351 n. 19
Jakob Unrest, Austrian chronicler
   (d. 1500)   201, 214, 216, 225
Jakub Świnka, Polish Catholic priest, the
   Archbishop of Gniezno (d. 1314)   8, 116,
   131, 174, 180–181
Jan Długosz, Polish chronicler (d. 1480)   136,
   154, 156, 179
Jan of Czarnków, Polish chronicler
   (d. 1387)   142, 146
Jerusalem   28, 32–33, 36–37, 145
Jesus Christ, central figure of Christianity
   (d.30/33)   29, 36, 369
Johann I Albert, King of Poland
   (d. 1501)   216, 355
Johann of Posilge, Chronicler of the
   Teuthonic Order (d. 1405)   322–323,
   334–340, 344, 346, 348, 352

Johann of Viktring, chronicler and political advisor to Duke Henry of Carinthia (14th c.) 200, 203–204 n. 52, 207, 210, 218–220
Johann Staindel, German chronicler (d. 1518) 201
Johannes Froben, Silesian chronicler (15th c.) 316, 318
Johannes Kungstein, German chronicler (d. c. 1405) 198, 204, 211, 222–223, 225
Johannes of Winterthur, German (Swiss) chronicler (14th c.) 197, 203, 209–210, 216, 221
John of Salisbury, English philosopher, diplomat, educationist, bishop of Chartres (d. 1180) 72 n. 45, 81, 87, 325
John of Worcester, English chronicler (d. c 1140) 58 n. 3, 62–68
Judith of Suabia, German Princess, Polish Duchess, wife of Władysław Herman (d. c. 1102) 108 n. 24, 240
Julius Caesar, Roman general and statesman (d. 44 BC) 115, 129, 143, 234

King of Prussia, figure of German heroic poetry 285–286
Kinga, St. (Kinga of Poland), wife of Polish Duke Bolesław the Chaste, Poor Clares nun (d. 1292) 174–175 n. 38, 176–177, 180
Klemens Janicki (1516–1543), Polish Renaissance poet 371
König Rother, figure of German heroic poetry 275, 277
Königsberg 323 n. 5, 326–327 n. 20
Konrad Bitschin, head of the city chancellery from Chełmno (Kulm), chronicler 348–349
Konrad Gesselen, chronicler of the Theutonic Order (14th c.) 340
Konrad II, German King, Roman Emperor (d. 1039) 107, 192
Konrad of Masovia, Polish Duke (d. 1247) 330, 332, 350
Konrad von Wallenrode Grand Master of the Teuthonic Order (d. 1393) 339
Krak [Grakch], fictional (legendary) ruler in Kracow 112, 128
Krakow 8, 14, 112–114, 126, 128, 130, 135–139, 141, 148, 150–152, 154–155, 163, 169, 172, 174–175, 178–179, 182, 204 n. 51, 205–206 n. 65, 66, 209 n. 85, 210 n. 89, 211–212 n. 105, 221–223, 226, 241, 254–257, 306, 308, 315, 332, 334, 338, 343, 350, 357–372
Kriemhild, figure of German heroic poetry 279–285 n. 87, 296
Kudrun, figure of German heroic poetry 275 n. 52

Ladislaus Herman (Władysław I Herman), Duke of Poland (d. 1102) 107–108, 238, 240, 299
Ladislaus Jagiello (Władysław II Jagiełło), King of Poland 225
Ladislaus Jagiello (Władysław II Jagiełło), King of Poland (d. 1434) 147, 151–152 n. 124, 165 n. 179, 211, 216, 223, 254, 325, 336, 339–340, 344–346, 352, 361, 364
Ladislaus the Elbow-High (Władysław I Łokietek), Polish duke and king 223
Ladislaus the Elbow-High (Władysław I Łokietek), Polish duke and king (d. 1333) 136, 141, 146 n. 96, 181–182, 198, 203, 207, 209, 221, 328, 330–333, 340, 342–343, 345, 357–359, 363, 368–369
Laurin, figure of German heroic poetry (dwarf King) 292
Legnica (Liegnitz) 218, 240, 306, 308, 317
Lestek, legendary/fictional?/ Polish Duke 115, 129, 143–144
Lestko the Black (Leszek II Czarny), Polish Duke (d. 1288) 135, 176, 330, 332, 371
Lewko, Jewish banker in Krakow (14th c.) 364–365
Lindau Johann, chronicler from Gdańsk (d. c. 1480) 353
Lipienko (Leipe) 350
Liutici (Liutizen) 190
Lohengrin, figure of German Arthurian literature 276
Louis I of Hungary, king of Hungary and Poland (d. 1382) 204–206, 223, 252–253, 337, 364
Lübeck 8, 198–199, 203–204, 209, 211–213, 221, 223–225, 265, 362
Lubiąż (Leubus) 133 n. 43, 139, 171, 308–311, 314, 320

INDEX OF GEOGRAPHIC NAMES AND HISTORICAL PERSONS 431

Ludolf of Żagań, Silesian chronicler
  (d. 1422)   202, 207, 213, 314–315
Ludwig von Erlichshausen, Grand Master of
  the Teutonic Order (d. 1467)   352, 354
Ludwik I (Ludwig/Louis I of Brzeg and
  Legnica), Silesian Duke (d. 1398)   220

Magdeburg   74, 118, 145, 169, 188, 190 n. 33,
  196, 199, 211–214, 221, 361–362, 364
Mainz   63–64, 68, 72, 76, 137, 169, 197–198,
  204, 211, 213
Manfred of Sicily, King of Sicily, son of
  Emperor Frederick II (d. 1266)   52
Marianus Scotus (M. Scottus of Mainz), Irish
  monk and chronicler (d. c. 1083)   63–65,
  67
Marienburg (Malbork)   214, 325–327, 334,
  338, 343
Mars, the Roman god   309
Martin of Tropau (Martin of Poland, Martin
  of Opava), Czech/Polish?/ chronicler,
  archbishop of Gniezno (d. 1283)   138, 143,
  145, 161, 197, 327 n. 23
Matthias Corvinus, Hungarian King, King of
  Croatia, Bohemia (d. 1490)   318, 352,
  355
Matthias of Neuenburg, German chronicler
  (d. c. 1370)   197, 215, 218, 220–221, 225
Mieszko I, Polish Duke (d. 992)   10, 104, 127,
  140, 159, 189–190, 205, 239
Mieszko II, Polish Duke and King
  (d. 1034)   106–107, 125, 127, 160, 192, 248
Milan   52, 164 n. 174
Minden   199
Montbéliard   45
Muhammad, Arab religious, social and
  political leader, founder of Islam   26, 31
Munich   200–201, 226

Nicolas Jeroschin, German chronicler of the
  Teuthonic Order (d. 1341)   323, 328, 335,
  340, 352
Nikolaus Tempelfeld, Silesian scolar and
  politician (d. 1474)   315

Orderic Vitalis, English chronicler,
  Benedictine monk (d. c. 1142)   63–67

Otto III, German King, Roman Emperor
  (d. 1002)   104–106, 113, 124, 127, 140, 144,
  160, 170, 172–173, 180–181, 218, 224
  n. 199, 229–230
Otto of Bamberg, bishop of Bamberg,
  missionary of Pomerania (d. 1139)   191,
  228, 230–231, 233–240
Ottokar of Styria (Otacher ouz der Geul?),
  Austrian chronicler a. poet (d. c.
  1322)   45–46, 197, 200, 207, 219

Paschal II (Paschalis II), pope
  (d. 1118)   60–61 n. 6, 62 n. 11, 66
Passau   201, 280
Peter of Dusburg, chronicler of the Teuthonic
  Order   322–323, 326, 328–333, 335–336,
  340, 348, 350 n. 16, 352
Peter Suchenwirt, Austrian poet a. herald
  (d. 1395)   243, 247, 250–253, 259
Petr Žitavsky (Peter of Zittau), Czech
  chronicler (d. 1339)   117, 202, 204 n. 52,
  209, 215, 222–223
Pfaffe Konrad, German epic poet
  (12th c.)   276
Philippe de Beaumanoir (de Rémi), French
  jurist and royal official (d. 1296)   52
Piotr of Byczyna, Polish-Silesian chronicler
  (14th c.)   306, 308
Piotr Włostowic [Piotr Dunin], Polish count
  (1153)   116
Poland   1, 3–4 n. 9, 6–10, 69, 101–104,
  106–114, 116–118, 122, 124–126, 130,
  132–136, 138, 140–143, 145–147, 150–152,
  154–154, 157, 159–160 n. 159, 161–163,
  167–170, 172 n. 22, 174–175, 178, 180–182,
  185, 187–191, 194–204, 210, 212, 214–218
  n. 157, 220 n. 162, 221–223, 225 n. 210,
  226–228, 230, 232–236, 238, 240–243,
  248–250, 253–259, 261, 263, 268, 272,
  274–279, 284–290, 292–293, 295–297,
  299–300, 302, 305–308, 317, 320–322,
  324–325, 328–329, 331–332, 334–341,
  344, 346–351, 353–354, 356, 358–360,
  363, 365, 367–368, 371–372, 382–384,
  386–387, 391
Poles   2–5, 7–9, 11, 13–14, 89, 93, 102–103,
  112, 115, 120 n. 3, 125–126, 128–129, 132,
  134–136, 139–141, 143, 150–151, 154–156,

Poles (cont.)
　158–160, 162, 165–166, 172, 176–179, 183, 185, 187, 189–194, 198, 235, 238, 263, 268, 272, 274–275 n. 52, 276–277, 279, 281, 283–285 n. 87, 286–289, 292, 296–297, 299, 301–303, 305, 307, 317–319, 324, 328–337, 340–342, 345–346, 348–356, 358–359 n. 7, 380, 382–384, 386, 389–391, 399, 422
Pomerania　10, 118, 147, 161–162, 227–228, 230, 232–234, 236–242, 334, 349, 352, 356, 358
Prague　82–83, 85–86, 88, 90, 95–96, 146, 169, 202–203, 208, 210, 215–216, 228, 232, 235, 240, 314, 334, 360, 362
Premysl Ottokar I, Czech Duke and King (d. 1230)　299
Přibík Pulkava of Radenín, Czech chronicler (d. c. 1380)　83, 202, 222, 307
Prussia　14, 124, 149–150, 211 n. 95, 214–214, 222, 227–228, 232, 234, 239–241, 285–286, 321, 325–330, 334–335, 339–339, 342, 347–350, 352–356, 383
Przemysł II, Duke of Greater Poland, Polish King (d. 1296)　118, 207, 215, 223–224

Ralph de Diceto, English chronicler, dean of St. Pauls Cathedral in London (d. c. 1202)　62, 70, 74–75
Ramung, figure of German heroic poetry　284, 287–288
Regensburg　87, 201, 205–206, 211, 213, 219 n. 161, 221–222, 230
Reinbold Slecht, German chronicler (d. c. 1422)　197, 222
Robert de Torigni, Norman chronicler, abbot of Mont Saint-Michel (d. 1186)　70, 77–79
Robert the Monk (of Reims), Frenchprior and chronicler (d. c. 1120)　34, 38
Rüdiger, figure of German heroic poetry　288–289
Rudolf Losse, counsellor to the elector-archbishop of Treves (14th c.)　43
Russia (Ruzzia)　189, 234, 275, 277–277, 281, 379
Rycheza, Polish Duchess and Queen, niece of Otto III (d. 1063)　106, 113, 125 n. 20, 127, 160

S(c)lavi　91 n. 43, 143–144, 159, 188–189, 192, 307 n. 11
Sącz (Stary Sącz)　174–177, 181, 369
Salomea, St., Polish princess, Poor Clares nun (d. 1268)　175, 177 n. 51, 178
Salzburg　72, 200, 206–207, 223
Saracens　30–31
Satan (Devil), figure of Christnian, Jewish and Islam religions　33 n. 58, 318
Seifried Helbling, Austrian poet (d. c. 1300)　301
Seljuks　30–31, 36
Sigebert of Gembloux, chronicler a. hagiographer (d. 1112)　50
Sigehêr von Vlâchen, figure of German heroic poetry　284
Silesia　10, 14, 117–117, 136 n. 61, 139–140, 145, 162, 168, 173, 202, 207, 213, 215, 220, 227–228, 232, 235, 238, 240–241, 301, 305–306, 310–314, 316–320, 325, 359
Simon Grunau, German (Theutonic Order) chronicler (d. c. 1530)　356
Sorbs　194
Spytihněv II, Czech Duke (d. 1061)　85, 87–88, 90, 93
Stanislaus, St. (Stanisław), bishop of Krakow (d. 1079)　134–135, 137, 168–169, 171–173, 180, 226, 241
Stanislaw Ostroróg, Polish politician and political writer (d. 1477)　153
Stanisław, Polish hagiographer (14th c.)　178
Straßburg　197, 212, 215
Stricker (der) – pseudonym of an anonymous German itinerant poet (13th c.)　276 n. 55
Švitrigaila, Grand Duke of Lithuania (d. 1452)　205, 349, 351
Syrians　30

Tannhäuser, mythologized medieval German poet　300
Theodoric the Great, Ostrogoth king (d. 526), prototype of Ermenrich　279
Theutonici – see Germans　81–82, 84, 86–91, 116 n. 67, 133, 143, 146, 366
Thietmar of Merseburg, German chronicler (d. 1018)　11, 185, 187–190, 194, 196

INDEX OF GEOGRAPHIC NAMES AND HISTORICAL PERSONS   433

Thomas Ebendorfer (d.1464), Austrian historian, professor, and statesman   201, 205, 207, 213 n. 124, 126
Tomasz (I), bishop of Wrocław (d. 1268)   117, 171
Treves   43, 46
Trzebnica (Trebnitz)   312
Turks   29–31, 166, 323, 355, 380

Ulrich Füetrer, Bavarian chronicler (15th c.)   200, 217–218, 225–226

Vienna   8, 151 n. 118, 165 n. 179, 201, 217, 243, 252–253, 256–257, 280
Vincencius of Prague, Czech chronicler (d.1167)   83, 90
Vincent Kadłubek, Polish chronicler (d. 1223)   9, 111, 113, 115, 126–127, 129–130, 138, 306, 365
Vratislav II of Bohemia, Duke of Bohemia (d. 1092)   85, 87
Vytautas, Grand Duke of Lithuania (d. 1430)   151–152 n. 124, 214, 225, 349

Walber ûz Türkîe, figure of Geman heroic poetry   284
Walberan, figure of Geman heroic poetry   292
Walerian Nekanda-Trepka, Polish satirical writer (d. c. 1640)   372
Walter the Chancellor, French crusader chronicler (d. c. 1122)   36
Wanda, fictional/ legendary?/ daughter of Krak [Grakch]   9, 112–113, 115, 128–129, 143, 158
Wenceslaus I, King of Bohemia (d. 1253)   299

Wenceslaus II, King of Bohemia a. Poland (d. 1305)   141 n. 78, 298
Wenceslaus, St. (of Bohemia), Duke of Bohemia (d. 935)   299
Wenezlan, figure of Geman heroic poetry   250, 259, 289–292, 297–299
Wigand of Marburg, chronicler of the Teuthonic Order (d. 1409)   222, 322–323, 336, 339–342, 344–346
Wilhelm (William), duke of Austria (d. 1406)   205–207, 253–256, 337–338, 342, 351
William of Tyre, chronicler of crusades (d. 1186)   26 n. 36, 33 n. 58, 37
Wincenty of Kielcza (Kielce), Polish hagiographer, composer a. poet (d. c. 1261)   137, 169–171, 181
Witelon, Silesian scholar (died ca. 1270–1314)   305
Witowt, see Vytautas   341, 344
Władysław I the Elbow-high (Łokietek), Polish Duke a. King (d. 1333)   208 n. 80
Władysław II Wygnaniec (the Exile), Polish Duke (d. 1159)   114, 127, 140, 145, 161–162, 306
Władysław II. Jagiełło (Jogaila), Grand Duke of Lithuania, king of Poland (d. 1434)   205, 213 n. 128
Wolfhard, figure of Geman heroic poetry   289–292
Wrocław   113, 117, 127 n. 28, 139–140, 146 n. 96, 148, 168, 171, 202, 204, 214–216, 220, 224–225, 233, 257–258 309 n. 18, 315–317 n. 46, 334, 361–362

Znojmo   87